THE CONTINENT

0   100   200   300   400 M.
0   100   200   300   400 K.

ATLANTIC OCEAN

North Sea

ULSTER

Dublin

FRIESLAND

London
Canterbury
Calais   Bruges   Sluys   RHINE
        FLANDERS   Ghent   Antwerp
        ARTOIS   Cologne   GERMANY
Montreuil   Lièges
SEINE   PICARDY   HAINAULT
Brest   OISE AISNE   Crécy   LUXEMBURG
Castle   Reims
BRITTANY   Paris   MARNE   Châlons-sur-Marne
LOIRE   Brétigny   Strasbourg
        BURGUNDY   Basel   DANUBE

Poitiers
                            Berne
        Limoges   Lausanne
Santiago   AQUITAINE   Geneva   L. Léman (Geneva)
de Compostela   Bordeaux   SAVOY   (Great) St. Bernard Pass
LEÓN   Milan
  León   FRANCE   Dax   PO   Pavia   Padua
                                    LOMBARDY   Venice
PORTUGAL   Pamplona   Avignon   Genoa
    Valladolid NAVARRE   Lucca
            Nájera   Pisa   ARNO   Florence
        ARAGON   TUSCANY
    CASTILE
    Madrid   ITALY
    Toledo   Rome

SPAIN

Seville

Cadiz   Naples

MEDITERRANEAN SEA

KINGDOM OF SICILY

Ascherl

CHAUCER

CHAUCER

HIS LIFE
HIS WORKS
HIS WORLD

DONALD R. HOWARD

A William Abrahams Book

E. P. DUTTON   NEW YORK

Published in the United States by E. P. Dutton,
a division of NAL Penguin Inc.,
2 Park Avenue, New York, N.Y. 10016.
Published simultaneously in Canada by
Fitzhenry & Whiteside Limited, Toronto.

Library of Congress Cataloging-in-Publication Data

Howard, Donald Roy, 1927–1987
Chaucer: his life, his works, his world.

"A William Abrahams book."
Bibliography: p.
Includes index.
1. Chaucer, Geoffrey, d. 1400. 2. Poets, English—
Middle-English, 1100-1500—Biography. I. Title.
PR1905.H58   1987   821'.1 [B]   86-32899
ISBN 0-525-24400-X

COBE

DESIGNED BY EARL TIDWELL

10 9 8 7 6 5 4 3 2 1

Contents

vi
Contents

SIXTEEN PAGES OF ILLUSTRATIONS FOLLOW PAGE 236.

Acknowledgments

Above all I am in the debt of several generations of scholars, especially John M. Manly, Edith Rickert, and Lilian J. Redstone, who compiled the 493 known documents pertaining to Chaucer's life, edited in the original languages with learned commentary and annotations by Martin M. Crow and Clair C. Olson and published as *Chaucer Life-Records* (Austin, Tex., 1966). I am deeply grateful to Professor Crow for his interest and encouragement. His answers to my letters have been a fountain of wisdom and of technical learning possessed by no one else alive at the present time.

Before I decided to write this book, while it was still no more than a subject for conversation, I had occasion to talk many times with the late Christopher Isherwood about how to write of the self and the other, of a world that was long ago, and of a writer whose personal life is almost erased from history. "Make it like a seance," he would say; or, "if you can see something he saw or hold in your hand something he touched, it will speak to you." I wasn't sure I knew what he meant, but I know now.

I began writing on a fellowship from the National Endowment for the Humanities in 1978 and was further assisted with two fellowships from the John Simon Guggenheim Memorial Foundation; the project fell together in my thoughts during a month at the Rockefeller Foundation's center at Bellagio, Italy. I am grateful to these foundations for their support, to Stanford University for research funds, and to the staff of the Green Library at Stanford, especially William Allen.

So many individuals have helped me without knowing they did so that I won't try to list them. Such a list would include the participants in three NEH Summer Seminars for College Teachers offered at Stanford in 1978, 1981, and 1984; and to hundreds of colleagues and students. And audiences: during the years I was writing, I gave talks at Ohio State, Boston University, the University of Virginia, Williams College, Berkeley, and Stanford, among others, and came away from each occasion in various ways encouraged or enlightened.

All but the earliest chapters were written on a computer, so I must express my gratitude for a project of Stanford University (named "Tiro" after Cicero's secretary, inventor of a form of shorthand), financed chiefly by the Pew Foundation and IBM. Its purpose was to help humanists cross this technological threshold by supplying for a modest fee computers, programs, classroom instruction, and advice. For the latter I'm especially grateful to Thomas Goodrich, of Stanford's Instruction and Research Information Services, without whose tutelage I should long ago have thrown the monster out the window.

My principal research assistant was Thomas Moser, Jr., who did routine and complex tasks with flair and intelligence; he was most useful as a gifted and skilled researcher, as a sounding board and counselor.

Parts of the manuscript, sometimes very large parts, have been read by Professors Morton Bloomfield, Judith Brown, John Fyler, Wesley Trimpi, the late Charles Singleton, and David Wallace. The entire manuscript was read by Professors William Askins, Jack Collins, Sherron Knopp, John Protsko, Daniel Silvia, Paul Strohm, Charles T. Wood, and Christian K. Zacher. There can hardly be a more devoted act of friendship than to read a book this long in a cumbersome typescript and offer detailed comments; I am grateful to them all.

To these I will add with gratitude, in what is my greatest debt, the name of my editor and friend, William Abrahams.

Stanford University
October 31, 1986

Preface

Of all writers Chaucer has had the greatest influence on English literature; he stands at its beginning, the father of English poetry, as Dryden and Arnold called him. And no writer in all our literature is quite so companionable. When we read him he speaks to us across the gulf that divides medieval from modern, beckons us into his inner world, makes us want to think his thoughts and feel his feelings even as he masks these behind multiple ironies and leaves us guessing at them. This quality, which at once invites and eludes, is so much an aspect of his style that no literary biography focused on his works can escape an effort to see into his mind.

It is hard enough even with those we know intimately to see inside their minds, for we know them only in relation to ourselves. We have to look inside our own minds to see such a relationship, and most of us but slenderly know ourselves. For Chaucer's mind we have the stunning evidence of what it produced—on which we see the mark of genius. But genius is the most elusive of qualities—it is the part of a subject's mind we can least hope to grasp or understand. So we are back again with his works.

And here, a tangle in the evidence. The records of Chaucer's life tell us about the affairs, largely the comings and goings, of a Geoffrey Chaucer

who served the king's court. There is nowhere in them any indication that
this Geoffrey Chaucer is the same one who became famous even during
his own lifetime as a poet, writer, translator, and scholar. One could
almost suspect there were two Geoffrey Chaucers, as in a metaphorical
sense there were. The argument for his oneness is an argument from
silence: if there had been two Chaucers in the king's court, one a courtier,
diplomat, and public official, the other a poet, both with the rather
unusual Christian name of Geoffrey, someone surely would have noted
the coincidence. There is, for hard evidence of his oneness, a single
passage in his poetry (*The House of Fame*, lines 652–660) where the poet,
called "Geffrey" by the amusing Dantesque eagle that carries him into the
sky, almost certainly refers to his duties as Controller of the King's Custom and Subsidy of Wools, Hides, and Wool Fells in the Port of London.

Virtually all the documents that provide us with facts about Chaucer's life were collected and assembled long ago and are published with
a few others as *Chaucer Life-Records*, ed. Martin M. Crow and Clair C.
Olson (1966). These records tell us chiefly about Chaucer's public life; of
his domestic or private life we know almost nothing. But then, even with
recent writers, the records of their private lives have often been destroyed
or made unavailable.

Chaucer—unlike most writers, I fear—led an interesting life. He
fought in the Hundred Years War and was engaged in the war of the
Spanish intervention. He traveled all over Europe, to Flanders, France,
Spain, and three times to Italy. He saw Florence during the "second
democracy," while Petrarch and Boccaccio were still alive and Italian
humanism was established and observable, and he returned to England
to write a poem about what was the chief obsession of the Italian humanists—fame. He met or saw most of the crowned heads and great nobles
of his time, and many of the great figures in politics, arms, and literature.
He served on commissions of major political importance, such as those
negotiating loans from Florentine bankers, or the use of an English port
by Genoese merchant ships, or the marriage of King Richard II. He would
be a good subject for a biography had he never written a line of poetry.
But he did, and most of his poems reflect events of his time and of his
life, both public and private.

If Chaucer's works are our best evidence of his inner world, of his
development and genius, this fact brings an element of subjectivity into
the picture. We know the poems, each of us, as they have taken shape,
upon reading them, in our minds and feelings; yet they have the power
to evoke different ideas and feelings in different readers, and of this
Chaucer was well aware. There is no scientific method for determining
a right way to read them, though there have been endless discussions of

"methodology." In a biography we want to establish a reading justified by the background of events and knowledge that swarmed about and within him as he wrote. We want to know what he *thought* he was writing. The power of his works to grip us six centuries later is what allows us into his thoughts, and perhaps by hindsight we can see qualities of which the poet himself might not have been aware. But, empathizing with him through his works in this way, we do not all see the same reality.

When I began writing, people informed me that I would be going to Europe to find new facts. I knew I would be staying home. Not that there are no new facts to be discovered: while England has been turned upside down for materials, no one to my knowledge has made a systematic search of archives in all the Continental cities Chaucer visited—in Florence, yes, but in Genoa, Milan, and elsewhere, no. One document found in Spain a century ago was overlooked until recently because of the unfortunate way it spelled "Chaucer" in French; probably there are more such documents. But I leave the search to others. A scholar might spend a decade finding two facts, and one of those would likely be wrong: facts about the Middle Ages are in short supply, and their status is often suspect.

And facts, like everything else, go out of fashion. In the 1960s it was reckoned a fact that "the drought of March," referred to in the opening lines of *The Canterbury Tales*, was a purely rhetorical convention drawn from the literature of Mediterranean countries where March is a dry month; England, hardly ever dry, certainly suffers no droughts in March. It was one of the best facts going, and it produced a corollary fact, that Chaucer's poetry, like all medieval poetry, is bookish and conventional— we must not expect actualities in it. These facts were printed in textbooks and taught in universities; I taught them myself, alas. Then it occurred to one scholar that March in England may be dry *in some places*; to another that weather may have changed since Chaucer's day; and to another that the word "drought" in Middle English meant not total lack of rain but only dryness. Actually, Chaucer lived in the "Little Ice Age," which came over Europe early in his century and lasted until the end of the seventeenth century. It brought a shorter growing season. March was dry, in some places still is. Farmers counted on this relatively dry period for planting; it was, a folklorist discovered, as proverbial in England among farmers as in Mediterranean countries among poets, and so were April showers. Realism, banished from the opening lines of *The Canterbury Tales* for a decade or so, was permitted reentry. The drought of March became a fact again.

It is the same with the date of *The Book of the Duchess*. Until the 1970s it was the only firm date we had for any of Chaucer's works. The poem is about the death of the Duchess Blanche, and four chroniclers reported that she died in 1369. The poem must therefore have been written in that or the following year. Then a scholar proposed that the poem was not written at once upon her death but for one of the annual commemorations of her death—a conjecture that might explain an otherwise inexplicable line mentioning the passage of eight years. If it was written for the eighth annual commemoration, it would put the completion of the poem ahead to 1377. But while this bold idea was still being grumbled about, a new document came to light—a letter dated 1368 with some plans for John of Gaunt's remarriage, persuasive evidence that the duchess, his first wife, was already dead. Scrutiny showed that the old date, 1369, had in fact been an error. The four chroniclers were found to be interrelated and thus only one authority, and that authority was wrong. So we are now comfortably certain of the date 1368 for the duchess's death—as we were before of 1369—and as much in the dark as ever about when the poem was written, when finished, and when presented.

Or again, the day of Richard II's coronation: all chronicles but one call it the eve of Saint Kenelm, the boy king and martyr; one alone says "the morrow of the translation of St. Swithun." So the eve of Saint Kenelm it has been; even Sumner Ferris, a great stickler for facts and vastly learned about the documents of the time, reports it without a footnote as common knowledge. But Charles Wood has lately shown that John of Gaunt, who chose the date, named the morrow of Saint Swithun in his official report of the coronation; unfriendly chroniclers substituted the martyred Saint Kenelm as a subtle threat.

My account of Chaucer's life rests to a large extent on such conclusions about dates. A literary biographer wants his subject's works in order so that he can examine a development in them, and the modern idea of when a work is finished is the date of publication. But this very concept is the child of the printing press; a medieval work was copied by hand, and the writer might go on revising as long as he pleased—no two copies need be the same, and almost never are. There is sufficient evidence that Chaucer revised often, that at times he worked on several pieces at once, that he put pieces aside, sometimes picking them up years later and rewriting them, sometimes forgetting about them or leaving them unfinished. His development was the more complex, not the less so, because he lived before "print culture."

So Chaucer's life was lived and his works written in a world vastly different from our own. Medieval ideas of individuality or personality were themselves different from ours. This doesn't mean the medievals "didn't have personalities" or didn't differ from one another, as obviously they did, but it means that if we are going to make a medieval person, in Mark

Schorer's phrase, "live in a living world," we must give more weight to, take more trouble with, that world.

Until ten years ago I believed that for want of facts no one could write a life of Chaucer. In 1968 I wrote, "no real biography of Chaucer has ever been written or can be written. We do not know enough. To have a biography, even a 'portrait,' we need to know about a man's family and education, his marriage and domestic life, his beliefs, his attitudes, his friends, his work and amusements"—and I went on to list the numerous things we do not know about Geoffrey Chaucer. But by the time the passage was published, in 1976, I had come to doubt it. Two biographies, those of John Gardner and Derek Brewer, had since appeared, and they seemed as real as any other. Neither was a literary biography. Gardner set out to write a literary biography but then sequestered his treatment of the poems in a separate book, *The Poetry of Chaucer* (1977). And in his account of Chaucer's life, being a novelist, he fictionalized details unknown. Brewer's volume, *Chaucer and his World* (1978), also put the poet's works into the background and adopted about his life a personal, conjectural manner; Brewer's enthusiasm for Chaucer's world, his wonderful selection of pictures, his wealth of descriptive detail, and his personal, thoughtful treatment are what distinguish his book.

I found I had changed my estimate of what a "real" biography is. I had been thinking about those older biographies that focused on the private (or secret) life of a public figure. But if we had the wherewithal to write such a biography, would anyone say it revealed the "real" Chaucer? No, in a modern biography of a medieval figure we want what Barbara Tuchman calls a "prism of history," and for a poet we want what Hugh Kenner calls an "X-ray moving picture." How do we know Geoffrey Chaucer at all? Because he extricated English literature from the medieval, instituted in English those accomplishments and effects that have *meant* literature to us since. Surely this is the real Chaucer, more real than Chaucer the Controller of the King's Custom and Subsidy, or that more perplexing Chaucer who is said to have beaten a Franciscan friar in Fleet Street, or raped one Cecily Champain—more real because we can read him still and take the measure of his place in history.

A biography is more than a life. As I have written this book I have performed ongoing experiments writing about my own life and the lives and selves of persons I have known with various degrees of intimacy. I think I now believe that a self is a hopeless jumble of selves and that a life moves, shapeless, from day to day. One can write about both, but to write a biography one must find a figure in the carpet whether there is a figure there or not. And yet we do not find anything without knowing first what we are looking for and why it is worth finding.

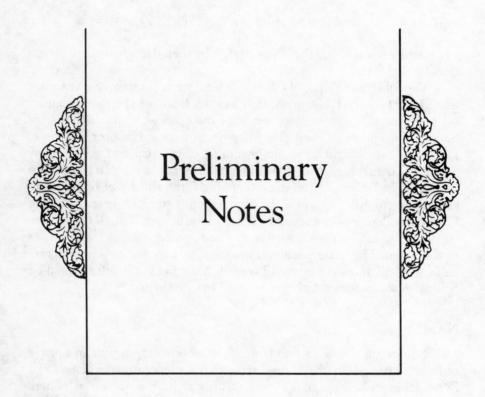

Preliminary Notes

REFERENCES

References, given at the end of the book by page number and catch phrase, chiefly indicate my sources and the sources of unfamiliar quotations. The notes are now and then skirmishes or excursuses peripheral to the text and addressed to my fellow Chaucer scholars. Substantive notes that explain or add or define appear in the text at the bottom of the page. Matters that I take to be common knowledge are not footnoted.

DATES

Dates are given as best I have been able to glean them from my sources. In Chaucer's time the Julian calendar was still in use. Because it calculated the solar year as being eleven minutes and fourteen seconds longer than it really is, the date of the vernal equinox, set in the fourth century A.D. as March 21, had by the fourteenth century fallen ten days behind. The error was to be corrected by Pope Gregory XIII in 1582, but this "Gregorian calendar" was not accepted in Protestant England until

1752, when it was called the "New Style"; by then dates had fallen eleven days behind.

The Old Style dating of Chaucer's time started numbering years not usually on January 1 but on March 25, the Feast of the Annunciation ("Lady Day"). Still, as we can see from the opening scene of the poem *Sir Gawain and the Green Knight,* written during Chaucer's lifetime, January 1 was thought of as the beginning of the year and called "New Year's." To make all this more impossible, years were often given in "regnal years," those of the reign of a king ("the third year of the reign of our present King"), and days given as saints' days or as feasts of the Christian calendar ("the second Tuesday after Easter"); such feasts were often "movable"—that is, varied from year to year according to the phases of the moon. Then, too, medieval numbers, usually roman numerals, are easily misread and were often miscopied. Most medieval dates should be read with an imagined "plus or minus" before them.

NAMES

Names, on the other hand, are given not as they appear in sources or follow rules but as they sound right to the modern reader. Chaucer's father, though he appears in some records as John le Chaucer, is here called John Chaucer as he would be today and probably was in the spoken language of his own time. Noble and royal titles are eschewed when they are confusing. Nothing is to be gained by calling John of Gaunt "the earl of Richmond," especially when at a certain point we must then start calling him the duke of Lancaster; there is no reason why, for "historical accuracy," the names in a book like the present one should be made as troublesome as those in Tolstoy. I am aware that John of Gaunt was never called "Gaunt" until Shakespeare called him so—that, historically speaking, it is like calling Joan of Arc "Arc." But if Shakespeare had called her "Arc" the English-speaking world would know her by that name.

QUOTATIONS FROM CHAUCER

Quotations from the text of Chaucer are from *The Works of Geoffrey Chaucer,* ed. F. N. Robinson, 2nd ed. (Boston, 1957) unless otherwise noted. But the punctuation is my own, and the spelling has been normalized by using the Middle English spellings closest to modern spelling according to the principles described by James Dean and myself in *The Canterbury Tales: A Selection* (New York, 1969). Obsolete or difficult words or phrases are marked with a degree sign (°) and glossed to the right. This way of quoting Chaucer should make his Middle English quite understandable to the reader with no previous experience of Middle English; in cases where this might not be so, I have paraphrased or translated.

Line numbers of passages quoted are given when they are thought useful to the reader. They are not given when the passage is identified in a phrase ("the last lines," "the speech that follows") or when a nearby line number has been cited in preceding quotations. Lists or clusters of line numbers are banished to footnotes or endnotes for aesthetic reasons, and for brief passages only the opening line number is given.

On the pronunciation of Chaucer's English, see Appendix A, pp. 513–516.

OTHER QUOTATIONS

Quotations from the Bible are generally from the Douay-Rheims version, as being closest to the Latin Vulgate used in Chaucer's day. Some common phrases known to English-speakers in the words of the King James version are so given.

Translations are my own unless otherwise noted.

Part One

Into the King's Service

(1342-1372)

1

Memories

In the autumn of feudalism, when the old ideals lay in tatters but boys still dreamed of being knights, Geoffrey Chaucer of London, son of John Chaucer the vintner—fourteen or so years of age—was sent from his native city for a stay in a royal castle, to learn the rhythms of chivalry.

The earliest record of Chaucer's life, 1357, declares in clerkish Latin that on the fourth of April, for *Galfrido Chaucer Londonie,* four shillings were paid for a tunic and three more for hose. In the same account, in May, for one Philippa Pan of London, 2s. 6d. were paid to have a tunic made for a feast (she, if "Pan" means Paon, was the lady Chaucer would marry). The record is from the household account of Elizabeth, countess of Ulster, wife of Prince Lionel. Two trimmed-down sheets of parchment, numbered 2 and 101, are all that have survived of her ledger; it was torn apart in the next century and its pages used as filler for bookbindings. In our time such old bindings have been carefully deconstructed, their stuffings of waste unglued and treated by expert craftsmen for what trace of the past they may reveal—in the present instance, a time capsule telling us all we know of Chaucer's adolescence.

Chaucer was sent to the Ulster household as a part of his education.

The countess had her own private staff with its own budget (hence the ledger), and young Geoffrey officially served her as a page, alongside ladies in waiting, esquires, yeomen, a chaplain. He was to learn the niceties of highborn conduct and the arts of war—to learn how things were done among the nobles and the royals. It took connections, powerful ones, to place a youngster in such a household, and the Chaucer family had such connections. About this part of Chaucer's upbringing or any previous part we know only what we can assume from a knowledge of the times, but we know the outcome: he was sent to war in France, 1359, at sixteen or seventeen, the age young men were usually sent to war, assuming there was a war. He was captured and taken prisoner; his ransom was paid by the king—£16, about the going rate for a *valettus*. After that he became a bureaucrat, and our information about his life begins then. Still, we can take the measure of what led up to this turning point and say something probable about his birth and family background, his education, and his memories.

Birth and Childhood

The only evidence of Chaucer's birth is in a deposition he made in his forties for a trial before the High Court of Chivalry. (The register of the family's parish church, Saint Martin in the Vintry, where we might look for a record of his baptism, perished with the church itself in the Great Fire in London.) The trial, which went on for five years, had to do with which of two families, Scrope or Grosvenor, had the right to bear a certain coat of arms. Chaucer's deposition, the last of twenty-two taken down on October 15, 1386, begins, in law-court French, *Geffray Chaucere esquier del age de xl ans et plus armeez per xxvii ans*—"Geoffrey Chaucer, esquire, forty and some years of age and armed for twenty-seven years." The age is a formalized guess made by the royal clerk, who gave the deponents' ages in round numbers and got most of them wrong. But he appears to have taken down Chaucer's answers accurately, and he gave a specific number for what was in this trial the more relevant detail, that Chaucer had borne arms for twenty-seven years; soldiers were considered armed from the time they were, as we would say, "commissioned," which meant the first time they were sent on a campaign, and this almost never happened before they were sixteen. The record of the Ulster household shows that he was there in April 1357, and a young man wouldn't have been sent away from home before he had reached "adolescence," that is, puberty, which in the Middle Ages was reckoned to have begun by fourteen, on the authority of ancient books. Twenty-seven years before

1386 would be 1359, and indeed the records show that in the later part of 1359 Chaucer was sent to France with the English army. So if he was fourteen in April 1357 and sixteen in late 1359, he was born no later than the early months of 1343, and possibly a year or so before.

The poet's father, John Chaucer, was about thirty when Chaucer was born. He was a prominent and well-to-do citizen of London, a vintner (an importer and wholesale merchant of wines), as his own father had been. Chaucer's paternal grandmother, Mary, was married three times—to John Heron, then to Robert Chaucer, and then to Richard Chaucer, a relative of Robert's. Chaucer's grandfather, Robert, died when John Chaucer was an infant; John was raised by his mother and her third husband.

As a child of about twelve John Chaucer had had a bizarre experience: he was spirited away at sword's point on a December night by his aunt, Agnes Westhall of Ipswich, and one Geoffrey Stace (later her second husband), with the idea of marrying him to his cousin Joan, her daughter. The purpose of this rash act was to secure his inheritance from his own father and so keep in the Westhall family certain properties in Suffolk. The boy's stepbrother (his mother's son by her first husband, John Heron) and his stepfather (his mother's third husband) rode to Ipswich, entered the house, liberated him, and—so Agnes claimed later—seized goods worth £40. There followed a trial and numerous appeals. In the end, Aunt Agnes was imprisoned in the Marshalsea and fined £250—a considerable sum if you consider that even a century later one could live modestly on £5 a year. The amount was paid in full to John Chaucer by the time he was eighteen, and his Aunt Agnes, now Mrs. Stace, ended up buying the property she had tried to seize.

Such an experience at an impressionable age might have made John Chaucer a cautious, wary person, or on the other hand might have set him an unfortunate example in the violent ways of the world. Probably both were true. Property and inheritance were abiding concerns—obsessions, really—in the late Middle Ages, especially among the merchant class to which the Chaucers belonged; and armed seizure, kidnapping, and trumped-up lawsuits were not uncommon ways to gain possession of them. Englishmen of Chaucer's day were not like the stereotypical stiff-upper-lip English of modern times, who are the children of the Enlightenment and the Empire; they were more like their Norman forebears, hot-tempered and given to extremes when among equals (they cultivated reserve before inferiors or superiors). They wept freely in public, flew into rages, swore copious and imaginative oaths, carried on almost operatic blood feuds and endless legal battles. The mortality rate was high in medieval times and life more precarious; we find more recklessness and terror, more resignation and despair, and more gambling with fortune. More violence, too, or violence of a more vengeful, ostentatious kind: decapitated heads displayed on spikes or bodies hanging from a gibbet was their style, where mug shots in the post office is ours.

This quarrelsome and litigious community left behind countless records of indictments, suits, pleas, writs, inquests, trials, and battles. In three of these a John Chaucer appears as a mounted warrior on an unsuccessful English expedition against the Scots, 1327; in the next year as a ringleader in an attack on the abbot of Saint Edmund (the band kidnapped the abbot and seized his valuables); and in January of the year following, 1329, as a participant in an attempted coup for which he was outlawed. Whether the John Chaucer of these records was Chaucer's father or a relative, one can't be certain: John Chaucer had a cousin of the same name and maybe a stepbrother too (who should, however, have been called John Heron). If this swashbuckling young warrior *was* Chaucer's father; politics, not youthful rapacity, was the reason for his exploits. In the background were the events that followed the deposition and murder of King Edward II. Edward's son and successor, Edward III, was only fourteen. Behind the young king on the one side was his mother, Edward's widow, Queen Isabella, and her lover Mortimer, both instrumental in the defeat of the dead king (they were supported by the hapless abbot of Saint Edmund). On the other side was Henry of Lancaster, chief of the council of regency, he too a leading force in making Edward II give the unwieldy scepter from his hand. In the power struggle between Mortimer and Lancaster that ensued, Lancaster won. Mortimer, judged a traitor, was hanged and drawn; his earldom perished, and his estates fell to the Crown.

So John Chaucer, briefly outlawed during a setback, was fighting on the winning side, the Lancastrian side—as were his stepbrother Thomas Heron and others of the Heron clan. Ten years later, 1338, John Chaucer was doing military duty in the army of King Edward III on an expedition into Flanders, the beginning of the Hundred Years War. It would be interesting to know if in later years he ever told his son Geoffrey old stories about the fall of Edward II and its attendant events, for in the last years of Chaucer's life, when England saw another deposition, that of Richard II, those events of more than seventy years ago came rushing to men's memories. The house of Lancaster was dominant in both depositions. Chaucer's father and his kinsmen had been firmly allied with the duke of Lancaster and King Edward III. John of Gaunt, one of Edward's sons, became Duke of Lancaster through marriage. Chaucer in his capacity as a royal esquire served Edward III and his heir, Richard II; his last known poem, "The Complaint of Chaucer to His Purse," written after the fall

of Richard II, is a witty request for the renewal of his grants addressed
to the new Lancastrian king, Henry IV, John of Gaunt's son.

John Chaucer from his mid-twenties was a busy member of the
London merchant community. We find him—age thirty—backing a law
against bad wine sold in taverns, shipping wheat to Flanders. At thirty-five
he was deputy to the king's chief butler in the port of Southampton, then
shortly customs collector on exports of cloth and beds from five ports—
appointments he held only a few years, not unlike appointments his own
father and grandfather had held and his son Geoffrey would hold at about
the same age. And real estate: when Geoffrey was a child, John Chaucer
was busy with properties inherited from various kin wiped out by the Black
Death. These were extensive, income-producing properties—at one time
or another he owned buildings and land in London and Middlesex, a
brewing establishment, twenty-odd shops outside the city wall of London
at Aldgate, ten and a half acres nearby, and various properties in Middlesex and Suffolk.

Some of these properties came into the family through Chaucer's
mother, née Agnes Copton. John and Agnes married about 1340, when
he was in his mid-twenties. She seems to have been married before to a
nobleman named Northwell, with whom she had a son, and may through
him have had connections at the royal court. The Coptons were a London
family, comparable in rank and wealth to the Chaucers. Apart from what
dowry she brought to the marriage, Agnes Copton—whose father had
been killed when she was very young—inherited the estate of her uncle
Hamo, a maker of coins who worked in the Tower of London, when he
and his only son died in the plague. These income-producing properties
provided security to a merchant family if the head of the household died;
much stock was put by them, and by "marrying well" into a family of good
status and wealth.

London was a merchant city, a major port and mercantile center. It
held a royal charter and was to a surprising extent self-governing. In 1377
its population was between 30,000 and 40,000; of these about 4,000 males
were franchised "citizens" (the number rises to 16,000 when wives and
children over fourteen are included). Another 7,000 males were unenfranchised "foreigns," as they were called—workers, servants, apprentices,
and such—and there were perhaps 2,000 aliens living in the city, mostly
Italian, Flemish, or German, plus a free-floating population of students,
numerous clergy of every conceivable kind, many a lawyer and many a
client attending sessions of the courts, nobles and their retinues, and
miscellaneous gawking visitors. The franchised citizens or "burgesses"
were themselves very stratified. They were great joiners: each craft had

its guild, and there were parish guilds or fraternities of a religious character with their own customs, officers, and liveries. The craft guilds had varying degrees of prestige, and within each there were ranks. The lowest were craftsmen too poor to rent a shop in a better district; they carried their wares to a common marketplace. The highest were the great merchants of the powerful companies, who had many employees and owned much property, and, as one might expect, tended to be elected wardens of companies and aldermen of the city. From among the aldermen the mayor was elected, and such offices of course afforded special status and privileges, though not salaries. One might picture their community as a mercantile elite ("merchant" was a term of dignity) made up of many small gradations—beneath it a descending population of unenfranchised workers, servants, peasants, and escaped serfs (who could gain their freedom if they managed to stay in the city a year and a day); above it an ascending order of knights, nobles, and the great baronial and royal families. The merchant society was based on "small-group solidarity," on special interests and intense family ties, and the basis for determining rank was complicated and subtle.

Chaucer's father was not an alderman or, so far as we know, a warden of the Vintners' Company, and since wealth and status went hand in hand, one can infer that he wasn't among the wealthiest. Yet his status among his fellow vintners must have been high: in 1356 the "wealthier and wiser" of them appointed him a collector of a subsidy to be raised in the city to finance two warships. At various times he witnessed deeds, served on juries, and stood surety for friends and associates when they were accused or sued or otherwise involved with the law. (In surety, of which "mainprise" was the most common kind, a responsible citizen would undertake to vouch for another's good conduct, appearance in court, payment of a debt, and such. If the person mainprised did not show up in court, say, the "mainpernor" was expected to appear in his place and usually pay a fee. In the early stages of a legal action, it was a formality —so much so that fictitious names were used, sometimes funny ones like Cat, Rat, Mouse, or God, Help, All, Men.)

In one intriguing document dated December 9, 1364, Chaucer's father stood surety with four others for Richard Lyons, vintner, guaranteeing that "Alice Perrers would be safe from any danger and might go where she pleased and do the king's business or her own." Alice Perrers, who was to become, if she was not already, the notorious mistress of Edward III, must by this time have been lady-in-waiting to Queen Philippa, though she was only about sixteen. Richard Lyons was one of the wealthiest merchants, in later years an alderman. Of illegitimate birth, he was ambitious, crafty, and unscrupulous; he was much hated for his monopoly on sweet wines. He lived the opulent, flamboyant life of the nouveau riche, many a scandal dogged his career, and he died by violence in the Peasants' Revolt of 1381. If John Chaucer stood surety for him, they must have had some association, though this doesn't argue for equality of status: members of the merchant community had easy relations with one another in spite of rank, and on the whole with the "foreigns" beneath them and noblemen above them as well. Perhaps John Chaucer was reckoned a proper person to stand surety because he was more substantial—with wealth going back several generations and of a better and older family— than the *arriviste* Lyons. Chaucer himself knew Alice Perrers; her father (if he was Sir Richard de Perrers of Essex, as is thought) had supported Lancaster at the time of Edward II's deposition and could have known Chaucer's father from those old, troubled times.

Such ties show that Chaucer by no means came from obscure origins. While his family were not *very* rich, neither were they newly rich. They lived at a time when wealth and status had come to have a tenuous but definable relationship: already there were *bourgeois gentilshommes* and impoverished nobles, untitled professionals like the Man of Law described in *The Canterbury Tales* who gained wealth and bought up landed property, and landed gentry outside the city, "country squires" like the Franklin who owned estates and held public office. In the next century they would all have titles, including Chaucer's descendants. By the fourteenth century Europe's economy was a money economy, in large measure a credit economy. An ordinary wholesale merchant, if he was an importer, would borrow money, buy goods, hire a ship, import and sell his cargo, and pay off his debts at high interest. If all went well, he got rich; some of the wealthiest merchants kept reinvesting their capital this way and owned no land at all. If his ship went down, as ships had a habit of doing, he was ruined. To escape his creditors he might take sanctuary or go on pilgrimage; or he might borrow more, whence it was desirable to keep the amount of one's debts to oneself. The Merchant in the General Prologue of *The Canterbury Tales* (not a Londoner) has this kind of circumspection about what he owes; and the Shipman tells a sordid tale of a merchant engulfed in such touch-and-go borrowing who is swindled by his clothes-crazy wife and a lascivious monk. One could suspect a certain condescension in these vignettes, for the Chaucers, though they borrowed and owed like anyone else, were a good cut above such speculating. They owned landed property, *inherited* property that produced income, and on that account were considered "gentry."

Forty and some years later Chaucer left us a capsule picture of a Londoner's world, this "bourgeois" world he grew up in. It is buried in the cross section of English life that is the overture of *The Canterbury*

Tales. At the top rank among the Londoners described there is the eminent Sergeant-at-Law, a judge—one of twenty holding such appointments—possibly identifiable as Thomas Pynchbek, who served as justice of Common Pleas, 1391 to 1396. As a legal dignitary Pynchbek would have lived in London much of the time, but he was not a citizen: coming from a landless family, he was a great purchaser of land, as Chaucer notes, but that land was in Lincolnshire. At the bottom rank among the Canterbury pilgrims is the Manciple, a steward at one of the Inns of Court, very clever at cheating his masters: as a servant he would have been one of the "foreigns" and not a citizen either. The Host on the pilgrimage, named Harry Bailly, is an innkeeper and was an actual living contemporary who did in fact own a tavern across the Thames in Southwark, not in London; he was fairly close to Chaucer in rank, even serving as a member of Parliament. The "Cook of London," named Roger Ware, an actual contemporary too, owns a shop of his own and so must be a citizen and belong to a guild, but he is very much lower on the social scale; the Host, with cruel jocularity, gives an unappetizing picture of his warmed-over pasties, the flies on his food, and the indigestion of his customers. Later, when he is so drunk he can barely stay on his horse, the Manciple openly ridicules him.

Such scattered scenes afford authentic glimpses of city life among folk far beneath the Chaucers in status, a cluster of small-time tradesmen who know each others' names and compete with bluff and raucous humor. Harry Bailly and Roger Ware, though not equals, behave to each other with rough familiarity. The Cook is little better than a servant; he has been hired by a group of five Guildsmen (described at line 369) to go along and feed them—a haberdasher, a carpenter, a weaver, a dyer, and a tapestry maker. They wear the livery of a "solemn and a great fraternity," probably a parish guild, and have in common membership in the nonvictualing trades, chiefly lesser guilds than the Vintners. They are smartly dressed, decked out pretentiously with silver knives. Each seemed, we read, like a splendid burgess who might be sitting on a dais in a guildhall; each for his wisdom deserved to be an alderman, for they had the property and income that the law required to qualify for the office:

Well seemed each of hem a fair burgeys°   *burger*
To sitten in a yeldhall° on a dais.   *guildhall*
Everich°, for the wisdom that he kan°,   *each / knew*
Was shapely for to been an alderman,
For catel° hadde they enough and rente.   *possession*

Their wives, we learn, would have liked that very much: it is "full fair" to be called "madame"—as aldermen's wives were called, rather than the usual "goodwife"—and march at the head of a city procession with a mantle "royally borne" behind them. One may sense in the passage a Londoner's, or a courtier's, raised eyebrow, or just traditional male drollery over wives putting on airs, but *these* were the kind of people Chaucer came from.

The family home on Thames Street in the Vintry Ward was comfortable and, by the standards of the age, large. The wine business was on the premises. There would have been wine cellars, a shop, and perhaps a tavern, and above these the family's rooms: a hall, a kitchen and pantry, two or three chambers, a sollar or sollars (lofts or rooms on an upper story, often overhanging), a yard where some poultry were kept, and a garden of vegetables, herbs, and flowers. The construction was the familiar wattle-and-daub of fourteenth-century towns. There might have been before the house a sign bearing a coat of arms, one of the pretensions of mercantile families; these might be legitimate arms claimed from an ancestor or procured from a herald. There were, in addition, coats of arms that signified the nature of the family business. Some families had both kinds.*

Inside, the walls would have been whitewashed and hung with wool hangings, possibly some tapestries. Rugs were not yet in use, and the stone floors were strewn with rushes sprinkled with sweet-smelling herbs. The wooden furniture was simple, but there were colorful cushions everywhere, embroidered, often, with heraldic or religious symbols. Beds were elaborate affairs, canopied for privacy and fitted with embroidered covers and hangings; the family usually all slept in one room, private rooms being a newfangled taste. Heat was provided by fireplaces or braziers. Candles, though expensive, were among their luxuries, along with embroidered tablecloths, silver dishes, silver-gilt cups. There might have been two or three household servants, apart from the apprentices and employees of the business.

Thames Street was a block from the river, and the houses had paths leading to the quays. Between the street and the river was a waterfront chaos of small houses and shops. On the other side of the property from the street ran an open stream, the Walbrook, that served conveniently as a sewage system, despite complaints of its unhealthy vapors. The Vintry was one of the more prestigious wards of the city—within it four parishes, each with its church. London, like any such medieval city, was walled; the gates were closed at sundown, the streets were policed, "nightwalkers" were prosecuted. The areas outside the walls—the "suburbs"—were sparsely inhabited and disreputable, for thieves and outlaws lurked there in secret after dark. For its inhabitants London meant the merchant city,

*The Chaucer coat of arms is known only from its use by Chaucer's son Thomas in the early fifteenth century, but John and Agnes Chaucer both had seals.

not the seat of British government as it means for us: the king and the royal court were outside the city wall in Westminster; only the house of Parliament was inside. There were within the walls about a hundred churches, most of them with bells and some with mechanical clocks, an invention of the previous century, that chimed the hours. By day it was bustling and noisy with its hubbub of iron wagon wheels, peddlers' cries, city dwellers' shouts—and also with what are to us country noises, horses neighing, barnyard clucking, bird songs, the barking of ubiquitous dogs. At night the curfew rang at eight, nine in summer, and there descended an awesome silence complicated by the rhythms of bells.

The Black Death

Foremost of Chaucer's childhood memories was the one he shared with all his generation: the Black Death of 1348–1349. This international epidemic of bubonic plague (and its pneumonic and septicemic varieties) was, by one historian's reckoning, "the nearest approach to a definite break in the continuity of history that has ever occurred." For such a generation history imposes a shape upon memory, and for the next generation, too, who only hear about it—as when in our time we speak of "the Great War and modern memory." The plague came from the Near East, swept from Sicily north across the Continent, following the trade routes, and came to England in August of 1348.

Chaucer was about six when the Pestilence, or the Death, as it was called ("Black" Death is a modern term), appeared first in the southern ports, then spread west through Somerset and Devon and northeast to London. His family was in Southampton: his father went there early in 1347 as deputy butler, when Geoffrey was only about five. His memories of the London of his childhood were shadows—the plague was his first "big" memory, the first public event he would recall. He would always remember what he saw of it and how people talked of it with terror in their eyes. The plague returned five times in Chaucer's lifetime, not counting minor episodes, and the threat hovered over England like a fog well into the seventeenth century, but the greatest disaster was the plague of 1348–1349, which depopulated the country by a third (some say a half) —it is said to have wiped out 200,000 villages in Europe. The result was a shortage of labor, an upheaval in the economy, inflated prices, higher taxes; then, partly the result of all this thirty years later, the Peasants' Revolt. Throughout the century people dated events *ante pestem* and *post pestem*, as we might say before and after the First or the Second World War. The *feeling* of the times, too, reverberated from the plague—the penitential gloom, the forebodings of the world's end, the religiosity and spirit of reform; the drawings of the Dance of Death and the writings on the Art of Dying that seem to date from this period; and, on the other side, the wildness and loose living, the breakdown of class lines and formalities, the reckless gaiety, the undertone of hysteria.

Their deepest scars, for those who lived through it, were memories: the bonfires of dead bodies; the priests (those who dared) wandering about giving the last rites; the prudent who, like Boccaccio's storytellers in the *Decameron,* fled into the country, some deserting their families, or nobles who sat within doors and avoided contact with the outside; the thieves and plunderers who dared rob the corpses (and were infected and struck down). And the rumors, in terrorized whispers, of whole villages wiped out; ships with rich cargoes floating aimlessly at sea, their crews dead; houses inhabited by wild geese. And the speculation of cures, of miracles, of efficacious charms, of the sins for which this scourge was laid on them and of the penances required. The cause (a bacillus) they didn't know, nor the carrier (a particular kind of flea, transported chiefly on black rats). Avicenna in his medical writings noted disturbances in the animal world, when "mice and animals living under the earth fled to its surface and were disturbed as if they were drunk," but that was as close as they came to the truth. From experience they knew something passed from victim to victim—vapors, putrid air; the pope at Avignon sat between two roaring fires for protection. They knew that even to speak with an infected person was dangerous, or to touch corpses with ungloved hands or gaze upon them with naked faces, or enter a house where a victim of the plague had lived, or touch anything the victim had touched. Some towns that had not been visited by the plague kept their citizens from contact with towns where plague had been. And they seemed to suspect that those few who had recovered from the disease would not catch it again.

The most learned doctors of the age could do little more than observe and speculate. The physician to the pope at Avignon, Gui de Chauliac, who himself caught the plague and recovered from it, wrote in his book on surgery that "it was so contagious, especially that accompanied by spitting of blood, that not only by staying together but even by looking at one another, people caught it, with the result that men died without attendants and were buried without priests. The father did not visit his son, nor the son his father. Charity was dead and hope crushed." If the cause of the disease was putrid air, what had putrified the air? Astrological influences were the most respectable explanation, especially lunar eclipses or conjunctions of the planets. But it might have been gases escaping in the earthquakes of 1347, or irregularities in temperature, winds, and rains, or fumes from decaying manure, swamp water, rotting plants, or unburied corpses on battlefields. Apart from air, the disease could be contracted direct from infected bodies, clothes, beds, even by the exchange of a look, through the "aerial spirit escaping from the eyes."

How was the disease to be prevented? First, by flight. That was the doctors' universal answer. After that, avoiding contact with the sick, or holding the breath if near them (good advice for the pneumonic form of the disease, which *was* communicable by contact). One should go to a low place away from vapors, stay indoors, seek out mountain air. Rose water was efficacious, and sweet-smelling plants. People were counseled to carry smelling-apples containing herbs, camphor, and such nostrums; to eat figs with filberts before breakfast; to use the standard remedies against poison (theriac, mithridate, bol Armeniac, terra sigillata) or best of all powered emerald, so potent against poison that if a poisonous toad looks at it, its eyes crack. One should keep the body in good health with proper food, white wine mixed with water (*boiled* water was sometimes recommended), massage, chastity (because sex heated up the body), and only light exercise, no hot baths, sleeping at night (not after meals), and, ah yes, inevitably, bleeding. But a healthy frame of mind was recommended as well: not to weep, or speak ill of others, or think too much, or stay awake, or be gloomy or frightened or anxious—all this was understood to contribute to health, for the medievals knew that "the body is often moved by imagination alone."

Physicians knew the symptoms and the dangers, but they knew no cure—never knew one until our century, when a serum was developed. Bleeding was the standard treatment; large quantities of blood were drawn from the inflicted to remove impurities, and if the patient fainted, the bleeding was delayed until he or she was revived. The boils were opened with a knife, sometimes cauterized; plasters might be applied to draw out the poison. And some patients recovered, though the futility of these treatments in most cases couldn't be overlooked. Many physicians, however, took fat fees for offering what they understood to be vain hopes or slim ones, and so grew rich upon the corpses of their patients. The Physician in *The Canterbury Tales* is one of these: we are told he had saved what he earned in time of pestilence. He is depicted as a learned, skillful, and solemn practitioner who "loved gold in special" and whose vast book learning "was but little on the Bible." This was somewhat a stereotype, but, chillingly, when it is his turn to tell a tale, he tells a "moral" tale from Livy about a father who, to save his daughter's threatened virginity, murders her in cold blood.

The symptoms of the plague were a boil on the thigh or upper arm, at first the size of a lentil, which grew to the size of an egg; headache, shivering fits, fever, violent pain through the body, weakness, vomiting blood. When people felt them coming on they confessed their sins at once, knowing they would be dead in three or at most four days; and their confessors, sometimes, died with them.

The sights of the plague: the boils, the bloody vomit, the wasted corpses; the closed-up houses; the black-hooded and well-paid servants who carried bodies to distant burial mounds; the villages left without a living soul, ghost towns, some of which rotted into the soil (and have been discovered in our time through aerial photography); fires burning to kill the evil vapors; the living at prayer, in church if they dared to go abroad; the tall candles in churches, some as tall as the church itself, perpetually burning as a charm against the pestilence; funeral processions.

The sounds of the plague: the sacring bells of ceaseless masses, the passing bell for the dead (silenced in some cities so as not to disturb the sick or instill fear), the imprecations and outcries of survivors, vomiting, groans. But also the silence: the silence of houses, signaling that all within were dead, the silence of evenings when none dared stir abroad for fear of the vaporous night air, the hush of terror, whispered news, breathed surmises; the silent eyes of people, big with dread and terror. And the smells: vomit, smoke, corpses.

The dominant feeling of the plague, for those who remembered it, was suspicion—suspicion of everyone (for anyone might contract the headaches and shivering at any moment and at once begin passing on the noxious vapor). And, too, fear of the unknown and the abstract: the plague, a personified figure called "the Death," was imagined as a black giant stalking the streets, a walking skeleton, a horseman on a black horse, a secret thief. Curiosity, moreover, for any bit of news that might raise hope or stir terror. And, for some, in the face of that terror, hilarity, drunkenness, and lewd abandon. "Others," wrote Boccaccio, "maintained that an infallible way of warding off this appalling evil was to drink heavily, enjoy life to the full, go round singing and merrymaking, gratify all of one's cravings whenever the opportunity offered, and shrug the whole thing off as one enormous joke. Moreover, they practiced what they preached to the best of their ability, for they would visit one tavern after another, drinking all day and night to immoderate excess."

For Boccaccio it was a recent memory: he was thirty-five when the Black Death came, and his majestic introduction to the *Decameron,* which hovers over the whole delightful book as a grim symbol of earthly tribulation, is thought the greatest eyewitness account of it—though in typical medieval fashion it is modeled on a passage from Paulus Diaconus. For Chaucer it was an early memory: he was a child when the plague came to England, just at the age from which we have our earliest memories— at the age when children, as Piaget has shown, are fixated upon symbols,

dreams, and fantasies. On that account Chaucer's memory was deeper;
in the last years of his life, for that Canterbury pilgrim who is the most
vivid and frightening of them all, the Pardoner, he selected a tale of Death
personified in the time of the pestilence. Three wicked revelers, drinking
in a tavern early in the morning, hear a bell and see a corpse carried to
its grave. They ask their servant who the dead man is. The boy tells them
it is an old fellow of theirs, slain while drunk and sitting upright on a
bench, by a privy thief that men call Death, who smote his heart with
his spear and went his way:

> He hath a thousand slain this pestilence,
> And, maister, ere ye come in his presence,
> Me thinketh that it were necessarie
> For to beware of swich° an adversarie: *such*
> Beth ready for to meet him evermore . . .

This mythic dread of Death, pictured and personified, stalking the
land may have been the most profound and enduring result of the Black
Death. To be always prepared to die was standard Christian teaching, but
death had never, since the early times of the martyrs, been so real, its
terrors never more specific. The knee-jerk interpretation held of course
that it was the wrath of God, a punishment for sins, and from this
viewpoint the only prevention or cure was penance, prayer, and resignation before an inscrutable Providence. It may be symptomatic of this state
of mind that Chaucer translated into English Boethius's *Consolation of
Philosophy,* a work that seeks to show how one should bear misfortune
in patience because in God's universal plan all is for the best; or that he
ended *The Canterbury Tales* with a treatise on penance. During the Black
Death, a quotation from Saint Augustine became a popular catchword:
"Nothing is more certain than death, nothing less so than the hour of its
coming." This notion of penitence as an unremitting state of mind easily
became hysterical. At Avignon the pope, sequestered in his palace, recommended to the people of the city devout processions and singing the
litanies. As many as two thousand attended, barefoot, wearing sack cloth,
some covered with ashes. Mass hysteria brought the crowd to wailing and
shrieking, tearing their hair, whipping themselves with scourges. And the
pope, the elegant Clement VI, revolted by these excesses and aware that
they could only spread the disease further, put an end to the processions
as hastily as he had ordered them. He became the enemy of public
demonstrations. When the Flagellants appeared by the thousands all over
Europe in the following year, dancing in grim processions through and out
of towns, scourging one another, near naked, with their terrible spiked
thongs, picking up new brethren along the way, bloody, weeping, singing,

often in defiance of church discipline and doctrine, the pope clamped down. A papal bull—October 20, 1349—denounced them and ordered prelates to stamp them out, using force if necessary.

Death, having been an obsession, became a fad. From this period arose the treatises on the "art of dying" universally read and studied by Christians into the eighteenth century. There was renewed interest in treatises on "contempt of the world"—Chaucer himself says he translated the classic work on the subject, *On the Misery of the Human Condition*, written 150 years earlier by Pope Innocent III. Visual images of this period just after the Black Death were the "dance of death" and the "memento mori"—the dancing skeletons beating drums, leering, shrouded in black or carrying a spear. These images were ready at hand, going back to the early thirteenth century when the orders of friars had developed them, in mural paintings, as a form of illustrated sermon. But now they took on a grimly humorous and satirical spirit. In Italy in the fifteenth century the skeletons are friendly and jovial while the living are reluctant and demure; there were often darkly comic captions ("Come, fat Bishop"); at Grossbasel one artist of a Dance of Death included himself and his family among the victims. Displayed bones or a skull, the skull and crossbones worn sometimes in jewelry as a reminder of the imminence of death, or represented in painting and sculpture, are traditions that date from the fads of this period.

If such graveyard humor was one way of accommodating the Grim Reaper, another was to find a scapegoat. The plague was blamed variously on Arabs, lepers, even—at Narbonne—on Englishmen. Inevitably the Jews, the traditional moneylenders of medieval Europe (though not, as is often thought, the only ones), were at hand on the Continent (they had been expelled from England in 1290) to be accused of poisoning wells. They were tortured and burned in many cities, especially in Germany. Chaucer's contemporary, the chronicler Jacob von Königshofen, described the burning of the Jews at Strasbourg:

> On Saturday—that was St. Valentine's Day—they burnt the Jews on a wooden platform in their cemetery. There were about two thousand people of them. Those who wanted to baptize themselves were spared. . . . And everything that was owed to the Jews was cancelled, and the Jews had to surrender all pledges and notes that they had taken for debts. The council, however, took the cash that the Jews possessed and divided it among the working-men proportionately. The money was indeed the thing that killed the Jews. If they had been poor and if the feudal lords had not been in debt to them, they would not have been burnt.

After this wealth was divided among the artisans some gave their share to the cathedral or to the Church on the advice of their confessors.

To fear and greed were added the self-justifications of guilt. There was a revival or continuance of the old slander about Jews murdering Christian children. A story about such a murder of an innocent Christian child by "the cursed Jews" crops up in *The Canterbury Tales*, where with disturbing irony it is told by that reserved and elegant lady, the Prioress.

All this was the dark side of the plague's aftermath. The other side was more promising: as life was threatened, it was valued. The opinions of medieval physicians about the causes of the epidemic, however wide of the mark, were in the aggregate an assertion in favor of learning, knowledge, and human effort. Because the clergy were depleted and the schools and universities in disarray, there was in the air an impulse to endow institutions, build memorials. In his foundation charter for a new college, the archbishop of Naples wrote that he had been thinking how all men die but once, fleshly glory fades like a flower and turns to dust, the life of man is like vapor. But he hastened to add that he was not himself expecting death, and in endowing his college he was giving it his name. This hope of providing oneself with a measure of earthly immortality in the stream of successive human lives, though it had its medieval background in ideas of knightly honor and reputation, is really the beginning of what we think of now as the Renaissance spirit. We cannot say the plague *caused* the Renaissance any more than we can say it caused the Peasants' Revolt or anything else, but it hastened and reinforced such tendencies. And, of course, one form of earthly immortality was the enduring words poets wrote about earthly deeds.

Apart from such indirect influences there is a direct connection between the Black Death and literature. Medieval doctors, as we have seen, took a holistic approach to the prevention and treatment of disease. Medieval medicine, taking its cue from ancient medical writers like Hippocrates and Galen, looked upon health as a natural state and upon disease and affliction as an aberration from nature. Nature was the great healer. The doctor's role was to prepare the patient so that nature could restore health. The doctor could set a bone and wrap it in linen (plaster of Paris is a modern invention), but nature made it heal: the ancient medical texts tell with perfect accuracy how long it takes each bone to mend. In the same spirit the medieval doctor cast his patient's horoscope to determine the time for treatment. But a doctor also had to take into account what were known as the "non-naturals"—influences on health not entirely under nature's sway, over which the individual could exert voluntary control. The air we breathe, the food we eat, our habits of rest or elimination all affect our health, but we must exert discipline over them.

Among these "non-naturals" were the *accidentia animae*—the patient's emotional and mental state. It was understood that a bad frame of mind was inimical to health, that anxiety, fear, or gloom made the body vulnerable to infection or less amenable to healing and recovery. So it was desirable to banish such feelings, maintain a temperate, cheerful attitude, avoid morbid gossip and the sights and sounds of the plague, and cultivate recreation, distraction, ease. A man might go hunting because it would occupy him, "take his mind off his troubles," and afford pleasure. Good food, pleasant conversation, nice clothes, and various entertainments thus promoted health; physicians recommended music, songs, and stories. So literature had value apart from the didactic or moral value of the written word. We can learn from what we read, yes; and therefore, as Saint Paul allowed—in a sentence Chaucer quoted in two crucial places—"all that is written is written for our doctrine." But the entertainment value of poems and stories had uses too: stories keep us in a healthy frame of mind, which is of course also a virtuous, never an intemperate or immoderate or licentious, frame of mind. They have therapeutic and hygienic values, which in turn make the reader or listener more susceptible to whatever moral or spiritual value they may have.

These fourteenth-century justifications of literature as a kind of medicine do not, according to their discoverer, Professor Glending Olson, "celebrate pure aesthetic pleasure or . . . promote literary enjoyment as an end in itself." They are "pragmatic, claiming physical or psychological or ethical benefits that make the gaining of pleasure from stories rationally acceptable." As we will see later, the most startling embodiment of this hygienic estimate of literature occurs in Boccaccio's *Decameron*, where the storytelling takes place during a flight from the plague and is part of a regimen explicitly intended to keep the participants healthy. Such hygienic regimens were much on people's minds in the fourteenth century; even when the plague had disappeared, its memory never did, and there was always the danger that it might, as several times it did, come back again.

Early Education

While Chaucer's father was deputy butler in Southampton, he left his business in the charge of his stepfather, Richard Chaucer, and his stepbrother Thomas Heron. They both died of the plague and he inherited their properties. So he had to give up the deputy butlership and bring his family back in haste to London. Perhaps the family's absence from London was after all what saved them, for Southampton, much less populous and cramped, held less danger of contagion. They returned to the crippled city to find their families on either side all but wiped out. They may have viewed with perplexity and distress their own safety among so many dead. They may have been the objects of resentment from the poorer classes, because they could afford to flee.

London was nothing like what it had been when they left it two and a half years before. Prices were unstable, some down, some drastically up; wages had almost doubled. Laborers had an advantage they had never had before, and there was a cheeky, saucy way about them. Fashions had changed—tighter hose, more bosom. You could sense impudent loose morals in the way some swaggered and wenched and drank: the immorality of the period was to be blamed on the pestilence for fifty years to come —as the pestilence in its time was blamed on immorality. Beneath this madcap abandon, scarcely suppressed, was the grief of mourning, the dreadful memories and awful dreams, the guilt survivors feel, and terror —anything might spring the floodgates of hysteria.

Chaucer began his schooling under these unpromising circumstances. At home, turbulent emotions mixed with a curious exhilaration born of activity: his parents were busy, preoccupied—wills had to be found and executed, lawyers consulted, the business started anew. With so many dead, the daily work that kept the city going was not getting done. The city government was vainly trying to fix the cost of labor. Nevertheless, the schools were opened up again and the children herded off.

Chaucer probably started his schooling late. There were clear ideas about when the parts of a life started: boys were "infants" until seven and "children" until puberty. Infants were considered irrational creatures, selfish and unruly, as of course they are. "They think only of the present and have no thought of the future," Aristotle had informed posterity; "they always want what is bad for them. . . . They are quick to laughter and quick to tears, continually shouting, chattering, and laughing. . . . As soon as they are washed and cleaned they get dirty again, and whilst they are being washed by their mother or having their hair combed, they struggle with all their might to get away." Puberty, at fourteen, ushered in the first stage of adulthood, "adolescence." This idea that adolescence is part of adulthood is in such matters the most striking difference between the medievals and ourselves; to us, adult life begins only after adolescence. But in the Middle Ages, until adolescence began, a child was "under the yard"—subject to being beaten with a stick or boxed on the ear. At fourteen he was "free" and adult responsibility was expected of him.

It is hard to show that childhood was notably different in the Middle

Ages from what it has been at any other time. It isn't true, as some say, that medieval parents suppressed parental feelings. Infant mortality was very high, to be sure, but it was, then as now, an extravagant woe to cry out "as doth the mother whan the child shall die." There is abundant evidence of maternal feeling, in the text of Chaucer among other places —witness the towering sorrow of the patient Griselda on the supposed death of her children, or the mother in the Prioress's Tale seeking her lost son "With mother's pity in hir breast enclosed, . . . as she were half out of hir minde." Children born deformed were cared for with devotion, and while there was probably as much physical abuse of children as there is now, excessive or cruel punishment was frowned on; there are stories of abused children tenderly pitied and protected. Infants were swaddled to make their bones grow straight; the practice went on into the nineteenth century, but it had no long-term effects on personality, as some have said. Infants of well-to-do families like Chaucer's were given over to wet nurses and other servants for weaning and care, but they were not on that account in want of parental attention any more than middle-class children of later times.

Little children of merchant families were taught the alphabet from a *tabella* (a hornbook) at a quite early age—as early as three or four—and might be set to practice writing letters on wax tablets. Part of such elementary learning might be accomplished in the home before children were sent to a school. They learned to read from a primer, which would typically contain the alphabet, the Our Father, the Hail Mary, the Creed, the Ten Commandments (some of these they might already have memorized), and such items of a religious character as an explanation of the Seven Deadly Sins. At seven they reached the "age of reason" and—with characteristic medieval regard for hierarchies—graduated from infancy to childhood, at which age a boy might be sent to school. While in aristocratic families this could mean being sent away to another nobleman's castle, in mercantile London boys lived at home and went to one of the schools in the city.

From our point of view, the most important part of Chaucer's early education was something he almost certainly learned at home: French. After the Norman Conquest, French was the language of the ruling class, and for several centuries England was a bilingual nation. The original Norman French of the conquerors came to have a "colonial" character, and the resulting dialect is called Anglo-Norman. During the thirteenth century there was an influx of Frenchmen who spoke the dialect of central France, and the French spoken in England became further differentiated into a dialect best called Anglo-French. Anglo-French was the subject of much mirth and condescension in France; the English themselves felt it

to be inferior, and it and French were no longer quite mutually compre-
hensible, so some families sent their youngsters across the Channel for a
purifying. When Chaucer comments that the Prioress spoke French
"after the school of Stratford atte Bowe" and knew no "French of Paris,"
he means that she's a small-time provincial aristocrat: she speaks the
French of nice ladies who have no occasion to go abroad.

Until the middle of the fourteenth century, it would have been hard
to say what *was* the language of England. The royal family spoke French,
but from the time of Henry III (1216–1272) English kings could speak
some English; Edward III (1327–1377) is thought to be the first who
spoke it well. In the thirteenth century a good many noblemen whose
native language was French began for practical reasons to have a go at
speaking English, and under this circumstance large numbers of French
words poured into English, giving it the hybrid quality that accounts to
this day for its richness of vocabulary and its infinite suppleness of expression. At the time Chaucer was born, French was still the language of the
royal court, of the Parliament, of lawyers and the law courts, of public
records (virtually all the records of Chaucer's life are in French or Latin),
of schools, of letter writing when Latin wasn't used, and of town councils
and guilds. By 1300, even in noble families, people grew up speaking
English as their native language, but French was expected of anyone with
any pretensions to education or social status, and those who didn't learn
it growing up needed to learn it in school or with a book and a tutor. In
1332, Parliament decreed that "lords, barons, knights, and honest men
of good towns should exercise care and diligence to teach their children
the French language in order that they might be more able and better
equipped in their wards."

This continued use of French in England was not just a matter of
tradition: France was considered throughout Europe the model of the
chivalric society, and French was spoken at the courts of most European
nations—it was the international language of diplomacy and chivalry. For
merchants it was the international language of trade. But the real importance of Chaucer's knowing French lies in the fact that it was the language of the model courtly society and throughout Europe was the major
language of courtly literature. There was of course literature in Latin, and
a vernacular literature in every country, but French songs and church
music, French love lyrics, French romances and *lais* of chivalry, and
French popular or bourgeois stories (fabliaux) were known everywhere.
They were known the more in England because England had scarcely any
native literary tradition. Old English literature, known to us in works like
Beowulf, had been lost: so much had the language changed that Old

English was unreadable. And after the Norman Conquest little was written in English until late in the thirteenth century. So Chaucer's earliest *idea* of literature was French. As a young boy he heard or read some English poems on religious and chivalric subjects in alliterative verse, perhaps, or metrical romances, or songs. But in later years he ridiculed or slighted some of the native verse, and he would have been aware that much of it did in fact imitate French models.

Then, just at the time Geoffrey reached the "age of reason" and was ready to attend a London grammar school, the role of French in England changed, though by this time the chances are he spoke French fluently. There was a new spirit of nationalism in the realm. Since 1338 England had been intermittently at war with France—Chaucer's father had himself taken part in the initial battle of what we call the Hundred Years War —and the famous English victories at Crécy (1346) and Poitiers (1356) brought surges of national pride. The depopulation following the Black Death made the English-speaking working class more important in the economy; and it may have decreased the use of French in schools for want of able teachers. By 1385, John Trevisa, scholar and translator, could observe that children in grammar schools now learned their lessons in English, not French, regretting that they knew "no more French than can hir left heel." In 1362 Parliament had decreed that lawsuits be conducted in English. By the end of the century, French was still in use at court and in Parliament and some law courts, still known among nobles, still used in correspondence. But it no longer came naturally: we find a letter to the king written in 1403 signed "Escript a Hereford, en tresgraunte haste, a trois de la clocke apres noone"—and the writer is no jokester, nor no clod neither, but the Dean of Windsor. About thirty years after Chaucer died, English came to be the official written language of the Parliament and so the official language of the Chancery. The clerks of the Chancery, basing their language in part on the London dialect, were to develop a standard prose style that would then remain in general use for plain expository writing until about the time of Defoe.

These changes in English habits of reading and writing—and of speaking—were happening throughout Chaucer's life. They explain why he *thought* of literature as French but *wrote* it in English, why he translated French works into English, and why, discovering a new kind of literature in Italy, he "Frenchified" it in form and mannerisms while adapting it in his native tongue. The year Chaucer left for the Ulster household, 1356, a writer calling himself Sir John Mandeville completed an immensely popular book called *Travels*; born around the turn of the century, Mandeville was an Englishman writing in England, but he said

that he wrote in French, not Latin, because more people knew French.*
Chaucer's friend John Gower, born in 1325, wrote ballades and a long
poem in French, another long poem in Latin, and—about the time
Chaucer was starting *The Canterbury Tales*—a long poem, the *Confessio
Amantis*, in English. To Chaucer, almost twenty years younger than
Gower, it seemed natural to write in English.

Geoffrey, having reached "the age of reason" during the time of the
Black Death, could not have begun school in earnest until it was over, in
the early months of 1350, when he was at least seven. At seven a boy
ceased to wear the infant's frock and dressed as adults did, in hose and
tunic. By then he would have had makeshift schooling in an indulgent
home atmosphere, would have learned to read, write, do simple arithmetic. Merchant families were by no means book collectors, but the Chaucer
family probably owned a few books, collections of romances and such, and
reading aloud, as well as telling stories, was an evening pastime. So was
singing songs, which would be memorized; and some of these, perhaps
most of these, were in French. Learning to play an instrument was
another worthy accomplishment acquired at home.

But at school, when he finally began to attend it, there was disarray.
The plague, being the first of several during the century, proportionately
struck more older people than would be the case in the later plagues, when
the ranks of elderly survivors had already thinned out. So the number of
experienced teachers was lessened out of proportion to the number of
pupils. There was generally a decline in the quality of education in small
local schools (much less so in the universities). Traditional ways of doing
things were readily dispensed with. There was a make-do atmosphere:
lessons were construed (which is to say, Latin was translated and parsed)
not in French but in English, to save time and perhaps relieve a strain
on teachers, or on some teachers' French. This happened, so Trevisa said,
in "all the grammar schools of England," and there may have been a spirit
of adventure about it. A medieval grammar school was a dungeon of rote
learning. The day began before sunrise (students had to provide their own
candles) and went till mid-afternoon, with two two-hour recesses for
meals. The schoolmaster's rod was his chief educational tool. And things
to be learned—grammar, arithmetic, Latin—had little to do with a child's
curiosity. The school met in one large room divided by curtains into four
parts—one a chapel, the other three for beginning, middle, and advanced
pupils. Perhaps for Chaucer this chaos of the schools just after the plague
was a blessing. It may be that the hurry-up atmosphere was a stimulus he
wouldn't have had otherwise. It may be that the abler students were put

*His Anglo-French original was soon translated into English, Parisian French, and Latin,
and other languages as well.

on their own, and perhaps here lay the beginning of what we know was his life-long passion, reading. Perhaps here too he formed what was a deeper habit, of *not knowing things with security.* Reading without the reassurance of a teacher's frequent assent, or with only such reinforcement as might be given by a teacher with little experience, or little time, or too many students, he could have formed that habit of doubting, questioning, wondering, which we find in his writings, and call skepticism.

Scholars favor the Almonry School at Saint Paul's cathedral as the one Chaucer attended, deciding the matter from its proximity (it was about a three-minute walk from the Chaucer home), its prominence as the cathedral school, and its books. Founded as a school for poor boys, it was by this time for young Londoners of the middle classes. The school for younger boys was a choir school, and it is intriguing to think that Geoffrey's early schooling might have been centered in music. Across the churchyard was the grammar school he would have attended when a little older, with probably a small number of schoolmates, and it happens that we know the name of one schoolmaster there who survived the plague, William Ravenstone. He died in 1358 and left his books to the school, eighty-four items bound in forty-three volumes, quite a large library for those times. That he was "almoner," dispenser of alms, as well as master suggests the tradition, going back a century and a half, that cathedrals provide a grammar school run by a master with his own benefice, for clerks and poor scholars. An earlier teacher who held the same position, William Tolleshunt, left his books to the school in 1328—books of general information like Isidore's *Etymologies,* of grammar, sermons, logic, natural philosophy, medicine, and law. His library reflects the characteristic interests of the universities of the time, the philosophy and science of medieval scholasticism.

But Ravenstone, who, being in charge of Saint Paul's school in Chaucer's day, may after all have been Chaucer's teacher, had literary and classical interests—he could be called a "prehumanist." His books reveal interests markedly different from those encouraged at the universities. From his will one gets the impression of a cultured man of the world, accustomed to luxury—generous to his boys, if one considers his bequest of an annual small gift to each student, and concerned about standards, if one considers his proposal of fines for incompetent teaching. His library, by a rough count, included twenty-five works on grammar and fourteen on words (Latin word lists, definitions of terms, and the like, for there were no alphabetical dictionaries until later). There were twelve books of hymns or prayers, a concordance of the Bible based on subjects, books on allegories of Bible stories, on jewels and their powers, on natural philosophy, on education, and on music. The remainder of his collection, some

twenty items, had to do with literature and chiefly with the ancient
classics: three copies of a treatise on accent in poetry attributed to John
of Garland, three copies of selections from Cato and lesser-known ancient
writers, two copies of Juvenal, two of Persius, Ovid's *Metamorphoses*,
Horace's *Satires* and *Ars Poetica*, Virgil's *Georgics*, Book 12 of Statius's
Thebaid, another work by Statius (probably the *Achilleid*), Lucan, Aristotle, Claudianus, Avianus, Theodulus, and Maximian. Many of these are
named or echoed in Chaucer's works. The books were intended for the
boys—they could borrow them and keep them in the dormitory or common room (a chest was provided), and the rules of the library allowed
them to borrow some books after they left school.

The emphasis on ancient Latin poets, and on reference books needed
to read those poets, is what stands out. The other books reflect the Seven
Liberal Arts of medieval educational theory: grammar, rhetoric, and logic
(the *trivium*); arithmetic, geometry, music, and astronomy (the *quad-
rivium*). These subjects were taught in English grammar schools, and their
divisions and order represented a process, or rather two processes. In the
trivium, grammar came first because it embraced the knowledge and
practice necessary to read Latin; it was learned from *The Eight Parts of
Speech* by Donatus (any grammar book was familiarly known as a
"Donat" by English schoolboys), a book in use since the fourth century;
it was the first book printed by Gutenberg. Along with it such ancillary
works as a grammar in verse might have been used as an aid to memoriza-
tion, for example the *Magnum Doctrinale* composed by Alexander de
Villa Dei in 1199—Ravenstone's library had five copies and a gloss on it
as well. The student then began memorizing *The Distiches of Cato*, a
collection of proverbs and sayings, and studied the *Institutiones Gram-
maticae* by Priscian. Rhetoric depended on a knowledge of grammar; it
was the study of figures of speech or, more broadly, the art of persuasion,
and it was learned from works like the *Ars Rhetorica* attributed to Cicero
or, in Chaucer's time, the *Poetria Nova* by Geoffrey of Vinsauf, a treatise
in verse that Chaucer quotes in the *Troilus* and makes fun of in the Nun's
Priest's Tale. Then one proceeded to logic or dialectic, of which the great
master was Aristotle; this discipline provided the technical grounds for
argumentation and was the basis of scholastic philosophy as pursued in
the medieval universities—a discipline William Ravenstone evidently
didn't care for. A second process began with arithmetic, which was admired in the merchant class for its practical value; children learned to do
their reckonings with an abacus, and possessed at least one permanently
useful skill. The more advanced student proceeded to more intellectual
and less usable arts: geometry, music (the harmonies of music had their
base in mathematics), and astronomy, and for these subjects he used

textbooks by Boethius, Euclid, Pythagoras, and Ptolemy, all of them cited knowingly by Chaucer.

Ravenstone's library slighted many of these subjects in favor of ancient literature. Tolleshunt's library, left to the school some thirty years before, had shown entirely different interests that had since passed out of fashion. A new trend was taking shape, and if Chaucer did not imbibe the spirit of this trend at the Almonry School of Saint Paul's, he imbibed it elsewhere. We can call it humanism.

The Old Humanism and the New

What we know as "Renaissance humanism" was only just beginning in Italy during Chaucer's lifetime and, in an embryonic manner, in England and France as well. To understand these beginnings—and the understanding is important to everything that follows—we must go back two centuries to the event that historians call the Renaissance of the Twelfth Century.

This earlier renaissance was a cataclysmic change in human history, a change so great that it makes the later renaissance of the fourteenth and fifteenth centuries seem a mere aftershock, as in fact it was. Kenneth Clark, in *Civilisation,* believed that the Renaissance of the Twelfth Century was one of three times in human history (the others happened about 3000 B.C. and 600 B.C.) when mankind "made a leap forward that would have been unthinkable under ordinary evolutionary conditions." He claimed it happened throughout the whole world, though most dramatically in western Europe. What caused it, no one can say. One theory holds that the development of the horse-drawn plow, by improving crop rotation, improved nutrition especially in northern Europe, and raised the level of actual physical energy. Another theory holds that the end of the world was expected in the year 1000, and when it did not come there was a surge of interest in the secular realm. The generations following the one that lived through the millennial year—the ones that lived in the middle and later years of the eleventh century—experienced a rush of hope for the future; and indeed it was then that the change began. Whatever the cause, the effects were profound and sweeping. There was a growth of towns and of commerce. The Crusades, beginning late in the eleventh century, brought improved communication (and trade) with the Near East—and kept European noblemen from fighting among themselves. The Gothic cathedrals were begun at this time. The universities, developing from the older cathedral schools, came into being. Translation—from Greek and Arabic into Latin—brought the learning of the ancient and the Arabic-speaking worlds into European thought. There was a rise in vernacular literature, new forms of poetry, an increase in the writing of history, a revival of Roman jurisprudence. Science and philosophy were reintroduced into Western thought, and great advances in technology began to be made. Some of these advances touched the concerns of literary culture: late in the twelfth century paper was introduced into Europe, making books cheaper and more readily available than they had been when written on parchment, and in the thirteenth century eyeglasses were invented.

Interpenetrating many currents of thought in the Renaissance of the twelfth century, and probably central to them all, was a view of mankind's place in the world that the historian R. W. Southern has called "medieval humanism." At base it was a belief in the dignity of human nature and of nature itself, a belief that man was able, through reason, to understand the laws of nature and thus to understand himself as central to the universal order. Until the middle of the eleventh century, Christian thought was inhospitable to such beliefs; what dignity and order there was in the world lay in the supernatural realm—in sacraments, symbols, ritual. Fallen man was insignificant and sinful, utterly dependent on divine and supernatural aid, his reason too weakened by original sin to grasp the laws of nature, and nature itself fallen and disordered.

But the eleventh century saw a new optimism. A notable manifestation of this change took place in the monasteries. In previous times monks imagined themselves living their life in imitation of the angels; an elaborate symbolism reminded them that the scapulars they wore were comparable to angels' wings, their singing of the divine office comparable to the choirs of angels, and so on. Now, this "angelism" of monastic tradition was supplanted by an emphasis on the human Christ. The crucifix, until now the rigid, clothed figure of Christ the King—the divine Christ—became humanized into the naked suffering figure familiar to us. Monks almost in frenzy expressed their devotion to this figure of the God-man, and imagined themselves imitating Him. One monk left an account of how he climbed upon the altar to embrace in tears the corpus of Jesus on the cross. And no doubt because humanity—to them, male humanity—had taken a new position in their thought and feeling, friendship became an ideal: the monks might love one another as they loved Jesus, and this human "love of friendship" could be considered a natural step in one's progress toward the Everlasting.

Outside the monasteries, a similar development: at this time the idea of "courtly love" appeared, almost simultaneously with the cult of the Blessed Virgin (her image in art was imported from Byzantium). But for our purpose the most significant of such changes occurred in education.

Early in the twelfth century there arose among certain thinkers a convic-
tion that man can collaborate with God in restoring fallen nature. The
means by which he could do this was reason; reason could show him how
the traits of human nature—the elements and humors and vital spirits
within his microcosm—are linked to the natural forces of the universe,
the macrocosm. "Man, being the epitome of the universe, is built to
understand the universe." And the means to be used by reason in accomplishing this end were the Seven Liberal Arts—the skills of language and
numbers through which the mind could rise to an understanding of
universal causes and harmonies.

Many of the names and most of the writings of these twelfth-century
thinkers would have been unknown to Chaucer. In the first half of the
twelfth century, Abelard, Hugh of Saint Victor, William of Conches,
Thierry of Chartres, and Bernard Silvestris were the principal figures, and
none of them is ever mentioned in any of Chaucer's writings. They were
the pioneers of an intellectual movement still in its youth: their contribution was, Professor Southern writes, "partly a ground plan and partly a
castle in the air." Later generations, in the second part of the twelfth
century and in the thirteenth century, had something more specific and
disciplined to offer. On the one side, we find "medieval platonism," an
effort to put together an integrated account of the natural order using
books: Plato's *Timaeus* for cosmology, Galen (recently translated into
Latin) for physiology, Macrobius, Martianus Capella. On the other side,
we find "scholasticism," an effort to put together an integrated account
of the natural order using *logic*: the logic was that of Aristotle, long
available and there were other Aristotelian works newly translated, via
Arabic translations, into Latin. Chaucer never mentions any of the names
of these later thinkers either, even the greatest of them, Saint Thomas
Aquinas (1226–1274), though he evidently knew some of their ideas.
They succeeded in applying learning and Aristotelian logic to the innumerable paradoxes of the Bible—succeeded to the extent of producing
throughout Europe a burst of intellectual excitement that lasted nearly
two hundred years.

These achievements belong to what Southern called "scientific"
humanism, a humanism based upon the application of *scientia*, of knowledge. We will call it the Old Humanism. It had many reverberations
outside the realm of theology and philosophy. Applied to government, it
produced a concept of a human (rather than a symbolic or quasi-sacerdo-
tal) ruler, an administrating king whose powers depended upon the community; ideas of the "common profit," of the "rule of law," of a political
community and a majority opinion were its products, and Chaucer, as we
shall see, held such ideas with fervor. Applied to law, the Old Humanism

took advantage of the revival of Roman jurisprudence, as in theology it had taken advantage of the revival of Aristotle, especially the *Ethics*: trial by combat and ordeal were replaced by a legal system based on argument and testimony, rhetoric and evidence—by Chaucer's time it was everybody's favorite toy. Applied to economics, the Old Humanism did away with "medieval communism," the notion of the primitive church that all property should be held in common—an idea barely separable from feudalism, which held that all property was in the keeping of king and emperor; instead, it established a justification for private ownership. In much the same way, the ancient Christian idea that profit is sinful was displaced by the theory that all goods have a just price, that profit and risk (and therefore interest) can be justified by law and reason.

All this sounds like progress, and it was. Of its ill effects, we can see hints enough. Warfare and capital punishment were justified by the same sorts of distinctions. Nevertheless, the Old Humanism had been a great soaring and expansion of the human spirit, and its lasting accomplishments were much greater than is generally thought. From the period of its heyday, the thirteenth century, we find as symbols of its optimism and wonder those circular designs that try to encompass all parts of knowledge in a unified schema—curiosities, as they seem to us now, that equate the humors, the winds, the elements, the stars, the virtues, the "ages of man." Such schemata are still known to us in the "rose window" designs of Gothic churches, and they retain even now some of their original sentiment and power. They express the impulse that existed behind all this intellectual activity, behind the development of the universities, behind the great theological *summas,* behind the Gothic cathedrals—the impulse to codify and equate all knowledge, to express the harmony of the universe. In literature, the highest achievement of this impulse and this tradition, completed in the very last years when it still meant something, was *The Divine Comedy* of Dante Alighieri.

And then, as gradually and subtly as it had taken shape, the Old Humanism passed out of fashion. "Europe then entered a period," writes Southern, "when the optimism which had buoyed up the efforts of the previous two centuries was abruptly destroyed: the flow of new intellectual materials came to an end; the forward movement in settlement and expansion came to a halt; the area of disorder in the world was everywhere increasing; everything began to seem insecure." Why? Perhaps like all fashions it had simply outlived its time. Or perhaps it fell of its own weight, out of the complexity of its own elaboration. A harbinger of its fall occurred on the Feast of Saint Nicholas, 1273: Thomas Aquinas, while celebrating mass, experienced a vision, or if we prefer to think so the symptoms of a breakdown, and never wrote or dictated another word. "All that I have written," he said, "seems to me like so much straw compared to what I have seen and what has been revealed to me."

If the system fell of its own weight, this was because its materials were "authorities"—old books of theology and science—and by now those materials were exhausted. But it was also because the medieval mind, credulous as it was of books, always acknowledged the superiority of an unmediated experience of God. In the end, as is dramatically shown at the end of Saint Thomas's life, learning would give up its place to spirituality and reason surrender to revelation. Petrarch, writing while Chaucer was still a child, concluded his imaginary dialogue with Saint Augustine, the *Secretum,* by making the bold statement that he "had not the strength to resist that old bent for study altogether," then praying that he might "hear the Voice that calls me, . . . hear the world grow still and silent, and the winds of adversity die away."

The decline of the Old Humanism was occurring during the time of Chaucer's grandfather; by the time his father was a young man, it was already old-fashioned. If Chaucer as a young man saw manuscripts of scholastic works from the previous century, as undoubtedly he did, they would have seemed to him formidable and uninviting—the script, illegible enough in its own day, would have been the more so for changed fashions in handwriting and for its innumerable specialized abbreviations. The pages would have looked cramped, the margins groaning with commentary less legible even than the text itself, and the paper—rather than parchment—on which so many such manuscripts were written would have made it all seem the more ephemeral. The terminology of scholasticism was no more inviting; it's not surprising that in the two places where Chaucer used some pet scholastic terms ("substance" and "accident") he put them into the mouths of glib, sophistical manipulators, Pandarus and the Pardoner. The very subjects argued about—"how many angels can dance on the head of a pin," in the modern cliché—seemed foolish: people lost sight of how specific the cases were and how large the issues ("whether angels have bodies" sounds even now like a perfectly acceptable subject to argue about in an age when no one questioned the existence of angels). Nor is there anything, even in the generally somber realm of philosophical discourse, quite as lacking in humor or style or wit as scholastic philosophy. We understand now how penetrating Saint Thomas's intellect was and with how much illumination he settled so many issues that had been so widely debated; and of course scholasticism won out in the end as the official philosophical instrument of the Roman Catholic Church. But by Chaucer's time scholasticism seemed formalistic and abstract, frigidly academic, and irrelevant to the realities of life.

The Old Humanism left, however, a heritage, as most systems do when they collapse. No one could or did escape it, because it was taken for granted. The belief in the dignity of human reason and its capacity to understand the natural order would never pass out of European thought. And man's central position in the order of the universe continued to be acknowledged even after the Copernican revolution would seem to have discredited it. The reverence for "authorities" and "sentences," for what was to be found in ancient books, remained a habit of mind. And the distinctions and definitions of the Old Humanism in politics and economics—the common profit, the rule of law, the just price —were by now indispensable ideas. All this was part of the intellectual atmosphere when Chaucer was a schoolboy. That the New Humanism of his time was built upon the old explains why the change, which to us seems like a sudden collapse, was to them so slow and so unfathomable. In English universities during Chaucer's lifetime a new philosophical current, nominalism, was making the first step away from scholastic authority toward observation, experiment, skepticism: whether Chaucer knew nominalist ideas or only shared its attitudes via the temper of the times is an enigma. The New Humanism didn't yet quite exist. Men felt regret at the obsolescence of the Old Humanism, a system many of whose parts were still familiar, and they bristled at the first glimmering interest in classical antiquity even when they embraced it—as we may bristle at socialism, or as our grandfathers bristled at universal suffrage.

The Old Humanism was not to be *obsolete* until men stopped thinking about it altogether, until a new system restored coherence. The old books were still on the shelves, tons of *quodlibets* and *disputationes* had accumulated, university students were still learning about "arguments," poets were still writing allegories about the Goddess Nature. It was only *obsolescent,* and obsolescence is in our heads and hearts, not in books and objects, things that have no soul. We can understand better through a comparison, fortuitously apt, with "classicism." The classical humanism that was just coming into vogue at the end of the fourteenth century became the center of the university curriculum in the sixteenth century and remained so until the beginning of our own century; it became obsolescent for us over fifty years ago—about as many years as the Old Humanism had been obsolescent in Chaucer's time. But it is not yet obsolete. All those editions with scientific-looking textual notes, all those philological disquisitions (and dissertations) line the shelves of libraries; there are still Classics Departments in our colleges, and classical scholars, and a smattering of students who can read Latin and Greek. It is only that where once Classics was the essence of a university education, it is now a specialized eccentricity, like playing the krummhorn. We experience this obsolescence as Chaucer's age experienced the Old Humanism: we still acknowledge Classics and are fearful for its future. One aspect of obsolescence is renewal. Periodically we try to bring the classical poets alive again, in translation. We scold at how classicists killed their subject by selling out to science, making philology compete with physics, turning their backs on "values." And who is to say that in time Classics might not be restored to what some still think is its rightful place?

A part of obsolescence is nostalgia. Having rejected the Old Humanism, men missed the ideas it had refined out of existence, in the same way that we may feel the loss of Cicero and Virgil, or the loss of classical ideals and values—heroism, duty, decorum. In Chaucer's time we find poets and intellectuals talking about the common ownership of property, or the Three Estates, or the taintedness of "meed" (reward or profit) as if these ancient sentiments about an ideal Christian commonwealth, dating from before the twelfth century, had never been scrutinized or doubted. There was nostalgia, too, for the sense of coherence and order in the universe: people wanted the feeling of it without the system that had produced the feeling. The old designs, rose windows and endless knots and circles-within-circles, emblems of the complexity and interrelatedness of the universal order, never lost their magic. And there was a slight throwback to the platonistic writings that had been in vogue before Aristotle became the rage: Chaucer always names Plato with respect, mentions the platonistic Alain de Lille with reverence, is forever mindful of platonistic Boethius whose *Consolation of Philosophy* he translated—but his few references to Aristotle and scholasticism are wry.

So it was natural that, during Chaucer's lifetime, intellectuals should turn to the ancient writings. During the 1340s, when Chaucer was an infant, the famous book collector Richard de Bury, bishop of Durham, then in his last years, was completing a treatise to which he gave a Greek title, *Philobiblon*, "the love of books." He was of the generation of Chaucer's grandfather and had had some influence on Edward III's education. During the 1330s he met Petrarch at Avignon—Petrarch left a brief, respectful comment on de Bury's love of arcane learning (they talked about the legend of Ultima Thule) and his knowledge of letters. Although the catalogue of his library has been lost, Richard de Bury said in so many words that in collecting books he preferred the ancients to the moderns; he mentioned the ancient poets often, and he wrote in a decorative Latin that could be reckoned humanistic.

Such interests already existed in England, then. And William Ravenstone, master of the Almonry School at Saint Paul's, shared them.

The decade when Chaucer would have been attending Saint Paul's school, the 1350s, was the decade when Boccaccio first met Petrarch. What was growing up then was a spirit that would in time take the place of the Old Humanism. Its interest was in the learning and accomplishment of the individual, not in universal order; and it saw the source of that learning and accomplishment in an idealized image of classical antiquity derived from classical literature, "humane" (as opposed to "divine") letters. Whereas the clergy and the international world of the medieval universities had been the home of the Old Humanism, the home of the new was for about a century to be the courts of noblemen. A group of friends sharing a love of learning and cultivating individual *virtù*—moral virtue and personal virtuosity combined in a cherished mystique—was the central idea of the New Humanism. And literature, in classical Latin or, later, in Greek, and in the vernacular, was its chief inspiration. Where the Old Humanism had aspired to grasp and systematize all knowledge, the New Humanism sought through literature and art to cultivate personal style, wisdom, and decorum. The aspirations of medieval chivalry—personal virtuosity, glory, fame—were adopted by the New Humanism, whereas the Old Humanism had been clerical: the "courtier" as scholar, poet, and soldier became the new cultural ideal.

But these were just hints of trends to come; it was too soon for them to seem like the beginning of a new era. In Chaucer's younger days the English had more of a sense of decline. People looked back with nostalgia, for example, at the great fairs of earlier decades; improved commerce had made them less necessary, and though they were still held they were, or seemed, less grand and exciting. So with the great speculative financiers of earlier times—Chaucer's acquaintance Richard Lyons was the last of them. The tournaments of former times were thought to have drawn more of an international audience, and present-day ones seemed provincial by comparison. English glory in war and in court life was also a subject of nostalgia; Edward III's program was to revive it—to play on fourteenth-century nostalgia, make men think a new era of glory was being born. And they did believe this, until England's luck ran out.

Memories at Fourteen

When Geoffrey Chaucer of London, fourteen or so years of age, was sent off to be a courtier, he was sent for complex reasons having to do with status and duty and his future, not with literature. Let us contemplate his memories as he makes the journey, the most important of all his travels, as it may be, from his native London to the household of Elizabeth, countess of Ulster, and her husband, Lionel—*Prince* Lionel, for he is the king's second son.

Of purely personal memories, their roots in the past and the unconscious, we can say nothing. Even the biographer with a living subject, or the autobiographer with himself, must fumble in such matters. With Chaucer we might do as Derek Brewer has done, guess at his relations with his father and mother by applying psychoanalytic canons to our impressions of his mature personality. But such guesses are the more uncertain because Chaucer was exceptional. Perhaps he seemed an intelligent, high-strung, sensitive child. But perhaps not. Perhaps his gifts made him seem a remote, withdrawn youngster (like a hermit, he would say of himself in his thirties), inattentive or unruly. Talents such as his may be a genetic accident or, in considerable measure, a quality of character and motive: perhaps there was a tension and challenge in his childhood that kindled his talents. But it can equally be the case that his talents made him seem like a creature from another world, or that as yet his talents had gone unnoticed.

The London of his earliest childhood, even by the time of the plague when he was in Southampton, was a jumble of remembered persons, scenes, stories. His step-grandfather Richard Chaucer, his grandmother Mary (if she was still alive), his father's elder stepbrother Thomas Heron, his mother's Uncle Hamo, and Hamo's son Nicholas all died in the Black Death. He remembers, and will always remember, his grandparents' house, the old shop on Watling Street that came into the family from his grandmother's first husband, John Heron, the pepperer (spice merchant). And no doubt remembers certain old stories of the family—how, long ago, the family owned taverns in Ipswich; how his grandfather Robert Chaucer, whom men also called Robert Malyn, first came to London; how various of his relatives had fared and perished, like his Uncle Simon, Richard Chaucer's brother, who got into a street fight, its cause forgotten, and was brought home to Watling Street to die, his head bashed in with a doorbar. Remembers, too, various of the grocers his family knew, and the pepperers, among whom were a good many Italians, and, from early times, remembers hearing the sonorous, bubbling Italian spoken in nearby streets.

Chaucer had a sister of about his own age, Katherine. Such at least was the local tradition of Kent: she married a young man of a prosperous Kentish family, Simon Manning of Cudham (his wife, it was recorded in 1619, was "sister to Geoffrey Chaucer, knight, famous English poet"). From contemporary documents we know that there *was* a Simon Manning, that he did have a wife named Katherine, and that Chaucer himself signed as mainpernor for him when he was sued for debt in November 1386. Simon and Katherine were already married when Chaucer was in his early twenties, and probably not newlyweds: in 1366 Katherine inherited a property in Greenwich (Chaucer's father died early that year) and the property was sold to a business associate of Simon Manning's. If they had been married several years, they were married when Chaucer was still in his teens: and since girls of the merchant class were married before seventeen as a general rule, most often at thirteen or fourteen, Geoffrey and Katherine must have been close in age.

An only sister is a considerable memory, and the marriage of a sister close to one's age can be a major and often a threatening moment in a young man's life if he is not yet married himself. A lifetime companion is given up—given away to someone else, which is worse. And Chaucer at fourteen left her behind in London, whether married or not. In Chaucer's writings there is almost nothing about the relationship between brothers and sisters, but there is a great deal—it is one of the dominant images in his work—about women sent off from their homes, *good* women, who are then at the mercy of an unpredictable world. Derek Brewer believes this preoccupation was an expression of Chaucer's own alienation as one of the "new men" of his society, and it may be. But the feeling behind it—very intense, if one thinks of Criseyde leaving Troy, Griselda banished in her shift, Constance set adrift—might have been energized by his memory of this parting from his sister, when a kind of love, a special kind of untroubled love that he could never know again, passed out of his life forever.

For the rest of us such memories are just part of the pathos of life, the universal experience of growing up. For a poet they are like flax touched to flame.

But of course this is all supposition, based on the premise that one's life is molded by relations with parents and siblings. Going on such premises we must admit that even if we had a personal statement by Chaucer himself, much of the emotional content of his memories would have been repressed along with much of the specific detail. We are dealing, then, with something demonstrably real that by its nature leaves only circumstantial evidence. But the subject is worth guessing about; we know from his works that his great theme was love, that women fascinated him. He lived in a man's world, but not in his mind or heart. All kinds of women fascinated him—vulnerable women, women victimized, or untimely dead, or cast on their own; admirable, heroic women; famous women of history; enigmatic and complicated women, like Criseyde and the Wife of Bath; wicked women; and stereotypical women, too, sluts and frumps and hussies—all get into his works. But the vulnerable, lost, and victimized stand out: everyone remembers and is amused by the sexpot Alisoun in the Miller's Tale, but it is Criseyde or Griselda that *haunts* us. We can suppose that the feeling had its wellspring in his experience of women—in good measure his early experience. Now, while he is on his way to meet his lady the Countess Elizabeth, women are on his mind, the women in his life; and the experience of women possessed by most boys of thirteen or fourteen—which is pretty much the same—has more to do with mothers, sisters, cousins, and aunts than we like to admit when we have left them all behind.

One other memory, the most recent and in the forefront of his thoughts, is of the planning and disputation that have gone into his present journey. Whether he *wants* to be a page in a royal household, after that a squire, and perhaps eventually a knight, is not for us to know. We can think he *thinks* he wants to do this, and does not think he wants to be a vintner. Whether both his mother and father were entirely favorable to the venture, we can know no better; but they must have arranged it. There was pressure on merchant families to "take up knighthood" and become soldiers for the king; Chaucer's father in his younger years had done military duty. But there was great resistance to that pressure, for being a soldier was an expensive luxury; in wartime, when military service might be demanded, you could hire someone to go in your place. Still, the court was an avenue to position; and the avenue to the court was a military career, at least the beginnings of one. Since the plague, opportunities for advancement were greater: there was a shortage of young men to fill significant posts, and over their heads the continuing threat, almost a certainty, of further war with France.

His schoolboy memories, now that he has left school behind, are like any schoolboy's. Events in his own family sink into the background. Several years before, his father was charged with assault in the court of Common Pleas by a certain Geoffrey Darsham, who testified that John Chaucer had beaten and wounded him at Iseldon, just outside London. Even now, as he is leaving home, his father is being sued for debt. But fights and lawsuits were quotidian affairs.

Certain important events of the time, much talked about, come to the fore because all such events have to do with the royal family, and he is about to enter its service. In 1350, when Chaucer was about eight, the king organized a fleet, enlisting in the venture all the great English nobles, against the Castilian ships that had been menacing English merchant vessels, and they did battle off Winchelsea in Sussex. The king's eldest son, Edward, brother to Prince Lionel and the military hero of the age, was rescued by Henry, duke of Lancaster, "the Good Duke." John of Gaunt, age ten, was permitted to go along, for his first taste of battle. Five years later England was at war in France again, and the famous victory at Poitiers came in September 1356. Everyone knew the details. Three divisions of French met the English army. One, under the dauphin, was defeated, and one fled. The third, led by the king of France himself, King

Jean, ran into the fire of the English archers with no archers of its own to back them up; he ordered his knights to dismount, and thus vulnerable they were surrounded by armed horsemen. A French knight banished for murder and now fighting for the English as a mercenary, Sir Denys de Morbeque, pushed through the throng—according to Froissart's account—and said, "Sire, sire, surrender yourself."

The king turned to him and asked, "To whom shall I surrender myself, to whom? Where is my cousin the Prince of Wales? If I could see him, I would speak to him."

"Sire," replied Sir Denys, "he is not here; but surrender yourself to me, and I will lead you to him."

"Who are you?" asked the king.

"Sire, I am Denys de Morbeque, a knight from Artois; but I serve the king of England, because I cannot belong to France, having forfeited all I possessed there."

The king handed him his right glove and said, "I surrender myself to you."

The knights present, greedy for the ransom, crowded about, each claiming the king as his own prisoner. King Jean, recognizing the danger he was in, said to them, "Gentlemen, gentlemen, I pray you conduct me and my son in a courteous manner to my cousin the prince; and do not make such a riot about my capture, for I am so great a lord that I can make all sufficiently rich."

Then two barons appeared, pushed through the crowd by force, and ordered the unruly knights aside on pain of death; dismounting, they advanced to the king with deep bows, and conducted him peaceably to the Prince of Wales. Thus the king of France himself was taken prisoner the year before by the Black Prince—the greatest conquest in all the history of England, men said. A two-year truce, the Truce of Bordeaux, would be signed on March 23, 1357, and in May the king would be brought in ceremony as a prisoner to London. Chaucer would by then be with the Countess Elizabeth, and the records show she was in London for this season. So about midday on a spring morning he would see, and never forget, the king of France crossing London Bridge on a white charger amid the rejoicing throngs, the Prince of Wales riding by his side with ostentatious humility on a small black hackney, and proceeding slowly, proud and chivalrous, through the city to the Palace of the Savoy, John of Gaunt's residence, built by his father, where he would lead the comfortable, hospitable life that chivalry dictated for highborn prisoners. The victory was in everyone's heart and on everyone's tongue. The Englishness of a Londoner had acquired a new dimension. It was not a good year for a gifted boy entering adulthood to be learning his father's wine business when he could be learning to serve his monarch.

The Ulster Household

Chaucer's years as page and yeoman in the Ulster household were intended to acquaint him with a way of life. From one point of view the years were one long repetition of endless routines and rituals; from another, every day of those years contained important experiences, and the events of greatest importance would only stand out later. Of such events there would be two.

The first occurred at Christmas, 1357. John of Gaunt, the earl of Richmond—Lionel's younger brother, third son of the king—came to Hatfield Castle in Yorkshire with his retinue. Geoffrey Chaucer of London received 2s. 6d. for necessaries against the feasting. This was the first time Chaucer met Gaunt in circumstances where any kind of interaction was possible. Gaunt was then seventeen, Chaucer about fifteen. They were, however, very far from each other in rank, and on this account it is stretching a point to say that they were ever to be friends. The young earl of Richmond came from another world entirely, that of the royal family. The year after the plague was over, when Chaucer was first having grammar beaten into him at Saint Paul's, John of Gaunt, age ten, was permitted to go on the sea battle off Winchelsea against the Castilian ships, along with his elder brother and all the great lords of England. At fifteen he was with the English army in France, was already knighted. King Edward III had negotiated for his marriage, sending no less a figure than Henry, duke of Lancaster, the most powerful baron in England, across the Channel to treat with the count of Flanders for the hand of his daughter. This had been in 1351 when John of Gaunt was eleven, but the negotiations came to nothing and the young earl was still unmarried. So Chaucer would have known all about John of Gaunt, earl of Richmond, the king's son, but John of Gaunt would have known little at best about a certain John Chaucer and his family.

The other great event occurred on Sunday, May 19, 1359, not four months before Chaucer was sent to the wars in France. This was the marriage of John of Gaunt to Blanche, duchess of Lancaster, daughter to Henry, "the Good Duke," who had been sent eight years before to negotiate for Gaunt's marriage in Flanders. Henry had no male heirs, and Blanche shared the inheritance with her older sister, Matilda, who was married to the duke of Zealand. The Duchess Blanche was one of the

great ladies of the time and John of Gaunt loved her deeply. The marriage
was held at Reading, and the Countess Elizabeth and Lionel, Gaunt's
brother, were there, with their retinues.

For Geoffrey Chaucer this would have been a memorable occasion
even if he never saw John of Gaunt again. England was at peace, and the
marriage was celebrated with extravagance. A ruby ring worth £20, a belt
garnished with rubies, emeralds, and pearls worth £18, and numerous
other rich gifts were forthcoming for the occasion, and three days of
jousting followed the ceremony. Then the whole company proceeded to
London, where another three-day tournament was held. The legend is
that twenty-four knights wearing the arms of the City—sheriffs, aldermen, the mayor himself—entered the lists and declared they would hold
the field against all challengers for three days. When they made good their
challenge, they threw up their visors and the crowd beheld not the City
officials but the king himself with his four living sons—Edward, the Black
Prince, Lionel, John of Gaunt, and Edmund—and nineteen of the chief
barons of the realm. A London legend, probably, whose substance is just
sentiment about the association of City and Crown, or, let us say, of
merchants and the court. But only a grand occasion could produce such
a legend. Or perhaps it is true: the royal gesture might have been paving
the way for getting city funds to subsidize a coming war. Whatever the
facts, it was the great royal wedding of its time, and the Duchess Blanche
as a young bride would have lived long in the memory of any Londoner:
"so fair," Chaucer would write of her, "so fresh, so free, / So good. . . ."

2

A Young Man's World

Between the ages of about fifteen and twenty-three the mind has a special resilience—what we learn then seems to go deeper and stay longer. Chaucer spent those years learning the amenities of the noble life and the brutal arts of medieval warfare, being packed off to France with an army, running errands as an international courier, and at length attending the Inns of Court for schooling in law and business. His efforts were designed to get him a place in his world, a new kind of place made possible by changing times. He was to be one of the "new men" of the late fourteenth century, valued for their practical attainments. If he had come from a noble family, he might have been such a "new man" as the Squire in *The Canterbury Tales,* not a soldier of fortune and a crusader of the old school, like his father the Knight, but a courtier with a courtier's accomplishments and graces. If he had come from the country, he might have been like the Franklin, a landowner and "country squire," affable, public spirited, inquiring. Or, if he had gone to a university, he might well have been like the Clerk, as in part he was anyway, an enthusiast of the New Humanism; or like the Man of Law, a valued professional who holds a royal appointment and is an amateur of literary art.

Yet in those years Chaucer must have learned much that is of value to a poet, because by the end of them he was quite able to write a superior poem. Evidently he read as much poetry as he could lay hands on and find time for, and he must have written short poems or songs of his own. In the retraction he put at the end of *The Canterbury Tales* he mentions having written "many a song and many a lecherous lay" that he cannot remember, by which he means courtly songs about earthly love: not "dirty" songs, as is commonly thought, but those that from a religious point of view would tend in the direction of "lecherous"—that is, amorous—feelings, the kind of songs admired in courtly circles. In those years he also learned what the world he lived in was like, what its people were like in different walks of life and at different social levels—a most usable skill for an administrator and public official but hardly usable for a court poet, though later he turned it to account in *The Canterbury Tales*. And, while it was *au fond* a native gift, he learned how to see into people's thoughts and feelings.

The Training of a Courtier-Poet

Pages continued some sort of schooling under a chaplain or clerk, though nothing so extensive as the long hours of a grammar school. While Geoffrey must have read more works in Latin, he was done with the Seven Liberal Arts—if he had gone instead to a university he would have kept at them with a vengeance, being required even to speak Latin with his classmates. As things turned out, he was only a passable Latin scholar by the standards of the age. He read Latin works throughout his life and translated at least one Latin author, Boethius, into English, but he never *wrote* Latin as Petrarch and Boccaccio, or his friend John Gower, did. In some passages in his poems translated out of classical Latin, he has been caught out in two mistakes that an expert Latinist would not have made —oh, the shame of it—and he may not have read as widely in ancient Latin authors as he makes it sound. Getting your hands on a copy of Cicero or Livy or Juvenal was not easy in the Middle Ages, and if you borrowed a work by one of them you might find it in an anthology with ten other authors as well, whom you might then read, perhaps hurriedly, knowing you might never see them again. There were, too, *florilegia*, collections of passages from various authors; better to read a little Seneca in such a collection than none at all. Or you might find your Seneca quoted by an author, since medieval authors loved to quote old books. Chaucer, for example, mentions Seneca so often that one feels he read him extensively, but it has been shown that all the passages he cites are quoted in one work by the learned friar John of Wales. And he read other classical Latin works in Italian or French translations: he may even have used Jean de Meun's French translation of Boethius in making his own translation.

No, what literature he encountered in the Ulster household was in French, and it was polite entertainment—short lyrics meant to be sung, in set musical forms like the ballade, the roundel, or the virelay, and stories, romances, tales of knightly adventures and of love, that were read aloud. All this was a matter of performance, something to be enjoyed in the evening, talked about, sometimes discussed or debated: Which of the characters in a tale was the most truly generous or chivalrous? What was true *gentilesse*? How ought such-and-such a knight or lady to have behaved or talked in love? Chaucer may have been called on to sing such songs or read such tales aloud, and just at this time when Englishness was a matter of pride, and France the enemy, he may have been asked to translate or imitate such literature in English.

Courtly literature was not intended to be read silently or studied, like the Latin classics. It reflected and therefore taught the manners and ideals of a privileged class, and was intended for an audience who shared the mentality of that class; it performed a morale-building function. Not that Chaucer didn't read such literature silently, or didn't read works of a moral and religious character; no doubt such moral works were sometimes read aloud to an assembled company—in Lent, say. But whatever he read in this courtly milieu was chiefly what he wanted to read, not what he was told to. His interests and motives were called into play, and could have been indulged abundantly: the prince and countess, like all the great royals, were always on the move. They traveled with their retinues from one of their own castles to another, or to visit other royal residences, and one can imagine that young Geoffrey knew exactly what books were available where.

Do we have any idea what sort of songs or lays he might have written at this time? None from his youth have survived, but if we assume his best early successes were with simple forms, like the roundel, we can find an example or two from his later works that could have been written in his youth. Here for instance is a roundel on the traditional courtly theme "the lover's wound." The knight in the poem is wounded by looking into his lady's eyes, and only a kind word from her will heal his wound, otherwise he must die. (No, it is not sillier than other songs; wait.) The basic roundel form, of which there were many variants, was a refrain repeated three times with two intervening verses, and using only two rhymes. The challenge of the form was to make the repeated lines sound natural and dramatically feasible.

Your eyen two will slee° me suddenly;   *slay*
I may the beauty of hem not susteene,
So woundeth it throughout my hearte keene.°   *sharply*
    And but° your word will healen hastely   *unless*
    My hearte's wound, while that it is greene,°   *new*
Your eyen two &c.
    Upon my trouth, I say you faithfully
    That ye been of my life and death the queene;
For with my death the trouthe shall be seene.
Your eyen two &c.

It is not a great poem, but if you imagine it being sung, it might have had that moving and haunting quality that we experience when we hear good songs performed.

Or, here is a similar roundel written for Saint Valentine's day, when by tradition all birds find their mates. It occurs at the end of his poem *The Parliament of Fowls* (*fowls* meaning "birds" in Middle English, not "poultry," as it has come to mean). The lines state that the "note" (i.e., tune) was made in France, and some manuscripts have in the margin the name of a French song, "Qui bien aime a tarde oublie" ("he who loves well will not forget soon"); the tune isn't known, but Chaucer's poem can be sung to characteristic French music of the day like that of the composer and poet Machaut.

Now welcome, summer, with thy sunne softe,
That hast these winter's wedres° overshake   *weather(s)*
And driven away the longe nightes blacke.
    Saint Valentine, that art full high on-lofte°,   *above*
    Thus singen smalle fowles° for thy sake: *birds*
"Now welcome, summer, with thy sunne softe,
That hast these winter's wedres overshake."
    Well han they cause for to gladden ofte,
    Sith° each of hem recovered hath his make.°   *since / mate*
Full blissful mowe° they singe when they wake,   *may*
"Now welcome summer, with thy sunne softe,
That hast these winter's wedres overshake
And driven away the longe nightes blacke."

If anything was to be learned from such courtly songs, it was a way of life and a frame of mind. By the time he entered the king's service, Chaucer knew how the royals and the nobles of the realm led their lives and conducted their affairs, could recognize them all, knew exactly what titles each had, how each was to be addressed, how each ranked, who was married to whom, who was related to whom. And he understood what they valued and believed. Whether this means he put alongside the mercantile attitudes of his upbringing the attitudes of this more prestigious class, or adopted those attitudes in preference to his "middle class" ones, is a difficult question. To some extent he was expected to do this: the upper commercial gentry like his family wanted their children to learn how to behave like aristocrats, to "learn gentilesse." And he needed to do this if he was to be an esquire in the royal household. To the extent that he succeeded in adopting the values of the aristocracy, he gained distance on the values of his mercantile background; hence the irony with which he treats members of the merchant class in *The Canterbury Tales.* On the other hand, he never *belonged* to the aristocracy and so never had occasion to *use* their values, which gave him distance from them; hence the irony with which he treats so many of their notions. It has been said that his status as one of the "new men" of his society made him an alienated man, one who did not feel he belonged to any established segment of the society. And, so the theory goes, this alienation produced the detached, ironic, and sometimes satiric spirit of his later works, along with his comic way of referring to himself as not quite fit, say, for "courtly love."

The other side of the coin is that he really knew what was in these knights' and ladies' hearts, and wrote about it as if it were the most important thing in the world. He was able to make the timid, elegant noblewoman of ancient Troy, Criseyde, as credible as any English lady of his day, and to make Prince Troilus, the king's son, as sympathetic and human as, let us say, Lionel, duke of Clarence and earl of Ulster. Most of his works until *The Canterbury Tales* are about nobles and royals and use courtly forms. It is generally believed that they were written for a courtly audience. Reading them, you would never guess the author came from a mercantile family.

Just how Chaucer adopted the values of the nobility after continued exposure to them might be clearer if we think about a specific example: property. Back in London, a dispute over a piece of land was something to take to the law courts or fight about in the streets, something, at an extreme, to kidnap your nephew for. But such goings-on were beneath the dignity of the royals and the nobles. They *had* their land, by feudal tradition enfeoffed to them by the king and passed down through their families, or in the right of their wives or husbands, complete with titles. The income came from tenants who farmed the land, and was collected by a bailiff in charge of that land. If their right to a castle and its land were challenged, the case was brought before the king; or if challenged by force, they fought over it as armed warriors. Escalated to a national level, most medieval wars were based on just such principles. The king of

England in Chaucer's time claimed a dynastic right to land in France; he raised an army and fought in France to protect his claim, which of course the king of France denied. The "title" by which a nobleman was called (duke of Lancaster, say) was in theory identical to his "title" to Lancaster itself. Almost any war was fought over such a title, which was viewed as a matter of principle, of right, and of honor.

Now Chaucer understood all these chivalric and noble attitudes and probably believed in them. But he himself had no "title" of any kind. When his mother died about 1380, he inherited the house on Thames Street. What did he do? He sold it, something a nobleman would never have dreamed of doing with the family property. It was bought by Henry Herbury, a wealthy vintner and London citizen who had leased it from Chaucer's mother. The house carried a quitrent (rent for the land it stood on) of 60s. a year due to the convent of Cheshunt—which Henry Herbury didn't bother to pay. After two years, the prioress of Cheshunt herself—Tiffany, her name was—came in person to the house and seized Herbury's hangings and curtains, basins and ewers in lieu of the rent. There followed, of course, a trial, and Madame Tiffany, proving that she had received 60s. a year from John Chaucer, won the case. What would Chaucer have thought about such typical city behavior? Nothing, perhaps, being used to its ways from birth. But after some years in genteel surroundings, he probably considered Herbury a churl for not paying the £3 per annum that was due, as his own father had done. But he might have thought it ridiculous that the lady prioress came *herself* with some hirelings and scurried about gathering up household possessions. Moreover, it was *infra dig* for Herbury to go to court over the incident: if he had had an ounce of gentilesse he would have admitted the money was owing—he knew perfectly well it was. In a word, it was petty. And undignified. No real matter of principle, or right, or honor was involved, only money; it was not genteel to quarrel over small amounts of money, only over titles, and lands, and perhaps large amounts of money, or money with a chivalric claim behind it, like a ransom. Yet Chaucer, as we know from his writings, saw amusement and considerable irony in the relativity of such matters. If a duke could fight a battle over land he claimed as his due, if a knight or squire could make a fuss over a ransom not paid for a prisoner he had taken, why *shouldn't* Madame Tiffany have scraped together some basins and ewers from the Herbury household in lieu of her convent's rent? And who was he to scorn their "bourgeois" way of behaving when after all he himself, like any bourgeois, had sold the property for ready cash?

This equivocal way of thinking, the thought of someone who lives between two worlds—which can be viewed as a conflict of values—may have been the single most important result of Chaucer's training in the Ulster household.

Life in a Royal Household

At court, people were playing a role in history and destiny, whereas London merchants played a role only in business affairs. Grandeur and glory were in the air: the ceremonies of everyday life at court were more portentous and more pervasive than anything Geoffrey had known in London.

Not that merchant life wasn't ceremonious enough. If we could be transported into medieval London, we would observe all kinds of bowing and scraping, hear everywhere titles of address, "sir," "master," "good-wife," "madame." People dressed to reveal their status, and there were unenforceable laws to keep them from dressing above their station. Bright colors, silks, jewels, silver daggers or swords, and gold, lots of gold, were symbols of rank; the "foreigns" of the city dressed in drab colors. Rank was observed in microscopic distinctions: parishioners even went to the altar to present their offerings according to rank—the Wife of Bath, we read, was "out of all charity" if any other wife preceded her. There were ceaseless processions and ceremonies associated with saints' days and holy days; with government, guilds, wars; with baptisms, marriages, deaths, even payments of rent or renewals of contracts.

But at court it would not be an exaggeration to say that everything was ceremony. Courtly life was a series of rhythms within rhythms. It would be like putting a dozen ticking and chiming clocks in a room, each running by its own pendulum and weights and chiming at its intervals, all of them interweaving in a pleasant cacophony that becomes part of the life of that room and a matter of course for its inhabitants. Every tournament, or hunt, or meal had its prescribed form and its traditional inner workings, and each day was a rhythmic progression of these ceremonies. The rhythm of the week (fasting on Friday, feasting on the Sabbath) was part of the larger rhythm of the liturgical year, with major seasons marked by feasts—Easter, Pentecost, Christmas, Epiphany. And each year was elaborately planned in advance with progresses from one royal castle to another, where lords and ladies and their retinues would celebrate those feasts and pass those seasons. They were constantly on the move. While Chaucer was with the Ulster household, records show an Easter spent in London, Saint George's day at Windsor, Pentecost at Woodstock, Christmas at Hatfield, Epiphany at Bristol, and you could add Reading, Stratford, Campsey, Doncaster, Anglesey, Liverpool. In what records survive we get fleeting glimpses: an excursion to the Tower of London to see the lions, cushions of tapestry ordered for the tournament at Smithfield in London, new liveries or shoes at Christmas or Easter. At the end of each planned sojourn they would pack all their necessaries: clothes, spices, kitchen equipment, eating utensils, even some favored items of furniture, dismiss extra servants or undesirable ones, and move on.

Prince Lionel, third son of King Edward III, next eldest to Edward, Prince of Wales since the second son died in infancy, was eighteen or nineteen when Chaucer joined the Ulster household. Arrangements for his marriage had been made in keeping with the king's policy of securing heiresses to enrich the royal family: at the age of three he had been betrothed to the nine-year-old Elizabeth de Burgh, countess of Ulster, heir presumptive to the enormous estates of the de Burghs and the de Clares, which included nearly half the territory of strife-torn Ireland. Lionel had been born in 1338 at Antwerp—hence you may find him called "Lionel of Antwerp," for the royals had a habit of naming children for their birthplace, for example John of "Gaunt" (born in Ghent) or his son Henry of Bolingbroke (born at Bolingbroke Castle), or his nephew Richard of Bordeaux (the future Richard II, born at Bordeaux in France). Lionel may have been named after the Lion of Brabant, the name celebrating the alliance of England with the queen's native land; or after a character in the Arthurian romance *Lancelot,* in accord with the king's wish to restore to England the spirit of King Arthur's days. Whichever is true, the name was extravagant and romantic, and indicates his parents' emotions. Queen Philippa had seen her eldest son swept at birth into the role of future king, then lost her next son; Lionel became her adored favorite. As second eldest male, he was appointed Keeper of England at the age of eight, officially the regent in the absence of the king or the Prince of Wales. At nine he was invested as earl of Ulster; at twenty-four he was to be made duke of Clarence, the name derived from "Clare" but with a possible Arthurian overtone. By the autumn of 1359, when he came of age and was about to go off to war with everyone else, there was evidently an official marriage as between adults, and at this time his and the Countess Elizabeth's finances were reorganized and their two households combined, after which Geoffrey Chaucer would officially be in attendance upon the earl himself.

So the Countess Elizabeth, six years older than her husband, was about twenty-five when Chaucer became her page. She was a decade older than he—a grown woman, a great heiress. Elizabeth was an only child, an orphan from infancy, although her grandmother, the lady of Clare, lived on till 1360. Queen Philippa had taken the poor baby under her wing at a time when she herself had just lost a daughter, Blanche of the Tower, and it may be supposed that she had a compensatory maternal feeling for Elizabeth. Queen Philippa acted as guardian of the girl's huge inheritance and saw to it that she was granted an annuity of £100 when she was twenty-one until lands of comparable income came into her hands. The alliance with her favorite son must have been a satisfaction to Philippa. Elizabeth and Lionel's only child, a daughter, was not surprisingly named after the queen; little Philippa was betrothed to Edmund Mortimer, earl of March, while Chaucer was in Elizabeth's service, and he must have observed the preparations and attended the ceremony. Of Elizabeth's character there are barely indications: she was an orphan, yet she was excessively loved by the dear, kindly queen, well provided for, well married. They were a handsome couple, "in their first age"—Lionel was gallant and dashing like all the men of his family, tall like his father, truculent, spoiled—at the dawning of what promised to be a life of grace and luxury, oblivious to the fate that lay before them.

In a royal household servantlike actions performed for a prince or his lady were a gentleman's duty and an honor, not menial or demeaning but a ceremonial function, a form of recognition. While Chaucer was in the Countess Elizabeth's retinue, he belonged to a hierarchy of officials in charge of the establishment: a steward to oversee the household, under him bailiffs, a butler, a chamberlain, a keeper of the wardrobe, and so on —many of these, in a royal household, being noblemen in their own right; a chaplain, a doctor, a barber who was surgeon and dentist as well, and squadrons of cooks, bakers, laundresses, grooms, clerks, kitchen boys, chambermaids, artisans. The young *domicelle*, "damsels," were companions and personal servants to the lady of the castle, a gaggle of lesser noblewomen and daughters of gentry were her ladies-in-waiting. The pages were adolescents of similarly good families, in an apprenticeship that would lead them up in a rhythm from page to *valettus* ("yeoman"), from yeoman to squire, perhaps to knighthood. The Countess Elizabeth at this time still had her own household or *familia*, some dozen personal servants. The thing Geoffrey had to learn first was to be part of this hierarchy and be attuned to its rhythms.

Each noble household was a world unto itself. In London, you bought bread at a bake shop, fish at a fishmonger's, meat at a butcher's, but in a nobleman's castle bread was baked daily, fish stocked in fish ponds, meat acquired by hunting. There were large numbers to be fed and cared for, in an isolated, usually rural setting, a self-sufficient village. The principal concern of nobles and royals, when they were not at war or occupied with government, was to keep the world about them, and the larger world of their peers, ticking along in its appointed way.

A strange world to a boy raised in the city, but a glamorous one where the knights were the chief culture heroes of medieval society, and knightly deeds were glory itself—"glory" was a conjure word to the nobility. Because the business of the medieval knighthood was war, their amusements were mostly warlike. Hunting, for example, was a mock battle waged against the animal world; its purpose was to get game to be eaten in hall, but in a larger sense its purpose was to exercise the horses, keep up one's horsemanship, release one's competitive urges, play at exercising power. Hunting was, like everything else in the noble life, a ritual with prescribed rules and strategies. The hunt, or the "chase," culminated in the butchering of the animals caught, with certain parts of the kill fed to the dogs, the rest trussed up and brought back to the cooks. Every aspect of the chase had an elaborate lore of perennial interest to the knightly class; the author of *Sir Gawain and the Green Knight* took some forty lines to describe the butchering of the deer. Knights loved to hear about the chase, since it meant hearing about themselves, and there were handbooks that codified its rituals and lore.

This interest did not escape the attention of court poets, especially in France, where the hunt for the stag was often given a symbolical or allegorical treatment, sacred or profane. The hunter might stand for Christ or the devil seeking man's soul, or for a knight facing death in battle or pursuing some instructive purpose. The possibility most often exploited was to make the chase stand for love. The lover's pursuit and "conquest" of the lady was represented as the hunter pursuing his quarry, both pursuits having form and tacit rules (both were called a game), and both being part of the noble life, of gentilesse. Or the hunter might symbolize love itself, the stag the lady, the hounds the lady's thought, feelings, and desires, so that the kill symbolized amorous fulfillment—a feast for those allegorical hounds, a noble end for the lady, with suggestions of sexual surrender and climax. Or this allegory might be stood on its head, with the stag symbolizing the male who in a process of maturing succumbs to the power of love. In England, this allegorizing of the stag hunt received a modest literary boost from the English pun on "hart" and "heart." Precious, overwrought, artificial—all these charges may with reason be brought against this tradition. But in its best examples, like Chaucer's *Book of the Duchess*, or like the unicorn tapestries (circa 1500) now in The Cloisters Museum in New York, or its companion tapestries in the Musée de Cluny in Paris—where the stag hunt and the capture of the unicorn symbolize on one level Christ's Incarnation and man's Redemption and are on the other level an allegory of courtship and marriage —it still has the power to move us and fill us with awe. Stand before those breathtaking tapestries and you see how the hunt was, for the medieval nobility, a glorious objectification of their way of life.

If hunting was a surrogate for war, there were more explicit surrogates reserved for special occasions. Tournaments were mock battles, sometimes involving a hundred or more combatants and drawing spectators from all the knighthood of the kingdom and even from abroad. They were grand festive occasions that acted out and celebrated the preoccupations and values of the knightly class. They were accepted unhappily if at all by the church; unless, and even when, they were conducted with blunted weapons, they led to useless deaths that were technically murder. And they were an extreme form of conspicuous consumption that drew horrendous condemnations: knights and ladies "expended and laid waste their wealth" on ostentatious equipage, expensive war horses, "lewd dress," and made the tournaments, which might go on for days, occasions for every vice and corruption. While in the countess's household, Geoffrey saw tournaments—for example, the one described earlier, in 1359, to celebrate John of Gaunt's wedding, where the king and his sons are supposed to have masqueraded as London citizens and held the field against challengers. And, for a Londoner in his teens and a page in a royal household, it is safe to say he enjoyed these spectacles. Thirty and some years later, as Clerk of the King's Works, he would be assigned to supervise the building of scaffolds and the preparations for a major tournament of that time, and by then his feelings may have changed.

Or jousting, a mock hand-to-hand combat on horseback with a lance: the lances, very long and massive, were lowered into position and affixed against a support on the knight's armor, whereupon the opponents charged their horses at each other in a fury. In an actual joust or list, the object was to run your opponent through; in the sport of jousting, it was to knock him to the ground. The combatants watched each other's eyes through the slits of their helmets to see where the other was aiming; aim and timing were all, for a knight in full armor on an armored horse, his lance in position, was by this time a ponderous war machine, a missile with the firer inside it, and once set off there was nothing to do but be out of its way. Or, at home on an ordinary day, you could for amusement and practice "joust at a fan" or "quintain," charging a target affixed to a hinge, with a beam or metal plate on its opposite end, so that if you hit the target the device would swing around and hit you from behind. The object was to hit the target and maneuver your horse quickly out of the way, a good exercise in horsemanship and agility, probably rather funny to watch. Hawking and falconry were another warlike sport, akin to hunting since the trained birds were birds of prey, by nature hunters, like the knights themselves. In the lore of the period, birds of prey were thought the aristocrats or knighthood of the bird world: knights and their ladies viewed their pampered predator birds as alter egos, counterparts of themselves but with what would be for warriors an overwhelming advantage, the ability to fly.

Indoor pastimes could be warlike too. The great medieval game, inherited from the Near East and played everywhere in Europe by the thirteenth century, was chess, a series of warlike strategies with kings and queens, bishops, knights, and castles, whose object is to capture or "check" the opponent's king. Chess must have had a special luster in England just at this time, when the French king himself had been taken prisoner. Games of chance—but gambling was forbidden as sinful—were dice and "tables" (backgammon). And cards were being introduced into Europe at this time, Tarot cards and other kinds of decks, the ancestors of ours, with kings and queens and with numbered cards standing for ordinary soldiers.

Another indoor pastime: conversation. They loved discussions and hypothetical arguments about warfare or abstract questions of honor and privilege, and the favorite topic, because it was of interest to the ladies, was love—"the game of love," as it was called. Such conversation could be elaborate, ritual flirting of the kind Romeo and Juliet engage in at their first meeting, or in a group it could be the discussion of how knights and ladies of various ranks should behave to each other in imagined circumstances or suppositional cases. To speak well about love was a valued skill: "Can he well speak of Love?" asks Criseyde of her uncle, on her first glimmer of interest in her suitor Troilus.

The rhythms of a day in a fourteenth-century castle began at sunrise, when everyone in residence rose, washed hands and face, dressed, and went off to the chapel to hear mass. After mass they ate a bit of bread with a little wine or ale, or a "sop"—bread dunked or soaked in wine, sometimes cooked as a porridge. After this, Geoffrey and the other pages were probably sent to their lessons with the chaplain or his clerk, or schooled by a squire or knight in horsemanship or weaponry. In the morning the whole castle was bustling with routine activity—laundering, cleaning, cooking—while the knights hunted and the ladies embroidered, sewed, and chatted. Dinner was served in the late morning—a large, ceremonious midday meal, with music and entertainment. In the afternoon the pages were allowed recreation of some kind. Supper was served around 5:00 P.M. and was a lighter meal—usually a main dish of meat or fish, cooked vegetables, cheese, and wine, ale, or cider. Wine was the more prestigious, because more expensive, beverage: it was imported from France or Spain in barrels and served in pitchers, and it was drunk new, not aged. They hadn't learned to cork bottles in the Middle Ages, so there were no vintages: any wine over a year old was vinegar. Nevertheless, there were distinctions to be made in flavor and strength and quality, and such distinctions must have been made with acumen by a vintner's son. One gets the impression that a good bit was drunk in the evening; there are very funny accounts of household and guests drunkenly saying goodnight and stumbling off to bed. Sometimes a little food was taken at bedtime, or even a late supper, and a nightcap of spiced wine, the *voidee,* was served in the lord's chamber before the curtains were drawn for privacy about his bed and those who didn't belong there were dismissed ("voided") from the room. Prayers, of course, punctuated the day—before meals and after, on rising, on retiring.

Pages were expected to make themselves useful and were assigned to help in various ways designed to teach them the workings of the noble life. Otherwise they were expected to keep out of the way and behave themselves, and courtesy books of the period suggest that they were as unruly as any adolescents, if one can judge from the *don'ts.* Don't quarrel, don't point, don't whisper, don't speak improperly of women, don't tell lies, don't scratch or make faces or yawn, don't pick your nose or blow it too loud, spit too far, belch, "fire your rear guns," pick your teeth, gape, pout. One might think such books were really meant for children, and some were; remember, noblemen's children were sent to a castle for training sometimes as seven-year-olds. But the most complete, John Russell's *Book of Nurture,* written (in verse) in the mid-fifteenth century but based on earlier works, is a complete manual for the running of a noble household, addressed to a hypothetical young adult who wants to be a "butler, . . . panter, or chamberlain."

The precepts in such courtesy books were ideals to be learned by youngsters, perhaps youngsters who needed to elevate their social class. Some of the don'ts (don't blow your nose on your napkin, don't wipe your teeth on the tablecloth) are fairly ludicrous and might have been included as jokes; one can imagine adolescents giggling at them, but surely one cannot imagine a youngster from a merchant gentleman's family wiping his teeth on the tablecloth? The do's were to stand up straight, look directly into the face of anyone who speaks to you, speak cheerfully, keep your opinions to yourself, obey, keep promises, trust your friends and be loyal to them, laugh discreetly, be silent among the ladies, and so on. Not that the nobles themselves always behaved so. They were given to outbursts of temper and harsh words, and their sexual mores were loose; the king himself had a mistress, as did his sons, and little effort was made to keep this quiet. But the young had to learn how nobility were *supposed* to act.

In such courtesy books almost nothing is said of sex. The young ladies in the castle were closely supervised and the young gentlemen kept at a distance. Not that there weren't prostitutes, and not that it wasn't fair

game to tumble a serving wench. But there was little privacy to be had
in a medieval castle, except outdoors. And puberty came later then, so
precociousness in matters of sex is not to be expected. Boys might sleep
several to a bed, but about sexual play or masturbation discreet silence
seems to prevail in books about conduct. Repression was likely a concomitant to an upper-class education then as now, for discipline and control
were above all being inculcated.

The larger rhythm of any day in a medieval castle was marked off
by the two main meals. For Geoffrey these occasions were different from
anything he had known in London. The whole household dined in the
castle hall. Tables were set up on trestles for each meal and dismantled
after, the fixed table in a permanent setting (*table dormant*) being at this
time a showy new fashion. They were spread with white cloths and set
with dishes and goblets of pewter or silver-gilt or gold, a silver or gold
spoon at each place—the fork would not show up in England for another
century. Knives, sharp ones for cutting meat, usually belonged to the
guests themselves, who cleaned them up on a piece of bread and put them
away at the end of the meal; otherwise one knife was provided for each
two people. Salt was placed in a fancy dish, often shaped like a boat, near
the lord, and small containers of spices—mustard, brown sugar, sweet
basil—were placed at intervals along the table. Setting the table was a
ritual in its own right, and Geoffrey and his fellow pages would have been
taught to lay the cloth and set the places. People entered, were seated,
and left by rank, with the lord, his family and guests at a head table on
a dais, others at side tables, all disposed according to a complex order of
precedence that the pages had to learn. John Russell's explanation begins
"The Pope hath no peer" and goes on through emperor, king, cardinal,
prince, archbishop, duke, and so on down to merchants (who sit with
squires), doctors, aldermen, and masters of crafts.

There are few aspects of medieval life so well documented as eating.
From courtesy books, household manuals, and recipe books, from paintings and illustrations and literary descriptions we get a vivid picture of
feasts and regular meals, the cuisine, the company. Before and after each
meal, and between courses, a servant called the ewerer ceremoniously
pours warm scented water over each guest's hands into a basin, offering
a towel. He pours from a ewer or aquamanile of gilt or bronze or silver,
or of enamel, sometimes handsomely crafted as an animal's head with the
water spouting from the mouth. Grace is said at the beginning and end
of the meal. While the highest in rank dine singly, most places are set in
pairs, each diner sharing dishes with a partner, the man serving the lady,
or the lesser in rank or age serving his or her superior or elder. Portions
are taken from a bowl and placed on a "trencher," a good-sized round slice

of bread cut, and sometime squared off, from loaves three or four days old (but the king's trenchers are of fresh bread); the trenchers soak up the juices and are then eaten, or given as alms to the poor, or used for sops next morning.

Food is served to a serving cupboard or *aumbry*, from there to a "surveying board" for finishing touches. A battalion of servers is overseen by specialized officials, the Sewer in charge of the dishes, the Panter in charge of trenchers and bread, the Butler (the word is from "bottler") in charge of wines and ales; these, in a prince's household, are not "servants" but persons of rank. The carving of a roast is a ceremony by itself, and the carver is a knight or squire of the lord's family who holds the knife with thumb and two fingers and is master of numerous operations, each with its own name, performed with an armory of special knives and tools. Food is eaten, at this time and on this level of society, with great *delicatesse*. Meat is cut into pieces with a knife and conveyed to the mouth with fingers; one wipes one's lips usually on a large napkin worn over a shoulder (but many paintings do not show napkins at all); one does not put so much in his mouth that he cannot talk. Such at least are the counsels of etiquette books. Chaucer's Prioress, who lets no grease float onto the surface of her wine when she drinks, never gets sauce on her fingers when she dips her food in it, reaches for things delicately and spills nothing from lips or fingers, obeys all the rules to the letter—more so, probably, than those who were secure in their gentilesse.

John Russell describes a dinner for a fish day consisting of four courses:

First Course: *musclade* of minnows, salmon belly, eels, a potage of porpoise and peas, baked herring sprinkled with sugar, a fish such as pike, lamprey, or sole, roasted porpoise, baked lamprey, a *leche* (a jellied dish of meat, eggs, fruit, and spices), and a fritter.

Second Course: dates in comfit, some fish like salmon in a syrup, three or four more fish dishes, another *leche*, and a fritter.

Third Course: cream of almond *jardine*, melmeny (a stewed dish, sweet-and-sour), a fresh sturgeon, bream, or perch in jelly, shrimps and other small fish, a "*leche* fritter," and a tansy (fruit pudding).

Fourth Course: baked apples and pears with sugar candy, ginger *columbine*, wafers, and hipocras (warm spiced wine).

When he writes "or," it is not clear in all cases whether he means that both dishes are to be served or only one. If both, the courses contain as many as fifteen items. It is clear that sampling small portions of many dishes was the essence of such dining: one chose from among them, not necessarily tasting all. The food was a feast for the eye as much as for the palate, for it was handsomely garnished, arranged, and colored with food colorings, gold and red and green. Illusion was part of the pleasure, illusion and surprise: a pheasant might be served with its own feathers covering it as if it were alive, candied fruit might be growing on a little silver tree, dishes might be made to look like castles or animals, a silver fountain might be spouting wine.

This particular meal must have gone on a very long time and been a special occasion, for each course or "service" was a separate event ending with a "subtlety." Subtleties were devices or sculptures made of paper cut out or shaped while wet, or of *papier-mâché*, or sugar, or marzipan, and were sometimes eaten. One was brought out for display at the end of each course, and they had a theme. With the fish meal just described, the first course ended with a subtlety of *Sanguineus*, a young, gallant man, piping and singing, standing on a cloud and representing springtime; the second was a warlike man named Estas, or "summer," rough, angry, standing in a fire; the third, named Harvest, was a man holding a sickle, wrapped in a gown and looking weary, standing in a river; and the fourth was Winter, gray-haired and feeble, sitting on a stone, with a heavy countenance. These, it is explained, represent the Ages of Man under the guise of the four humors and the four seasons: youth is sanguine and like springtime, maturity choleric and hot like summer, the "third age" phlegmatic and sluggish like autumn, and the fourth melancholy like winter. Each has a Latin verse inscribed on it, a rhyming couplet in lame meter, naming conventional characteristics of each age (youth is amorous, laughing, singing). There were similar sequences of decorations on religious seasonal themes, and it sounds as if such contrivances were sometimes stored and used again "with other sights of great novelty," but they were by nature ephemeral art that left no traces. They were conversation pieces—in this instance a simple-minded allegory about the passing of time, harmlessly didactic, not without a religious moral for those who cared to find one, but at base a curiosity to ooh and ah over. Between courses, too, there were "interludes" of music or entertainment, and courses were announced with trumpet fanfares. Not that every meal in a medieval castle was as elaborate as this, nor does this account by John Russell in the mid-fifteenth century tell exactly what the entertainment for a special occasion would have been like back in Chaucer's time; but we know from other documents, like the Parson's dour scolding at the end of *The Canterbury Tales*, that there *was* "excess of divers meats and drinks, and . . . dish meats burning with wild fire, and painted and castled with paper," along with "too great preciousness of vessell" and "curiosity of minstralcy."

What is most relevant for our purpose is the entertainment held during and after such dinners and suppers, and in the evening, of which unfortunately less is known than of the food. We do have a good sense of music at this time, know what a rebec sounds like, a krummhorn, a tambour, a portable organ (with two small weighted bellows lifted alternately, that blow a steady stream of air as they fall), recorders, flutes, trumpets. We know songs of the period in Latin, French, and English that would, or could, have been sung in an English castle, and for some we have melodies preserved in the musical notation of the age. Who played the instruments? At court, professional musicians, no doubt, yet playing an instrument was an admired accomplishment. Nicholas in the Miller's Tale, a well-to-do student at Oxford with his own income and the unusual luxury of a private room rented from a local burgher, can play a psaltery, a harplike stringed instrument; Absolon, the local parish clerk, somewhat of a bumpkin despite his airs, plays the less prestigious guitar; the Miller plays the low-class bagpipe, and it sounds as if the Squire in the General Prologue plays the upper-class flute. All of them can sing. In France, center of chivalry, knights themselves composed and sang songs of love. So it seems likely that the young pages and damsels of the Ulster household played and sang. If Chaucer had an inclination to compose songs or lays this early, he was in an environment that would have encouraged it.

Reading aloud was another courtly entertainment. A noble or royal household was, among other things, a veritable museum of possessions on display, and books—handsomely copied books, on fine vellum with gorgeous illuminations and paintings, bound in supple leather and fitted with crafted metal clasps to hold them shut—were among such objects of ostentation. Less expensive books were borrowed by courtiers (and sometimes pilfered), but large, well-made books were to be "placed on a high desk and read aloud by a standing lector." If we can judge from a famous passage in Chaucer's *Troilus* (2: 81–84), ladies read aloud to each other, and there is abundant evidence that oral reading after dinner (and sometimes before) was a medieval pastime. Before the printing press, reading took more time and effort: every scribe's handwriting required an adjustment, there were numerous abbreviations, light was poor, eyeglasses inefficient. This meant that *all* reading was done aloud or at least with moving lips. Making such an effort when someone could make it *for* you was as pointless as, well, typing one's own letters. Yes, nobles could read; but why should they? Froissart reports that he read his poem *Meliador* aloud in installments before the count of Foix (who commanded silence, boasts the author). And in a very handsome copy of Chaucer's *Troilus*, made shortly after the poet's death, a stunning painted frontispiece shows a courtier at a lectern before a court, in a garden. It is widely assumed the courtier is Chaucer and the court Richard II's, but even if it is merely a stylized drawing, it tells us something—as does the poem itself, addressed often to an audience—about the social role of literature in Chaucer's England.

Of entertainments other than song and story, there were acrobats and jugglers, dwarfs, jesters, and illusionists—magicians or sleight-of-hand artists, like the famous Englishman, Colle, whom Chaucer describes in *The House of Fame* as doing an amazing trick, concealing a windmill under a walnut shell! There were, moreover, mimes, puppet shows, short secular plays. But you never hear of a young squire or damsel doing stunts of this sort—it wouldn't have been genteel. For a description of late-fourteenth-century polite accomplishments, it's traditional to cite the passage on the Squire in the General Prologue: singing, playing the flute, making up both the music and the words of songs, dancing, "portraying" (drawing, probably), and writing. The Squire is a delightful youngster of about twenty, with curly hair and embroidered fashionable clothes, and it isn't hard to see why some find in the passage a touch of nostalgia on Chaucer's part for his own youth; but the Squire is the son of a knight and a soldier, not of a merchant. Like the Squire, though, Chaucer was able to make up the words of songs, and we can be virtually certain that his talents were nurtured, possibly discovered in the Ulster household. The matter is important because everything he wrote until *The Canterbury Tales* was written for such a milieu, a royal household that enjoyed, among other entertainments, hearing songs sung and stories read aloud, preferably after dinner.

The Medieval World Picture

Here we must ask a virtually impossible question: What was going on in young Geoffrey's mind at this time in his life? With our own contemporaries such a question narrows to personal details—friends, love affairs, studies, avocations, escapades. For the medievals, we have little evidence of such particulars. Letters, journals, and the like were rarely written and few would have survived anyway. But a young man of the fourteenth century, raised in mercantile London and then plunged at fourteen into the shimmering world of his nation's aristocracy, would have had his thoughts about his world radically altered. And this part of his mind we can see, in part.

Geoffrey came to the Ulster household fresh from his schooling, in his head a storehouse of lore and rote learning organized into structures. Memory itself was different when books were scarce and paper expensive, before there were alphabetical dictionaries or index cards: educated people practiced an "art of memory" by organizing materials into images visualized in *places*—for example, on the doors or windows or columns of a remembered building. It was a way of training the memory (expressions such as "in the first place" are fossils of it), and through the visual arts it became more generally a habit of mind. So a fourteen-year-old boy had a highly visual picture of the universal order. Above his head was heaven; under his feet, inside the round unmoving earth, was hell. Beneath heaven swirled the seven planets, creating the heavenly harmony described by Boethius, in the variable cycles and epicycles described by Ptolemy—at their outer edge the *primum mobile*, which sets the whole in motion, next under it the sphere of the fixed stars, below this the planets within concentric spheres, Saturn, Jupiter, Mars, the Sun, Venus, Mercury, and, closest to Earth, the inconstant Moon, the realm of time and change. The positions of these heavenly bodies at each person's birth, then day by day and hour by hour throughout his life, had an influence decipherable through the science of astrology. In heaven and throughout creation were the seven choirs of angels, named in Holy Scriptures, who might appear, visible or invisible, in the lives of mortals; in heaven, too, gathered in the sight of God, was the communion of saints, each known to us through the legend of his or her holy deeds, to whom we can pray for intercession; in hell were the souls of the damned, and the devils (who might appear among humans at any time to tempt us); in purgatory, souls awaiting the Last Judgment.

Man was in the center, a bone of contention between the opposing forces of heaven and hell. On the scale of creatures he was halfway between the heavenly powers and inanimate matter. The fifteenth-century travel writer Felix Fabri, marveling at a workman who repaired his ship under water, wrote, "how he could strike with his hammer there, and how he could remain so long in the salt water, I cannot understand. But this much I know, that the human mind has dominion over fire and water, even as the stars have dominion over the human mind." Man was the microcosm, with interior harmonies of function in tune with the greater harmony of the universe, the macrocosm. But seen another way man was like a fly in the wanton palm of providence, confronting the opposing forces of order and disorder.

On the side of order, man was subject to nature, "the Goddess Natura"—an active, normative principle with laws man must obey: procreation and self-preservation were parts of natural law, for example, so that sodomy or suicide was "against nature" as well as against the revealed law of Scripture. Marriage—or better, mating—was part of nature's way, and doctors said that rest was nature's cure.

But on the side of disorder, man was subject to fortune, "the Goddess Fortuna," pictured turning a wheel on which men climb, rise, and then fall. Fortune was really a figure of blind chance—from man's point of view random, unpredictable, meaningless, but from God's point of view part of a master plan that He sees as in a timeless moment. Fortune meant that man could not count on any outcome in the corrupted currents of this world, but that every chance occurrence, when it happened, was *meant to be.* If you wanted fortune's gifts—wealth, power, pleasure—you might or might not get them; if you got them, they might be taken away from you. There was no certainty or justice in it; it was the way things were, and the only lesson in it was that to escape Fortune, you did not climb upon her wheel.

Such "goddesses" were not official doctrine, but they were perfectly compatible with Christianity when understood as metaphors. Fortune, for example, was best explained by Boethius in *The Consolation of Philosophy*—of *philosophy,* not theology: theology was concerned with abstract dogma, and philosophy was merely its handmaiden. The great debates that kept Christianity intellectually alive were unsolvable matters of faith, like the freedom of the will. If man's will is free, how can it be said that God governs all things? Religion's answer is that it is one of the mysteries of dogma, to be accepted on faith. Boethius's answer, using earthly philosophy, is that in governing all things God made man's freedom—*inner* freedom—part of His universal plan: God of course knows in advance every choice everyone will ever make, since He sees all in a timeless present, but His foreknowledge does not *make* us choose as we do. And this reasoning was a comfort for over a thousand years. It meant that freedom of the will operates only in our inner, moral worlds; if the ceiling falls on my head, this is the result of nature, fortune, the stars, or other influences that are part of God's universal plan, and my freedom is to accept the necessity of the ceiling's collapse with patience, knowing that all is for the best in the end. "Patience makes virtue of necessity" was their maxim. Thus much from philosophy; from religion I know I can hedge my bets by praying for safety, beseeching the patron saint of ceilings to pray for me, going on a pilgrimage and venerating a saint's relics, or getting some of the powerful holy water from his shrine, doing penance for my sins, getting indulgences, doing good works like visiting the sick or giving alms to the poor or to the church.

Medieval religion gravitated to these opposing impulses. On the one side, religious practices like receiving the sacraments, praying, venerating relics, going on pilgrimages. On the other side, "taking things philosophically," with resignation, self-abnegation, and contempt for the transitory world. This makes the freedom of the will seem of small moment, no doubt, and on the whole the medievals *were* very necessitarian in their thinking. But we should not forget that they envisaged free will as something in operation every moment of their lives, not just when ceilings fall. Free will, you might say, dogged their heels. Was it a sin of gluttony to salivate over a beefsteak? No, because salivation was involuntary. But yes, because you can control salivation by not looking or sniffing at your beefsteak with lusting thoughts, by eating it in a rational way (natural law requires that we feed our bodies) without taking an excess of pleasure that might tempt you to further sensual indulgence. Saint Thomas Aquinas said that it was a sin of omission when reason did not exert control over the "movements of sense" in any area where reason can hold sway. Freedom of the will, seen that way, is a relentless responsibility—one could say a burden.

"Blind beasts" lacked both reason and free will, and followed Nature's laws by instinct. They had no immortal souls, knew neither right nor wrong, were not subject to original sin. For of course original sin was the outcome of man's original freedom. Adam and Eve were created with the ability to follow God's commandments, but in their freedom they allowed themselves to be tempted by the devil; rather, Eve was tempted by the devil, Adam by Eve. The woman was the weaker sex by her creation, for God made her of Adam's rib—Adam's *crooked* rib in medieval lore—and her reaction to the serpent's suggestion was "delight"; Adam's sin was greater because he gave rational "consent."

The result of the Fall of Man was a punishment visited on all creation. Nature was corrupted. The planets now turned at different speeds, seasons changed, the very weather was capricious, beasts became hostile. The human body was punished by sickness and death, the will by concupiscence, the reason by ignorance. Adam and Eve were expelled from paradise, commanded to go forth and multiply; she would bear children in pain, and their progeny would grow weaker, the race would decline, and the world "grow old."

While evil came into the world in the Garden of Eden, it had come into the *universe* long before, when the angel Lucifer and his followers waged war in heaven against the Almighty and were cast into hell. A superior race of extraterrestrials, the angels, thus produced a fallen race superior to man in powers, but malevolent and damned. They—Satan, as he was now called, and his henchmen—wrought the first temptation of the first man and woman, and could appear on earth at any time in any guise: in the Friar's Tale an agreeable yeoman dressed in green and coming from the north (both traits of the devil in medieval lore) meets up with a Summoner and announces, after friendly overtures, "I am a fiend, my dwelling is in hell" (the evil Summoner, as the Friar maliciously depicts him, answers with nonchalance, "Ah, what say ye"). And there were creatures as well who might or might not be devils—incubi (who impregnate women in their sleep, producing de- mons), succubi (comparable female spirits), ghosts, elves, hags, giants, nymphs, good and bad fairies, goblins; Hamlet, on seeing his father's ghost, asks if he is "spirit of health or goblin damned." These creatures were part of popular belief, not church doctrine, but the two were rarely in conflict. Such creatures lived in dark and hidden places and were only sometimes glimpsed by mortals—some of them unfriendly hags and de- mons, some "little people," some with human shapes. Who were they? Perhaps a separate rational species falling between men and angels; or angels who had been, so to speak, celestial fence-sitters who neither joined Lucifer nor sided with God, and who were not damned but ex- iled; or ghosts of dead souls; or souls not truly dead but taken away by fairies; or descendants of Cain; or freaks and sports of nature resulting from the Fall; or spirits of the four elements—earth, water, fire, air; or, of course, devils. Or witches, yes; but the great age of witchcraft was not to come until the Renaissance.

When Chaucer arrived at the Countess Elizabeth's door, he already knew all this, and nothing he learned in her retinue altered any of it. For it was the lore of the age, as strong at court as anywhere. Perhaps there were superstitions among the peasantry that would have been scorned at court; the carpenter in the Miller's Tale, seeing his student lodger in a trance, recites a meaningless charm,

> For nightes very, the white *Pater-noster*!
> Where wentest thou, Saint Peter's soster?

—and evidently we're supposed to think it funny. But the traditions of courtly culture were often as meaningless. Think of heraldry, with its arcane symbolism and abstruse terminology, its boastful mottoes and cherished concepts. Or the old feudal ceremonies of coronation or hom- age admixed with pagan symbols and ritual practices whose meaning was shrouded in history. The superstitious carpenter in the Miller's Tale, or the Miller himself, might have thought it no less funny that the Scrope and Grosvenor families spent five years at trial in the Westminster refec- tory before the king and the High Court of Chivalry, with Chaucer himself giving testimony, over which one had the right to bear a particular coat of arms.

But while such lore would have been unaltered by the Ulster household, the traditions and mentality of the court, which Chaucer learned there, would have altered his sense of history and of conduct.

History looked, in the Middle Ages, like a straight line divided into parts, with a beginning and an end. To us, time goes into an infinite past and forward into an infinite future; it is the modern habit to see time itself as a process—the notion began in the eighteenth century, when people commenced to number years backward from the birth of Christ. To the medievals, time began with the seven days of Creation and ended with Doomsday, and the past consisted of stages marked off by great events. These stages of history were not a progress or evolution, as we would see them, or even a process; they were cycles, mere repetitions, and anything like a process in them was a process of decline.

The earliest period of history was the "Golden Age" or the "Former Age" (Chaucer wrote a short poem about it, based on a passage in Boethius's *Consolation*): it was the period before the Fall when Adam and Eve tilled the primordial garden and the age of their first descendants, cast upon fallen and hostile nature but still retaining some of their primeval grandeur. In that Golden Age, men were larger and stronger, and lived longer. In their primeval simplicity, they led, in one view, a "soft" existence, eating natural food, wearing simple clothing, needing little; in another view they led a "hard" existence, facing the elements and the wilderness, surviving by ingenuity. The ingenuity required of them became the civilized arts, which helped, as Milton put it, to repair the ruins of the Fall.

The two great events of history were the Fall and the Redemption. They divided the past into two parts: from the Fall to the Coming of Christ, and from Christ to Doomsday. The Redemption, that pivotal moment in history when God became man to offer fallen men salvation, gave meaning not just to what came after but to what had gone before. All the history contained in the Old Testament had new meaning when seen in the light of the New Testament, for the Coming of Christ fulfilled all the laws and prophecies of the Old Testament. Where the New Testament told a literal truth and gave a single teaching, the Old Testament consisted of types and shadows. Its literal, true history had a deeper figurative meaning, called "typological" or "allegorical"; Noah's flood, which really happened, was itself a sign or "type" of the washing away of sins in Baptism—and also a sign of the destruction of the world on the Day of Judgment. So, the manna from Heaven in Exodus, chapter 16, was a type of the Holy Eucharist, and the Song of Songs—a marriage hymn, quite explicit about the physical side of marriage—was an allegory of the mystical marriage between Christ and His church.

The Old Testament law of Moses was a true law, the law of the "old dispensation." Before the law of Moses, men followed the law of nature and the "God of Nature." So there was a notion of *three* ages: the Age of Nature (or the "Age Before the Law"), the Age of Law, and the Age of Grace. Beyond this division, there was a division into *seven* ages, corresponding to the seven days of Creation in Genesis, chapter 1. The first age was that of Adam, the second of Noah, the third of Abraham, the fourth of Moses, and the fifth of David; the sixth age was that of the Coming of Christ, and it would continue until the Second Coming, which would be the Seventh Age of the World, comparable to the sabbath of the week of Creation, when the world would be subsumed into the timeless universe.

Throughout history a series of civilizations had risen, flourished, and fallen—like the cities of the Old Testament (Babylon, Jericho) or the cities of the ancient world (Thebes, Athens, Troy), each new civilization rising from the ashes of a dead one. When Troy fell, Aeneas escaped and founded Rome, and Aeneas's descendants spread out over Europe, settling various parts that succeeded Rome—Ticius to Tuscany, Longabard to Lombardy, Felix Brutus across the English Channel to England. On this account London was known in Chaucer's time as "new Troy" and England as "Brutus' Albion"—Albion, from Latin *alba*, "white," referring to the white cliffs of Dover as the first sight of England seen by a Continental discoverer. The history of civilization, viewed this way, was a history of failures: what had happened to Thebes and Troy was to happen to Rome, and sooner or later to any civilization. The process was not cumulative, only repetitious. And nothing was to be learned from it except that earthly life is unstable.

Alongside this myth of the past was a body of legend. Legends were authentic bits of history, and for Christianity this meant chiefly the lives of saints, plus apocryphal stories like the notion that Noah's ark came to rest on Mountain Ararat or that Judas Iscariot committed suicide. Each saint's life was a discrete story representing some aspect of Christian heroism or martyrdom or self-abnegation, and, given the subject matter, each saint's life taught a lesson. Nevertheless, the legends had interest for their own sake. Each was a unique instance of the extreme case, often with a striking visual image that identified the saint. Telling stories of saints or reading them aloud seems to us drab entertainment, but the way painters treated these themes shows even now their inherent excitement: Saint Veronica holding her veil with the image of Christ's face, Saint Catherine immolated on her wheel, Saint Sebastian naked, pierced with arrows—each is a vivid, dramatic, often violent episode, and each death came about as a result of a heroic moral choice made under unique circumstances, all of it vibrant with horror, drama, and an ultimate glory.

If there were two cultures in medieval society, the courtly one was itself imbued with and inseparable from Christian culture, as to a lesser extent Christian culture, with its own nobility and property and its great war, the Crusades, was imbued with courtly ideas. But the international courtly culture of the late Middle Ages had a cultural ideal and a historical mythology of its own—not a whole myth of universal history, as Christianity had, but a mythology about Love (of which more later) and mythic notions of chivalrous conduct, of the ideal ruler, knight, lady. Where part of the Christian myth involved the Ten Commandments, the Cardinal Virtues, the Seven Deadly Sins—lists of qualities to be cultivated or eschewed—courtly culture developed, after the twelfth century, a comparable set of mythic concepts. The great popularity of the *Roman de la Rose,* some of which Chaucer translated, was largely owing to its way of codifying and allegorizing them. Chaucer's famous description of the Knight in *The Canterbury Tales,* that he "loved chivalry, / Trouth and honour, freedom and courteisye," conjures powerful notions—mystiques, as they actually are—that were as potent in courtly culture as "faith, hope, and charity" were in Christian culture.

The knight who followed the ideal of courtly culture possessed *chivalry,* etymologically "horsemanship," which meant the whole body of conduct proper to a male member of a knightly milieu. Its components can be defined by us in cold, practical ways. "Prowess" was your ability to subdue a foe in battle. "Truth" (better, "troth") was your ability to make good all vows and obligations owed in a hierarchical world—to God, to your overlord, to all oaths you had made, to your lady, to your vassals. "Honor" was honorable conduct, especially with allies, foes, prisoners, or those with whom you had a bond or obligation. "Freedom" was generosity, the giving of appropriate gifts and the willingness to relinquish possession or privilege out of fairness or bounty or charity. Courtesy was "courtliness," good manners. "Glory" was the fame of a knight and his reputation or "good name," the just reward of noble deeds, a measure of immortality in the stream of successive human lives; to love glory for its own sake was a sin of "vainglory," but to fight for glory was part of chivalry. (Knights fought for booty too, and intellectuals could squeeze out a justification: in a just war, one's opponents were the wicked and the wicked didn't have the right to own property. But booty never gets included with magic words like honor and glory; since greed was so indisputably present the less said of it the better.) In defining such terms in this practical spirit we mustn't forget that they were potent honorifics, as "gentlemanliness" or "bravery" or "responsibility" were among us a generation ago, or as "integrity" or "autonomy" might be today—words too charged with feeling to be defined in specifics. When we talk about such words, we find ourselves in heated, convoluted discussions that come to no conclusion: we define them best by telling stories.

As Christian culture had a body of legend, bits of true history, illustrative and celebratory, courtly culture had its legends too, old stories of fabled nobility and heroism, of great battles and leaders. Since old books inspired so much reverence in the medievals, legend (from Latin *legenda*, "things to be read") constituted legitimate, true history. And this legendary history of the world, seen from the vantage point of courtly culture, was much closer to history as we conceive it in modern times: a history of nations and leaders, wars, and decisive battles. There were legends of such civilizations as Troy or Rome, Antioch in the time of Cleopatra, France in the time of Charlemagne, England in the days of King Arthur. And legends of such leaders as the Nine Worthies: three Jews (Joshua, David, and Judas Maccabaeus), three Gentiles (Hector, Alexander, and Julius Caesar), and three Christians (King Arthur, Charlemagne, and the crusade hero Godfrey of Bouillon). So when Chaucer found a story of the fall of Troy among the works of Boccaccio, the story of Prince Troilus's love for Criseyde, he would have seen it as a new piece of the "matter of Troy," a story of courtly love between a royal prince and a noblewoman in the last days of London's ancestral city.

In the court of Prince Lionel and the Countess Elizabeth, Chaucer encountered, more than he would have had he stayed in London, this body of chivalric legend. It was part of the lore of courtly life, much of it written down but much of it, in all likelihood, preserved in memory and told or recited. It was the folklore of a privileged caste. If folklore is by definition an oral tradition, there *is* no medieval folklore, only evidence that some lore was recorded and an assumption that more must have existed. In courtly society, where clerks could be set to writing things down, such lore was more likely to be recorded, but much of it was oral and so has vanished. For convenience, we can call it "knightlore."

This knightlore was a large part of what Chaucer learned in the Ulster household. It would have included verse romances and songs, remembered and performed by minstrels or by courtiers themselves. Some of these, especially the romances, were written down and read aloud, and when thus preserved they are a literature based on knightlore. There were romances of great heroes and wars and adventures, and great loves— "storial thing that toucheth gentilesse," Chaucer styled them. Not that the characters in romances aren't very often Christians, or that their values and adventures aren't often Christian too. Knighthood itself was Christian in the sense that a knighting ceremony involved vigils, prayers, and sacraments, that knights commended themselves to Christ before battle, that they always thought the cause they championed was just, that some wars were sanctioned by the pope, and so on. But in romances it was possible to have pagan heroes, pagan backgrounds—pagan gods, too, like Mars and Venus, who were conveniently planets as well, and in love stories Cupid, god of love, busy with his arrows.

There were romances of every conceivable kind on every conceivable subject, even for different audiences. There were "bourgeois" romances in which the knightlore is watered down, tailored for an audience of merchants or burghers; Chaucer was to make fun of these in a parody, the Tale of Sir Thopas, which is amusingly enough the tale *he* tells on the way to Canterbury, so dull the Host makes him stop, says his rhyming isn't worth a turd. The going notion about romance subjects was that there were three "matters"; the notion derives from a remark by the poet Jean Bodel, who said, in rough translation, "there are only three matters that have anything to do with anything—of France, of Britain, and of Rome the Great." He had in mind romances about Charlemagne, about King Arthur and his knights, and about the heroes of the ancient world like Alexander. But there was much more: there were tales of native English heroes, tales of Oriental adventures, tales of magic. There were funny romances, tragic romances, even rather intellectual romances. And religious romances: alongside the magic love potions and the wicked dwarfs, there is the quest for the Holy Grail.

Such knightlore young Geoffrey in his teens would have found glorious and inspirational. From it—the disillusionments would come later—he imbibed that feeling the medieval knighthood cherished and cultivated, the feeling, in Othello's words, for "the plumed troop, and the big wars, / That make ambition virtue." This is what soldiers get from memory and story; what Chaucer would get from war itself, in a few years, might be otherwise. But it will repay us to consider that most of what he was to write may be seen as a development of such knightlore. Except for *The Canterbury Tales* all his longer poems are courtly forms, dream visions or romances. All are about knights and ladies except *The House of Fame*, which is about himself in search of "love-tidings," courtly stories to write about. And *The Canterbury Tales*, which contains half a dozen bits of romance matter involving various degrees of parody, begins with the Knight's Tale, a high-minded romance of ancient Athens in the time of Theseus.

Now, in the 1350s, the English knighthood, at war with France, had had two victories to make ambition virtue. Brutus's Albion had a new historic dimension for this generation of English knights, and the young page from London—"new Troy"—was intensely aware of England's past. National history wasn't taught in schools or valued as a category of formal learning in the Middle Ages. From his father Chaucer might have heard of the days of bad King Edward II and the early days of Edward III. And he would have known the great English kings who had made a mark for some reason—Henry II, say, because he was Saint Thomas à Becket's antagonist, because he did public penance after Becket died his martyr's death, because you could see stained-glass windows on the way to Canterbury and at Canterbury, and pictures in books, depicting these events. Of English history before the Norman Conquest, Chaucer probably knew very little: a few of the kings whose names the church preserved, like Saint Erkenwald or Saint Edward the Confessor, perhaps, but the memory of Anglo-Saxon England had been obliterated by the Conquest.

What was known of early Britain was legend, preserved in a twelfth-century book, *The History of the Kings of Britain* by Geoffrey of Monmouth, whom Chaucer mentions once as "English Gaufred"; in it we may read of King Cole, King Lear, and King Arthur, but the author leaves off in the seventh century, referring the reader to other historians, like William of Malmesbury, whom Chaucer never mentions. Chaucer probably could name the kings since William the Conqueror (there were mnemonic verses for schoolboys), and he no doubt knew stories (there is a romance about King Richard the Lion-Hearted, and one about a fictional English king, Athelston—both written in his century). But in courtly literature, the great heroes and deeds remained chiefly of the long ago and far away; the greatest British king, Arthur, went back very far indeed, and whenever Chaucer mentions the Arthurian legends his references sound a trifle deprecatory, as if to suggest he didn't believe they were true stories. He has the Squire mention Lancelot, adding quickly "and he is dead," and refer to Sir Gawain "though he were comen again out of fairye"—i.e., if you could bring him back from the land of enchantment. Or here is the Wife of Bath beginning her Arthurian tale:

> In the olde dayes of the King Arthour,
> Of which that Britons speeken greet honour,
> All was this land fulfilled of fairye.
> The elf-queen, with hir jolly compaigny,
> Danced full oft in many a greene mede.°   meadow
> This was the old opinion, as I rede°—   believe
> I speek of many hundred yeers ago.
> But now can no man see none elves mo° . . .   more

We would expect that our young poet, whose most famous poem is of English pilgrims on the national English pilgrimage to the shrine of the English saint, was stirred by English heroism, but if we can judge from his writings, he was not. The remembered past—as opposed to the recorded past—was all about him in buildings, artifacts, things that belonged to one's grandfather or great-grandfather. The bloodlines of the noble families receded back to the time of the Conquest. And wars, yes, there had been wars in England, and glorious international wars, the Crusades, going back into the dimness of history. Books could be dated by the fashions in handwriting, illumination, binding—some scribes even put a date on a work when they finished copying it. For those of Chaucer's time, this living sense of the English past felt its way back into the thirteenth century, not quite into the twelfth. A "renaissance" in the twelfth century was invisible to them; they could not see the great cultural changes that we can see, and in England the twelfth century had been the century after the Conquest, a time of turmoil. To us, the centuries of the Middle Ages each have character; to them, they were only strings of years receding into darkness and fragmentary legend.

In that time of English victories, there was a surge of interest in stories of native English chivalry; the greatest English romance, *Sir Gawain and the Green Knight*, a tale of King Arthur's court, was written in the northwest midlands during Chaucer's lifetime. Yet Chaucer never took any interest in writings about English heroes of former times. Actually, Edward III promoted a fad for King Arthur, even had a Round Table built at Windsor Castle. But by the time court poets were ready to pick up the subject, Edward's court was in decline and the fad had disappeared —or might have seemed out of place. Then, too, Chaucer's education predisposed him in favor of ancient times, of deeds celebrated in ancient Latin poems: the *real* English past—not mere fables of elf-queens and "fairye"—only stretched back into the century before, but knighthood, glorious knighthood, went back to pagan antiquity, and one could read about it, in prestigious Latin, in the books of ancient writers.

The Siege of Reims and the Treaty of Brétigny, 1359

In 1359 the glory of English knighthood was put to the test again: the Truce of Brittany expired in March and King Jean, still a prisoner in England, came to an agreement with King Edward. If Edward would renounce his claim to the French throne, he would be given most of northern France plus four million gold crowns as King Jean's ransom; princes of the blood would be held as hostages to insure payment. While the king of France went on with his pleasant life in captivity, being moved with his large personal retinue from castle to castle to prevent escape, hunting, hawking, entertaining his English captors in lavish fashion and being entertained by them, the French Estates General flatly rejected the humiliating terms in a harsh reply, and Edward declared war on August 12.

Since the victories at Crécy and Poitiers, Edward III was acknowledged the military genius of his age, and soldiers of fortune from all over Europe, glory and plunder in their hearts, flocked unbidden to Calais to join the English army. There they spent their money, sold or pawned their possessions, and grew surly. Henry, duke of Lancaster, was sent ahead to organize them, pay their debts, and lead them marauding through the north of France, joining the main army when it arrived at Calais. The army required hundreds of ships; as it embarked at Dover, in late October, the king spoke stirringly of his purpose, gave his oath he would die sooner than fail—to cries of "God and St. George!" France being devastated by war and famine, the English were prepared to provision their army with a vast equipage (it took over a thousand carriages to transport), down to portable ovens and small leather boats for catching fish in rivers. The nobles, many of them, brought their hawks and hounds.

Edward's master plan was to separate the army into the customary three divisions, one led by him, one by the Prince of Wales, and one by Henry, duke of Lancaster; these would cross France by separate routes and join near Reims. They would capture Reims, that sacred city where French kings were by tradition crowned, and there Edward would take the crown of France to which he claimed title. Then they would proceed to Paris and capture it, and so, they imagined, all of France. The king and his followers were confident, too confident, after their great previous victories. They did not count, for example, on the relentless rains of that season; had not, despite their plans, brought enough provisions; did not foresee the difficulty of pillaging fortified towns for food. The three divisions came together by accident on November 29, ten leagues before the appointed place, and their leaders met in council. Then they divided again. The division led by the Prince of Wales evidently had with it at this time the prince's brothers, John and Lionel; with Lionel, it is assumed, marched Geoffrey Chaucer, now a *valettus* or yeoman.

They passed Montreuil southeast through Hesdin, crossed the Somme near Amiens, passed Nesle and Ham to Saint Quentin, crossing the River Oise, and proceeded to Rethel, twenty-odd miles northeast of Reims. They found the enemy prepared for their coming. The French burned Rethel as the prince's division approached it, sooner than have it be of use to the invader. They deserted Autry, thirty-odd miles east of Reims, and Manre, fifteen miles further east. They strengthened the fortifications of Reims, put nearby castles in defense or else destroyed them. They razed the Benedictine Abbey at Saint Thierry and other monasteries. The English occupied what monasteries and towns were left about Reims, intending to block passages into the city and besiege it. Expecting a glorious battle in the field, like Crécy or Poitiers, they found

instead an ominous silence. They waited. Roving bands of English soldiers
made forays on towns as far as fifty miles away. At Cernay-en-Dormois,
thirty miles east of Reims, followers of the duke of Lancaster and others,
when the inhabitants taunted them from the walls, crossed the double
moat, scaled their way to the top, put to death what inhabitants had not
fled, and burned the town. It was the last day of 1359. Meanwhile at
Cormicy, ten miles northwest of Reims, followers of Prince Edward and
John of Gaunt took the town in a night attack, despite its double moat
and strong wall, but the tower within stood firm. They began to dig up
the tower's foundations until, on January 8, it stood only on wooden props.
The lord of the castle, under safe conduct, was shown, with a display of
chivalrous courtesy, the unpromising circumstances of his keep, and he
at once surrendered with a no less chivalrous display of gratitude; then the
wooden props were set afire and the tower tumbled. Three days later, on
January 11, the English, having done as much destruction as they could
and knowing they would never be able to take Reims, marched off in
chagrin, south into Burgundy, until the middle of March.

What Geoffrey Chaucer, yeoman, was doing during these months,
we can only suppose. Like any junior officer, he did as he was told. He
was armed with sword and dagger and was assigned to a knight, perhaps
Lionel himself, carried his lance and did his bidding, supervised common
soldiers and the *garciones*, grooms or serving boys. Derek Brewer gives a
wonderful imagined picture of wet clothes and boots, an iron helmet and
body armor of chain mail and plate, the tedious routine of lighting fires,
checking horses, arming his knight, sleeping on the ground in tents or in
commandeered houses or monasteries, enduring the wind, rain, and cold,
hearing stories of former wars told by old soldiers after nightfall. Geoffrey
was sent, we can be certain, on foraging expeditions: getting food had
become a serious problem. Or he went hunting or hawking with the
nobles, or riding off for adventure with his fellows. Medieval warfare was
predatory in the extreme—looting, wanton destruction, rape and murder
of defenseless civilians were taken for granted. And, too, in any skirmish,
small bands of warriors might get detached and be ambushed. While
engaged in such activities, probably in a small group, Chaucer was captured and imprisoned. The accounts of the Keeper of the King's Wardrobe show that on March 1, 1360, while the army was in Guillon, £16
was given by the king as his ransom; the amount is in line with other
ransoms paid for yeomen.*

*In the same account, Richard Stury, king's esquire, was ransomed for £50 ($15,000 or
more in today's currency), and two *garciones* ransomed on the same day as Chaucer were
worth 27s. (about $400) apiece. One of these was named Thomas of Chester, which
happens to be the name of a poet who later wrote the romance *Sir Launfal*, possibly

Years later, in 1386, Chaucer testified in the Scrope-Grosvenor trial
that he had seen the Scropes bearing the disputed arms before the town
of Rethel and thereafter throughout the campaign until he was captured
(*"par tout le dit viage tanqe le dit Geffrey estoit pris"*). So he was captured
sometime between the arrival of Prince Edward's division at Rethel in the
first week of December and March 1, when he was ransomed. If he was
captured before the army marched south in early January, he was doubtless held prisoner in the area of Reims for about two months, rejoining
the army at Guillon when he was freed. *Where* he was held prisoner,
where *anyone* was held prisoner, is not recorded. Soldiers of rank, when
captured, were treated chivalrously, with hospitality and great courtesy;
they were under house arrest in a nobleman's castle, with reason to hope
for "good deliverance," usually by ransom. Chaucer's captivity—he being
yeoman to a prince of the blood—could have been a pleasant respite, a
time to converse and read, hear songs and stories. And, among numerous
places where he might have been detained, is Reims itself.

The possibility is intriguing (otherwise it would be too remote to
mention) because in Reims at the time lived the greatest composer and
poet of the day, Guillaume de Machaut, a canon of the cathedral, now
almost sixty, whose poetry was to influence Chaucer profoundly. With
Machaut was his protégé, perhaps his nephew, Eustache Deschamps,
fourteen or fifteen years old, who would influence Chaucer too, even
address a flattering ballade to him. To suppose that these three great poets
of the age met briefly at Reims in wartime, two of them still in their teens,
seems too romantic to have happened, but one detail supports it. In
Chaucer's *House of Fame* the description of Fame's palace bears a certain
resemblance to the façade of the Maison des Musiciens at Reims. It was
a banker's house and shop, with five sculptures on the second floor depicting musicians—or a musician, perhaps the banker himself—playing various instruments. It is a most curious, and unique, edifice, and so is
Chaucer's description. He might have found sculptured musicians in
niches elsewhere or thought up the idea by himself: but if he'd seen the
Maison des Musiciens he would not have forgotten it. It is just possible
that Chaucer as a prisoner of war spent some time gazing at the curious
structure and remembered it well enough to elaborate on it almost two
decades later.

Chaucer's testimony that he had seen the Scropes at Rethel and

influenced by Chaucer, whom Chaucer may have satirized in "Sir Thopas"; but it would
be a long shot to say this was the same Thomas of Chester. Another of the men ransomed
two months earlier had been with Chaucer in the Ulster household; his name is given as
"George, *valettus* of the Countess of Ulster," and the sum is £10, the lack of a last name
and the amount suggesting he was lower in station.

throughout the campaign until he was captured seems to suggest that he did not see them thereafter. Other witnesses were asked if they had seen the Scropes at Paris; Chaucer was not asked this question. So it is possible to infer that Chaucer was with some division that did not proceed to Paris. And there *was* such a division, that of the earl of March.* March was mortally wounded at Rouvray, near Guillon, at the end of February just before Chaucer's ransom, and those of his men who were captured at Rouvray were ransomed, paid off, and sent home. Possibly for Chaucer this was the end of the war.

The army, with Geoffrey or without him, went on to Paris, laid siege to the city, and challenged it on April 6. On the following Monday, April 13—"Black Monday" it was called—the English army was hit near Chartres by a sudden freak storm of terrible wind and rain, with cold so severe that men died of it and hailstones large enough to kill men and horses: "it seemed," wrote one chronicler, "as if the heavens would part and the earth open and swallow up all." The English, terrified by the storm and fearing it betokened God's wrath, decided to accept France's terms of peace—so the king vowed to the Blessed Virgin during the storm. In the Treaty of Brétigny, drafted on May 7, Edward reduced his territorial claims and renounced his claim to the French crown, King Jean was freed and his ransom reduced—hostages would be sent to England to insure its payment. Even so, the English had brought mighty France, flower of chivalry, to a settlement, laid her low with destruction and universal deprivation. They returned home as if victorious, in the merry month of May.

The Inns of Court

The Treaty of Brétigny was worked out in detail and ratified at Calais the following October. The French king went over to Calais in July under escort; the Prince of Wales, the duke of Lancaster, and others went over in August, and they were joined in October by the king himself and Prince Lionel. The treaty was dated October 24, 1360; the English all returned home at the end of the month, taking with them the French hostages, some twenty-three great nobles, princes of the royal blood and powerful barons like Enguerrand de Coucy. During these last two weeks of negotia-

*At the siege of Reims March's retinue was with John of Gaunt's, and the Scropes served Gaunt. Prince Lionel had a family connection with March (his infant daughter was betrothed to March's son) so it isn't out of the question that Chaucer might have served with him rather than with Lionel. Gaunt's followers, though normally in the king's division, marched with Prince Edward on the way to Reims but not thereafter. Only the prince's division was at Rethel.

tions King Edward III gave a spectacular supper in the castle of Calais
for the king of France, and on the next day King Jean went on foot, with
the Prince of Wales and his brothers Lionel and Edmund, to Our Lady
of Boulogne to give thanks. Whether Chaucer saw any of these festivities,
we cannot be sure, but we know from Lionel's account book that late in
October he was sent with letters to England. These were letters touching
personal matters or family business; if they had been official letters pertaining to the treaty, they would have been sent by one of the king's
esquires and paid for out of the Privy Wardrobe. We do not know if he
returned with a reply. Chaucer was now approaching twenty, old enough
and experienced enough to be entrusted with a responsibility, but it does
not appear that this trip across the Channel was of any special significance. It is the first recorded instance of his traveling as a courier or envoy;
on any such mission he might not have known what was in the sealed
letters he bore, and if he knew he would not have told.

At this point, at the end of the year 1360, Chaucer disappears from
sight. He does not really emerge again in the records until late July 1368.
He has a passport in his hand. He is about to sail from Dover. He is over
twenty-five, the age thought to mark the end of adolescence and the
beginning of full-fledged adulthood. He is named in the king's warrant as
"nostre ame vallet Geffrey Chaucer." His career has begun.

It may be (but there is no evidence) that for some part of these years
he was with Lionel in Ireland when Lionel was viceroy there; the post
involved putting down military uprising. There is one bit of evidence that
for some part of these years he attended one of the Inns of Court, the
Inner Temple. The great Renaissance editor of Chaucer, Thomas Speght,
writing an account of Chaucer's life in 1598, recorded that "not many
years since, Master Buckley did see a Record in the same house [the Inner
Temple], where Geoffrey Chaucer was fined two shillings for beating a
Franciscan friar in Fleet Street." Master Buckley was evidently William
Buckley, keeper of the records of the Inner Temple in the 1560's and
1570's, so we must give some credence to this reported record. Chaucer
had been recently a soldier, had taken part in a wantonly violent war, and
might be pressed into military service again. He was at home in London,
where street fighting was an everyday affair: his Uncle Simon had died in
a street fight, and his own father, respectable vintner that he was and now
close to fifty, had been dragged to court for fighting in the streets some
ten years before. In what records of the Inns of Court have survived,
three-fourths of offenses recorded against students are for disorderly conduct; the fine of two shillings was usual. And Franciscan friars were a
nuisance. The ideal was that they should travel in pairs, begging and
giving their gains to the poor. By Chaucer's time they were corrupt.

Chaucer's contemporary, William Langland, who was just beginning *Piers Plowman* at this time, satirized the friars savagely, making the reform of the four orders of friars a symbol for the reform of the Church itself. And Chaucer's own satire of a friar in *The Canterbury Tales* is a masterpiece of invidious wit. Perhaps, after all, it is not so unimaginable that Chaucer as a law student had attacked a friar on a city street, either because the friar was a pest or because the law student and his companions, ex-soldiers, were behaving in a drunk and disorderly manner like typical students of the day.

If Chaucer attended the Inns of Court, it was in the normal course of things, and he probably had little choice in the matter. He was now in or on his way to the royal household, received a stipend, lodging and board, a clothing allowance, plus gifts of money at Christmas and other occasions. The royal household offered its own education to its young squires, part of which might be to send them as special students to the Inns of Court; records show the king's esquires admitted without having to pay for meals except those they actually took (for of course they took their meals chiefly in the royal hall) or observe rules requiring study in vacation. They needed to know enough law and business to serve the court in an official capacity, and what they needed to know was prescribed by tradition and precept. The path to officialdom was a well-marked one.

Chaucer's fellows in the Ulster household, who must have been his friends and companions for some years, followed the same path he did, though none went as far. Alice Dawtry and Philippa Roet (if she was Philippa "Pan") both went into the queen's service: Reginald de Pierpont, never heard of again, probably died in the war. For the rest, Edmund Rose became valettus to the king, married Agnes Archer, damsel of the queen's chamber; in 1369 he is listed alongside Chaucer as an esquire of the royal household. Geoffrey Stukely, valettus to the Countess Elizabeth in 1354, is valettus to the king in 1356, still in the royal household in 1368 when he is listed alongside Chaucer as an esquire; in 1374 he is sent as envoy to Flanders. "George," valettus to the countess of Ulster, as we saw earlier, was in the war with Chaucer, ransomed in January 1360. John Prior, possibly the son of a London merchant, is recorded as bringing news to the Prince of Wales of the birth of his second daughter in 1358. John Hinton, in 1366–1367, received an annuity from Lionel, duke of Clarence, as having been the Countess Elizabeth's esquire before her death. That Chaucer was transferred to the royal household sometime between 1361 and 1368, that he moved up from valettus to esquire, that he was sent abroad, even perhaps that he married a damsel of the queen's chamber, is part of a completely predictable picture.

But the exact nature of a courtier's education in the late fourteenth century is dim for want of facts. The royal household, or Prince Lionel's for that matter, had the capacity to teach its squires most of what they needed to know. This was categorized as "noriture" (comportment) and "lettrure" (book learning), much of which they learned in the normal course of court life. "Noriture" included dancing and music and manners, and such skills, but not warlike skills, were taught at the Inns of Court: we read that they had dancing, singing in harmony, study of Scripture, reading chronicles that teach virtue. To what extent the Inns had really evolved into educational establishments in Chaucer's day is debatable. They may as yet have been little more than clubs for lawyers; but they existed, and eventually they would offer an elite kind of education for the well-to-do, who could learn polite accomplishments and business skills without formally studying law.

With Chaucer it was the other way around. He could learn his "noriture" and most of his "lettrure" at court, but could the court teach him common law? The legal side of education at the Inns, at least as it developed in the next century and a half, involved "bolts" and "moots" as well as "readings." The "readings" were lectures on the statutes and cases, delivered in the hall with solemnity, by the leading lawyers of the realm. They were historical investigations intended to keep subtle inventions and distortions from creeping into the interpretation of the law. (Chaucer reports of the Man of Law that "In termes had he caas and doomes alle / That from the time of King William were y-falle"; i.e., he knew all the cases and decisions since the time of William the Conqueror, and knew them "in terms," which probably means he knew them in chronological sequence as they were recorded in the annual terms or sessions of the courts; otherwise it means he owned a set of the *Year Books*.) In addition to such rote learning, law students attended the sessions of the Court of Common Pleas as observers, where they sat in a special section called "the crib" and had certain procedures explained to them by the judges. They debated doubtful cases and questions in "moots"; they wore black gowns and caps, sat before the senior members ("benchers") who acted as judges, and argued the case of the plaintiff or defendant, after which, evidently, the benchers argued it for them correctly. "Bolts," which probably developed after Chaucer's time, were in effect practice moots. The fine for absence from the moots ("mootfail") was 13s. 4d., almost seven times greater than for beating a friar. One can imagine that Chaucer acted as an "inner barrister" and argued cases in this way, and probably enjoyed debating the moot points. It does not follow that he was a lawyer; his route was laid out by the royal household.

The Inns of Court were so-called with reference to the king's court, not the law courts, and the chances are they first became educational institutions by being called upon to provide legal training for the king's esquires. They became finishing schools for the gentry later, precisely because the king's esquires were already being trained there. Chaucer— according to this interpretation of the evidence—attended the Inns of Court at an early stage in their development, when they were still in essence clubs that provided chambers for lawyers and served only second- arily as schools, at the behest of the royal court. If they offered anything in the way of "noriture," Chaucer and his fellow squires would not have needed it, for this aspect of the education offered by the Inns developed in imitation of the royal court. The Inns provided for others who could afford it what the court provided for its esquires.

That Chaucer *had* legal training there can be no doubt. The late Professor Rickert's rhetorical question remains persuasive after fifty years: "Take, for example, the Genoese mission of 1372, in which Chaucer's only associates were two Genoese. The business concerned the establish- ment of a seaport in England for Genoese citizens and merchants, and the 'franchises, liberties, immunities, and privileges' associated with such a grant. Are we to believe that the English interests would have been left in the hands of one unfamiliar with the law?" And there are a dozen other questions relating to Chaucer's career that are no less provocative. We know the court was turning for its appointees from those clerically edu- cated to those educated in the common law. He might have learned his law from a tutor or a book, but then why is there that joke on lawyers in *The Canterbury Tales*, about the Manciple, the steward "of a temple," who has thirty masters all so learned in the law that they could run the estate of any lord in England, but he can still cheat them all? Why is it introduced with so much rhetorical flourish and obvious relish? It really sounds like an insider's joke, a *student's* joke.

The question of Chaucer's legal education is important because it was to have a bearing on his ideas about literature, particularly about "fictions." The kind of legal education he would have had meant he would have acquired a feeling for "legal fictions." The cases students tried or debated were often imaginary ones, and the way laws were understood was by applying them to hypothetical or fictional cases. The method had ancient precedents. Such cases didn't have to be true stories, they only had to present a problem, raise a question about the law, ultimately about justice and right. For example: the *law* is that if a woman is raped she can choose whether the rapist be executed or marry her; the *case* is that a man rapes two women in one night, one woman chooses that he be executed and the other chooses that he marry her. Every story, seen as a "case," has a possible intellectual significance apart from its relation to "the facts."

This way of looking at fictions as *cases* encouraged the development of a particular linguistic skill, for cases involved ambiguity; because circumstances alter cases, a meaning applied to one case will be different in another, and what is *said* about those circumstances is therefore always open to scrutiny. Ambiguity was to be a hallmark of Chaucer's mature style. He developed a way of saying only and exactly what he meant—and seemed to be implying something more, precisely because he said no more than what he did. The technique produced those ambiguous characters who are so lifelike because we know them as we know real people, incompletely: the Wife of Bath, with her unrecounted (but evidently significant) youth and her apparent childlessness; the Merchant, of whose indebtedness no one knew anything; the Prioress, who emulates the appearances of the court. And Chaucer was drawn to ambiguous stories, stories that end in a question, a twist, or a surprise. Ambiguity of this kind is not something one finds in medieval literature; one finds mystery and wordplay, and sometimes a playful tone on the author's part, but not this spare, inscrutable presentation of facts, themselves ambiguous, that are limited as evidence, invite questions—are, in the traditional phrase, *moot.* Cases are reported happenings about which the inquiring mind seeks to pass a judgment, inquire out a meaning. Cases may or may not be fictions, but fictions are always cases, and cases make us think about the world.

3

The Best
of Times—
the 1360s

The Court of Edward III

When the Treaty of Brétigny was signed, the English party returned from Calais with their French hostages. Among the party was a young poet from Hainault, Jean Froissart, twenty-two, on his way to seek Queen Philippa's patronage. And with them too may have been Geoffrey Chaucer, about seventeen, now a veteran of the wars in France. A few weeks after their return, King Edward III reached his forty-eighth birthday. He had reigned now thirty-three years, and on the whole reigned well. A king's court, and from it the nation, took its character from the king himself; his tastes and quirks, let alone his personality and convictions, were imprinted on the group that hovered about him in the Chamber and indirectly on the swarms that hovered about them.

Edward's character is difficult to get at, and his childhood may or may not explain it. His father, Edward II, could have been little more effective in a paternal role than he was as king or husband; and Edward's mother, Queen Isabella, had taken a lover, Mortimer, with whom she engineered her husband's deposition. Crowned at fourteen, with his fa-

79

ther in a dungeon, Edward III had been called upon to mature in haste;
he was but a puppet king caught between opposing factions, his mother
and Mortimer on the one side, the earl of Lancaster and his party (for
whom Chaucer's father had fought) on the other. Three months after
Edward took the throne—January 1327—his father was removed to
Berkeley Castle and, in September, secretly murdered in a plot of Mortimer's devising. The method reportedly used to slay him, lacerating his
innards with a red-hot iron inserted through the anus, was not consciously
chosen as symbolical retribution to a reputed sodomite but (according at
least to historical traditions) because it left no visible marks. He was
discreetly reported to have died of natural causes. There was a stately
funeral, which his widow attended, and he even enjoyed a short career as
a saint.

    Lancaster, knowing that he like others could be put to death on some
trumped-up charge, had organized a plot against Mortimer and had a
retainer secure the sanction of the pope and enlist the young king; secret
correspondence between pope and king, with a password to forestall
forgeries, is preserved still in the Vatican. In the autumn of 1330, Mortimer and Queen Isabella, sensing conspiracy, retreated to Nottingham
Castle under constant guard, with new locks on the gates, but the conspirators, with young Edward's assistance, gained admittance through a
secret passageway. While one of Edward's knights took a sword to two
of Mortimer's men and the queen begged her son hysterically to have pity
"du gentil Mortimer," Mortimer was seized, conveyed to London, and
condemned by Parliament. He was hanged and disemboweled for a traitor; by the king's command his body was left hanging two days from the
gibbet.

    A few years later Edward II's murderers were brought to trial; two
of them were found guilty and the third an accessory, but they were
allowed to escape—the accessory, Maltravers, in 1351 had his sentence
commuted and his estates restored along with his seat in Parliament, and
he lived on happily in England into the 1360s. Queen Isabella's role as
hated Mortimer's cohort was benignly overlooked; her royal son settled
a luxurious annuity on her and she lived grandly, moving about as she
pleased, hawking, reading romances, entertaining. In her last years she
took the habit of the Poor Clares, and when she died in November 1358
—the year after Chaucer met her grandson, John of Gaunt—she was
buried as a nun. Chaucer, then about sixteen, may have attended her
funeral in the Countess Elizabeth's retinue.

    Edward had learned the skills of kingship—to protect his interests,
choose advisers, form alliances, fight back, make compromises—under the
pressure of these terrible events, at an impressionable age and from prac-

ticed mentors who then became supporters. By eighteen he was prepared to declare his majority and take the reins of government. His development belies modern ideas of psychology. He had—according to the claims of the time—a weak, ineffectual, and possibly homosexual father, an intense eccentric with common tastes, prey to male favorites, hysterical, and foolish. He had a domineering, treacherous, unbalanced mother ("the she-wolf of France," she was called), a troubled childhood, and a tumultuous adolescence. Yet he grew into a virile, secure, outgoing man, gallant, fair, honest, and chivalrous in his dealings with friend and foe, an excellent father, able enough as a statesman, a military leader of genius. He was a handsome, large man—six feet tall, it is said, in an age when average height was about five-foot-three—humorous, high-spirited, a ladies' man. Perhaps the explanation of his unneurotic character is an early triumph, as he might inwardly have conceived it, over an unloving father (which may explain his indulgence toward his father's murderers) and a triumph over his mother's consort, Mortimer; having seen his father's and potentially his own principal antagonist dispatched, he could afford charity to his mother and her allies. If Oedipal conflict counts for anything in character development, his had a happy resolution.

Indeed, Edward's mother had provided him, out of no particular solicitude, with what may have been his greatest source of strength, his wife. The court of course had an eye out for brides while he was still a child, and Philippa of Hainault was on their list; they sent the bishop of Exeter to report on her and her sisters when Edward was nine. In 1325 Isabella went to Paris to seek military aid against her husband's party from her brother, the king of France, and she took Edward with her. When France said no, she pushed on to Hainault, a small Flemish-speaking principality on the French border, and sought the aid of her cousin William, count of Hainault. He struck a hard bargain: mercenary troops and an early payment on the dowry in return for the marriage of one of his daughters to the Prince of Wales. Edward, just fourteen, met the daughters, the second of whom, Philippa, was his age; later chronicles claim, in gushy language, that Edward and Philippa took to each other, that he said he preferred her to the others, that she wept on his parting. These stories are almost certainly reminiscences of Queen Philippa herself in later years, colored by time and her own full-bodied sentiment, and recorded by courtier-historians, but they may be true for all that. Her happy marriage and happy memories of it suggest that Edward and Philippa fell in love as two fourteen-year-olds might. Their vows, the terms of the settlement, were exchanged by proxy that year, and shortly Philippa came to London amidst "great rejoicings." There were tournaments and elaborate celebrations. Then she proceeded north in cold January to York, where the young king was. It is said she got out of her carriage at each town and rode through it on a palfrey, greeting the eager citizens. The religious ceremony was performed in the cathedral in January 1328, snow flurrying into the still unfinished nave.

Everyone loved Philippa when she first came to England, and everyone seems to have loved her throughout her life. There was hardly a family in England that didn't name a daughter for her. The English were glad enough to have their king married, and they were overjoyed at Philippa's warm, outgoing personality. For her, the marriage was an exceptionally favorable one; in the normal course of things she could hardly have expected to be the queen of England, and she must have set her mind to doing it right. Her heraldic motto in her native Flemish meant "I work hard," and she took the idea to heart: she was always tirelessly devoted to her husband, her children, her retainers from her native Hainault, and her whole English family. She never allowed her court, as foreign royalty often did, to become a haven for pickthanks and sycophants from her native country. In her first years on English soil she stood beside her husband—they were sixteen then—during that most difficult time following the murder of his father when he had to take a hand in the defeat of his uncle Mortimer and his mother. In October 1329, after more than a year's worrisome delay, she was pregnant; and, safely pregnant, indeed six months gone, she was crowned queen of England at Westminster Abbey the following March. In June she gave birth to the future Prince of Wales, Edward—whom history two centuries later would call "the Black Prince" after his legendary black armor of burnished steel.

That she was constantly with her husband during these years, knew Mortimer, knew Isabella, watched each painful event that led to their downfall, meant that she understood Edward. She had shared his most difficult, most formative experience, and he was the closer to her because of it. Thirty-five years later he still used a pet name for her in her native Flemish, *myn biddinye* ("my little helper"). She often accompanied him on military expeditions, even when pregnant—not unprecedented, yet it was not expected of her. And she was generous to a fault. Orphaned children of her huge, extended, English family, like Elizabeth, countess of Ulster, she raised as if they were her own. She packed the household with *domicelle*, "damsels," young girls of good families—among them Chaucer's wife, Philippa (formerly damsel to the Queen's foster daughter and daughter-in-law, Elizabeth) and Alice Perrers, a young woman of indeterminable origin, possibly an orphaned daughter of a nobleman or one down on his luck, who later became the king's mistress—and she clucked over this brood, wheedling marriages and properties and annuities, showering gifts. She was a great patroness, too, of arts and learning;

her chaplain, Robert Eglesfield, founded Queen's College, Oxford (she is the queen it is named for) with funds she raised. When her youthful countryman from Hainault, the poet Jean Froissart, came seeking her patronage in 1360, she took him on as her secretary, fostered his writings, among them the enormous *Chronicles*, which remain the most complete record of her age, if not the most reliable; but Froissart's sticky nostalgia for the old chivalric virtues, his gargantuan exaggerations, his biased, sentimental fictionalizing, are a reliable barometer of the feeling she inspired.

And to this royal household, sometime in the 1360s, when Philippa and Edward were in their fifties, Geoffrey Chaucer came to be attached.

Queen Philippa was a large, motherly woman in her mature years, broad-hipped, plump, and double-chinned, if one may judge from her tomb effigy. In youth she had dark-brown hair and a fairly dark complexion, a high, broad forehead (very fashionable at the time), deep-set brown eyes, a broad nose, full lips, white teeth with the lower ones protruding slightly, a well-formed body. She and Edward both liked money and luxury, and whether because it was her nature or because her staff were careless and inefficient, she was a terrible spendthrift. There were protests about her large debts, and she laid claim to properties not really hers, of which she was at least once unburdened by Parliament; in 1362 Edward was forced to pay off what she owed. Of Edward's marital infidelities, she was patient. He is supposed to have loved (one chronicler says raped, describing the incident in grisly detail) the beautiful "Countess of Salisbury," Alice Brotherton, his cousin. He is supposed to have had a mistress at Calais, whose dropped garter he recovered, sometime in the 1340s, from a dance floor, with the gallant—or possibly pointed—remark "*Honi soit qui mal y pense,*" evil be to him who thinks ill of it. This is the legendary beginning of the order of the Garter; its actual founding was otherwise. It is even said, perhaps not wrongly, that Philippa in her last days of illness saw to it he was provided with a mistress from among her own *domicelle*, Alice Perrers, then about twenty.

Philippa, like all medieval queens, was kept busy bearing children, in her case at intervals of a year or two. After Edward, Prince of Wales, there was a daughter, Isabella, and another, Joan, who died at fifteen; a son William who died in infancy, followed by Lionel and John of Gaunt; a daughter, Blanche, who died in infancy; Edmund of Langley; two daughters, Mary and Margaret, both of whom married well but died in their teens; a boy named William after her lost second son, who died in infancy too in 1348, the year of the plague. After the Black Death she had only one more, seven years later, in 1355, Thomas of Woodstock, in later years the infamous earl of Gloucester, Richard II's antagonist. She bore her eldest at eighteen, her youngest at forty-three. She wanted her children's marriages to be as sound and happy as her own, and matching them up properly was her abiding concern.

Her two eldest children took their time about marrying, and both married for love. As the Prince of Wales, Edward, the Black Prince, would have been expected to marry for diplomatic and dynastic reasons, but negotiations to marry him with a Portuguese princess and a daughter to the duke of Brabant failed. At thirty he had some bastard children, but he was still unmarried, an almost unprecedented circumstance. He had fallen in love with the Countess Joan, "The Fair Maid of Kent," two years older than he, one of the great beauties of the age. She was Edward III's first cousin, had already been married twice (the prince himself was godfather to one of her children), so penances and papal dispensations were in order. After the death of her second husband in December 1360, they were married, in October 1361. King Edward initially opposed the marriage because it offered no political advantages, and Queen Philippa was less than happy with it: she probably didn't like Joan of Kent very much, may have disapproved of her checkered marital career, not to say her earlier relationship with her own husband, or his with her, if indeed this was the case. Since their first son would be heir presumptive, she may have feared that Joan of Kent, being past thirty, might not produce a healthy child. And Joan gave birth to a son, inevitably named Edward, in 1364, who in fact may have been retarded or deformed. In January 1367 she had another son, a perfectly healthy one, Richard, born at Bordeaux—the future Richard II.

Philippa's eldest daughter, Isabella, resisted all efforts to marry her; she had been jilted by one suitor and had spectacularly jilted another. At thirty-three she was in love with one of the hostages for the king of France's ransom, Enguerrand de Coucy, and became his wife in 1365. The match was very pleasing to King Edward, who may have arranged it, and not displeasing to Philippa. Coucy was eight years younger than Isabella, a great lord in his own right, of a courtly and elegant demeanor. He was in due course made the earl of Bedford and admitted to the order of the Garter in hopes that he would settle in England. But in the year before their marriage, one of the French hostages, the French king's second son, had fled, and the king of France returned voluntarily to London, as he felt honor required. What his other motives may have been is a mystery—escape, pleasure, hopes of arranging a peace or reducing the ransom are all quite possible. His chivalrous return was greeted with much feasting, which doubtless contributed to his death that very year, at the age of forty-five. A magnificent funeral was held in Saint Paul's and his body was then sent to his native soil. But since the ransom had not been paid, the hostages remained. Some bought their freedom, some escaped, some took leave and stayed away on the strength of lame excuses. Enguerrand de Coucy, now of the English royal family, left with his bride for his home in France, and there he chiefly remained. Isabella returned to England after the birth of her first child and there *she* chiefly remained. She had been the adored eldest daughter, insanely indulged since childhood, and like her mother she was a great spendthrift—outdid her mother, really, for her extravagances amounted to a sickness.

As Philippa had a special fondness for Isabella that had plainly spoiled the girl, she had a similar fondness for Lionel. She had, as we have seen, arranged early for his marriage to her beloved ward, the Countess Elizabeth. In the 1360s Lionel was sent to Ireland to take charge of the situation there, something he did with ill success. He was there five years and accomplished next to nothing except the passage of the repressive Statutes of Kilkenny, 1366, which set English policy in Ireland for two centuries to come. Whether Chaucer was ever with him in Ireland we do not know, though Irish libraries and archives have been sifted for a clue.

In 1363 the Countess Elizabeth died suddenly of an unknown illness —a sorrow all the deeper to Queen Philippa because she had lost two of her own daughters, both recently married, the year before. She sent for Elizabeth's eight-year-old child, Philippa of Eltham; it is possible that "Philippa Pan" (who had been raised by the queen) returned with the young girl and joined the queen's household at this time. To the queen there was a further worry: her dear Lionel, at twenty-five, was without a wife, and a suitable one would have to be found.

Several years earlier, in 1359—before the Black Prince and the Princess Isabella were married, before Lionel was sent to Ireland as king's lieutenant and Chaucer began to study law—John of Gaunt, the king's third son, married Blanche, the daughter of Henry, duke of Lancaster. Of all Philippa's children he was the brightest, the most intellectually inclined, and his marriage, as things turned out, was the most advantageous. Like his elder brother and sister, he married for love, but he married earlier than they, at nineteen; he was the first of the sons to marry except for Lionel, who was betrothed as a child.

Blanche was the daughter of the most powerful and most eminent baron of the realm and, by virtue of his great estates—he was earl of Derby, Leicester, and Lincoln, in later years Moray, as well as duke of Lancaster—the richest. The son of the old earl of Lancaster, "blind Henry" (who in opposing Mortimer and Isabella had really established Edward on the throne), Duke Henry was a knight of the old school— idealistic, dutiful, pious. He gave of his vast funds to support colleges and monasteries and build churches, and to aid the poor and the oppressed.

Universally loved, he was known as Henry, the Good Duke, and for the
best of reasons. He was, virtues aside, an accomplished man, with a literary
bent, who during an illness wrote in French a devotional work called
Mercy, Grant Mercy, in which he summed up his sins and blessings, and
another known as *Le Livre de Seyntz Medicines.* He went on crusades,
in a day when crusading had lost its luster, in Lithuania, Algeciras,
Rhodes, and Cyprus (two of these are mentioned in connection with
Chaucer's Knight). But he was preeminent as a warrior for the crown, was
really Edward III's chief companion in arms; we have already seen him
heading one of the three armies that marched to the Siege of Reims,
alongside the Black Prince and the king himself. And he had been rewarded abundantly, having almost royal powers in his Lancastrian estates.
From the proceeds of a fief in France granted by the king, he built the
great palace of the Savoy in London and filled it with treasures—it was
the showcase of the realm and in the early 1360s was serving as a decent
enough prison for the captive king of France. In one respect only he was
a poor man—and this could not have escaped King Edward and Queen
Philippa—he had no sons. His estates were to be divided between his two
daughters, Maud and Blanche. In 1361 the plague, never wholly absent
since 1348, struck England again—it was called the Second Pestilence—
and Duke Henry fell victim to it on May 23. The eldest daughter, Maud,
now married to William of Bavaria, duke of Zealand (it was her second
marriage), was sent for and in due course set sail for England to claim her
half of the inheritance. But she too fell victim to the plague and died, on
April 10, 1362. Thus the entire estates of Lancaster fell to Blanche and,
in the right of his wife, to John of Gaunt, earl of Richmond—and now
duke of Lancaster.

Until then Gaunt's career had been for the most part military; at
court he was overshadowed by the Black Prince, ten years his senior and
the hero of the age. Gaunt had been on two campaigns in his teens, was
knighted at fifteen; he was evidently not at Poitiers, but he served well
enough under his elder brother at the Siege of Reims. It was not just the
illustrious tradition of the House of Lancaster that raised him to a new
prominence after 1362. Both his older brothers were away—Lionel in
Ireland; the Black Prince, who had been made Duke of Aquitaine eight
years before, in France with his new bride. John, duke of Lancaster, was
thus the eldest of the royal princes present in England during these years,
and he was now gloriously installed in the Palace of the Savoy. He was
first summoned to Parliament in 1360 as the earl of Richmond, and took
an active role in Parliament thereafter: in 1362–1363 he stood behind a
bill that made English the official language of the law courts. He was, too,
behind Parliament's rejecting Pope Urban V's claim to suzerainty over

England. John Wyclif, an Oxford scholar, a priest in his early forties, and a royal chaplain, gave the official defense of the position, and we can date Gaunt's acquaintance with Wyclif from this time. During these years of peace there were numerous tournaments and feasts, occasions for a significant member of the royal family to be prominently on display; and England in its time of victory had become an international center of chivalry and diplomacy. In 1363 it happened that three kings came to England at the same time, and they were entertained by Gaunt and the Duchess Blanche at the Savoy—the kings of Denmark, of the Scots, and of Cyprus; the last, Pierre de Lusignan, was urging a crusade, and since his treacherous murder by his own liegemen is recounted in Chaucer's Monk's Tale, it is often supposed that Chaucer saw or met him on this occasion. The French hostages were entertained at the Savoy too, and in the next year King Jean stayed there until his death in April.

In September 1364 Gaunt was sent to Flanders on his first diplomatic mission, a mission of the greatest international importance. He was to arrange a marriage between his younger brother, Edmund, and Margaret, only daughter of the count of Flanders and widow of the duke of Burgundy. She was the greatest heiress of the age, with an inheritance embracing vast estates in Flanders and France; an alliance with her would have given the English a hold in France greater than war had gained them. And the mission was a success: a marriage treaty was ratified in October. But Edmund and Margaret, like most European royals, were related in one of the forbidden degrees of consanguinity (in their case the third). A papal dispensation would normally have been a mere formality, but the papacy was at this time established in Avignon, and the pope, a Frenchman, favored France. The dispensation was denied, the marriage postponed, elaborate diplomacy pursued. Gaunt awaited the outcome in London, but the pope never agreed to the marriage, and it was never held.

Chaucer's "ABC"

During this time when John of Gaunt was so visible as the chief representative of the royal family in London, Chaucer came to have a place at the Lancastrian court (which some call patronage and some friendship) that he enjoyed throughout his life. We know this because arrangements touching Chaucer's marriage, which occurred during these years under the sponsorship of the queen, involved John of Gaunt. We do not know how the relationship began or whether Chaucer's poetry had any bearing on it, but there is reason to believe that one of Chaucer's earliest poems dates from these years. It is an adaptation of a passage from Guillaume Deguileville's

Le Pèlerinage de la Vie Humaine, written in the 1330s; the passage is a prayer to the Virgin Mary in which each stanza begins with a successive letter of the alphabet, and it is for this reason called "An ABC," a title given to it in the fifteenth century by the poet Lydgate. It survives in twelve complete manuscripts and a printed text, plus three fragments. When it was first printed in Speght's second edition of Chaucer (1602), Speght reported that it was "made, as some say, at the request of Blanche Duchess of Lancaster, as a prayer for her private use, being a woman in her religion very devout." Speght was a reliable scholar, so one may suppose he had his information from his manuscript (he seems to have used one different from any now known), or from some tradition of his time.

The notion could have been the error of someone with *The Book of the Duchess* on his mind, or a mistake for some other lady, but it is not, as such notions often are, drawn from a misreading of something in the text itself: there is not a word in the "ABC" that could suggest the Duchess Blanche. So we should lend some credence to Speght's report; Blanche could have requested it, or John of Gaunt requested it for her as a gift. What commentators overlook is the relation between writing the poem and making it a presentable object. A medieval noble, asking for a prayer to be translated, would have expected it to be copied by a scribe and made or incorporated into a prayerbook. Those initial capitals, one for each stanza in alphabetical order, would have cried out for the illuminators and artists of an atelier devoted to producing fine manuscript books, and the surviving manuscripts bear this out.

Imagine, then, a handsomely prepared prayerbook with an illuminated capital at the beginning of every eight-line stanza, each page elaborately decorated with paintings and gold leaf, the margins overflowing with floriations and drolleries. It would have been a very valuable Gothic book that would have perished when the Palace of the Savoy was destroyed in the Peasants' Revolt. Such prayerbooks were among the rich possessions of many fourteenth-century nobles (the famous books of hours of the duc de Berry would be an example), who saw no contradiction between their religious purpose and their ostentatiousness. Then, too, this was the generation of English nobles whose native language had become English. John of Gaunt, judging from his voting record in Parliament, particularly favored the use of English—the sentiment was part of the national feeling of the time, a direct result of the English victories over France, given greater impetus just now when French hostages were still in London, and when the pope had sided with France against the marriage of Prince Edmund to Margaret of Flanders. The time had come to pray in English. As for Blanche's being devout in her religion, a number of entries in the papal registers of the time show her petitioning the pope for various dispensations and permissions (to have a portable altar, for example), for herself and others, which do suggest more than a routine concern with the faith; and one remembers that her father had been a devout churchman.

The *Prier à Nostre Dame* is the more authentic title of the manuscripts (that titles were still given by scribes in French shows how tenaciously French lingered). It is a very free translation—an adaptation, really. Its alphabetical organization was a tradition of medieval poetry and most of its content remains, by the nature of the case, unaltered, but Chaucer transformed it in every other respect. The original is in the standard eight-syllable line of French medieval verse, arranged in twelve-line stanzas with a rhyme scheme that affords only two rhymes per stanza. In English this would have been a tall order, for rhymes are more abundant in French, which has more standard endings. Chaucer reduced the demand of rhyme by adopting an eight-line stanza and a rhyme scheme that affords three rhymes for one-third fewer lines. This decision would have reduced the sheer number of words by a third, and though Chaucer adopted a ten-or-eleven-syllable line, having one more metrical stress than the French (an "iambic pentameter" line, as we conceive it, and one of the first in English), he still reduced the number of words per stanza, promoting concision. This new verse form encouraged him to divide up the long periodic sentences of his original into shorter, more pointed utterances. Here, for example is his opening stanza:

> Almighty and all merciable queene,
> To whom that all this world fleeth for succour,
> To have releese of sin, of sorrwe, of tene°,   *trouble*
> Glorious Virgin, of all flowres flow'r,
> To thee I flee, confounded in errour.
> Help and releeve, thou mighty debonaire,
> Have mercy of my perilous languour.
> Vanquished hath me my cruel adversaire.

The French version divides stanzas into triplets, most of which enclose one clause or sentence. This sounds natural in French because rhymes come so naturally; the more obtrusive rhymes of English, if they enclose clauses or sentences, tend to give a thumping emphasis—sometimes very useful, but not when addressing the Virgin Mary. To soften this effect, Chaucer divided the stanzas into quatrains, and in about half the stanzas he made grammatical units spill over past the end of a quatrain, or past the rhyme words at the ends of lines or the couplets made by the rhyming fourth and fifth lines.

The result is a poem having an appropriately modulated effect. And yet its actual content of diction and image is more heightened than in its original. Chaucer kept Deguileville's initial words for the letters of the alphabet when they were strong words, nouns mostly, that tripped off a clear image or concept: *fleeing, glorious, Moses, temple.* In most other cases, he substituted similarly vivid words: *almighty, bounty, comfort* (for Deguileville's bland *à, bien, contre*). Thus he arranged to have the first word of each stanza—especially important if it were to begin with an illuminated capital—fix an image in the reader's mind that could be developed in the stanza itself. Everything is more concrete and specific: where Deguileville referred abstractly to the Annunciation, Chaucer introduced the figure of the archangel Gabriel.

Poetry is an art form; prayer is not. It would be inimical to the spirit of prayer to use a poetical prayer for self-display; here, art must conceal art, and the effect must lend dignity and thought. Irony, wordplay, or humor would be out of place, and while Chaucer was a master of these, they are not to be found in the *Prier à Nostre Dame.* Its language is heightened, its manner meditative. It may owe a debt to medieval traditions of mystical devotion: its thought is not sequential or logical, but what might be called centrifugal—it focuses the mind on the image of the Virgin and, using repeated names of praise, associates that image with fundamental Christian dogmas. It is not lacking in intellectual content. It calls on the tradition of typology, the notion that stories of the Old Testament are symbolic "types" of the truths in the New Testament, as for example in the striking stanza at line 89, which makes Moses' burning bush a symbol of the Blessed Virgin, and also of hellfire:

> Moises that saw the bush with flambes rede
> Brenning° of which there never a sticke brende   *burning*
> Was sign of thine unwemmed° maidenhede.   *spotless*
> Thou art the bush on which there gan descende
> The Holy Ghost, the which that Moises wende°   *believed*
> Had been afire, and this was in figure°.   *symbol*
> Now lady, fro the fire thou us defende
> Which that in hell eternally shall dure.

The poem does not view religious devotion as part of a process of spiritual growth or development. It repeatedly has the speaker "flee" to the mercy of the Virgin; he can only "resign his welfare into her hand." If Chaucer himself chose the passage to be translated, it reveals him early in his life favoring a way of religion that he would follow until he died —a religion of resignation rather than of growth.

By its nature the *Prier* is a circumscribed poetical task, not of itself terribly demanding. But Chaucer's translation is a better piece of religious verse than other such English poems of the fourteenth century. It incorporates the art of French and Latin hymnody into an English poetic form that was not to reach this level of performance for another century.

His Marriage to Philippa Roet, 1366

On September 12, 1366, a letter in Latin assigned in the king's name, to "our beloved Philippa Chaucer, one of the *domicelle* of the chamber of Philippa, Queen of England, our consort," an annuity of 10 marks (a mark was two-thirds of a pound). It doesn't *say* she is the wife of Geoffrey Chaucer, but it gives her his name, and a similar letter written eight years later does call her Geoffrey's wife. Perhaps he had been married long enough by then that his wife's maiden name had receded in the royal clerks' memories; in some records a woman goes on being called by her maiden name a year or two before her married name is taken note of— dealing with the royal bureaucracy was rather like dealing with a computer. But probably Geoffrey and Philippa were married in 1366 and the annuity to her was a wedding gift. Nine months later Chaucer too was given an annuity, very likely upon the birth of a child, in recognition of his parental responsibility.

Philippa was the daughter of Sir Gilles de Roet, known as "Payne" or "Paon," which meant "usher": he came from Roet in Hainault and had been an official of protocol in the household of Marguerite, empress of Germany and countess of Hainault, Queen Philippa's sister. He accompanied Queen Philippa to England when she came as a girl to marry Edward, was in attendance on her at the Siege of Calais, 1347, and held, according to his tombstone inscription in Saint Paul's, a position in the college of heralds as "Guienne King of Arms," i.e., the record keeper of genealogies of the noble families in Guienne (Aquitaine). It sounds as if he was a widower. At some point he returned to Hainault and Marguerite's service, leaving his son and three daughters in England in Queen Philippa's care. The son, Walter, was placed in the retinue of the Black Prince. The eldest daughter, Elizabeth, was placed in a convent in 1349 when she was about thirteen. Philippa and Katherine—Katherine was the youngest—were raised by the queen.

Queen Philippa kept a motherly eye on the infant daughters of her old retainer from her native land, and when they grew older she saw to it—for it was her métier—that they were appropriately married. She placed the older girl, Philippa, in the service of her foster daughter, Elizabeth, countess of Ulster, and took her back into her own service when the countess died in 1363. She placed the younger girl, Katherine, in the service of Blanche, duchess of Lancaster; about 1366 or 1367 she arranged for her to marry Sir Hugh Swynford, one of Gaunt's retainers. At about the same time, she arranged for Philippa to marry Geoffrey Chaucer.*

All the documentary evidence about their marriage has to do with money. In 1366 Philippa was granted the annuity for life of 10 marks as a *domicella* in attendance upon the queen. In 1367, Chaucer received a similar grant of 20 marks; by then he was in the king's household, is called (probably by mistake, or in a generic sense) *esquire*, for the records show him a *valettus* until 1372. The picture is of a typical marriage between two members of the royal household, one in the king's service, the other in the queen's until the queen's death. Subsequent records show that while Geoffrey often traveled for or with the king, Philippa traveled often with the queen or, later, with the second duchess of Lancaster. So it appears that some part—perhaps some considerable part—of their married life was spent away from each other. In 1372 Philippa received an annuity of £10; in 1374 Geoffrey received a royal grant for a pitcher of wine daily (its cash value was 20 marks a year, just under £14). On June 13, 1374, the day after Chaucer took the oath as Controller, he and Philippa received from John of Gaunt another annuity of £10. In the aggregate they were a prosperous couple, and the more so because Philippa received further grants from John of Gaunt in her own name.

Then, in the early months of 1366, Chaucer's father died. Chaucer's mother leased the house in Thames Street to Henry Herbury, and by July she was remarried to one Bartholomew Chappel, London citizen and vintner. This may sound as if her marriage followed hard upon, but such marriages in merchant families were often contracted to secure property or the continuance of a business. Chaucer's sister Katherine seems at this time to have inherited property in Kent from her father, and Chaucer must have inherited something too. His mother lived on about fifteen

---

*It does appear that she was the "Philippa Pan" who was Chaucer's contemporary in the Ulster household. The "Pan" of the household records has an elevated dot after it, indicating an abbreviation or contraction. This is sometimes thought to stand for *panetaria*, "keeper of the pantry," but that position was generally held by men and the word is normally abbreviated *panet'*. It might stand for Pantolf, a wealthy family from Puddelsden in Shropshire ("Pullesdon" is mentioned once in connection with Philippa "Pan"), or for the name Panetrie, a London family that had certain connections with the Chaucers. But neither of these fits the picture as Philippa Paon de Roet fits, and there was a sixteenth-century tradition that Chaucer married the daughter of "Sir Payne Roet." "Pan" probably derived from the diminutive "panetto" or "paonnet" by which Sir Gilles had been known when he was a lesser official, an assistant usher, as it were; the o in "Paon" had no phonetic value. There is no doubt about who Chaucer married; what is at issue is whether the two had known each other since early adolescence.

years, but of his relationship with her or with his stepfather nothing is known.

Geoffrey and Philippa had, as it appears from scanty and often mysterious records, four children.

The eldest would have been Elizabeth "Chausier," who entered the elegant convent, Barking Abbey, in 1381.* She was first sent to the Black Nuns, in Bishopgate Street, London, near Chaucer's quarters at Aldgate. John of Gaunt paid £15 8s. 2d. for her admission. If when she entered the abbey in 1381 she was in her teens, the usual age, she would have been born in the mid-1360s, shortly after Chaucer's marriage, and have been the oldest child. How can it be she wasn't named Philippa?—it was her mother's name and the queen's name, and by this time no family was without a daughter of that name. The answer must be that she was named for the Countess Elizabeth, who had died in 1363, in whose service Geoffrey and Philippa apparently first met.

The eldest son, Thomas, was born in 1367. In the next century he had great wealth and position; his daughter became duchess of Suffolk. He was known in his own time as the son of Geoffrey Chaucer, and he served in the retinue of John of Gaunt.

A second son, Lewis, is known only as the boy sent to Oxford about 1390 at the age of ten, for whom Chaucer wrote his *Treatise on the Astrolabe*; he is addressed as "my little son" (though this could be a figure of speech for, say, the poet's godson, the child of Sir Lewis Clifford). But there is a record of Thomas and Lewis Chaucer bearing arms in 1403.

Finally there is an Agnes Chaucer listed as a damsel-in-waiting at the coronation of Henry IV; she was listed with Joan Swynford, probably Joan Beaufort, the daughter of Katherine Swynford by John of Gaunt. Her name, Agnes, it will not escape notice, was Chaucer's mother's name. Still, if she was a *domicella* in 1399, she could have been born as late as the mid-1380s and might have been the poet's grandchild.

One notes the presence of John of Gaunt in many of these family dealings. Shortly after his first wife's death Gaunt took Katherine Swynford, Philippa's sister, as his mistress, and made no secret of it; she remained so after his marriage to the Princess Costanza of Castile. Her place at court was dignified with the position of governess to the duke's children; her husband, Sir Hugh Swynford, regarded the arrangement with complacency, but as Gaunt's retainer he had little choice. In 1372,

---

*She was, assuming an Elizabeth "Chausir" is the same nun, still alive in 1397, on record as swearing obedience to a new abbess. It is sometimes thought she was the poet's sister or half sister, but Agnes Chaucer was *at least* forty when Elizabeth was born, and one would be hard pressed to explain John of Gaunt's involvement.

the year after Gaunt's marriage to Costanza, Katherine bore Gaunt an illegitimate son (in the same year, Philippa was granted an annuity of £10), and there were other acknowledged children. Twenty-four years later, after the death of the Princess Costanza, Gaunt married Katherine, in 1396, thus legitimizing his children by her. All these circumstances are well known, and since the affair went on for over twenty years, it must have been taken in stride at court out of habit if nothing else.

Chaucer's connection to Gaunt and, through his marriage, to Katherine Swynford, has suggested to a few scholars with a collective nose for scandal that Thomas Chaucer, who was so well favored in future years— and who took his mother's coat of arms rather than his father's—was the bastard son of John of Gaunt by Philippa Roet, and that Chaucer was used (and favored) to cover up this fact. Heady with such a surmise, the same scholars have made out poor Sister Elizabeth, she of Barking Abbey, to be Gaunt's bastard daughter. The evidence is very arcane: it has to do with dates, which could be coincidental, with coats of arms and their symbolism, which is often ambiguous, and with Gaunt's payment of Sister Elizabeth's dowry to the convent and his favors to Thomas Chaucer. One might ask, from the simple vantage point of human nature, why Gaunt would have been at such pains to cover his tracks when a few years later he made no bones about having Katherine for his mistress. Until 1368 there is a reason to believe he had no mistress at all: he still had the Duchess Blanche, with whom, by all indications, he was deeply in love. If he had had a child by Katherine or Philippa while Blanche was still alive, he *would* have had a reason to cover his tracks—and the more he loved Blanche, the more reason he would have had; by the time Blanche died, Philippa was married to Chaucer, and Gaunt could, some say, have fathered a child or two on her during the early years of her marriage, which would put Chaucer, as B. J. Whiting wryly observed, in the "pretty role of contented cuckold." Of course one must admit if Chaucer had been assigned such a role he would, like Sir Hugh Swynford, have had little choice but to play it. Yet those who believe this bit of scandal never entertain the obvious corollary, that he would have had to be contented *perforce,* and that with his swallowed pride would have seethed a deal of swallowed resentment and rage—which we would then be obliged to regard as the heated wellsprings of a habitual irony.

But gossip it is, and modern gossip; there is no record of any such talk at court in Chaucer's day, though Speght and others in the sixteenth century reported doubts that Thomas Chaucer was Geoffrey Chaucer's son. True, if there had been such talk it would have had to be in whispers. All we can say is that it's possible Chaucer's marriage was unconventional in this way, that he made an honest woman of Philippa—or that he and

Philippa made an honest woman of Katherine. Or that he married Philippa and *then* was cuckolded by his friend. Or that for political advantage he played pimp to a powerful royal with his own wife. Or that he didn't know, or knew and didn't care. Any of these possible interpretations gives an unsavory and curious picture, though a very interesting one. All are guesses; none can be ruled out.

If we ignore the gossip and assume that Chaucer's was a perfectly legitimate marriage to an estimable lady who had a questionable younger sister, we get a more palatable and more consistent picture—not that medieval life was any more palatable or consistent than modern life is. Chaucer himself did not lack connections with John of Gaunt, and in later years the fact that the duke truly loved Chaucer's sister-in-law may be reason enough why he granted financial favors to Chaucer and Philippa. Chaucer's eldest son used Chaucer's coat of arms at first, then took his mother's coat of arms because it was more prestigious—he was a snob, not a bastard. As for the quality of Chaucer's domestic life, it may have been anything from a tender idyll to open war. One biographer, the late John Gardner, reasoned that because so much good is said of marriage in Chaucer's writings, his own marriage must have been a happy one—even though, as he believed, Chaucer *was* a contented cuckold. But one could as easily argue the opposite case, that so much ill is said of marriage in Chaucer's writings that his wife must have been as great a shrew as the Wife of Bath at her worst, or as shameless a baggage as May in the Merchant's Tale.

What must be remembered is that Chaucer *married well*, and the marriage brought him advantages of status, connections, and annuities. At this we have no occasion to raise an eyebrow, for such advantages were in the nature of medieval marriage, as to some extent they are in the nature of marriage still. In the Middle Ages marriages were contracted not just by the two partners but by their families—as one historian says, "the transaction was not one between two individuals but between two groups." In this case the queen herself was acting on behalf of the young lady's father. Precisely what advantage Philippa would have had from the contract must be a matter for earnest conjecture. Perhaps she was shy and withdrawn in contrast to her forward sister. Or perhaps not pretty. But it is equally possible that the advantages were as much if not more on her side. She was marrying a young man of great ability and promise, a man of parts, from a family not that far beneath her own in rank, and perhaps in better financial circumstances. And an amusing man, given to writing poems in his spare time.

A marriage in the late fourteenth century between such families was business, and the business began with a discreet feeler. If one family saw

a possible advantage, they sent a letter or messenger to find out the
inclinations of the other family; with Geoffrey and Philippa this may have
been done by the merest word from the queen. The wishes of the young
man or woman might be consulted as well. If the parties were agreed,
certain conditions had to be seen to: one had to be sure, for example, that
the couple were not within the forbidden degrees of consanguinity or were
not betrothed elsewhere. A marriage contract was then drawn up, dealing
almost exclusively with financial matters. First, the dowry. The lady's
family were expected to put up a sum of money or property that she would
bring to the marriage. But the young man, too, was expected to come to
the marriage with means and property. Then arrangements were made for
the inheritance of these combined assets if either party died. In particular,
if the wife survived the husband—not unusual in a warrior society—there
were provisions for a "dower" (that part of his property she would inherit)
and a "dower house," a place other than his family home where she would
live if he died and which would revert to his family upon her death. At
the very top ranks of society the lady often had an inheritance, budget,
and retinue of her own, and brought to her marriage her own little empire.
But at the level of society to which Chaucer and Philippa belonged a
relatively simple agreement was enough. The agreement was repeated
before the church door as a part of the marriage ceremony, and before
witnesses too (the Wife of Bath's famous five husbands, taken "at church
door," were chiefly rehearsing a financial settlement there). After this the
wedding party went inside the church for the wedding and the nuptial
mass. Then, as now, there was a wedding reception, but its purpose was
to accumulate a body of witnesses lest either party were to claim the
ceremony had not been performed. Secret marriages, though there were
many, were discouraged for this reason; it was too easy to repudiate them.

What kind of marriage did Geoffrey and Philippa have?

There is a reason why their marriage might have been more than this
characteristic medieval settlement, and certainly more than a *mariage de
convenance* for John of Gaunt's benefit. This reason we must intuit, and
intuit from Chaucer's later works—a procedure fraught with dangers but
in this case justified. *Chaucer liked women.* He had what was for his day
an unusual kind of interest in women, and he had unusual insight into a
woman's mind. The evidence in support of such an assertion is overwhelming: he was the first male writer since the ancient world who was
successfully to see inside the mind of a woman, successfully to portray a
woman's thoughts and feelings. He may have been the first *writer* since
the ancient world to see inside the mind of the sex opposite his or her
own, though Marie de France and Héloïse could be reckoned exceptions.
Other exceptions, like Chrétien or the authors of the *Roman,* had but

limited success. Chaucer had no models to follow, and there was, as we shall see, little to lead him into this accomplishment but his own interest and ability. On what, then, could that ability be based? In part, so the argument of future chapters will run, on his capacity to see in previous literature possibilities for literary techniques by which he could do something never done before. But, more than that, he had the interest, and the *motive,* to portray women, and he would not have had it without some predisposition to do so—which we must find in his temperament or character.

Chaucer was what may be called an androgynous personality. He lived in a man's world, achieved eminence as a public figure and a writer in a man's world, yet he had no difficulty at all seeing the world through women's eyes. "Androgynous" in this sense does not suggest any physical anomaly or any characterological limitation. It is simply the ability to see things from the viewpoint of either sex; Coleridge said a great mind must be androgynous. In the Middle Ages it must have been the case that many men lived so much in a man's world of knighthood and warfare, hunting, tournaments, and the like, that the women in their lives were mere necessities; they were the subjects of song and story, the objects of desire or emotional dependency, indispensable in family and dynastic alliances, but never companions or friends, certainly not equals. Of course there have always been some men who get on better with women than with men, and in a warrior society where rivalry among males was so fundamental, this may often have been the case. But the androgynous personality is not limited in either way.

It is hard to imagine how Chaucer could have succeeded in portraying Criseyde or the Prioress or the Wife of Bath if he did not have, androgyny aside, the ability to be a companion and a friend with women. And if it's true that Philippa Roet was an acquaintance he had known since adolescence, perhaps early adolescence—they would have had an acquaintanceship stretching over nearly a decade now—it is hard not to imagine that at the time Chaucer married Philippa he was already close to her as brothers are close to sisters, as friends and longtime companions are close, in a kind of closeness few husbands during any age can truthfully claim to enjoy.

But while this is safe enough to say about Geoffrey, we have no basis on which to say anything similar about Philippa. Chaucer liked and understood women and must have found them easy companions. The similarity between Chaucer the narrator, in *Troilus and Criseyde,* and the character Pandarus has often been remarked upon, and it may be that Chaucer himself possessed the quality that he depicts in Pandarus, the ability easily to associate with women, talk and banter with women, second-guess their thoughts, share their world, take them aside, gossip, chitchat, enjoy their company, and make them enjoy his. But none of this means that Philippa Chaucer had anything like that ability to relate to men. She might have resented his way with the ladies. In later years Queen Anne herself, it would appear, was to banter and discourse with Master Geoffrey, and it could be that his androgynous qualities served not at all to promote domestic concord. Between friends and companions can grow rivalry; the easiest companionship in the world can go sour. We know only that they remained married for some twenty years and had children, and that after Philippa's death Chaucer never remarried. But we know too that they were often apart. We know (but we will treat it later) of a curious document relating to the rape of one Cecily Chaumpaigne by one Geoffrey Chaucer, Esq. For the rest we can only say of Chaucer's marriage that we are in no worse position than we are with many a living couple that we can observe daily at first hand: from all that strikes the eye, they may appear a model of domestic concord, and unless we are very intimate with one or the other partner, or with both, we never know more than that except from inconclusive hints, from virtually unreadable signs, or—what is by its nature unreliable—from gossip.

Was the Marriage Unhappy?

The unanswered question about Chaucer's domestic life is whether he loved Philippa, whether he knew love at all from personal experience. For he does in his poems very often speak as if love was outside his ken and marriage was a burden. "It seems impossible to put a pleasant construction on these passages," one writer concluded. "It is incredible that they have no personal significance. The conclusion clearly is that Chaucer was not happy in his matrimonial relations." Such passages are often ironical, however, or occur in conventional antimatrimonial comedy. Moreover, sex, love, and marriage are three different, if interrelated, subjects—what Chaucer said about one cannot be used in evidence about another.

Perhaps, all the same, we can get from his writings a clue about Chaucer's private life from his writings, if only through intuition. Some of the relevant passages are too ambiguous to have a meaning all can agree upon. For example, in *The Book of the Duchess* Chaucer speaks of a "sicknesse / That I have suffred this eight yeere" (lines 36–37) and says his cure is no nearer: there is only one physician who can heal him. Then he brushes the whole matter under the carpet: no more of that, let us pass over it until another time, what will not be must be left behind. What can this mean? It is apparently the conventional "lovesickness" of French poetry—the details are based on poems by Machaut, including the specified number of years. The one physician who can heal him is of course the lady he loves unrequited. It is probably all a fiction and no such lady ever existed. Poets, even "bourgeois" ones, wrote as if they were courtly lovers, by the same kind of conventional dictate that makes present-day popular singers, even those who come from England and Australia, pronounce the words of songs as if they came from Tennessee. On the other hand, the passage *could* have a relationship of some sort to Chaucer's life. One scholar even came up with the suggestion, not entirely implausible, that the lady was none other than Joan of Kent, whom the king had loved and the Black Prince married. Rather ambitious for a vintner's son, but it would mean that she was a "poetical mistress," a lady to whom such poems were addressed in a nonpersonal way, for the sake of art and patronage. It would be serious, but not factual. It can't be a joke—a joke would be out of place in this context, and so would a veiled reference to his wife. The specific reference to eight years is the real puzzle; for the rest, the best explanation is that the passage is conventional, deliberately vague, and only intended to serve an artistic purpose.

This is almost the only place in his poetry where Chaucer seems seriously to speak of himself as being a "courtly lover," except in some of his songs, and these are conventional too—love songs about the lover's longing, or the lady's beauty or nobility, or, in one case, her faithlessness. What we find more often in his poetry is the suggestion that he knows nothing about love except for what he reads in books. This might seem less than complimentary to Philippa—but not really if it is a joke. In *Troilus and Criseyde,* in what is undeniably a serious context (1: 15–18), he says that he, who "serves the servants of the God of Love," does not dare to pray to Love for help, because of his unlikeliness—"so far am I from his help, in darkness." What is this darkness? It is the lack of that light the God of Love could shed on him, and he is without it, he says, because he dares not pray to him. It is implied that if he *did* pray to the God of Love, his prayer would not be heard because of his "unlikeliness": the word (this is its first recorded appearance in English) means improbability or unsuitability, but he does not indicate why he is "unlikely." In his later songs the idea is a joke: he is too fat, or too old, or bored, or is in decline. It may be implied (but is never stated) that he is not high enough on the social scale to expect to participate in "courtly" love, and possibly his purpose was to forestall that objection by denying his likeliness on other grounds, or ambiguously. But as this picture of the "unlikely" narrator emerges, it *is* funny. He "serves the servants of Love," a formula that makes him like a pope in Cupid's religion. And his purpose in taking the pose is to "distance" himself, to keep himself out of the poem and make the reader, whom he flatters as a *true* courtly lover, feel the more involved in it.*

In spite of his frequent pose as an outsider to love, Chaucer *did* understand a great deal about passion and sex. He represents these feelings in his characters vividly, with compassion and insight, and in realistic detail—in passages added to the material of his sources. He knew what it was to fall in love, to experience unbearable longing as Troilus does, or thwarted love as Pandarus does. He knew as well healthy sexual urges and knew how they could be fulfilled in raunchy, fly-by-night ways without vows or commitments—just for fun, as with Nicholas and Alison in the Miller's Tale, or fun mixed awesomely with aggression and revenge, as with those two lusty Cambridge clerks in the Reeve's Tale. But the fact that he knew these and many other varieties of experience doesn't mean he knew them firsthand. In fact, that argument is disproved by his keen insight into the young widow Criseyde's cautious, self-concealed desire, or the much older Wife of Bath's indomitable zest, her yearning, her nostalgia. He cannot have experienced at first hand the emotions of these two very different kinds of women, yet he *knew* their emotions, else he could not have represented them so powerfully. Then what do these literary accomplishments prove about Chaucer the man himself? Nothing. They only prove that he was, in Keats's phrase, a "chameleon poet," capable of an imaginative reach into experiences *other* than his own.

Even so, his own experience must have been considerable. He was human, he was married, he fathered children; and almost all his readers, feeling empathy with him, believe in their hearts that he really had a good deal of firsthand experience in passions, affections, and sex. That intuition must be evidence of a sort. No one has ever suggested that Chaucer was at base a repressed celibate, like Henry James, say, whose deep understanding of human emotion was an imaginative feat of thought, observation, and empathy. It is impossible. His range of experience was greater than James's—you can't imagine James writing the Miller's Tale, or the raucous prologue of the Manciple's Tale, let alone the tale of patient Griselda. Ezra Pound said Chaucer knew more about life than Shakes-

*There may be a serious undertone to this passage at the beginning of *Troilus*: the suggestion may be that he dares not pray to the God of Love because he is a Christian and the God of Love is a pagan god, Cupid. From this point of view, his unlikeliness ought to be shared by the audience. Both the comic and the serious meaning come out later in the poem. The narrator can be a very funny figure who at one point naïvely cries, with envy at the lovers' blissful night, "Why n'ad I swich one with my soul ybought"—why didn't I buy such a one with *my* soul? (3: 1319–1320) But the undertone of meaning, confirmed explicitly at the end of the poem, is that such joys *are* enjoyed at the peril of one's soul.

peare, which is true: Shakespeare's knowledge of life was largely based on an actor's experience—he got it in the greenroom.

But there must have been one side of Chaucer's personality that *can* be described as "repressed." His literary accomplishment was in large measure an imaginative feat of *reading,* of imitating and adapting, of trial and error. This is a solitary accomplishment, the work of a withdrawn, inward-turning person whose experience comes vicariously from books. And in fact very often when Chaucer refers to himself, he refers, humorously, to just such a person. In *The House of Fame,* written when he was in his thirties, he has the comical eagle describe him:

> But of thy very neighebores
> That dwellen almost at thy doores,
> Thou hearest neither that ne this.
> For when thy labour done all is,
> And hast made all they reckeninges,°   *accounts*
> Instead of rest and newe thinges,
> Thou gost home to thy house anon,
> And, also° dumb as any stone,   *as*
> Thou sittest at another book
> Till fully daswed° is thy look,   *dazed*
> And livest thus as an heremite°,   *hermit*
> Although thine abstinence is lite°.   *small*

A decade later the Host in *The Canterbury Tales* says to him,

> . . . What man artow°?   *art thou*
> Thou lookest as thou woldest find an hare,
> For ever upon the ground I see thee stare.

then, turning to the others,

> He seemeth elvish° by his countenance,   *abstracted*
> For unto no wight doth he dalliaunce.
> (7: 1885–1894)

And there are other such passages, that must be taken seriously as self-humor pointing to a quality in himself that, if it had not existed or he was unaware of it, would not have been something for him to joke about.

This withdrawn side of Chaucer evidently came upon him as he grew older. We can suppose that it was there *in embryo* when he was a young man of affairs, newly a part of the royal household and newly married. But he was kept very busy in those years, was ambitious, was physically vigorous (one did not travel abroad if one was not), and was intellectually alive. He was often separated from his wife, and even when they were together there is no hard evidence that before 1374 they had a private residence to live in; they might have lived with relatives, who cared for their children when they were both traveling or occupied at court, though Philippa might have brought the children with her when she was at court. The chances are, their marriage was happy in its earlier years.

Where then is all the purported evidence that Chaucer was not happy in his marital relations? *The Book of the Duchess* celebrates a marriage for love, and *The Parliament of Fowls* celebrates marriage (better, mating) in the abstract. *The House of Fame* has to do with "tidings of Love" and a royal betrothal; it is the one place where Chaucer makes explicit references (there are two of them) to his domestic circumstances. One is the passage quoted above where he returns home to spend the evening over a book, something Philippa may or may not have complained about; but Chaucer could have been thinking of times when she was not with him. The other is a very funny passage in which the great hovering eagle shrieks at him "Awake!" (in Middle English the word makes a birdlike, quacking sound) in, he says, "the same voice used by someone I could name." It must be his wife who thus rudely wakes him, some argue, because Geoffrey and Philippa were by this time living together in the pleasant residence at Aldgate. And he adds (lines 565–566) that "it was said in a pleasant way, as was not usually the case." Isn't this a joke between married people who are genuinely fond of each other? Imagine Chaucer reading the poem at court, with Philippa present and scores of mutual acquaintances; even if it was read out of her earshot, it can't be sarcastic—the context is too effervescently comical for him to have spoiled it that way. If the "one I could name" is Philippa, the passage is tangible evidence of Geoffrey's and Philippa's playful and affectionate regard for one another at this time, fifteen years into their marriage.

Nor is there evidence about his marriage in his later masterpieces. *Troilus and Criseyde* is about a deliriously happy love affair—a secret marriage, some think—in a pagan setting, which ends with bad fortune, a forced parting, and a jilting. It is one of the saddest poems ever written, but it expresses no discontent over marital relations—it's about the transitoriness of love, and possibly after twenty years of married life Chaucer had some thoughts on that subject. Even in *The Canterbury Tales* much of what is said about marriage is stock humor about shrewish wives, henpecked husbands, cuckoldry, adultery, and other tribulations of married life. The Wife of Bath's tale of "woe that is in marriage" is a high-spirited reflection upon married life—and she is, after all, looking for a sixth husband. There are bitter stories of marriage, but they are stock comedy. There is the Clerk's idealized tale of patient Griselda bearing the yoke of her marriage to a sadistic husband—sympathetic aplenty to the woman's side of marital woes, and not a funny story but one of immense pathos that could, we know, move medieval readers, *male* readers, to tears. There is (in the Knight's Tale) a chivalric romance that ends in a happy marriage, and (in the Second Nun's Tale) a saints' legend of a saintly marriage chaste and dedicated.

What we must remember is that when Chaucer wrote all these conflicting views of marriage in *The Canterbury Tales,* his wife Philippa had been dead for several years.

Chaucer's treatment of marital woes in *The Canterbury Tales* is rich and many-sided and contradictory; and in this it does indeed seem to have personal significance. But it reveals complex feelings, of which unhappiness is but a part. In 1396 he wrote to his friend Bukton, who was about to marry in his forties, "God grante you your life freely to leade / In freedom—for full hard it is to be bonde." It was then a decade since Philippa's death, and he had written the Wife of Bath's prologue and tale in the interim. Perhaps there is discontent expressed in this remark about bondage, but the context is humorous ("read the Wife of Bath about this matter," he advises) and the ending is a resolve not to remarry, not to fall again into "the trap."

Courtly Love

Though sex and marriage belonged to everyone, "love" in Chaucer's time belonged to the upper classes. A bumpkin like Absolon in the Miller's Tale, who apes courtly conventions of song and poetry and upper-class mannerisms of "dalliaunce and fair language" is uppity and affected—ridiculous because he misuses courtly language in hilarious malapropisms. "I mourne as doth a lamb after the teat" (line 3704), he sighs, in a metaphor of his own devising—for lambs longing for the mother's teat don't show up in courtly tradition. When Chaucer refers to himself as an outsider to love, this stock ineptitude may be a part of the humor. For example, he wrote a song called "To Rosemunde" in which he proclaims his love for a lady whose name (*rosa mundi,* "rose of the world") is grandly symbolic and encompassing, like the "mapamounde," he says, the map of the world. But as the description of her emerges, she has round red cheeks and a squeaky voice, and he, the lover, is wallowing in tears like a cooked fish in a galantine sauce—and calling himself "Tristan the second." Well, Tristan might have described himself as a fish caught on a hook, for this *was,* if you can believe it, a conventional image, but a fish in a cooking utensil was not. The joke is two-sided: the "courtly lover" here gets the conventions wrong, but on the other side his mistakes make us see that the conventions themselves are something we can laugh at.

When Chaucer in more serious poems takes the pose that he knows nothing about love except from books, he violates one of the courtly conventions. The poet was expected to speak as though he too were a lover. All the French poets did so; Dante, Petrarch, and Boccaccio did so; and Chaucer did so in *The Book of the Duchess*. A young squire in the royal household was expected to know about such things, not profess ignorance. Talking about love was a great evening pastime, and talking about it well was a recognized skill. In this verbal aspect of courtly tradition Chaucer must have been exceptionally brilliant, so part of the humor in his pose came from its being incongruous, rather like the famous mathematician who says he can't add. In some ways it is just part of Chaucer's strain of self-humor about his being withdrawn and abstracted, always with his nose in a book. It is very hard to imagine that anyone took the joke as unkind to Philippa.

Such jokes would have made no sense if people didn't know the conventions. Everyone has heard of "courtly love," and almost everyone has heard of C. S. Lewis's four characteristics of it, "humility, courtesy, adultery, and the religion of love." To Lewis, courtly love was "a revolution in human sentiment," a courtly or aristocratic tradition, in large measure literary, which altered men's and women's attitudes and feelings about the relation between the sexes. This is but one of many interpretations, and nearly all have a measure of truth: that it was based on the bond between the feudal vassal and his overlord; that it was a revolt against Christian doctrine and so a heresy; that it was a "morale-building ethos" among a lower echelon of knights faced with a shortage of marriageable heiresses; that it was an allegory meant to condemn cupidity. It existed more in song and story, in fantasy, and in conversation than in everyday behavior, but it was not any the less a part of experience for that. Still, the historian Georges Duby has shown that it did influence the actual behavior of aristocratic families in France in their dealings about marriage. "Courtly" is, by the way, a modern attributive for it; in its own time it was simply called "love," or in France, *fin amor*.

In the court of King Edward III this tradition, by then two centuries old, was still taken seriously, still talked about and written about, still part of chivalry and gentilesse. By now it was in people's bones, or anyway in noblemen's bones, and was known at a popular level too; it was on its way to becoming a classless social norm, as (with certain changes) it remains to this day. By the end of the fifteenth century, in the letters of the Paston family, we find one of the family's servants, Richard Calle, addressing the family's daughter (with whom he was, to their horror, in love) in the traditional language. "Love" was predictable behavior in the male, who is "the lover." The lover and the lady are expected to be highborn and young. The lover is at first indifferent to love, then smitten by Cupid's arrow. He suffers and pines; the lady is remote and distant. He must find a means to make her aware of his existence—through a go-between, a serenade, a letter—and he must never despair. She on her side must not acquiesce too soon, nor yet be proud. In the end, if all goes well, she will accept him and he will rejoice. And love, whether requited or not, will have an ennobling effect on him, make him a better knight, a greater warrior, more courteous, more gentle, more generous. Love is for nobles, and it makes them nobler. It is, too, for the young. Older men looked with amused skepticism on the amorous excesses of youth, including their own; Chaucer in a late poem says, "While I was young, I put it forth in press, / But all shall pass . . . ," rather much as Polonius, seeing Hamlet mad for love, says "and truly in my youth I suffered much extremity for love; very near this." Any violation of these norms—if the lady falls in love with the man, or if the man is hypocritical or fickle, or old—is either funny or unseemly.

In a civilization dominated by the church, it is not surprising that love was described in the language of religion. The "religion of love" was modeled on Christianity: the lover sought "grace" from the lady, did penance, asked mercy, carried about in his mind always an image of her beauty (like a monk meditating on the Virgin or the crucified Lord). He must be faithful, like Christians in marriage, patient like Christians in adversity. If she grants him "grace," he will find himself in "heaven's bliss." But the lady is not the deity in this pseudoreligion; the deities are pagan ones—Venus and Cupid—and the lady more like a saint. In this respect courtly love was a form of pseudopaganism, a fantasy of returning to the religion of the ancients, to the "Age of Nature." The lover prays to the God of Love, Cupid, to forgive him any former irreverence and to help him. There is a nonvirgin and child, Venus and her son Cupid, and sometimes saints and martyrs. The God of Love's arrows, shot through the eye into the heart, are impulses, what medieval theologians called "the first movements of sense," suggestions that may take root in our hearts, may delight the will and entice the reason. The pattern by which love comes into the lover's life is in fact modeled on the pattern by which medieval moralists described the occurrence of sin: reason is overcome by passion, and a wrong choice is made. Reason is thus an enemy in the antiworld of courtly love, and its sensible, true dictates are cavalierly brushed aside. But it is often implied that reason will triumph in the end, that the whole amorous enterprise is but a temporary truancy or game.

How could medieval Christians play at paganism and antirational licentiousness? Everyone knew that the church valued chastity most highly and counseled marriage—best, marriage only once—to fulfill the biblical command, "Go forth and multiply." That anything beneath that was sinful, there was no question in anyone's mind. Some think the "religion of love" was an actual heresy, something the church opposed, a serious effort of medieval man to shake his fist at the ascetical strictures of Christian morality. But although the church didn't like it, and did condemn some literary works about it, if it had perceived courtly love as a serious heresy it would have have crushed it. When in the early thirteenth century the church found itself menaced by the Catharist heresy, it mounted a crusade, promised the knights booty and indulgences, and let them wipe out the rich civilization of Provence.

Yet in this "religion" of love adultery was the norm. Not literally, of course: adultery would have been a difficult norm in a world where people rarely slept in a room by themselves, where nobles were forever surrounded by servants and retinues, where women were never without companions. Adultery in this context—which is a clerical context—means sensuality. The only righteous alternatives to marriage, as prescribed by the clergy, were chastity or widowhood. Anything else in the sphere of male-female relations was reckoned adulterous, even the passionate love of one's own wife, and anything outside that sphere was "unnatural." Marriage was thus constrained, regulated, and one-sided: producing children was its end, among nobles it served economic or dynastic goals, the woman was sworn to obey the man. None of these conditions was friendly to love, for love was an "inborn suffering" that should be unconstrained and mutual. Some writers, with willful irony, insist that love *must* fly in the face of religion. They flatly declare that love and marriage are incompatible, that the true lover serves Venus (i.e., pleasure) alone. It was understood that procreation is incompatible with love; love was not entered into for such practical purposes, and in literature it was not allowed to have such results. The "tragic love" that issues in an unwanted or illegitimate child is a middle-class story belonging to a later age. Tragic love in medieval literature was love frustrated by the husband's jealousy or the lady's fickleness or the knight's unworthiness—by inward failures or by conflicts within their code, as between love and honor, or by fortune.

One writer, John of Garland, in his treatise on poetry, distinguished three *styles* for dealing with love: one for those who hold court, one for city dwellers or burghers, and one for rustics. He said that for courtiers love can be adulterous but also can occur within marriage. Such writers —and medical writers too—agreed that there could be an *inordinate* love that overcomes reason and makes a man love's captive; physicians viewed this, the *amor heroes*, "heroic" or "noble" love, as a peculiar aberrance of the nobility. The ideal was a love in which honor transcended utility.

Such an ideal of love had been, since the twelfth century, part of courtly culture. As such it was part of a man's world and was seen from a man's viewpoint; but because it elevated the lady into a position of prominence, ladies liked and fostered it. Poets often said they were writing "for the ladies"—Dante and Boccaccio both say this. In part the expression meant only that they were writing in the vernacular; what was written for the ladies was not perhaps to be taken very seriously, for there was a whole other kind of work, written in Latin and for men, and to such works Dante, Petrarch, and Boccaccio devoted a large measure of their endeavors. But what poets wrote for the ladies had more force and more imaginative play, and on this account it is the side of medieval literature we still read for pleasure; we read the rest out of duty if we read it at all. Not that noblemen didn't find the tradition every bit as entertaining as the ladies did, but for them it was only half a life. For the medieval knight the larger and more important half had nothing to do with ladies, it had to do with battle. The God of Love was *said* to be irresistible, but for men love was a choice. Some knights were lovers and some were not. In Sir Thomas Malory's *Morte d'Arthur,* the cynical knight Dinaden is asked in a perfectly matter-of-fact way if he is a lover: "Marry," he answers, "fie on that craft."

Medieval love was at base a sensibility, a mystique. To understand it you had to be to the manner born—well, unless you were a poet—and part of what you had to understand was that its excesses could be silly; it had almost from its inception a humorous and ironic aspect. Its variousness was what gave it power. It could rise, as in Dante, so high as to symbolize the union of the soul with God in the beatific vision, or sink as low as Chaucer's hypocritical Damian in the Merchant's Tale, making hasty love to slatternly May in a tree. It could be an elevated, tragic sentiment, which raises human experience to a peak of joy and idealism but sees that this peak must, like all earthly things, pass away. It could be a love crowned by a marriage, successful both as love and as the union of two noble houses, shattered only by death. It could be long-suffering and self-sacrificing, a love between rivals where one rival may die and in dying cede the hand of the lady in marriage to his rival. All of these variations are in fact depicted by Chaucer. But he depicts, too, the excesses and the absurdities, the pretensions, the hypocrisies, the debasements, and he ridicules those who take it too seriously, or who take it seriously for the wrong reasons. Doubtless along with other aspects of chivalry it improved the manners and sensibilities of a warlike aristocracy, but knights who at home loved the songs and the stories and the banter were still capable of hideous cruelties. And this was no more seen as a contradiction than being a devotee of Venus and yet a Christian.

Whether courtly love raised the position of women is arguable. For any but those of aristocratic families it did nothing. And the women of aristocratic families already *had* status: they were valued pawns in the important business of marriage, and came to their alliances with their own retinues and property and networks of family connections. In their lord's absence, when he was at war, they were in charge of the castle. In the long run women must have benefited from medieval love, at least because it made communication between the sexes easier, gave women a new role in social life, and gave them a new relationship to art (they could be patrons). All the same, if Chaucer's observations are any testimony, medieval love, even in the fourteenth century, did not make substantial changes in the position of women. In Chaucer's later works we see Criseyde, a gentlewoman, a member of the nobility, treated with great deference and courtesy; but she is lied to and deceived, badgered and bamboozled by her uncle with the assent of his friend the Prince. At the end, when Troilus is jilted and in despair, Pandarus observes with complacency that she can be replaced. The Wife of Bath, from the successful sector of the middle class, a weaver with her own shop and probably her own employees, not to mention legacies from four husbands, obviously has considerable status, but it is based on work, on money, and on what she calls her "sturdy hardinesse." One cannot imagine any woman having much higher status in her peer group than the Wife, in Chaucer's time or for some centuries after. But this did not come her way because of courtly love, and love in this sense is never in her thoughts.

Chaucer's own marriage was not "courtly." He did not really belong to the social group in which courtly love was appropriate, nor perhaps strictly speaking did his wife, and their marriage may have been arranged in too businesslike a way to be thought romantic. He was the *poet* of Love, and his love poems all make a joke of his inappropriateness in the role of lover.

4

The Wheel Turns

England's Disasters

The medieval conception of Fortune's Wheel does sometimes really seem an accurate description of medieval history. Chaucer learned the lore of the courtly world in the English royal household during the 1360s; by the mid 1370s, when he had just turned thirty, that lustrous, colorful world, peopled with almost legendary figures, was at its height. Then, beginning in 1368, the wheel began its downward course.

For Chaucer a harbinger of this turn was the Countess Elizabeth's death in 1363. She had been the first great lady he had known and though she died far away in Ireland and after he had left her service, her death made the Ulster household and the whole world of his adolescence seem more than ever in the past. All the great ladies of the age had, in the intervening years, come within his purview, Queen Philippa herself, the Duchess Blanche, the Princess Joan of Kent, and the Princess Isabella among them. In 1363, at twenty, he belonged to a world of great palaces and paved parlors, of courtly ceremony and gentilesse, a world in which young esquires like himself were, in the words of one account, "accus-

tomed winter and summer in afternoons and evenings to draw to lords'
chambers within court, there to keep honest company after their cunning
in talking of chronicles of kings and of others' policies, or in piping, or
harping, [or in] songings. . . ."

It was an age of ambition and an age of spectacle. As far back as he
could remember, English glory and chivalry were in the air. The royal
household of his younger days was heady with the great victories of the
age—Sluys in 1340, Crécy in 1346, and that most stunning of victories
at Poitiers in 1356 when the French king had been taken captive. Even
the campaign of 1359–1360 that he had been on, though it failed in its
grandiose goal of making Edward III king of France, was *perceived* as a
victory: France was weakened, its lands devastated, and the Treaty of
Brétigny was reckoned a triumph (later, in the 1370s and 1380s it came
to be seen as a diplomatic betrayal). The extravagance and ostentation of
Edward and Philippa were part of the vibrancy of those times; When the
nation was not at war, spectacular tournaments were held—in 1347, the
year after Crécy, there had been nineteen, and there were many in the
1360s after the Treaty of Brétigny. There had been great royal weddings
like those of the Black Prince in 1361 and the Princess Isabella in 1365;
the famous visit of the three kings in 1363; the spectacle of King Jean's
return to London in the following year, and his no less spectacular funeral.
The nameless herald of Sir John Chandos, in his *History of the Black
Prince*, wrote of King Jean's time in London, "They danced, hunted,
hawked, jousted, and feasted, just as in King Arthur's reign."

King Edward III meant his reign to be a golden age of chivalry.
When Chaucer was still an infant, the king had commanded a Round
Table built at Windsor and set out to revive the glories of King Arthur's
days; he meant to bring nostalgia and sentiment into the service of his
reign. The order of the Garter was one product of this policy. Its legendary
beginning, as a royal whim entertained over a great lady's dropped garter,
was an opportunity seized to execute something long mulled over. Probably the felicitous phrase itself, *honi soit qui mal y pense,* was what made
this the right moment, for noble thoughts were indeed the heart of the
chivalric ideal. And because the chivalric ideal was French in origin, and
France the hub of the chivalric universe, England's triumphs had an
almost mystical significance. It is not surprising that in the flush of their
triumphs young Englishmen, in spite of their nationalism, let their hair
grow and shaved off their beards in the French manner and adopted
French fashions in dress. The English remained great Francophiles
throughout the century, though continually at war with France.

That it was an age of spectacle is revealed most dramatically in
clothing. After the Black Death, the spirit of abandon that followed the

plague expressed itself in outlandish fashions. The art of tailoring had
been invented late in the thirteenth century; until then men and women
alike wore draped, loose tunics. Tailoring marked the beginning of "fashion" in the modern sense: the creation, by constant variations in design,
of varying "looks" expressing attitudes. Before that the fundamental sexual distinction in clothes had been *drawers*. Men had worn underdrawers,
but there was a taboo (which lasted into the nineteenth century) against
any garment coming between a woman's legs. With tailoring, men's
underdrawers evolved into outer garments: tailored tunics became form-
fitting, open at the neck, cinched at the waist, with shoulders and sleeves
molded into the shape of the body. As the tunic became shorter, hose and
pants became visible. After the plague, men wore tight hose, a different
color for each leg, and short tunics—which preachers ranted against—
that revealed buttocks and genitals. Sleeves became long enough to touch
the ground, and draped fabric continued to be worn as outer garments for
conspicuous display. This was the age when men wore long, pointed
leather shoes, *poulaines*, so long their points often had to be attached to
the upper calf with a silver or gold chain; as one can imagine, they
promoted a mincing gait that was reckoned decadent. Hats were various
and elaborate, of fur or stiffened fabrics. Women's headdresses grew
larger, their décolletage deeper; they plucked their eyebrows and hairlines,
dyed their hair, used powder and rouge. Jewels and furs were worn by both
sexes. Such ostentation was picked up by the "middle" classes, and there
were futile efforts to regulate their dress by law. Clothes came to be a
language in which messages could be read, or by which statements could
be made or fictions composed, and Chaucer (in the General Prologue) was
perhaps the first writer to see the literary uses of this language. Most of
these extravagant fashions were French in origin; they spread about northern Europe (the Italians were more conservative) and the English particularly aped them. They had set out to out-French the French.

French chivalry, the very tradition that made France the center of
fashion, was in a curious way a major cause of England's military ascendancy. Under Edward III, the English had a practical streak that the
French considered unchivalric; and it was true, such expediency in warfare
was to bring the end of chivalry. At Crécy and Poitiers, everyone knows,
it was the English longbowmen, foot soldiers, who saved the day. The
French had archers too, but they didn't deploy them with the shrewd
tactics the English developed: at Crécy the French knights, in much
larger numbers than the English, had appeared in grand array prepared
for the traditional pitched battle. The vanguard, when the French king
ordered a halt (to delay the fight until morning), misinterpreted the
command; they had "glory" on their minds, and, thinking they were being

deprived of their honored position, indignantly continued their advance, the rest of the army following. The English bowmen fired their arrows into the advancing vanguard, which collapsed in a heap of dead horses and knights and sent the army retreating in disarray.

The French, with overweening pride in their chivalry, could never admit that lower-class archers defeated their knights; they blindly ascribed the victory to the two phalanxes of knights on foot that protected the archers against a cavalry attack from the sides. Ten years later, at Poitiers, they had learned nothing. They had their enemy in a plateau with only a single access and could have starved them into submission. But no, "glory" was more important. They charged the English with three hundred horsemen leading phalanxes of knights on foot, which they supposed was what had won Crécy for the English; the English archers calmly shot down the horsemen as they entered the pass, and those who survived retreated pell-mell into the army behind them, the English pursuing. After Poitiers, the French did not for some years deign to fight with the English; they shut themselves up in their castles while the English raided and burned unprotected villages and towns.

France's defeats were in this way a matter of attitude, and the attitude was inherent in the chivalric ethos itself. At the heart of chivalry, from one vantage point, was an aristocratic ideal of glory, honor, and esteem, based on noble thoughts and good motives and self-sacrifice; but the noble ideal was always on the edge of falling *en décadence*. The English chronicler Geoffrey Baker referred in an almost matter-of-fact way to "the usual and inbred pomp of the French race." But it was easier for the English to see this in the enemy than in themselves. The dark side of chivalry was that, as a code for a warrior caste, it was based on caste solidarity. The elaborate courtesy was only owed to other nobles; social inferiors were unworthy of it, couldn't understand or respond to it—if the poor or the lowly were treated well, as happened once in a while, it was rather out of charity than chivalry.

Even among nobles, chivalry was often a matter of noblesse oblige proffered by a victor, anticipating ransom and booty, to social equals who had little choice but to respond in kind. When the king of France had been captured, it will be remembered, he was not willing to speak with a lesser captor than "my cousin the Prince of Wales." When they took dinner together, the prince served the king at table because the king was of higher rank, and assured him in humble terms—and assured him he did not say it for flattery—that his feats of arms on that day won the prize and the chaplet, "if you please to wear it." The king on his side consoled himself that "like a stout-hearted soldier ready to live and die for a just cause, we were taken on the field by the judgment of Mars." Even leading his captive into London, the year Chaucer went to serve the Countess Elizabeth, the Black Prince, dressed in soldier's garb, rode a hackney while the king in his full regalia rode a great white destrier. *Before* a battle there might be similar displays of chivalry, but more often there were arrogant challenges, mockery, and taunts, descendants of the old *flytings* of pre-chivalric knighthood; in 1369 the king of France sent his challenge to the king of England by a common servant, to signify his contempt. At the heart of chivalry was violence—instinctual male competitiveness, primitive, vainglorious, sullen. In such moments, when battle was in the offing, base emotions, pride, bloodlust, ambition, could becloud the nobles' judgment. And greed: booty and ransom were an acceptable part of war—knights did not think the profit motive conflicted with honor, any more, say, than modern physicians or lawyers think taking fees conflicts with professional ethics.

The Spanish Intervention

The Black Prince, the chivalric hero of the age, lived by the code of knighthood and was its exemplar. The pages of the chronicles are filled with stories of his prowess, his humility and courtesy, his generosity. He even, like the knights of romance, married for love. His father groomed him for this role and, with generous paternal pride, allowed him his share of victories and glories. At Crécy, when a knight urged the king to go to the prince's rescue, the king is supposed to have said, "Let the boy win his spurs; for I am determined, if it please God, that all the glory and honor of this day shall be given to him, and to those into whose care I have entrusted him." It is hard to find a single instance where Edward III seemed to be competing with his son. But the son, intent on living up to ideals of warrior conduct and kingship, was in some sense competing with his father: he was, as future king, driven to match or outdo him—driven by the code itself, by his father's dedication to it, and by his own striving temperament. It would tell us something that he fell in love with Joan, the "Fair Maid of Kent," if it were true his father loved her first.

In 1367 the Black Prince led an army into Spain and recaptured Castile for its deposed king, known as Pedro the Cruel. The prince consulted all his barons and sent to England for the king's advice, but the decision was still a poor one, and the brilliant victory at Nájera was in the long run a defeat. The decision was made chiefly out of chivalric considerations. Because Pedro had been brought down by his illegitimate half brother, Don Enrique de Trastamare, he seemed the rightful, legitimate ruler. Moreover, he was an ally in distress—Edward III had had a strong relationship with Pedro's father. And Enrique, who had been raised in France, was predisposed in France's favor. It may be true that if the English could have stripped the scales of honor from their eyes, they would have seen Pedro as an unprincipled tyrant who had ordered the deaths of many Spanish nobles, even his new wife, a French princess whom he repudiated for some inscrutable reason the day after they were married. And because he was on good terms with the Moorish king of Grenada, the church considered him its oppressor—the pope had excommunicated him, legitimized his bastard brother Don Enrique, and encouraged Enrique to take Castile by force. The French, remembering the repudiation and death of their princess, had joined the alliance, in part to secure a powerful ally against England. It was this alliance that defeated Pedro in March 1366, and Pedro now sought the protection of the Black Prince.

Why did England take up Pedro's cause? First, probably, because the French took up Enrique's, as did the pope. More important, the English wanted to keep the powerful Castilian navy out of France's service, perhaps even put it in their own. Then too England was in possession of Aquitaine; the Black Prince, as duke of Aquitaine, was installed in a glittering court at Bordeaux, and Aquitaine lay on the border of Spain, the small kingdom of Navarre separating it from Castile, the largest Spanish kingdom—with which Aquitaine had a traditional alliance. And, since June 1362, there had been a political and military alliance between Don Pedro and the king of England; it had been celebrated with a ceremony in London, was ratified by Edward III in February 1363—but by the desultory Pedro not until a year and a half later, in September 1364. Idealism, it can be argued, won out over common sense. The English should have made friends with Enrique de Trastamare; instead, they fought for tradition, the principles of rightful inheritance and chivalric alliance, and closed their eyes to Pedro's character. On the other side, it can be argued that Pedro's character was blackened throughout Europe by a campaign of propaganda from his enemies—Enrique, the king of France, and the pope. "Pedro the Cruel" may not have been so much the villain as is thought.

Seven years later, when Pedro was dead, John of Gaunt married Pedro's daughter Costanza (1371) and thereafter saw himself as Pedro's rightful heir; it is for this reason that Pedro's memory was colored favorably in English eyes. Chaucer, whose wife was a damsel to the Duchess Costanza, heir to the Castilian throne, commemorates him in the Monk's Tale—"O noble, O worthy Pedro, glory of Spaine"—in two crisp and powerful stanzas as "worthy king" whose "pitous death" was an act of perfidy. And perhaps Chaucer was right.

Chaucer appears and disappears rather puzzlingly in Navarre a month before Pedro's defeat. He was issued a safe-conduct by the king of Navarre on February 22, 1366, preserved in the archives of Navarre in Pamplona. It was good for twelve weeks and permitted him to travel in Navarre with three companions plus their servants, horses, and baggage. It appears that he was in charge of a secret diplomatic mission; he alone is named but not his three companions, which means that he was in charge—or that they were traveling incognito. He was about twenty-four. It is inconceivable that he was fighting for Enrique de Trastamare, as the discoverer of the safe-conduct believed, for he would have been flying in the face of English policy; and it is unlikely that he was making a pilgrimage to St. James of Compostella during Lent (the season for pilgrimages being after Easter), at a time when the nation was on the brink of war.*

Why was he sent to Navarre as the French were preparing to invade Castile? King Charles of Navarre, "Charles le Mauvais," had at first sided with the French—he was French himself and was also duke of Normandy —on promises of certain Castilian lands that Navarre claimed; but the French then turned about and agreed to a scheme whereby Aragon would conquer and annex Navarre. Hearing of this plan, the king sided again with Pedro, but in December was bought off by Aragon. Possibly Chaucer was sent two months later to try to dissuade or buy off the slippery king of Navarre.

The other possibility is that he was sent in an effort to keep certain English knights from getting involved with the invasion of Castile. The English were in no position to oppose the invasion with a military force. To do so might reopen the war with France at a time when England was at a disadvantage, for France had already bought up the available companies of mercenary soldiers. These companies—sometimes called just "companies" and often "Free Companies," in awesome capitals—were organized groups of professional soldiers from virtually all European countries, including England; their interest was to get pay and booty and to fight for the sheer love of fighting. Chivalry interested them not at all; they stole, plundered, raped, mistreated prisoners barbarically, pillaged and destroyed churches and monasteries, abused and murdered priests,

*The language of the document, which says he may "enter, stay, move about, turn around and go back," somewhat discourages the notion that he was passing through Navarre to Castile. He mentions the mountains of Spain once in *The House of Fame*, line 1117— in the first line of a couplet, where he is not in need of a rhyme—while describing a castle made of ice high on a rock; this may suggest that he had crossed the Pyrenees by the pass at Roncevalles in Navarre and remembered the height, the steep drops, the winter ice, a monastery or castle seemingly hanging in the clouds. But then, he could have read or heard of these, or passed there later with the English army, or had another mountain range in mind.

imprisoned noblewomen, kidnapped children. When they were unemployed, they were a scourge to any nation where they were rousting about, and there was little for that nation to do but expel them by force or find employment for them, or sit still and hope someone else would hire them. The pope himself had cause to fear them. They had become one of Europe's major problems, the more so because no war could be waged without them.

England had used these Free Companies in all its major battles. Just now, when a French invasion of Castile had been launched and no English military involvement seemed contemplated, certain English soldiers of fortune, along with some Gascon knights from Aquitaine, were planning to join the army invading Castile—not quite as mercenaries but, let us say, as hired or borrowed leaders. This was specifically prohibited in England's treaty with Don Pedro made in 1362, and in December King Edward had sent a letter to five Englishmen of renown warning them, in the strongest language, that he had heard some knights of English allegiance were planning to march against Pedro and that any who did would be punished. The letter evidently failed to reach them in time, and Chaucer was (so it's conjectured) sent into Navarre to intercept them. Whether he succeeded isn't known, but the following year all the five knights to whom the letter had been addressed obeyed the Black Prince's command and rejoined the English forces.

The battle of Nájera, in which Chaucer may have participated, was, in the great tradition of English victories, won by the archers. The English bribed the eminently bribable king of Navarre, still pledged to Don Enrique, to let their army pass through his kingdom, and set out from Bordeaux on January 10, 1367; they had bought up the available Free Companies, many of which had previously fought against Don Pedro. The army's departure was delayed for the baptism of the Black Prince's second son, Richard, known as Richard of Bordeaux. At Dax they waited a few days for the arrival of John of Gaunt and his troops.

The enemy was backed by the French army under the generalship of Bertrand du Guesclin, a military genius of obscure origins (peasant origins, it was said, though Froissart reports that he himself claimed descent from an African king in the time of Charlemagne). He was a Breton of medium height with dark skin, thick lips, and green eyes, broad shoulders and long arms, uncouth in his behavior and noticeably ugly. It was this gangling, unattractive Breton who would save the French from their own chivalry. He was himself a mercenary, or at least was so perceived by the Free Companies, and chivalry was very little on his mind. He won by tactics and guile, putting expediency first, as the English had done with their archers. But unlike the English he took little care of honor, and so made treacherous acts a part of the tactician's skill.

The English crossed the Pyrenees by the pass at Roncevalles— famous in *The Song of Roland*, a story Chaucer alludes to in his stanzas on Don Pedro—and passing through Navarre encamped near the enemy at Nájera. The Black Prince sent his challenge, that he had come to restore the rightful heir to the throne; the reply came back that Don Pedro had no support, that his defeat had been God's will. But then the Spanish made an error rather like the errors of the French in previous battles. They had the English in a position where the mountain passes could be blocked off; they could cut off their supplies, starve them into a retreat, and attack them when they retreated. But the Spaniards, buoyed up by a few small successes and hungry for glory, spread out their army for battle. At sunrise the two armies came in sight of each other, their armor glistening beautifully (says Froissart) in the morning sunlight. The Black Prince, praying aloud, reminded the Almighty, "Thou knowest that in truth I have been solely emboldened to undertake it in the support of justice and reason, to reinstate this king upon his throne, who has been disinherited and driven from it, as well as from his country." The English let loose a rain of arrows, and the foe, after rallying thrice, fled across the river, which it was said flowed red with blood—as it may have done, in this case, being small. Du Guesclin, refusing to flee, was taken prisoner. It was March 28, 1367, the day before Palm Sunday.

After the battle they proceeded about sixty miles west to Burgos for tournaments and feasting, and in a month or so another sixty miles southwest to encamp around Valladolid. The prince had trouble cooling down Don Pedro's desire for revenge and more trouble with the Free Companies, who, not yet paid, were pillaging the countryside. Don Pedro had promised to pay the cost of the campaign when he was restored to the throne; the prince assumed he would keep his promise. Now he claimed he would have no money till he reached his treasury at Seville; if the prince would wait, he would bring it. He never returned. In the summer he sent word that he would send the money if the prince would dismiss the Free Companies (they were hardly dismissable while the prince owed them their wages); the prince knew then that he would never be paid. In the summer heat, disease broke out—amoebic dysentery, probably—and large numbers died. The prince contracted the illness, from which he was never to recover; within three years he gave over his command of Aquitaine and returned to England, in nine years he was dead. Pedro's treachery and the sickness changed the prince's character as they changed the course of his life, for he, who had been the flower of chivalry, now became morose, bitter, and given to fits of rage.

Lionel's Second Marriage

In the year after the Spanish invasion of 1367, a marriage was arranged for Prince Lionel, a propitious and adventurous marriage, but an ill-fated one. The negotiations had been initiated by Galeazzo Visconti, lord of Milan, on behalf of his daughter Violante. He, with his brother Bernabò, had tyrannized northern Italy and now held more than sixteen cities there. The settlement, completed at Westminster about the time the Black Prince was encamped at Valladolid, gave Lionel various territories in Piedmont, towns and cities guaranteed to produce 24,000 florins a year, a payment of 100,000 florins to King Edward and almost 200,000 to Lionel and Violante (a staggering sum) plus innumerable gifts of jewels, garments, and vessels of gold and silver. Lionel was approaching thirty; Violante was about thirteen. Little is recorded of her appearance or character; the Visconti, who were blonds for the most part, were known for their good looks, and given the ferocity of the young girl's family and the unhappy short life she was to endure, one can imagine in her a certain depth and complexity.

Lionel left for Milan in late March or early April of 1368 with 457 men and 1,280 horses; the party proceeded into France, arriving in Paris on April 16, where it was met by all the great lords of France—among them Enguerrand de Coucy, Lionel's brother-in-law, and Count Amadeus VI of Savoy, known as the "Green Count," Violante's uncle and likely the chief mover behind the marriage negotiations. Lionel stayed in a magnificent apartment in the Louvre, and there were four days of feasting, which the king himself, Charles V, joined. All these nobles and the king too were about the same age, and their conviviality was great (as they feasted, English mercenaries were marauding Champagne, but this was overlooked). The French king, on their departure, gave Lionel and his companions gifts said to be worth over 20,000 florins (the price once put on the city of Arezzo). The wedding party proceeded across France, through Chambéry, where they spent three days, being feasted at every stop and gathering up more wedding guests along the way. Once in Italy, they stayed at Pavia, where just the year before Galeazzo Visconti had completed the building of the enormous Castello, one of the greatest palaces in all of Europe. Then they traveled the twenty miles to Milan, arriving on May 27. They were met by Galeazzo and his wife, Bianca, his son Gian-Galeazzo, age sixteen, who was married to Isabella of France, and an enormous train—among them eight ladies dressed alike in embroidered scarlet gowns with gold belts, and thirty knights with thirty squires dressed alike and riding tilting-steeds.

The ceremony was held in the cathedral on Monday, June 5, the bride attended by her two uncles, Amadeus of Savoy and Bernabò Visconti. The wedding feast was held in the courtyard outside the cathedral, the Piazza dell'Arengo, at two huge tables, one for men and one for women—some hundred guests, served by nobles and watched, one assumes, by a horde of spectators. The meal was elaborate even by medieval standards: there were eighteen courses, each, save the last two, being a double course of meat and fish,* and after each course gifts were presented to the couple. The gifts, meant to please Lionel, as will be seen, would by the end of the meal have amounted, in mere summary, to something like this: eighty-six hunting dogs of various kinds in pairs or dozens, each group in matching appurtenances (gold collars, for example, with silk leashes); six goshawks, twelve sparrow hawks, and six peregrine falcons, with creances (the leashes used in training them) having silver-enameled buttons—the falcons had velvet hoods adorned with pearls on top; six small coursers with gilded saddle and equipage (including lances, shields, and helmets), six large coursers similarly equipped, six small steeds having equipage of gold and green silk with red buttons and tassels, and six great tilting steeds similarly equipped; twelve each of steel corselets, tilting panoplies (with saddles, lances, and helmets), and war panoplies; twelve pieces of cloth of gold and twelve of silk; two large decanters of gilded and enameled silver, with matching bowls and goblets; a doublet and hood of satin covered with pearls, and a matching ermine-lined cloak; a large silver basin with a clasp or handles decorated with an emerald, rubies, and diamonds; a ring set with a large pearl; five silver belts, gilded and enameled; twelve fat cattle, two handsome coursers, and—oh, yes—seventy-six horses and numerous other gifts, like silver belts or cloth of gold, distributed to the duke of Clarence's barons and gentlemen, in amounts according to rank, plus robes and money to the mountebanks, minstrels, and acrobats who had entertained them.

Imagine a thirteen-year-old girl, the center of attention at such a wedding feast, on such a June day, under the hot Italian sun. Yet she is only a symbol; attention is on her father and her uncle, on the tall

*For the curious reader, the menu in bare outline was: (1) suckling pigs, gilded, with fire in their mouths; porcelain-crabs, also gilded. (2) Hares, gilded; pike, gilded. (3) A large calf, gilded; trout, gilded. (4) Quails and partridges, gilded; roasted trout, gilded. (5) Ducks and herons, gilded. Carp, gilded. (6) Beef and fat capons with garlic-and-vinegar sauce; sturgeons in water. (7) Capons and veal in lemon sauce; tench in lemon sauce. (8) Beef pies with cheese; large eels in pies. (9) Meat aspic, fish aspic. (10) Meat galantine; galantine of lampreys. (11) Roasted kid; roasted garfish. (12) Hares and kids in a chive sauce; various fish in chive sauce. (13) Venison and beef in molds; fish turned inside out. (14) Capon and fowls in red and green sauce, with oranges; tench turned inside out. (15) Peacocks, with cabbage, French beans, and picked ox tongue; carp. (16) Roasted rabbits, peacocks, and ducklings; roasted eels. (17) Junkets and cheese. (18) Fruit, wine, confections.

handsome foreign prince, now her husband, and his entourage of English lords. For attention in such a marriage was focused on the alliance it created. The Visconti were climbers, who had not stopped at climbing over each other. Their ambitions in an English alliance involved trade, power, prestige; the gargantuan wedding feast was a statement, and it is impossible the English didn't know what was being stated. The Visconti's power scarcely went back thirty years: their ancestor, Azzo Visconti, had purchased Milan from the emperor in 1328, and annexed ten other cities. When he died without an heir in 1339, the kingdom passed to his uncle, Luchino, who ten years later was poisoned by his wife, then to Luchino's brother Gian, archbishop of Milan. By 1354, when Gian died, it consisted of sixteen cities in Lombardy, and was inherited jointly by his three nephews: the eldest was poisoned by the younger two, who divided Lombardy up between them and held Milan in common.

These two were Bernabò and Galeazzo, the hosts of Lionel's wedding. Of the two, Galeazzo, Violante's father, was supposedly the less vicious, yet it was he who made the notorious edict against traitors— which meant anyone who in his opinion opposed him—that they be tortured for forty-one days, every other day, recuperating on the alternate days, in a barbaric sequence beginning with four days of the strappado, then the flaying of the soles of the feet (the victim then being made to walk on peas), the rack, one eye gouged out, the nose cut off, the hands and feet cut off one by one, the flesh torn with pincers, until at last the victim was broken on the wheel. Stories of his brother Bernabò's atrocities included these: he had a man's eyes put out because he was found on a private street, had a woman burned to death by her own husband, shut two of his chancellors in a cage with a wild boar, and made an unsuccessful effort to poison his nephew Gian-Galeazzo. When Pope Urban V, in an attempt to stop Bernabò's incursions upon Tuscany, sent a bull of excommunication, Bernabò forced the two papal legates to eat it in his presence —first the parchment, then the wax seals. When Galeazzo died ten years later in 1378, his son Gian-Galeazzo succeeded him, living a bizarre life of prayer and fear, keeping himself under constant guard. In 1385, pretending to be on pilgrimage, he visited his uncle Bernabò, dismounted, and while embracing him signaled his German mercenaries to seize him; Bernabò died in prison the following December, presumably poisoned, and is coldly commemorated in Chaucer's Monk's Tale as "the scourge of Lombardy."

There is good reason to believe that Chaucer accompanied the English party, of which no complete record survives, that he saw Lionel's wedding, was sent to England to report, and was then sent back to Italy almost at once with a reply. The journey took about five or six weeks, and the records show that on July 17, exactly six weeks after the wedding, he left England and did not return until the last day of October. Although there were other affairs in Europe he could have been attending to, the odds are that he was sent to Milan. He had been in Lionel's service. He knew Italian. There survived into the sixteenth century a tradition that he had attended Lionel's wedding. And the timing is right: allowing six weeks for travel, he would have arrived back in Italy late in August, stayed two weeks, and left for England in mid-September.

It is not especially important that Froissart was at Lionel's wedding, for Chaucer had other occasions to meet him. But it is important that Petrarch was there. He arrived in Pavia a day or two after Lionel did, summoned to act as an intermediary between the Visconti and the pope. He was suffering from an injury to his shin that had become infected. He did attend the wedding feast, but on that very day his grandson died in Pavia and he was overcome with sorrow. Clearly he was in no condition to be glad-handing the English squires; we have to conclude that Chaucer did not meet him. Petrarch was sixty-four and acknowledged the greatest man of his age; Chaucer was in his twenties, completely unknown, a mere valettus of the English royal household. Such a meeting could have taken place only if Petrarch had been much in circulation, and he was barely in circulation at all. But Chaucer may have gazed at him from afar: someone must have pointed him out, told of his works, answered Chaucer's questions. And possibly this reverent glimpse of a distant luminary is in part what we find expressed, years later, in the awed, enthusiastic encomium of the Clerk's Prologue to "Franceys Petrak, the lauriat poete" whose sweet rhetoric has "enlumined all Itaille of poetrie."

What may have impressed Chaucer more was the touching figure of Violante, thirteen years old, by no choice of her own the pawn in this display of wealth and power. In later years he would have remembered a timid, confused blond girl dressed in a lady's rich gown and jewels, bravely or stoically acting her role in these men's affairs, entering an unimaginable future. The memory would emerge as a constituent of his fascination with long-suffering, victimized women, like Constance or Griselda or the ladies in *The Legend of Good Women*. What he would learn of Violante in future years would call up and reshuffle that memory, for she was to be married three times before she died childless at thirty-one. Her second husband, the marquis of Montferrat, was fifteen when he married her. He was a maniac who raped and brutalized those about him, was accused of murdering one man and cutting off the leg of another; the chronicles in unfriendly exaggeration say he killed men, boys, and even children from among his own retinue. He was slain early in the second year of the marriage by one of his own German soldiers as he was strangling a serving boy. After this, Violante was married, at the insistence of her brother Gian-Galeazzo and against her will, to her first cousin, Lodovico, son of Bernabò Visconti; four years later, in 1385, when Bernabò was seized, Lodovico was seized with him. Violante died soon thereafter, never seeing Lodovico again.

Chaucer might have received from this trip another kind of impression, of a reverse or negative kind. Even if he came with Lionel's party and attended the wedding, he was in Lombardy very briefly—about a week in early June, two weeks in September. The glimpse of Italy might have roused his curiosity, left him dissatisfied and eager to see and know more of the rich commerce and culture, and the strange ways, of the Italians. Five years later he was sent to Italy again for a longer stay, in Florence, and this short earlier trip may have helped him get more from the later one. We could compare the experience of the travel writer Felix Fabri, who in 1480, after a short, disappointing pilgrimage to Jerusalem, wrote that the things he had seen there seemed to him "shrouded in a dark mist, as though I had beheld them in a dream," and swore he would return: "I regarded this pilgrimage as merely the preamble to that which I intended to make."

After the wedding Violante returned to Pavia and Lionel went to Alba, the principal city in his new Italian territories, about sixty miles to the southwest. He took part in a tournament on August 16. At some point in late August or September he fell ill and returned to Pavia for a few days, then went back to Alba. Quite where he was when Chaucer arrived back from England in early September, and whether he was or had been ill, is impossible to say. Chaucer left Italy for England about September 15, bearing messages known, probably, not even to himself.

When he got back home in late October, he learned the devastating news: the Duchess Blanche was dead. She had died on September 12 and lay buried in Saint Paul's Cathedral. Until recently it was believed her death occurred in 1369, and since there was an outbreak of plague then it was assumed that was how she died; now that we know she died in 1368, we are in the dark as to the cause. She was in her late twenties. She had borne five children, of whom three survived: two daughters, Philippa and Elizabeth, and a son, Henry of Bolingbroke, the future king Henry IV. In 1368 Gaunt appears to have been in England, so the likelihood is that she died at the Savoy Palace in the Strand with her husband at her deathbed.

John of Gaunt's grief at the death of his wife was enormous. He ordered an effigy in alabaster to be placed on her grave in Saint Paul's, ordered perpetual masses for her soul said at an adjoining altar, gave instructions that he be buried beside her (as indeed, more than forty years later, he was), and commanded that a commemoration of her death be held in Saint Paul's each year. These annual commemorations were held, and after Gaunt's death they were continued by his son. Within three years of Blanche's death he would be married to the Princess Costanza of Castile, and would take a mistress, Katherine Swynford, sister of Chaucer's wife. He had been nineteen when he and Blanche were married; now he was twenty-eight. Her death, coming as he approached his thirtieth year, wrought a change in his character. He was to be thereafter a man possessed by his ambitions: at the end of the century he would be "time-honored Lancaster," powerful over all English barons, father of the next king, Henry IV. It was sometimes thought, quite unfairly, that he was aiming for the crown; after his marriage to Costanza he styled himself king of Castile, and the populace wryly called him *Monseigneur d'Espaigne*. His eldest son by Katherine was to be the ancestor of Henry VIII. Had Blanche not died, his character might not have taken this turn toward seeking power. His grief at her death was of the extravagant medieval kind. Medieval knights of royal lineage are often depicted as unfeeling military leaders whose relationships with women were exploitative and wanting in sentiment; yet they could love their wives with towering and noble emotion, and grieve as powerfully in mourning. Richard II, upon the death of Queen Anne in 1394, was to order the manor house at Sheen—beloved by her, for him now laden with anguished memories—torn to the ground; he was nearly the same age as Gaunt was when Blanche died.

And this grief of Gaunt's can touch us still, for it was to be the subject of Chaucer's poem *The Book of the Duchess*. Chaucer began working on the elegy at once; one scholar argues that it was completed by November, others that it was not presented to the duke for several years, possibly was read at one of the annual commemorations of the Duchess's death as much as eight years later. But its intensity of feeling argues that it was conceived and begun while her death was still a painful memory.

Queen Philippa wasted no time finding Gaunt a new wife: she wrote to Count Louis de Male, father of Margaret of Flanders, the greatest heiress in Christendom, for whose hand John of Gaunt himself had treated on behalf of his younger brother Edmund of Langley. On December 1, she sent her ambassador, Sir Richard Stury, a friend of Chaucer's who had fought with him in the wars. Sir Richard returned on Christmas Day bearing a letter in which Count Louis, with great courtesy, regretted that the marriage between his daughter and Edmund of Langley had been foiled by the pope's withholding the dispensation. He said he had waited two years, lest the pope change his mind, before proceeding with other plans: "In the circumstances, beloved lady, I pray that you will excuse me from entering into other negotiations while the present talks are in progress." The talks were with France, and they were well along: Margaret married Philip of Burgundy the following June. Probably the queen's proposal was an effort on Edward III's part to forestall a marriage that would bring Flanders under French control—a rather desperate effort, at that, for no one had any reason to think the dispensation denied to Edmund would be forthcoming for his brother.

Then, toward the end of November, word reached England from Milan that Lionel was dead. On October 3 he had made out his will, and had died at Alba on October 17 while Chaucer was still on his way home. The nature of his illness is indicated only by the circumstances: he had been indulging in endless feasting since he left England, was leading an extremely strenuous life, was in a foreign country during the hottest months of the year. The heat, the food, the water, the exertion—any of these could have conspired to give him amoebic dysentery, cholera, an infection, a heart attack. Or else Fortune had prepared some ironic, inexplicable death. The grief of Galeazzo Visconti was said to be great, hardly surprising in light of the enormous hopes he had put in the marriage. But there was talk that Lionel might have been poisoned by Galeazzo, poisoning being so much a way of life among the Visconti. The suspicion was raised in skirmishing between Sir Edward Despenser, second in command at Alba, and Galeazzo, but the conflict was settled through diplomacy—by Amadeus of Savoy, the "Green Count," who had arranged the marriage in the first place—and suspicion was cleared when Galeazzo took an oath. The possibility that Bernabò Visconti or Gian-Galeazzo might have been behind a poisoning seems not to have arisen, though they had more motive. Lionel was buried in Pavia, but in later years his body or some part of it was sent home to England and buried in the abbey church at Clare, next to the Countess Elizabeth.

The End of an Era

The following year, 1369, which began under the somber cloud of these two deaths, was as dark a year as any Englishman could remember since the Pestilence. England's fortunes had turned, and the wheel was on its downward course.

On March 23, the victory won at Nájera was turned to a defeat: Don Pedro was killed and Enrique de Trastamare regained the throne of Castile. Worse, this happened through an error of judgment on the Black Prince's part: after the prince had returned from Spain to Aquitaine with his prized prisoner, Bertrand du Guesclin, and John of Gaunt had returned to England, du Guesclin played on him what might be called a chivalric trick. The prince, according to Froissart, asked du Guesclin one day how he was.

"My lord," replied Sir Bertrand, "I was never better: I cannot otherwise but be well, for I am, though in prison, the most honored knight in the world."

"How so?"

"They say in France, as well as in other countries, that you are so much afraid of me, and have such a dread of my gaining my liberty, that you dare not set me free; and this is my reason for thinking myself so much valued and honored."

The prince, knowing that there was some truth in the taunt, answered, "What, Sir Bertrand, do you imagine that we keep you a prisoner for fear of your prowess? By Saint George, it is not so; for my good sir, if you will pay one hundred thousand francs, you shall be free."

It was a very steep ransom, but du Guesclin replied, "My lord, through God's will, I will never pay a less sum." When the prince heard du Guesclin's reply, Froissart thinks, he knew already he had made a mistake. In fact the mistake was put to him by his council, but he took the chivalric position that he had given his word and must keep it. In fact, denying ransom (as we learn in the Knight's Tale) was thought excessively cruel—the French resorted to it sometimes, but the English never.

Du Guesclin was released on ransom and rejoined Enrique, who was already leading an invasion of Castile. Pedro's army was defeated and Pedro himself, at Montiel, was surrounded. He offered to du Guesclin a large bribe to let him escape, and du Guesclin, pretending he would take the offer, invited Pedro to his tent. There Pedro, seeing his half brother, fell upon him, and Enrique ran him through with a knife.

That summer there was an outbreak of plague, large enough to have been called "the third pestilence." There was in addition a terrible murrain of cattle. Heavy rains the year before had brought the worst harvest in half a century. And there was a slump in the wool and cloth trades.

Sorrows came, in Shakespeare's phrase, not single spies but in battalions. The queen was sick all that year, and it had become clear she would not recover. On August 15 she died at Windsor castle of what contemporaries called dropsy, probably congestive heart failure. Froissart reports that when she felt her end approaching, she extended her right hand from beneath the bedclothes and said to King Edward, "We have enjoyed our union in happiness, peace, and prosperity: I entreat therefore of you that on our separation you will grant me three requests."

The king, sighing and with tears, replied, "Lady, ask: whatever you request shall be granted."

In death as in life her heart went out to others: "My lord, I beg you will acquit me of whatever engagements I may have entered into with merchants for their wares, as well on this as on the other side of the sea. I beseech you also to fulfill whatever gifts or legacies I may have made, or left to churches, here or on the Continent, wherein I have paid my devotions, as well as what I may have left to those of both sexes who have been in my service. Thirdly, I entreat that, whenever it shall please God to call you hence, you will not choose any other sepulcher than mine, and that you will lie by my side in the cloisters of Westminster."

The king in tears replied, "Lady, I grant them."

Then she made the sign of the Cross, recommended to God her husband the king and her youngest son Thomas of Woodstock, who was present in the chamber, and then gave up her spirit—"which," says her countryman Froissart, "I firmly believe was caught by the holy angels and carried to the glory of Heaven; for she had never done anything, by thought or deed, that could endanger her losing it."

She was buried, as she requested, in Westminster Abbey, in the chapel of King Edward the Confessor, that holiest place in the old church. Eight years later Edward III was buried beside her, and there they rest still in their great Gothic tombs beneath their effigies—hers a white marble sculpture made by Hennequin of Liège during her lifetime, his of gilded bronze cast the year he died.

The most famous story about Philippa of Hainault, which may be legendary, was of how she had saved six citizens of Calais when the city fell to the English in 1347. Obdurate in his threats against the citizens, at whom he felt great anger, the king was finally prevailed upon to pardon them; but he demanded that six of the principal citizens "march out of the town with bare heads and feet, with ropes around their necks, and the keys of the town and castle in their hands. These six persons shall be at my absolute disposal, and the remainder of the inhabitants pardoned." Six of the leading citizens bravely volunteered. All wept at the sight as the king eyed them in anger and they pleaded for their lives. He ordered them beheaded, and was deaf to the chivalrous entreaties of his captains. Then, says Froissart, "The queen of England, who at that time was very big with child, fell on her knees, and with tears said, 'Ah, gentle sir, since I have crossed the sea with great danger to see you, I have never asked you one favor: now, I most humbly ask as a gift, for the sake of the Son of the blessed Mary, and for your love to me, that you will be merciful to these six men.'

"The king looked at her for some time in silence, and then said: 'Ah,

lady, I wish that you had been anywhere else than here: you have en-
treated in such a manner that I cannot refuse you; I therefore give them
to you, to do as you please with them.'

"The queen conducted the six citizens to her apartments, and had
the halters taken from round their necks, after which she new clothed
them, and served them with a plentiful dinner: she then presented each
with six nobles, and had them escorted out of the camp in safety."

Probably it is apocryphal but it has in it this kernel of truth, that her
great human kindness and the great love between them restrained and
ennobled Edward. He was fifty-six when he lost her, whom he had called
his "little helper," and the loss wrought an unhappy change in him.

In honoring her request that he make good her gifts, Edward headed
the list of orders to the Exchequer with a grant of 10 marks yearly to Alice
Perrers. The year before, she had received from the king the revenues
from the manor of Arlington in Berkshire. Possibly Edward had already
taken her as his mistress; possibly, as is sometimes thought, the noble
queen in her sickness had commended her to him. On the queen's death,
similar grants were made to others of her ladies, and gifts of liveries for
mourning were made to members of the royal household, including Geoffrey and Philippa Chaucer.

Alice Perrers had, shortly before this, borne a child, a daughter
named Blanche, who was rumored to be the illegitimate child of John of
Gaunt, for whose support the king settled £20 a year. After the queen's
death, Alice Perrers prevailed on Edward to give her a gift of land, the
castle at Wendover. She was just past twenty. She had the capacity, or
the shrewdness, to take the queen's place not just in the royal bed but in
Edward's life. He seems to have become emotionally dependent on her
as he had been on Philippa, for which no one could blame her; but she
was young enough to be his granddaughter, she was greedy, she was not
above cheating him. He was beguiled, one could say besotted by her, and
in years to come acted the fool with her before the very eyes of his court,
a court that had adored his queen. There were to be scandals, Parliament
was to become involved, it was to be said he had been bewitched by her,
or had fallen into dotage.

That year, the wars with France began again. The Black Prince had made
himself unpopular in Aquitaine with a tax designed to recoup his enormous losses in the Spanish war. By the time his council persuaded him
that it was a disastrous policy, it had done its harm: the king of France,
appealed to by the nobles of Aquitaine as their "overlord," summoned the
Black Prince before him as if he were his vassal, though by the Treaty of
Brétigny he assuredly was not. The prince took up the challenge, said he

would go to Paris but with his helmet on and with sixty thousand men, and unchivalrously threw the king's messengers into prison; the king in turn sent his challenge to the king of England by a "common servant," who was politely told he had done his work well and allowed to leave. King Edward once again claimed the throne of France, and sent John of Gaunt with an army to ravage the enemy's countryside, from July to November 1369; Chaucer was with him.

In June 1370 Chaucer went abroad again, not with Gaunt: the letters of protection for Gaunt and his men were all good for a year, whereas Chaucer's was good only till Michaelmas, and this suggests some different, shorter mission, perhaps touching a treaty with Flanders or negotiations with Genoa, for the letters allowed enough time to get to Genoa and back. In this campaign Sir John Chandos, one of the great knights of the age, was slain, a terrible blow to England, and his death was less than glorious: fighting on foot, with his visor up (though he had lost an eye five years before in a hunting accident), he slipped on the frosty ground, became entangled in the long surcoat he wore over his armor, fell, and while thus groveling on the earth was run through by a French squire.

France sent two armies into Aquitaine, under the dukes of Berry and Anjou, with Bertrand du Guesclin in the service of the latter; they captured, among numerous other cities, Limoges. It was surrendered by its bishop, in whom the prince had absolute trust, who had indeed baptized the prince's son, and this was reckoned an act of dire treachery. The prince, lying on his sickbed at Bordeaux, fell into a rage, swore on his father's soul he would take the city and have vengeance on these traitorous subjects. Too weak to mount a horse, he was carried at the head of his army on a litter. They found Limoges prepared for a siege, the people shut within strong walls and well provisioned. He determined to mine the walls; offered a pardon to all rebels who would renew their allegiance to him; swore he would never leave until the city fell. In a month the walls were mined, the mines filled with combustibles, and the combustibles set afire. When a section of the wall collapsed, filling the ditches, the English rushed in over the rubble while others attacked the gates. The prince, borne in on his litter, watched while the soldiers, on his orders, ran about killing the citizens—men, women, and children. When those near him begged for their lives, he turned a stony face away from them. The knights of Limoges defended the town, their backs to a wall, determined to fight to the death. The duke of Lancaster and the earl of Cambridge and their men dismounted and fought on foot, to be on an equality with the brave enemy. The three French leaders fought on while the Black Prince watched. He looked on the combat, says Froissart, "with great pleasure, and enjoyed it so much that his heart was softened and his anger appeased." At length the French surrendered, their leader Sir John de Villemur saying, "My lords, we are yours: you have vanquished us: therefore act according to the law of arms."

John of Gaunt replied, "By god, Sir John, we do not intend otherwise, and we accept you for our prisoners."

Evidently Froissart meant to imply that the prince's softened heart kept him from insisting the knights be put to death, rather than taken prisoner and ransomed by the traditions of war. Even so he added, "But the business was not here ended, for the whole town was pillaged, burned, and totally destroyed." The traitorous bishop was dragged from his palace and the prince, eyeing him indignantly, told him he would lose his head and ordered him from his presence. Later, John of Gaunt asked him of the prince and ultimately spared his life at the behest of the pope.

This was the last battle of Edward the Black Prince. In January 1371 his eldest son, Edward of Angoulême, who would have been heir to the throne, died at Bordeaux at the age of six. The prince had loved the boy dearly; it would be interesting to know whether the implication made by Stow in the sixteenth century ("the death was not too soon, it was said") has any validity, for one wonders if the prince could have loved a sickly or deformed or retarded child. But he was too ill to attend the funeral. On the advice of his physicians he put his rule of Aquitaine into the hands of John of Gaunt, bade farewell to his barons, saw them do fealty to the duke of Lancaster, and set sail for England with his wife, Joan, and his little son Richard, now heir presumptive. Here the Black Prince disappears from the pages of Froissart save a brief entry recording his death in 1376.

Historians have argued endlessly over the Black Prince's conduct at Limoges. True, his sickness left him in frustration and rage, which he loosed on the rebellious city. It has been conjectured that his debilitation was exacerbated by cirrhosis of the liver, and it is not out of the question that in his days of frustration he drank to excess. He had other reasons to be frustrated. All his striving had been for an impossible dream; he had been betrayed by his Spanish ally, to whose aid he had come, and now by his companion the bishop of Limoges. It is true, too, that chivalry itself explains why he was moved by the bravery of the French knights but not by the agony of innocent townspeople, even women and children. He had sent messengers, who told the people of Limoges that they must put themselves at his mercy, but so Walsingham observed, "the undisciplined populace wished to hear nothing of them"—not that the populace had a choice; would one expect their leaders to have sent them to the polls? In our time, we feel that killing innocent women and children is an atrocity but killing soldiers, even conscripted soldiers, is not; in the Middle

Ages nearly the reverse was the case—ordinary citizens were shamelessly slaughtered in wars, almost routinely so when a city was taken by storm, but the "law of arms" protected nobles. Nevertheless, Christian charity dictated pity. We may allow Froissart, who adored prowess and chivalry almost foolishly, and sang the praises of the English royals, to have his say:

> It was a most melancholy business; for all ranks, ages, and sexes cast themselves on their knees before the prince, begging for mercy; but he was so inflamed with passion and revenge that he listened to none, but all were put to the sword, wherever they could be found, even those who were not guilty; for I know not why the poor were not spared, who could not have had any part in this treason; but they suffered for it, and indeed more than those who had been the leaders of the treachery. There was not that day in the city of Limoges any hearts so hardened, or that had any sense of religion, who did not deeply bewail the unfortunate events passing before their eyes; for upward of three thousand men, women, and children were put to death that day. God have mercy on their souls! for they were veritable martyrs.

Chaucer, in the coming years, looking back would see that the prince had fallen short of the highest ideals. His friend Gower, addressing himself to Richard II in the *Vox Clamantis,* commented on the prince's ferocity ("his sword was often drunk with the blood of the enemy . . . a torrent of blood slaked the thirst of his weapons") and by the 1380s Chaucer would have agreed.

The Black Prince returned to England to die, though despite his illness he remained active in Parliament. John of Gaunt stayed in Aquitaine. After the battle of Nájera Don Pedro had given his three daughters as hostages against his promise—made on the gospels before a high altar —to pay the Black Prince what he owed him. The daughters were still at Bordeaux, abandoned by their father for the price of his war debts. The eldest had entered a convent and then died; the next eldest, Costanza, became heiress to the throne of Castile and León from the "legitimist" point of view that the English espoused. The following year, September 1371, John of Gaunt married her and brought her back to England. By that time he had taken up with Katherine Swynford, younger sister of Philippa Chaucer, who bore him a child, named John, some two years later. Costanza was sixteen when they married, Gaunt was thirty-one, Katherine twenty-one.

Costanza, obsessed with her father's murder and the lost throne, lived a withdrawn, prayerful existence among her small retinue of faithful Spanish retainers. In the first year of the marriage she had a child, a daughter, and it must seem odd that the little girl was named Catalina (Katherine); but Katherine Swynford was the governess of the duke's children, the marriage was an entirely political affair, Costanza was still an adolescent, and altogether a foreigner. Probably she had a cordial, possibly close relationship with Katherine Swynford and was in her heart grateful that she needn't "pay the marriage debt" except to produce heirs; she produced only this one, for a son born two years later died in infancy. At about the time Costanza's daughter was born, Philippa Chaucer entered her service, and one assumes that Chaucer had a chance to observe the lonely young Castilian heiress closely.

In June 1372, the Black Prince's successor in Aquitaine, the earl of Pembroke, was sent to take up his duties; but the English fleet was intercepted by the powerful Castilian navy off La Rochelle, Pembroke was taken prisoner, and the ships that had not been sunk were captured, among them the ship containing the funds for the campaign. At once a retaliatory campaign was planned, which it was hoped would reverse the English losses in France and save the besieged city of Thouars, one of the few English cities that had not fallen to the French; it could not hold out beyond the end of September. Late in August a fleet of 400 ships, with 4,000 men-at-arms and 10,000 archers, set out, with the king and John of Gaunt aboard, and the dying Black Prince, carried on a litter; but now "the king's weather," the good winds that always seemed to favor royal expeditions, failed them. For six weeks the fleet was buffeted by winds gone mad, again and again was blown off course, until at last the sailors gave up and turned the ships back to England. The futile venture cost £900,000, almost twice the price of King Jean's unpaid ransom, and left England on the brink of a fatal defeat in Aquitaine.

In the wake of this disaster, hastily in November, Geoffrey Chaucer was sent abroad with two Italians on an important mission. He was first to go to Genoa to treat with the Genoese for the use of an English port, then to Florence to deal with the large loans England had been negotiating with the Florentine bankers. He left on December 1, 1372, and would be gone almost six months. When he returned the following spring, he would see, the more clearly for having been away, that England was never again to be the land he had known.

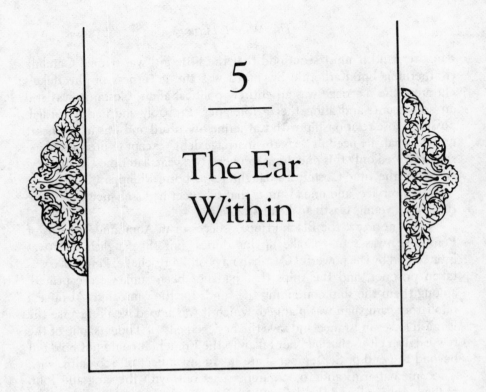

5

The Ear Within

As England's fortunes declined, something unrelated to them, more important in the long run and of more far-reaching consequence, was occurring in Chaucer's mind, in that sequestered place where sounds are heard, words and phrases remembered, the structures of language stored: a process, unconscious or semiconscious, of poetic development, which we can follow by observing its results in his work and knowing its ultimate effect on English literature.

That poetic achievement, the lens through which we see a poet's life, throws out of focus its other sides, public or private. Writing poetry is a solitary occupation, carried out by a private self that may have little to do with one's other selves. Northrop Frye, adapting Aristotle, observed that lyric ("pure" poetry) is made of *babble* and *doodle*—*melos* and *opsis*, inner streams of the ear and eye, bearing noises and shapes. Poets have an overdeveloped sensitivity to such stimuli, and the resulting inner streams, made of habit and memory and some quirk of the brain, are the instrument they play on. True, rhetorical convention was the essential art a medieval poet learned, but this didn't make him a mere copyist; rhetoric developed his instincts. A good poet, in the Middle Ages as now, was different from other people in some constitutional way. Rudolf Bing, late of the Metropolitan Opera, characterized opera singers as having an abnormality of the vocal organs; poets might be characterized in the same cold spirit as having an abnormality of the "ear" (we will include with "ear" whatever whole part of the brain transforms outer stimuli to inner poetic force, and we will speak of the "eye" later).

How to listen to what was happening in that "ear"? By taking soundings from the finished poems, comparing lines, phrases, passages. With a modern poet we have, often, wonderful wastebaskets of drafts and canceled versions, along with journals and letters—evidence of what "wouldn't work," of false starts, failures of imagination and nerve. These can give a scholar a clear sense of what the poet was and wasn't after, but only when one sees the result in the finished work. With all the wastebasket evidence in the world, we still are looking for that inner road that leads from one poem to another, from minor work to masterpiece. Not an easy road to follow, but poets themselves, when they talk about their work, rarely give a better itinerary than their biographers or critics: they are too close to all their changes of heart, and their developed "ear" is based on taste and habit, hence barely conscious. And too, theirs is self-criticism; their judgments are based on *doing,* the critic's on observing, comparing, evaluating.

And here we must face a difficulty we needn't face with more recent poets: we do not fully know how Chaucer's poetry sounded. After Chaucer's time the pronunciation of English changed so much that by Shakespeare's time Chaucer's poems no longer sounded right. He was admired for his eloquence and "philosophy," and as the "first finder of our fair language," but by the sixteenth century his rhythms were a puzzle and his rhymes did not seem true. Some writers, a few, believed that Chaucer's meter was regular, but from about the time of Queen Elizabeth I Englishmen began to admire him for the wrong reasons and *tolerate* his "rough verses." People condescended to Chaucer in the fault-finding spirit endemic to literary discourse: one Henry Peacham, writing in 1622, generously found, "under a bitter and rough rind," a kernel of "conceit and sweet invention." People liked Chaucer for recording the manners and "humours" of his age but thought him weak in "numbers," that is, meter. Dryden said there was in his verse "the rude sweetness of a Scotch tune" —it was "natural and pleasing, though not perfect."

Only in the eighteenth century did it cross anyone's mind that one could grasp Chaucer's meter by reconstructing his pronunciation. Thomas Gray, writing about 1760, suggested that the final *e*'s within words were pronounced in Chaucer's day, and that pronouncing them made his verses scan. The editor Thomas Tyrwhitt, 1755, saw the value of "a more complete theory of [the] author's versification." These ideas were found valid in the nineteenth century; not only different pronunciations but a different system of rhythm had existed in earlier English verse. We still do not know in every detail how Chaucer's poetry sounded, but we know it was not "rough" to the ear.

French Court Poetry

When Chaucer began to write poetry, still in his teens or early twenties, he would have had in his interior ear *two* systems of rhythm. One was the natural rhythm of spoken English, his native language, which was fundamental to the rhythm of native English poetry. The other was the rhythm of French poetry, the poetry he knew and admired. Chaucer, like everyone of his station at the time, was bilingual, and there can scarcely be a doubt that when he first tried his hand at writing songs or lyrics, he wrote them in French. None of his poems in French has survived, but there are French poems that *could* be by him, even some—in a manuscript of the University of Pennsylvania—which appear to identify the author as "Ch."* By his time, as was mentioned earlier, the French spoken in England was no longer "Norman" but a dialect peculiar to Britain best called Anglo-French. It was barely understandable to a Parisian, but people who traveled in France, as Chaucer did, knew "French of Paris" too. Poetry, *good* poetry, in Anglo-French doubtless retained the native rhythms of French verse, because it continued to be modeled on works by contemporary French poets. And in Chaucer's time this meant the great genius of the age, the poet and musician Guillaume Machaut. Some of Chaucer's earliest verse is based on, in fact virtually translated from, his poems. Machaut was of the previous generation—he was born in 1300 and was to live until 1377. Among the other French poets whose works Chaucer knew, Deschamps, Froissart, and Graunson were all about Chaucer's age and not at this point a major influence, though he had met Froissart by now, and knew his poems.

Chaucer's early ideas about poetry were derived from these French writers, all of them court poets. If you asked him, in his twenties, what kinds of poems he was writing, he probably would have answered, "ballades, roundels, virelays, dites," and so on—that is, he would have named particular forms, each having rules for its verse form and rhyme scheme,

*University of Pennsylvania Ms. French 15, dating from the period of Chaucer's lifetime, contains 311 poems in French; fifteen of these have the intriguing heading "Ch" that seems to indicate authorship. They were discovered in the 1970s by Professor James I. Wimsatt.

or *kinds* of poems, like the dream-vision or complaint, having set conventions of subject and manner. They wouldn't have excluded religious verse: Machaut was famous for his religious poems and for religious music, too (his Masses remain masterworks of medieval music), and Chaucer, as we have said, did write the *Prier à Nostre Dame* or "ABC," drawn from the French poet Deguileville. It's hard to say much about his early lyrics; we have only twenty-two of his short poems, four of doubtful authorship, and most are from his later years. But one can't understand where Chaucer *started* without having a picture of French courtly poetry; fortunately, a picture of it emerges in Chaucer's own poems because his debt to it was so great. That debt, however, had its reverse side. By the time he was in his thirties he was prepared to make fun of it and was making fun of it and looking for something new. If this was a "revolt" it was only half a one: when he found something new to imitate, in Italy, he turned it in the direction of Machaut, Deschamps, and Froissart, because their tradition was in his blood: he wasn't able to escape it.

Why would he have wanted to escape it? Perhaps because he learned about it in the golden age of the 1350s and 1360s; by 1370 that age was over, England had fallen into desperate times, there was disillusionment and panic in the air. People looked back on a day when such court poetry had an audience that was confident, fashionable, enthusiastic; had they not, only a decade before, been talking about reliving the age of King Arthur? And now most of the great knights and ladies of those days were dead, the king himself had gone dotty, outrageous Alice Perrers dominated the court, under which domination it was very far from the days of King Arthur. Those highly wrought French poetic forms suddenly had become a poetry of nostalgia—bitter nostalgia, that revealed how bad everything had gotten, and left the reader asking why.

French court poetry implied an image of the poet's role and status at court. This image became bitter too. The poet presented himself as a valued member of the court whose duty it was to speak to the prince, or the lady, or the assemblage of courtiers, most often saying what they wanted or expected to hear, saying what he was bidden to say or what he deemed would please. The poet's place at court was as an adjunct, and it wasn't necessarily an honored place: patronage was bestowed capriciously, admiration and rewards were given but meanly. The poet Martin le Franc, having presented to Philip the Good as fine a bound copy of his poem *Le Champion des Dames* as he could afford, wrote that it was not only ignored but used by various members of the court for a mat or a footstool. The poet was there to entertain, to enlighten, to encourage or inspire, to console. His "matter" was given to him by courtly fashions and events: love and chivalry and deeds of arms were his subjects, or dreams that spoke obliquely to an occasion—a royal birth or marriage, a death, a departure. With the right prince and the right circumstances, courtly poetry sought promising occasions and new treatments. The French hostages going off to their palatial English prison offered such an occasion, and Machaut wrote a poem about it that Chaucer knew. If the court loses its dignity or its glamour, the poet loses his share of these; such poetry turned to dust when a court was down on its luck.

We get an idea of this poetry from one of Chaucer's ballades that probably did come from his younger days, named (by Skeat) "Womanly Noblesse." Its difficult meter is handled with skill, and the poem is untypical in certain ways: aside from a missing line in the second stanza, the last line of each stanza isn't a repeated line, as was usual, and the *envoy* doesn't begin with the customary "O Prince." It's a tour de force of rhyming, having but two rhymes throughout. Some commentators think its virtuosity and its unconventional features mean it comes from Chaucer's mature years, but he was skillful and unconventional enough in youth. It makes better sense to say that it must have been written while the English court still had enthusiasm for its conventions. In it the poet puts himself in the role of the courtly lover, asks the lady's "pity" and "grace," reminds her of his lifelong "service," his "buxomnesse" (obedience), his "pains" and "heaviness," praises her beauty, her comportment, her "gentilesse." It's a compendium of standard motifs, the sort of thing Chaucer in more mature years retreated from, took liberties with, or made fun of. But it sounds as if, when it was written, the poet took it seriously and anticipated an audience that was au courant. Here are its third stanza and envoi:

Considering eek° how I hang in balaunce   *also*
In your service, such, lo, is my chaunce,
Abiding° grace, whan that your gentilesse   *awaiting*
Of my greet woe liste do allegeaunce,
And with your pite me some wise avaunce,
In full rebating° of mine heavinesse,   *abatement*
And thinketh by raison that womanly noblesse
Should nat desire for to do thee outrance°   *injury*
Theras° she findeth none unbuxumnesse°.   *where / disobedience*

        L'envoy
Auctour° of norture°, lady of pleasaunce, *model of / comportment*
Soveraigne of beauté, flow'r of womanheede,
Take ye none heed unto mine ignoraunce,
But this receiveth, of your goodliheede°,   *goodness*

Thinking that I have caught in remembraunce
Your beauté whole, your steadfast governaunce.

The Translation of the *Roman de la Rose*

Chaucer's earliest known labor as a poet of courtly love was to translate into English verse some part of the *Roman de la Rose*. The *Roman* was read all over Europe into the Renaissance and left its mark on any courtly writer. It's conventional to refer to it as a single poem, but in fact it is a poem in two parts, each by a different author. The first part is an unfinished narrative of 4,058 lines, in French octosyllabic couplets, by Guillaume de Lorris, of whom nothing is known but his name. He is believed to have died in 1237, leaving the poem incomplete. His part is a personification-allegory depicting the beginnings of a love affair. After his death, some unknown writer added a brief, entirely unsatisfactory ending. Just how popular the *Roman* was during the remainder of the thirteenth century is hard to determine. No extant manuscripts date from this period before Jean de Meun's continuation, but Guillaume's poem enjoyed a vogue in its own generation and survived into the next.

Here, in bare outline, is the action of Guillaume's part:

The poet dreams he wakes in May and, walking out, comes upon a walled garden, the Garden of Mirth. On the outside of the wall are painted figures representing qualities inimical to Love: Hate, Felony (vice), Villainy (lower-class behavior), Covetousness, Avarice, Envy, Sorrow, Old Age, Pope-Holy ("prudery"), and Poverty. He is admitted by a maiden, Idleness, who brings him to the lord of the garden, Mirth. Dancing in Mirth's company we find Gladness and Courtesy, and the God of Love himself, accompanied by a bachelor named Sweet-Looks and six ladies—Beauty, Richess, Largess, Fraunchise, Courtesy, and Youth. The Dreamer rests beside a well, the Well of Narcissus, whose story is inscribed on it; then, looking into the well, he sees two stones of crystal (the lady's eyes) that reflect the garden. Now we find that this well, with its "Mirror Perilous," is the Well of Love; in the mirror the Dreamer sees a rosebush and selects a rose. The Rose is, of course, the young lady, and the experience at the well is that of falling in love: the God of Love's arrow presently passes through his eye into his heart.

Yielding to the God of Love, the Dreamer receives instruction— "here the Romance improves," we are told. The God of Love cautions him against villainy, pride, meanness; tells him to serve and praise women, be well dressed and clean, merry, and steadfast in love; and instructs him about love's woes and pains. Then, more specifically, he tells him how to approach the lady, advises him to tip her servant well, and commends him to Good Hope, Sweet-Thinking, Sweet-Speech, and Sweet-Looks. The God of Love then vanishes, and the Lover, left alone with his wound, attempts to approach the Rose.

The Lover is joined by Fair-Welcome, son of Courtesy. But, approaching the Rose, he finds three opponents. One is Daunger (the lady's haughtiness, represented as a loud-mouthed *villain*: it probably represents a saucy adolescent snub, before which Fair-Welcome, who stands for her ability to be nice to him, flees). The second opponent is Wicked-Tongue (gossip, traditional enemy of lovers). The third is Reason. Reason tells him he has made a mistake in yielding to the God of Love and should drive Love away. But he repudiates this advice, and Reason skulks off.

Now he encounters Friend, the male companion who can serve any lover as sounding board and go-between; with Friend's encouragement he makes a covenant with Daunger, that he may love as he pleases so long as he keeps his distance from the Rose. He gains as allies Fraunchise and Pity, who persuade Daunger to bring Fair-Welcome back; with Fair-Welcome he is permitted to gaze upon the Rose, and at once desires a kiss. The enemy of his desire is Chastity; but he gains a new ally, Chastity's principal antagonist, Venus. With her aid he attains a kiss, and at once confronts new enemies: Shame, Wicked-Tongue, and Jealousy.

Jealousy (who probably stands, in plain terms, for the young lady's parents) makes a tower and imprisons Fair-Welcome, builds a wall about the tower and mans it with Shame, Dread, and Wicked-Tongue. In the tower he sets an Old Woman, who is the young lady's Duenna or Nurse. The Dreamer is here found in despair, thinking how Love, like Fortune, is forever changing and how comfortless life must be without Fair-Welcome. On this wretched note the poem breaks off.

Even this brief summary reveals the fascination (and extravagance) of the work. Precious as it may seem, it invited medieval readers into its world as active participants: one can imagine them arguing over the true meaning of the various figures, or about the propriety of the Lover's desires and moves, or the remedies for his setbacks. But no summary can reveal the *Roman*'s richness of description and inventiveness of detail. It is as various and highly wrought as a tapestry or a goldsmith's chalice—rereading it, remembering passages, finding new details, lingering over its sheer decorative lushness was part of the experience it offered. But in addition, the essential mystery of the inner experience it described, the moral ambiguity of Reason's flight, the Lover's dolorous predicament, the tantalizing absence of an ending—these set readers to guessing, posed an intellectual challenge. And underlying all was the enticing aura of courtliness itself, the style of life shared by its audience.

Forty years after Guillaume's death, his poem was read by Jean de Meun, a master of the University of Paris, who wrote a continuation of it. He was the author of many translations into French and of a witty *Testament.* Because he is called *magister* in records, it is assumed that he taught at the University; he was an academic, not a courtier, and as a city dweller he can be called "bourgeois." His mentality has little to do with courtly culture. His poem is what might be called a "university poem"— the kind of poem that springs out of a milieu devoted to study and books. It is digressive, discursive, replete with stray bits of learning, forgotten names, lost causes, petty quarrels. Whether one has a taste for Jean de Meun's continuation, which runs to 17,722 lines, depends on whether one has a taste for poetry of this kind. At its best it is witty, ironic, outrageous; at its worst, chaotic, tedious, and parochial. But it is a world apart from the shorter and more aristocratic work to which it is a gigantic appendage, a continuation run wild. It is as if some poem written in the earlier part of our century, some poem by Eliot or Yeats, say, were to be picked up forty years later by a university wit and expanded into a Nabokovian parody five times the length of the original. The resulting hybrid could enjoy enormous popularity among a quite various audience. Those who had no taste or understanding for the academic's wit and irony, and the arcane learning of the continuation, could still take an interest in the earlier poem and in certain sections or aspects of the addendum.

This is apparently what happened to the *Roman,* for it was widely read, and the numerous manuscripts give the work in its entirety. It was not the case that its earlier part enjoyed one readership, a courtly one, and its later part enjoyed another, academic readership. Jean de Meun's part would have been accessible to any intelligent reader or hearer; while a few passages mention personages or causes célèbres in the university world of his time, for the most part its treatment is broadly humorous and extravagantly inventive. It proceeds on the standard principles of medieval rhetoric—*amplification, digression, exempla,* and the like—and thus grows organically from its original. Guillaume's remark about tipping the lady's servant—and his providing her with a Duenna in the tower—is picked up thousands of lines later and turned into a garrulous monologue on lovers' tricks and secrets spoken by the Duenna, a prototype of the Wife of Bath. One can imagine that it gave infinite delight to all kinds of people—read, as it must have been, aloud serially before a group.

Then, too, the whole book in both parts was a picture book. Virtually all manuscripts of it are illustrated, the larger number of them gorgeously so. They were the possessions of noble families, families that could afford a big, sumptuous book. The pictures are lively and elegant, and cumulatively afford an expansive vista of medieval court life: they are a testimony to the enthusiasm of courtly culture for its own richness. They focus on clothes and decor and manners as they illustrate the speakers, incidents, and stories woven into this complex literary tapestry. A moral is there in the early part by implication: the lover rejects Reason, but it is clear that in the end Reason would have had its say and fleshly love been defeated. In Jean de Meun's continuation moral and religious considerations are explicit—Reason *has* its say and Nature, as a part of God's will, triumphs. But the book was popular not because it had a moral; it was popular because Guillaume's original poem codified a set of circumstances under which courtly behavior was possible, specifically under which a young aristocratic male could fall in love. To the extent that the *Roman de la Rose* did this, it was like a courtesy book or etiquette book. And it would have enjoyed a vogue if it had been only that. What gave it its additional magic was its extravagant, wry, thoughtful, and wildly funny continuation. Here, for those who had an interest in gentilesse, was God's plenty.

How much of the work did Chaucer translate? The Middle English translation has survived in two versions—one printed by Thynne in 1532, based on a manuscript owned by the Hunterian Museum in Glasgow. The whole of this Middle English translation comes to only about a third the length of the original, but it translates all of Guillaume de Lorris's part. Its translators must have selected these passages, unless the remainder was lost. The Glasgow manuscript dates from the first quarter of the fifteenth century, and possibly its compiler selected with an eye to the interests of readers at that time; if so, he preserved the seriously courtly part and omitted much of what is "academic."

The translation breaks into three fragments, and the first, consisting of 1,705 lines from Guillaume's part, is generally believed to be by Chaucer. It is in the same London dialect as his poems, and its rhythms and diction sound like his; the other two fragments sound less like Chaucer's dialect.* In any case we *know* that he translated some part of the *Roman.* The poet Deschamps, addressing a poem to Chaucer in 1385, says in so many words that Chaucer, the "grand translateur," translated the *Roman*

---

*They are translated from a different French text than the first, and the dialect is northern. Various experts, poring over these texts, have concluded that Fragments B and C were by a northern translator but were then revised along with Fragment A by someone who spoke the London dialect. This reviser collated the three fragments with a third French text, added material, and cleaned up the dialect by removing as best he could the northernisms. What relationship if any Chaucer had to Fragments B and C, we can never know: there is an off chance that they were originally by him and were copied and adapted by the mysterious northerner; or that the mysterious Londoner who removed the northernisms was Chaucer himself.

de la Rose. And Chaucer himself, in the Prologue to his *Legend of Good Women,* has the God of Love say to the poet that he has translated *The Romance of the Rose,* "that is a heresy ayainst my lawe / And Maketh wise folk fro me withdrawe" (line 330). This remark suggests that Chaucer had translated some of Jean de Meun's part, for the earlier courtly part by Guillaume de Lorris is no "heresy" against Love's law; Jean's critique of it is what was reckoned "heresy." In the two other places where Chaucer gives a list of his works—the Man of Law's Prologue and the Retraction at the end of *The Canterbury Tales*—he says nothing about translating the *Roman,* which may suggest that he didn't take it very seriously as a part of his oeuvre. It is traditional to regard it as an exercise of his poetical apprenticeship. The translation, like its original, is in octosyllabic couplets, which Chaucer abandoned in later years, and the part of the translation that sounds authentically Chaucerian contains some very wooden passages, though it contains as well some very lively ones. He probably started it in his twenties and worked at it off and on until he found other things to write.

This poetical exercise had an unexpected impact on his development: it helped him to portray characters. What must be remembered about the *Roman* is that it describes an interior event. We are told that we are in the Garden of Mirth, where we encounter a number of personages; but what this means is that we are inside a young man's psyche. We are watching him fall in love with a young lady who is flirtatious but coy; and she is protected by a Duenna, her parents, and her own reserve. He must contend with the problems of any young lover: with people gossiping about him, and with *reason,* which warns him away. This psychological allegory is truly an effective way of seeing into the mind of another. To the extent that medieval thinkers were concerned with psychology, they were concerned with what happened in the soul when it made a good or bad choice. And in making such an analysis they were concerned with *faculties* of the mind—with reason, intellect, will, passion, memory. This "faculty psychology" is based on the notion that the mind has separable functions—it is the ancestor of modern constructs like superego, ego, and id. It is sometimes objected against the *Roman* that while most of its personages are mental qualities like "Fair-Welcome," some are individuals like the Friend or the Duenna; but even the individuals are mental qualities in the sense that they represent the dreamer's experience of people, not the people themselves.

Part of the delicacy and the intellectual acumen that the *Roman* fostered in its readers for over three centuries was an ability to examine, as under a microscope, the interior events that take place in our little worlds of consciousness and feeling. The actual plot of the *Roman* is that of any love story; it is the minute scrutiny of the interior world that accounts for its excitement. And in Jean de Meun's part there is the further, and telling, conclusion that the lover must take by storm the tower in which Fair-Welcome is imprisoned, as the English took castles in France; the wall is broken down, the tower set afire, and the young man not only gets the young lady but gets her pregnant! In the end, Nature triumphs, and the love affair has the happy ending—procreation—which the church itself prescribed.

Chaucer's immersion in this literature of psychological allegory during his early years gave him the ability to put on paper insights about people that he had from observation. His elegy to the Duchess Blanche or his story of Troilus and Criseyde follow precisely the psychological pattern of the *Roman* and use its conventions to describe falling in love, but "psychological allegory" is abandoned: the characters are not faculties or qualities of the mind but people, people who seem to walk before us as on a stage. We know their interior worlds because we are told, by the author or through soliloquies, what they think and feel, or because we are provided with details of gesture or behavior that help us intuit their mental states. That is a large step in the direction of modern literature; but the step could not have been made if its author were not writing for an audience schooled in the allegorized psychology of the *Roman*.

An Ear for English Rhythms

Imagine him, then, in his twenties, back from the wars, with the *Roman de la Rose* open at his elbow, turning the French verses into English ones. The speech rhythms of French, or any romance language, are different from the rhythms of English, and these different speech rhythms affect the rhythm of verse. The romance languages are "syllable timed": speakers hear the syllables of words as units of a sentence. But English, like its sister languages of the Germanic family, is "stress timed": speakers hear syllables as parts of word groups in the sentence, and the word groups are marked off by major stresses. In English there are more levels of stress, and stress coincides more exactly with emphasis, though this is a matter of degree; one can emphasize by stress in French, but switching the word order or the accent within a word is the more likely way. When you say a phrase in French—*la porte de la cité*—it sounds staccato to an English ear, like *ta-taa-ta-ta-ta-ta*. In English the same phrase, "the gate of the city," comes out with two major stresses: *ta-TA, ta-ta-TA-ta*. To an English ear, French and Italian when spoken sound like a machine gun; words and phrases don't seem to come forth with definition—the timing seems so regular that one has trouble hearing where words and phrases, even sentences, leave off. Heaven only knows what English must sound like to a French or an Italian ear—like a series of irregular explosions, perhaps, or Morse code.

Because of these differences in speech, verses in French move along in a regular tum-tum-tum-tum, and a poet counts the number of syllables, not the number of stresses. With English verse it is the opposite: the line may accommodate extra syllables so long as the number of stresses is unequivocally right. Here are the opening lines of the *Roman de la Rose* in the French of the time:

> Maintes genz dient que en songes
> N'a se fables non et mençonges;
> Mès l'en puet tex songes songier
> Qui ne sont mie mençongier. . . .

The eight-syllable lines mark off grammatical structures—phrases and clauses. Pauses occur naturally at the ends of lines, and the rhyming couplets therefore have a binding effect: they "frame" word groups. All moves along with definition and dignity; it is not monotonous, because it does not violate the natural rhythm of the spoken language. It is as if one were speaking—orating, perhaps—but in measured phrases, and in rhymes. There is no problem of its being "singsong": "singsong" means regular and unvaried, and to a French ear there is for such verses no other way.

But translate these lines into a comparable poetic form in English, and you have stumbled on a difficulty. Here is Chaucer's translation:

> Many men sayn that in sweveninges°   *dreams*
> There n'is but fables and lesinges°,   *lies*
> But men may some swevenes seene
> Which hardely that false ne beene. . . .

This, one must admit, is singsong. As best he could, Chaucer was imitating the sound of his original, but where in the French the eight syllables string themselves off with fluid suppleness, in English there must be four metrical stresses in each line:

> Mány men sáyn that ín swevenínges
> There nýs but fábles ánd lesínges. . . .

As one naturally speaks the lines, the "major" stresses required by emphasis make a counterpoint to the metrical stresses required by poetic form. The major stresses, depending on the performer, would probably be:

Many men sáyn that in swevenínges
There nys but fábles and lesínges. . . .

Since English is "stress timed" in this way, with one major stress per word
group, the lines break up in what to a French ear must sound like fits and
starts. The result is that the caesura (pause) in an English line is more of
a hiatus than in a French line (in French octosyllabics there really *is* no
caesura). And with phrases differentiated in this more abrupt way, the
"framing" of grammatical structures within rhyming couplets, graceful
and natural in French, imprisons those phrases in English, making them
seem heavy-handed and monotonous. And there is this irony, that the
more a poet tries to imitate the sound of the French original, the more
he gets that singsong, natural in French, that is boring and artless in
English.

Thus Geoffrey Chaucer, in his twenties, struggling to get life into his
Frenchified verse:

Now this dreme wol I ryme aright
To make your hertes gay and light,
For Love it prayeth and also
Commaundeth me that it be so.
And if there any aske me,
Whether that it be he or she,
How this book the which is here
Shall hatte°, that I read you here,   *be called*
It is the *Romance of the Rose,*
In which all the art of love I close.

This passage—from Fragment A of the *Roman,* lines 31–40—is not a
promising start for a poetical career. The lines mumble along two at a
time, ticking off clauses and sentences, in despite of the usual variety of
our spoken language. The rhymes are uninspired—desperate, one might
say: *also* and *so, me* and *she, here* and *here* (both used in the same sense,
very undesirable). There are clichés and tag phrases to plump things out
—"gay and light," "whether that it be he or she," "this book the which
is here"—none of them in the French.

And yet just ten lines before this passage Geoffrey did much better.
Starting out on a verse paragraph, it sounds as though his enthusiasm,
before it got bogged down in what are after all routine matters, took him
momentarily off the ground:

Within my twenty yeer of age,
Whan that Love taketh his carriage°   *toll*

Of younge folk, I went soone° *early*
To bed, as I was want to done,
And fast I slept; and in sleeping,
Me mette° such a swevening° *I dreamed / dream*
That liked° me wonders well. *pleased*

Here the rhymes are natural, not forced. And every word contributes to the meaning; there are no clichés or tags. But apart from that, the verse *sounds* better. It seems to have energy, it sounds not like mumbling but like *speech*—strong, thoughtful speech that progresses from one point to another, goes somewhere. How does it get this effect? By variation, by *ir*regularity, which would be inimical to the French. For example, there is no caesura in the first two lines, but one falls strongly in the third, where there is a natural pause; in the fourth line, another caesura after "To bed." So, too, pauses at the ends of lines or couplets come irregularly here; we have *enjambement* (running a phrase past the rhyme into the next line, as in the second and third lines). Tumbling on past the rhymes that way makes the rhyming couplets much more palatable to English ears; otherwise the heavier stresses of English make them hammer away at the reader, as in French they do not.

Moreover—and this would be unheard of in French verse—the number of syllables varies from line to line. While the basic scheme is four beats and eight syllables, the second line in the quoted passage has ten syllables, the last only seven. But both have four stresses and scan perfectly.*

Another feature that gives these lines luster is alliteration. "Slept . . . sleeping" in the third from the last line produces a repeated consonant cluster that offers some force, and the *s* from the cluster is picked up again in the next stanza ("such a swevening"), framed before by "me mette" and after by "wonders well," themselves both alliterating phrases.

It was by instinct, one could say, that Chaucer happened to get it right here though he got it so wrong elsewhere. And anyone who goes through the first fragment of the Middle English *Roman,* or *The Book of the Duchess,* will find the verse uneven in this way. There are passages

*In the second line, "carriage" was pronounced cà-ri-á-ge. The scansion of the last line may be explained in two ways. One is that "me" has a long vowel and, coming just before the caesura, provides a rhythmical space (*x*), like "syncopation," equivalent to a metrical beat:

Thât lík-'êd mé 'x̂ wónd'êrs wéll.

The other involves the theory (see Appendix A) of sounding final consonants with audible release:

Thâtê lí-' kêdê mé 'ẃondêr- 'sê wéll.

that are energetic and grand, others that are tedious and bumbling. His instinct was right at times, but as if by accident; he had not learned to sustain the best possibilities of this verse form. Where did his instinct find the techniques that gave it power? It found them in spoken English: he could hear them as possibilities in the way things were said. But he probably recognized those possibilities in speech because they had already been realized centuries before in native traditions of English verse, the traditions Chaucer was, if not revolting against, ignoring.

In this native tradition there was what we call "alliterative verse," in which every line had four basic stresses with a caesura in the middle after the second stress. The line might have any number of syllables. At least one of the stressed syllables on one side of the caesura had to alliterate with at least two on the other side; there were variations and exceptions, but this was the basic pattern. The form, standard in Old English, survived into Middle English. During Chaucer's lifetime there was a revival of it, and some of the masterpieces of his century—*Piers Plowman*, the alliterative *Morte Arthure*, *Pearl*, and *Sir Gawain and the Green Knight*, to name only four—belong to the revival. Chaucer probably knew such poetry was being written in his time, but he appears not to have liked it. Nevertheless, such verse had the effects he needed. It invited the poet to divide up phrases as they naturally occur in speech, without having to count syllables. In English it was easier to find words that alliterate than to find words that rhyme, and natural word groups could tumble along with alliterations that enhanced their groupings, as here in the opening of *Piers Plowman*:

> In a *s*ummer *s*eason, when *s*oft was the *s*unne,
> I *sh*ope me° in a *sh*roude, as I a *sh*eep were,   *dressed myself*
> In *h*abit as a *h*eremit, un*h*oly of workes,
> *W*ent *w*ide in the *w*orld, *w*ondres to seen.*

At its best it is not at all monotonous, because the caesura in the middle of each line is sometimes a strong pause called for by the sense of the sentence, sometimes only a metrical pause, scarcely noticeable. In the same way, phrases do not have to break off at the end of a line: enjambement comes naturally in alliterative verse. Nor is it bombastic: the repeated letters weld groups of words, and the changes from one letter to another ring changes in syntactical and rhythmical units. For grim destruction and chaos, listen to the deliberate rhythm and the four alliterations in the opening lines of *Sir Gawain and the Green Knight*:

*In Margaret Williams's translation: "Once in summertime, in the soft sunlight, / I dressed up in shaggy clothes, just like a shepherd. / Fitted out as a hermit of not-too-holy life, / I set out for the wide world, looking for wonders."

Sithen the sege and th'assaut watz sesed at Troye,
The borgh that brittened and brent to brondes and askes . . . *

But the same form can be delicate and subtle when the alliterating letters
fall on words that don't have a strong semantic stress:

Well negh in all the wele° in the West Isles . . .   *wealth*

And while the number of syllables is fluid, it isn't without consequence.
You can gain emphasis or dignity in alliterative poetry by reducing the
number of syllables, or you can increase them into an excited rush of
verbiage. A wonderful verse form—perfectly and naturally suited to English.

Thus Chaucer, without knowing it, found in the farthest reaches of
his ear possibilities that would have escaped or horrified the Francophile
in him. He would find something like it in Italian verse when he began
to read it. One cannot say for sure that he disliked alliterative verse; in
the one place where he mentions it, at the very end of *The Canterbury
Tales*, he has the crusty Parson protest that he will not tell a tale in verse
but only a sound story in prose (it turns out to be a "meditation" on
penance!), and what he says is,

. . . I am a southren man,
I cannot geste° *rum-ram-ruf*, by letter.   *tell a story*

He adds that he holds rhyme but little better, an opinion Chaucer would
not have shared. Chaucer was a "southern man" as well, and by the
fourteenth century the alliterative tradition was probably considered in-
digenous to the north by people in the south. To someone from London,
and a courtier, it would have seemed rustic. Nevertheless, it rang in his
ear (once, in the Knight's Tale, at line 2599, he even lapsed into an
approximation of it to simulate the clashing and banging of medieval
battle, and he did the same in his Legend of Cleopatra). The native form
gave him, perhaps without his knowing it, the means to create in English
a forceful, natural replica of French octosyllabic couplets.

The Book of the Duchess

When Chaucer returned from abroad in 1368 to find that the Duchess
Blanche had died, he was able, thanks to the techniques he had by that
time developed and mastered, to construct a poem on her death, *The*

*In Marie Borroff's translation: "Since the siege and the assault was ceased at Troy, / The
walls breached and burnt down to brands and ashes . . ."

Book of the Duchess, in which he could sustain for more than 1,300 lines
this energetic use of four-stress rhyming couplets. He was writing now
with his personal feelings fully engaged. He was moved by the elegist's
purpose, to express grief, and the courtier's purpose to show sympathy for
the bereaved duke, to help him face the future. These purposes held his
interest, which had lagged when he was just translating.

  The Book of the Duchess has often been charged with what are
reckoned flaws: that its characters are wooden, that its narrative lacks
proportion, that it has extraneous elements and a weak conclusion. But
in recent years scholars have compared it closely with the poems in French
that it is drawn from or is similar to—its sources and analogues—and
seeing it beside these makes us realize that it belongs to a particular
literary kind. It is a poem of consolation. Such poems were almost never
used as elegies, but there had been one, by Jean de la Mote, consoling
Queen Philippa and her relatives on the death of her father, William of
Hainault; Chaucer probably knew it, though it was written before he was
born. Chaucer's poem, like these predecessors, is a very "Gothic" kind of
poem: like medieval tapestries or the elaborately illuminated capitals in
late medieval manuscripts, it is the product of a highly conventional,
stylized, ornamental tradition. If we see it in these terms, which are its
own terms, we see how well it succeeds in what it sets out to do. To see
it in *our* terms would be like comparing a fourteenth-century tapestry with
Picasso's *Guernica*.

  Chaucer surely began the poem at once upon his return to England,
while grief was still in the air and the court was still in mourning. It is
entirely possible, as one scholar thinks, that he completed it within a
matter of weeks. Or completed at least a draft of it: there is almost nothing
in it that seems to want revision or suggest haste. Chaucer considered it
one of his major works, for he named it among his poems every time he
listed them; almost twenty years later, in *The Legend of Good Women*
(F Prologue 418), he called it, very specifically, "The Death of Blanche
the Duchess." If one does not consider a poem finished until the poet is
through tinkering with it, it may not have been finished for some years,
but the thesis that it was *written* some years after Blanche's death is
untenable: one offers consolation to a bereaved friend and speaks earnestly
to him of facing the future in the weeks or months that follow his
bereavement, not years later. By September 1371 John of Gaunt was
remarried, and though the marriage to Costanza was only a practical
affair, the poem, if written at this time, could have been misconstrued as
a criticism of Gaunt's second marriage. By this time Gaunt had taken
Katherine Swynford as his mistress, which suggests that his bereavement
was substantially reduced; and even if he was still grieving for Blanche,

would Chaucer have written a poem of sympathy praising Blanche after his own sister-in-law had taken Blanche's place in his bed?

So the poem must have been *begun* at once in late 1368 and *written* in some early form shortly thereafter; when or how it was *presented*—or *if* it was presented—is another question. The image of Chaucer reading it aloud at court hovers over all discussions of this matter, perhaps because there is that famous picture, in a manuscript of the *Troilus*, showing (it seems) Chaucer standing at a lectern before the court of King Richard II. But there is no evidence that he presented *The Book of the Duchess* aloud before the court of Edward III or to John of Gaunt. Poets some-times presented such poems to a patron in a bound copy; that may be as much of a presentation as it ever had. We can suppose that the duke read or heard it, and that it was known in court circles, because Chaucer named it years later among his works and because copies of it were made. Three manuscripts have survived, not a large number, plus an early printed edition based on a fourth manuscript now lost. But its presentation may not have been the great court event we'd like to think. Chaucer may have given Gaunt a copy late in 1368 or early in 1369, then for his own satisfaction kept it about, revised it further, and read it to some friends who asked to make copies.

It has been suggested that Chaucer might have presented his elegy at one of the annual commemorations of the duchess's death. But Gaunt was out of England during September of each year until the sixth anniver-sary, 1374. Such anniversary services, very common in medieval life, would have been held anyway whether Gaunt was present or not, and it's possible Chaucer was asked to read his poem in one of these years—but it's very unlikely: the poem is addressed quite personally to Gaunt, is trying to persuade him to leave his grief behind, take consolation from his happy memories, face a new day. Are we to believe that he read such sentiments to the king, Alice Perrers, the Princess Costanza, Katherine Swynford, and Gaunt's children *in Gaunt's absence?* Of the sixth anniver-sary, the first Gaunt attended, we happen to have a detailed description. It was rather more elaborate than other commemorations, judging from the cost. On the eve of the anniversary, alms were distributed to prisoners and the poor, wine and sweetmeats were served to the company and the cathedral chapter after vespers for the dead. On the anniversary itself there was a solemn high mass at Saint Paul's. The church was draped in black, and forty newly made candles burned about the duchess's tomb, with six of the thick candles known as mortar-lights on the tomb itself. Twenty-four men dressed in the Lancaster livery stood about the tomb holding torches. A rather modest supper was then served to perhaps sixty or seventy people at the Palace of the Savoy. Nothing is said of poems read or other entertainments. And there are no records of any gift or grant to Geoffrey Chaucer from John of Gaunt at that time that might be thought a reward for the poem.

The earnest elegiac words of *The Book of the Duchess* would surely have seemed a period piece six or more years after Blanche's death. That the poem made no acknowledgment of the queen's death in 1369 might have been thought an anomaly. And its courtly manner and conventional motifs could have seemed out of place in the mid 1370s when England's great age of victory and chivalry was so clearly a thing of the past. Then why all the fuss about its being read at an anniversary of the duchess's death? It is because of the vexing passage beginning at line 36, where the poet explains why he cannot sleep:

I hold it be a sicknesse	
That I have suffred this eight yeere,	
And yet my boot° is never the neere°,	cure / nearer
For there is physician but oon°	one
That may me heele—but that is done.	
Pass we over until eft°.	later
That will not be mot need be left.°	must be ignored

This is the conventional language of "lovesickness" and might refer to any number of things, but explanations are unnecessary. The passage is there to throw dust in the reader's eyes: it establishes the poet, conventionally, as a fellow lover or fellow sufferer, a counterpart and foil to the grieving Knight of the poem. Eight is probably a quite arbitrary number that could have symbolical significance (in religious symbolism it meant a return to the beginning after the seven days of the week or of Creation, hence eternity or resurrection). And the simple fact is, Chaucer got it out of Machaut.

When Chaucer sat down to write the poem he took to heart the advice of the rhetorician Geoffrey of Vinsauf in the opening lines of his *Poetria Nova*. Chaucer translated these lines in *Troilus and Criseyde*, representing them as a thought crossing Pandarus's mind while he plans the love affair:

For every wight that hath an house to founde°	build
Ne runneth not the work for to beginne	
With rakel° hand, but he will bide a stounde°	rash /
	wait a moment
And send his herte's line out fro withinne,	
Alderfirst his purpose for to winne°.	attain

He who builds a house should *not* rush into the task helter-skelter but hold back, send out the plumb line of his heart, and take measure of his purpose; as with a house, so with a poem. Chaucer's purpose was to offer consolation to the duke, consolation and encouragement, perhaps advice; and to eulogize the deceased duchess, to make a memorial for her in words and images as lustrous as a tombstone effigy. To do this, to speak well of the dead and speak earnest words to the bereaved, is a formidable task over which the greatest poets have stumbled. Words of eulogy grow quickly absurd at the least hint of pomposity or contrived eloquence; and sympathy is best expressed in earnest silence, least well in platitudes. The model Chaucer did *not* want was the bombastic, repetitious verses given as a sample by Geoffrey of Vinsauf, on the death of Richard I ("O sorrow! O greater than sorrow! O death! O truculent death! would you were dead, O death!"); he would later make wicked fun of the passage in the Nun's Priest's Tale. What he wanted was an effect like that of the dream vision, where inner feelings are dealt with as such: not an allegorical vision like the *Roman* with personified figures like Pity or Grief, but simply one in which a royal patron is offered comfort.

And he knew such a poem, the *Dit de la Fonteinne Amoureuse* by Guillaume de Machaut, written for the duke of Berry. In 1361 under the Treaty of Brétigny the duke, recently married, was obliged to be separated from his wife when he was sent to England as one of the hostages for King Jean's ransom. Machaut wrote the poem, in stanzaic form, to offer comfort to both parties. The poem begins with the Dreamer overhearing a Knight's complaint: the Knight must part from his lady, and she is not even aware of his love. He remembers the story of Ceys and Alcione and, remembering that Morpheus, god of sleep, helped Alcione, wishes he would help him too. The Dreamer, taking note of what he has overheard, accosts the lover. They go off to a park and, falling asleep beside a fountain, both dream the same dream. In this shared dream, Venus appears, brings the lady to the knight (who has turned out now to be a prince): the lady offers him kisses and kind words, and the prince awakes comforted.

From this poem Chaucer took the basic elements of his poem, as will be seen from a summary:

1. The narrator, unable to sleep, reads the story of Seyx and Alcione, then wishes Morpheus would help him sleep.

2. Falling asleep, he encounters the emperor "Octovien" leading a hunt. A little dog, lost, comes to him and leads him into a wood, where he comes upon a Knight dressed in black. He overhears the Knight's lament, then accosts him, asking him what is his loss.

3. The Knight tells his story at length; the dreamer, uncomprehending, asks again what is his loss, and the Knight tells him how he won his lady's love.

4. The narrator for the third time asks the Knight what is his loss, and the Knight says, "She is dead." The narrator replies, "Nay, is that your loss? By God, it is routhe [pity]." The hunt is ended and the Knight goes off to a castle on a hill. The narrator says he decided to make his dream into a poem, and now it is done.

Not only is the plot modeled on Machaut's poem, but long passages are virtually translated from it. For the impending separation of the lovers, Chaucer substituted the lady's death. And he omitted Venus's appearance and the lady's words of comfort; the comfort in *The Book of the Duchess* really comes from the narrator's simple realization that she is dead and from his simple expression of pity. Chaucer added long passages from another poem by Machaut, the *Jugement du Roy de Behaigne,* in four-line stanzas. It is a debate between a knight and a lady: the lady's lord has died, the knight's lady has deserted him, and they debate whose grief is greater. Much of the discourse of the Black Knight and the Dreamer in *The Book of the Duchess* is drawn from it—their conversation, the Black Knight's complaint, his narration of his love affair, and his description of his beloved. Machaut's dreamer, like Chaucer's, is naïve, befuddled, and obtuse—a comic figure removed from the action and so not in a class with the noble personages of the poem itself.

For other passages Chaucer drew from a half-dozen other poems.* According to one editor's count, 914 of its 1,334 lines show a direct debt to another poet's work. This way of writing poetry seems by modern standards slovenly and disingenuous; the poem seems to us a derivative crazy quilt by a young poet not ready to approach his work with a firm hand. But originality wasn't prized in the Middle Ages as it is in modern times; *soundness* was prized. They hadn't our idea of "literary property": a successful poem belonged to everyone. If another poet had written passages of merit that could be used in constructing a poem, it was an advantage to the poem and a compliment to the other poet. It wasn't stealing or butchering. It was closer to what we might call adaptation or allusion—their attitude was closer to ours about musicals based on plays, or about nonobjective painting. Besides, *The Book of the Duchess* in no way suffers from its borrowings: the tone and style are completely consist-

---

* The Black Knight's complaint against Fortune, the list of moral virtues he found in the lady, and some details of his story are from still another poem by Machaut, the *Remède de Fortune.* The lines describing Flora and Zephirus, who overlook the garden (lines 402ff.), are from Jean de Meun's part of the *Roman de la Rose.* The lines that describe the dream setting and come just before the Dreamer falls asleep are modeled on the *Roman,* with an assist from Froissart's *Paradis d'Amour.*

ent, and there is scarcely a line that *feels* translated from a foreign language or seems to belong in another poem. This may be so because the poet did not, as we imagine, sit down and copy out of other books; it is more than likely that he had long passages from these poems by memory.

And the conception *is* original. Using the traditional courtly poem of consolation for the purposes of an elegy had been done only once before, in the poem by Jean de la Mote mentioned earlier. Poems for the dead in medieval literature were more likely to be barefaced laments in elaborate language; Chaucer wanted to lament Blanche's death in an understated way. Unlike his sources, which are in stanzas, his poem is in couplets. Stanzas were more formal and courtly, being thought the proper form in which to address royalty; and stanzas parcel out material, shape it, and therefore distance and heighten it. Couplets are more conversational, less in the high style, hence more suitable to narrative: each couplet sets up no expectation beyond the succession of further couplets, makes events seem to flow as in time rather than to be organized as in memory. The choice was right for the simplicity Chaucer wanted to achieve.

The result is one of the great elegies of the English language. It deserves a place beside *Pearl* or Milton's *Lycidas* or Shelley's *Adonais*— and it may be a better poem than they are. The elegy presents the poet with two almost unavoidable traps: he may, like Shelley, overpraise his subject in extravagancies that invite parody, or, like Milton, focus upon his own woe and hence upon himself in such a way as to absurdly ignore the deceased. Chaucer's poem avoids both pitfalls: the Duchess Blanche does not rise as a star into the sky, and the poet does not babble on about current events or wax solemn about pastures new. The focus is on the grief of the deceased lady's *husband*, the Black Knight of the poem, who is of course John of Gaunt. The poem is a quite conventional French dream vision, and the dreamer-poet appears, as in such poems, befuddled and confused. These conventions are no more stylized, certainly, than those of the pastoral elegy that were to become standard in later English literature, used by Spenser, Milton, Shelley, and Matthew Arnold. One could make a case that the conventions of the French dream vision are more suitable to the purposes of elegy than are those of pastoral: a befuddled dreamer in a surreal world is a more promising device for expressing the feelings we have when we mourn than are shepherds tootling their pipes while their sheep munch in the pastures.

And Chaucer managed to make the world of his poem, as was not always true in dream visions, successfully dreamlike: events happen in what seems no rational order—there is the selectivity of real dreams here, and what Freud called condensation. The dreamer's horse appears in his bedroom and later disappears unaccountably from the picture; a dog appears, leads the dreamer into the next scene, and is forgotten; the lady is at once a remembered person and a pawn in a chess game; a bell chimes noon and midnight at the same time.

The opening section of the poem, in which the Dreamer reads and recounts the story of Seyx and Alcione before falling asleep, continues to be faulted as "extraneous." But Chaucer took the story of Machaut's poem and deliberately removed it to the beginning of his poem for a purpose: the story is a mirror image of Blanche's death. In the story, Seyx the king goes abroad and dies in a shipwreck; to his wife at home Morpheus sends a messenger disguised in the body of Seyx who tells her he is dead (line 209):

> And farewell, sweet, my worldes blisse,
> I pray God your sorrow lisse°—   *lighten*
> Too little while our blisse lasteth.

Within three days she dies of grief. In life, it was the lady who died; she was at home, not away; her death was seen by Gaunt, not revealed to him; her body was starkly there to be buried in Saint Paul's, its likeness carved in alabaster; and John of Gaunt was left with a grief he must not die of but survive. From this point of view, the purpose of the poem is to warn the bereaved against such an excess of grief. The simple words of the deceased Seyx to the living Alcione were no less applicable to John of Gaunt: "Let be your sorrowful life. . . . Too little while our blisse lasteth."

The narrator, suffering from insomnia, myopically takes note of Morpheus: I never heard of gods that could make people sleep or wake, he says, "for I ne knew never god but one" (line 237). So he offers them —just for fun ("in my game")—a fine bed with rich gold appurtenances if they will make him sleep. And at once he grows weary, drops off, dreams "so inly sweet a sweven" that hardly anyone would be able to interpret it. He says, "This was my sweven": the rest of the poem recounts the dream—at the end he says again, "this was my sweven, now it is done."

The poem consists of a series of contrasts. Its early scenes are "extraneous" in the sense that once we have read them and experienced them, we can forget them; they are going to work upon us in a sublime way. For each element of the poem prepares us for a counterpart to follow. When we come to that counterpart it seems like a déjà vu, and its contrast with its remembered counterpart gives it definition. Thus the narrator's sleeplessness and unnamed sorrow contrast with the Black Knight's precisely defined sorrow. The narrator's naïveté contrasts with the poet's own clarity and simplicity: at the end he will say, "This was my dream, it had something to say, I decided to write it, now it is written." So too, the narrator chooses to read a "romance" (line 48) for diversion—for "play," to "drive the night away," he says—and his romance takes place during the pagan Age of Nature, "while men loved the law of Kinde"; but all that follows is for instruction and comfort, not diversion, and it has reference to a Christian world, not a pagan one.

To such contrasts, Chaucer added a very funny one, probably a private joke. Throughout the dream every word is adorned with the elegances of medieval rhetoric, the verse is crisp and varied, the diction forceful, the images pellucid. But in the story of Seyx and Alcione, at its key moment when Juno commands Morpheus to go to Alcione disguised as Seyx, Chaucer has her speak sixteen lines of the most stupid verse imaginable (lines 136 ff.)—awkward, cliché-ridden, with tag lines like "it is no nay," redundancies like "full pale and nothing roddy," "go now fast, and hye thee blyve"—which may be translated "very pale and not ruddy," "go fast and get going quickly." She might be a fourteenth-century house-wife sending the servant after vegetables. Her ridiculous speech makes the narrator's "romance" seem like a badly written book—again, in contrast to what will follow.

In the dream the narrator finds himself awakened on a May morning by birds singing sweetly, like a "thing of heaven," and his chamber set with windows of glass in which is wrought the story of Troy and walls on which is painted the *Roman de la Rose*. He is in a world of song and story, and it is ambiguous whether what he sees are words or images. Suddenly he hears a hunt—a hunt for the hart, the symbolical courtly hunt, with the courtly pun on "heart." He takes his horse (which appears to be in the room with him) and leaves the chamber. He asks someone, "Say, fellow, who shall hunte here?" and is told it is the "Emperor Octovien" —presumably the Roman emperor of that name, probably with a compli-mentary reference to King Edward III. The hart is found, but then escapes, and the dogs lose its scent. Now the narrator's horse has disap-peared, he is on foot, and he encounters the lost puppy: it creeps up to him, holds its head down, puts its ears together, and lays its hairs back, then escapes when the narrator reaches out to it. The little dog is present for only eight lines, yet, if we may trust the dozen critics who have explained him, he is fraught with multiple significance. He is a conven-tional animal whose function is to lead the narrator to a significant place; he is a symbol of domestic or marital harmony, or of reason and dialectic; he is sympathetic and lost, like the mourning Black Knight; he is menac-ing and mysterious. He leads the narrator down a path through a surreal forest scene in a green springtime wood filled with animals, until he comes upon the Knight in black.

The Knight is sitting by an oak tree (the oak was associated with death); the narrator comes up behind him, so that the Knight does not

see him. The narrator overhears him recite to himself a "rhyme"—a "lay"
or "song," it is called—without a melody: a poem. Its genre is twice
specifically identified as a *complaint*. The complaint was a French courtly
form, having no particular rhyme or stanzaic pattern, usually a monologue
in which the speaker laments his unhappy state and wishes for a remedy.
This is what he hears:

> I have of sorrow so gret won°   *plenty*
> That joye get I never none,
> Now that I see my lady bright,
> Which I have loved with all my might,
> Is fro me deed and is agoon.
> Allas, Death, what aileth thee,
> That thou n'oldest° have taken me,   *wouldn't*
> Whan thou took my lady sweete,
> That was so fair, so fresh, so free,
> So good, that men may well see
> Of all goodness she had no meete°!   *equal*

The narrator observes the Knight's sorrowful sound and appearance: It
seemed a wonder, he says, that nature could suffer any creature to have
such sorrow and not be dead. The remainder of the poem consists of a
dialogue between the narrator and the Knight in which the narrator asks
him what his sorrow is and the Knight responds by telling his story.

On the surface of things it seems absurd that the narrator cannot
understand what is so plainly stated in the complaint, and critics of a
previous generation reckoned this a flaw because it seemed improbable.
But what the narrator hears is an entirely conventional verse, the complaint of a forlorn lover; there is no reason for him to suppose it states a
fact or explains, rather than expresses, the Knight's sorrowful mood. What
the narrator cannot understand is that beneath the conventionality of the
verse lies a stark reality. Why should he? If you came upon a cowboy in
a field singing to himself a typical cowboy song about death, would you
conclude that someone had really died? That is exactly the narrator's
circumstance: he wants to know why the knight is sad, wants to help him,
tells him it may ease his heart to tell his story, but doesn't see that the
conventional song stated the facts. This central moment in the poem
serves as an instruction to the reader about how to read the poem: we must
seek beneath—or *in*—its conventionality its core of human feeling and
human truth.

Throughout the ensuing discourse the Black Knight speaks entirely
in conventional indirections, in personifications and metaphors and traditional images. He says that Death has made him naked of bliss. He says

that he is Sorrow and that Sorrow is he. He tells in a lengthy passage how
he has played a game of chess with Fortune and Fortune has taken his
queen. The narrator, as literal-minded as a computer, says that no one
would make such woe over a chess queen. Some think the narrator's
literal-mindedness is the conventional obtuseness of dream poetry, others
that it is a sort of psychotherapeutic ploy to keep the knight talking.
Whichever is true, it is certainly a ploy on Chaucer's part, and it does its
work, for the Knight goes on to say, at line 743,

> Thou wost full littel what thou menest;
> I have lost more than thou wenest

—"little do you know what you mean; I have lost more than you suppose."
He will say this twice again, and each time, when questioned, will tell
more of his story. But the story comes out in the conventional terms of
courtly love: In youth, he says, he gave his service to Love, then in time
saw a lady of great beauty but found her distant and indifferent. He
describes her in the conventional language, praises her appearance, her
soft and eloquent speech, her dignity of behavior, her goodness, wit and
"trouthe," then describes his reactions to her, how vastly he loved her,
loved her *without repenting*. The narrator asks him to tell how he first
spoke to her, and asks again what he has lost. Again the knight says, "I
have lost more than thou wenest," and goes on to tell how he dared not
approach her but only to compose songs to her, of which he recites the
first, at line 1175:

> Lord, it maketh mine herte light,
> Whan I think on that sweete wight°   *creature*
> That is so seemly on to see;
> And wish to God it might so be
> That she wolde hold me for hir knight,
> My lady, that is so fair and bright!

He then tells how in fear and trembling he approached her, unable to do
more than hang his head and say "Mercy!" At length he declared his love
and swore to be steadfast, and she came slowly to trust him and take pity
on him, at length accepting him and giving him a ring as token (line
1289):

> Our hertes weren so even a pair
> That never nas that one contrayre
> To that other, for no woe.

In this long, conventional description, nothing is said of marriage.
The poem has dealt so far only with love, with the feeling between them,

and that only in traditional ideal terms. This may disappoint a reader with
a bent for realism, but it could not have disappointed the English court.
At such a time one does not want to be reminded of quotidian realities;
one wants to think that things went according to the myths and ideals
of one's class or culture. The description of Blanche is highly conventional, though with a few details that might be thought particularizing;
but probably she, like most medieval ladies, was at pains to conform to
the age's ideals of appearance and conduct, and to the extent that she did
so the description would seem appropriate, would probably strike a grieving audience as a true picture. It is the same with the Black Knight. It
is hard to imagine the blustery duke hanging his head and saying
"Mercy!"—but that is what lovers in poems did, and if a young man at
nineteen did not take such poems as a model for behavior, he might as
a mourner at twenty-nine like to believe he had.

But now this conventionality and sentimental idealism are dispersed.
The narrator bursts forth with a question: "Sir, where is she now?" The
Knight replies (line 1304) that *that* was the loss he mentioned before:

> "Bethink how I said here-beforn,
> 'Thou wost full littel what thou menest;
> I have lost more than thou wenest'—
> Got wot, alas, right that was she!"
> "Alas, sir, how? what may that be?"
> "She is dead." "Nay!" "Yis, by my trouthe!"
> "Is that your loss? By God, it is routhe°!"   *pity*

This conclusion says in the plainest language what any mourner finds
hardest to say: *She is dead.* And the narrator says all any sympathetic
friend can say: *It is routhe.* Everything that has gone before has prepared
for these primal, irreducible responses, and they are the end of the long
dialogue.

It is only in the remaining twenty-three lines that Chaucer permits
himself an allusion to their marriage. Suddenly, the horns blow and the
hunters move on: the hunt for the "hart" is over. "All was done, / For
that time, the hert-hunting." This king,* we are told, rode homeward to
a place not far away:

> A long castel with walles white,
> By Saint John! on a rich hill.

* The "king" is the Black Knight; or, possibly, the leader of the hunt, Octavian, who was,
however, called Emperor. The Black Knight seems to be equated here with the King Seyx
of the introduction and with the king in the game of chess, in which the queen was lost.
It is not necessary to assume that when the passage was written, John of Gaunt had already
begun to style himself king of Castile.

The lines are an anagram: "long castle" means Lancaster (sometimes called Longcastel), "white" means Blanche, "rich hill" means Richmond (-*mount*). They present virtually a heraldic image of the two houses joined in marriage: Blanche, duchess of Lancaster and John, earl of Richmond. That image owes itself directly to the values of courtly culture, reminds the reader that this marriage had, beyond the great love it contained, those values of rank and dynasty that were the essence of marriage for princes of the royal blood. And this reminder would have been for them a very considerable and moving consolation. The marriage had joined two houses in such a way as to confer status and wealth greater than either house had of itself, and had brought forth issue that would inherit those entitlements. None knew then that their son would be King Henry IV. History made Chaucer's ending right.

With that, a bell in the castle rings the hour of twelve. In the dream the hunt has been in the morning, so the hour struck is noon. But now the dreamer wakes and finds himself in bed at night, his book of Seyx and Alcione still in his hand: the hour is midnight, a new day is beginning. The implication of the ending, which is as much as one can say to hearten those who mourn, is that the future lies ahead.

This is the consolation of the courtier to a patron, and its courtly meaning is manifest and explicit. One might expect in medieval times a religious consolation, and in fact there is a religious message. If the Knight lost his queen to Fortune, this means he lost her to one of those chance occurrences that must be accepted with resignation and patience as part of God's universal plan. To indulge in an excess of grief at such a loss would be prideful and self-centered, lacking in Christian resignation and patience; and he whose grief was excessive in this way needed to be restored to spiritual health. All of this, too obvious to say outright, is present by implication. The narrator's "sorrowful imaginacioun" is no more a healthy state in spiritual terms than in psychological ones, and the "physicien but one" that can heal him is, from this viewpoint, God. The stated lesson of the story of Seyx and Alcione is the familiar Christian one of mutability: "too littel while our blisse lasteth." The hunt for the hart had a Christian meaning, since the captured hart could symbolize the crucified Christ or the soul of man. Fortune is specifically a Christian concept. And the lady's beauty is in essence an inner virtue of character and their love at base spiritual.

This religious level in Gothic art can be quite arcane: since everything in the Old Testament was thought to prefigure the message of the New Testament, anything mentioned in the Old Testament—a king, a lion, an onion—had a hidden meaning, usually more than one. Some of these symbols were familiar in the iconography of medieval art and would have been easily recognized when used as symbols. Many still are: the crown of thorns, the shepherds, the lamb. Others were esoteric and known only to the learned. In poetry there is a wide margin for coincidence and no method of verification; if you find an onion in a poem, you may suspect it brings with it a connotation of biblical symbolism that could be discovered in medieval exegetical writings, but such writings often provide many meanings of varying applicability, and one must always suppose some onions in poems are only onions. Is Octavian mentioned because he was emperor when Christ was born? Is the king who returns home at the end of *The Book of the Duchess* the risen Christ? Is the "long castel with walles white" really a reference to what Chaucer in the "ABC" called "that palays that is bilt / To penitents"—the palace of heaven? Well, perhaps, at one level. But the king is obviously a figure in the hunt, and he rides home to a "long castle" and a "rich hill," obviously Lancaster and Richmond. If the poem has a subtext of religious symbolism, that subtext is secondary, and might have been perceived by a medieval reader quite unconsciously. The existence of such symbolism in medieval art has appealed in our time to a kind of sensibility that likes to claim a hidden message as the true one. The argument is that the true hidden meaning of all medieval poems is the unitary message of Christian charity, and that medieval readers were monklike automatons who looked only for that message.

Nevertheless, it is true that Chaucer—this early in his career, and now more than later—wrote in this Gothic style, introducing symbolical allusions to beliefs taken for granted. That style, especially in these troubled years, made *The Book of the Duchess* much more than an occasional poem: after Prince Lionel and the queen had died, and the Black Prince's son Edward, and when everyone knew the Black Prince would never recover, it became a poem about the transience of earthly bliss.

Chaucer at Thirty

Imagine him then on a certain day in October or November 1372, summoned to the king's chamber or before some officer of it to be told he will go to Italy on the king's business. He is approaching thirty. It is now four years since the Duchess Blanche died: John of Gaunt is married to the young Princess Costanza, that remote, sad girl with her pious ways, and calling himself king of Castile; Katherine Swynford has that year borne the duke a son, John. The Countess Elizabeth has been dead nearly ten years, Prince Lionel and the Duchess Blanche four, the queen three.

Chaucer's father is dead, his mother remarried. The French wars have begun again, and Gaunt is steadily abroad. The Black Prince is back in England, mortally ill. The king is in his dotage, Alice Perrers is forever about him, the court is gossiping shamelessly: there is cynicism in the air —cynicism about chivalry, cynicism about marriage. The picture of domestic bliss preserved in *The Book of the Duchess,* of marital love won in the old courtly way, idealized and gorgeous, and enriched by a sense of loss, seems now old-fashioned, seems about the deaths of many, about the passing of a way of life that is itself, now, like a dream.

Chaucer has been married six years; is father, it appears, to a girl and a boy. He may take satisfaction, love and fatherhood aside, in the status of his marriage: his wife was daughter of a knight of the dead queen's retinue, was herself a damsel of the queen's chamber, and is now damsel to the Princess Costanza. She is often at court, often with her sister Katherine, who is very much at court. Geoffrey and Philippa are together but fleetingly, have as yet no private lodgings of their own; one can imagine them in the early years of their marriage scurrying to Westminster, cloaks flying—black cloaks of mourning, often, in those years—across the paved tile floors, before the great roaring fires, past the uniformed guards, clad in the liveries of king and queen, parting, going about their separate duties; now, parting at home or in the street, Geoffrey to the palace or to Windsor or, increasingly, abroad, Philippa to the Savoy in the Strand or traveling with Princess Costanza's ladies.

Master Geoffrey, esquire of the king's household, but not of the king's chamber, is by now fully trained for specialized duties. Coming into the Ulster household with the urban prejudices of a merchant family, he must never seriously have thought of taking up knighthood, but he has done his service as a soldier and as king's messenger; has attended in some way—and to whatever extent they were already schools in his day—the Inns of Chancery and the Inns of Court; can write the fair, proper hand approved for the keeping of records, in the right bureaucratic Latin or French as occasion requires; knows the standard practices of commerce and finance; knows the law as an official of government must know it. His education has in the main been an internship supervised by the royal household; he has traveled already in the king's service to France, Flanders, Spain, Italy; can speak, read, and write Latin, French, and Italian. "Nouriture"—comportment—has been a part of this training; the elaborate codes of precedence and deference are now second nature to him, and public speech is a part of this, for all negotiations and diplomacy were carried out with a high-flown rhetorical art, in elaborate tropes and dignified periphrases—the art of which Polonius was master. As for book learning, "lettrure," the reading of Latin classics and French verse was encouraged at court: to talk about feats of arms and heroes of olden days, and of love, and to compose poems about these, were valued skills.

As he approaches thirty, his thoughts about how old he is are somewhat different, only somewhat, from modern thoughts. Because the Bible said man's life was threescore and ten, thirty-five was reckoned the peak of life. Ten years on either side of that peak marked off "manhood," at least by Dante's reckoning of it, so Geoffrey has recently entered maturity. Almost all authorities agreed that adolescence, the first stage of adulthood, ended at twenty-five. The change was as major a one as puberty, for it entailed a physiological permutation of humors: adolescence was hot and moist, maturity hot and dry. A change of diet was called for, and of attitude; the desirable traits of an adolescent, Dante thought, were sweetness, obedience, sensitivity to shame, grace of body, whereas manhood called for temperance, bravery, love, courtesy, loyalty. Now over twenty-five, Geoffrey is fully entered into the world of adult responsibility, which as one might suspect had gradations too: by one reckoning you were in *juventus*, young manhood, till thirty-five, and in *virilitas*, full manhood, till fifty.

In our time it has been observed that young men in their twenties are moved by a desire to set out on their own, gain freedom from their families, establish an identity and career and domestic life of their own. It is a period of striving, learning, adapting. In their early thirties this driving force gets off its track and one enters a period of uncertainty and doubt, of questioning. Not that medieval men necessarily had identity crises or life crises as modern men evidently do, or had them at comparable ages; yet their way of dividing up the stages of life is surprisingly like modern observations, and they must have faced turning points as they advanced from stage to stage.

As Chaucer approached thirty, England's fortunes must have wrought many crises among the royal esquires. Young men in their twenties, it is said, are likely to have an older man in the picture, a mentor from whom, as they enter their thirties, they tend to withdraw. For Chaucer, Lionel and John of Gaunt would not quite have qualified as the authority figures of his twenties, for they were not appreciably older than he, only higher in rank; besides, Lionel died halfway through the period, and Gaunt was out of the country more than half those years. If Geoffrey had such a mentor in his twenties, it was probably an older man, a poet as well as a courtier: John Gower.

Chaucer had met Gower by now; they met, tradition holds, at the Inns of Court. Gower, some dozen years older than Geoffrey, is at this time writing ballades in French and the *Mirour de l'Homme* (he will not write in English for fifteen or more years yet); Chaucer belongs to a new generation for whom English is naturally their language, to speak and write. How rich a friendship they had, it is not possible to say, but for want of another significant English poet it may have been at its richest now when Chaucer most needed a poetical mentor. The French poets of the day, Machaut especially, were Chaucer's poetical heroes; Froissart, whom he met, one assumes, in the 1360s, and who has toadied about the English court off and on during these years, is probably no more than an acquaintance; if more, one would think garrulous Froissart would have memorialized the friendship. He has not met Deschamps, judging from the manner of Deschamps's later poem to him, dated 1385, for one does not write hyperbolical, servile praise to an old friend, or call him by his full name. But Gower was there in London, a kindly, dedicated man, an excellent poet. That Chaucer was writing in English may have been an alienating circumstance, may have put him on his own, for it is hard to know what other poets writing in English he could have known at this time. William Langland, author of *Piers Plowman,* has only just completed the earliest version of his vast, shaggy alliterative poem. John Clanvowe is Chaucer's age, Thomas Usk approximately so, but they won't know Chaucer till later. Thomas Hoccleve is two years old. Gower and Chaucer have followed the French tradition, writing for the same courtly audience, sharing materials. In the future their major poems will have certain fundamental principles and characteristics in common. Both will begin writing "frame narratives" at the same time, though of very different kinds. And Chaucer's independence of Gower does begin at this time, as he turns thirty.

It is psychologically the right moment in his life for new models, and the right time for doubts. Whether his career was the right one, whether he was going anywhere in it, whether he would find anything further to write about or write in English any better than he has—these would have been the questions he was asking. The answers were to come in a surprising way. He was to be abroad six months. He was to return to palpable rewards in his career and a settled life that afforded time to write. And he was to have had a head-spinning glimpse into a new world of letters and a new kind of life.

Until now Chaucer has made one major accomplishment as a poet: he has mastered in English one mode of French poetry. He has done something no other English poet had done, brought the French courtly dream vision and French lyric forms successfully into English. He has (but there is a question about the date) written in English one piece of religious poetry, the "ABC," that is far above the level of English religious verse written in his century. He has translated the *Roman de la Rose.* And he has written *The Book of the Duchess.* If he had done only this, we would know him as the author of *The Book of the Duchess*, and it would be reckoned a masterpiece among the Francophile court poems in English. One wonders if up to this time he has felt any impulse to disturb the bonds of courtly solemnity, or developed much of a sense of humor. Little of the muted humor in *The Book of the Duchess* promises the extravagant comedy of his later years, unless it might be the narrator's vow to Morpheus or the goddess Juno's bumbling, verbose instructions to her underling. He seems not yet to have discovered irreverence.

Nor does there appear, at first glance, much promise of the "novelistic" realism and psychological insight of later years; but the basis of it is present. In the descriptions of *The Book of the Duchess*, even phrases that are highly traditional and were already clichés, like "hair of gold," come in passages like lines 848–865 that successfully evoke the experience of seeing the lady for the first time, of recording first impressions. Then, too, the picture of the lady thus evoked is a *memory*: it is an inward experience of her possessed by another, the poet's imaginative projection of the Black Knight's interior world. Dialogue comes into these works—not much that harbingers the great dramatic scenes of the *Troilus*, yet in the exchanges between the Dreamer and the Black Knight the two *sound* like people talking, and their feelings come out in their words. Chaucer could have learned this from translating the *Roman*, for while the characters are allegorical personifications, they talk like living people, and this quality of living speech gets into the translation at times—though as much in the parts that are not thought Chaucer's as in the part that is: when the Lover approaches Fair-Welcome, in lines 3086–3116, you can really believe you hear a young man intent and breathless, pouring his heart into what he wants; and you can hear Fair-Welcome's cool and slightly pompous reply.

Above everything else, one major point in Chaucer's development stands forth in these early works: in the ending of *The Book of the Duchess* he has found that underplayed, discreet manner, that restraint, that seems the essence of his style.

Chaucer never turned his back on these early accomplishments. There is not a single later work that doesn't bear the imprint of French court poetry. Yet nothing he did in later years could have been done in France. None of his major works after *The Book of the Duchess* is really like Machaut and his followers even when it is borrowed from them, or anything like his English contemporaries. Geoffrey had to go through a transition to get from the one point to the other; and part of this transition was emotional. He is about to enter a period of storms. His work changed, everyone knows, after he fell under the influence of Italian poets; he made their kind of poetry more French than they would have wanted it, in a way that would have pleased the French but little. One can suppose that something in his makeup, and some of the emotional storms of this period, would have led him, anyway, where we know he went: in the direction of *fiction*. But as things happened, he went in these directions only after he returned from Italy in the spring of 1373.

Part Two

To Italy
(1372–1380)

6

Florence, 1373

The trip was ordered suddenly, in the dead of winter, when the days are shortest and the route across the Alps most treacherous. Chaucer was to leave on December 1, 1372, in the company of two Italians, Sir James de Provan and John de Mari, to give the anglicized names of official records, along with two Genoese crossbowmen for protection, three of the king's messengers, and probably a few more soldiers and servants. His two companions were eminent merchants both in King Edward's service. Giovanni del Mare, from Genoa, was the senior member of the party; he was empowered to contract for mercenaries. Jacopo Provano, a native of Carignano, who had been granted a life annuity by King Edward the year before, was the king's agent for purchasing ships from the Florentines, and he would go on with Chaucer as far as Florence. His son Saladin (the name of the sultan of Egypt who captured Jerusalem, a curious name for a merchant's son) went with the party.

Their mission was, first, to arrange with Genoa for the use of an English port; a treaty of free trade between England and Genoa had been signed the previous September after two or three years of negotiations. No records show these arrangements concluded, but they must have been,

since Genoa and England continued to carry on a flourishing trade.
Another part of their business in Genoa was to hire Genoese mercenaries;
Giovanni del Mare and others were to hire them in the king's name. From
Genoa Chaucer went on to Florence; his business, which was secret, had
to do with finances—in the previous August the king had contracted for
loans with the Florentine Bardi and other bankers. Negotiations recorded
at Florence were also afoot to provide England with eight or ten ships,
and Jacopo Provano, as Edward's agent, had been a party to the agreement.

War was in the air. In the following year, Edward III was to launch
another invasion of France, and this was now being planned. In the
previous June, the English fleet had been defeated by the Castilian navy;
then in August a fleet of four hundred ships had set out against France
only to be defeated by unfavorable winds. England's losses were enormous, so there was no hope of venturing against the enemy again without
replenishing the coffers, and this meant dealing with the Italian banks.
Edward had been doing just that since the very first years of his reign, and
benefited from it in more ways than from the money: it had given him
freedom to pursue his ambitions without imposing heavy and unpopular
taxes. Almost thirty years before, he had defaulted on loans amounting
to £230,000—worth a kingdom, the Florentine historian Villani said—
and this had been a major cause, though not the only one, for the
downfall, in 1345, of the great Florentine banks, the Bardi and the
Peruzzi. So Chaucer's first major assignment must have been a delicate
one; England's credit was not good, and the amounts needed were great.
He must have brought it off, however, because in the following year
England waged its war and Chaucer, back in London, received substantial
rewards.

Setting out on a mission devoted to commerce and finance, Geoffrey
Chaucer at age thirty could never have guessed the real importance of this
journey. He was to return from Italy, his mission accomplished, with the
inevitable flood of impressions about Italian culture and with three or four
books, or at least a knowledge of them, works of recent Italian literature
that he might never have heard of if he had not been to Italy. These books
—which he may not have possessed or borrowed until later—were to
change the whole direction of his poetry and, ultimately, the course of
English literature. We know exactly what they were and how they entered
into his work. It is not really ironic that we know nothing of the negotiations with the bankers.

Chaucer was chosen for this mission because he was young and
vigorous and could withstand the arduous winter travel, because he was
trained at court and raised in a mercantile environment, and because he

could speak Italian. There was a colony of Italians living along the London waterfront, including a community of Genoese with a quay of their own, with whom his father had had particular business associations. As a member of Prince Lionel's household, he must have been expected to refurbish what Italian he had on the assumption that Violante and her Italian train would come to England. Although in his translations and adaptations there are some errors (which could however have been in his originals), and although he sometimes used French versions of Italian works, it has been demonstrated beyond any question that he *read* Italian with great accuracy. How well he *spoke* Italian we cannot be certain. It was not a language the English spoke constantly, like French, nor one like French or Latin whose literature was part of their education, but one assumes that Chaucer spoke it well: in medieval diplomacy, eloquence and tone were important. In whatever language, the post was an excellent one for a poet.

Midwinter Journey

The mission got off to an unfortunate start. An advance payment of £50 had been made on November 23 to del Mare through one "James Jackaman," or "Jakemyn," probably Jacopo Jacomani, a Florentine merchant, and Jackaman failed to turn the money over. Word of his intentions reached the court at once—he was probably being watched—and before nightfall the sheriffs seized his property. He was bound to the king for a large sum, possibly payment for those Florentine ships, and it now appeared he was about to make off with the funds. Perhaps the explanation is that the king owed him money for some loan previously made, and he had chosen to pay himself with the money put in his keeping; it had happened before. A summons was issued for the money and del Mare given a second payment, this time directly. The following January, while the party was en route to Italy, "Jackaman" appeared before the Exchequer, admitted he had kept the money, and after a trial was imprisoned in the Fleet, where he seems to have disappeared from history.

The route was dictated by the military situation on the Continent. Because of the war with France, taken up again in 1369, Englishmen were being detained in French territory. So they took the Rhine route through Germany, called "the Dutch way": from Calais through Bruges, Ghent, Maastricht, Aachen, and Bonn or Cologne, up the Rhine past Mainz, Speyer, and Strasbourg to Basel, then southwest to Lausanne on Lake Léman. From here they had to choose a pass across the Alps that would keep them away from the wars then being waged in Milanese territory: either the Great St. Bernard pass (through Geneva and Chambéry) or the

Mount Cenis (through Martigny and Aosta) would lead them safely through Savoyard territory and deposit them near Turin.

Crossing the Alps was the worst part of the journey. In the Middle Ages, the Alpine passes were kept open in winter through extraordinary efforts: Savoyard guides piloted parties through them, and monks cleared paths, kept a lookout for those in distress, provided aid and shelter, and in the springtime gathered up the bodies of the unrescued. The hardships of medieval travel are almost unimaginable; the very word, from the French *travail*, meant "toil." What we do in two comfortable hours by plane took a laborious month for medieval travelers. Moving along at some thirty miles a day in good weather, and less otherwise, in a caravan of horses and mules, they had to worry about everything—the animals, the weather, the baggage, the road, whether they were getting lost, whether they would reach a hospice before nightfall, whether if they did not they would find a safe place to sleep. And there was the omnipresent danger of robbers: travelers had on their persons all the money they would need for a journey, with letters of credit good at their destination, so it was inevitable that highwaymen swarmed the major routes. Chaucer himself in later years was robbed while traveling. Travelers often had to dismount and lead the frightened horses. We read of horses' eyelids frozen in the cold, of horses falling by the wayside of exhaustion. Crossing through a mountain range in winter meant wearing goggles or a mask against the snow, being dragged while the wind howled about you over unnegotiable places on a bed of branches secured by ropes, called a *ramasse*, coaxing along the horses, keeping up your courage and your hope, or sometimes being pushed along in terror. Adam of Usk, crossing the Alps the year after Chaucer died, in early March, said he was "drawn in an ox-wagon half dead with cold and with mine eyes blindfolded lest I should see the dangers of the pass." Even in warm weather there was often rain; travelers must have been wet much of the time, dirty all the time. And tired— riding for hours is boring, strenuous, hard on the back; they slept out of exhaustion. Each morning when they set out they prayed to Saint Julian, patron saint of hospitality, for *bon hostel*, a place to stay the next night, knowing that if they did not find one they might die of exposure.

The way they *pictured* a journey to Italy was different, too, in the Middle Ages. When we travel from England to Italy, we see ourselves as moving "down" a map from north to south toward Africa, and "across" Europe from west to east toward Asia. But for medieval travelers there were no usable maps. You moved from one place to the next, inquiring the way and consulting an itinerary that gave directions, distances, advice about practical matters like overnight stops or changes of money. There were mariners' charts but no usable land maps; the earliest "road map" was made in England during Chaucer's lifetime—the so-called Gough map—and it was just a novelty, not meant to accompany a traveler. Maps were still the products of artistic ingenuity, intellection, and book learning, not of scientific observation, or measurement, or exploration. Chaucer evidently knew, because he once refers to it, a *mappa mundi* of the kind still to be seen at Hereford Cathedral, a huge depiction of the *orbis terrarum* with labeled countries and places; it depicts Scotland as an island separate from England, something no Briton would have taken as a fact —it was an abstract political idea. Such maps, derived from the earlier "T-O" maps, showed the earth as a circle with a T or cross inscribed in it. The top half of the circle is "Asia," the bottom left quarter "Europe" and the bottom right quarter "Africa." The vertical staff of the T represents the Mediterranean, and the two horizontal staffs the Dnieper (some say the Danube) and the Nile:

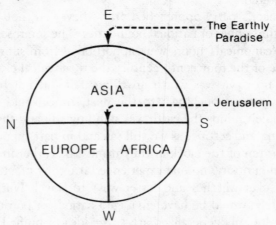

The diagram shows all the basic medieval facts about the world. The Garden of Eden or Earthly Paradise, far in the east, was at the *top* of the world, closest to heaven. The north, where in medieval folklore the Devil was said to dwell, is on the "sinister" side, the left side. There are three continents because the world reflected the Trinity, and its divisions formed a cross. Jerusalem, where Christ died, is the center of that cross: on some such maps a figure of Christ is represented behind the world, with arms outstretched, as if being crucified on its T. Monsters are often shown in the outlying seas.

So when Chaucer traveled from England to Italy, he would have supposed himself moving *up*: up toward Rome, toward Jerusalem at the center of the earth, and beyond that (for a few travelers, missionaries, and merchants) up the mainland of Asia toward the Earthly Paradise at the "end of the East," closest to heaven. He would have understood that he was moving across the "Island of the Earth" (*orbis terrarum*) that sat on the globe surrounded by ocean. Aristotle held that at the equator was an uninhabitable and impassable torrid zone. On the underside of the earth were the controversial "antipodes," an opposite hemisphere that some believed was inhabited and some believed did not exist—the *utopia* ("nowhere") of later literature. The Bible said all mankind descended from Adam; if there was an uninhabitable and impassable zone at the equator, as Aristotle said, how could Adam's descendants have crossed it? And there were to the north and south frigid zones, also uninhabitable. To man was left an intermediate "temperate" zone. These received ideas were based on ancient authorities often in conflict with one another. In the next century, the discovery of America was largely an intellectual feat— an "invention," one scholar calls it—in which such ideas were reexamined and slowly altered.*

As Chaucer's party approached Italy they were not aware, as we would be, of time zones or national boundaries. The sun rose and set daily, and the old "canonical" hours were apportioned from sunrise to sunset. By the middle of the fourteenth century the mechanical clock had swept Europe, and no town was worth anything if it did not have one; but traveling slowly from one town to the next, time would have seemed stable. In people's minds the earth was standing still and the sun moving about it—rising and setting, as we still say and in part suppose. The idea that when it is ten of the clock in Italy it must be earlier in England was an intellectual curiosity; no one experienced it in any practical way until there were pocket watches and faster ways to travel. Nor, as Chaucer approached Italy, would he have envisaged nations or borders. "France" and "Italy" were only generalized areas; the idea of unified nations with boundaries was not yet a habit of mind. As he descended from the Alps, Chaucer would not have thought "I am entering Italy" but "I am passing from Savoyard into Genoese territory." He would have thought of their *language* as Italian, however, and he understood that Italian was, as he later expressed it, "a manner Latin corrupt."

Some say the medievals took no pleasure in landscapes or nature, but

*Medieval men knew, of course, that the earth was round. Sir John Mandeville, writing while Chaucer was still a child, claimed to prove it could be circumnavigated. Their estimate of the earth's circumference, derived from the ancients, was accurate. Columbus, working out a circumference by a method of his own devising, mistakenly thought the earth smaller and so believed the westward route a feasible way to reach the "end of the East." When he arrived in the Caribbean he took it for the Orient, even believed he was nearing the Earthly Paradise, which he theorized was a protuberance on the top of the earth shaped like a woman's breast. It was Vespucci who deduced that there must be a fourth continent, which, shockingly, meant the earth could not be in the image of the Trinity.

this can't be true. Pope Innocent III in his treatise *On the Misery of the Human Condition* chastises people who climb mountains to look at the terrain as guilty of sinful curiosity.* If medieval travelers ignored the scenery it was because in their "travail" they hadn't the time or inclination to gaze at it. At about Christmastime, Chaucer's party crossed the Alps; later they would have recalled vivid moments when they stopped and looked about at the snowy peaks, sheer cliffs and steep drops, a river or lake visible far below, here and there a house or town or church tower; or moments of warmth and shelter and cheer. The simple pleasure of getting in out of the cold, of hot food however plain, of a little wine however ordinary, would have been moments of exquisite delight, memorable by contrast. The contrast is depicted in *Sir Gawain and the Green Knight*: the hero, riding through the forest alone on Christmas Eve, having slept outdoors in his armor, prays with amusing modesty for shelter and a place to hear mass on Christmas Day and at once comes upon a glorious castle of the very latest fourteenth-century design (though he is living in the days of King Arthur!), where he is clothed in luxurious warm garments and showered with plentiful food and drink—a medieval traveler's fantasy.

So, as he arrived in the north of Italy at about New Year's, Chaucer must have felt a kind of joy he had scarcely known before. The travail at a certain point was behind him. Descending slowly through the foothills of Savoy, the party at last came down into temperate lowlands where there was no snow, where the days would have seemed longer than in England —and were getting longer since the winter solstice, which fell on December 11 by the old Julian calendar. It can be unexpectedly warm on a sunny day in January in the north of Italy, especially at midday, and to an Englishman just down from the icy mountains, bundled in his furs and English woolens, it would have seemed like spring.

Coming then into this wintertime oasis, having seen from the mountaintops the valleys and houses and towns below as a soaring bird might see them, Chaucer found that here, near Turin, trees and shrubbery to a surprising extent remain green in winter. There were not just evergreens with needles but trees and shrubs like the holly familiar to Englishmen, strange and lovely nondeciduous plants along the wayside that he could stoop to touch and admire, and ask their names of his Genoese companions, plants having lush red berries and crisp pointed leaves, and here and there even winter flowers of bright yellow and winter roses of white. He

*St. Bernard is said to have ridden along the shores of Lake Léman with his eyes closed to shut out the glories of the world. But this was said *about* him (he was probably in pain, and able to induce a trancelike state). The conclusion his companions reached about his motives shows how aware they were of the scenic glories.

would have looked back at the forbidding snow-capped promontories his party had just negotiated: they seemed distant and inscrutable, a world of ice suspended in the sky. Of the geology behind such a landscape, medieval man knew nothing; it was because of "untamed" nature, the decay of the world attendant on the Fall of Man, that man's place on the Island of the Earth was so far less hospitable than the Garden of Eden had been, and this hostile world could be tamed and inhabited only by human ingenuity, by the arts of civilization.

Genoa

As the party proceeded from Turin to Genoa, they had to avoid the wars going on in Milanese territory. In January, a papal army under Enguerrand de Coucy in alliance with Count Amadeus of Savoy—the "Green Count"—joined, near Parma, with the English mercenary Sir John Hawkwood and his terrifying private army. (Hawkwood had his soldiers polish their armor to a forbidding mirrorlike gloss, which dazzled and frightened opponents and in a bright sun impaired their vision.) These military forces were just now moving toward Milan. The complex war, to be won that spring in what seemed a miracle by the outnumbered papal forces under Coucy, was waged against the Milanese tyrants, the Visconti, allied with the marquis of Saluzzo and two large companies of mercenaries who after the manner of mercenaries had just changed sides; Hawkwood had changed sides too in the other direction. For Chaucer these were all familiar figures: he had seen and probably met Coucy in France, or in England while he was hostage for King Jean, and he had seen the Visconti and Count Amadeus of Savoy at Lionel's wedding.

The unfavorable time of year, the dangers of crossing the Alps in winter, the necessity of avoiding the warring forces—everything that seemed to put a cold hand upon their mission—helped to prepare Chaucer psychologically for the time he spent in Genoa and Florence. It was his first extended encounter with a foreign culture; France wasn't really foreign to a fourteenth-century Englishman, nor was nearby Flanders, and his stay in Spain, exotic then as now, had been brief. His short visit to Milan five years before may have given him that special receptivity to a foreign land that one attains from an earlier visit cut short. And he was just at that age—thirty—that lies beyond youthful dependency. To be out of danger, to be in warmer weather and more attractive surroundings, to have the sense of accomplishment that travel afforded in the Middle Ages, to look forward to seeing more of Italy—all this meant that he arrived in Genoa with a particular exhilaration, of a kind known to modern travelers only after a long hike or an automobile trip fraught with inconveniences, and otherwise only in the negligible exhilaration that is a component of "jet lag."

Genoa, when Chaucer saw it, was one of the great cities of Europe. The major Italian cities—Genoa, Florence, Milan, and Venice—were the most powerful economically. Paris was much larger than any of them but less significant in trade and politics; probably the great Flemish seaports like Ghent and Bruges were their closest rivals. Genoa was about the same size as London, just under 40,000 inhabitants; Florence was bigger, closer to 50,000. These centers of maritime trade had an organic interrelationship, the one supplying what the other needed. Wool, for example, was the chief English product and export, and its greatest imports from Genoa were alum (Genoa had a virtual monopoly on it, because it possessed the great mines at Foglia in Asia Minor), and other essential ingredients of dyes.

While Chaucer would have been struck by Genoa's importance in trade, this wouldn't have made him feel that London was inferior. After all, London was the center of a nation: the king and Parliament were there, industry and trade were centered there. Italy had no comparable city, had no king, no parliament; each Italian city was a state unto itself, had its own government, laws, foreign policy, taxes, and coinage, and these city-states were forever at war with one another—two wars were going on right now. The Visconti of Milan, in Chaucer's phrase the "scourge of Lombardy," controlled some dozen cities. Genoa was a small empire with colonies stretching as far away as the Crimea and North Africa, and in control of Corsica; the year Chaucer was there it occupied Famagusta. Six years later it was at war with Venice, its ancient enemy, and went down to a humiliating defeat; in the treaty of peace, 1382, Venice gained control, and Chaucer must have remembered Genoa in later years as another example of worldly glory vanishing away.

In the Italian mercantile cities government had passed, most notably in Florence, from the old feudal aristocracy into the hands of the merchant class, and the leadership was elective. In Genoa, the first doge—a merchant, Simone Boccanegra—was elected just a few years before Chaucer was born. He was elected again in 1356, by which time the nobles and the Milanese too had been driven out; in 1363 he was poisoned while entertaining the king of Cyprus, Pierre de Lusignan, one of the three kings entertained that same year by John of Gaunt at the Savoy. During the time of Chaucer's mission to Genoa, the doge—with whom Chaucer must have dealt direct—was Domenico Fregoso; he had only recently deposed his predecessor, Gabriele Adorno, known to us as the hero of Verdi's opera *Simon Boccanegra*.

As a native of a merchant city, Chaucer was fascinated by this early kind of democracy, with its "mercantile ethic" and new ideals of good government, and from his work we can see he went on thinking about it for many years. But as an official of the king's court he must have thought a good deal, too, about the advantages of a strong centralized monarchy, and his sympathies lay in that direction. What England had that Continental nations didn't was an alliance between the burghers and the nobles, sanctioned by the Crown. The English "gentry" was really the product of this alliance. The royal government needed the support of the burghers for taxation and military service, and often for support in the Commons against powerful baronial forces in the House of Lords. Prominent burghers intermingled with the lesser nobility and often intermarried with the younger sons or the daughters of peers. The English nobles, through this "gentry," had an essential sympathy with commercial life. In Italy, a similar process was occurring: the nobles and the burghers—the "patricians" and "plebeians" of nineteenth-century opera—were undergoing a reciprocal adjustment.

Genoa was not a cultural center as Florence was; it had only a negligible tradition of lyric poetry and song, though its architecture was distinguished. It was a great supplier of mercenary troops, its soldiers being expert at the crossbow. But its accomplishments were mostly commercial: it was the originator of maritime insurance and (though it's disputed) of double-entry bookkeeping. The Genoese were a practical, rather stolid people, and to the English or French, or the Florentines, they must have seemed dull. But the English thought them more serious, or less frivolous, than the Florentines or Venetians, probably because they exported useful products, not luxuries. The city was, as it still is, wedded to the sea. A traveler can to this day get a sense of what medieval Genoa was like by wandering about the old port and the old section of the city with its tiny narrow streets, like Venice without canals. There even remains standing a section of the old city wall, one of the gates of the city, as it actually was, the Porta dell'Olivella; in the third generation after Chaucer's brief stay there was born to the warder of this gate a redheaded son, Christopher Columbus.

Chaucer never mentions Genoa or anything specifically associated with it, but then he never mentions Florence either, though it clearly made an impression on him, and rarely mentions contemporary Italy. Since he had been to the north of Italy before at the time of Prince Lionel's wedding, he was prepared for the way Italy looked. The Italians used stone and brick for their buildings, whereas London was largely made of wooden structures, only churches and public buildings and palaces being of stone. An Italian city of the fourteenth century must have seemed to a Londoner monumental, substantial, grand. Little of the London that Chaucer knew is still standing, so much of it having been wiped out by fires, but in Italian cities we can still see and touch and traverse a good deal of what was there in Chaucer's time. In Genoa the cathedral church of San Lorenzo remains (if you close your eyes to the baroque additions) the imposing Gothic structure he gazed at, with its alternating horizontal stripes of light and dark marble, so characteristic of northern Italy, which even today seem breathtaking and extravagant to a northern or transatlantic visitor. We have no idea where the negotiations for the use of an English port by the Genoese were carried out— probably in the doge's palace.

It's useless to guess what Chaucer as a *poet* saw and remembered of Genoa. As an ambassador he saw the public buildings in their official grandeur and as a tourist, if he had the time, he saw the churches, the palazzi, the port, and—for him most important, one imagines—the people. Perhaps here or in Florence he saw particular folk arts, like Italian street drama, theatrical farces that would be the remote ancestors of Punch and Judy shows, raucous popular entertainments different from those of England or France, and perhaps these were salted away in his memory to emerge as an influence on his more raucous tales. But there is little in his writings that furnishes a clue to his immediate experience of Italy. A poetical genius in a foreign land might ignore the standard sights the rest of us would gawk at and be taken up by peculiar small details. Of course he would have admired the great rose window in the cathedral of San Lorenzo with its twenty-odd radiating petals and its large aperture in the middle, more like a daisy than a rose. But he had seen rose windows all over England and France, and might for all we know have studied with greater fascination the little church of San Donato, a romanesque structure of brick and stone built in the tenth century and rebuilt in a Gothic style in the twelfth century. It has on its façade a circular window surrounded by alternating stripes of light and dark marble into which is set what looks to be a metal wheel, an eight-spoked wheel with a hole in the middle, as an actual wheel has a hole for an axle. Not a rose window, but a more homely curiosity: a wheel window, or, depending on how you looked at it, a window wheel.

Florence

In March, Giovanni del Mare was back in Bruges hiring mercenaries, so Genoese affairs must have been settled some weeks before. The party probably arrived in Genoa during the second week of January, and the relatively uncomplicated business couldn't have taken long. The business in Florence being more important and complex, they pressed on as soon as possible and could have been there by February. The normal route—it took a week or less—was along the shore road, then east to Florence from Viareggio or Pisa. One would like to have had them see Pisa, with its grand Gothic churches and sculptures, and its magnificent baptistry. The famous tower, about twenty years old, was already leaning. On the south wall of the Camposanto was the startling fresco *The Triumph of Death*, painted—we now know—before the Black Death, showing (in one scene) a company of youthful aristocrats not unlike Boccaccio's, three young knights confronting their own corpses, Death as a dark-winged female with a scythe. In its way it is an encyclopedic representation of Death in the universal order, complete with angels and devils, the Last Judgment, and the Inferno, and owes some of its conception to the Old Humanism. It strangely captures the feeling of postplague Europe, and if Chaucer had seen it he would have been startled—nothing like it was to be seen in England. But he might as easily have gone inland to Florence from Viareggio.

Chaucer was accompanied to Florence by Jacopo Provano, who had been negotiating with Florence in the purchase of ships. But the bankers were the big worry and probably chiefly Chaucer's responsibility. As he rode, he may have been rehearsing or memorizing his speeches or planning his arguments, "recording" them, in the Middle English phrase, like Troilus before his first meeting with Criseyde, thinking "*Ma fay,* . . . thus will I say, and thus."

London and Florence had in common the wool trade: the manufacture of woolen cloth was the major industry here. Chaucer's business was with members of the guild second in prestige after the wool guild, the bankers. The Florentine bankers were not just moneylenders but major financiers and entrepreneurs—an Italian, and originally Florentine, phenomenon. The church of course forbade usury, and from its basic position it never budged. But in the previous century, in the days of the Old Humanism—the early days of a money economy—there came into the service of Christian businessmen in Italy that delicate weapon of social change, the Subtle Distinction. It was agreed, with reason, that there was a just price to be charged for services and an allowable profit to be made on transactions, and that this was to be distinguished from what could properly be called the sin of usury, *excessive* interest. It came about that *modest* interest rates—of up to about 20 percent—were reckoned within the realm of licit enterprise, and anyway interest could be disguised by making the principal loaned less than the face value, or by calling it a penalty for late payment or a fee for risk. This revised definition of a sin opened a major and profitable industry for Christians (moneylending had hitherto been a monopoly of non-Christians). Florentine merchants began the banking enterprise by lending money to bishops and nobles and taking their land as security; by the mid-fourteenth century the Tuscan countryside around Florence had thus passed, through manifold defaults, into the hands of the merchant bankers, who became the new aristocracy. Aristocrats in turn took up business to survive.

Money itself—the hard, chinking coins that were the objects of avarice then, before wealth came in a credit economy to have a spectral quality—was a Florentine *specialità*. Medieval money in all European nations was based on the value of a pound of silver. The basic coin was the silver penny (*denarius* in Latin, whence *denaro* in Italian and *denier* in French, whose "d." remained until 1970 the abbreviation for the English pence). Twelve pennies were worth a *soldo* (French *sou*, the English shilling), and twenty *soldi* were worth a *libra*, a pound. The *soldo* and *libra* were theoretical units of value, not coins; but the Florentines had the remarkable notion, in the eleventh century, of minting silver *soldi*, and in 1252 they took the even more astonishing step of issuing a gold coin, the *fiorino*, or "florin," so-called because it bore on one side their coat of arms, the lily (on the other side, their patron saint, John the Baptist). In the next century some fifty cities had minted coins imitating it, some of them barefaced counterfeits: by Chaucer's time minted coins had various names and values, had reputations and prestige—"the Katherines of the one lordship," travelers were warned, "will not go in the next lordship." Florence was a great financial center in part because its coins of silver and gold set a European standard.

The Bardi were the principal firm Chaucer was sent to deal with, and while they remembered Edward III's default and their subsequent bankruptcy, and must have been leery of English loans, it had all happened almost thirty years ago, before the Black Death. The bankruptcy had been elaborately settled by a committee of "syndics" appointed by the Commune of Florence, and the Bardi were in business again. England in the meantime had been making gestures of repayment. There was much else to complicate the discussions. The Florentines depended on England for the raw wool needed in their major industry, clothmaking, and there was an elaborate history of trade relations between the two nations. Bardi merchants got special treatment from Edward III and enjoyed a privileged position in England—some advantages lay on their side. And, however great a risk English kings had been, the Florentine bankers were in the habit of thinking in huge sums, loans and trade had gone on since the famous bankruptcy, and the amount of the default, which had seemed "worth a kingdom" twenty-eight years before, seemed less now—it was, for example, less than half the ransom asked for King Jean, never paid in full, and nearly a fourth of what England had lost in its disastrous venture against France the year before.

Chaucer was in Florence at what we now know was a major turning point in European history. That whole frame of mind that we call humanism (the term was used but rarely then, though they spoke of *studia humaniora*) was beginning to take shape here before it took shape elsewhere, and Chaucer must have been aware that some sort of intellectual and cultural ferment was going on, though he would have stumbled at describing it. To us, humanism was essentially a step in the direction of secular values; to them, at first, it was a fad in reading. It was the study of humane, as opposed to divine, letters, and this meant ancient books by pagan authors, books of philosophy as opposed to theology, or books touching upon the arts of civilization. The interest in books from pre-Christian antiquity was not of itself new. It had been a component of the Old Humanism, as we have seen, and in its new renascent literary form it went back a generation or so to the earliest glimmerings of the New Humanism; Chaucer's teacher, William Ravenstone, was an early enthusiast of it, what we would now call a "prehumanist."

But in Florence they had made a further step. Some works by ancient writers, as had always been known, were lost, and Petrarch had been conducting a deliberate search for these—and finding some in obscure libraries, often in monasteries. In their reverence for such texts they desired to preserve them with the greatest accuracy, and to that end they were developing a script, "humanistic" script, in which each letter was carefully rounded so that it could not be mistaken for another—a striking improvement over the crabbed Gothic hands of the time, the first tendency toward uniformity in reproduction, which was to provide an impetus for the printing press. And in the same spirit, their reverence for the ancient texts led Petrarch and Coluccio Salutati to write Latin not in what they saw as the barbaric patois of medieval schoolmen but in imitation of ancient, classical Latin, the prose of Cicero or the verse and metrics of Virgil or Ovid.

This fascination with ancient writings led the Italian humanists of the fourteenth century to another interest: Greek. To Chaucer, reading Plato or Homer in the original tongue would have seemed a most arcane accomplishment; what little of Plato was known in his time was in Latin, and Aristotle was read in Latin translated from Arabic translations. In later years, mentioning Plato in *The Canterbury Tales* with the customary reverence, he added, with eyes askance, as one might say, "whoso can him read"—meaning that while everyone cited Plato as an authority, most of his works weren't readable in western Europe. In Florence, he saw the first shimmer of an impulse to change that. Both Petrarch and Boccaccio studied Greek, and Petrarch learned to read Homer haltingly. His teacher, the Basilian monk Barlaam, was very learned in the ancients. Boccaccio had a much less effective teacher, Leontius, a pupil of Barlaam—ugly, ill-kempt, slovenly, as Boccaccio described him, though Boccaccio arranged for him to teach Greek at the university in Florence in the early 1360s, and won out over the merchant community, who wanted modern colloquial Greek, tradesmen's Greek, to be taught. But scruffy Leontius was not much of a success; Boccaccio never learned any Greek to speak of, though Leontius did produce a translation of both of Homer's epics, and of some Aristophanes and Aristotle, with a commentary. By the time Chaucer visited Florence, Leontius was gone and Greek was not to be taught there again until 1396.

Humanism, as we see it, was a movement—a revolution in attitudes and values, in education, in literature, and in art. But Chaucer wouldn't have seen it this way; he would have seen each tendency as something separate, though he might have pondered a connection among them. The classical scholarship and philology, the study of Greek, the searching for ancient texts, the imitation of classical Latin—that was only one side of it. On the other side, Boccaccio had written lyric poetry and romances and even prose works in his own vernacular tongue, the Tuscan dialect of Italian, as Chaucer was writing in the London dialect of English; these works, the *opere minori in volgare*, were of a very secular character, some of them about heroes of ancient Troy or Greece or Rome. Petrarch, though he had written his famous sonnets and other poems in Italian, was scornful of the vernacular; while Boccaccio adored Dante, Petrarch was, to his discredit, indifferent to the great Tuscan poet.

Literature aside, Chaucer saw much building in progress. There was, too, a new and different kind of painting and sculpture, puzzling compared to what he had seen in other countries. And there was another tendency, what we call "civic" humanism, having to do with the government of a city-state dominated by the merchant community—a *theory* and an *ideal* of government that came about later but whose foundations, partly visible now, would have held immense interest for a Londoner. But while *we* see the integrity of this Florentine spirit, and see in it the dawning of the modern world, Chaucer would have seen nothing of the sort. To him Florence was a foreign city in a foreign world, its new fads and interests puzzlingly different from its former ones; and much that he observed was only just getting under way. As with any traveler, the experience led him to compare the way things were at home and speculate about the future, and some of his speculations were skeptical.

Italy, despite all its newfangledness, might have seemed to an Englishman rather dowdy and conservative, even backward. It had no royal court, no national unity, no gentry; its nobility had no political power; court life of the kind Chaucer knew must have seemed not to exist here. Food was predictably different (pasta was eaten, supposedly introduced from the Orient by Marco Polo but probably much older), and upper-class Italians ate with a strange new instrument, the fork. Some women dressed in a restrained, old-fashioned style in collarless draped garments held by loose, low cinctures, with long sleeves, wore headbands rather than the elaborate headdresses of the French and English, wore little jewelry. The lewd extremes of dress that the English had adopted, outdoing the French, were less prevalent in Italy. As in England, sumptuary laws opposed fancy adornment. The men dressed like merchants and artisans, for that is what they were; they did not vie with the nobility in fashion because the nobles weren't in power. Italian men were not to become fops for another century. The nobility were not entirely out of the picture—they still took precedence on ceremonial occasions, if only because they had flashier costumes. Yet the Italian burghers had adopted many of the ideals of chivalry and gentilesse—as, in a different way, had the humanists.

What Chaucer saw was a pre-Renaissance Florence hard for us to imagine. Petrarch and Boccaccio were old men now—both would be dead within two years—and the leading humanist of the next generation, Coluccio Salutati, ten years Chaucer's senior, was already writing his learned and influential treatises and was employed as a notary. He did not become chancellor of Florence until 1375 and didn't write his most famous work, *De Seculo et Religione*, until 1381, and it doesn't appear that Chaucer came into any memorable kind of contact with him. Leonardo Bruni of "Aretino"—i.e. of Arezzo—was only three years old.

As in Genoa, many of the buildings Chaucer gazed at are still standing, but he saw them without the Renaissance or baroque additions that characterize them today. He saw the work of the earliest Renaissance artists in Florence—Giotto, Cimabue, Andrea Pisano, Daddi. He saw the particolored cathedral, Santa Maria del Fiore, begun some hundred years before and just five years from completion, but it lacked the noble dome built by Brunelleschi, who wasn't born till four years later. He saw the Badia, the ancient monastery with its hexagonal campanile built in 1330; the Church of Santa Margherita, where Dante's Beatrice worshipped; the Badia di Santo Stefano, where Boccaccio was to lecture on Dante that same year (but he wasn't invited to do so until after Chaucer had left for England, though Chaucer could have heard about the plans to invite him). He saw the old Dominican church, Santa Maria Novella, where Boccaccio's seven young ladies and three young gentlemen formed their *brigata* in the *Decameron*, an elaborately Gothic structure built in the previous century; when it acquired a Renaissance façade by Alberti in the fifteenth century, and was remodeled by Vasari in the sixteenth century, its medieval character was obliterated. He saw Or San Michele, by his time abandoned as a grain mart, rebuilt, and dedicated as a church. He strolled across the Ponte Vecchio, which had been rebuilt in stone by Neri di Fioravante in the 1340s; it was about sixty feet wide, had forty-three shops, must have looked to Chaucer somewhat like London Bridge.

The medieval Florence he saw was in a perpetual state of change. It had originally 275 tall structures—some of them steeples and campaniles, most of them towers. The towers had been built by noble families as places of refuge during the frequent riots of the previous century, and as such they were symbols of power, wealth, and status; they had at one time risen as high as 230 feet. Late in the thirteenth century, when Florence had become a merchant city, they were required by law to be cut down to less than a hundred feet. By this time those not razed had been intricately combined with other or newer structures. All this convoluted medieval accretion was to be swept away or covered over by the builders of the Renaissance. To envisage the Florence of 1373 we must imagine it without so much as a hint of the baroque and with only a glimmer of the new spirit in painting, sculpture, or architecture: a simple walled city, a city of stone, its skyline punctuated with the leavings of numerous abandoned towers. The closest you can come today to the Florence Chaucer saw is probably San Gimignano, a fourteenth-century town with a medieval wall and gates, and with tall (and sometimes leaning) "towers of nobility" such as those once erect in Florence. Like any medieval city it was, and seems to remain, permanently on the ready against battle, siege, or civic disturbance—unadorned, majestic, stark.

Chaucer had grown up in a city governed by merchant and craft guilds and he himself was now an official of a national government. The way Florence was governed, then, surely interested him—and he had been briefed about it already. He had come to the Florentine republic during a period that historians call a "democratic interlude," a period of representative government during which as one historian declares, "shopkeepers and artisans actually sat in the seats of power." The twenty-odd Florentine guilds, like the London guilds, were stratified into major and minor companies of greater or lesser importance. Each guild had a college of consuls who held office for six months and were expected to seek the advice and consent of a city council. The city priors and other officials were chosen from these guilds, but the head of the Florentine chancellery held a permanent post. What made the system work was an oligarchy of the upper guilds with their greater power, money, prestige, experience, and, it could be supposed, wisdom. But in 1373 this oligarchy was not in control. Five years before, about the time Chaucer had been returning to Milan with messages for Prince Lionel after his wedding, there had been in Florence an uprising of workers, the dyers, followed by "something so novel and ominous that it may be set up as a landmark": a strike—the beginning, one may observe, of a flourishing Italian tradition. Five years after, there was to be, in the summer of 1378, the famous uprising of the *ciompi*, the ordinary workers—often compared with the uprising of the Jacquerie in northern France (1358) or the Peasants' Revolt in England (1381), but in Florence it was an uprising not of peasants but of what we would call urban blue collar workers. This was government by mob rule, a government of the incompetent, as it seemed to some: Boccaccio never missed an opportunity to speak of such government with contempt. For him, as for other humanists, special qualities of mind were to be expected in those who occupied the seats of power: intellect and reason, yes, but also qualities that had been the hallmark of medieval chivalry.

The merchant bankers with whom Chaucer had his business, raising enormous sums for an English war, were men of substance and prestige, of an old and powerful Florentine guild. These were cultivated people, and it may be assumed that they showed the young emissary from the English king a handsome degree of hospitality. He would have been lodged and entertained lavishly. He would have been shown, with ostentation, their acquisitions—plate, jewels, paintings, books. And he would have heard their conversation, an art and a diversion in medieval Italy. In the evenings after dinner, along with such entertainments as song or dance or reading aloud, there was talk—about books, sometimes about a book or poem that had just been read from aloud, and about writers, and tales.

Florentine Literary Culture

Chaucer's knowledge of Italian literary culture probably began in talk of this kind. Before he found any books he didn't already know, he found a new kind of readership—not courtly but "bourgeois"—that took an active interest in vernacular poetry, admired Dante's poems and idolized Petrarch as a man of letters. The Florentines had—what Londoners did not—a university, where the writings of the ancients were being taught, where Greek had been taught (if briefly and badly), where later that year Boccaccio, chief Florentine man of letters, would discourse on the *Divine Comedy*. This Florentine literary enthusiasm was different from the more scholarly literary culture of which Petrarch was laureate, which put Latin over the vernacular and the ancients over the moderns. In London you might find similar groups of men from the guilds and professions interested in vernacular literature, but in Florence the interest was more active and widespread, and the works being written were of a different kind.

Chaucer knew some Italian literature before he came to Italy. There was a stream of educated Italians coming to London, some of whom would hold high positions in the English court. Walter de Bardi, King's Monnaier under Edward III and Richard II, came from the Florentine banking family—he was supposedly related to Dante's Beatrice Portinari. Such people knew the *Divine Comedy*; there were surely copies in England. And a stream of Englishmen went constantly to Italy on business or pilgrimage; Prince Lionel had even married a Visconti. There is every reason why Chaucer could have read Dante before he ever set foot on Italian soil, and other Italian works as well. True, Dante's influence does not show up in Chaucer's work until after the voyage of 1373, and Boccaccio's and Petrarch's influence later still. But this assumes that the influence of one writer on another is instantaneous, that writers don't ponder, absorb, reread, mull things over, change their minds. The influence of Italian literature on Chaucer's writings came not immediately upon his reading the books, but slowly, after being there in Florence in 1373, returning to Milan in 1378, and in the interim reading and rereading them, revising and rewriting his poems. And he left a record of this period of confusion in that confusing poem *The House of Fame*.

It is often assumed, too, that the Italian influence on Chaucer began with his *buying* books—a notion, no doubt, of academicians with happy memories of bookstalls abroad. But buying books in the fourteenth century would have been more like buying paintings or jewelry today, and it's hard to imagine that Chaucer, furnished with the standard travel allowance for one of his station, would have had the funds to purchase many books. He might have arranged subsequent purchases and deliveries through an intermediary, but in those days none but the very rich bought as many books as they read. One borrowed or rented a book, or read it in somebody's library, or made a copy, or copied or memorized a significant part.

However it came about, the three great Italian poets of the fourteenth century did in the long run influence Chaucer's work, each in a different way.

Dante had been dead more than fifty years when Chaucer came to Florence and was already the revered master. He was as distant a figure, and as established, as Henry James is to us. Petrarch and Boccaccio, old men now, had been infants when Dante was in his last years, living in exile; and already then, Dante was an object of veneration and awe—"the man who had seen hell," they called him, whispering that his cloak bore stains of smoke and flame.

Petrarch and Boccaccio were Chaucer's elder contemporaries. Of Petrarch's works Chaucer knew, as far as we can tell, scarcely any. He acknowledges in so many words, and with lavish praise, that the Clerk's Tale is Petrarch's; he does not say that Petrarch's version was a translation into Latin of Boccaccio's Italian original, the last story of the *Decameron.* He follows Petrarch closely save for a few alterations made perhaps to suit the Clerk, and the lavish praise comes after all from the Clerk, not necessarily from Chaucer. Petrarch's Latin translation of the story was circulating in Italy by the time Chaucer returned there, in 1378, so he could have seen it then and made or purchased a copy. There is, too, in the first book of *Troilus and Criseyde,* a translation of Petrarch's sonnet "S'amor non è," presented as "Troilus's first song." This is the only hard evidence that Chaucer knew Petrarch's writings, but he must have read more than the one story and one sonnet: as we shall see, he might have known the *Trionfi,* the *Africa,* and the *Secretum.* Petrarch was already a legendary figure throughout Europe. He had been crowned laureate poet a year or two before Chaucer was born, when he was thirty-six, after an examination by Robert, king of Naples, in a manner Petrarch imagined was based on ancient precedents; during the examination among other things he discoursed upon the art and end of poetry and on the properties of the laurel. At the invitation of the Roman senate he was thereafter crowned with laurel in the hall of the Senatorial Palace on the Capitoline —he chose this invitation over a similar one from the chancellor of the University of Paris—wearing the robe of honor given him by King Robert. After a blare of trumpets, Petrarch gave his oration, in the form of a medieval sermon but on a text from Virgil, with quotations not from the Bible but from the ancients. His theme was the difficulty of the poet's work, the hidden or allegorical significance of poetry, and the poet's rewards. As he was crowned with laurel, he was declared "poet," "master," indeed "professor," of poetry and history, with appropriate professorial rights and privileges, and he was given blanket approval of his writings, the right to crown other laureates, and Roman citizenship. It was from one point of view the most colossal feat of self-promotion in literary history, and it made Petrarch "the most famous private citizen then living." From another point of view, the examination before a royal patron, the oration, the crowning in the Roman senate, all of it was part of a program to raise the status of the poet, to magnify the significance, the *power* of poetry, and to revive the values of the ancient world.

Chaucer knew Petrarch's reputation as "Laureate Poet," who had "enlumined" Italy with his poetry, and this fame could not have failed to impress Geoffrey Chaucer at the age of thirty. In Milan, at Prince Lionel's wedding, he had seen the man himself, if only from afar; had heard had felt the whispered awe. Of Petrarch's scholarship, his greatest contribution to Western culture, Chaucer appears to have known almost nothing.

So in *The Canterbury Tales* he has the Clerk of Oxford—though he represents him as a learned, dedicated university student—speak glowingly of Petrarch as a *poet* rather than a scholar. We can't assume Chaucer didn't know that the Clerk's tale, which he says the clerk learned from Petrarch, was originally by Boccaccio: Boccaccio's version ends with Dioneo's cynical commentary, whereas Petrarch's moralized version is very clerkish. But while Chaucer used Petrarch's moralization, he then added the Clerk's song, cynical enough itself and possibly inspired by Boccaccio's ending. The Clerk has, like Chaucer himself, come into contact with Italian humanism in its early days—he's been to Padua and has learned the story from the great man himself, whom he names and eulogizes. This is a detail in the presentation of him, like the Wife of Bath's husbands or the Knight's crusades or the Prioress's gold brooch— something out of his past that makes him who he is. And who is he? He is a young member of the international world of the medieval universities, which went back to the days of the Old Humanism. He has come into contact with what Chaucer recognized as the very beginnings of a revolution in higher education, and he is fired with enthusiasm for it. In the same breath with which he praises Petrarch's poetry and "sweet rhetoric" he praises Giovanni di Legnano for philosophy and law and "other art particular." Had the Clerk been to Florence instead and been fired with enthusiasm for the complex figure of Boccaccio, great scholar and author of the *Decameron,* the Clerk would seem a very different kind of fellow. Nevertheless, his enthusiasm is, like Chaucer's, for Petrarch's poetry, not his "humanism."

While Petrarch the man, the living legend, struck a responsive chord in Chaucer, Boccaccio the man seems to have interested him not at all. He never once so much as mentions his name. This is a great puzzle, because in the sheer number of works—number of *lines*—involved, Boccaccio's influence on Chaucer was greater than any other. Chaucer does sometimes name and praise writers who were his contemporaries, and Boccaccio's name in the late fourteenth century, though occasionally confused with others' names, was widely known. What's more, Chaucer *emulated* Boccaccio in a way he did not ever emulate Dante or Petrarch: he made direct adaptations of two of Boccaccio's Italian poems and followed him throughout the rest of his career in the *kinds* of works he wrote. Yet in each instance he altered what he found, tried to improve upon it. To understand that influence, we will need in due course to see as best we can what Boccaccio was doing in both his poetry and his prose, though he is an enigma of literary history. And we will need to see how Chaucer *understood* what Boccaccio was doing, even if Chaucer was wrong.

Whether Chaucer met Petrarch or Boccaccio in 1373, in the last years of their lives, has been debated endlessly. Chaucer was in Florence from about February until late in April; Petrarch was in Padua, 120 miles away. Chaucer could have made the four-day journey to see him, and returned to Florence or gone home by way of Padua rather than through Genoa as he had come. But while the route through Genoa was still safely out of military zones, the route through Padua was not. There was a war between Padua and Venice, and the Paduans were manning forts throughout this region. In March, Venetian cavalry raids had come within ten miles of the road Chaucer would have had to take, and the road was occupied by troops. A sea attack by Venice on the Paduan defenses was imminent, and news traveled slowly. He could have taken certain back roads with a guide, or traveled with troops, but any way was dangerous. Is it likely that the king's diplomatic representative in Florence, on his way home to render account of his mission, risked his life to visit a celebrity? And if he did, how was he to be sure that Petrarch, one of the most important men in Europe, now very busy, old, and in ill health, would (unless elaborate plans had been made) have been willing or able to receive him? There is one further argument against the visit: Petrarch in his letters commented extensively on everything that happened to him day by day, but he left no record of such a meeting.

It is curious, but almost surely coincidental, that just at this time, when Chaucer was in Italy, Petrarch was working on his translation of the Griselda story. Chaucer wrote a version of it and later used it in *The Canterbury Tales* as the Clerk's Tale, but there is no reason to think he learned it—as he said the Clerk did—from Petrarch himself.

Beyond these historical circumstances, which make a meeting with Petrarch virtually impossible, the Clerk's extravagant praise of an idealized Petrarch sounds like praise of a public figure whom the writer *hadn't* met. When we are young, our heroes stand up best at a distance. Nothing is more disappointing, when we are thirty, than watching our admired elders spill their food, wander off in their thoughts, display their aches and pains or their failing memory or drifting attention. We want our heroes to be heroes. When we meet them, we are more often than not puzzled, surprised, subtly let down—and sometimes brutally disillusioned. Suppose Chaucer *had* met Petrarch. Petrarch we know was in failing health, had lately suffered from scabies as well, was burdened by work and preoccupied by the nearness of death. And Chaucer we know was observant of and sensitive to others' behavior. Petrarch might have risen to the occasion and memorably impressed the unknown young English squire who had risked his life to visit him; but if he had been up to such a performance, can we believe that the young squire—not to mention the laureate's performance—would have received no mention in those voluminous letters?

This line of reasoning, whatever it may be worth, is more convincing as an argument that Chaucer did meet Boccaccio. It might explain why he never mentions his name. Chaucer was in Florence for as much as ten weeks. During this time Boccaccio was at Certaldo, about twenty miles from Florence, and often made trips into the city, where he was an eminence. Chaucer's business was with the merchant bankers of Florence, with whom Boccaccio had connections: his own father had belonged to this guild. It is hard to imagine that Chaucer's interest in letters did not come up in conversations, and harder to imagine that the Florentines did not bring up Boccaccio's name. Boccaccio was known in mercantile circles as the writer of the *Decameron,* which one critic calls a "mercantile epic," written, as its text reveals, *for* a merchant-class audience and taken up by them with enthusiasm. Chaucer might have heard some of the stories read aloud as an entertainment, or might have looked cursorily at its beginning and end, as Petrarch did, and read a few of the tales. In 1373 the *Decameron* had been circulating nearly twenty years, and early copies of it are written in mercantile hands. A year or two before Chaucer's time in Florence, Boccaccio had made a revised or improved version of it, carefully copying it himself in the handsome holograph manuscript preserved now in the Hamilton collection at the Berlin Staatsbibliothek. Surely Chaucer, having heard of this living Florentine writer, would have been interested in meeting him, and surely among the merchant bankers with whom he had official dealings some had the wherewithal to arrange a meeting.

Suppose, then, that such a meeting took place. Chaucer was thirty; Boccaccio was sixty. Boccaccio was in ill health, suffered from obesity, had had a "dropsical" illness, intestinal and respiratory ailments, violent abdominal pains. From these illnesses he had partly recovered, but he was still going through stages of depression. Like Petrarch, he had had scabies a year before—a most uncomfortable ailment in the Middle Ages, difficult to treat, slow in being cured or overcome, whose painful itching, worse at night, promotes sleeplessness, nervousness, and irritability. By all accounts Boccaccio was a touchy, oversensitive man, and he was worried about his own health and Petrarch's, and about approaching death. It

seems quite probable that if a meeting with Chaucer took place, it was
not a success. There would, for one thing, have been the language barrier.
Unless you speak a foreign language very fluently, it's dreadfully frustrating to try to carry on an intellectual conversation. If Chaucer's Italian
wasn't up to this, they could have resorted to French, in which Chaucer
was more at home than Boccaccio, or Latin, in which Boccaccio was more
at home than Chaucer. Beyond the barriers of age and language lie those
that always exist between foreigners: they had less to talk about than
countrymen do. They might have talked about ancient poets or the
ancients in general, in which case Boccaccio could have talked rings
around his young English visitor. Perhaps Chaucer had by now read
something of Boccaccio's, but it is never easy for a young writer to talk
with an older one about his works, especially when he has read but few
of them. One can imagine the conversation turning to an easier subject:
other writers. And here, of course, Petrarch would have come up. Boccaccio was very emotionally dependent on Petrarch, his authority figure
and role model: speaking of his mentor, he would have spoken as of one
much older than he, more famous and significant, whom he called "magister" and "pater" even in his old age! And it's interesting that such a
reverent encomium to "my sovereign maister deere" is exactly what Chaucer put into the mouth of the Clerk.

The assumption has always been that if Chaucer and Boccaccio met,
the meeting was all cordiality and fascination, sparkling with literary
discussion and shared enthusiasms. Not that Boccaccio wouldn't have
seen the crisp intelligence and ready wit of the young Englishman, and
not that Chaucer wouldn't have recognized at once the immense learning
and grave talent of the Italian master. But he would have found him very
different from the figure he might have imagined—fat, nervous, gloomy,
sickly, uncommunicative. And who is to say if in Boccaccio's eyes the
young Englishman didn't seem overconfident or cheeky, or too Frenchified or courtly, or with spotty reading in the Classics. Such uneasy meet-
ings get shelved in our memories. We do not necessarily forget or "block"
them, but they remain a source of discomfort that we manage to keep in
the darker recesses of consciousness. The possibility would explain why
Chaucer, spending years adapting Boccaccio's *Il Filostrato*, making it
burgeon into a poem longer, more detailed, more shimmering with philosophy and religion and human warmth, more exciting, more dramatic than
its Italian prototype, would have expropriated the legendary name "Lollius" to serve as a mask for Boccaccio. How convenient to push the recent
Italian poet back into the world of books, and ancient ones at that,
identifying him with an obscure writer of the Trojan war, called the
greatest of them all, a writer (the product of a copyist's error, as "Lollius"

actually was) whom no one had read, whose work was thought lost. It would explain too why, fifteen or twenty years later, in the Monk's Tale (line 2325), Chaucer refers to Boccaccio's famous work, *De Casibus Virorum Illustrium*, and says it is by Petrarch: a kind of Freudian slip, it may be, or a willingness to believe a preexisting error, for the two *were* sometimes confused. And it might be one explanation of why, in all the places where Chaucer lists and praises authors, as for example in *The House of Fame*, he never includes Boccaccio. True, he never mentions Machaut or Froissart either. But a meeting in which Chaucer somehow felt himself demeaned, or condescended to, or disappointed—a meeting that he left with the uneasy feeling that he had met the great man at the wrong time, or had failed to put his best foot forward, perhaps a meeting in which his own embarrassment and diffidence had made him an unlikely and foolish-seeming companion—all this could explain why he admired Boccaccio's books but ignored the man himself.

The really important event that happened in Florence, on a certain day in the spring of 1373, was that Geoffrey Chaucer got his hands on the books of the foremost Florentine man of letters. Chaucer was a booklover. Again and again he talks with humorous enthusiasm about his passion for reading—"and other bookes took me to, / To read upon, and yet I read alway," he says, winding up one poem, or, starting another, "On bookes for to read I me delyte, / And to hem yive I faith and full credence," or "there is game none / That fro my bookes maketh me to go." He talks about *collecting* books, about reading at night until his appearance, or his vision, is dazed, about living like a hermit. Yet we must respectfully assume that Chaucer didn't waste much time in Florence reading. When May comes and birds begin to sing and flowers bloom, he declares in *The Legend of Good Women*, "farewell my book." It *was* spring, and Florence at that time was the most exciting city in Europe. Nevertheless, there must have been an occasion when he was invited to browse in the library of one or more of the prominent Florentine guildsmen. A tale or two of the *Decameron* he might already have heard read aloud, but the book itself, if he ever saw a copy, was awesomely long, containing as it did a hundred stories, and it was in prose, a curious, decorative prose, modeled on the medieval *ars dictaminis*: in Italian it is called *prosa d'arte*, and Boccaccio was its inventor. For a foreigner it would have been difficult, and besides, as much as the Florentine merchants loved the *Decameron*, Chaucer wanted to see Boccaccio's *poems*. If he had a shelf of Boccaccio's works before him, he would have passed over the prose works in favor of poems, and been drawn to poems that seemed to resemble the French poetry he knew, like the *Caccia di Diana* or the *Ninfale Fiesolano* for their classical mythology, or the *Amorosa*

Visione because it was a dream vision. Certain of Boccaccio's works set in contemporary Italy, with unfamiliar allusions and in traditions he didn't know, would have been less attractive, like the *Elegia di Madonna Fiammetta*, puzzling enough still. But when he came upon a long epic poem about Theseus, *Il Teseida*, comparable to Statius's *Thebaid* and set in ancient Greece, he would have been attracted at once. Boccaccio obviously shared his interest in the ancient world, and Chaucer would have itched to read those poems on classical themes: the "epic" *Il Teseida*, and what appeared to be a romance, called *Il Filostrato*, set in ancient Troy, legendary ancestor of London. Having read these two works, he would have had a further reason for never mentioning Boccaccio, but we will come back to that later.

It is probably true that Chaucer never in his life set eyes on all of Boccaccio's works—unless during a visit to Boccaccio, however disastrous otherwise, the master himself had memorably displayed them. At this particular time, we happen to know, Boccaccio was working on a revision of the *Genealogia Deorum Gentilium* ("On the Genealogy of the Gentile Gods") and finishing *De Casibus Virorum Illustrium* ("On the Falls of Famous Men"); these learned works, written in Latin, dauntingly long, were known to Chaucer in later years. And yet when he has the Monk mention *De Casibus*, later, he has him say it is by "my master Petrarch," and we know Boccaccio did call Petrarch "master." Perhaps Chaucer had misunderstood and thought it *was* by Petrarch. Chaucer had a special penchant for stories from classical mythology; but it doesn't appear that he really cared much about this kind of classical scholarship. When *he* wrote a work on the "falls of famous men," he made it a casual series of short poems; and when in later years he resurrected them for *The Canterbury Tales*, he put them in the mouth of the pompous, defensive Monk, who with his scholar's hoard of a hundred "tragedies," the same number as the tales in the *Decameron*, might be an unconscious portrait of Boccaccio.

Chaucer knew, from however hasty a survey of Italian writings, that something was happening in literature here, though he didn't yet know what. He could not have purchased more than a book or two, would not have had time to make copies of more than scattered passages, could have read only a little of what most interested him and barely glanced at the less intriguing items, which he may then never have seen again. Yet Boccaccio's oeuvre made an impression. Chaucer took an interest in the surprising *range* of Boccaccio's works. In later years Chaucer liked to think about his own total output, and he several times lists his titles and mentions what he wrote "in youth." And his last three major poems all have counterparts among Boccaccio's: *Troilus and Criseyde* is a direct adaptation of Boccaccio's *Filostrato*, *The Canterbury Tales* is a frame narrative after the manner of the *Decameron*, and *The Legend of Good Women* is a collection of stories comparable to Boccaccio's *De Claris Mulieribus*. In addition, the Monk's Tale is a *De Casibus Virorum Illustrium*—is even called that in some manuscripts—and the very first of the Canterbury tales, the Knight's Tale, is a condensed version of *Il Teseida*.

Leaving Florence, Chaucer had a great deal to think about. But he needed to know more and read more of Boccaccio before he would have any clear thoughts about this author or his works. He did not see how many ideas he could, and would, get from Boccaccio. And possibly he never saw the magnitude of his debt with objectivity.

Looking Back

By the time the negotiations in Florence were complete, messengers had been sent back to London three times, presumably to report on progress; the results were evidently favorable. While we don't know what was said in the talks, we can imagine something about their manner or style, knowing as we do that diplomacy in the Middle Ages was based on the arts of oratory and letter writing. It was, as to some extent it still is, a matter of speechmaking. You did not merely present letters or offer arguments; you explained them and commended them. A treatise called *The Art of Speech and the Art of Silence*, by Albertano of Brescia, was so widely read that we can assume Chaucer knew it, as he knew (and translated) an adaptation of another of Albertano's works, the "Melibeus." "When speaking," Albertano recommends, "employ language that is cheerful, honest, clear, and simple; speak with an undistorted mouth, a tranquil expression, calm face, and without unseemly jeers or loudness." In diplomacy, he recommends "first, at the appropriate time and place," a salutation. Then, "commend those to whom the diplomatic message is directed, indicating that the dispatch is from an associate of yours who may have dictated his message to you." Next, "deliver the exhortation, using eloquent language suitable to the person from whom the message is sent." Requests, he says, should be made in a solicitous manner and analogies should be introduced. A sufficient reason should be provided for anything mentioned in passing.

One can imagine Chaucer carrying out these recommendations with grace, but one can imagine too that several weeks of adopting this stance would have been wearing. Perhaps it was this elocutionary aspect of his career that made him, in his writings, commend the second part of Albertano's art—silence—and show an impatience with needless talk. In the 1380s the poet Deschamps sent a verse epistle to Chaucer through their mutual friend Sir Lewis Clifford, addressing him "great translator," in which he praises among other things his brevity of speech. His diplomatic career would have commended concision in speech, as perhaps his temperament fostered a certain defensive reticence. If he was chosen for the Italian mission because he knew the language, diplomacy in a foreign language must have developed in him an ability to read facial expressions and gestures, to *sense* a drift of thought or receive clues to what others are thinking. And we see these skills, in his longer narrative poems, in the language of gesture the characters use with each other and in their ability to surmise and second-guess each other's thoughts.

The long trip back to England, with his mission successfully behind him, was just the time to mull over and sort out his experience of Florence. The weather that year was good if one may judge from the records of grain prices, and traveling back to England in late April and May, crossing the Alps when they were passable and green, when there were springtime flowers blooming, and when people's spirits soared, would have been the most propitious occasion on which to confront and assimilate what he had learned. Easter that year fell on April 17, exactly six weeks before the day Chaucer's arrival home is recorded, so he must have left on the five-week trip just after Easter, when by tradition pilgrims set off on their springtime travels. By coincidence, probably, April 17 is the date when the pilgrims of *The Canterbury Tales* set out.

And what was he thinking about as he traveled back to England?

Chaucer had seen what was undeniably a superior culture: Italy, in his day, led Europe in the arts of civilization. It had the largest, most commercially powerful cities, a new and seemingly effective form of city government; it led Europe in medicine, in scholarship, in art; it was the center of banking and finance. It had a new spirit in literature, and a literary culture unlike anything anywhere else in Europe. It had Dante—even ordinary people knew and recited Dante's poem. It had a "mercantile epic" in prose that people were reading and talking about. In every aspect of life, it had hope, it had excitement. And in part this was *because* there was no centralized government. The Italian city-states Chaucer had seen were republics, with elected leaders, governed by men of the merchant class. They were, if one thought of it, what London might be were it not for "England"—were it not for the feudal system brought by William the Conqueror, which was the basis of its national government, its aristocracy, and its monarchy.

Much of what Chaucer had seen was the product of the movement we call humanism. But much that he saw was a concomitant, not a product; it was a new sensibility accompanying other trends, neither a cause nor an effect. In the visual arts there was a greater expressiveness and attention to detail, what we call realism, that must have seemed very advanced, or very strange, to an Englishman, even one who had traveled in France and Flanders. In painting and sculpture, he would have seen tendencies that could in England be observed only in manuscript painting, in the miniature pictures that foreshadow Renaissance art. Along the Rhine, passing through Germany, he would certainly have seen some of the sculptures of the period, with extraordinary, lifelike faces whose expressions show discernible emotions: smiles with crinkling facial lines, taut muscles, glinting eyes. The art and sculpture of Florence revealed similar tendencies. He would have seen the frescoes by Giotto and other works that were the first tendencies in the direction of an artistic revolution. But he would have seen a countertendency that might have impressed him even more and had a more profound effect: after the Black Death, even before it, Italian art developed a somber, monitory strain, of which Orcagna's fresco painting *The Triumph of Death* in the Church of Santa Croce in Florence is a prime example. It was painted just after the Black Death, and there's not a doubt that Chaucer saw it. The painting of the same name at Pisa, which Chaucer may have seen, was painted *before* the plague, but what contrasts one can make between them are very subtle. They seem to show us that a feeling about death had swept through the area before the Black Death did.

Even in these grim and didactic works, as in more worldly and optimistic ones, there is a curiosity, in trecento Italian painting, about everyday life—an interest doubtless befitting a democracy in a mercantile center. It is important not to overemphasize this as an Italian development, for an interest in domesticity was in the air throughout Europe. Derek Brewer points to the significance of the *Meditationes Vitae Christi*, written in Italy early in the fourteenth century, translated into English in the fifteenth century but perhaps known there earlier. It tells the life of Christ by deemphasizing the supernatural and theological, by making his life seem like an ordinary person's life—we see him learning his lessons like any schoolboy, see the Virgin Mary sewing like anybody's mother. This tendency came into painting: a Virgin and Child painted late in the fourteenth century at Hamburg shows the Blessed Virgin knitting a shirt, using four needles. Such "domestic, quotidian realism," the "realism of the everyday" in Erich Auerbach's phrase, had already appeared, but minimally, in literature. What Chaucer saw of the visual arts on the Continent might have reinforced observations he made elsewhere. His temperament gave him a special receptivity to detail, individual feeling, and the realities of daily life; his literary inclinations gave him a greater interest in how such tendencies were appearing in *books*. His experience of Europe and especially of Italy promoted that most striking, perhaps most painterly, characteristic of Chaucer's style, his attention to everyday detail—from Pandarus's house or Troilus's seal ring, to the Prioress's broach or the wart on the Miller's nose.

In Italy he had encountered too something new in the art of telling stories, a new kind of story in poetry, and stories told in prose. Telling stories is a universal impulse, and the better part of stories are gossip and anecdote, the quotidian, dispensable stuff of conversation. Of stories that survive and are passed on in speech or writing, some celebrate heroes or events of former times, and these we call *legends*: their meaning lies in their claim to preserve the past. Other stories spring from the impulse to explain phenomena, and these we call *myths*: their meaning lies in their claim to show that the world makes sense—they teach the hidden meaning that we want to believe lies beneath appearances, and on this account, unlike legends, they are open to allegorical interpretation. Until Chaucer's time, medieval stories were mostly of these two kinds. What he had encountered in Italy were stories, of the sort people tell every day, that make no claim to preserve history or explain phenomena, that do not instruct, do not have a "use." They please us, or interest us, or amuse us; they satisfy an emotional need, ease our minds by recreation. They exist for their intrinsic interest. The characters depicted in them belong to a different "mode": they are no longer, as in myths and legends, our superiors and forebears, or as in romance our heroes, but our inferiors—characters like ourselves on whom we can look with irony because we see their ordinariness, their foibles and errors. The discoverer who set sail on this uncharted sea was Boccaccio. The locus of the discovery is the *Decameron*. The discovery in a subtler form is to be seen in his earlier poems, among them the *Filostrato*, a poem from which has been excised, as by a surgeon's scalpel, all that might give it the aura of legend or myth. It is, in modern parlance, a *fiction*.

The moment in literary history Chaucer had witnessed (but not yet understood) was the moment when *fictions* took their place in the realm of literature.

But with this he also witnessed the moment when the poet or writer was assuming a new role in society. The humanists believed the writer spoke not just to the prince or the court but to humanity—to posterity. In France and England, the poet's role was to please the court and the prince, and he could exert no influence without doing that first. But in Italy, the humanist and writer Coluccio Salutati was soon to be chancellor of Florence; Petrarch and Boccaccio, though both officially of the church, held positions of importance and respect among those in political power. There were, in Italy, to be sure, despots like the Visconti, as there were influential nobles like the Green Count of Savoy; and the great mercantile families in cities like Florence absorbed the values of the old nobility and in time became—witness the Medici—princes. Yet poets in these mercantile city-states were treated with greater deference than poets in monarchical France or England, and had a greater expectation of rewards.

Of these rewards, one in particular struck Chaucer: fame. The humanists held fame to be the reward history confers on the writer. Like the "glory" knights won for deeds of arms, the poet could lay claim to his share of worldly luster. Petrarch's coronation as poet laureate was an effort to put this ideal into practice. In later years, in his *Secretum*, Petrarch dutifully reminded himself that fame is "nothing but talk about someone, passing from mouth to mouth of many people": it is akin to gossip, and like all temporal things it will perish.

But Petrarch *believed* in fame, thirsted after it. Twenty years earlier he had written an allegorical dream vision in Italian, the *Trionfi*, depicting Love and Chastity, Death and Fame. Its idea was that fame triumphs over death—that fame is a measure of immortality in the stream of successive human lives. The *Trionfi* is one of those works Chaucer might have glanced through while in Italy, and later remembered in part. In the early 1370s, about the time Chaucer was in Florence, Petrarch added another section to the poem, on Time and Divinity, which concludes that all is vanity in the end. The poem consists of a procession of military heroes chiefly from ancient times, among them an unspecified duke of Lancaster who fought in France, probably Henry, the Good Duke, the Duchess Blanche's father. Chaucer could hardly have failed to note this passage, might even have fancied it referred to John of Gaunt. And alongside these famous warriors in Petrarch's poem he would have found poets, philosophers, and historians of antiquity, who owed their fame to their works.

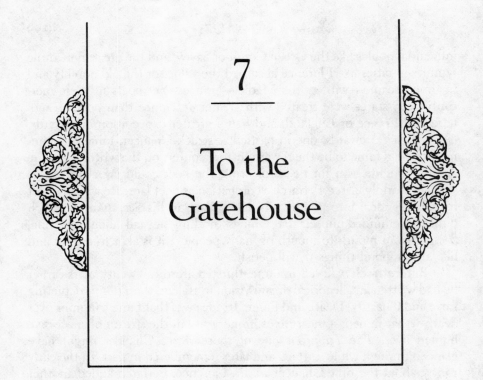

7

To the Gatehouse

England, 1374

When Chaucer arrived back in London, on Monday, May 23, he found everything in turmoil. The ships commandeered to make a transport fleet were assembling at Plymouth. Money had been raised, horses had been purchased, an army of mounted soldiers, almost half of them archers, had been enlisted and paid in advance to bolster their morale. But the ships were slow in gathering, and because a change in the battle plan required a change in the port of embarkation, they were being rerouted to Dover and Sandwich. The commander in chief was John of Gaunt.

Tutbury Castle had been prepared for the queen of Castile, now twenty. There, and in other northern castles, Costanza would wait out the war with the duke's children, her baby daughter, Catalina, and her retinue, among whom, of course, was Philippa Chaucer. Since the embarkation had been planned for May, the duchess and her ladies may already have left for Tutbury. The fleet was not ready until the end of July, and the army, having thus wasted the summer months, did not begin its march into France until August 4.

The duke had organized the expedition to perfection. The king was too old and the Black Prince too sick to join it, and Gaunt was for the first time wholly in command. Glory in France, however, was but a secondary motive: he was planning the conquest of Castile. Costanza and he had formed an alliance with the king of Portugal against Enrique of Trastamare, and just before the army left he offered pardons to "rebels," hoping to gain for his side any fence sitters among the nobles of Castile. He had already begun negotiating for other Castilian allies. "Lancaster's midsummer madness," his biographer calls it: Gaunt fancied that he was going to march through France victorious, then proceed into Spain, defeat the usurper, and be crowned.

Most of the coming year Chaucer was at court and busied himself trying to collect the money owed him for his expenses in Italy. The payments on his and Philippa's annuities were seriously in arrears, though at one point he managed an advance of £10. He needed, perhaps badly, the funds the government owed him, and the bureaucracy of the Exchequer was maddeningly slow. He had been paid a hundred marks (£66 2/3) on leaving London to cover expenses at the going rate for an esquire of his rank, 13s. 4d. a day, and had received 220 florins (£33) on March 23, in Florence, advanced by Jacopo Provano; on the debit side, he had paid out traveling costs for his men and horses and the three messengers sent from Florence. He rendered his accounts shortly after his return, though they haven't survived; we know from later documents that the government owed him £25 6s. 8d., about twice what he was paid annually. But there was nothing to do but borrow and wait. Five months passed. On November 11 a mandate was recorded at Westminster under the king's Privy Seal, in French. "To the treasurer and the barons and chamberlains of the Exchequer, Greetings:"

> *Nous vous mandons qe vous acontez par soun serement ouvesque nostre ame esquier Geffrey Chaucer du viage quel il fist nadgaires en nostre service alant vers les parties de Jeene et de Florence pur aucunes noz secrees busoignes . . .*

—and so on. It was all written out with a quill pen on a scroll of parchment into the Memoranda Rolls of the Exchequer, where it is still preserved, some 250 graceless words in all, from which we learn that he was to be paid:

> for the whole of the said voyage from the day that he departed from our city of London for that purpose until his return . . . reasonable expenses for his passage to and fro across the sea,

and also for messengers that he sent on that account to us to
report to us on our aforesaid business . . .

Below, in Latin, an endorsement that the writ was delivered to the
Exchequer, and that the accounts of the heretofore inscribed Geoffrey,
made in the service of the king, in pursuit of the king's business in the
territories of Genoa and Florence, in the forty-seventh year of the reign
of King Edward III, were enrolled in the forty-seventh roll of the Rolls
of Accounts.

So there it was. A few days later there appeared in the Foreign
Account Rolls, in Latin, a document nearly twice as long, going through
all the same details once again, with multiple references to the territories
of Genoa and Florence, and the aforesaid Geoffrey, and the secret business of the king, with a detailed summary of payments and expenses, an
accounting of the sum owed, and directions that it be paid. Three more
months passed. On February 4 of the following year, there appeared on
the Issue Rolls a writ in Latin of fifty-odd words stating that to the said
Geoffrey had been paid into his own hands £25 6s. 8d. for expenses in
the king's service on the king's business in the territories of Genoa and
Florence, and so on, the amount being named twice. This means it had
passed the audit and been paid out. It had taken eight months—which
was rather fast.

We can guess that sometime during those months the said Geoffrey
made the four-day journey north to visit his wife and child, or children,
at the duchess's court, but of these domestic affairs there is not half a
sentence in any language. His son Thomas would have been born about
this time: if Thomas's age on entering military service or marrying was
typical, a probable date for his birth is 1373–1374. Those who argue that
Thomas was the illegitimate son of John of Gaunt would have us believe
that Gaunt seduced Philippa in Chaucer's absence and Chaucer returned
to find himself a cuckold. Gaunt had had one bastard child before his
marriage to the Duchess Blanche, and his only other known bastards are
the four children he had by Katherine Swynford. John Beaufort, eldest of
these, was born about this same time. It makes more sense to conclude
that Philippa became pregnant with little Thomas before Chaucer left for
Italy or just after he returned.

Late in August he was assigned to go to Dartmouth and obtain the
release of a Genoese ship being detained in the harbor there, the *Seinte
Marie et Seinte George*. Its master, one "Johannes de Negris," of Genoa,
was under arrest. A decade earlier di Negro seems to have been captain
of a ship called the *Seinte Marie* traveling between Genoa and London
for "the king's merchant," Giovanni del Mare—Chaucer's companion to

Genoa. It wasn't unusual for someone to seize a ship, or anything else, if he thought he could get away with it, and Dartmouth had a bad reputation for such goings-on. But the captain of the *Seinte Marie et Seinte George* had connections at court and Chaucer was sent, almost certainly with an armed guard, to liberate the vessel by the king's command.

It's often thought that while Chaucer was in Dartmouth he learned about a wealthy merchant-shipowner, John Hawley, whose ships were robbing Genoese vessels, and that the portrait of the ship captain from Dartmouth in *The Canterbury Tales* is owing to this experience. The Shipman's vessel is called the *Maudeleine,* and in later years there *was* a ship with that name sailing out of Dartmouth; its master, Peter Risshenden, was associated with Hawley and was involved in the piratical sort of activity ascribed to the Shipman. More significant than anything Chaucer might have remembered a dozen years later is the fact that he was chosen to deal with the Genoese vessel: he was now an expert on Genoa, on trade with Italy, and was soon to be appointed to the Wool Custom in part because of that expertise. For a dozen years he was to be attached to this maritime world, the world of imports and exports, of international shipping; the smell of salt air and the creak of ships' rigging was a preponderant part of his life during what turned out to be his most formative and productive years as an artist. He must have known a great many ship captains and merchant seamen, known the tricks they brought to the customs office and the dangers they faced on the high seas, heard many tales of storms and pirates and thievery aboard ship, and many sailors' yarns, and encountered many colorful characters. Yet nothing of this international world of maritime commerce gets into the works he wrote while he was involved with it, and almost nothing of it gets into *The Canterbury Tales* beyond the portrait of the Shipman and a few lines in the description of the Merchant. His literary ideas came from literary works; if he went "direct to life," as people used to say, he did so very selectively—yet he knew much more about life than what shows in his writings.

The court during this winter, dominated as it was by the king's mistress, was a dispiriting milieu. The men who were fit were off to war, and most of the ladies were in attendance upon the Duchess Costanza. The Black Prince, intent on having his son succeed to the throne, came from his estate in Berkhamsted and took his seat in the House of Lords, but was too ill for social life. The Princess Isabella was in France. The queen's role in court life had increasingly been usurped by Alice Perrers. Like the king himself, Dame Alice loved possessions, money, and display. She had gotten Edward to give her an estate at Wendover, situated near

estates of John of Gaunt and the Black Prince, with both of whom she
managed to be on good terms. She purchased a house in the city from
Richard Lyons, the flamboyant vintner, at a low price, with the understanding that she would use her influence in his favor. Nine years earlier
she had had dealings with Lyons of such a kind that he had been ordered
by the king to desist; Chaucer's father had stood surety for Lyons and she
had been guaranteed freedom of movement without hindrance. Now, she
and Lyons were friends again. They must have had something to gain
from each other.

    Alice Perrers's knack was to make friends with influential gentlemen
who could be useful to her. She couldn't have been the vulgarian she is
sometimes depicted as. She was a knight's daughter and a onetime damsel
of the queen's chamber, and if she was acquisitive, this gave her something
in common with the men around her. As allies she had figures of no less
significance than Lord Latimer, the king's chamberlain, and Sir William
of Windsor, the king's lieutenant in Ireland, and with their aid and advice
she purchased more London properties. She put up the ransom for Lord
Fitzwalter, imprisoned in France, and took his family castle at Egremont
as security. The money for these ventures came as loans or gifts, mostly
from Edward: she borrowed funds from him and got him to cancel the
debts as they came due. He ceded to her, in writing, the jewels and
personal possessions of Queen Philippa, which she paraded about in public
—not the happiest spectacle for a court that had so adored the dead queen
—and some of which she sold. He bought her jewels from merchants; it
was said she would then lay out before him the very jewels he had bought,
claiming they were on loan from merchants against a decision to purchase
—and Edward, his memory failing, would buy them a second time. She
took a sizable portion of the funds given to William of Windsor when he
was sent to Ireland, probably in return for useful information; he earned
the king's rebuke for his outrageous exploitation of the Irish, by which he
made up his deficit, and the king was never the wiser. She purchased the
manor of Oxhey from Thomas Fitzjohn, out from under the Abbot of
Saint Albans, who claimed it as a legacy. The abbot had met his match;
but he became one of her many enemies in the church who would cry
out against her when the time was right. She was a shrewd, charming
beauty who in short order became one of the richest women in England.
She was not yet thirty.

    One of Alice Perrers's friends was Geoffrey Chaucer. She was a few
years younger than he and had been a damsel of the queen from about
1359. They had by now been in the royal household together more than
a decade, and it can be demonstrated in impressive detail that they

traveled in the same circles and knew the same people. Her father was Sir Richard Perrers, several times sheriff of Essex. She was married in her teens to an older man, William Champain, a well-to-do London baker who had died in 1360; she had with her at court, it was said, a daughter, Isabel, and that was indeed the name of one of William Champain's daughters. Another of his daughters, by a previous wife, Agnes, was Cecily Champain, who must have been Alice's stepdaughter. Alice Perrers is believed to have been secretly married to Sir William of Windsor, some years her elder, with whom she had been in such profitable cahoots, and it is true they lived together after the king's death. She had several children out of wedlock, one by the king, a child whom he knighted before his death; a record dated July 1374 mentions a "Geoffrey Perrers" in a long list of men to be arrested, which has raised a feeble conjecture that she had had a son by Chaucer. For whatever reason, she did Chaucer certain favors: the house he would move into at Aldgate the following May could have been arranged by her, and her friend Richard Lyons was Collector of the Petty Custom and Subsidy, when Chaucer was appointed controller.

Throughout the winter they heard the perplexing news from France. In September the English army had reached Troyes, in October it was in Burgundy; from there it headed south through the Auvergne, then, in the dead of winter, westward to Bordeaux. The French, as they had done before, refused all challenges to battle, kept themselves closed up in walled towns; the English, profiting from time wasted in years gone by, raised no sieges. John of Gaunt was not the strategist his father and elder brother had been and never succeeded in forcing the enemy to a battle. A French army pursued them into the Auvergne and harried them from the rear, but abandoned pursuit when the weather turned, seeing the English effort was doomed. Men and horses died, wagons had to be abandoned, food ran low. By the time the army reached Aquitaine almost half of it was lost, and many of those who survived left dead horses along the way and arrived in Bordeaux on foot. Men began to desert, in large enough numbers for the king to order, on January 8, that soldiers returning to London without permission be arrested. The venture had accomplished nothing. Leaving behind them a trail of slaughtered peasants and burned villages, they took not a single town nor regained a foot of soil, and never even approached Castile.

The English may not have fully understood the futility of the campaign. The army, having passed through France unchallenged, could fancy the enemy cowering in their castles and themselves proceeding in triumph. In December the chancellor had reported to Parliament that the army "by their good and noble governance and deeds of arms has wrought great damage and destruction to the enemy." In the spring the pope intervened, there were threats of excommunication, a truce was declared. But it is hard to imagine that anyone, least of all the seasoned warriors at court, could have seen it as a victory. The people began to grumble against John of Gaunt. When he returned King Edward is supposed to have reprimanded him, and he to have brooded ten months in his northern castles.

And yet, in the first week of April, when Lent was over, while the army was on its way back to England, the king declared a week's tournament at Smithfield as if there were something to celebrate. They were going to celebrate the sun. Alice Perrers, as the Lady of the Sun, rode in procession in a chariot; the other ladies, on foot, held the silver bridles of the knights' war horses; young women above rained flowers on the pageant as it passed. Alice Perrers, center of this chivalric spectacle, went bedizened in a leather cap encrusted with jewels, a russet gown with white lining, trimmed with ermine and embroidered with pearls, and a cloak, lined in red, that had been made in Italy from cloth of gold.

The Gatehouse at Aldgate

John of Gaunt had landed at Dartmouth by April 26 and was at the Palace of the Savoy on May 1, where he remained until mid-July. The Duchess Costanza and her retinue must have come to join him, and Geoffrey and Philippa must have been reunited. Soon after this, Chaucer was set up all at once with an income, a dwelling, and a position, so it is often assumed that the duke had a hand in improving his fortunes. But the first reward Chaucer received, an unusual one, came while Gaunt was still crossing the Channel.

April 23, the feast day of Saint George, was the Feast of the Garter, and the king celebrated it at Windsor, which he had rebuilt for his famous round table. On this chivalric occasion, which hearkened back to the old days of England's luster, Chaucer was granted a pitcher (probably a gallon) of wine a day for life. The writ of privy seal, in French, and the patent in Latin, say he is to pick it up from the king's butler "every day in the port of our city of London."

There are other such gifts on record for an amount of wine per *year*; an amount per day is rare. Such grants went to very significant figures, but rarely to the royal esquires; and Chaucer, oddly enough, received more than some members of the royal family had—though, not so oddly, less than a third of what went to Alice Perrers. His was, incidentally, the only gift recorded at Windsor on that day.*

Whether he was being rewarded for a poem, or belatedly for his service in Italy, or for something else, it's notable that the grant directs him to collect it each day at the port, a unique provision. It seems less than convenient for one of the king's esquires to be scurrying off to the waterfront daily for more wine than he could drink; and this oddity suggests that when the grant was made it was already known that he would *be* at the port daily as controller of the Wool Custom. There is something festive and slightly jocular about the gift: an unusual, extravagant gesture perhaps with a congratulatory intent and a sly hint that Master Geoffrey will be expected on the job daily—and in a position to offer wine to his associates. Does it sound like hush money or recompense paid to a cuckold, as some have said? No, it sounds like an old-fashioned display of royal largesse. The gesture contained a message: future preferment. As a gesture it was a colossal piece of conspicuous waste—Richard II commuted it to cash a few years later, after its message had been forgotten.

A fortnight later, on May 10, Chaucer received a lease, also for life, of the apartment over the city gate at Aldgate; a month after that, on June 8, he was appointed controller of the Wool Custom. If these preferments were celebrated with the gift made on the Feast of the Garter, the plan had been made before John of Gaunt ever returned from France. Not that he wouldn't have approved. His mistress was Chaucer's wife's sister, and the sisters were in attendance upon the duchess, with whom Chaucer may have taken occasion to ingratiate himself. Chaucer and Philippa were low on cash; their annuities were still in arrears, and Chaucer had waited long even for the settlement of his accounts. Slow payment was a way of life at court, and in these years Edward had become forgetful, negligent, befuddled. Someone had to get his ear and argue Chaucer's cause. It could have been Costanza herself. Or Alice Perrers might have arranged with the king, as well as with Richard Lyons, for Chaucer to have the customs post and a comfortable place to live about ten minutes' walk from his work. Dame Alice owned extensive properties in the neighborhood of

*It has been suggested that this was a reward for presenting a poem at the celebration of the order of the Garter, but there's no known poem by Chaucer written at this time. John Gardner suggested "The Book of the Lion," the lost work Chaucer mentions in his Retraction at the end of *The Canterbury Tales,* probably a redaction of Machaut's *Dit du Lyon.* The poem might indeed have been appropriate to the court of Edward III during his years with Alice Perrers, for it deals with *losengeours,* the malicious talebearers and gossips who were reckoned a threat to courtly lovers. Some very early version of *The House of Fame,* with its emphasis on gossip and reputation, could have been similarly appropriate.

Aldgate and had the influence to secure the dwelling for her protégé, even without the king's intervention. Richard Lyons knew Chaucer's family and was to be Chaucer's superior in the Customs. The mayor, Adam de Bury, whose name appears on the lease, was a family friend. And Chaucer's family evidently had connections with the group of Hainaulters that had surrounded Queen Philippa, among them Chaucer's father-in-law. The war was over and the army on its way back, lessening the drain on finances. All that was left for Edward was the grand gesture.

The gatehouse at Aldgate was in the gift of the city. There were a handful of such dwellings, some of which—witness Newgate—were used as prisons. During this period five of them had tenants, mostly officials of the city, often sergeants empowered to make arrests and keep the peace. Several times the king had asked the city to give one to one of his esquires. Chaucer, like other tenants, agreed to keep the property in good repair and relinquish it if it was needed in the defense of the city; the city agreed to keep no prisoners there and exact no rent. Judging from the men to whom gatehouses were leased—Chaucer's friend Ralph Strode held the one at Aldersgate, for example—they were respectable, prized dwellings. Because the leases in Latin use the word *mansio*, "quarters," they are sometimes described as palatial mansions, but really they were two-room apartments with a storeroom or cellar below.

Chaucer's new prosperity came about in this way, through connections, and he may well have asked these influential people to help him—perhaps, as he did in later years, by writing poems to them. He received the appointment to the controllership on June 8. The job in the Wool Custom paid £10 a year plus a bonus (*regardum*) of 10 marks, and there was probably a further stipend for the Petty Custom—not a large sum, but there was money on the side, as we shall see. Here John of Gaunt enters the picture: on the day after Chaucer took the oath of office, Gaunt matched the salary with an annuity of £10 for life, for his services and "also for the good service that our well loved Philippa, his wife, did for our honored lady and mother the queen, whom God pardon, and for our very beloved companion the Queen [of Castile]. . . ." Five days after that, Gaunt ordered alabaster for the Duchess Blanche's tomb in Saint Paul's; since the year she died he had been out of the country much of the time, and now he was thinking of her—so it's possible that the annuity was, at least in part, a reward for *The Book of the Duchess*.

On July 6, ten days before Gaunt left for the north, Geoffrey and Philippa collected the arrears on their Exchequer annuities, which came to nearly £20—Philippa's hadn't been claimed in over three years. If they were broke before, they were now suddenly prosperous. Between them they had nearly £70 a year in annuities and wages,* plus certain fees and gifts, a rent-free dwelling, and—oh, yes—a gallon of wine a day.

Chaucer lived in the gatehouse at Aldgate for some dozen years, and they were his most productive ones. During this time he wrote *The House of Fame, The Parliament of Fowls, Troilus and Criseyde,* and other, lesser works, and he conceived the idea of *The Legend of Good Women* and of *The Canterbury Tales,* writing certain tales or passages that became parts of each. It is the only one of his residences that we know much of; happily, it is the most important. If today you get off the underground at Aldgate, there is nothing of Chaucer's world for you to see. Even the parish church at Saint Botolph-without-Aldgate was built in the eighteenth century; the old church standing in Chaucer's time just outside the walls, where his father owned property, was judged unsafe and torn down in 1744. The gatehouse was a small dwelling actually built into the wall above the gate. There is a plan of Aldgate based on an Elizabethan survey, which shows the gatehouse incorporated into two circular towers about twenty-six feet in diameter on either side of the twenty-foot road. The dwelling on the upper story, approached by a spiral staircase, appears to consist of two U-shaped rooms measuring about twelve feet by twenty feet, connected by a smaller rectangular room. The larger rooms apparently had small windows, one on either side, looking out along the wall. The neighborhood was chiefly of tradesmen who owned houses with shops, many of which had gardens.

Not a bad place to live, Aldgate, but it may not have been a good place to write. Underneath it, through the gate, passed an endless stream of iron-wheeled carts carrying foodstuffs, or the entrails of slaughtered beasts, or dung. It was a principal gate of the city, and several times when London was threatened by a French invasion its atmosphere became military; at such times it was locked at 6:00 P.M., an armed watch set at 8. There were complaints that such residences were given to favored persons to live in, which was true enough; but Chaucer was a public official, and not without military training—he may have been expected to have a hand in the policing of the gate. We have no idea how much he was alone here, but his wife and children were often away. It appears that he wrote at night. In *The House of Fame* there is that famous passage, quoted earlier, where he describes spending the day over his accounts, then coming home to another book and working over it at night —and at night, after curfew, the city was silent enough to please any writer. There is in the same poem mention of the difficulty someone had waking him up in the morning.

*The value of it can be judged from the fact that about this time an esquire's wife and her servant had board and lodging with a London alderman for £10 a year.

It is pointless to speculate whether Chaucer, by day or night, was given to looking out windows, or to guess what he saw if he did so. As I write this, I can see the city of San Francisco spread before me, gemlike beside its bay—but I do not look at it; or, if I look, my mind is elsewhere. On the other hand, if suddenly I heard sirens or an outcry, if there were a fire or accident or, God forbid, an earthquake, I would put down my pen and watch. Only a monster would not—and at that, he would be a monster for his lack of curiosity, something no one could accuse Chaucer of. From the gatehouse, moreover—or from the city wall it was built on (for the apartment itself had but two small windows looking out along the wall) he had a Janus-like view: on the one side the teeming life of the city, on the other what were called the "suburbs"—a most disreputable locus, where by Chaucer's own description (in the Canon's Yeoman's Prologue) "these robbers and these thieves, by kinde / Holden hir privee, fearful residence, / As they that dare not shewen hir presence."

Aldgate was, we might add, the gate through which the rebels entered the city during the Peasants' Revolt of 1381: it was opened for them at night, allegedly by an alderman named William Tonge. Chaucer was in London at the time, and an eyewitness to the Revolt—from an excellent vantage point, if a frightening one. Then, too, and this is probably the most important fact about it, Aldgate was a main thoroughfare through or past which moved all sorts and conditions of men (and woman too), visitors from out of town, thieves and wretches from the suburbs, and travelers on their way to London Bridge—among them, pilgrims to Canterbury.

The Controller of the Customs

On Monday, June 12, Chaucer went to the palace in Westminster and was sworn in as controller before the court of the Exchequer, in its offices upstairs, outside the Great Hall. The oath required that he live in the port of London and carry out his duties in person or by a satisfactory deputy, receive no gifts, undertake that the king lose no revenue due him, and submit accurate accounts without error or fraud in any particular, "so help you God and His saints." The appointment stipulated that he keep the accounts in his own hand; he was allowed a deputy only later. He was controller of the Wool Custom (a permanent duty on exports of wool, wool fells, and leather), the Wool Subsidy (a secondary, larger duty voted by parliament for particular periods of time), and the Petty Custom (a duty on other merchandise).

The controller acted as an auditor of the collectors, who were the major officials. They supervised the accounts, paid the controller's salary (which was half as much as theirs), and received a commission on amounts collected. They were prominent, wealthy, powerful citizens, and they showed up at the customhouse rarely. In Chaucer's time the most famous of them, apart from the notorious Richard Lyons, were William Walworth, who was elected lord mayor of London that very year, 1374; John Philipot, mayor in 1378; and Nicholas Brembre, mayor in 1386, hanged in 1388 on a trumped-up charge of treason. All were rather questionable when it came to ethics, though we can never be sure how much of what we read was concocted by their enemies. The collectors were such major figures because wool was the major export and the taxes on it a major source of revenue. The wool trade, through the Staple, was a monopoly; the purpose of the Staple, a corporation of wool merchants working out of designated ports at London and Newcastle, was to cut off direct trade between sheep farmers and foreign merchants. Through a series of compromises between the Staple and Parliament, the government had established taxes on these exports; the merchants passed the taxes on by paying lower prices to sellers and charging higher ones to buyers. By now these taxes could be counted on, and so the king could borrow on them; wealthy merchants lent him large sums and were paid off direct from incoming taxes. For example, when Chaucer came to the Customs, Richard Lyons was the "farmer" of the Petty Custom and Subsidy; he had paid £3,000 to the Bardi in the king's name and lent the king £6,000; the king promised to pay at a rate of 2s. per tun of wine and 6d. in the pound on merchandise. In 1374, with Richard Francis, Lyons lent the king 8,354 marks, and with John Pyel £10,000. Nicholas Brembre and William Walworth lent similar sums. Needless to say they were all collecting interest; Richard Lyons was later accused of taking 50 percent, a high rate, but within reason.

The monetary gains for a controller were considerable. In 1376, for instance, Chaucer received £71 4s. 6d., the proceeds from the sale of smuggled goods that had been seized; this may have been a reward for informing on the smuggler. We know that controllers and collectors did take bribes, and we know that the collectors under whom Chaucer worked were powerful men, all of them profiteers, whom he could not afford to cross. In 1376 Richard Lyons was accused of extortion while he was farming the Custom and Subsidy, and went to prison for it. Chaucer must have had to look the other way often enough, and perhaps, as some argue, he could hardly have avoided profits that would seem to us like graft. But he served in the office twelve and a half years, longer by far than the average term at that time, and though accusations of corruption flew about freely there is no hint that his probity was ever called in question.

Because Chaucer in *The House of Fame* represents himself in the controllership as a harmless drudge, we tend to think it a routine and boring job; actually it was a quite responsible one and probably rather interesting. There were officers separately appointed who moved and weighed cargo and others who searched for tax evaders; he oversaw these operations, interpreted the laws applying to taxation, adjudicated disagreements, and kept the accounts. He was given a seal with which he stamped indentures written on parchment—one copy going to the payer as a receipt, the other to the Exchequer. This was a double or "cocket" seal, constructed in such a way that the wax could only be imprinted with both parts. A tablet of wax was put on the lower part, ribbons (to be attached to the document) were laid across and another tablet of wax put over them; then the top part was attached and the two pressed together. The collectors held one part of the seal and the controller the other, so all goods had to pass through both officials or their deputies; in fact, the collector's seal was kept in a bag sealed by the controller and vice versa. It was in the nature of Chaucer's position that he imposed the duties and kept the books himself. The customhouse was on the wool quay; in 1382 a new house was built, with a tronage hall (for weighing cargo) and cellars downstairs, a countinghouse and latrine upstairs. The next year a third floor was added with two more offices; probably this construction entered into Chaucer's responsibilities. He had to inspect the books of the packers and porters, who kept separate accounts of their own, and be in touch with the searchers, who went about in boats with an armed guard looking for illegal movements of funds or smuggled goods. Any of these officers might be offered a bribe, and if they were accused or caught Chaucer had to go off to the Exchequer and be involved in the hearing of their case. Sometimes his seal was surrendered to a merchant as security for a loan to the Crown, and then, in order to use it, he had to have dealings with that merchant, sometimes a foreigner, or with his agents. There was great variety in what he had to do, and he came in contact with a variety of people. He must have seen infinite venality, witnessed colorful subterfuges, heard improbable and ridiculous dodges and lies and excuses. Nor could the job have been terribly time consuming: he was assigned other duties as a royal esquire, and, during these years, he probably read and wrote more than at any other time of his life.

His training in the royal household especially suited him for the post: he had legal expertise, he had served abroad in matters touching commerce and finance, he knew the byzantine workings of the Exchequer and the government, including its vastly complex system of accounting, still not fully understood. The records of his service in the Customs are more extensive than any other kind of life records we have about him, and the administration of government in his time has been studied in vast detail. Unhappily, this wealth of information tells us little of his life. It isn't hard to imagine that after some years of government service he grew impatient with the cumbersome machine of which he was a part. Just collecting money owed him meant hours of finagling, waiting patiently for writs and documents to be copied and enrolled and audited. Everything else proceeded with the same pomp and snail-like complexity. English administration of the period is sometimes called the most efficient in Europe, and perhaps they did make bureaucracy work better than other governments did. But it was still bureaucracy, and it had already the classic features of bureaucracy: passivity, indifference to the individual, waste of effort, the loss of any sense of a reason for doing things as they are done. Like all bureaucracies, it was self-perpetuating and self-serving, it afforded a haven for hundreds of pompous little men in love with small-time power, and it couldn't be escaped or avoided or changed—you couldn't quit it, you couldn't revolt against it, you couldn't alter or improve it. It cannot have been the best milieu for a poetical genius, and we have to assume it took its toll. He could go home to the gatehouse and read or write in solitude, but in some of what he wrote during those years we sense a deep frustration and disillusionment.

The language of bureaucracy, too, was something he was schooled in and accustomed to, and that language was, then as now, empty and repetitious, a ritual jargon of pat phrases and formulaic diction that rarely said what was meant in a direct way. One memorandum in French, sometimes thought to have been composed by Chaucer himself and written in his own hand, is exceptional: it's short and to the point—one sentence long. It may have been as a reaction against this feature of his official life that he came in his later works so often to praise silence; to ridicule long-winded bores, glib manipulators, and rhetorical flourish; and to develop, in the General Prologue, a literary style in which he says exactly what he means, no more and no less—an abstemious concision, which we read as irony.

Chaucer and Books

Chaucer's finances continued to improve. In the last two months of 1375 another source of income came his way. Certain orphaned minors who were heirs of tenants-in-chief remained wards of the king until they were twenty-one; these wardships, which could be purchased, were sometimes granted by the king to his courtiers—with the right of overseeing and consenting to the ward's marriage, for which otherwise a fee was paid. The custodian was expected to see that the heir was appropriately maintained and his properties kept up; he collected rents, paid wages, and kept accounts. With large estates he turned over accounts and was paid a fee; with smaller estates he received surplus proceeds and paid a rent to the Exchequer or the Chamber. In November Chaucer was appointed ward of Edmund Staplegate, heir of a wealthy Canterbury merchant, and in the next month ward of William Soles, heir to a manor in Kent. The total compensation Chaucer received isn't known, but at one point he was paid the large sum of £104 against the Staplegate property. Eventually he was in a position to purchase property, and he purchased it in Kent. That his wards came from there isn't necessarily significant, however, for his family owned property in Kent and his married sister lived there.

In these improved circumstances it appears that Chaucer began to buy books in earnest. He was in daily contact with merchant shippers from Italy and elsewhere with whom he could arrange for the procurement of particular books, possibly—since he was an official of the port—at a very good price. Chaucer speaks often and warmly of his love of books, but such a love was a different feeling then. The modern booklover comes to be inundated—books overflowing the shelves, books piled on their sides, books in the kitchen, books in the bathroom. One loves them as objects —precious objects if they are "rare," very nice ones if they are art books or fancy editions or have good bindings. But much in any modern library is ephemeral. And the value is spectral. A first edition of a novel is nothing until there is a second, but a first edition of a dictionary is valueless unless it is very old indeed. Medieval books, however, were all copied by hand, the best on vellum gorgeously illuminated and bound. Each was a unique product: there were no "editions" of multiple copies. All books were rare, and all were precious: it is said a good book on vellum would have cost as much as a burgher's house, and the value was stable, visible to the eye —dependent on the quality of parchment and writing, the amount of illumination, size, workmanship. For someone of Chaucer's income this meant the greatest selectivity, meant buying books written on paper, copying one's own, borrowing, visiting someone's collection, listening to a book read aloud. It meant that one's memory of books was vivid. *No* books were ephemeral; all were meant to last. The learned clerk Johannes Tritheim complained that while a book written on vellum would last a thousand years, one written on paper would only last two hundred years —and even at that, he was wrong. Paper had been introduced into England less than two hundred years before the year he wrote this, 1492, but good rag paper it was, and many books on it survive handsomely today.

Chaucer said in the later version of the Prologue to *The Legend of Good Women*, written in the mid-1390s, that he owned sixty books; it was a large investment, part of one's property to be left to one's heirs, best kept locked in chests (shelves were for the very rich or for libraries, and anyway shelved books at the Sorbonne and elsewhere were chained to the shelves). One looked with awe on the likes of Richard de Bury, bishop of Durham and later lord chancellor of England, who died two years after Chaucer was born. Said to have vast learning, he had at all events vast wealth, and he collected books like a man possessed, by purchasing them, or getting them as gifts from religious houses currying favor, or borrowing and not returning them or having them copied, illuminated, and bound in his palace. Men said that his quarters were so laden with books one could barely walk through them; that it would take five large wagons to hold them all; that his books filled all the libraries of all his various residences; that he owned more books than all the other English bishops put together. His collection, a modern scholar observes, dwarfed any other English collection of his day. How many books would this have been? About 1,500, by the same scholar's estimate. Little wonder if Bishop de Bury died in poverty and the books were sold to pay his debts.

Today you could collect that many books just about Chaucer.

So a contemporary in the fourteenth century might be forgiven a little smirk at a prelate who owned 1,500 books, for he could never read them all in a lifetime. Avarice, as much as love of learning—avarice, and superfluous curiosity, and the exhibition of vanity—must have been what moved him. And the bishop did write a book, *Philobiblon,* in which he described his purposes and methods as a collector, praised books and learning, and recorded the complaints of books against abuses (he has the books themselves speak), defending himself against his enemies and critics who charged him with those sins—in ornate Latin, very bookish itself— and denying that he loved books as objects, if one can believe him. He was an early humanist who had met Petrarch at Avignon, and Petrarch must have understood his love of books perfectly: one can imagine Petrarch reminding him that it is in the nature of books to be objects. The bishop left his library to his Oxford college for the books to be lent to students—he made a great point that they were not to be chained, either.

But the ordinary man of letters had to buy with care books he knew he would read many times, or books he proposed to use in the making of another book, or to translate or to adapt; or, if he traveled abroad, he had to think about books of importance that he might never see at home. To a medieval booklover, spending money on books was in a worthier category than spending money on, say, clothes—though wives, as Chaucer makes plain several times, did not agree. Books contained new learning and old wisdom, and were, Chaucer said in an apt phrase, "the key of remembrance." As objects they were worldly goods and worldly vanities, but their use was spiritual: unlike clothes, which symbolized status, or jewels, which had quasi-magical properties, books contained *truth*. "Truth," it was sometimes said, "by whomever spoken, comes from God," although in honesty one would have wanted to add that books afford pleasure too.

It is on account of this medieval (and Renaissance) notion about the truth in books that "plagiarism," as we have said before, was unknown to the Middle Ages. The idea of literary property and authors' rights came long after the printing press; in Chaucer's day an author was a steward of what could be learned or enjoyed. And, too, books were an uncharted ocean. For us, bibliographies and catalogues chart our course: we can find out pretty nearly all the books written on a subject, if we care to. But in Chaucer's day an intellectual might write a sound treatise on, say, the virtues and vices, and it might never be read or known outside the town in which he wrote it. No one knew how many treatises there were on such important subjects; if you found a good one known to few, you were doing a service to snatch it from oblivion, adapt it, improve it, combine it with another treatise—Chaucer's Parson's Tale combines two rather well-known works on just that subject. Hence two medieval works by two different authors may turn out both to be in large measure borrowed from a third, or one may in large measure be taken from the other. A work has to be identified by its incipit, the opening line of text, for titles were rarely standard or unique. It was good to know authors' names and read their books, but the books were common property and their texts were often inextricably intermingled.

As he accumulated books, Chaucer spent his spare time reading and thinking about them, and making abortive adaptations or translations of some. After his return from Italy he had a notion of something different he wanted to do in poetry, but for some years he could not get the hang of it. All that is left of this period are fragments and suspected early versions. For example, possibly about this time he began a work that he later referred to as "The Life of Saint Cecile," which was inserted into *The Canterbury Tales* as the Second Nun's Tale. It was a saint's legend, actually based on the *Acta Sanctorum*, about an early Christian martyr, a Roman noblewoman who gave her life and dedicated her chaste marriage to the propagation of the faith. It was most appropriate for the Second Nun, the Prioress's companion, who is never described, but originally it must have been written for a religious occasion (in the early 1380s an English prelate, Adam Easton, was made cardinal priest of the Church of Saint Cecilia in Rome) or for a religious person, and likely a woman —who but the Duchess Costanza? Perhaps some of the "tragedies" that turned up later in the Monk's Tale date from this period; one of them, as we've noted, celebrates Don Pedro of Castile. Some of the "legends" in *The Legend of Good Women* might have been written this early. Quite possibly, too, there was an early version of what was to be the Man of Law's Tale, that saga of a Roman emperor's daughter married to a foreigner and cruelly set adrift in alien lands. It would have moved the Duchess Costanza, the more so because the heroine is restored to her family in the end; perhaps it is no coincidence that the heroine's name is Constance, her dominant virtue *constantia*, steadfastness. One theory is that Chaucer wrote the Man of Law's Tale in the early 1380s to promote John of Gaunt's invasion of Castile. The story is based on the Anglo-Norman *Chronicle* of Nicholas Trivet, written forty years earlier; John Gower wrote a version of the same story in the 1380s.

These works, still essentially French in character, show an incipient Italian influence: the "Life of Saint Cecile" has an invocation drawn from Dante's *Divine Comedy*, and we will see Dante's influence in the *Complaint unto Pity*, the *Complaint to his Lady*, and *The House of Fame*. We will see, too, works that reflect Boccaccio's influence—the *Complaint of Mars*, for example, and the unfinished *Anelida and Arcite*, part of an experiment that would ultimately become the Knight's Tale.

"The King Is Dead, Long Live the King"

For Chaucer, this was a tranquil time; for England it was not. There were droughts in 1374 and 1375 and another outbreak of plague. Taxes were high, prices were up, foreign trade had dropped off. Popular discontent was reaching a fever pitch, and there were ugly tales abroad about Alice Perrers and others of the court. John of Gaunt, because he was the leader of the royal family in these years of Edward III's folly and the Black Prince's decline, became a scapegoat for everyone's unhappiness. Stories began to circulate that he had designs on the throne; that he was plotting against the rightful heir, his nephew Richard; that he had poisoned his first wife's sister for her inheritance; that he was really a changeling substituted at Ghent for a daughter of Queen Philippa.

Until the spring of 1375 Gaunt remained in retirement, though he came to London in October for the seventh anniversary commemoration of the death of the Duchess Blanche, the first he had been able to attend. The following March he went to Bruges for three months to negotiate peace with France: he had concluded that any continuation of the ongoing war would only keep him from the throne of Castile, and he was prepared to negotiate. The dukes of Anjou and Berry represented France; Gaunt, representing England, doggedly styled himself king of Castile,

though the French dukes, still allied with Enrique de Trastamare, declined with equal determination to recognize the title. Negotiations
dragged on, and a truce, not lasting peace, was the upshot. The duke went
again to Bruges the following October for some five months; this time the
Duchess Costanza accompanied him, and, upon her returning from a
pilgrimage to Saint Adrien de Grammont, gave birth to a son at Ghent,
inevitably named John and therefore, with typical medieval superfluity,
to be known as "John of Gaunt"; whose death in infancy may be reckoned
a convenience to historical writers. On March 12, 1376, the truce was
prolonged for another year. It began to be plain that peace with France
was only to be obtained through a royal marriage between one of the
French princesses and the heir presumptive, now age nine.

Just after Gaunt returned to England, on Monday, April 28, Parliament was convened for the first time since 1373. This was the famous
"Good Parliament," which came forth with such sweeping measures and
gave such virulent expression to the discontents of Edward III's last years.
The king himself was present at the ceremonial opening in the Painted
Chamber of the palace; thereafter Gaunt presided. The Commons, meeting in the chapter house of the abbey in a state of great agitation,
proceeded to draft 146 petitions that touched every conceivable griev-
ance. At the heart of all was taxation. They were of course being asked
to grant further taxes to support the war and keep the peace, and they
complained, with justice, that taxes granted before had been embezzled
or misspent. A committee of bishops and lords was chosen, with the king's
approval, to hear their complaints; chief among them was the complaint
that certain councillors and royal appointees were dipping into the king's
revenue. When John of Gaunt asked who these were, they named Lord
Latimer, the chamberlain, and Richard Lyons. What Chaucer may have
thought about these charges we would like to know, but we do not. He
had been appointed since the last barrage of such complaints in the
Parliament of 1373 and was never to anyone's knowledge the object of
subsequent ones, but in future years he referred more than once with
impatience to the "noise of people" in parliamentary sessions.

This session did in short order become noisy indeed. They demanded
the arrest of Richard Lyons. They demanded that Alice Perrers be banished from the court. They demanded the replacement of the king's
councillors. And to these demands Edward had no choice but to agree.
When Lord Latimer demanded to know who brought the charges against
him, the spokesman of the commons, Sir Peter de la Mare, declared that
he and all his fellow members did so, and there followed a trial—the first
instance of an impeachment. When Latimer was found guilty, a string of
others were disposed of in the same manner, among them Richard Lyons,

who went off to prison. In the end, only the wool subsidy was granted, and that only for three months and with the proviso that it go unrenewed for three years.

In the fall, after Parliament was dissolved, John of Gaunt took his revenge. He called a meeting of the Great Council at Westminster. It ruled that the Parliament just dissolved was not a true parliament and declared its acts null and void. William of Wykeham, the wealthy and influential bishop of Winchester, who had opposed the court party, was tried on charges of misconduct during his chancellorship ten years before, deprived of his temporalities, and banished from the court. Peter de la Mare was thrown into prison. Alice Perrers was permitted to return to court, and Lord Latimer was restored to his seat on the Council.

When Parliament met again in 1377, it was on the whole compliant. It petitioned for, and received, a pardon for those impeached—in fact received, in celebration of the king's jubilee, a pardon for all offenses civil and criminal. In return for this virtual bribe it voted a poll tax. Gaunt made an exception to the pardon in the case of his enemy, William of Wykeham; but the bishops rallied to Wykeham's support, voting a poll tax on clergy only after he was admitted to their convocation. When Gaunt still refused him a pardon, the bishops in retaliation brought charges against John Wyclif, Gaunt's protégé. Gaunt provided Wyclif with four ecclesiastical defenders, doctors of divinity, and attended the trial himself, with armed retainers; it turned into a free-for-all of insults and threats—Gaunt in a fit of temper muttered that he would drag the bishop of London out of Saint Paul's by the hair, and in the ensuing melee, a near riot by the furious London citizens, he and his followers fled for their lives to Kennington. There young Richard and his mother were staying, and on their account the mob forebore to pursue Gaunt's party; the Princess Joan did her best to act as intermediary. The Londoners rioted outside Gaunt's London palace, the Savoy, hung his arms upside down to signify treason, and chased those wearing his livery out of the streets. New rumors circulated about his illegitimacy. Gaunt demanded reprisals.

It could not have been a happy time for Philippa Chaucer, or for Geoffrey either. After huge labors of peacemaking, in February 1377, the king pardoned the Parliament and the next day dissolved it. Then, in what were to be the last months of his reign, he pardoned William of Wykeham and restored most of his temporalities—at the intercession of Alice Perrers.

During the session of the Good Parliament, the Black Prince died, on June 8, 1376. As he lay dying in his chambers at Westminster, he called his son Richard to his side and had him swear to respect all gifts he had made, exactly as his mother had done on her deathbed. Devoted especially to the Trinity, as others might be devoted to a particular saint, he contrived to die on Trinity Sunday at 3 P.M. While the bishop of Bangor was administering the last rites, an enemy of the prince, Sir Richard Stury—a friend of Chaucer's—entered the chamber; the prince flew into a rage on seeing him, and Stury slipped out. Yet his last words are supposed to have been, "of all mortal men who willingly or ignorantly I have offended, with all my heart I desire forgiveness."

His embalmed body lay in state in Westminster hall for four months. On September 30, both houses of Parliament joined the court at Westminster, and in full mourning followed the coffin, drawn by twelve black horses, through the London streets, past the Palace of the Savoy, past Saint Paul's, and across London Bridge; the prince's wish was to be buried at Canterbury, the shrine to which he had always had a special devotion. Chaucer was in London at the time and, as one of the royal esquires, would have joined the solemn march through Southwark and out the Old Kent Road along the route he was to have his Canterbury pilgrims follow. At the cathedral Prince Edward was buried not in the crypt, as he requested, but in a place of greater honor, behind the high altar near Saint Thomas's shrine. His effigy in gilded bronze, showing him with hands clasped in prayer, survived the Reformation, when Saint Thomas's shrine was destroyed; over his tomb were hung his shield, helm, jupon, scabbard, and gauntlets—probably those he had used in battle, for the helm has the marks of blows—and these ancient "honours," replaced by bright-colored replicas in 1956, may be seen there still, displayed separately in a glass case.

The prince in his last months had been at pains to assure his son's claim to the throne. The succession was not so clearly defined then as in modern times, and for a boy of ten to succeed posed problems. Parliament, at the Black Prince's urging, acknowledged Richard as successor, managing into the bargain to make it look as though the rumors of Gaunt's ambitions were true. But whatever Gaunt's secret desires, there is no evidence that he made any effort to secure the crown for himself. He saw to it that Richard was made Prince of Wales, duke of Cornwall, and earl of Chester; that he received Wykeham's seized property; that he was sent to preside over Parliament. The Black Prince had appointed his brother Gaunt one of his executors, and Gaunt now began to instruct his nephew in the arts of kingship. When it became plain that Edward III was dying, a deputation of Londoners begged the young prince's support, fearing reprisals from John of Gaunt.

Edward III died on June 21, 1377, a Sunday, in the palace at Sheen, in the fifty-first year of his reign. At once the deputation of Londoners went to Sheen, and Gaunt in their presence kneeled before Richard and begged him to pardon the London citizens, promising to do likewise. In the same spirit he let Richard take credit for a public reconciliation with William of Wykeham; and Peter de la Mare was pardoned and released. In April the king had managed to hold the Feast of the Garter at Windsor, on which occasion he knighted his grandson Richard, his own youngest son Thomas of Woodstock, the "son of Dame Alice Perrers," and some others, among them Gaunt's son by the Duchess Blanche, Henry of Bolingbroke, then eleven. He had made his will the previous autumn, naming John of Gaunt his executor; Alice Perrers, already rich enough, was not named. On his deathbed he talked to Dame Alice of hunting and hawking, as if he would recover, but was confessed and given the last rites; his last gift to her was the same as his first, two tuns of Gascony wine. When he died, it was later charged, she stripped the rings from his fingers, though in charity one must assume she took or was given a keepsake. She was not admitted to his funeral. He was laid to rest two weeks later in Westminster Abbey, beside his queen, in the chapel of Saint Edward the Confessor, and there he lies still beneath the great sculptured tomb.

The ten-year-old Richard was crowned on July 16, a Thursday rather than the traditional Sunday. Richard did, just before his coronation, fulfill his promise to visit the pardoned citizens of Chaucer's native city, and the Londoners received him in jubilation. The day was chosen by John of Gaunt, steward of England, because it was "the morrow of the translation of Saint Swithun"; Swithun had been tutor to King Egbert's son Ethelwulf, who later rewarded him with the see of Winchester. Dressed in a white robe embroidered with gold (the white symbolized his innocent youth) Richard rode from the Tower down Fleet Street on a white horse, the duke of Lancaster, as steward of England, heading the procession alongside Henry Percy, the marshal. From the palace to the Abbey, John of Gaunt walked beside the king, bearing the great sword "Curtana"; before him went his other uncles and the earl of March, behind him the archbishop of Canterbury. Trumpets blared, fountains ran with wine, houses were hung with cloth of gold and silver and bright colors; a scarlet cloth laid down by the king's almoner covered the path they walked. There was a castle made of stiffened canvas with towers and a belfry, with maidens throwing gold coins to the king and an angel holding a gold crown, gesturing to him. About the young monarch marched the great barons and bishops of the realm, all of them dressed in white, each performing some traditional coronation service, each one's right having been decided in the court of claims, held the week before by John of Gaunt, high seneschal of England.

In the abbey, the king, on a scaffold so all could see, took the coronation oath, to keep the faith and the laws, do justice and have mercy. Each step in the long coronation was punctuated with anthems, psalms, and prayers. He was led to the high altar, where *Veni creator spiritus* was sung, the king kneeling. The archbishop of Canterbury then blessed and anointed him, and he was invested, one by one, with the tunic of Saint Edward, the sword, the bracelet, the robe, the spurs. The crown was placed upon his head, the coronation ring upon his finger, at last the scepter given into his hand. Then he was led to the throne to hear the coronation mass. Certain changes in the ceremony underscored his royal power. The archbishop asked the people if they gave consent after he had taken the oath, not before; and the peers' touching of the crown after the coronation was publicly explained as an agreement to aid the king. At length there was the dramatic appearance of the king's champion, mounted and in full armor, to answer challengers.

The protracted ceremony, tiring enough for an adult, left the boy exhausted. He was carried on the shoulders of his tutor, Sir Simon Burley, home to the palace to rest. On the way he lost one of the ritual coronation slippers of Edward the Confessor, sewn with floral designs of jewels and pearls, which were too large for him; some reckoned the loss an ill omen. Later, before the banquet, he created four new earls and nine knights in a gesture intended to glorify the monarchy and look in hope to the future. During the long banquet that followed, the *coronne à manger*, the crown the king wore at meals, too heavy for him to support, was held above his head.

Secret Missions: Lombardy, 1378

During Richard's minority the realm was governed by an unofficial regency—no actual regency was declared—whose chief movers were John of Gaunt and the king's mother, Joan of Kent. The truce with France was about to expire, and the government was at once taken up with efforts to provide funds for a war or, what would have better suited Gaunt's ambitions in Castile, to renew the truce or make a permanent peace. The best way to peace was a royal marriage with a French princess, and for the next several years this goal was pursued with vigor by numerous emissaries, among them Geoffrey Chaucer.

Two days before Christmas in 1376, Chaucer had gone abroad on secret business in the company of Sir John Burley—brother of Sir Simon Burley, the king's tutor—with funds sufficient for a short trip, but the records give no hint of a destination. Possibly they were sent to Bruges, where ongoing negotiations for a treaty with France were being held

(John of Gaunt was there at the time), or to France on related business touching a marriage between Richard and the Princess Marie, daughter of the king of France. The following February, 1377, Chaucer was sent to Flanders with Sir Thomas Percy—a figure of some importance, at that time admiral of the north, later made the earl of Worcester—then on to Paris and Montreuil, returning March 25. Two weeks later he was paid for "divers voyages," and since records are sparse for this term there were probably more than the two recorded. On the last day of April he was ordered back to France; on May 10, in a document again mentioning his frequent trips overseas, a deputy was appointed to carry out his duties at the Customs. A later document indicates he was in France for fourteen days and back by June 26, five days after Edward III's death.* Froissart says that among his companions on this mission were Sir Guichard d'Angle and Sir Richard Stury, that Enguerrand de Coucy was among the French ambassadors, and that a marriage with the Princess Marie was discussed.

Since these negotiations dealt with peace between England and France, the king's marriage was a related issue. Chaucer made one other trip, early in 1378, treating for a marriage between the king and "a daughter of his adversary of France." Three later missions (1378–1380) made by various dignitaries, great lords and prelates, treated for peace with France via a marriage alliance; no records indicate that Chaucer was connected with any of these, though they could have been among his "divers voyages."

It took four years of diplomacy before a royal marriage was arranged, and there were exasperating setbacks. But its importance was enormous. The Black Prince, the king's father, back in England's heyday, had not married until thirty and then married for love, but no such impractical course was open to King Richard, whose marriage could bring peace to England or, failing that, secure it a great ally. Negotiations with France, begun in 1376 for the hand of the Princess Marie, then five years old, faltered upon the question of England's controlling a dozen cities in Aquitaine, and the disarming of Calais. Then in 1377, as a treaty was about to be ratified, the Princess Marie died suddenly. In the following year negotiations were resumed for a marriage with her younger sister, Princess Isabel, but Isabel died in February and the French king's one remaining daughter, a tiny infant born that very year, became the object of negotiations.

*That Chaucer was not listed among those receiving mourning attire for Edward III's funeral suggests he was not in England at the time. Froissart says that on Edward's death the ports were blocked to keep the news from reaching France until the succession was assured; so one cannot assume Chaucer rushed back on hearing news of the king's death.

The Great Schism brought these talks to a halt. Two popes, one in Avignon and the other in Rome, claimed the triple crown; the French declared their support of Clement VII in Avignon, the English supported Urban VI in Rome, and Anglo-French relations were broken off.

The papacy had moved to Avignon in 1309. Shortly before that, in a political struggle between the pope and the king of France, the French had actually conducted an assault on the pope, Boniface VIII. A few years later, one other pope intervening, the French managed the election of a French pope, Clement V; claiming that he feared Italian reprisals, he never went to Rome, establishing instead the papal court at Avignon that became such a center of simony and graft and luxury, which Petrarch and others found so loathsome. The following six popes were all French, but the last of them, Gregory XI, became persuaded, in part at the urging of Saint Catherine of Siena, that reform of the church could only be accomplished if the papacy returned to the see of Saint Peter, and this Gregory had the courage to do early in 1376. He died in March 1378.

Pope Gregory's chosen successor, Urban VI, was a Roman. He appeared before the Roman populace, who acclaimed him ecstatically and then, according to the peculiar custom of the time, rushed off to sack his palace. Pope Urban, crowned on Easter Sunday, proceeded to pack the curia by creating twenty-six Italian cardinals. In response, the cardinals who had elected him, most of them French, set up an antipope, Clement VII, which left the nations of Europe and the Italian city-states to take sides. Possibly the English saw such a division in the offing, for just after the coronation of Urban VI a commission was sent to Milan to treat with "the lord of Milan, Bernabò," and with Sir John Hawkwood, about "certain affairs touching the expedition of the king's war." They probably wanted to win Visconti support for a Roman pope against French rivals and thus foster an international alliance against France. The mission was sent in two groups, a group of ten men headed by Sir Edward Berkeley and another of six headed by Geoffrey Chaucer. The negotiations involved a possible alliance with the Visconti through a marriage, and an effort to obtain Hawkwood's services.

On May 16 Chaucer appointed a deputy to handle his affairs in the Customs, Richard Barrett, a colleague who had been in the Customs fourteen years. The memorandum, as mentioned earlier, is a pointed, one-sentence statement, sometimes thought to be written in Chaucer's own hand. He had already received letters of protection, and in the following week appointed two attorneys to act on his behalf in his absence. This was a necessary precaution: when you went abroad, a lawsuit could be brought against you and you could lose it by default. One of those receiving Chaucer's power of attorney was Richard Forester, an esquire of the king's chamber who, records show, received from the king numerous grants of money and land. Unless there was more than one Richard Forester, he was a professional attorney, who took over the tenancy at Aldgate when Chaucer left it. Chaucer's other attorney was his friend John Gower, the poet; Gower, the year before, had moved into the priory of Saint Mary Overeys across the Thames in Southwark and was living there in semiretirement—he was about forty-six, and had still not started writing in English.

Chaucer's party and Sir Edward Berkeley's left London on the same day, May 28, and probably traveled together. Sir Edward was a knight of the king's chamber, an older man—he died just a few years later—and of greater standing than Chaucer, as we may judge from his title and larger daily stipend. Since 1376 he had been appointed to various commissions treating for peace with France, once with John of Gaunt; King Richard while still Prince of Wales had granted him £50 a year, very likely at Gaunt's urging. He and Chaucer were appointed as companions and their mission was the same, to treat with Bernabò Visconti and Sir John Hawkwood on matters touching the war. Whether the appointment of two separate parties was simply a matter of status or accounting, or whether it suggests there were certain secret matters one or the other was to be concerned with, no one knows. But as we shall see, a marriage alliance between King Richard and Bernabò's daughter Caterina was to be explored.

Milan in the fourteenth century was a showcase of Visconti grandeur, perhaps the wealthiest capital in Europe. Standing walled in Lombardy's fertile plains, it looked to the west upon the foothills of the maritime Alps, through which two passes made it accessible as a center of trade. Wool, armor, agriculture were its principal industries. In population it was as large as, perhaps larger than, Florence. It was said in the previous century to have 6,000 fountains, 150 hostels for visitors, 300 public ovens (private ones were forbidden, to prevent fires), 10 hospitals; there were 10,000 monks, 1,500 notaries, 150 surgeons and 28 doctors, 70 private teachers, 40 copiers of manuscripts, and, to its glory, 8 professors of grammar. By Chaucer's time it had gained, among moralists, a reputation for decadence: men wore tight clothes like Spaniards, women curled their hair and bared their breasts, the numerous whores were taxed (the proceeds helped maintain the city wall), men and women alike dressed up in silk, cloth of gold, and pearls. Under the Visconti there were sumptuary laws forbidding such extravagances, possibly enforced with more success than elsewhere; the historian Sachetti described the Visconti policemen chasing women up and down the streets to inspect their attire.

Dominating the city, at gates on either end of it, were the palaces of Bernabò and Galeazzo. Bernabò's was larger, more ostentatious and vulgar, much more a seat of political power and military strength, but no less handsomely appointed. Galeazzo's palace of brick, the stolid edifice now called the Castello Sforzesco, with walls twelve feet thick and great interior courtyards, was more a center of culture and refinement. In the ten years since Chaucer had been in Lombardy for Lionel's wedding, Bernabò Visconti had gained ascendancy over his brother Galeazzo. He was the more politically inclined and the more ruthless; Galeazzo was an invalid, suffering from a family illness, gout. Galeazzo's daughter Violante, wife for three months to Prince Lionel, was now twenty-three; the year before, after nine years of widowhood, she had been married to the fifteen-year-old marquis of Monferrat, Secondotto, already notorious for having driven away the "gentlemen, counselors, and servants of his father" and taken up with dissolute companions. Rapes and murders were charged against him, and there were wild stories about his fits of rage. At the time of his marriage, he had fallen into a quarrel with his regent over the city Asti, a town in his possession that had somehow escaped annexation by the Visconti. Violante's brother, Gian-Galeazzo, came to his new brother-in-law's aid, and Secondotto in a flush of adolescent gratitude made him governor of the town. Meanwhile, the marquis's cousin Amadeus of Savoy, the "Green Count," demanded payment for his past military and financial aid unless (he said) the young marquis would leave off his vices. Thus things stood while Chaucer was in Milan. Having seen Violante ten years earlier married and widowed in a season, he could hardly have failed to observe the ill omens of her second marriage. The following autumn, when the English party was back home, the matter of Secondotto's supposed debt to the Green Count was put to Gian-Galeazzo as arbitrator; with characteristic treachery he took the Green Count's side, in fact made a treaty with him, permitting the count to annex properties belonging to Secondotto and helping himself to Asti. The marquis, seeing he had been tricked, flew into a rage, rode off to Milan hoping to gain Bernabò Visconti's aid, and on his way was murdered, "stabbed through," as Stow put it, by "a base horsekeeper"—or, what seems much more likely, dispatched on orders from Gian-Galeazzo.

Treachery and violence were quite literally the Visconti emblem. Their ensign they appropriated from the city of Milan itself when it was a free commune: a serpent—symbolizing the city's patron saint, Ambrose —standing upright in seven ascending coils. They made it more dragon or viper than serpent, and placed in its mouth the figure of a man being devoured feet first, his arms outstretched in horror.

Yet the brothers Visconti, united though they were in tyranny, were markedly different in character. Bernabò, with whom Chaucer and Berkeley were to have their dealings, was warlike and obsessed with power, an open enemy of the papacy, famous for tantrums of rage during which only his wife Regina could approach him. He was a clever man, said to be "learned in the Decretals," that is, in canon law. In his education and frame of mind, he was a product of medieval traditions and ideas, in some measure of the "Old Humanism." Justice was his passion. But in pursuit of it he shook his fist at religious and moral values: ferocious, vengeful, and pathologically cruel, he was given also to rapacious lust. He had by his own reckoning thirty bastards in Milan; his house was compared by a contemporary to the seraglio of a sultan. It was he who had made the Vatican emissaries eat the papal bull they brought, both parchment and seals. It was he who told the archbishop of Milan, when he came with a complaint, "Don't you know, fool, that I am pope and emperor and lord in all my lands and neither the emperor nor even God himself can, in these my territories, do that which I do not wish to be done." And it was he whom Chaucer called "god of delite and scourge of Lombardie."

Bernabò had the year before allied himself with the English mercenary Sir John Hawkwood by marrying him to one of his illegitimate daughters, the child of his favorite mistress, Donnina Porro, daughter of a Milanese nobleman. Hawkwood kept up surprisingly good relations with his father-in-law even while as a professional soldier he waged war against him from time to time. He was about sixty years old when Chaucer met him. Born in Essex, he was the younger son of a good family, who took up arms, and, it appears, fought at Crécy and Poitiers; after the Treaty of Brétigny, in the early 1360s, as England's glory was fading, he joined one of the companies of English mercenaries that were forming in France. By 1361 he was fighting in Italy against the Visconti, in a battle financed by the pope. From this time dates his private army, known as the White Company, with its banners, flags, and vests of white and its formidable gleaming armor (polished with the bone marrow of goats); he was chosen its captain-general in 1364. The company had a large following of women, including some nuns carried off by force. In time it had headquarters in several estates given to Hawkwood by the pope.

Hawkwood fought for various Italian cities, notably Florence, and for the papacy. His distinction was in part based on scrupulous loyalty, a transmuted sort of chivalry: when he had entered into a contract he fought with unswerving devotion and, unlike other mercenaries, would never take a bribe. He was hardheaded, humorless, and driven. He is supposed to have cried at two friars who wished him peace, "Is not begging your profession and is not war mine? If you wish me peace how shall I live? So I say—God take away your alms." He was one of the great military figures of the age, in part because he brought to Italy the English

technology of war: the longbow, dismounted cavalry, and what he called
the "lance," a mounted team of knight, squire, and page wielding lances.
His English soldiers, accustomed to cold weather and able to fight in
winter, seemed to the Italians almost superhuman. They were described
as "warm, eager, and practiced in rapine and slaughter," having "little
care for their personal safety but in matters of discipline very obedient to
their commanders." Hawkwood always remained a loyal subject to the
king of England, and it must say something that the king, in the very
documents sending Chaucer and Berkeley to talk with him, called him
"our dear and loyal John Hawkwood."

When Chaucer and Berkeley arrived in Milan, Hawkwood was with
his army at Monzambano, near Mantua, about seventy-five miles to the
east. He came up to Milan during the second week of July, about two
weeks after Chaucer's arrival, and didn't return until August 5. He was
probably in Milan most of this time.

While Chaucer was in Milan, on August 4, Galeazzo Visconti died.
His court was in Pavia, some twenty miles south, in the imposing palace
completed three years before his daughter had married Prince Lionel.
Though overshadowed by his brother, Galeazzo left a more enduring mark
on the Visconti empire: while Bernabò had conducted himself on the
model of the ancient or medieval tyrant, Galeazzo was a despot of a
different mold, closer to a Renaissance prince. He was a patron of the arts,
a collector of books, the founder of the great Visconti libraries. It was he
who had been Petrarch's patron for eight years, between 1353 and 1361;
and Petrarch after his departure from Milan returned to spend each
summer with Galeazzo at Pavia. Chided by Boccaccio for playing courtier
to a monster (he called him Polyphemus), Petrarch replied that he only
lived on the Visconti's land, not in their house. But while this was true,
Petrarch was Galeazzo's literary adviser and his friend, and through him
Galeazzo met the scholars and poets that came to visit the laureate. He
imbibed from him the spirit of the New Humanism and passed that spirit
on to his son Gian-Galeazzo. To the extent that he could, at least when
it came to collecting books, he passed it on as well to his brother Bernabò.

Galeazzo had built at Pavia a second, larger palace, its walls a hundred feet high, its towers fifty feet higher, where Petrarch spent his
summers and to which Galeazzo moved his remarkable library. Pavia
indeed became the cultural center of the Milanese empire; once the great
palace was completed, 1365, Galeazzo deserted Milan for the ancient and
enormously more pleasant city on the banks of the river Ticino. Like
Florence and San Gimignano, Pavia was dominated by "towers of nobility," some hundred fifty of them, useless and decaying, that had been built
by noble families in previous centuries as refuges from civil strife. Chaucer

had seen the palace at Pavia in 1368, with Lionel's party, and would have heard of the famous library, assembled under Petrarch's tutelage. He might have been expected to go out of courtesy, or have gone to visit Lionel's grave, or to attend Galeazzo's funeral. An inventory of the library has survived; the library itself was seized by the king of France at the end of the next century, and about a hundred of its 988 volumes exist today in the Bibliothèque Nationale at Paris. It is estimated that Galeazzo himself had owned about four hundred volumes, among them various Italian works, some of which Chaucer might not have been able to see elsewhere. The library had a collection of "Troy books," mostly in French. It had Dante's *Divine Comedy* and his *De Monarchia*. It had nine works by Petrarch. It had seven works by Boccaccio, among them the *Filostrato*, the *Decameron*, the *De Genealogie Deorum Gentilium*, *De Claris Mulieribus*, and *De Casibus Virorum Illustrium*—all but one of the works Chaucer is thought to have known.

Even if Chaucer never saw the library at Pavia, he surely saw during these six weeks Bernabò's library at Milan. When Bernabò was seized by Gian-Galeazzo in 1385, there were riots: the Milanese sacked Bernabò's palace and then set it on fire, destroying the records of his government and the library. Not a trace of it remained. We know there was a library in the palace containing the books of his predecessor, the Archbishop Giovanni, books chained to the shelves with silver chains, along with "many other authors and volumes." We can suppose that these included classical and Italian literary works, augmented with the collaboration of Galeazzo and, at least indirectly, of Petrarch. If there were works by Petrarch and Boccaccio that Chaucer hadn't seen yet or didn't own, he may have read them or gotten copies here—for it was his last time in Italy. "Chaucer," writes an expert, "may not have obtained the bulk of his Italian material until he went to Lombardy, and . . . the Visconti may have owned the very manuscripts in question." Some of these could have been works he already knew or knew about: what Chaucer had learned of Italian letters five years earlier in Florence gave him a sense of what to look for in the Visconti libraries. It is sometimes argued that because the Boccaccio manuscripts in Milan do not identify the author, Chaucer must by sheer coincidence have picked several works all by Boccaccio; but the Visconti librarians would have been able to identify the author.

But would the tyrant of Milan have permitted the English emissary to browse through his library and copy as he pleased? Yes, and in fact there is reason to believe he would have encouraged it. Ostentation was as deeply part of Bernabò's nature as greed or lust or cruelty. He was renowned for hospitality and gifts. If the young Englishman liked books, the library would have been opened to him. There was, according to one record, a *cancellaria*, a chancery, in the palace, where copies could be made. And there was a family tradition of generosity in such matters: in the next century the library at Pavia was open to visitors and it happily made copies for them if they wished—a remarkable fact in an age when books were guarded as precious objects. It may be in one of the Visconti libraries that Chaucer made a copy of that sonnet by Petrarch, "S'amor non è," which appears in *Troilus and Criseyde*, and a copy of the Griselda story—Petrarch's version of it is contained in his letters, and there were volumes of Petrarch's letters in Pavia. The works of Albertano of Brescia —four copies, in Latin and French—were there, and may have been where Chaucer found the *Melibee*. It is quite possible that Bernabò's munificence produced for Master Geoffrey a gift of copied works, works he wished to possess, such as Boccaccio's *Il Teseida* and *Il Filostrato*. Their influence on him dates, as we shall see shortly, from the years immediately following the Milan journey.

And it may be that such a gift and such hospitality colored Chaucer's memory of Bernabò, so that when he heard the news of his death seven years later, it grieved him. In 1385, Gian-Galeazzo, known as "the Count of Virtue," took control of the Milanese empire by having his uncle Bernabò seized while pretending to visit him on his way to a shrine. Bernabò languished in prison with Donnina, Sir John Hawkwood's mother-in-law, but Hawkwood failed to rescue him: he had already sworn homage to Gian-Galeazzo for a thousand florins. True, Chaucer refers (in *The Legend of Good Women*, lines 374–375) to "tyrants of Lombardie / That han no reward but at [i.e., through] tyrannie." But when Chaucer called Bernabò Visconti "god of delite and scourge of Lombardie," he was not necessarily calling him a tyrant. "Delite" meant delight or pleasure in a neutral sense—a "god of delight" might be devoted to the pleasure of others, whence generous. And "scourge" meant an instrument of punishment—not necessarily a tyrant, quite possibly an instrument of chastisement or reform. The phrase is ambiguous, the context impartial, detached. Chaucer says—or has the Monk say—that he will tell of great Bernabò's misfortune, and proceeds to accuse his nephew. Gian-Galeazzo, Violante's older brother, was five years younger than Chaucer, and he was present both times Chaucer was in Lombardy; Chaucer had an impression of him. Of Bernabò's death he wrote:

> Thy brother's son, that was thy double ally,
> For he thy nephew was and son-in-lawe,
> Within his prison made thee to die.

—adding only that he knew neither how nor why.

The diplomatic outcome of the negotiations with Hawkwood was slight, perhaps nil. We know only that the following December, just before Christmas, two friars, one an Englishman, arrived with messages from Hawkwood; they were rewarded rather meanly with ten marks to the one and five to the other—and Hawkwood remained in Italy until his death in 1394. He never fought for England. He had been exhorted twenty years before by Saint Catherine of Siena to turn from "being a servant and soldier of the devil" and go to Jerusalem to fight the infidel, which he courteously promised to do. But he went on fighting for various Italian cities (he fought for Florence against Gian-Galeazzo), planning to keep his promise to Saint Catherine of Siena and then return to England. In his seventies, he retired to a quiet life in Florence, where in gratitude for his services the Florentines gave him a pension, built him a marble tomb in the Santa Reparata, and bought up his property to finance his return to England. He died before setting out. He was given a state funeral, the Signoria providing a hundred large wax torches along with banners and shields. His corpse was robed in cloth of gold and the remains were sent, at his request, back to England to his king. His portrait in the Duomo at Florence may still be seen.

The marriage negotiations were more promising. Two Milanese ambassadors returned with the party, bearing to King Richard the offer of a marriage with Caterina Visconti and a staggering dowry. Then in December, a few weeks before Hawkwood's messengers had delivered their message, two messengers from Bernabò arrived in London and were grandly rewarded by the king with 200 marks in gold and two silver-gilt cups. It is clear they bore good news. Chaucer's mission was, in this respect, a success. The following March, 1379, King Richard appointed a royal commission to treat with Milanese ambassadors for a "marriage contract between our person and the lady Catherine, daughter of the great and powerful Lord Barnabo, lord of Milan."

8

The House
of Fame

In the early years at Aldgate, Chaucer wrote his most puzzling poem, *The House of Fame*. He worked on it, so it is generally believed, for several years, revising it often and, for whatever reasons, leaving it incomplete. It was his first comic poem, and like all comic masterpieces it has a profoundly serious dimension.

The House of Fame reveals an element of struggle—over the poet's hopes and goals, over certain literary ideas and models, and, it appears, over discontents in his personal life. Chaucer was in his early thirties when he started it; at thirty-five he reached, by medieval reckoning, the middle of life's journey. He had a future in the royal household, a wife and family, a better than modest income. Yet he may have found his choices limited and his future without challenge. Seen as a personal document, *The House of Fame* was the by-product of such a period of settling down.

The House of Fame was written after Chaucer returned from Florence and received the controllership (the job is mentioned at lines 652–660), after the summer of 1374. And since it concerns the announcement of a royal marriage, it very likely dates from the period starting in 1376 when he was serving on commissions to negotiate a marriage for King

Richard. As we will see, 1379 is the best guess for the date when Chaucer finished or abandoned it.

The Plan

The House of Fame grew in layers, each embodying an idea that could have produced a separate poem. What came first, the skeleton of the poem, was a medieval dream vision in the French manner intended to announce and celebrate a piece of news significant at court. The festive tone suggests news of a marriage, and the poem does resemble—and is in large part based on—Froissart's *Le Temple d'Onnour,* which celebrates the coming wedding of an unidentified couple.* It begins in the usual roundabout way with an invocation—"God turn us every dream to good!" —and a short meditation on the kinds and meanings of dreams. The poet says he will tell us a dream he had on the tenth day of December, mentioning the date twice. Giving a date was conventional in courtly poetry, but something significant *did* happen on December 10, 1379.

In the dream, the dreamer finds himself in a temple made of glass, Venus's temple, and he sees on a wall, written on a "table of brass," Virgil's story of Dido and Aeneas. As he reads Virgil's words—"I will now singen, if I can, / The armes and also the man"—they become moving images. But it is not Virgil's story of Aeneas's mission as founder of Rome; it is Ovid's love story, in which sympathy lies with the forsaken Dido. Chaucer chose this initial story of an ill-fated love as a mirror image (like that of Ceys and Alcione in *The Book of the Duchess*) of the propitious royal match to be announced. On its completion, the dreamer is snatched up by an eagle and brought into the sky to the House of Fame. He watches the goddess Fame holding court, bestowing good and bad fame on various petitioners, and is then carried off to a nearby House of Rumor from which come the "tidings" fame is made of. He hears a noise in a corner where people are telling "love-tidings," sees a great crowd running up, and sees a man who seemed to be "a man of greet auctoritee." There the poem breaks off. Evidently the man of great authority was to announce the news the audience was anticipating. Or, rather, *suggest* it: when a court poet presents news already known at court, he *hints.* That is what Froissart had

*Another opinion holds that *The House of Fame* treats in a satiric way some piece of court gossip, about Chaucer himself or some prominent person like John of Gaunt, in order to discredit it. But no such rumor is evident, and no source supports the idea as Froissart's poem supports the celebration of a royal marriage. It is true that during this period John of Gaunt was unpopular and his enemies were clicking their tongues over his supposed indiscretions, and the foolishness and inconsequentiality of such loose talk may constitute a running theme in the poem.

done, and it is beyond a doubt the effect Chaucer was aiming for in the ending.

He began the poem hoping to present it at court when negotiations for one of the French princesses or Caterina Visconti had come to a successful close; but the "tidings" it was to celebrate failed to materialize. The nature of these tidings is clearly indicated. The talkative eagle explains that Jove has taken pity on Chaucer, whom he condescendingly calls "Geffrey," because he has long served Jove's nephew Cupid, as well as Venus, without reward; he's done his best ("though there's very little in your head") to make books, songs, and *dites* praising Love's art—in which, the eagle adds, the poet takes no part himself. Jove has learned that he "has no tidings of Love's folk" to write about, neither news "from a far country" nor even gossip from the neighbors and when he finishes his work, instead of rest and "new things," he goes home to his house and sits "as dumb as any stone" in front of another book. So Jove has arranged for him to hear tidings, both true and false, of every conceivable kind—new loves commenced and old loves won, accidental loves, loves renewed or exchanged, merriment, fuss, jealousies, gossip, deceptions. Later, in Fame's palace, the poet is asked by a stranger why he is there, and he answers (at line 1886) haltingly,

Some newe tidings for to lere°,	*learn*
Some newe thinges, I n'ot what	
—Tidings, other° this or that,	*either*
Of love, or suche thinges glad.	

The stranger asks him, "Well, then, what are these tidings that you bring here, that you've heard?"* The implication is that the poet has come to hear news he already knows or knows about. And in fact he says this just at the end, as the tidings are about to be announced: he is there (line 2134)

. . . a tiding for to heare,
That I had heard of some countree
That shall not now be told for me—
For it no need is, redely;
Folk can sing it bet than I.

The reference fits perfectly Chaucer's circumstances as a member of a marriage commission. What he knows from a far country is to be announced now at home, and there's no need for him to tell it because others can, and will, tell it better. Then comes the uncompleted ending:

*Lines 1907–1909, which may have been meant to read "What are these tidings *that bring you here,* that you've heard?"

Atte last I saw a man,
Which that I nevene° nat ne can,   *name*
But he seemed for to be
A man of great auctoritee. . . .

In future years Chaucer named the poem among his works, calling it *The House of Fame* in the Prologue to *The Legend of Good Women* and "the book of Fame" in the Retraction; so he saw it, finished or not, as a poem that deserved to be known—and *was* known. He calls the third book, which is almost as long as the first two combined, "this littel laste book," and it does lead up to an ending. Most scholars now agree that there are perhaps just a few lines missing at the end, a single speech or short exchange.* Some think it was meant to end the way it does as a joke on the court, a sort of shaggy-dog story.

But it's possible that Chaucer did finish the poem and the ending got detached.† For instance, in later years he might have wanted to replace the dated courtly ending with a more ambitious one, better suited to the poem's religious and philosophical implications and to its character as an inquiry into the nature of literature, but he never got around to it. The remaining puzzle, the "man of greet auctoritee," has invited some dozen or two guesses. One writer, thinking the poem a religious allegory, identifies the man of great authority as Christ; another, thinking it a "Boethian" vision, identifies him as Boethius—strange figures to be showing up in a whirling house of twigs where men are yelling and stomping! A critic who sees in the ending the germ of *The Canterbury Tales* identifies him as a harbinger of Harry Bailly, the host on the Canterbury

*An older opinion was that the poem as it stands was a prologue, meant to introduce a collection of tales (the "tidings" he is to hear), and was abandoned in favor of *The Canterbury Tales*.

†No manuscripts of Chaucer's poems date from his own day; all are fifteenth-century copies. There are twenty of the *Troilus* and over eighty of *The Canterbury Tales*, but there are only three of *The House of Fame* (plus Caxton's and Thynne's printed versions), and their terrible condition suggests that the poem wasn't widely circulated during Chaucer's lifetime: it was a court poem written for a single occasion and then forgotten. As an intellectual *jeu d'esprit* it interested other poets and some of Chaucer's intellectual friends, who may have made makeshift private copies. Such a copy, with a page missing at the end, might have been the prototype of the two most nearly complete copies, which go as far as the "man of great authority." The manuscript, now lost, from which Caxton printed his version, had sixty-four more lines missing at the end, and the other surviving manuscript had 315 more lines missing, even stopping in midsentence. All these versions have dropped lines and gross errors; they must have been made from corrupted and mutilated old copies. Some *did* have pages missing at the end; and the fifteenth-century copyists of the two most complete manuscripts left blank pages in case an ending came to light—one left two, the other six. Caxton made up twelve lines to round out his version, carefully indicating that they were his own and adding "I find no more of this work toforesaid." This disclaimer got detached in later printings and his twelve lines were thought to be Chaucer's until the nineteenth century.

pilgrimage. Boccaccio, the God of Love, and the poet in the abstract as authority have all been suggested. Yet obviously he was meant to be anonymous, like the other figures who address the poet. The narrator says he is "a man, / Which that I nevene nat ne can"—a man "whom I can't name," or "whom I don't know," and we have to take him at his word: if he had been going to turn about and identify him, he would have said, in the past tense, "whom I *didn't* know."

What apparently happened was that Chaucer began a characteristic dream vision announcing a royal marriage. The king for whom he was writing was a child not yet twelve, and he had the sound instinct to appeal to a boy of that age with humorous figures (a schoolmasterly eagle), fantasy (a flight in the sky), and curiosities (an explanation of how sound travels). But in this fantastical material he found a way to explore topics that were on his mind, and fame or reputation was one of these. In Froissart—and in Dante too—he had found the equivalent of the phrase "new things," which translates into modern English as "news" and into Middle English as "tidings." He saw that such news was the stuff of reputation, and this reminded him of Ovid's passage on a "house" of Rumor (*Metamorphoses* 12: 39–59, given here in Rolfe Humphries's translation):

> There is a place
> At the world's center, triple boundary
> Of land and sky and sea. From here all things,
> No matter what, are visible; every word
> Comes to these hollow ears. Here Rumor dwells,
> Her palace high upon the mountain-summit,
> With countless entrances, thousands on thousands,
> And never a door to close them. Day and night
> The halls stand open, and the bronze re-echoes,
> Repeats all words, redoubles every murmur.
> There is no quiet, no silence anywhere,
> No uproar either, only the subdued
> Murmur of little voices, like the murmur
> Of sea-waves heard far-off, or the last rumble
> Of thunder dying in the cloud. The halls
> Are filled with presences that shift and wander,
> Rumors in thousands, lies and truth together,
> Confused, confusing. Some fill idle ears
> With stories, others go far-off to tell
> What they have heard, and every story grows,
> And each new teller adds to what he hears.

Miniature of Chaucer reciting Troilus to the court

London at the time of Chaucer's death

Edwardus iij
R̄ qynqꝰ

¶ Anno dn̄i m̄o CCC xxxij xxo
ffebrua̅ fuit coronatꝰ Edwarde iijꝰ qm̄ e
ꝓgen e̅ iuxta q̅ ꝰ ad wytꝰ temulꝰ
ꝓ... nutus

A̅fter him regned his son ful ryȝt
The prudde Edward ꝑat doughti knyȝt
C onrys he HARꝶ well here.
T hat to him were bothe lese + dere.
fꝰt ꝑe kynge ꝶid A Ꝫiete maystrey.
Atte Sclure he breuuid A Ꝫrete stede.
Atte Sꝛesse ye ffuuȝht ꝑere a ȝayn.
The kinȝ of Beme ꝑer was sleyne.
And ye kinȝ of ffrunce put to flyȝt
So lenȝer ꝑan durst he ffoȝe.

A Sege at Salice he les bi fore.
T hat lested Alkelle mounethe and more.
And as he thens wuld ȝo.
he wanne Salice And rollme mo.
At the bataille of ꝑeitohe bi ordenaunce
was take ꝑn the kinȝ off ffrince.
At Westmestre he lioth ꝑere.
he regnid alle most ffy ȝere.
All for him Veꝶ ꝓrince edwarꝶ
Whiche had A son that ȝete Richard.

Edward III

The marriage of Edward III and Philippa of Hainault

Knights jousting

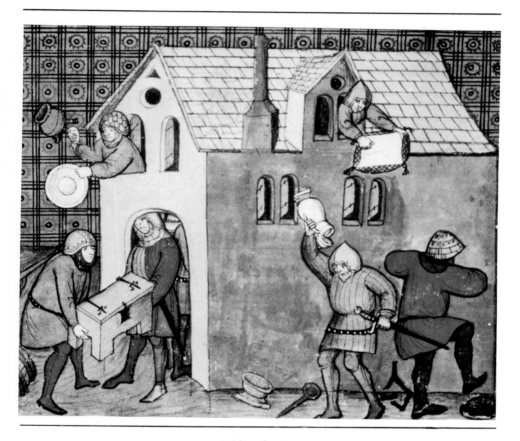

Soldiers looting:
the Hundred Years War

Patient and doctors during the Black Plague

Top: *Man warming feet* Bottom: *Man in stocks*

Top: *Butchers preparing meat*   Bottom: *Breadmaking*

Tavern

*The Peasants Revolt: Two of the leaders, John Ball on horseback,
Watt Tylers on the left, identified by names on their coats*

*The Peasants Revolt: Richard II, right, speaking to the peasants, and,
at left, the murder of Watt Tyler by the Lord Mayor of London*

*Edward III, Richard II,
and Henry IV*

"Then longen folk to goon on pilgrimages. . ."

In Virgil he found a similar figure, Fame (*Aeneid* 4: 182–191, given here in the translation of Robert Fitzgerald):

> Pinioned, with
> An eye beneath for every body feather,
> And, strange to say, as many tongues and buzzing
> Mouths as eyes, as many pricked-up ears,
> By night she flies between the earth and heaven
> Shrieking through darkness, and she never turns
> Her eye-lids down to sleep. By day she broods,
> On the alert, on rooftops or on towers,
> Bringing great cities fear, harping on lies
> And slander evenhandedly with truth.

The passage occurs in the story of Dido and Aeneas—which was probably how Chaucer came to use that story as an introduction. Fame, according to the ancients, was the reward of poets—it was, like the "glory" of medieval warriors, a measure of immortality on earth. Chaucer had encountered in Italy the humanists' fascination with that reward, and we must assume it was on his mind. Poets could, moreover, *confer* fame: the claim was a tradition of courtly poetry, holding out a promise to a patron or prospective patron. Judging from the evidence of the poem, he must have had at least a glance at Petrarch's *Triumph of Fame*, possibly in the early version where Fame triumphs over Death, and a glance at Boccaccio's description of the triumph of glory in the *Amorosa Visione*. He might have seen Petrarch's very funny dialogue between Joy and Reason in *De Remediis Utriusque Fortune* where Joy doggedly insists on writing to have fame in the teeth of Reason's admonishments. Fame was the theme for the last day of the *Decameron* and the moral of *Il Teseida*, and it was the Italians' pet obsession. Rather than have his dreamer go to a temple of Honor, as Froissart's dreamer did, Chaucer decided to have him go straight to a temple or palace of Fame, and it must have crossed his mind, with amusement, that a journey into the realm of Fame would be like Dante's journey made in Virgil's company.

Dante

When Chaucer had to get his dreamer out of Venus's temple and into the palace of Fame, he remembered the place in Dante, at the beginning of *Purgatorio*, Canto 9, where in a dream an eagle snatches the poet up from a wasteland "as far as the fiery sphere." With that in mind, Chaucer had his dreamer go outside the temple to see where he was and there find himself in a wasteland "withouten town, or house, or tree," like the desert of Libya, he says, sacred to Venus and Jove. There (line 496) he looks to the heavens with devotion:

Tho° was I ware, lo! at the laste,	*then*
That faste by the sun, as hye°	*high*
As kenne might I° with mine eye,	*As I could see*
Me thought I saw an eagle sore°,	*soar*
But that it seemed muche more°	*larger*
Than I had any eagle seen.	
But this as sooth as death, certain,	
It was of gold, and shone so bright	
That never saw men such a sight,	
But if° the heaven had y-wonne	*unless*
All new of gold another sunne.	
So shone the eagle's feathers brighte,	
And somewhat downward gan it lighte.	

The astonishing lines, virtually translated from Dante, do successfully capture the solemnity and dignity of the *Divine Comedy*, and its sense of wonder. "Had Chaucer been able to sustain this note, he would have been a different poet," writes John Fisher, adding "But we prefer to have him Chaucer, as he evidently preferred to be."

Turning the page, we find the beginning of Book 2 and the language becomes colloquial:

Now herkeneth, every manner man
That English understande can . . .

After a short proem invoking Venus (and another Dantean echo, "Thought, that wrote all that I mette"), we witness a scene that would have delighted a young boy: the eagle snatches the poor fleeing poet up and begins a long, tedious lecture with a command that sounded in Middle English exactly like an eagle's cry: "Awake!" The fact that the heavenly creature borrowed from Dante turns out to be a *funny* eagle, who talks "in manne's voice" and whose first word is a squawk, has made some observers believe that the passage, indeed the whole poem, is a parody of *The Divine Comedy*. Chaucer says the voice is the same as that of someone he could name, though it speaks in a "goodly" way that wasn't usual, and some assume this voice is a reference to Chaucer's wife. Gower's biographer believes the eagle is a parody of Gower. Everyone senses satire or parody here, but of what?*

*It's an appealing fantasy of some Chaucerians that Chaucer may himself have been a wonderful mimic. The eagle's voice, "the same voice as somebody I could name," may,

Whatever else may be parodied, there is a substratum of reference to the *Divine Comedy*. It is going much too far to say that because the poem is in three books it is itself a parody of the *Comedy*. After all, Froissart's *Le Temple d'Onnour*, the closest model of the poem, is in three parts too, as is Petrarch's *Triumph of Fame*. The parody is centered in the solemn, speaking eagle that Chaucer took from Dante and made a compulsive talker and a pedant. Eagles in medieval lore were noble birds —as birds of prey, they were the knights of the bird world, and they were said to be the kings of the air. It was thought they could gaze at the sun direct without blinking, that they could soar out of human sight and still see fish in the sea, so that their clear vision symbolized contemplation and philosophy, and might also symbolize rhetoric. Moreover, golden eagles might be seen in churches as lecterns holding up the Scriptures—they symbolized Saint John the Evangelist and stood for gospel truth. All this symbolism may have been in Dante's mind and was understood (and used elsewhere) by Chaucer. The Chaucerian touch was to make this elevated medieval figure funny. Where Dante's guide was Virgil, Chaucer's is a garrulous eagle. Where Virgil always speaks to Dante in tones of earnest instruction and high-minded respect, as to an equal, the eagle speaks to Chaucer as to an intellectual inferior. And where Virgil spoke pointedly, the eagle is a stuffy bore.

The greatest compliment we can pay a writer, so the maxim goes, is to parody him. And there are places in Chaucer, as in the *Troilus*, where he was influenced by Dante as a pupil by a master. Dante's *Comedy* is one of those ultimate and pivotal works that come at the end of an era; it was the literary triumph of the Old Humanism, written in the last years before it fell out of fashion, rather as Milton's *Paradise Lost* was written in the last years of Renaissance humanism. Chaucer saw that this was not the right time to emulate Dante's achievement; he was instead to emulate Dante's admirer, Boccaccio. He saw too that it was not in his temperament to write in Dante's manner—though at the end of the *Troilus* he achieved this, however briefly and in whatever different context to whatever different end. This side of Chaucer's response to Dante is not a statement about Dante at all; it is a statement about himself.

The other side of his response to Dante does reveal impatience. Chaucer sets out to explore the realm of earthly pseudoimmortality, fame and reputation, which he then discovers is based on gossip and half the time on lies. Chaucer puts his finger on something that has seemed

as he performed the poem, have been identifiable as the voice, say, of one of the king's tutors, like Sir Simon Burley—something that would have overjoyed the young king and set the court upon a roar.

unappealing to many: Dante would have his reader believe that in a vision, with a companion who happens to have been the greatest poet of ancient Rome, he perceived the ultimate truth of the universal order. He thus put himself in God's place, passing out eternal punishments to his contemporaries, not omitting to pay off certain personal debts. One can imagine Chaucer reading the *Divine Comedy* patiently over several years, without the glossaries we have to help us and a running Who's Who of medieval Europe at the bottom of the page, and we can imagine his awe turning to amusement sometimes, and sometimes to distaste. There is an incredible arrogance in Dante that we are schooled to overlook; but a reader of Chaucer's day, a Christian reader but a stranger to Florentine history and politics, might have looked up from the page now and again and thought wryly, "Judge not lest ye be judged."

Aside from this religious or moral objection to Dante's poetical undertaking, Chaucer could have had a philosophical objection. Medieval poetry was expected to convey the truth. It contained *scientia,* knowledge. Chaucer said that out of old books comes "all this newe science that men lere," that books were the "key of remembrance." Poems, it was understood, might show the truth under the figure of an imaginary world; a reader could find truth in a poem without accepting the poet's truth claim as fact. But Dante's claim strained this suspension of disbelief; God's judgments are known only to God—they are "forbidden knowledge." A reader of Chaucer's day could have reacted to Dante's claim with what we call skepticism, for there was in the air in Chaucer's time a current of philosophical thought termed nominalism that is akin to skepticism. It held that the "platonic ideas" or universals did not have a separate existence; we know a horse when we see one only because we have a cumulative experience of horses, and the "idea" of a horse is only a name for such an accumulation. Later skepticism answered the question, What do I know? by saying (as Montaigne did), I know only what I experience in myself, or (as nominalism and the scientific method did), only what I see or observe. Chaucer's answer was more characteristically medieval: I know only what I hear or read.

So Chaucer's trip into the other world of reputation or fame, in search of tidings, becomes a search for linguistic units—for language before it is written down, that is, for speeches. To this search the eagle's lecture addresses itself. He has been sent by Jove to bring "Geffrey" to the House of Fame, where he can learn tidings of love, and he explains (in a passage borrowed from Ovid) that all *sounds* pass to that house, which stands between heaven, earth, and sea. He then explains (line 729) the medieval doctrine of "Kindely Inclining," the equivalent of our law of gravity. To the medieval mind, all things had an inborn propensity to move up or down, a sort of homing instinct: what was light went up, what was heavy down. The eagle points out with relentless logic that speech is sound, that sound is "broken air," and that air, being light, goes up. He claims to prove this "by experience," and uses an analogy with the waves observed in water when a stone is dropped (this seemingly modern theory of sound waves came from Boethius's *De Musica*). The eagle then, with much repetition, draws the logical conclusion: every speech moves naturally up to the house of Fame.

And now the narrator, being hurtled through the sky, looks down and sees the earth below him, an aerial view of the kind Chaucer would have remembered from crossing the Alps or the Pyrenees, the eagle all the time instructing him in astronomy. At last (line 1027) they come to Fame's palace:

> . . . full of tidinges,
> Both of fair speech and chidinges,
> And of false and sooth compounded.

There is a great sound, a rumbling, like the beating of the sea against hollow rocks or the last reverberations of thunder.* The narrator is let down to take his chances in "Fame's place" and is told at last that every speech, when it comes here, bears the likeness of the creature who spoke it:

> When any speech y-comen is
> Up to the paleyce, anon-right
> It waxeth like the same wight°   *creature*
> Which that the word in erthe spake.

Chaucer playfully rationalized this world in the sky with medieval theories about the physics of motion and sound. The authoritative tone of Dante's guide, Virgil, is replaced with this droll fantasy, and Dante's solemn credulity is replaced too. Where Dante presented himself as a receptacle of divine truth, Chaucer presents himself as dubious, recalcitrant, indifferent. The eagle has said (line 699) he will bring him to Fame's house where he can hear all possible love tidings—can he believe this? No, Geffrey replies, it isn't possible. After his logical demonstration, the eagle has asked if he has not proved his point simply, without difficult language or matter; yes, Geffrey replies, and the eagle boasts (lines 865 ff.) that he can speak simply to a simple man—

*The detail comes out of Ovid, *Metamorphoses* 12: 53, quoted above (p. 236).

> Aha! . . . lo, so I can
> Lewedly to a lewed man
> Speke, and shew him swiche skilles
> That he may shake hem by the billes

—can show him arguments so palpable that he can shake them *by their beaks*! "How do you like my conclusion?"

"A good argument," Geffrey answers, "and probably right."

Later, flying through the sky, the eagle asks if he wants to learn something about the stars.

"No, certainly not."

"Why?"

"Because I'm too old to learn."

"Otherwise I'd have told you the names of the stars and the signs of the heavens," he says.

"It doesn't matter."

"Oh yes it does, by God. You know why? Because when you read poetry you read how the gods could turn birds, fish, and beasts into stars . . . but you don't know where they are."

"It doesn't matter," replies Geffrey, "I don't need to. So help me God, I believe what they say, those who write about this subject, as if I knew the places themselves. Besides, the stars shine so bright, it might hurt my eyesight to look at them."

"That may well be," says the eagle.

How much all this has to do with Dante remains a puzzle. Lydgate, a century later, said Chaucer "wrote also, full many a day agone / Dante in English, himself so doth express." Because he mentions other poems but not *The House of Fame,* this is often thought a reference to it. Kittredge, early in our century, called it a maddening phrase. Lydgate may have meant it as a general compliment, or had the ending of *Troilus* in mind. But *The House of Fame* is the one place in Chaucer's writings where he speaks of Dante as a poetical mentor. And it is the first time he did what he would do later many times: make fun of something he admired.

Fame and Rumor

In Latin, as in Middle English, "fame" meant both reputation and report. Chaucer probably set out to have Fame—who sifts the tidings that come from Rumor and bestows on each a "name" and a "duration" (line 2110) —make an allusive pronouncement about the king's marriage. Later, when the news changed or failed to materialize, he decided to have the pronouncement come from the less reliable but more fundamental source, and added or put at the end the fantastical description of the House of Rumor. But Fame remains central. The story of Dido and Aeneas told at the beginning of the poem makes two essential points, that fame can be based on false reports, and that it is not necessarily bestowed with justice. Aeneas, false and traitorous, goes down in history as a hero; but Dido, though she is true and forsaken, goes down in shame (line 345):

> O, wellaway that I was born!
> For through you is my name lorn°,   *lost*
> And all mine actes read and songe
> Over all this land, on every tonge.
> O wikke Fame! for there n'is
> Nothing so swift, lo, as she is.
> . . . .
> Eke, though I might duren° ever,   *live*
> That° I have done, recover I never,   *what*
> That I ne shall be said, allas,
> Y-shamed be through Eneas. . . .

The remainder of the poem, following the procedure of medieval rhetoric, is an *amplificatio* of this fundamental idea.

As we have seen, the medieval dream vision was structured so that each element prepared for the next. Chaucer began the poem with an account of the kinds of dreams that can and cannot be interpreted.* In a rather intellectual and private kind of joke, he calls Book 1 a "sweven" (Latin *insomnium*, line 79, the meaningless dream that repeats waking experience) as if to suggest it merely refers to what he had been reading. He calls Book 2 an "avisioun" (Latin *visio*, line 513, a vision of the future seen but not understood). The implication is that Book 3, with its "man of great authority," was to be an "oracle" (Latin *oraculum*), a meaningful dream in which a venerable figure gives advice or reveals the future.

This oracle would be the court news that the poem was to announce. Petrarch in later years added two more poems to *The Triumph of Fame*, adopting the characteristic medieval view that fame is among the world's vanities and in the end vulnerable to time and eternity. Chaucer had in mind the worldly, humanistic idea of fame; but what he gives us is a *skeptical*, and sometimes comical, view of that humanist idea, essentially a Christian view of it, not unlike Petrarch's later view.

Seen this way, *The House of Fame* belongs not to French but to

*The lines are based on a famous passage in Macrobius: they offer six categories arranged in three pairs, one of each pair having meaning, the other not.

Italian and Latin traditions, exemplified by Petrarch's *Secretum*, which was known as a treatise "de contemptu mundi." Chaucer's poem is, if there can be such a thing, a comical work on contempt of the world. The typical treatise on contempt of the world was encyclopedic; it tried to catalogue the world's vanities and show how everything we pin our hopes on—physical pleasures, or riches, or knowledge, or renown—will disappoint us in the end. Chaucer's poem narrows its focus upon one of those vanities, renown. It explores it in extravagant detail, as works on contempt of the world often did, for they *wallowed* in what is loathsome or unsatisfying about human experience. (Lothario dei Segni warned, of the man who is raised to greatness, that "at once his cares grow heavy, his worries mount up, he eats less and cannot sleep. . . . His strength is diminished, he loses weight." One wonders if he found it so a year or two later when he was raised to the papacy as Pope Innocent III.) The extravagant and bloated descriptions of worldly vanities in such writings brush up against the medieval carnival spirit—the Feast of Fools and other folk customs that parodied the church, the "goliardic" poems that mocked Christian rites and celebrated fleshly pleasure. This other side of medieval culture, which mocked official culture and celebrated worldly life, has a preponderant place in *The Canterbury Tales*. It was in large measure graveyard humor, like the grim overblown drawings of the Dance of Death with their taunting, wry captions—"Come, fat bishop. . . ." It was the tradition of medieval writing that would, at the close of the Middle Ages, come to fruition in Rabelais.

The description of Fame's palace typifies this spirit of extravagant comedy. It is a collage of conceptions, phrases, and images that Chaucer had culled from his reading, from the art of his day, and from observations made in his travels. A "house" or temple appeared in the two dream visions that served as his models, Froissart's *Temple d'Onnour* and Nicole de Margival's *La Panthère d'Amour* ("Love's Panther," a poem bearing many similarities to Chaucer's poem).* Chaucer has his palace built on a mountain of ice that looks like glass—a detail conceivably inspired by the passage in the *Roman de la Rose* where Fortune's gifts are said to be "like glass in their fragility." His substitution of Fame for Fortune, as we've said, was inspired by Italian humanism and probably by Petrarch's *Trionfi*, from which he may also have taken the image of the sun melting the ice.

The resulting allegory, for all its borrowings, is unique and wondrous. The castle stands on a mountain whose rock looks like glass but is then discovered to be ice. The dreamer thinks to himself that it is "a feeble

---

*These include a three-part structure surprisingly like his and a temple of Fortune. There were further details of a temple of Fortune in Alain de Lille's *Anticlaudianus*).

fundament" to build on. He sees engraved on one side the names of famous people, the letters melting away so that they cannot be read—"so unfamous was wox hir fame" (line 1146). On the other side—the north side, away from the sun—he sees

> How it was written full of names
> Of folks that hadden greate fames
> Of olde time, and yet they were
> As fresh as men had written hem here
> The selfe day. . . .

The image implies that the sun, passing like time, *melts* names as it does snow or ice. The characteristic medieval treatment of fame insisted that reputation, like all worldly things, *melts*: "Trust rather," says one widely known Latin poem of the Middle Ages, "in letters written in ice / Than in the frail world's vanities. . . ." But Chaucer introduces a distinction made in Petrarch's *Trionfi*: some ancient names are protected from time and mutability by poets and historians. But their reputations are given capriciously, the Goddess Fame being, as we learn, the sister of Fortune (line 1547).

The description of the castle introduces a further distinction, between writers and performers. On the outside are niches containing statues of minstrels and storytellers. This is the realm of oral and visual art, performed art: among its personages are musicians and what we may call illusionists, who appeal respectively to the ear and eye. Of musicians there are harpists like Orpheus and Orion, and others in a list that includes a Briton, the Welsh bard Glascurion, with smaller harpists sitting under them and imitating them "like an ape, or as art imitates nature" (the image distinguishes inspired from derivative or merely imitative performance), Dutch pipers playing dance tunes, and trumpeters playing war music.

In another group are jugglers, magicians, sleight-of-hand artists, witches, sorceresses. Chaucer had a fascination with such illusionists who can cast a spell as if by magic, and such figures show up in later works like the Squire's Tale or the Franklin's Tale; some of his greatest characters—like Pandarus or the Pardoner—seem to possess such powers through sheer glibness. He concludes his list with another British exemplar, a contemporary, "Colle," a sleight-of-hand artist who did in fact exist, and whom he sees perform a remarkable trick, a symbol of what artists do: he places a windmill under a walnut shell. The windmill stands for the cosmos, the walnut shell for the brain. The feat is precisely the magic that exists in literature: the author encompasses the world within the mind.

Fame's palace, on the outside of which these figures are carved, is made of beryl (a stone having the property of magnifying things) and embellished with gold. The interior walls are plated half a foot thick with gold and set with jewels, and on a throne made of a single carbuncle sits the goddess herself; like the goddess in Book 4 of Virgil's *Aeneid*, she grows from the height of a cubit until her head touches heaven, she has as many eyes as a bird has feathers, as many ears and tongues as a beast has hairs, has wings on her feet, and bears on her shoulders men of the very greatest fame, like Alexander and Hercules. From her dais to the door stretch two rows of metal pillars: each is of a metal sacred to some appropriate pagan god or goddess, and atop them are figures (statues, one assumes they are, though this is never said) of poets and writers, who bear on their shoulders the fame of past civilizations: that of the Jews is held up by Josephus, that of Thebes by Statius, that of Troy by Homer and others, including "English Gaufride"—Geoffrey of Monmouth. Last come "the Latin poet Virgil" and "Venus's clerk, Ovid," Lucan, Claudian, and other poets that bear the fame of ancient Rome. The hall has grown a thousand times larger and we see more writers than there is time to name, telling stories that would be "a full confus mattere" to hear. The point is that fame is given to individual poets only insofar as they belonged to a civilization, yet it is they who preserve the historical tradition of that civilization.

At the heart of this vision of Fame's palace is a passage of some 350 lines (lines 1520 ff.) describing a procession of petitioners who come to Fame's throne in groups, crying "Largess, largess!" The petitioners are granted good or bad fame or none at all. When the goddess decides each case, the god of wind, Eolus, bestows fame with a trumpet of gold called "Clear Laud" or one of black brass called "Slander." The black trumpet is said to be uglier than the Devil himself, its sound bursting like a ball from a cannon with black and colored smoke billowing ever larger and stinking like the very pit of hell. The sound of the golden trumpet smells, by contrast, like pots of balm among baskets of roses!

The first three groups to approach Fame have done good works and ask for good fame in recompense. To the first the goddess flatly refuses any fame at all. To the second she gives *bad* fame. To the third she gives good fame—in fact, she says, better than what they deserve.

The fourth and fifth groups have done good works too but say they care nothing about reputation. She coldly grants the one request—"Let your works be dead"—but turns on the other group in outrage, cries "Are you mad?" and gives them *good* fame.

The remaining groups are similarly paired. There are idle men whose deeds amounted to nothing and for whom women had only indifference, but they ask to go down in history as men whom women loved madly and who were worthy, wise, good, rich, and happy in love. She grants their request, almost with enthusiasm. When the next group asks the exact same boon, she delivers an angry tirade and refuses them.

The last pair are two groups of traitorous and wicked men. The first want good fame in spite of their deeds, and she turns them down: "although there's no justice in me, it doesn't *please* me to do this." The second want the bad fame they deserve, and she grants their request: "Gladly," she says, "Eolus, do you hear what they ask?" This last group alone contains an identifiable personage: its spokesman is that very "shrew" (blackguard) named Herostratus who set fire to the temple of Diana at Ephesus in 356 B.C. for no other reason than to go down in history; the incident is mentioned by Plutarch and Cicero, among others. Chaucer played him false by saying he burned the temple of Isis at Athens, the wrong temple and the wrong city—a wry example, though perhaps unintentional, of what can happen to anyone's fame.

This madcap scene gives the impression that it covers all possible contingencies, but it doesn't. No wicked men win good fame as Aeneas did, and the idle are not indifferent to fame as one might expect, but the implication is that anything is possible. The goddess admits there is no justice in her, then rages against those who think they needn't be deserving. Her replies are comically shrewish: she takes a leering, sadistic tone —"Wit ye what?" she begins, as she is about to give good men bad fame —and denies requests with sneering barbs like, "Go your way," "Fie on you." To the idle, who ask an undeserved good name, she delivers (line 1776) indignant insults:

> Ye masty° swine, ye idel wretches,   *lazy*
> Full of rotten slowe teches°,   *sluggish flaws*
> What? false theves!

She is like one of the queens in *Alice*, flaunting her inconsistency but expecting those who court her to *believe* she operates by just deserts— a picture of adult postures as children see them. At an intellectual level, the comic picture is at base the medieval argument that fame, like all worldly vanities, is untrustworthy and disappointing.

And now someone standing at the dreamer's back addresses him, in a kindly way, as it seems to him, and asks, "Friend, what is your name? Are you come here to have fame?"

"Nay, forsooth, friend," answers Geffrey, and goes on to say that he desires no fame, is satisfied if people leave his name alone, knows best himself how he stands.

"But what dost thou here?"

Geffrey answers, "Some newe tidings for to leere"—in a bumbling way, as if puzzled:

"I n'ot what,
Tidings, other this or that,
Of love, or suche thinges glad. . . ."

He who brought me here, he says, told me I'd see and hear wondrous things in this place, but *these* aren't the kind of tidings I have in mind.
     "No?"

No, he replies, because I always knew that some desired fame and praise and reputation, but I never knew how or where Fame dwelled or what she looked like or anything of her state or the manner of her judgments until I came here.

The man asks what tidings he's heard, then backtracks: "But never mind. I see what you want to hear. Come along, I'll lead you to another place where you'll hear many a one."

They go out of the castle, and Geffrey sees a structure even more outlandish than Fame's palace: the House of Rumor. It stands in a valley beneath the palace. It is constructed of twigs or wicker, like a basket, and is whirling about "as swift as thought." It emits so much noise that even if it stood on the River Oise it could be heard in Rome (a genuine memory trace, for he had crossed the River Oise twenty years before with the English army and here compares its sound with that of a stone hurled from a catapult during a siege). He declares that the *Domus Dedali,* called Labyrinth, was not so wonderfully made: in the Middle Ages, Daedalus was considered the archetypal builder or architect, and the labyrinth, called "the House of Daedalus," was a symbol of building, designing, or creating. There were, in certain Gothic cathedrals in France and Italy, and perhaps in England, mosaics inlaid on walls or pavements showing a maze, a circular maze that one traces about in many convoluted turnings (but with no blind alleys or wrong choices, as in modern mazes) until one arrives in the center. The center was sometimes labeled *ciel* or *Jérusalem,* the designs themselves were called *Dédales* or *chemins de Jérusalem* and one inscription says the labyrinth stands for "this world."* This whirling wicker structure, sixty miles long and shaped like a cage, has thousands of holes in its roof, and its numerous doors are left open day and night to let sound pass in and out. It is full of whisperings and janglings about every conceivable subject—Chaucer gives forty examples—and is built to

*It is thought the pavement labyrinths may have been used as symbolical pilgrimages, along which penitents crawled on their knees, and some architects put their names at the center to signify that they created the building as God created the world.

last as long as it pleases Aventure (Chance), who we learn is the "mother of tidings."

Now the eagle appears again, calmly perched on a stone, and reminds Geffrey that Jove has promised him "uncouth sightes and tidinges." Picking him up with his claws he flies through a window and deposits him inside—whereupon, says Geffrey, in a vivid experience of relativity, the house stopped moving.

And now he finds himself in a great crowd of people constantly whispering to each other, "Do you know what happened?" and all swearing what they say is true. Each hears a tiding, tells it to another but adds something to it, and so each tiding passes from mouth to mouth and increases like fire from a spark until it burns a city. These tidings pass every which way until each arrives at a window or a crevice in the wicker. Sometimes a false and a true one collide, so that neither can get out until they join forces and leave "compounded" as a single tiding. From the House of Rumor they proceed to the House of Fame, where their survival is decided by the senseless process we have already witnessed.

In the House of Rumor, Geffrey sees especially shipmen, pilgrims, and pardoners (line 2121). Pilgrims were notorious liars and exaggerators, as were sailors and pardoners, so it's not surprising to find the thought here; the passage is of particular interest because it may represent the earliest germ of *The Canterbury Tales*. At this point he observes in a corner of the hall, where men are telling love tidings, a crowd running up, crying "What thing is that," "I don't know," falling over each other, casting up their eyes and noses, treading and stomping on each other's heels—and he sees a man whose name he doesn't know but who seems to be a man of great authority.

"Tidings"

The conception of "tidings," the raw stuff of reputation and of history, is the heart of the poem. Chaucer put the House of Rumor last because it is a figure for the world. In it the things of the world become *reports*: Chaucer's fantastical image is of a giant whirling wicker basket full of crevices and doors from which tidings—the linguistic leavings of events, compounded of truth and falsehood—escape. When they reach Fame's house, if they do, they take on the image of the person who uttered them.

The houses of Fame and Rumor are not the physical locus of sound and speech where words are matched with things—though that is what the eagle says—but the *mental* world in which words are matched with thought. Chaucer is quite explicit about this. The place he flies to with his eagle is his own mind; his vision is a mental landscape. The idea is introduced in the proems or prologues that begin Books 2 and 3—both based rather loosely on lines from Dante. At the beginning of Book 2 (line 523) he represents thought as a writer and dreams as writings stored in his brain:

> O Thought, that wrote all that I mette°,   *dreamed*
> And in the tresory it shette°   *shut*
> Of my brain, now shall men see
> If any virtue in thee be. . . .

Flying through the air, he reminds himself (line 973) of Boethius's words:

> . . . A thought may flee so hye,
> With feathers of Philosophye,
> To passen everych element.

At the beginning of Book 3 (line 1102) he calls upon "divine virtue" to

>   . . . shewe now
> That° in mine head y-marked is—   *what*
> Lo, that is for to meanen this,
> The House of Fame for to descrive.

Later, he says the House of Rumor turns "as swift as thought" (line 1924). Where Dante had described the eternal realm that exists apart from the world, Chaucer describes a realm of thought that exists apart from but *in* the world.

And what he wishes to reveal of this interior realm has to do with the art of poetry. At the beginning of Book 3, in a proem inspired by the invocation to the *Paradiso,* he asks Apollo, god of knowledge and light, to guide him, adding to the passage (at line 1094) a notion not in Dante: "Not that I wilne for maistrye / Here art poetical be shewed"—not that I wish poetic art to be revealed here to display my skill in it—but "that I do no diligence / To shewe craft, but o sentence," that I don't show off my craft or artistry, but only show "sentence," meaning. And if he succeeds in showing what "in mine heed y-marked is," he will go like Dante "Unto the nexte laure I see, / And kiss it"—the laurel being symbolic of poetry or literature (the two were synonymous in medieval thought).

He wants, then, to examine the nature of literature. Because tidings are the link between present experience and future knowledge, the stuff of reputation and tradition, they are the stuff of literature. Chaucer associates them with "newe thinges" that one can hear, gossip or news. The phrase "newe thinges," which he found in Dante and Froissart, happens to have been the closest one could come in Middle English to a translation of Italian *novelle* (our word "news" didn't exist in Middle English). The term meant the kind of stories Boccaccio was writing in the *Decameron*, stories about things that happened. Chaucer apparently fancied that the *novelle* he encountered in Italy represented a first step in the making of literature, the step in which reported events are retold and preserved in writing.

Setting out to allegorize Fame, Chaucer hit upon the notion that literature exists in a tradition and is of a piece with hearsay—the legal term for evidence passed by word of mouth. His image of the names on the sunny side of the mountain melting into oblivion seems to allow that an entire cultural tradition can pass away and leave not a trace behind. But the image of the poets holding up the reputations of former civilizations suggests that, while all things will pass away in the end, what is celebrated in poetry and preserved in books will endure longest. What will endure less long is celebrated by the minstrels and "gestiours" on the outside of Fame's house, the merely oral performers.

The House of Fame is a humorous court poem written for a boy king about his impending marriage, but Chaucer tinkered with it until his own concerns began to appear in it. He was asking himself what literature is made of because he was looking for something out of which to make a literary work, and these concerns came into the fabric of the poem until they became in some manner a theory of literature. But in the end he adopted the pessimistic or "Boethian" view that finding something to write about and having one's writings endure are matters of chance.

There is chance, he thought, in poetic invention and poetic tradition. Following the rhetorician Geoffrey of Vinsauf, he held that conceiving a poem was like planning to build a house: the artist does not begin in a helter-skelter way but must (as Chaucer translated the phrase in the *Troilus*) "send his herte's line out from withinne, / Aldirfirst his purpose for to winne." Geoffrey of Vinsauf had in mind a builder's plumb line; Chaucer had in mind something closer to a fisherman's line, for he has the poet "send out" his line and "get" or "catch" (*winne*) his purpose, suggesting that the outcome depends on luck or accident. This is implied in *The House of Fame*. Works of literature are made of a common basic stuff, tidings; they survive as the works of the authors or poets (the surviving anonymous work is overlooked), and those authors or poets survive alongside others in a tradition. A literary or poetic tradition is at base a grab bag of tidings preserved by writers and given a direction by

Fame, the sister of Fortune. The tidings needn't be true or the direction just, for literary works happen by Aventure, and Aventure, we are told, is the mother of tidings.

What all this seems to say is defensive and pessimistic. Chaucer was looking for something to write about, but he felt he must wait as a passive recipient for the right tidings—a gloomy thought for a young poet to have.

The Record of a Personal Crisis

The House of Fame presents not a coherent, developed view of poetry's place in history, but the feelings and instincts, and the whirlwind fantasy, of a literary genius whose head was full of new ideas. Yet the poem may be the greatest poetical statement in the English language about the nature of poetic influence and poetic tradition. It affords, moreover, a surprising glimpse into a poet's inner world of thought. There is nothing like it before in English literature, probably nothing like it again until Milton's time or after. Chaucer's contemporary, Petrarch, comes closest to such a self-revelation in his letters, by sheer volume. With Chaucer, the glimpse is a lucky accident.

The House of Fame is ambitious, convoluted, searching—and confused. Two generations ago the estimable Danish scholar, Aage Brusendorff, called it "the most personal of all Chaucer's poems"; a recent and no less estimable English critic, A. C. Spearing, finds in it "the occasionally uneasy working out of a personal problem." The reader senses beneath the humor in *The House of Fame* an inner discontent, a lack of purpose or direction. The poet of love is without anything to write about, takes no part in Love's affairs, even *hears* nothing about them. Chaucer had now been married some thirteen years, had a home, had children, had means; yet his wife, in the duchess Costanza's service, was often away, and he, alone, lives, he says, like a hermit ("though mine abstinence is lite") in the comfortable apartment over Aldgate, where he could write something of worth if he but knew what.

Fame, the poet's reward, is on his mind. When the eagle swoops him up, at line 584, he cries out,

> O God! . . . that madest kinde°,   *nature*
> Shall I none other wayes die?
> Whe'r° Joves woll me stellifye   *whether*
> Or what thing may this signifye?

It is a ludicrous conceit, that Jove may turn the young poet into a star before he's written anything to speak of. And the humor of it is exploited:

he modestly objects that he isn't Enoch or Elijah, or Romulus or Gany-
mede, or any of those that were borne up directly into heaven. The eagle
archly disabuses him:

> Thou deemest° of thyself amiss.   *judge*
> For Joves is not thereabout—
> I dare well put thee out of doute—
> To make of thee as yet a sterre

—Jove isn't about to make a star of him *as yet.* The reader may sense a
touch of comic hope, or if you prefer of self-deprecating humor, in that
"as yet." Where the hopeful love poet ought by rights to be all eagerness
for the trip into the realm of Love's tidings, Geffrey is indifferent, hesitant, uninterested. He is too old to learn. It isn't important. And when
at last in Fame's house a kindly stranger asks him, "Friend, what is your
name? Are you come here to have fame?" (line 1071) the poet answers,
with emphatic oaths, that he is there for no such purpose:

> "Nay, forsooth, friend," quod I,
> "I came not hither, grant mercy,
> For no such cause, by my head!
> Sufficeth me, as I were dead,
> That no wight have my name in honde°.   *meddle with my name*
> I wot° myself best how I stonde.   *know*
> For what I drye°, or what I thinke,   *experience*
> I will myselven all it drinke,
> Certain, for the more part,
> As far forth as I can mine art."

Does the reader sense in this speech a kind of calm resolution, a
comfortable self-awareness, a secure sense of himself and his limitations?
Perhaps. He is *not* come to have fame, it is enough that no one meddle
with his reputation, for he knows best how he stands. Whatever happens,
he will *drink* it all—*as far as he knows his art.* "Drink it all"? Commentators believe he had in mind a proverb, "He who brews bad ale must drink
less well," and so means that he is prepared to take the consequences. But
note the qualification: "for the more part." That qualification isn't just
a filler chosen for the rhyme (no problem finding rhymes for "art"); it
must mean that he is prepared to take most *but not all* of the consequences. What we sense beneath any calm resolution here is ambivalence,
doubleness. If he knows his art he can hope that *some* of the consequences
will be favorable. "Drink it all" seems to mean taking the *unfavorable*
consequences: Chaucer several times uses the idiom "to drink woe,"
"drink distress," and such, but a cheery connotation ("drink joy") was

possible. Beneath these lines we discern a struggle within himself against discouragement or frustration: his ambition to gain recognition for his writings apparently has been thwarted in certain ways, and he has had to face a period when he was living like a hermit, in the eagle's words "as dumb as any stone," which may have meant "depressed."

What might he have been depressed about? Just taking the data of the poem itself—as a basis for divining things his intimates mightn't have guessed or he himself been fully conscious of—we can see a hint of loneliness and isolation. He had acquaintances at court, men and women he had known in some cases since adolescence, and he had had good preferments from the old king that had been continued by the new one. He had been redeployed in a way most favorable to a writer—he had security, privacy, and time. Nevertheless, that wildly farcical scene in Fame's palace, with the hoards of petitioners, Fame's malicious rejoinders, the blasts of stinking smoke from Aeolus's trumpet, the goddess's capriciousness and unpredictability, could be read as an indication of how Chaucer felt in the late 1370s. Possibly, once installed in the Customs and the house above Aldgate, he looked forward to a period of reading and writing only to find it interrupted, at altogether unpredictable moments, by assignments that took him abroad and therefore put him under the perennial handicaps of travel. Perhaps it was not his marriage, as some have thought, but his career that prompted those inscrutable lines, early in the poem, at line 115, about making a two-mile pilgrimage to the shrine of Saint Leonard, famous for releasing prisoners, "to make lithe of that was hard"—to turn something that was hard into something easy. And perhaps the discouragement was in his career as a writer, not as a courtier.

He had read Dante with admiration and concluded, for whatever reasons, that it was not for him to write in this vein. Since looking for something to write about becomes a theme in the poem, we assume he lacked a subject or theme, a "purpose," as he would have called it. But even given a purpose, he shows doubts about the *way* he ought to write. He had mastered the manner of the French dream vision, the manner in which he began *The House of Fame,* but he had encountered something in Italy that made him want to change this manner, yet left him, so far, not knowing how.

With the depression, then, went anxiety. He was looking for a model. Chaucer had not read Boccaccio extensively at the time he wrote *The House of Fame.* The first work of Boccaccio's that Chaucer read with care was *Il Teseida,* after which he had it constantly in mind; it was a work with which he "played almost as a child plays with a new toy . . . as if its appeal had been so irresistible that Chaucer found it hard to keep his hands off it." Its presence is evident in all his earlier works after *The Book of the Duchess*, until the Knight's Tale, which is an adaptation of it. But in *The House of Fame* there is only a single passage of five lines that shows a familiarity with it, the invocation to Book 2, mostly influenced by Dante but containing, like a fingerprint, a curious error, a reference to Mount Helicon as a "clear well," which Chaucer must have got from the *Teseida*, Book 11, stanza 63 (Boccaccio in turn must have gotten it from Guido delle Colonne's *History of Troy*). Unless Chaucer got the notion from Guido direct, it shows us that Chaucer had read through to—or browsed in—the next-to-last book of the *Teseida* by this time but had not yet fallen under its sway.

Chaucer could not have written about fame as he did without knowing the Italian humanists' ideas about it. Even if he did not read their writings he would have heard about their ideas in Italy: "Italy was," Professor Williams reminds us, "the one part of medieval Europe where fame was recognized as an incentive and a reward surpassing even political power and material wealth. . . . 'Fame was that goddess for which all Italy was sighing.' " But what Chaucer wrote was a *critique* of that notion: he saw that fame is based on "tidings" that are sometimes false. This wasn't an "insight" of Chaucer's, really, but a notion drawn from Ovid and Virgil. The insight he had was that "tidings," the reports passed by word of mouth, which are the stuff of fame, are also the stuff of *novelle*, the new kind of stories fashionable in Florence.

The anxiety in *The House of Fame* is about models. Until now Chaucer's literary model was French courtly poetry. If he had a personal model or mentor, it was probably John Gower. Not enough is known about their relationship for us to discern any cooling off: they seem to have had uninterrupted cordial relations for many years. But it is at this time that Chaucer's way of writing turns away from Gower's. He had gone out on his own. It wasn't necessarily his Italian experience that made him take this turn—people at his age often leave behind the mentors of their twenties. But Chaucer encountered in Italy the new model of the poet that Petrarch had fashioned, a model that revolutionized European literary culture and whose effects last to the present day. And he encountered, or would encounter, models for poems or kinds of poems in Boccaccio's works. But it was the *lack* of a mentor or model that caused him anxiety.

Chaucer had reached an impasse. The result of this impasse—of which we possess fossils in the poem, and would otherwise know nothing—was his discovery or recovery of his sense of humor, his ability to take humor out of its native element of intellectual display and psychological defense and make it a force in a poem. It becomes the force that manipulates the audience, and the performer too, into the acquiescent state of laughter. The poem, or the writing of it, worked for him as a kind of therapy. After this he could say he himself knew best how he stood; something in him had been laid to rest or had settled down or been resolved, something that had stood in his way.

The Historical Occasion

The House of Fame's ending, or lack of one, invites us to get lost in its intellectual and personal curiosities. Charles Muscatine is right that the poem belongs to "the decadence of late Gothic art," as he was right that it is Chaucer's "most flamboyant poem . . . colorful, varied to extremes, undigested." It's easy to forget that it is at base a humorous *jeu d'esprit* for a young king's impending marriage. No one can object that Chaucer worked at it so long, that so much of his reading and inner life got into it. But in working it over this way he let it get away from its purpose: as an occasional poem, its ending would have brought us back to its occasion.

The "houses" of Fame and Rumor are details Chaucer got from books and compounded in a process of convoluted and inconclusive thinking. They are the heart of its allegory, and they *seem* barely relevant to the poem's occasion. But they bear a remarkable resemblance to an actual cluster of buildings, the royal palace on the Ile de la Cité in Paris, which Chaucer had seen in the spring of 1377 with the commission sent to negotiate peace with France, which of course meant a royal marriage. This is a recent discovery by Professor Laura Kendrick. The palace was the residence of the king and the seat of the *Parlement de Paris.* Its Great Hall was the public center of the monarchical government, whence the palace was called the *Palais de Justice* (Chaucer's palace of Fame was notable for its *lack* of justice). The Great Hall had three rows of pillars on whose tops stood statues of the forty-seven kings of France who had reigned until that time, placed in chronological sequence, in postures as if they were supporting the roof—strikingly like the statues of poets and historians in Fame's house. It was an architectural feature unusual, perhaps unique, in a secular building. It had, in addition, a gilded, double-vaulted ceiling (Fame's hall, remember, was plated with gold) and a huge marble table that served as a dais.

Connected to the Great Hall by a long gallery was the Sainte Chapelle, that architectural jewel that stands there still, breathtaking with its sculptures and stained-glass windows; a contemporary wrote that it made him feel as if he had been "swept up to heaven"—and it may have inspired Chaucer's image of Venus's "temple of glass." Its vaulted ceiling was painted blue with gold stars, and like many chapels it had a gilt eagle lectern standing before the altar. In addition, there hung from its ceiling a trophy of a hero of the crusades, Godfrey of Bouillon: a leg bone and claw of an enormous vulture, with huge and terrifying talons—rather like the "grim paws" of Chaucer's eagle as he grasps Geffrey up "with his sharpe nailes longe."

These details, so much like those of Chaucer's poem, would be less impressive if the Great Hall of the French royal palace hadn't been connected to the Sainte Chapelle by the *Galerie aux Merciers,* the Gallery of Haberdashers, a long, narrow hall packed with merchants' wooden stalls. One stepped directly from the ceremonious and elegant Great Hall into this busy gallery, where lawyers and clerks carried on business and people gathered to gossip and haggle. One contemporary reported that "nouvelles et esbattements," news and diversions, were exchanged there, and there were rules to control its noisy hubbub while the court was in session. A cross section of Parisian society flocked to it; one historian remarks that "its walls reverberated with the cacophony produced by so many throats. Rumors flew and died, like sparks from a fire; altercations erupted and were submerged again in the general chorus; the shrill voices of innumerable street-traders shared a ceaseless litany. Other sounds besides the human voice were sometimes heard: . . . the trumpet blast preceding the publication of a royal ordinance."

These images from Chaucer's trip or trips to Paris are so like the three principal settings of the poem that they must have been part of its original conception. One can guess that Chaucer went to Paris with a commission that discussed the king's marriage to the French princess, got the idea of a dream vision celebrating such a marriage, and associated the royal palace where the discussions had taken place with the setting of his vision. When negotiations broke down, the poem had to be abandoned or altered. During such hiatuses Chaucer toyed with it aimlessly, not knowing what occasion, if any, it might serve.

Then in May 1378 he went to Milan in part to explore a possible marriage between the king and Caterina Visconti. He returned in September accompanied by two Milanese ambassadors empowered to promise Caterina's hand and a large fortune. Chaucer might have gone back to the poem expecting a marriage with the Milanese heiress. The following December messengers arrived from Milan with what appears to have been good news, and in March 1379 the king appointed a commission to discuss with Milanese ambassadors a marriage with the lady Caterina.

But in the months that followed, the Roman curia began to take an interest in an alliance between England and the House of Luxembourg. Anne of Bohemia, sister of the duke of Luxembourg, had been proposed a few years earlier and summarily rejected; but in the meantime her father had died and her brother, Wenceslas, now king of Bohemia, had the year

before been elected to succeed his father as Holy Roman Emperor. This
raised her status quite enough to get her back on the list of royal brides,
and negotiations were begun: Michael de la Pole and John Burley, already
in Rome, were sent on to Germany. The alliance would surround France
with enemies. For England it meant the possibility of defeating France,
for the church of crushing the Avignon papacy. Even so, the English,
leaving no stone unturned, also sent a commission to France to explore
once again the possibility of peace through a marriage alliance.

Finally news came from the Visconti, on December 10, 1379. The
date is important: "the tenth day of December" was mentioned twice at
the beginning of *The House of Fame*. Professor Larry D. Benson, reviewing independently the evidence about the date of the poem, concluded
from literary allusions and astronomical references that 1379 was the
likeliest year for its completion. On December 10 of that year payment
was made to two ambassadors from Milan and an ambassador from Cardinal Pileo of Ravenna, who was representing the Vatican in England's
negotiations with Wenceslas. The marriage with Caterina Visconti would
not take place; the Vatican had convinced the Visconti that its plan for
an English alliance with Luxembourg was in the best interests of all.
England had no choice but to agree, but there was grumbling. They had
lost Caterina's large dowry; impoverished Luxembourg, offering no dowry,
actually expected a huge payment in return for Richard's marrying Anne.
And, to their displeasure, the Vatican was in effect dictating English
policy.

These disagreeable conditions became, by default, the historical
background of *The House of Fame*. There is no evidence that the poem
was ever presented at court, but the presentation Professor Benson imagines perfectly expresses the spirit of the ending. He thinks that in 1379
Chaucer had the poem on hand, with a space at the end for the "love-
tidings," when suddenly, just before the tenth of December, the disappointing news arrived—especially disappointing to Chaucer because he
had traveled far and worked hard to promote the Visconti alliance. With
a diplomat's sense of what was entailed, he saw that England had now to
go ahead with negotiations for Anne of Bohemia. And seen this way the
news from Cardinal Pileo seemed comical and anticlimactic. The news
was that there was no news. Benson conjectures that at some court
occasion shortly after December 10 Chaucer presented the poem just as
it stood. It was conventional in dream visions that the dreamer wake at
the end, so the joke was a very bold one: "when Chaucer got to the final
lines about the one who 'seemed for to be / A man of greet auctoritee,'
he paused, turned, and slightly bowed in the direction of Cardinal Pileo's
nuncio"—who, having heard the poem in a language he couldn't under-

stand, vaguely smiled and returned the bow. Then the poet closed his book and sat down, and the court, slowly seeing the point, broke out in laughter and applause.

Whether or not this really happened, the unfinished poem breaks off with the mention of a "man of great authority." The phrase evokes the image of a mentor figure, which may have produced anxiety sufficient to make Chaucer "block" and set the passage aside. It reveals an inner need that made the young poet susceptible to influence, and that influence, whether or not he liked it or even knew it, was to be Boccaccio.

9

Reading Boccaccio

Chaucer must have begun reading the *Teseida* about the time he was finishing *The House of Fame*, and it must have been the first of Boccaccio's works that he read with care. It is a traditional inference of Chaucer scholarship that during the Aldgate years he wrote an early adaptation of it, conventionally known as "Palamon and Arcite," from which he later fashioned the Knight's Tale.* During those years, from

---

*In the Prologue to *The Legend of Good Women* (1386), where he lists his works, Chaucer includes "all the love of Palamon and Arcite / Of Thebes, though the story is known lite" (F. Prologue 420, G. Pro 408). It was assumed by Tyrwhitt in the 1790s that this had been "a mere translation" of the *Teseida*. William Godwin, writing in 1803, assumed that by "the story" Chaucer meant his own poem and was indicating that it had been a popular failure, as if it were a published book: "as Chaucer has informed us, near forty years after its publication [it] was 'knowen lite.' The poet, in sober confidence that his work, in its most essential particulars, was worthy of public notice, recast it in the front of his Canterbury Tales, and reduced it from about ten thousand lines, which is the length of Boccaccio's poem, to little more than two thousand. The consequence has been, that Chaucer's original work is lost, and, unhonoured, consigned to oblivion." In 1870 the scholar Ten Brink proposed that this "lost work" had been written not in couplets as the Knight's Tale is but in seven-line stanzas, a

about 1380, he was reading works by Boccaccio, imitating them, reacting to them, writing adaptations of them. By 1386, when he left Aldgate, he had completed the early version of the *Teseida*, completed *Troilus and Criseyde* (his adaptation of *Il Filostrato*); probably begun the short poems on the Falls of Princes that were to be the Monk's Tale, modeled on Boccaccio's *De Casibus*; planned and perhaps started *The Canterbury Tales*, arguably modeled on the *Decameron*; and planned if not begun *The Legend of Good Women*, modeled on *De Claris Mulieribus*. That is the sum of Boccaccio's impact on Chaucer. It all happened in less than a decade, and it touched virtually all of Chaucer's remaining work.

Chaucer knew best the two works by Boccaccio that he adapted, the *Teseida* and the *Filostrato*. He knew less well, perhaps in a fragmentary way, works like *De Claris Mulieribus* or the *Filocolo*, from which he used passages. Beyond this, we can assume he knew or knew about some works like the *Decameron* or certain of Boccaccio's Latin writings, which he imitated in broad outline; these he may have seen once fleetingly in Italy and never again, or heard read from aloud, or only heard described.

It was known from early times that Chaucer based the Knight's Tale on *Il Teseida*, and it was taken for granted that he knew the *Decameron*. Oddly, it was not known until the nineteenth century that he based the *Troilus* on *Il Filostrato*; Tyrwhitt discovered (or rediscovered)* it in 1775 but his discovery was ignored. In 1867 the debt was demonstrated in a doctoral dissertation by a systematic German, and six years later, nearly a hundred years after Tyrwhitt's discovery, a parallel-text edition appeared in which anyone could compare the two poems passage for passage. It must show us something about human nature, or at least academic nature, that once scholars had a sure thing visible in parallel columns they promptly denied any other influence: if Chaucer did not adapt or quote a work by Boccaccio, he had not read it. Anything that seemed to cast aspersions on Chaucer's originality met, and to a large extent still does, with massive resistance: if we *must* admit that he used the *Filostrato*, we will in retaliation deny that he even knew the *Decameron*.

---

notion since discarded. For all anyone knows, the early version could have been substantially identical to the Knight's Tale.

*It may have been known in Chaucer's day and then obscured. Lydgate, in the fifteenth century, said the *Troilus* was translated from a book called "Trophe," "in Lumbard tunge." Dryden said it was adapted from a book by "a Lombard Author." Godwin, writing in 1803, a generation after Tyrwhitt's discovery, mentioned a "version made by Boccaccio of the same story, probably from the same author," and Ralph Waldo Emerson went about saying in lectures that it was from a work by "Lollius of Urbino."

"Anelida and Arcite"

One of Chaucer's experiments from the early Aldgate years, which shows a small but certain influence from the *Teseida*, is the poem called "The Complaint of Fair Anelida and False Arcite." It is an experiment with metrical and stanzaic forms—a very successful experiment, one that has been called "the perfection of everything that had been tried," with passages "unsurpassed indeed anywhere in Chaucer's work." It consists of an introductory narration and the complaint of a jilted queen, Anelida. Its nine-line stanzas use only two rhymes each; the fifth stanzas of its two parts are roughly in the form of a virelay, having sixteen lines (still only two rhymes), and mixing eight- with ten-syllable lines. As if this weren't enough to tax the poet's ingenuity, the last stanza of either part has an internal rhyme on the second and fourth feet, like the leonine hexameters of medieval Latin poetry, an almost impossible feat in English. Here is Anelida despairing of Arcite's pity and fidelity:

> But wellaway! too far be they to fetche;
> Thus holdeth me my destinee a wretche.
> But me to rede° out of this drede, or guye°,   counsel / guide
> Ne may my wit, so weak is it, not stretche.

It is one of the passages in which Chaucer comes closest to pure lyricism, for it is a prosodical display describing only a shift of mood: the strophe ends with the hope that Arcite will come back and all will be forgiven, the antistrophe with the hopeless thought just quoted.

No one knows who Anelida was or where her story came from. Chaucer prefaced her complaint with an invocation adapted from the opening of the *Teseida*, then followed this with an apparently invented narrative explaining her circumstances; in line 21 he claimed (falsely) that he took the story from Statius "and after him Corinne." He began the main narrative with an epigraph taken from Statius (the same epigraph he would later put at the beginning of the Knight's Tale); the first four stanzas, describing Theseus's return from Scythia, are taken from Statius too; the setting and the name Arcite are from the *Teseida*. The story, reminiscent of Dido's, is a conventional tale of a lover's fickleness. Arcite wins Anelida's love, but when he finds her submissive and devoted he deserts her for another. The moral, stated at line 201, is that he valued her the less because she loved him:

> The kynde° of mannes herte is to delite   nature
> In thing that straunge° is, also God me save!   unfamiliar
> For what he may not get, that wold he have.

Ironically, his "newe lady," quite possibly acting on the same perverse principle, takes no interest in him. Some have argued that the poem refers to one or another episode at the English court, but the story itself is too stereotyped for such an identification and the evidence too slim.

The "Corinne" Chaucer names as his secondary source is unknown too—the Theban poetess Corinna, it may be, or a code name for Ovid or Boccaccio.* Chaucer calls his tale "This olde storie, in Latin which I finde" (line 10); a story had more dignity if it came from a Latin source, better yet an ancient Latin source, and for rhetorical reasons it could pay to make one up. It's possible he didn't know the author or the title of *Il Teseida* (they are missing in two of the manuscripts at Pavia from which his copy must have been made); but it's impossible he didn't know who Boccaccio was—he knew several of his works, not just this one, and he had been to Florence where Boccaccio, still alive, was a leading intellectual and writer.

"Anelida and Arcite" must have been fairly well known. It has survived into our time in eight manuscripts and Caxton's printed version, plus four manuscripts containing the complaint without the introductory narrative. Four of the manuscripts have a final stanza, somewhat awkwardly written, that takes up after Anelida's lament and purports to continue the story—probably spurious, though Chaucer might have planned at some point to add a matching complaint by Arcite.

Chaucer never mentions this poem in lists of his works, even when he includes unfinished ones; he probably saw it as one of "many a song" written for practice and abandoned. It shows him in control of a poetic virtuosity that is French in origin, and it shows him with the *Teseida* on his mind.

The Invention of the Five-Stress Line

Among the scattered and half-finished experimental poems that cluttered his desk during the years at Aldgate, we find, rather suddenly as it would appear, the ten-syllable or five-stress line that was to become the standard "iambic pentameter" of later English poetry. It had almost never been used in English before, but it was used in French and Italian verse and Chaucer had used it, perhaps for the first time, in his "ABC." His reading of Italian poetry was probably what made him see its advantages in English.

---

*One theory holds that "Boccaccio" in Italian means "bad mouth" and that Chaucer humorously or maliciously sought to conceal Boccaccio's identity with names that approximate this meaning; *corina* in Italian meant "wry-mouthed."

Until now, nearly everything he wrote was in "octosyllabic couplets," which, as was said earlier, did not sound in English as they did in French: English has stressed and unstressed syllables, and the number of stresses (not as in French the number of syllables) was what made a poetic line. We saw Chaucer in earlier days developing ways to avoid the monotony of four-stress lines in English by varying the number of syllables, changing the position of the caesura, using enjambement. But now he discovered that a five-stress line, having ten syllables or more, avoided monotony even better.

He discovered this not just by seeing it in Italian verses but by seeing it already immanent in the English poetic line he had been writing. Here are some lines from *The Book of the Duchess*:

> This méssagér took leéve and wénte
> Upón his wáy, and néver ne sténte
> Tíll he cóme to the dérke valléye
> That stánt betwíxen róches twéye.

Such verses in French or Italian would not sound as tum-te-tum as these do, and the curious thing was that the smoothest sound came where there were *not* eight syllables, according to rule, but nine:

> Upón his wáy, and néver ne sténte

—that extra syllable, "ne," gave a mysterious luster and variation to the phrase it occurred in, and may have inspired the switch to trochees in the next line. Too, at the end of the line, the natural pause made the ear (in Chaucer's time) hear the *e* on "stent*e*" even if strictly one did not sound it. And if you counted that syllable too you had not eight syllables but ten.

In other such passages one could count ten syllables and, by virtue of an internal pause (pauses being more ponderous in English), count *five* beats rather than four. In *The Book of the Duchess* he had written,

> . . . in the dawening I lay
> (Me mette° thus) in my bed all naked.   *dreamed*

Now that second line by count had ten syllables:

>   1 2 3 4 5 6 7 8 9 10
> (Mé mette thuś) iń mý bed alĺ nakéd

—but did it still have only four beats? Yes, in one manner of hearing it:

> (Me métte thús) in my béd all náked

But there was a pause after "thus" which could seem a part of the rhythm, like the non-strums between the strums of a guitar; for by delaying the strum the guitarist makes an extra beat of the unstrummed part (which we call syncopation). In that case the line (with the pause marked "*X*") would scan like this:

(Me métte thús) **X** ín my béd all náked.

But suppose that, in place of this pause or "non-strum" in the line, you inserted a one-syllable word, like *as*:

(Me métte thús) as ín my béd all náked

—why, then you would have eleven syllables and five beats rather than four, there would still be a pause after "thus," and the sound would still be regular and natural.

In English speech, some stressed syllables are stronger than others. There are three contrasting degrees of stressed syllables, besides unstressed ones, in modern English, and it was doubtless the same in Middle English; but in poetry all stressed syllables are equal for purposes of counting. The result in English—quite foreign to French or Italian—is a kind of counterpoint between spoken stress and metrical stress. To the English ear the five-stress line seems to sound more like a spoken utterance, suits better the rhythms of the spoken language, than the four-stress line. "To be or not to be, that is the question" sounds more like a man thinking grave thoughts than "Not to be, that is the question." "It droppeth as the gentle rain from heaven" sounds more like a young woman praising mercy than "It droppeth as the gentle rain" or "It droppeth as the rain from heaven." Why? Probably just because we're used to it. If you're writing a poem, there's no reason why you can't make four-beat lines sound like natural English speech; the problem comes when you're writing *rhymed* lines. In English the rhymes stand out more than in French or Italian, are too insistent, come too fast. Chaucer had already discovered ways to soft-pedal this quality of English rhymes; but an extra foot in the line accomplished it best of all.

In Chaucer's early poems—*The Book of the Duchess*, the translation of the *Roman de la Rose, The House of Fame*—he had used French-style octosyllabic couplets, and of course the rhymes of couplets are the most insistent. In these experiments of the late 1370s he was writing in stanzas, as the Italians did, and the stanzaic form, having fewer couplets or none, eliminates the problem. It wasn't until *The Canterbury Tales* that he took the obvious, natural step and wrote couplets in five-stress lines—a step that makes him the inventor of English "heroic verse."

Rhyme Royal and the Merchant "Puy"

In these experimental scraps the most common stanzaic form, "rhyme royal," is also thought to be Chaucer's invention. Stanzas were reckoned more elegant than couplets—the stanzaic form was the one appropriate to be read at court, as the name "rhyme royal" implies. In his Aldgate experiments these seven-, eight-, and nine-line schemes are used in more or less equal distribution, but the seven-line "rhyme royal," rhyming *ababbcc* won out: it was the form he used in *The Parliament of Fowls*, the *Troilus*, and four of the Canterbury tales whose tellers aspire to elegance. If Chaucer did not himself invent rhyme royal, he established it in England for two centuries as a proper vehicle for elevated discourse.

What we must notice about the poems Chaucer wrote in his so-called Italian period is how French they are. They were completed when he had copies of Dante and Boccaccio open on his desk, but they are only subtly colored by Italian literature. Take for instance "The Complaint unto Pity": it is a personification allegory—one of the few Chaucer wrote —in the courtly tradition of the *Roman de la Rose*, in rhyme royal (it may be the first poem in which he used that form exclusively), organized like the "Anelida" into a narrative plus a complaint. The complaint consists of nine stanzas, three groups of three stanzas each, each group ending in a common rhyme—a pattern modeled on the French ballade. The narrative tells how the poet, setting out to complain to Pity about Love's cruelty and tyranny, finds Pity dead and "buried in a heart" (line 14), surrounded by Beauty, Pleasure, Youth, and so on. Knowing that the letter of complaint he has written will not avail if Pity is dead, the narrator puts it away—but not without first telling us what it says. Addressed to the lady, or to "Pity" in her, it says (line 109) not unsurprisingly that he will lament her death and always be true:

> For well I wot, although I wake or winke°,   *sleep*
> Ye rekke° not whether I flete° or sinke.   *care / float*
> But natheless, yet my trouthe I shall sustene
> Unto my death, and that shall well be seene.

This sounds on the surface very French, and it is. Yet scholars whose ears may be trusted find in the diction subtle indications of an influence from the *dolce stil nuovo* and even from particular sonnets of Petrarch. Italian poetry affected Chaucer's style before it affected his taste in subject matter or poetic form.

From this period too comes a sheaf of verses so alike and so stereotyped that they can be—and have been—mistaken for a single poem, variously called "A Complaint to his Lady" or "A Ballade of Pity." They are in fact four (perhaps three) drafts on the same conventional theme. The first is two stanzas of rhyme royal. The second and third are in *terza rima,* the first known appearance of the Dantean verse form in English, a quite successful effort at a form hard to manage in our tongue:

> The sore spark of pain now doth° me spille°,   *makes / die*
>   This Love, that hath me set in swich a place
>   That my desire he nevere wol fulfille,
> For neither pitee, mercy, neither grace,
>   Can I nat finde; and yit my sorrowful herte,
>   For to be dead, I can it nought arace°.   *remove*
> The more I love, the more she doth me smerte°,   *hurt*
>   Through which I see, withoute remedye
>   That from the death I may no wise asterte.°   *escape*

The fourth of these fragments consists of nine ten-line stanzas (the second stanza has eight lines and a different rhyme scheme); it has several rhyme words missing, as if the poet hadn't found workable rhymes when he abandoned it. These are scraps from Chaucer's workshop—drafts for "The Complaint unto Pity" or some other poem, or trial runs with various verse forms. They are the only examples we have of Chaucer's work in progress. Evidently they were saved by mistake, perhaps by someone thinking they were part of the manuscript of the "Complaint unto Pity."

These fragments were experiments with more elaborate verse forms; they come close to the aristocratic traditions of troubadour verse, which were more important to Gower than to Chaucer, and it's possible they were written under Gower's influence. They may have been written, as Gower's and some of Chaucer's ballades may have been, for oral delivery before an annual merchant feast, the "Puy," which involved a contest of "royal songs"; here, in fact, may be the origin of the term "rhyme royal." The winner received a crown of laurel from the elected master of the feast, who was called the Prince; and here may be the origin of the convention by which a ballade is concluded with an envoi addressed "O, Prince." The contests were a case of the merchant class playing at royal and noble traditions, and were quite widespread. They were of French origin: they went back to the *Confrérie de Notre Dame de Puy* (Puy was, apparently, a town in the Auvergne), and they were common in the south of France in the thirteenth century. The records of the London Guildhall show that there had been a "Puy" established in London in the early fourteenth century, probably by men from some English-dominated part of France like Aquitaine; it was described as an all-male affair "for the crowning of a royal song," and the tradition apparently maintained itself into Gower's and Chaucer's day. A part of the movement away from courtly to "public" poetry, the Puy was courtly in its models and mannerisms, but was a merchant-class event—very possibly an ingredient in Chaucer's notion of his audience.

"The Complaint of Mars"

Another of these poems in nine-line stanzas, this one introduced by a narrative in rhyme royal, is called "The Complaint of Mars." But now Chaucer has read farther in *Il Teseida*. The story is taken from Statius and Ovid, but the subject reveals him suddenly interested in two of the pagan gods that figure in Boccaccio's epic. He views them not the way Boccaccio did, as actual gods in ancient mythology, but in the medieval way as *planets*. On the surface is the all too human (or anthropomorphic) tale of Venus loving and then jilting Mars, a stock situation in courtly poetry; under that surface is a body of astronomical references depicting a conjunction of Mars and Venus in the sign of Taurus.*

The poem was written for Saint Valentine's day, on which by a courtly tradition (possibly Chaucer's invention) birds were said to choose their mates. We hear a bird crying for the others to rejoice at Venus "risen among the red rays," warning lovers to flee, "lest wicked tongues you espye!" It is the moment of "dread" when the sun rises and lovers lament the ending of the night—the occasion of the conventional *aube* or "dawn song," as in *Romeo and Juliet* or *Troilus and Criseyde*. The lovers are Venus and Mars, who in mythology had an adulterous union, but Chaucer depicts them as *planets*: their conjunction in Taurus is a union in which they vow love to each other. Unhappily, Venus travels in her course twice as fast as Mars, so that when Phoebus the sun comes into the palace "with torche in hand," Mars arms himself, bids Venus flee, and is ludicrously left behind. Part of the humor is that certain technical terms of astrology were applicable to a love story in a literal sense. It sounds anthropomorphic enough, and has a true Chaucerian wryness and laconicism, when we are told (line 71) that

*Such an astronomical conjunction did not occur in England between 1369 and 1400, though one like it occurred in 1385. John Shirley, the fifteenth-century bookseller, appended a note that the poem was said to censure, on John of Gaunt's urging, an affair between John Holland, Lord Huntingdon, and the duchess Isabella of York. Others have claimed it censures Holland's seduction of John of Gaunt's daughter Elizabeth. These events happened in 1385–1386. The evidence is not strong, but it's possible the poem has such a topical reference—which would however make it something uncharacterisitic of Chaucer, a protracted jeer.

The greate joy that was betwix hem two,
When they be met, there may no tongue telle.
There is no more, but unto bed they go,
And thus in joy and bliss I let hem dwelle

—but it happens that the technical term for such a conjunction of planets was *copulare*. As Venus proceeds in her course she approaches Mercury, who receives her "as friend full dear." Mars, jilted, is left to bemoan his plight. The bird-narrator says he will rehearse Mars' complaint for us and then take his leave—first wishing every creature, because it's Valentine's day, joy of its mate.

Mars' complaint will be, we expect, the conventional one of the forsaken lover. But Mars talks like a bluff, plain-spoken soldier and phrases his complaint in a literal-minded, military way: the "order" of complaint, he says, is that if one is going to complain he must first have something to complain about, or else it will be thought he is complaining foolishly and pointlessly—and "alas! that am not I!" He announces that he gave Venus his true service forevermore—and adds "how dear I have it bought!" He complains that he has no one to complain *to*, since she is going to die heartbroken (she is well out of sight by now), and complains that *she* has no one to complain to either. He ends by asking knights, ladies, and lovers to complain on his behalf for the sake of Venus, who is ever ready to help them, "ensample of all honour" who "never dide but all gentilesse." The silliness of it is that while Mars the cuckold goes on with his fatuous complaint, we know Venus is in Mercury's arms and not complaining in the least: the *copulatio* of the two planets makes them like two ships that pass in the night, she traveling at twice the speed.

Did this poem contain some deeper admonition or moral lesson for Saint Valentine's Day? Perhaps, but in a lighthearted way. Saint Valentine was for no good reason associated with mating, and mating, for medieval Christians, meant either marriage or adultery—there was no in-between. The "complaint" is that of a self-deluded lover mouthing courtly sentiments, which are thus parodied. The poem commends the true and lasting union by ridiculing a fly-by-night one that is unhappy and unrewarding. Venus and Mars talk and react like sinful mortals, but what they do, being planets, is foreordained; it's rather like Boethius's idea that while we act freely, the outcomes of our actions are predestined, and Chaucer may have been translating Boethius about this time. Perhaps Venus wheeling away at double speed and embracing Mercury is distantly akin to Criseyde departing for the Greeks and turning to Diomede, and perhaps Mars left behind with nothing but literary conventions is a distant kin to Troilus; but we do not laugh at Troilus.

"Palamon and Arcite"

What inspired "The Complaint of Mars" was a reaction Chaucer had to
the *Teseida*. Boccaccio, writing an epic set in the ancient world, depicted
the gods of ancient mythology as real gods. He was vastly learned on the
subject, and the *Teseida* contains long displays of his erudition; he even
added glosses giving further information. Chaucer loved the ancient
myths and found all this instructive and fascinating, but his common
sense, or his sense of humor, got the better of him: Venus, Mars, and
Saturn were really planets, and what they did as gods undergoes a comic
sea change when seen from an astronomer's viewpoint.

Whether the early version of the Palamon story had this same comic
aspect, we don't know. But we know that in the later version, the Knight's
Tale, the gods are planets (talking planets, to be sure) and their powers
are planetary "influences." Not that Chaucer found *Il Teseida* unsatisfying: once he got into it he couldn't get it out of his head. But the *Teseida*
is long—twelve laborious books, with all the trappings of a classical epic
—and its elevated diction makes it hard to read. Boccaccio set out to write
a work modeled on Virgil's *Aeneid* and Statius's *Thebaid*; he even made
it come out to the exact number of lines as the *Aeneid*—or, in some
manuscripts, one stanza longer. In many ways the *Teseida* is closer to a
medieval romance, but it is of epic proportions in its grandeur and linguistic display. Imagine Chaucer struggling with it in a handwritten manuscript having no notes for a foreign reader, at a time when there were no
alphabetical dictionaries and at best rudimentary Italian-English word
lists.

Still more frustrating was the task of rendering the long poem in
English verse, and the result contains remnants of his frustration. For
example, Chaucer writes of Palamon's imprisonment (line 1457):

And eek thereto° he is a prisoner   *in addition to that*
Perpetually, not only for a year.

"Not only for a year" seems a redundancy coming after "perpetually," as
if it might have been chosen partly for the rhyme. In the lines that follow
Chaucer lets himself humorously remark on this:

Who coude rime in English properly
His martyrdom? forsooth it am nat I!
Therefore I pass as lightly as I may.
It fell that in the seventh year, of May
The thridde night (as olde bookes sayn,
That all this story tellen more plain). . . .

The humor is directed at himself: he is laboring not just to rhyme, but to understand, clarify, and condense. He is taking a romance epic of almost ten thousand lines not counting glosses, introductory sonnets, and the like, and turning it into a much less epical romance that will be just over two thousand lines. His omissions and condensations sometimes leave curiously abrupt phrases that seem anticlimactic. Were they meant to be funny? After Arcite's long love complaint for Emily, Chaucer tells us (line 1572),

> And with that word he fell down in a traunce
> A longe time—and after he up sterte.

Well, perhaps it just came out funny, and more so to the modern reader, but the word "sterte" suggests that the joke was intended. It isn't just that he fell down in a trance for a long time and afterward *got up* (there's no such stage business in Boccaccio, by the way)—he "started," jumped or bounded, up! Or again, when the two heroes, out of prison, encounter each other and fight, we are told (and neither is this in the original) that they are fighting up to the ankles in their own blood—a circumstance that would be alarming enough if they were standing in a tub. Chaucer, having made the remark, hurries on, leaving them (line 1660) in this ridiculous posture:

> Up to the ankle foght they in hir blood.
> And in this wise I let hem fighting dwelle,
> And forth I woll of Theseus you telle.

Still, this mock-epic quality in Chaucer's version is not necessarily parody. Chaucer liked the *Teseida*, and the many changes he wrought in it for his own purposes do not signify displeasure. To Boccaccio it was an epic that must, like all epics, have gods and divine intervention, fate, mortals struggling powerless against imperturbable forces. To Chaucer it was a romance; he weeded out the epic machinery and made it a story of character.

Arcite, devoted to Mars, is the warlike one; Palamon, devoted to Venus, is the lover. In Boccaccio, Arcite sees Emilia first. In Chaucer, this is reversed—the lover, Palamon, sees her first, and the warlike one, seeing her afterward, initiates a competition. In Boccaccio, Emilia is a realized figure, an innocent girl of fifteen who flirts with the two knights, who throughout the poem thinks, reacts, speaks. Chaucer reduces her to a cipher—we see her only through the eyes of the smitten lovers, eyes covered by the scales of love. Again Chaucer, with an eye to character, depicts Theseus as preternaturally cruel, allowing no ransom for his two noble prisoners, very harsh by medieval standards—perhaps faintly reminiscent of the Black Prince at Limoges. But he makes this change (Boccaccio's Theseus did not prohibit ransom) in order to show him later softened by experience: when he declares a tournament, he declares that the two sides should fight with blunted weapons (Boccaccio's Theseus makes no such declaration) and the people cry out in glee over his goodness.

Whether or not Chaucer tailored the story for the Knight, the exaggerations that sound like literary parody seem to come from Chaucer. For instance: dying Arcite commends Palamon to his lady and breathes his last word, "Mercy, Emelye!" It is a genuinely dramatic moment. Then Chaucer, departing from Boccaccio altogether, adds (line 2809),

> His spirit chaunged house, and wente there
> As I came never, I can not tellen where;
> Therefore I stinte. . . .

—"his spirit changed its place of dwelling and went there where *I* never came, I can't tell you where. Therefore I'll keep quiet." And he goes on: "I'm no theologian. I find nothing about souls in this table of contents, and I don't care to tell those opinions about them, though they write about where they dwell. Arcite is cold, may Mars guide his soul. Now will I speak about Emelye. Emelye shrieked. . . ." Is there not an intentional want of dignity here? Boccaccio gloriously described the flight of Arcite's soul into the sky; Chaucer omitted the passage (and used it later to describe the flight of Troilus's soul in *Troilus and Criseyde*). Yes, someone could argue that the Knight is himself an ironist, or a no-nonsense warrior who doesn't care to speculate about souls. But it seems very odd that he should be glancing through a "registre," the listed contents of a book— Chaucer was the one sitting in front of a book. One estimable critic calls the comic abruptness of these lines about Arcite's death a "deftly administered antidote for tragedy," and it's true, Chaucer's version avoids tragic, as it avoids epic, extremes. It is a work with a happy ending—a thoughtful, possibly a "philosophical" comedy. It remains "epic" in its way, but its epic pretensions have been brought down to earth.

The philosophy in Chaucer's earlier version of the *Teseida*, if we can judge from the Knight's Tale, was a mixture. At the end, lines 2748 ff., we get first the ruminations of Theseus's old father Egeus, that everything in life must pass away. The passage is memorable for its use of the commonplace that life is a pilgrimage:

> This world nys but a thurghfare ful of wo,
> And we been pilgrims, passing to and fro.
> Death is an end of every worldly sore.

But this is preceded by Egeus's remark, spoken by Theseus in the *Teseida* in a straightforward way, but turned by Chaucer into a bloated platitude, punctuated in mock deliberation with "quod he" and "he said":

"Right as there died never man," quod he,
"That he ne lived in earth in some degree,
Right so there lived nevere man," he seyde,
"In all this world, that some time he ne deyde."

And Chaucer wryly adds that he said "much more to this effect, full wisely. . . ."

This platitudinous wisdom is succeeded a page later with Theseus's philosophical speech about the First Mover and the Chain of Love, drawing the lesson that everyone should make virtue of necessity by accepting what cannot be changed. The passage is drawn from Boethius and added to the material of the *Teseida,* and it's impossible to know if it was added in the early version or added later. It might well have been thrilling to a medieval audience to hear an ancient pagan arriving at Christian moral doctrine by deduction: Boccaccio has Theseus say that it is wise to make virtue of necessity, but Chaucer shows him *reasoning* to this conclusion from ancient, platonistic premises.

It is often overlooked that Theseus tacks on to this speech a moral observation as if it were a corollary, though it is closer to a contradiction —and the passage *is* in Boccaccio, is indeed the great lesson of his work: that a man has most honor if he dies in the flower of his age at the height of his excellence, when his "good name" is assured (line 3055):

Than is it best, as for a worthy fame,
To dien whan that he is best of name.

This is the Renaissance ideal of fame; and Chaucer, having recently finished *The House of Fame,* could not have overlooked it. But it was also the older idea of "knightly glory," and this was what made the story appropriate to the Knight in *The Canterbury Tales*: the Knight is depicted as a crusader, but his story ends with military and chivalric notions that had become "humanist" ideas.

The Extent and Nature of the Influence

There are some half dozen of Boccaccio's Italian works that could have exerted an influence on Chaucer, but the evidence consists of similarities in plot or form, or parallel phrases, characters, and situations, most of them attainable from other works or from literary conventions. Chaucer might have read Boccaccio's *Filocolo,* a prose romance one part of which is a precursor of the *Decameron* and from which one story is thought the principal source of the Franklin's Tale. Three of the tales in *The Canterbury Tales* have analogues in the *Decameron,* but the *Decameron* versions cannot be shown through verbal parallels to be Chaucer's sources; still, Chaucer could have heard or read them in Italy and remembered the stories without having a text before him as he wrote. The same is true of the *Decameron* in its larger conception and plan. And Chaucer may have seen some of Boccaccio's works briefly and decided not to read them, yet they could have made random impressions on him that found their way into his poems without his knowledge.

For example, the *Corbaccio.* It has now and again been suggested that Chaucer knew it, but no certain influence can be shown. In 1387 a Florentine notary, Lodovico Bartoli, turning it into *ottava rima,* reported that Boccaccio himself hated the work. Imagine, then, Chaucer stumbling upon it. He would have seen at a glance that it was a dream vision in prose: the narrator, rejected by a certain woman, finds himself in a place variously called "the labyrinth of love," "Venus's pigsty," and "the valley of sighs and woes," where he meets a shade from the dead, the former husband of the woman who rejected him. The valley they are in, the shade informs him, is "what you call 'the court of love,' " and all the growling beasts in it are the "wretches—of whom you are one—who have been caught in the net of false love." The narrator tells how he revealed his love in a letter, assuming the woman would accept him or discourage him discreetly. Instead she gossiped about him, laughed behind his back, even showed his letter to another man, with whom she was in love, who is called "the second Absolom." The shade reminds him that it isn't proper for a man to love at his age, that love destroys the reason and harms the body, that women are wicked, foolish, a danger to men. From here the garrulous shade goes on with a swollen harangue against women that continues for the rest of the book: women are greedy, vain, lascivious—flirts, whores, connivers, thieves, liars. He maliciously describes his former wife as she was at close hand, fat and ugly, "swamp-faced," "sitting on her haunches in her lined mantle, brooding over the fire, with livid rings under her eyes, coughing and spitting great gobs of phlegm. . . ." In the end, the narrator declares he sees the duties of his age and learning, and the woman's baseness—and will avenge his outrage by writing about it.

Chaucer might have suspected this curious book was a joke of some kind, though its ending seemed serious. It contained references to Boccaccio's age and at least one to the circumstances of his life, but Chaucer would have known little about these, or about Florentine attitudes to women, or about the sumptuary laws passed in Boccaccio's time governing female dress and comportment. Maybe the work wallowed by design in lame arguments, was a tour de force of grotesque, exaggerated detail, drawing close to the body and regarding its secrets in obscenely comic enlargement. (There is a discernible path moving from such medieval works toward writers like Rabelais or painters like Bosch and Breughel, and there *was*—or was to be—this grotesque element in Chaucer, in the Pardoner, for example, or the portraits of some of the Canterbury pilgrims with their warts and running sores.) Or maybe the *Corbaccio* represented two mad passions, of a woman's former husband and her repulsed suitor, one heaping blame on all women and the other on this woman alone—two male defenses. Or maybe it really was an ironical attack on the excesses of fleshly love, or an act of revenge—the author mentioned several times that she showed his letter to others and mocked him, even repeating it again at the end, then in the epilogue to boot. Or maybe the narrator was the butt—the consoling figure from the beyond absurdly heaps coals on his rage, leaving him at the end as angry as before.

If Chaucer glanced through the book enough to raise such questions, he would have closed it in confusion. A decade later that snide phrase of Boccaccio's "the second Absolom" (referring to the Old Testament figure, who had perfect beauty) could have inspired his choice of a name for the aspirant suitor in the Miller's Tale; but it was a conventional name used to ridicule male vanity. Or he might have remembered the woman's harangue at her husband ("Do you think I'm fooled and that I don't know whom you're chasing, whom you're in love with, and whom you talk with every day? . . . By the Cross of God, I'll do to you what you're doing to me. Am I now so skinny. Am I not as beautiful as so-and-so? . . ."); it is a most striking speech—De Sanctis cited it as "language worthy of Plautus"—and one can imagine Chaucer being drawn to it. There was a whole tradition of such writing, and he could have created the Wife of Bath from such details half remembered, whether from the *Corbaccio* or not. There are other Italian works by Boccaccio that have been suspected of exerting such a subtle influence on Chaucer—the *Filocolo*, the *Ameto*, the *Amorosa Visione*, and more—but the similarities always belong to traditions Chaucer could have found elsewhere.

In Italy Chaucer was not looking for exotic or peculiar works, but for those whose traditions were familiar to him, and that he could understand and imitate. Of Boccaccio's other poems the *Ninfale Fiesolano*, a romance in *ottava rima*, and the *Amorosa Visione*, a dream vision imitating Dante, would have seemed of interest, and it is thought he may have read the latter, though again no certain influence can be shown.

But from the whole shelf of Boccaccio's works the two Italian poems about the ancient world—the stories of Troilus and Criseyde and of

Palamon and Arcite—were for Chaucer the most interesting.* Why? Because since his days at Saint Paul's under Master Ravenstone the ancient world itself interested him intellectually, even emotionally. It was why Italian humanism interested him. These two Italian works of Boccaccio's were tales of ancient Greece and Troy, themselves adapted from works he knew, like Statius's *Thebaid* and medieval "Troy books." A poem set in Troy was of special interest to an Englishman and a Londoner (to Boccaccio, Troy held little interest). Here was material he could *use*.

Among Boccaccio's Latin writings Chaucer found two works that were interesting for their conceptions and subject matter. One was *De Claris Mulieribus,* stories of famous women; Chaucer read at least some of it, for he used its story of Zenobia in the Monk's Tale and its story of Cleopatra in *The Legend of Good Women,* and the work as a whole furnished the idea of his *Legend of Good Women.* † The other was *De Casibus Virorum Illustrium.* Chaucer used bits of it in *The Legend of Good Women* and the Monk's Tale. And in the earlier antecedent of the Monk's Tale, he used the conception of it at least in part, and evidently used its title, for the words "De casibus virorum illustrium" are given in the manuscripts. Like the *Corbaccio* it was a dream vision in prose, which must have struck Chaucer as a peculiar, but perhaps reasonable, idea. Prose in the Middle Ages was, first, the language of Scripture, and after that the language of learned or practical discourse—of treatises, textbooks, documents. Most of these, and the more respectable of these, were in Latin. In Boccaccio's *De Casibus* the dreamer dreams that famous figures of history appear before him in his study; in a colloquy with the goddess Fortune they tell their stories, or Fortune tells them, or the narrator. It was essentially a learned treatise, a political treatise, not dramatic enough for Chaucer to want to make it a poem, but intriguing as a repository of historical information.

These stories of famous men who fell on Fortune's wheel were legends not of saints but of secular figures; they came from the body of "storial thing," what we call history—like the figures in Dante's

*In this choice lies a curiosity. In the *Decameron,* at the beginning of the sixth day, we are told that Dioneo and Lauretta sing a song about Troilus and Cressida. At the end of the next day, the seventh, we are told that Dioneo and Fiammetta sing a song about Palamon and Arcite. These are the only times in the *Decameron* when characters are said to sing songs about particular subjects, though the songs aren't quoted. And Boccaccio picked from his own works the same two stories Chaucer picked.

†The greatest of Boccaccio's collections was "The Genealogies of the Gentile Gods"; Chaucer must have dipped into it at least, for he used it, along with Ovid, for the story of Hypermnestra in *The Legend of Good Women,* but he showed no interest in imitating the concept itself.

Commedia. The dream-vision aspect of the work impressed Chaucer not at all: from the viewpoint of French traditions, a dream vision about power, rather than love, was an anomaly. But the figures themselves, and the notion of collecting their stories, were attractive. Chaucer got the idea of making his own collection of such tales but without the thesis or the framing device, telling them more briefly than Boccaccio had, and in verse. His plan was to start with the fall of Lucifer, then go to the fall of Adam, through the Old Testament and the ancient world—Sampson, Hercules, and so on—into Christian times. He wrote seventeen of them, in eight-line stanzas. The shortest are but a single stanza; the longest is the fall of a famous woman, Zenobia, queen of Palmyra, from Boccaccio's *De Claris Mulieribus.* He probably wrote some of these at first for the youngsters at court, possibly the young king himself, to hear or memorize; they are after all moral lessons about kingly power. After the first few, they come not in chronological sequence but haphazardly, as if he added stories as they came to him. The little collection has a fair amount in common with Boccaccio's, and it has the same title. Six of Chaucer's seventeen personages are in Boccaccio's work, but Chaucer got their tales elsewhere. Certain lines and passages, however, are from Boccaccio's *De Casibus* and others could be.

Almost exactly in the middle of Chaucer's collection are four stories of modern kings. The last was the least recent, Ugolino of Pisa (d. 1289), whose story is told in the opening lines of *Inferno,* Canto 33. Chaucer ends his version with a tribute to Dante—"for he can all devise / Fro point to point, not o word wol he faille"—in fact he didn't follow Dante on all points, so he must have used another source as well. The other three contemporary monarchs were men Chaucer had met or seen. Pedro, king of Spain, father of the duchess Costanza, gets a sympathetic treatment: Chaucer was writing for the royal court, and Pedro was John of Gaunt's father-in-law—indeed, Gaunt was Pedro's heir. Chaucer's references to "the field of snow with a black eagle caught on a red limrod" and "the wicked nest," which seem to us so unfathomable—and the explanations in footnotes so arcane—would have sent chills through his audience, for they knew the snow and the black eagle caught on a limrod of red was the coat of arms of the dreaded enemy Du Guesclin, and that "the wicked nest" was French *mau ni,* Oliver de Mauny, second in treachery, the very opposite of the chivalrous Oliver in *The Song of Roland*:

> O noble, O worthy Pedro, glory of Spaine,
> Whom Fortune held so high in majestee,
> Well oughten men thy pitous death complain!

Out of thy land thy brother made thee flee,
And after, at a seege, by subtiltee,
Thou were bitraysed° and lad unto his tente,   *betrayed*
Whereas he with his owne hand slow thee,
Succeeding in thy regne and in thy rente°.   *income*
    The feeld of snow, with th'eagle of black thereinne,
Caught with the limrod colored as the gleede°,   *live coal*
He brew this cursednesse and all this sinne.
The wicked nest was werker of this nede°.   *violence*
Noght Charles'° Oliver, that took ay heed   *Charlemagne's*
Of trouth and honour, but of Armorike
Genylon Oliver, corrupt of meede°,   *bribery*
Broght this worthy king in swich a brike°.   *trap*

Another of these contemporary monarchs is Pierre de Lusignon, king
of Cyprus, who had visited England twice; in 1369 he was murdered by
his own liegemen. In 1385, when Bernabò Visconti was murdered by his
nephew, Chaucer added the stanza about him—perhaps soon after news
of his death reached England. The stanza comes after the stories of Pierre
de Lusignon and Pedro of Castile, but *before* Ugolino and other figures
from earlier times. The order makes no sense, and one assumes he meant
to rearrange it, but he never did. The last story, of Croesus, was rewritten
to end with a closure device, the repetition of some lines defining tragedy.

A collection of stories may or may not reveal a common thread that
constitutes a theme or moral. Stories about the falls of the great—which
the medievals called "tragedies"—had the traditional moral that Fortune
topples the good and bad alike. The mutability of the world and its lack
of justice was their set theme. For Boccaccio, this moral idea inherent in
the genre was displaced by his interest in a process of justice and reason
working in history. Chaucer overlooked Boccaccio's intellectual purposes.
The only common thread is the set theme of the genre itself. Chaucer's
figures fall because of blind Fortune, some unjustly through the treachery
of others, some through pride or other vices as if Fortune were an agent
of punishment. There is no consistency in viewpoint. No thesis emerges.
They are *exempla* of kingly power, useful in themselves cumulatively for
a boy king to know and think about. Apparently Chaucer lost interest in
the collection and put it aside. When he started *The Canterbury Tales*
he must have asked himself whether he could use any of these "tragedies"
as tales, or if there was among his pilgrims anyone who would have had
a motive for *collecting* them. And for this Boccaccio-like role he singled
out the Monk.

Reading *Il Filostrato*

When Chaucer turned to *Il Filostrato* he found it a very different kind
of work. It was less grandiose than the *Teseida* and only a third as long.
It was not an epic but, apparently, a romance, though unlike any romance
Chaucer had ever seen. It was not an episodic, panoramic history like its
sources, chief among them Benoit de Sainte Maure's *Roman de Troie*,
and it was not interlaced in structure after the manner of French romances, but a single, discrete story, closer to what the Italians were calling
a *novella*. Chaucer may not have known that it was derived from a
peculiarly Italian form of popular entertainment, the *cantare*, and that
Boccaccio wanted to take this popular form and raise its literary status.

Il Filostrato would have looked to Chaucer, C. S. Lewis said, like "a
new bit of the Troy story": it shared in the spirit of legend. But here again
there was a difference, for it was domestic legend—"tidings" about a love
affair, lacking the most fundamental conventions of French love poetry:
the lover was not "sighing like furnace" (in Shakespeare's phrase), the lady
was not *dangereuse*, the affair was not idealistic and ennobling. On the
contrary, the lover was prompted, as the reader is told again and again,
by "hot desire," and the lady, cautious only of her reputation, was otherwise no less heated up than the hero. The affair was consummated with
most uncourtly dispatch: Troiolo goes at night to Criseida's chamber, she
having dismissed the servants, to an assignation arranged by his friend
Pandaro (the name meant "I will give all"), and she jilts him with equal
dispatch. Her reasons or feelings are not accounted for. The moral is that
young women are fickle. The lesson to be learned is addressed to the poet's
own lady. There is not a hint of Christian or philosophical *doctrine*.

The poem, Chaucer would have thought, was *stark*. It is not going
too far to suppose he was shocked by it, though intrigued as well. The
Filostrato recreated pagan sensuality in a pagan setting: its author seemed,
or claimed, to know what *carpe diem* really meant in the pagan world, and
in his prologue and epilogue he brazenly associated himself with his pagan
hero. You would never guess from his poem that he was himself a Christian. He seemed rather to be openly in revolt against Christian values, to
embrace the material world, the flesh, the appetites—to espouse classical
antiquity for its worldview, not its books. Chaucer probably found in it
something he could not have expected, something not to be found in
English romances: a separation without a restoration, and love without
marriage. He probably thought the poem coarse—lacking the *delicatesse*
that was the essence of the French courtly tradition. And this is one

possible reason why he never named Boccaccio: he must have sensed vulgarity here, a mind of great originality that did not understand the finer points of courtliness—not, as we shall see, an unfair estimate.

Whether Chaucer understood what Boccaccio was "really doing" in the *Filostrato* is an impossible question; we are not agreed among ourselves what he was doing. Chaucer might have believed he saw what Boccaccio was doing but have wanted to do (as he did) something different. Whichever was the case, C. S. Lewis was right that he must have thought while reading it, "this will never do." When he finished it he might have reflected that it was a deliberate fabrication—the reader was not expected to think it true. That the author associated himself with the hero only underscored its falseness; in the prose introduction he said the story was a shield for his own feelings, and in his epilogue he turned from his story to contemplate his own love life, which we now believe, and Chaucer might have sensed, was a fabrication too. The work was like a protracted rhetorical device—like *superlatio,* deliberate exaggeration, or *ironia,* irony: we are meant to see how starkly un-Christian the Age of Nature was, and so are meant to be turned back upon ourselves—to wake as from a dream and find ourselves in the Christian West during the Age of Grace.

The evidence for any such hypothesis about how Chaucer read, or misread, *Il Filostrato* is in how he adapted it. Where in the *Teseida* he had found masses of amplification that he wanted to omit, here he found much that cried out for amplification. He had reduced the *Teseida* to about a fifth of its length, but he made the *Filostrato* almost half as long again and his additions explain his intentions. Chaucer *supplied* the French conventions of love psychology. He *made* the hero sigh and weep, even faint in the lady's chamber; he *made* the heroine *dangereuse,* indeed made her constitutionally timid. He removed the stark paganism, representing it instead as an exotic polytheism, part of everyday life—and, more intriguing still, as a philosophy of life held by Pandarus, the lady's uncle. He obliterated the poet's association with the hero, supplying instead a bookish narrator (an amusing self-projection not unlike the "daswed" narrator in *The House of Fame*) who has an imaginary old book by a lost author, "Lollius." He added soliloquies that reveal Criseyde's thoughts and feelings, restored from Benoit de Sainte Maure (what Boccaccio had omitted) the heroine's pained and self-lacerating soliloquy about the jilting, added an epilogue in which the narrator rejects "pagans' cursed olde rites." He made the work less stark and overtly carnal, more puzzling and ambivalent, more psychological, more philosophical, and in the end more Christian.

Boccaccio's poem was, in the modern phrase, "distanced." The audience looks on it as from afar: the poet claims he wrote it to persuade his lady to pity him, and we are supposed to see it through his eyes. This device is the reverse of a truth claim: we needn't think the story true, but the author's feelings, expressed through the story, are true. Chaucer's greatest change was to downplay this distancing—to introduce a sense of intimacy between the narrator and his audience, and to promote the audience's direct involvement with the characters. It is thought in the English-speaking world that Chaucer improved *Il Filostrato* with these changes, but this is because he made it more like a modern novel, which is to say he made it more palatable to us. We do Boccaccio a grave disservice if we fail to ask why he wrote it as he did. Whether Chaucer understood why, even *felt* he understood, is a separate question, not really answerable.

Boccaccio's poem opened up in Chaucer's mind a vision of a romance, a tragic romance—and, perhaps as early as this, while he was still only thinking about it, a *philosophical* romance—unlike anything, as it would turn out, written before in England, or in France or Italy either.

Beyond Reading

At one time or another virtually all of Boccaccio's Italian works have been put forward as sources of works by Chaucer or influences on him. It was a fad at the turn of the century when his use of the *Filostrato* could no longer be denied; scholars systematically considered as influences each of Boccaccio's Italian works except the two Chaucer adapted, and rejected all. "We must," one author concluded, "continue to doubt the English poet's knowledge even of the existing person of the Italian writer"—and then tipped his hand: "The English poet served no apprenticeship to the Italian. He never became a literary disciple to him. He did not weakly imitate him as a master."

For years this was the accepted opinion. Chaucer's greatness would be diminished if Boccaccio were more than one of many negligible influences. But influence is something much more complicated than an apprenticeship or a discipleship. And imitation is not weak unless the poet is weak. Harold Bloom has shown us how far from mere imitation literary influence is, how much it is tinged with competitiveness, ambivalence, anxiety. Writers, emulating their literary mentors, envy and fear them, crave independence. Afraid that their debt will lessen their accomplishment, they react *against* their predecessors—they imitate them *strongly* by revisionism.

This model of poetic influence would have been unthinkable two generations ago. Sensible as it is, and as much as it squares with what we know now of human psychology, it created an agonized furor when it first appeared—then the shouting died down and it seemed obvious. Original- ity cannot be measured by the absence of borrowings; the most derivative works in the world show originality in style, treatment, insight. Chaucer's originality shows best in works based on other works, like the *Troilus*, where we can see how much he brought to what he was working with. Chaucer had to learn to "be unoriginal" when he passed from French to Italian models—had to learn to imitate productively.

It remains possible—many still believe it—that Chaucer didn't know even of "the existing person" of Boccaccio. But it is the greatest improba- bility, involving almost inconceivable coincidences. Believing it would mean accepting the following scenario: two, perhaps three, of Boccaccio's Italian works fell into Chaucer's hands by serendipity and he made adapta- tions of them; a few others fell into his hands and he quoted from them; several of Boccaccio's Latin works fell into his hands and he imitated the concepts of two and used passages from those two and others—but he did not know who wrote any of these works or that all were by the same author. And this though he had been to Florence while Boccaccio was alive and nearby and had met people like the Visconti who had known Boccaccio; though there was a community of educated Italians living in London; and though Boccaccio was famous in Italy, and outside Italy too in the twenty-five years between his death and Chaucer's. The far more probable scenario is that Chaucer knew about Boccaccio, had even possi- bly met him, knew more works than the few we can prove he knew, and knew or sensed enough about Boccaccio's remarkable career as a writer to think about it, be curious about any of his works he could look at even briefly, and compare what Boccaccio accomplished with what he was himself accomplishing or planning. Part of Boccaccio's influence on Chaucer, maybe the larger part, was on his sense of himself as an artist producing an oeuvre, his sense of his calling as a writer—as a *poet*. Chaucer's trip to Florence had taken him to the right place at the right time, and what he saw in Boccaccio and Boccaccio's mentor Petrarch was a major shift in literary history, one he barely understood.

10

Boccaccio
and the Birth
of Fiction

The two poems by Boccaccio that Chaucer chose to adapt would have looked to him like "courtly" literature, but the *Decameron* was a new kind of work—it embodied a new genre or "mode" with a new spirit and written for a new audience. Its plan and arrangement would have interested Chaucer, its sheer bulk, and its popularity in mercantile Florence. Yet it must have seemed to him exotic, written for and read by Florentines; you could write a work like it for Londoners, or Englishmen, but the *Decameron*, if translated, could not have in England the impact it had in Florence. And Chaucer was still too much a court poet to think about writing a work like it, even in verse. But it left an impression that he would seize upon when the time was right.

The Novella and the *Decameron*

The *Decameron* was the first major collection of *novelle* and the first significant specimen of fiction. The word *novella*—ancestor of our word *novel*—was already the name for such stories. There had been collections of them before, at least two in Italian. One is lost, and almost nothing is known about it save its title and author, the *Fiori di Novelle* by Francesco da Barberino, who died during the Black Death at the age of eighty-five. Another, called *Il Novellino* (later named *Cento Novelle Antiche* by its editor, with Boccaccio in mind), written in the late thirteenth or early fourteenth century, contained—like Boccaccio's—a hundred tales. It is a collection of impressive speeches and replies, courteous and valiant deeds, generous gifts; the stories are short, for the most part anecdotes, and are not held together by a "frame story." They reveal dramatically the connection the earliest fictions had with hearsay, news, or gossip, which Chaucer called "tidings."

From such a model Boccaccio made a literary masterpiece. By enclosing it in a frame narrative that recounts a game or ritual of storytelling, he gave it a significant form in which the tales are grouped by subject and constitute a "mercantile epic." In Chaucer's time it was imitated in Lucca by Giovanni Sercambi (1348–1424), in Florence by Giovanni Fiorentino in his *Percorone* (circa 1378–1385) and by Franco Sachetti (1335–1400) in his *Trecentonovelle* ("Three Hundred Tales"). These first instances of literary fiction, the Italian collections of *novelle*, were in prose—the earliest, the anonymous *Novellino*, in a language close to that of speech. Here is one of those stories in its entirety, No. 89:

> *This Story Is about the Courtier Who Began a Story*
> *That Never Came to an End*:
>
> A group of knights was dining one evening in a great house in Florence; and a courtier was there who was a great storyteller. When they had dined, he began a story which never came to an end.
>
> One young page of the household, who was serving and perhaps had not had much to eat, called him by name, saying:
>
> "Whoever taught you that story did not teach you the whole thing."
>
> And the other replied, "How so?"
>
> And he said, "Because he neglected to teach you the ending."
>
> Whereupon the other became ashamed and stopped.

This style is direct, unadorned, shorn of conventional rhetoric. Its emphasis is on events themselves, unshaped by the arts of expression (though the events may have to do with storytelling). Such a style was to become the language of the novel. Seen in this historical light, Boccaccio and Chaucer created two divagations in the development of fiction. Boccaccio elevated this natural style into "high" literary prose with syntactic inversions and long periodic sentences, based upon the Latin *cursus*, a form of rhythmical prose appropriate to elevated discourse. Here is a passage from the introduction to the First Day of the *Decameron*, where Boccaccio describes the Black Death, in the Payne translation as revised by Charles Singleton, the closest imitation of Boccaccio's prose in English:

> I say, then, that the years [of the era] of the fruitful Incarnation of the Son of God had attained to the number of one thousand three hundred and forty-eight, when into the notable city of Florence, fair over every other of Italy, there came the death-dealing pestilence, which, through the operation of the heavenly bodies or of our own iniquitous doings, being sent down upon mankind for our correction by the just wrath of God, had some years before appeared in the parts of the East and after having bereft these latter of an innumerable number of inhabitants, extending without cease from one place to another, had now unhappily spread towards the West.

This elevated manner, always a possibility in fiction, was the road taken by Proust or James, and in it Boccaccio created his masterpiece. Chaucer went in another direction. He took the material of fiction, these simple stories of things that had happened, didactic only as examples of conduct, and turned them into poetry. It never occurred to him to imitate Boccaccio's ornate prose. Chaucer's, like most medieval prose, is workaday and practical, clear, measured. It is the prose of a government official with a keen intellect who viewed prose as a vehicle for communication, not art. If he had chosen to write *Troilus and Criseyde* in such prose, he would have produced the first novel. He nearly did so as it is; in the *Troilus* he added to Boccaccio's original the domestic and personal detail, the dialogue, the interior monologues, the psychological scrutiny, all that we associate with fiction, and created what has been called the "first novel, in the modern sense." But it is in verse.

Boccaccio and His Book

Until recently, many of Boccaccio's Italian works, because they purported to be personal utterances, were read as a source for the facts of his life, and his works were then interpreted, by a great feat of circular reasoning, in the light of this "biography." Now it is understood that the "I" in his prologues and epilogues is essentially a fictional character. It used to be thought too—because he said as much in a letter to Petrarch—that in his middle years he renounced the salacious works of his youth and turned to scholarship. But here Boccaccio's actions speak louder than his words. He wrote the larger number of his Italian narratives in his early thirties (the two Chaucer adapted were among his earliest, written when he was in his twenties), but he completed the *Decameron* at about the age of forty, hardly part of youth. Moreover, these "salacious" works, under the microscope of modern critical inquiry, have appeared in various ways ironical and so quite adequately moral. Boccaccio saw them as courtly works, some based on popular forms, "written for the ladies" in the parlance of the day, which meant they were polite entertainments capable of being withdrawn by a retracting palinode or shrugged off as a mere bagatelle; the phrase was a device for evading responsibility. But what was "written for the ladies" had more force and more imaginative play than what was written in Latin for "serious" readers—males—and it is what we still read with pleasure; we read the rest out of duty if we read it at all.

Boccaccio never renounced these entertainments. About four years before his death—this has only been learned recently—he prepared a revised version of the *Decameron,* carefully written in his own hand. The manuscript has survived into our time and is preserved, in the Hamilton collection at the Staatsbibliothek in Berlin,* in Boccaccio's unique script, identifiable as the handwriting of his very last years.

Boccaccio was an illegitimate child raised by his father, a lesser functionary of the Bardi bank, a man remote in manner, stern, often away.

*The story of its discovery has a fascination of its own. In 1933 the Hamilton manuscript was sent from Berlin in a diplomatic pouch to the Laurenziana library in Florence at the request of the famous scholar Michele Barbi. He examined it and concluded, according to the later report of his assistant, "*E lui*—This is it, and it is not the handwriting of his early years but of his very last years." His judgment was confirmed by his colleague Giuseppe Vandelli. For reasons not entirely clear, Barbi never returned to look at the manuscript again; he and Vandelli took the secret to their graves—possibly thinking the information too explosive, for of course it showed that Boccaccio had not "renounced" his secular works. Barbi's assistant, Alberto Chiari, heroically putting a scholar's obligation to truth above personal loyalty, revealed the discovery to the world of scholarship seven years after Barbi's death, in 1948.

At this time the American scholar Charles Singleton was preparing an edition of the *Decameron* and had concluded that the Berlin manuscript, Hamilton 90, was the most authoritative. When he heard it was in Boccaccio's own hand, he brought to Berlin the ranking expert on Boccaccio's handwriting, Armando Petrucci, who sat before the manuscript turning pages for some time, then turned to Singleton and, echoing Barbi's pronouncement, declared, *E lui.* Singleton asked if there were not some idiosyncrasy in Boccaccio's handwriting never found in another's; well, yes, there was his odd way of making a final *s*, which, however, almost never occurs in Italian. Singleton thought of one or two proper names and foreign words in the *Decameron* having final *s*, and there it was, as conclusive as a fingerprint.

Boccaccio, sent to Naples in his teens to study canon law, fell in with the rich and sophisticated court of the Angevin ruler and remained there as an aspiring literary figure until he was twenty-eight. In this aristocratic milieu the son of a middle-class family could survive only by drawing attention to himself. In his extravagant early poems, written against the background of French courtly poetry—the Angevin court was French—and under the influence of Dante, they gained him the notoriety he desired: they were romances and dream visions in both verse and prose, all in the vernacular. They were about love, of course, but were focused daringly on the physical and sexual. Boccaccio was taking popular forms like the *cantare,* narratives recited aloud on streetcorners, and trying to raise their literary status; he did the same with the *novelle.* His efforts to write in the courtly mode in these early Italian works—at least some of which Chaucer knew—were often awkward and coarse. He never quite grasped the spirit of courtliness. Chaucer, raised from fourteen in a courtly world, would have discerned this failing in Boccaccio's early works, and this, so it has been argued, may explain why he never mentions Boccaccio by name.

Boccaccio returned to Florence in 1341. In April of that year, shortly after Boccaccio left Naples, Petrarch, then thirty-seven, was crowned poet laureate on the Capitoline in Rome. Boccaccio heard about the coronation and contracted at once a deep admiration for the laureate, even wrote an essay about him, and made overtures to him. Almost a decade later, in the fall of 1350, Petrarch, returning from a pilgrimage to Rome, stopped at Florence. Boccaccio met him at the city gate, gave him the customary gift of a ring, and entertained him as a guest in his house. Petrarch was nine years older, by birth rather much higher on the social scale, and a great deal more famous. Boccaccio was by now the acknowledged leader of Florentine culture, and he had probably written more than Petrarch had—he had written nearly all of the *opere minori in volgare* and had begun the *Decameron*—but he did not regard himself as the laureate's equal. While he had been playing court poet to a Neapolitan prince and writing saucy works in his native tongue, Petrarch had been traveling about Europe discovering manuscripts of ancient writers, and writing works in Latin. He had begun his epic *Africa,* which he never finished, and had written *De Viris Illustribus,* a learned work on famous men; the *Secretum,* a dialogue between himself and Saint Augustine, and the *De Vita Solitaria,* both high-minded works about the calling of the man of letters. And he had been crowned laureate after a public examination, like an ancient Roman. This was indeed someone for Boccaccio to admire.

And Petrarch with his enormous self-regard accepted the role in which Boccaccio cast him, of a superior and mentor. He acknowledged Boccaccio as his disciple and politely condescended to his Italian works and prose narratives; such were the snobberies of the day. Both had written epics about the ancient world, but Boccaccio's was in the vulgar tongue. Both were writing *rime*—"sonnets"—in Italian, but Petrarch thought of them as something he did with his left hand (by an irony of history they became his most famous and influential works). In the matter of writing in Italian, Boccaccio had the example of Dante before him— he was already a great student of Dante, was soon to begin a treatise on him—but about Dante Petrarch remained always indifferent and vague, never quite prepared to accept the universal judgment that Dante was the greatest Italian poet. In the year after their meeting, Boccaccio began writing the *Genealogie* in Latin, doubtless in response to Petrarch's urging. It reveals something about their relationship that in this same year Petrarch began the *Trionfi*, in Italian, modeled on Boccaccio's *Amorosa Visione*.

Both men were complicated personalities. Both had something to gain from and give to the other. Petrarch had single-handedly brought secular poetry—"humane letters"—and the role of the poet into high esteem, and Boccaccio revered him for it; what Boccaccio had done for prose was as great, but the accomplishment was ahead of its time— Petrarch could not have been expected to admire it. Boccaccio aspired to Petrarch's honors, envied them, strove for them. In 1353 Petrarch accepted the hospitality of the Visconti in Milan; Boccaccio in a letter begged him not to become a courtier to a tyrant. But not two years later Boccaccio himself was off to Naples to be a courtier, accepting the invitation of Niccolò Acciaiuoli, a friend from his youthful days in Naples, a fellow Florentine of the same class as himself, and illegitimate too, who through a propitious marriage had risen to enormous power in the Neapolitan kingdom. Boccaccio had spoken invidiously of him in poems and letters to friends; in a matter of months he was leaving Naples disgruntled, for what slight we do not know. Acciaiuoli, an arrogant, sarcastic, insensitive man, had probably heard of Boccaccio's hostile words about him; but then Boccaccio was extremely touchy and irascible—on his return he wrote an eclogue heaping abuse on Acciaiuoli, whom he called Midas.

The situation was the same eight years later. Petrarch was off to cross the Alps and visit the court of the Emperor Charles IV. Boccaccio urged him not to go—the journey was dangerous, he would be distracted from his work. But then Boccaccio went once more to the court of Acciaiuoli for another disappointment, worse than the last; this time he took his library with him, evidently expecting to stay, and got a "bed not fit for a dog" in a room "like a sewer," which he was expected to share. He had wanted a position of dignity, like Petrarch's among the Visconti; instead he got the crass insults recorded in his letters. Possibly his hopes were too high, possibly he saw slights where none were meant—he was emotionally delicate, everyone agrees: his friend Nelli, probably echoing a sneer from Acciaiuoli, called him "a man of glass."

In their friendship Boccaccio seems always the one to give, Petrarch to receive, or else refuse. In the year after their first meeting, through Boccaccio's efforts, Petrarch was offered a chair at the new *studio,* the university, in Florence. Petrarch, after accepting the splendid gifts that went with the offer, turned it down, to the fury of the university's officials. Boccaccio overlooked and forgave it. Two years later, 1355, Boccaccio sent Petrarch a magnificent gift, a manuscript of Saint Augustine's commentaries on the Psalms, and the next year sent him works he had discovered by Varro and Cicero, copied in his own hand. Petrarch wrote in the volume of Saint Augustine, "That distinguished gentleman, my lord Giovanni Boccaccio of Certaldo, poet of our age, gave me this immense work, which arrived from Florence April 10, 1355." The word poet (*poeta*) was the highest compliment. But Petrarch never, as it appears, thanked Boccaccio for any of these gifts. Acciaiuoli had lately bestowed extravagant praise on Petrarch and the laureate must have smelled honors in the offing; he may have felt he had something to lose by a display of friendship with a man Acciaiuoli scorned. When taxed by Boccaccio for his silence, Petrarch after some delay wrote a soothing letter in which he declared Boccaccio a *poeta,* and Boccaccio was humbly grateful.

It was always thought that a turning point in Boccaccio's life occurred in 1362 when he was forty-nine. He was visited by a fanatic from Siena with news that "the blessed Petroni," a religious figure who had a local cult there, had had on his deathbed a vision of Jesus, who told him Boccaccio and Petrarch were soon to die and must renounce poetry. Boccaccio, who was like Petrarch a clerk in minor orders, had received an ecclesiastical benefice the year before (he may in fact have been ordained a priest), and this perhaps stirred his anxiety or guilt, though they were always pretty high. He wrote to Petrarch, and Petrarch's reply, which contains all the information we have, suggests that Boccaccio was genuinely distressed. Petrarch was not: he encouraged his friend to continue his literary pursuits and urged him to give up any thought of retiring from the world or selling his library—not, however, without offering to buy it himself. Boccaccio went back to work, and his writings after this incident are not less "secular" than they had been before it. As he grew older he wrote less in Italian "for the ladies" and more in Latin for scholarly male readers; but his scholarship was still "humane" letters, and he still took an interest in improving his "youthful" works.

Petrarch was forever urging Boccaccio to be more serious, more scholarly. He never read the *Decameron* until the year before he died, and then read only a little of it, writing Boccaccio a patronizing letter:

> Your book, written in our mother tongue and published, I presume, during your early years, has fallen into my hands, I know not whence or how. If I told you that I had read it, I should deceive you. It is a very big volume, written in prose and for the multitude. I have been, moreover, occupied with more serious business. . . . What I did was to run through your book, like a traveller who, while hastening forward, looks about him here and there, without pausing. . . . If the humor is a little too free at times, this may be excused in view of the age at which you wrote, the style and language which you employ, and the frivolity of the subjects, and of the persons who are likely to read such tales. . . .

He goes on to relate his enthusiasm for the last tale and announce that he has translated it into Latin. The implication is that what he translated into Latin would have a claim on posterity that the original, in the vulgar tongue, would not. And indeed Petrarch's translation, which Chaucer in turn adapted into English, circulated all over Europe and drew international attention to the *Decameron*.

Boccaccio revered Petrarch, called him "magister" and "pater," even in old age. But while they played at master and pupil—perhaps more to the point, father and son—the two great humanists imitated each other, inspired each other, vied with each other. Boccaccio wrote his *De Claris Mulieribus* as an addendum to Petrarch's *De Viris Illustribus,* and his *De Casibus* in imitation of Petrarch's *De Remediis Utriusque Fortunae.* On the other side of the ledger, Petrarch wrote his *Posteritati* in response to Boccaccio's *Vita Petrarchi* and his *Invectivae* in response to Boccaccio's *Genealogie.* Petrarch's *Trionfi* were inspired by Boccaccio's *Amorosa Visione*; and in old age, when Boccaccio revised the *Amorosa Visione,* Petrarch revised the *Trionfi*.

Rely on Petrarch as Boccaccio did, long for attention, fall into gloomy moods, lose confidence or hope, fret over his finances or his future or the state of his soul, Boccaccio nevertheless knew exactly what he was doing, knew it with the secure instincts of a genius. And knew he had to do it on his own. He was never to have anyone for a father or, in fundamental respects, for a master; he only needed the *idea* of it. Petrarch several times invited Boccaccio, in the most explicit terms, to come and live with him. Boccaccio always refused. Under Petrarch's influence he had turned to learned writings in Latin, and his learning, as vast as Petrarch's, produced works that equaled the master's, perhaps surpassed them. If he had followed Petrarch's counsel, Boccaccio would have abandoned the *Decameron* when it was just begun. He began the *Genealogie* the year after he met Petrarch, yes, and it was the great repository of classical learning throughout Europe for four centuries; but he went on writing the *Decameron* for three more years, and then, almost two decades later, as an old man, sick, knowing he was facing death, rewrote the whole of it. During his middle years Boccaccio had stumbled on something that had made him famous, famous in a way Petrarch would never be famous. He, who had tried to be a courtier, writing courtly works for a courtly audience, had written a long work in Tuscan prose, *prosa d'arte,* for his own class, the merchant class of the Florentine commune, and they had received it with enthusiastic and respectful approval. Outside of Florence, in other city-states, the *Decameron* was known and admired; even Acciaiuoli sought a copy of it. When in the *Genealogie* Boccaccio distinguishes a kind of stories like "old wives' tales" containing no truth, and says they have "nothing in common with the works of the poets," the remark is often reckoned a rejection of all fictions including his own. But it only rejects them from the realm of poetry; in the realm of prose Boccaccio had made a place for them.

The *Decameron:* Contempt and Escape

What the *Decameron* did, and what Boccaccio at some level of consciousness meant it to do, was to alter the status of fiction. In giving his work a characteristic pseudo-Greek title supposed to mean "ten days," he highlighted the chief activity of his ten young people who flee the plague for fourteen days and spend ten of them telling stories. He gave it the subtitle "Prince Galeotto" (Prince Gallehault of the Arthurian legend, who introduced Lancelot and Guinevere) in a covert reference to Francesca's remark in *Inferno* 5: 137, *Galeotto fu il libro e chi lo scrisse,* "the book was a Gallehault, and he who wrote it." This is sometimes thought a declaration that he meant his book to be like a pander, but the word *Galeotto* did not have this low connotation in the Tuscan of Boccaccio's day; Gallehault was a friendly introducer, a go-between, but not a bawd. Besides, the word was a pun—*galeotto* also meant a pilot. Boccaccio seemed to mean that his book was a third party piloting or introducing the stories to the reader and the reader to the stories. It was, so he argued in his own defense, up to the reader to respond to them aright.

That was the attitude toward stories in traditional Christian thought. Stories were one of "the things of this world" to be renounced, but in the established Augustinian theology the things of this world were in themselves indifferent, good or bad only insofar as they were used well or ill. Stories, like pictures or jewels, were commendable so long as the story taught something, the picture prompted devotion, the jewel adorned a relic or a bishop. Some stories (what we've called legends) could be accepted on faith as authentic survivals of the Christian past: they were testimonials to the faith, exemplary or cautionary, that brought history to bear on the present. And some stories (what we've called "myths") could be accepted for their inner truth—interpreted mystically or allegorically for their hidden meaning.

Apart from these there must always have existed garden-variety stories about funny, curious, or amazing things that are supposed to have happened, preserved in gossip or lore and told for their interest. In the twelfth century, stories of this kind attained literary status in courtly romances, *lais*, fabliaux, and the like, all in verse. They had sometimes mythic and legendary significance, but if so they had more often to do with the chivalric than the Christian past. And perhaps on this account they came to be viewed by moralists with discomfort.

For morality itself had changed. While this new kind of writing was making its appearance, there were appearing too the gloomy treatises and poems on "contempt of the world." The psychology or frame of mind that lay beneath "contempt" was the very opposite of what lay beneath fiction. "Contempt" meant indifference, withdrawal, disdain for what is temporary and unsatisfactory, as opposed to what is eternal and perfect. The writings *de contemptu mundi* appealed to a particular sensibility, which was the dark, uneasy, pessimistic underside of the new secularism. Fiction appealed to the opposite sensibility: fictions amused people, let them live in others' lives as a temporary alternative to living in their own, embodied not contempt but *escape*. Fictions had beginnings and ends, had neatness and balance, made sense; real life, then as now, went on in helter-skelter fashion and most often made no sense at all. From real life one could draw the lesson of contempt for the world, but not from fictions—fictions made the world out as a state to be embraced.

Fictions ran counter to the prevailing pietistic utilitarianism, as we may call it, because they lacked "profit." One doesn't find heaped on them the vituperation reserved for lechery or gluttony or avarice, but fictions were denounced as vanities. Chaucer's Parson calls them "lesings," lies: "another lesing cometh of delight for to lie, in which delight they wol forge a long tale, and painten it with all circumstances, where all the ground of the tale is false." This was the hard line; subtler thinkers, like Saint Augustine, had seen that some kinds of truth can be grasped through falsehoods, that in the arts the more lifelike representation is the greater lie, that (in Saint Paul's words) "all that is written is written for our doctrine."

Boccaccio set out to rescue this subtler attitude, to promote a return to the older Augustinian view that a work of art is a thing indifferent, good or bad only as we make it so. In the *Decameron* he rejected the idea that a story must offer a "truth" or else be a "vanity." He claimed that we can read any story for good or for ill; the responsibility falls on us and has nothing to do with the content of the story. He says this in so many words at the end of the *Decameron*: "like all other things in this world, stories, whatever their nature, may be harmful or useful, depending upon the listener."

The *Decameron*, then, is a story about stories. The narrator is not a forlorn lover but an eager storyteller, and he introduces us to a group of ten storytellers in a setting of comfort and delight. They make a resolve to escape together from the plague and follow a regimen doctors actually prescribed: they eat good food and drink good wine in moderation, and take pleasure in songs, dancing, and stories. The purpose is to ease the mind and body as a hygienic measure. Doctors recommended flight to those for whom it was possible, and the group rehearse the reasons why they need not stay in the city precisely as they are outlined in medical treatises of the day. The stories have the same purpose as the songs, the wine, the trip itself: they give pleasure, bestow calm, afford relief from the cares of life.

The framing story of the group's activities invites us into this ambience, makes us participants. We become one of them during a luxurious two weeks, on ten days of which each tells a story, one acts as king or queen for a day, each day having a theme and ending with a song. All is as we would have it be. No part of the plan is ever violated. There are luxurious gardens (in which the tales are told), handsome country estates, servants, good food, wine, conversation, sport and pleasure, of which the stories are a part. Nothing occurs during the two weeks to darken this idyllic atmosphere, except a quarrel among the servants, viewed as an amusement by their masters. None of the characters is less than delightful —even the cynical Dioneo is a feisty, pleasing character; all are of the upper class; and though we are able to remember which is which and tell them apart, we do not have a strong sense of their individual personalities. Nor are the tales each tells especially suitable to his or her character— one never learns from the tale something revealing about the teller. The members of the group have generalized, not individualized, traits; their names are suggestive of character—Lauretta suggests Petrarch's Laura,

Panfile means "loves all," Filostrato "cast down by love"—but the meanings are a matter of disagreement among scholars and do not reward any
effort to make the work an allegory. We are never put in the position of
a detached observer of the ten participants' appearance or character; the
presentation of them leaves blank spaces, as one might say, which invite
us to project ourselves upon their somewhat spectral presences, join in
their genteel and pleasurable existence.

Their sojourn begins on a Wednesday and with interruptions on
Fridays (because it is a fast day) and Saturdays (so the ladies can wash their
hair for the sabbath) continues for ten days of storytelling through a
Tuesday; they leave Florence on a Tuesday and return on a Wednesday,
as if there had been no interruption in the week. On the first day they
travel but two miles out of the city to a palace in the country. On the third
day they travel to another two miles to the west (in a sort of anti-
pilgrimage, for one remembers that Jerusalem, the symbolic destination
of all pilgrimages, was in the *east*) to another palace having a walled
garden with a crystal-clear pool very reminiscent of the *Roman de la Rose*,
and we are told that "they all began to maintain that if Paradise were
constructed on earth, it was inconceivable that it could take any other
form." On the fourth day the author undertakes the famous defense of
himself, in the course of which he tells an incomplete tale of a boy
protected by his father from ladies. When he sees some ladies, having
been taken to Florence, his father tells him they are goslings; he asks to
take one home so he can pop things in its bill, and the father answers
"their bills are not where you think and require a special sort of diet," then
realizes his wits "were no match for Nature." The author's story is a
declaration that this is the world of Nature we are in, different from the
world of Grace; his modest defense is that in writing for the ladies he is
doing what is natural. At the end of the sixth day the company enters the
Valley of the Ladies, "perfectly circular in shape . . . though it seemed
the work of Nature rather than of man." In the epilogue the author
acknowledges that "the things of this world have no stability, but are
subject to constant change," and adds that this is what may have happened to his tongue, which he then characterizes as an instrument both
of storytelling and of kissing. The last image of the *Decameron* is this
dual-purpose tongue, very like the last image of *The Canterbury Tales* in
the last lines of the Manciple's Tale, the wagging tongue counseling
silence.

But at the end of the two weeks, when we leave this world of Nature,
what do we return to? To the city of Florence, which the company left
to escape the Black Death of 1348, described in detail at the beginning
of the work. And there is no suggestion that anything has changed.

History had given Boccaccio the stuff of an allegory or a *sovrasenso* with which to frame his work. The plague was something all his audience had lived through, and its message was clear: the world is mutable, filled with strife and terror. Storytelling is a pleasant and genteel game that allows us to escape this circumstance *for a time*.

Boccaccio's precedent in all this was the tradition of the *Roman de la Rose*, the courtly tradition of pseudopaganism that pretended to worship Venus, Cupid, and Nature. The tradition was that of "naturalism" —what Professor Aldo Scaglione has characterized as "revaluation of instinctive life in a rational framework"; in the *Decameron* this becomes "an appropriate introduction for a gentle opening of the mind—without a direct, sudden, and drastic exposure—to those subterranean phenomena of life, those forces of matter and of the unconscious, which, in their full bloom, could but frighten and repel the medieval mind." The world of Nature was a refuge from the strict ascetical morality of the church, a safe refuge because it was always to be understood that the claims of Nature must yield to the claims of Grace—in the end. The tradition of naturalism posited an ordered world: there was a law of Nature, a goddess Nature, and there had been, in the ancient times that the humanists admired, an Age of Nature.

This tradition gave Boccaccio a sort of immunity. He could always assert the claims of grace over those of nature and so retract his writings that were "of the world," like Petrarch in the *Secretum* allowing that "to things temporal things eternal will succeed." With that immunity he proceeded in the *Decameron* to tear away at the corruptions and hypocrisies of the church, to mock it good-naturedly, to make a joke at its expense. The very first tale is of a scoundrel whose brazen pretense of piety wins him sainthood. Perhaps it is true, as one critic thinks, that Boccaccio set out to desacralize the institution of the church as a necessary step toward its reform. Or perhaps he was taking the temporary license given to such customs as the Feast of Fools, adopting a satiric carnivalesque spirit.

For in the *Decameron* the world of story is a temporary antiworld; the real world has a plague to be escaped. Darker sides of human life come out in the stories, but they are only stories after all and for the most part funny ones. And they are told in an aura of moral neutrality. The outer frame, the flight from the plague, is static: it is an image of the transitory world, fallen and diseased. The stories are dynamic: they relate to one another, to their tellers, to their assigned topics, and belong to an indulged world, a world apart. To Boccaccio, this "world apart" existed for its own sake within the world of the everyday. It is available for a little time, is chiefly for the leisured and privileged, is its own reward, exists for no reason but escape and survival.

In this conception of fiction as a world apart from the fallen world
we inhabit lies the origin of our habitual idea that fiction is a mass, of
which a single instance must be called a "work" or "piece" of fiction. The
tales of the *Decameron* are held together, in Erich Auerbach's phrase,
"only by the common purpose of well-bred entertainment," but they
cohere as a mirror world or antiworld of the world they tell about. Critics
have labored hard to find an allegory or a grammar or a substructure of
themes that makes some message emerge from the antiworld of Boccaccio's hundred tales. But the message is *that there is no message.* From
them emerges, rather, an ethos. The reader gets a composite experience
of coping with the realities of life, and the virtues put forth are those of
the merchant class—wiliness, street wisdom, good instincts, common
sense, a quick tongue; on the other side of the coin idealism, love, hope,
patience, humor, disdain for hypocrisy or cant or sanctimoniousness. The
tales aren't told to *teach* this ethos; they are told, as all fiction is told,
because it is diverting—the ethos takes shape not in the tales but in us
as we read them.

Then at the end we are back in the city: "The three young men went
off in search of other diversions; and in due course the ladies returned to
their homes." In the epilogue the author himself emerges at the center
of all. His last words, addressed to the ladies, are. "If perchance these
stories should bring you any profit, *remember me.*" Fictions are part of
the world, and will pass away as the world will pass away, but while the
world lasts they can, whatever else they may do, *bring fame to their author.*
While its epilogue ends with this humanist preoccupation, the *Decameron,* like the *Filostrato,* presupposes the sensibility of contempt for the
world and expects the audience to see, in the group's return to an un-
changed city, the implication of mutability, vanity, imperfection. Boccaccio represents fiction as an escape, but he represents that escape as if
it were a dream in a bleak world against which we are powerless and which
in the end we must despise. At the end of the *Decameron* we return home
and go on with a life to be endured; the stories have a limited place in
the scheme of things and a limited value. In this, Boccaccio was more a
man of the Middle Ages than Chaucer. But just *because* he thought
fiction limited in this way, his fiction could afford to be more extravagant
and impudent than Chaucer's, less admixed with serious matter, and in
prose rather than verse.

And Boccaccio saw to the heart of the matter as, it may be, Chaucer
did not, recognizing that fictions are a separate kind of experience, one
that exists because it satisfies an emotional need. As a scholar Boccaccio's
stupendous accomplishment was recording and interpreting the myths
and legends of classical antiquity, and he believed such stories useful

because they had respectively a mystical or historical truth. He believed fictions are useful as recreation, as escape; that was an accepted medical and philosophical idea, and squares still with common sense. But he may have believed too, according to ancient precedents, that fictions were "cases" to be examined and argued about—were tools for thinking about human life.

The Uses of Fiction

That Boccaccio's art is an art of escape—that entertainment is its use— was the thesis of an article by Charles Singleton published in 1944, "On Meaning in the *Decameron*." He argued that Boccaccio "is interested in giving by artistic strategy, not by direct reasoning, a justification of his art," that he "had good reason to know that the art of his tales was an art of escape. He knew this in his own soul, and he knew it in his contemporaries. Here was an art completely bare and defenseless, for it could not claim to teach."

Boccaccio was commending, Singleton believed, a "moment of art," that moment for the reader in which a work is so compelling that "all else is put from the mind and art can exist with no other *raison d'être* than that in itself it is a consolation and a delight." The frame of the *Decameron* attempts to "justify and protect a new art, an art which simply in order to be, to exist, required the moment free of all other cares, the willingness to stop *going anywhere* (either toward God or toward philosophical truth)."

This sounded to specialists in Italian literature like "art for art's sake," a notion very little palatable on either side of the Atlantic, especially in universities. The specialists wanted the *Decameron* to be a work with a meaning, a "serious" meaning, intellectual, allegorical, moral. And it would not do to find this meaning in the frame: the book is a story about stories told by a group in the larger world of Florence during the Black Death, beyond which world lies the encompassing mind of the author, who at certain points may step outside his book to defend it. These framing devices indicate such earnestness about the tales that it is thought the real meaning must be in them, and there have been many attempts to find such a meaning, no two of which agree. One recent scholar, with endearing candor, concludes that "none of the attempts I have seen to fit the stories into definite and precise formal patterns of meaning has been successful, including my own."

Boccaccio in later years wrote a definition of narrative (*fabula*) in Book 14 of the *Genealogie* that is often thought to prove that he rejected the *Decameron*. He said that narratives, under the guise of invention, illustrate or test ideas: "As a story's superficial aspect is removed, the meaning of the author is clear." Borrowing from Macrobius, he distinguished four kinds of narratives. The first is manifestly false, as when animals talk; the second combines false and true, as when people are turned into animals for believable reasons. These are what we have been calling myths. The third "is more like history than fiction," as in Virgil or Homer, who tell events that "could have occurred, or might at some time": the authors "portray varieties of human nature and conversation, incidentally teaching the reader and putting him on his guard." These are what we have been calling legends, narratives having mystical or historical meanings. Then Boccaccio says: "The fourth kind contains no truth at all, either superficial or hidden, since it consists only of old wives' tales."* Of this fourth kind (what we have been calling "fictions") he adds that they have "nothing in common with the work of poets."

This remark is often taken as a rejection of the fourth kind of narratives that "contain no truth": Singleton himself thought Boccaccio "changed his mind" in later years. And yet Boccaccio, referring to his opponents, says "I count as naught their condemnation of the fourth form of fiction," though he chooses to say nothing in its defense. Now that we know Boccaccio revised the *Decameron* in old age, we know he did not change his mind about the tales he wrote in the *Decameron*, though clearly they *were* of this fourth kind. His view, consistent throughout his life, was that there exists a class of narratives that contain no truth but still have a use. In the *Decameron* the escape from the plague is a metaphor, which tells us that fiction is an escape from the world, a detachment from the world of a different order than "contempt." Contempt brings us to a spiritual distance, gives us renunciation; escape brings us to a rational distance, gives us perspective. In the *Genealogie*, speaking of narrative (*fabula*), Boccaccio tells us that it pleases the unlearned with illusions and the learned with hidden truths, that it teaches and delights "with one and the same perusal." He praises it for its *emotional* effects —for restoring minds to sanity or inspiring motivation to learn. About the fourth kind of narrative, that contains no truth and has nothing to do with poets' work, Boccaccio could have stated in the *Genealogie* what he suggested through an artistic strategy in the *Decameron*; but he did not, and we must divine his thoughts from the strategy.

Boccaccio suggests in the epilogue of the *Decameron* that histories

*Cum sit delirantium vetularum inventio, literally "since it is the invention of ranting old women." The notion is close, etymologically, to English "gossip," which implies the idle talk of older people such as godparents. In *The House of Fame*, as we have seen, gossip, "tidings," and *novelle* were equated.

are neutral, their value dependent on the reader. Various critics have argued that in the tales themselves he meant to promote a certain frame of mind appropriate to the mercantile class; or open the mind gently in areas where medieval thinking was rigid and circumscribed; or present an inductive program of training in leadership and responsible civic behavior; or extol fame (the subject of the last day's stories) as the reward of noble conduct, which can raise us from the level of animal instinct so often depicted in the tales. Critics have found patterns of themes in the tales, or identified abstract characteristics or virtues in the members of the group. All these interpretations are feasible, all are supported by the text. Yet the work in its complexity, like all masterpieces, defeats any effort to pin it down. The author meant the work to mean something, all agree, but none can agree on what he meant.

Recently, however, an American scholar, Wesley Trimpi, has discovered a connection between the fictions of Boccaccio's age and a body of ancient, traditional ideas *about* fiction—a connection he thinks Boccaccio saw or sensed. The discovery is so new that no one yet knows how it may color our estimate of medieval and Renaissance literature or literary thought. Trimpi has found something people had suspected or guessed but never seen, like a new kind of particle or a missing link. If it were a discovery in the sciences its discoverer would probably, in due course, win a Nobel prize.

Trimpi's purpose was to show how late medieval fictions were shaped by ideas inherited from ancient rhetoric. Rhetoric, intertwined as it was in the ancient world with other disciplines like philosophy, poetics, or grammar, had its origins in the oratory of the law courts. At base, rhetoric was a set of prescriptions for arguing a case—it was, as it remains, the art of persuasion, but it was tied particularly to persuasion in a court of law or before a legislative body. From the exercises in rhetoric described in ancient treatises the young orator learned his art in the spirit of a game before he went into the less relaxed atmosphere of court or forum. The ancient methods of argument became part of the elementary exercises in schools and were thus passed on to the Middle Ages and the Renaissance as the elements of literary education. When the ancient civilizations passed away, the social background of rhetoric changed but the treatises and terminology survived. Rhetoric remained in use in law courts, even while its connection with other disciplines was obscured, and so it remained part of education. The place of fictions in a system of intellectual inquiry, and their "immunity" as exercises or experiments of thought, were thus transmitted to the later Middle Ages.

At the center of the ancient system were the methods of examining motives. When we examine any act that has been committed, we want to know whether it really took place and what exactly happened, but we want most to know what was the character or quality of the act. We want to know whether a murder was committed in self-defense, was premeditated, was done in malice or in passion. And here *fictions* enter the picture. We argue such matters best by presenting fictional examples or hypothetical cases or by citing familiar stories, like those of Oedipus or Hamlet. In ancient rhetoric the "quality" of an act came to take precedence because the orator, as an artist, could dwell on the emotions involved and thus play upon the feelings of his audience—which was the best way of winning sympathy for his client. And fictions were the best means for doing this.

In addition, fictions were a means of adjudicating between general precepts and particular cases. To use a classic example, the amount of food an individual needs is a mean between too much and too little, but the actual amount must be adjusted to the circumstances of each case—a person's size, age, activity, and so on. Making a determination between the general and the particular in this manner—called "equity" in ancient thought—is achieved by attention to particular circumstances, whether true or not. When we *think* about such questions, we say, "if a man is of medium frame and works as a stonemason" and do not consider that we are telling a lie. "If" gives the fiction license. The fiction tests the application of a law: it isn't true in fact but true *in relation to its use*. Fictions were not lies because they were not intended to deceive; they were cousin to what we now call "legal fictions." When we say "truth is stranger than fiction," we have in mind the generalizing use to which fictions are put; an *actual* case often raises particularities that only muddy the issue of how a law should be applied, but a fiction gets precisely at the point.

So from the orator's point of view, a fiction was part of a constructed argument. Ancient writers, Cicero and Quintilian among them, distinguished three kinds of stories: a story without truth or verisimilitude, called a fable (*fabula*); a story based on events of the past, called a history or legend (*historia*); and a story that is fictional but bears a likeness to the truth, called in Greek a *hypothesis* (in Latin, *argumentum*). Such a hypothesis or argument—a "hypothetical" in modern parlance—was used in an inquiry by examining both sides of the case in an effort to arrive at the probable solution. This inquiring on either side (*in utramque partem*) does not presume that one side is right and one wrong; the dialectic establishes a middle ground, and that middle ground is the *image* of what is probable, right, and just.

In a court of law, then, there was a general proposition or thesis to be argued and a particular case to be examined. The general proposition pertains to philosophy; the case, with its particularity and ambiguity, and its questions about the quality of actions, pertains to rhetoric. And a fictional or hypothetical case was the best way to set out such an argument for discussion. Here is an example from Seneca. The law required that a priestess be chaste and pure. The case is of a young virgin captured by pirates. She is put up for sale and sold to a pimp, who puts her to work as a prostitute. But she asks each man who comes to her that he pay her (she must give the fee to the pimp) and not lie with her. A soldier comes to her, refuses to do what she asks, and tries to rape her—but she kills him. She is charged with murder, tried, and acquitted. Then she is sent back to her native country, where she applies to become a priestess. The question to be debated is, was she sufficiently chaste and pure for the priesthood?

In the presentation of such stories it was important that they seem real. The orator constructed a highly particularized version of the events in a hypothetical case. These constructions relied on what were called "colors"; the term was applied in a more general way to the coloring of events by devices of style—of toning down or highlighting guilt. The plot of the story is like a line drawing; the "colors" give it life, and are therefore the added, artful aspect of fiction. The term "colors" survived into the Middle Ages—it is used several times by Chaucer—and the idea itself has never disappeared: we still believe that detail and feeling are what give "life" and "color" to fiction.

Fictions worked by deduction. If we were examining real-life events, we would arrive by induction at certain general observations. But we examine a fiction armed with a prior body of adequate premises and come to probable conclusions about *one case*. It is an exercise of thought. One notion has been that *exempla* were the originals of fictions, and this may be; the medieval way was to state a principle like "murder will out" and tell stories that illustrate or prove it by example. But this medieval habit —which Chaucer loves to ridicule—was probably a degenerated form of the way fictions were used in rhetoric as "arguments" to test a general proposition. Chaucer ridicules piling them up so that the logical thread is lost; when his characters get to telling *exempla*, they become obsessed with the stories and forget the argument, which would have seemed funny to anyone with legal training.

This was what fictions were in the courtroom. In the classroom they were more playful and fanciful: they tended to split off from the ancient forensic tradition. The teller of the fiction had an "immunity" because he told his story in an indulgent atmosphere as part of his training. This context had been largely forgotten in the Middle Ages, but the playful manner had survived: fictions became the materials for hypothetical arguments in mock cases and fantastical ones. They were a game, not in schools alone but in the playful discourse of clerics in monasteries or cathedral chapters, or in the courts of nobles. And such traditions as the argument *in utramque partem* made these amusements the more delightful because the storyteller might playfully leave things up in the air.

A fiction, then, was neutral: it was told *as if* it really happened, but in a context that assumed an audience possessing a prior body of precept and a spirit of inquiry. Its ethical implications were not in the plot or in the "facts," but in the reactions of a participatory audience. This is in part what Boccaccio had in mind in the epilogue of the *Decameron* when he said that stories are harmful or useful depending upon the listener.

This gamelike atmosphere in which fictions existed is very like the atmosphere of much medieval literature—of its debates and dream visions, of the *Decameron*, of *The Canterbury Tales*. We leave the active life for the contemplative, leave the courtroom where one side must win for the playful, inquiring, open-ended spirit in which both sides can be viewed equally. Some medieval works, like the *De Amore* of Andreas Cappellanus, have always been puzzles because of their even-handedness and ambiguity, their "irony," but they are completely understandable when seen as arguments *in utramque partem*. There were "debate" poems that came to no resolution. In courtly poetry there were forms like the *jeu parti* that offered two sides of a question, and there was a tradition of *demandes d'amour* in which a love story ended with a question for the audience to discuss.

In both Boccaccio and Chaucer we find "questions" of this kind—the first part of the Knight's Tale is an example; so is the Franklin's Tale. This is something Chaucer did not need to get from Boccaccio, for both inherited the same traditions. In one of his earliest prose romances, the *Filocolo*, Boccaccio introduced a series of such questions, and the passage is generally thought the predecessor of the *Decameron*. And in the *Decameron* many of the tales lend themselves to such questioning.

How clearly medieval thinkers understood the ancient traditions of rhetoric, the place of fictions in those traditions, and the "immunity" of those fictions, we cannot be sure. Petrarch, Boccaccio, and Chaucer all had legal training, which may have given them a better sense of rhetoric than others had; and all knew the major rhetorical texts. Boccaccio shared with Dante and Petrarch a reverence for the poet and for letters; but unlike them he wrote fictions and was prepared to defend their usefulness. Petrarch, translating the last tale of the *Decameron*, the story of the patient Griselda, moralized it, made it a medieval *exemplum* of how we should bear adversity with patience. He had missed the point. Chaucer, in the Clerk's Tale, telling Petrarch's version and including Petrarch's moralization, has the Clerk add an envoy making light of the whole venture by admitting ironically that the ideal of patient wives isn't followed any more. Chaucer's envoy turns the story back into an argument *in utramque partem,* closer in spirit to Boccaccio's version than to Petrarch's.

There had appeared in Italy a fashion for stories that were only stories, that had no mystical or historical truth. In ordinary Italian, as we've said, they were called *novelle*—"new things." (The word had, in fact, been a term in ancient law: new cases that had not yet been brought under a generic heading were called *novelli*—it wasn't yet clear what premises would apply to them.) The earliest Italian *novelle* were sometimes merely anecdotes, and indeed in the *Decameron* some stories only recount a clever reply, though most have a plot. They existed because of their interest: each was open to discussion—each raised a question, and each could thus be put to a use. The birth of fiction occurred when such narratives were understood to have a role in a social and cultural milieu. It was a *re*birth to the extent that fictions had belonged to a realm of discourse in the ancient world, but their realm and context was now different. The continuity with ancient thought lay in their playful and heuristic uses in education, in their character as thought exercises. What a fiction *did* depended on the listener or reader. As a narrative it was morally neutral, but as a practice or experience fiction had the ability to make readers think and reason *about the world.*

Chaucer suggests sometimes that a narrative can speak for itself, that its value depends upon the reader, that he as the author is a mere reporter and not to be blamed if a tale offends or fails to please. When Chaucer represents the naïve idea that "fables" are wrong because they are lies, he puts it in the mouth of the crusty Parson (in the Parson's Prologue), who in the same breath disapproves of verse and rhyme. (The naïve idea shows up in the Parson's prose "meditation," where one assumes it is meant as sound morality.) Chaucer knew and used the kinds of stories that are an *argumentum in utramque partem,* and he knew from his days at the Inns of Court that such fictions are tools of inquiry about what is just and right.

Chaucer's writing would not have been the same if he had never gone to Florence. But the Florentines were only making their first exploration of this phase of literature and literary theory. When Chaucer returned to England, he would begin to make such exploration of his own.

Part Three

Into Our
Time

(1380-1400)

11

Chaucer
at Forty

The Parliament of Fowls

By the beginning of 1380 England had opened negotiations with the
House of Luxembourg for the marriage of King Richard II with Anne of
Bohemia. The goal, conceived by the Vatican and supported by the
Visconti, was to enclose France with enemies. It went against the grain
that the church was meddling in the royal nuptials, and Luxembourg,
which would normally be expected to proffer a large dowry, instead demanded enormous funds—twenty thousand gold florins in English coin
plus a loan three times that great and nine thousand gold nobles for
Anne's expenses. Nevertheless, a mission was sent to Germany in June
1380, a marriage settlement was signed on May 1, 1381, and Anne
became queen of England the following January.

Chaucer at once began a new poem to celebrate the forthcoming
marriage. *The House of Fame* had gotten too long, too digressive, and too
intellectual for a court poem. Besides, it had been written for an adolescent, and now the king was nearly an adult. Chaucer had a better idea:
a dream vision containing a love debate among birds (*fowls* in Middle

307

English) who are choosing their mates on Saint Valentine's day. It would be called *The Parliament of Fowls*. It contained the same elements as Chaucer's other dream visions—the dreamer reads a book, falls asleep and dreams of an allegorical scene, encounters a figure or figures (Venus and Nature), and overhears a dialogue. Like other poems of this period, it is in rhyme royal stanzas and has a decasyllabic line. While no principal source for it is known, we can see how Chaucer pieced together materials in the characteristic medieval way. By now he was further along in his reading of Boccaccio's *Teseida*, and he took from it a long allegory of Venus and her temple. From Alain de Lille's *De Planctu Naturae*, which he mentions in the poem, he took a corresponding description of the goddess Nature.*

The Parliament of Fowls is a Valentine's Day poem, like "The Complaint of Mars," or the early lyric "The Complaint d'Amours," and, later, *The Legend of Good Women*. It has always been assumed that the English court held a festival on Saint Valentine's day, but there are no records of such festivals until after Chaucer's time, and then only in France. The feast day of Saint Valentine, February 14, coincided with the Roman fertility rites of the Lupercalia, and in twelfth-century writings the saint is once or twice associated with fertility and nature; otherwise there is no reason why he should have been associated with love or mating. In fact it may be that Valentine's Day as we know it was invented by Chaucer. For there was another Saint Valentine, Saint Valentine of Genoa, a purely local saint that no Englishman could have been expected to know about. But Chaucer had *been* to Genoa—he may well have been there on Saint Valentine's day, February 14, 1373, and learned then about the other, local Saint Valentine, whose feast day was May 3. He mentions that date at key points in several poems, the Knight's Tale and *Troilus* among them. It may be that Chaucer himself was the mythmaker, introducing at the English court a special courtly-love Saint Valentine with an annual festival not unlike the popular one we still observe, for it has recently been shown that May 3 was the day Richard was betrothed to Anne.†

His idea for a Valentine poem on the royal marriage was better suited to present conditions. Since the king was approaching adulthood, a poem with more "philosophy" was called for. And Chaucer had lately read a book that perfectly served his purpose, *The Dream of Scipio*, the epilogue

---

*The allegory of Venus is lines 183–294; that of Nature is lines 298–364. Alain is mentioned in the latter passage, line 316.
†May 3 had further meanings associated with love: it commemorated the finding of the true Cross by Saint Helena (for which it was said a church was built on the site of an ancient temple of Venus), and in Ovid the date is assigned to the goddess Flora, "ministress of Venus," whose celebration was notably libidinous.

of Cicero's *De Re Publica* that had been lost in medieval times except
for this one passage preserved in Macrobius's commentary on it. As the
epilogue of a work on the *res publica,* the "common good," *The Dream
of Scipio* summed up the work's thesis, so it could be read—and Chaucer
chose to read it this way—as a "mirror for princes," a statement about
the place of the prince's government in the order of things. This is what
the narrator is reading when the poem begins; it tells how Scipio's grandfather appears in a dream, takes him into the heavens and shows him
Carthage, and affirms that any virtuous man who loves the common good
("common profit") shall have eternal joy, that the dead have eternal life
in another place, and that this world "nis but a manner deeth." Showing
him how small the earth is in relation to the nine spheres with their
heavenly harmony, he tells his grandson that "he ne shulde him in the
world delite": at the end of time every star will return to its first place and
all worldly deeds will pass into oblivion. Those who work for the "common
profit" will enter that eternal place; those who break the law or delight
only in the body will whirl about the earth in pain for many ages before
they are forgiven.

When day ends and he must stop reading for lack of light, the
narrator goes to bed, full of "thought and busy heavinesse." His sorrow
or alienation is underscored by a puzzling statement, in lines 90–91, that
he had what he did not want, and did not have what he wanted:

For both I hadde thing which that I n'olde,
And eek I ne hadde that thing that I wolde.

And now he falls asleep and dreams that Scipio Africanus comes to *him*
and leads him to the Garden of Venus. He stands before its gate with two
inscriptions (a detail Chaucer took from Dante and the *Roman de la Rose*),
one in gold promising "all good aventure," the other in black warning of
"Disdain and Daunger." When the dreamer stands before this gate in
dread, Scipio grabs him and shoves him in, remarking that the inscriptions
aren't meant for *him*: he is only going to *see* what he can't experience
—and, like the eagle in *The House of Fame,* Scipio promises that he will
see "matter of to write."

The two entrances to the Garden of Venus, with their inscriptions
in gold and black, stand for happy and unhappy love. If all goes well, love
will lead to the "well of grace," where "green and lusty May shall ever
endure." But if the lover encounters Disdain and Daunger—the lady's
scorn and aloofness—it will lead to a place where trees bear no leaves or
fruit: the only remedy is to avoid it.* The passage implies that love must

*Because happy love is described as fertility and unhappy love as sterility, the distinction
sounds like the medieval idea that virtuous love leads to procreation and sinful love does

happen by free choice and mutual consent, which is the theme of the poem.

Inside the garden the dreamer sees a breathtaking allegorical scene representing the "two Venuses," good and sinful love. The garden is a green world with every kind of tree, flowers of all colors, fish, birds, small gentle beasts, music, spicy air—all the plenitude of beneficent Nature: it represents the good Venus who serves *Natura pronuba et procreatrix*—the Venus who, in harmony with Nature, encourages marriage and procreation. Here we find the god of Love, Cupid, and an array of relevant allegorical figures, Will, Pleasure, Courtesy, Gentilesse, and so on, including Foolhardiness, Flattery, Desire, Message-Sending, and Meed (bribery). But now the dreamer comes upon a temple made of brass (line 231), sacred to Venus, with women dancing about it, from which come sighs engendered by desire: here we see Jealousy, the gods Priapus, Bacchus, and Ceres, and in a dark corner Venus in a gold bed, naked to the waist —the traditional iconographic representation of the lustful Venus. On the temple's interior walls are the broken bows of maidens who lost their virginity "in despite of Diane the chaste" and the stories of various tragic loves.

Back in the garden, the dreamer encounters the goddess Nature as Alain de Lille described her in *The Complaint of Nature*. Nature's complaint was that all creatures obey Nature's law and use sex for procreation; man alone abuses sex with sportive or self-indulgent practices, known as *sodomia*—sexual acts that do not lead to procreation. ("Sodomy" in medieval thought was a violation of nature, "adultery" a violation of marriage.) The goddess Nature is presiding over the annual pairing off of birds, who are pictured in a social hierarchy: birds of prey, being like knights, are the highest, then birds that eat worms, birds that live in the water, and birds that eat seed (line 323). Each species of bird had a sort of stock role in medieval lore, and in thirty-five lines Chaucer gives us a catalogue naming thirty-four species—the dove with meek eyes, the jealous swan that sings when death approaches, the scornful jay, the turtledove whose heart is true, the stork ("avenger of adultery"), the wise raven, the crow with voice of care, and so on. Each bird is going to choose its "formel or its mate."* The meaning, borne out later in the poem, is that the aristocratic birds serve a "lady," a courtly ideal, whereas lower-

not, but the two distinctions are separate: love, whether happy or unhappy, might be virtuous or sinful, but the lover who encounters Disdain and Daunger and does not choose the remedy of avoidance is the one more likely to fall into a sinful state.

*"Formel" meant "female" when applied to eagles, and the female eagle, being larger and therefore superior for sport, may have been reckoned the "form," that is, the ideal.

class birds only choose a mate. The goddess Nature, "vicar of the almighty Lord," holds on her hand "a formel eagle" (line 373):

> . . . of shape the gentilleste
> That ever she among her workes fond,
> The most benign and the goodlieste.
> In her was every virtue. . . .

Birds choose their mates on Valentine's Day, she says, because she "pricks them with desire," and adds that the most worthy, the Royal Tercel (the male eagle), will choose first. The rest will follow by order, and the males' choices of a companion ("fere") must be agreed to by the females. But the Royal Tercel chooses the Formel for "my sovereign lady, and not my fere," his *lady*, not his *companion*. The four-stanza speech is a lyrical flight of decorous love rhetoric with not a tinge of irony. He declares he is hers entirely, and that she should be his because none loves her as well. It is a very gracious speech, and one can easily believe the speaker is Richard II.

While the Formel is blushing sweetly and Nature is urging her not to be afraid, Chaucer introduces two other male eagles "of lower kinde" who speak up in rebuttal. "That shall not be!" cries the first,

> I love her bet than ye don, by saint John,
> Or at the least I love her as well as ye. . . .

He claims to have loved her *longer* and protests that if she find him false or unworthy, "do me hangen by the hals!"—*hang me by the neck* (hanging, one must remember, was lower class), adding that if he fail to serve her well and save her honor, "Take she my life and all the good I have!" The second eagle, who might be thought the Hotspur of the bird world, talks like a bluff warrior blurting out his sentiments without courtly adornment: his image of her hanging him if he fail to honor her and then gathering up his possessions is a good deal less than courtly.

The third eagle has a conciliatory, logic-chopping manner. He must die for sorrow unless he speaks, though the birds and Nature are in a hurry to be done. He cannot, he says, boast of long service, but he could die for woe as well "as he that hath been languishing / This twenty winter." He concludes that although he can do no service that will please her, he is her truest servant and would most *like* to please her.

The argument sets intensity of devotion against length of devotion, and sets the genuine courtly humility of the royal eagle against the boastfulness of the one and the self-effacement of the other. We get what *could* have been a serious love debate, but the brusque tone of the second eagle

and the contrasting *delicatesse* of the third dispel the seriousness—as the
eagle in *The House of Fame* dispelled the Dantesque grandeur by grab-
bing the fleeing poet in his claws and addressing him "in mannes voice."
And now the ordinary birds demand a hearing. The different classes of
birds *talk* differently: it is a curious fact that Chaucer, the first great
master of dialogue in English literature, learned the knack with talking
birds. The birds sound off in rough-hewn English, "Have done," "Let us
wende," "Come off" (which we may translate "Get it over with," "Let's
go," "Come on") and their impatience degenerates amusingly at line 499
into "Kek kek! cuckoo! quack, quack!" The female Goose cries "All this
nis not worth a fly!" and boldly claims to have a remedy. All agree that
the Royal Tercel is the right match for the Formel, and they speak in a
cheeky, down-to-earth way that would have tickled a courtly audience.

The female Turtledove is by contrast so self-effacing that her speech
(at line 509, a difficult passage endlessly commented on) says only that her
has no business saying anything. "Ye may abide a while yit, parde," she
begins, and then says, "If it be your wille / A wight may speke, him were
as fair be stille . . ." (which we may translate, "if it be your will that a
creature speak who might as well keep still")! Then she talks her way out
of speaking at all: she is a seed fowl, one of the unworthiest, and "it is
better for a creature to keep quiet than to meddle in things he can't speak
or sing about; whoever does that is overstepping a bound, for an office
performed when not asked for is often an annoyance."

Nature cries, "Hold your tongues there!" ("in an elegant voice") and
rules that one speaker represent each group. Here the "parliament" begins. It consists of four speeches, the last three by lower-class birds who
are rudely put down by birds of the upper class. The arguments are
whether the Formel should marry the eagle who loves her most or marry
the one of highest rank (line 540), and whether the royal eagle, if she
rejects him, should choose another (line 563) or love her unrequited (line
582). Their arguments represent upper- and lower-class attitudes. The first
speaker, the noble Tercelet, offers a measured, reasoned discourse. His
tone is aristocratic: he follows a logical order, his sentences seem longer,
he uses more connectives and qualifiers. The question is so complicated
and there are so many different views, he says, that it can't be settled by
argument; it seems as though it must be settled by battle. At once the
eagles cry out—as warmongering English knights would, Chaucer implies
—"All ready!" The Tercelet protests with great courtesy that he is not
finished, then declares that the Formel should choose the one who is the
most worthy in knighthood, has been knighted longest, and is highest in
rank and noblest in blood.

Next (at line 563) the waterfowl elect the female Goose as their spokeswoman. She talks somewhat like the Wife of Bath:

> Peace! Now take keep every man,
> And herkeneth which a reson I shall forth bringe!
> My wit is sharp, I love no tarryinge.
> I say I rede° him, though he were my brother,   *advise*
> But she wol love him, lat him love another!

The Turtledove, who according to medieval lore took only one mate in its life, speaks for the seed fowl, with such sentiment that she sounds by coincidence very courtly: a lover should not change but serve his lady until he is dead, however indifferent she may be. The female Duck scornfully calls this a joke and declares—like the Goose—that there's more than one pair of stars in the sky. In the end, the male Cuckoo says brusquely that so long as he can have his mate in peace (cuckoos lay their eggs in other birds' nests) he doesn't care how long they argue—let them stay single forever.

So the parliament, like some sessions of the English Parliament about this time, turns into a shouting match. Nature silences them all and declares (line 632) that the Formel herself will get to choose the suitor she wants:

> "If I were Reason, [she says] than wold I
> Conseil you the royal tercel take,
> As said the Tercelet full skillfully."

But she is not Reason, she is Nature. The birds must make their own choices. As a picture of a discussion in which large numbers loudly participate without reaching a conclusion, it is good-natured ridicule of the government, court, and parliament. In it we glimpse Chaucer's own impatience and frustration: the marriage negotiations had gone on now for three years in a maze of turnabouts and dead ends, Chaucer had been sent abroad three or four times, there had been endless babble, and the young king was still unmarried. Yet the poet reassures his audience, and perhaps himself, of the importance of all this to-do: the common birds react impatiently with refreshing common sense—but they react this way because they do not understand. In the end the Formel, "with dredful voice," gently asks Nature that she be allowed not to decide until next year. Nature agrees, bids the three eagles stay in Love's service another year, and lets the rest of the birds choose their mates "by even accord," i.e., mutual agreement. They embrace with their wings and intertwine their necks (as swans in love were thought to do), thank Nature, and sing a roundel, then fly happily away with their mates. The noise they make wakes the narrator. He, turning to another book, hopes that someday he will dream "some thing for to fare / The bet"—meaning the Formel's favorable decision.

It had always been supposed that *The Parliament of Fowls* celebrated a court marriage; the question was, which one? The only clue is that the royal suitor has two rivals, and even at that the rivals could be a mere convention to supply the dialogue with a love debate. It is safe to suppose that the royal Tercel, whom the Tercelet and Nature favor, is Richard II. But did Anne of Bohemia have two other suitors?

It happens that she did. Over a hundred years ago one was identified as Friedrich of Meissen, to whom Anne had been betrothed for seven years, and in 1910 the other was identified as the son of the king of France, the future Charles VI. All were still children—the two suitors were both eleven, she about thirteen. Charles V had tried to stop the marriage to Richard by offering, in April 1380, his daughter Catherine to Richard, with Angoulême for a dowry; when England turned this offer down, he offered his eldest son to Anne. So the second tercel, who is of "lower kinde" and pleads length of service, is Friedrich, a minor German noble with no claim to a kingdom and no strong claim on Anne beyond the seven-year betrothal. The third tercel, the future Charles VI of France, who does indeed speak nobly, cannot claim length of service, having only just entered the field. He is not represented as a royal bird because England still claimed the crown of France. Richard at thirteen was the oldest of these suitors, so it was true, as is said in line 549, that he had been in knighthood longest (he had been made a knight of the Garter by Edward III in April 1377, three months before his coronation, when he was ten). The other two, being two years younger, mustn't have been knighted at all.

These facts were called into question in the early 1900s, first by J. M. Manly of the University of Chicago, the great authority on Chaucer's life and times, then in greater detail by his protégé, Edith Rickert. She claimed to show that the engagement to Friedrich had been broken off several years before, and gave reasons to doubt the much better documented suit of the French king. Her argument was just characteristic scholarly skepticism, but—such are the vicissitudes of the scholarly world —it was enshrined in the notes of the standard edition of Chaucer, thus attaining the status of fact. The obvious historical background of the poem was in this way abandoned, and the attention of critics turned somewhat relentlessly to its content of ideas, its structure and unity, and its satiric intention.

In recent years—the results were published in 1982—Professor Benson reexamined all the arguments and the heaps of evidence behind them. The greatest doubt about the date of the poem, and therefore about the historical events behind it, was cast by an obscure astronomical reference (lines 113–119): Chaucer says Venus was visible in the north-northwest when he began writing his dream. Professor Manly claimed to show that Venus would not have been visible in the north-northwest in 1380, and this seemed to send the whole argument about the poem's date and occasion tumbling like a house of cards. In later years, his evidence was reviewed by Professor Hamilton Smyser, who concluded that Venus *was* visible in 1380, and Benson, producing a review of the astronomical evidence by the astronomer Alan Lazarus, confirmed Smyser's conclusions.

Benson also found that Friedrich *was* still officially betrothed to Anne in 1380 and the future Charles VI of France was still very much in the picture: while the English were sending their ambassadors to Germany in June, Wenceslas sent ambassadors to Paris in July with instructions that they should avoid the topic of marriage, which must mean the topic had been raised and he wanted a delay. In the poem, delay is the upshot. The Formel asks a year to think it over. The actual delay in finding a wife for young Richard, three years, must by now have seemed to English courtiers slightly ridiculous, and the poem makes a joke of these drawn-out proceedings at a time when the court had good reason to believe they would soon turn out favorably.

So *The Parliament of Fowls,* as an occasional poem, devoted itself to an occasion that had political and philosophical significance. A king's marriage was different from other marriages: it was a political commitment, an alliance of powers. If the king was the head of the body politic and God's anointed ruler, he was part of the universal order in a singular way. Cicero's *Dream of Scipio* was an appropriate introduction because at its heart lay a message about the moral obligations of a prince— indifference to the world and the body and devotion to the "common profit." But the poet's dream reveals too that in this world we must follow the temporal laws of the natural order. Marriage for procreation is the great law of Nature, and this law we see enforced by Nature on Saint Valentine's day. But for a king, following this law has another dimension, for he must produce not just offspring, like other creatures, but an heir, a royal line.

Chaucer introduces the conception of the "two Venuses" not to warn his sovereign against lechery but to present in its fullest implications the image of the good Venus, the Venus of marriage and offspring. The conventions of courtly love, which must otherwise be mere amatory conniving, are valid when put in her service. Chaucer depicts two abstract realms, of Venus and of Nature. On the side of Nature, the ordinary birds' contribution to the "common profit" is the propagation of the species, whence they see the debate of the noble birds as overrefined and absurd. But on the side of Venus is a world of scruples and ideals known to her noble and royal servants: in that world the love debate, the rival suitors, the lady's idealization, the lover's servitude, the high expectations and noble commitments have purpose and meaning because a king's marriage is a public example and a responsibility to the kingdom. As *The House of Fame* had declared, "The news is that there is no news," *The Parliament of Fowls* declares, "The decision is to delay the decision." The importance of the decision warrants the delay.

This was philosophical enough for a young man not yet fourteen. *The Parliament of Fowls* cannot, writes Muscatine, "support the theory that makes of it a sober philosophical tract." It is a court poem with an appropriate content of quasi-philosophical ideas: Chaucer grasped and applied those ideas so well that a philosophical position can be inferred from them, but *The Parliament of Fowls* remains a court poem, invoking for its purposes a concept about Nature that was by Chaucer's time a dead idea. That idea had come into being in the late twelfth century against the background of the Albigensian heresy. The Albigensians had held that matter is evil and spirit good, that procreation is wrong because it imprisons a pure spirit in an evil body, and that the race therefore ought to be allowed to become extinct. Against this heresy, which quite literally opposed motherhood, twelfth-century intellectuals argued that sexual desire is part of Nature's law. By Chaucer's time there was no longer any need for such a doctrine, but the old image of the goddess Nature survived because it was pictorial and unassailable, probably most of all because it implied the intriguing antithesis of raw sexuality, sexuality for its own sake, practiced for delight. There was an evil Venus who stood for such sexuality, a good Venus who stood for breeding. It was the safest idea in the world, utterly respectable and drab—a splendid plaything for poets to adorn and celebrate without fear of disagreement. But against this drab notion, the special character of a king's marriage was an earnest message for a young monarch about to wed.

For Geoffrey Chaucer, not yet forty, his poem's humorous evocation of class differences, attitudes, and speech, was—though he didn't know it—the germ of *The Canterbury Tales*. We see him here at the end of his poem, after the birds have sung the merry roundel and flown away, a solitary, alienated figure: the narrator or dreamer, now awake, turns to other books, hoping to read someday a book that will make him dream something that will be to his advantage. We are back with the solemn figure we met at the start, who had what he did not want and did not have what he wanted. Spring and love return to earth, but, as E. T. Donaldson observes, "To the wintry narrator that spring will never come." Chaucer represents himself as one closed off from experience who must, to find the thing he wants and doesn't have, turn to books, always seeking, never quite finding. Perhaps it was only an artistic device for illuminating by contrast the multivalent love the poem has explored. Perhaps. But in fact there *was* something Chaucer was looking for in books, and as yet he hadn't found it.

Cecily Champain

Early in 1380, about the time negotiations for the king's marriage with Anne of Bohemia were begun, and probably while *The Parliament of Fowls* was being written, Chaucer was involved in an incident that will never be explained unless new evidence comes to light. A document signed by a woman named Cecily Champain, "daughter of the late William Champain and Agnes his wife," released Geoffrey Chaucer from *omnimodas acciones tam de raptu meo tam* [sic] *de aliqua alia re vel causa* —"actions of whatever kind either concerning my rape or any other matter." The release is dated May 1, a date whose traditional connection with love affairs may or may not have amused Master Geoffrey. As witnesses to this release, Chaucer brought forth some very big guns indeed, which means he thought the matter grave: the chamberlain of the king's household, Sir William Beauchamp; Sir John Philipot, prominent merchant, then the collector of the Wool Custom (for whom Chaucer was controller), alderman, member of Parliament, lord mayor of London in 1378; Sir William Neville, knight of the king's chamber, admiral of the northern fleet; Sir John Clanvowe the poet, also of the king's household; and Chaucer's neighbor Richard Morel of the Grocer's Company.

The word *raptus* is what makes the document so tantalizing: it could mean either kidnapping or rape. It was not unusual for minors or wards to be kidnapped or abducted, to secure for example their inheritance through a forced marriage—as had happened to Chaucer's own father when he was a child. But Cecily Champain was not a minor. Her father had been dead for twenty-one years, and besides, if she were a minor or a ward her parent or guardian would have had to sign for her. In this sense *raptus* meant the seizure and abduction of her person; it was not a case where property was seized in lieu of the payment of a debt, and it wasn't an arrest made because she owed money to the Customs—*raptus* was the name of a particular crime. According to the opinion of an eminent legal historian, if she had been seized bodily, "the release would have proceeded from the injured party, viz., the feudal lord, parent, husband, or employer of Cecilia"—but it may be she had none of these. If there had been an abduction, it probably had to do with property. Say, for instance, she rented or sublet a property from Chaucer and failed to pay the rent; if he had her evicted bodily from the premises, she might through the usual escalation of lawsuits have called this an abduction. The document, one should add, is only a promise not to make the accusation; it doesn't indicate if it would or would not have been false. About the meaning of "abduction," it must be added that if all parties knew the act had been only that and not sexual rape, it seems that two poets, the king's chamberlain, the lord mayor, and the others—some with legal training—could have proposed a less ambiguous term.

This leaves us with "rape." Sometimes false charges of rape—a very serious crime—were brought against a legal adversary to put him at a disadvantage by getting him thrown in prison. This is the interpretation of Professor D. W. Robertson, and he cites such a case, though he doesn't really show it was a common practice. If word reached Chaucer that Cecily Champain or some accomplice was planning such a maneuver, it would explain why he marshaled his most powerful friends, perhaps not just to witness the document but to scare her into signing it. But then, he would have done the same if the accusation were true. Our legal historian thinks there is no evidence of rape—but then of course there is no evidence of anything: "that Chaucer seduced Cecily we may well believe. But there is nothing to suggest that she could have convicted him of a felony." This is essentially the same notion of accusations of rape that many current police officers and lawyers have, namely that the woman consented and regretted it later.

What has never been considered in this connection is the more or less recent discovery by Haldeen Braddy that Cecily Champain was Alice Perrers's stepdaughter. Such identifications are always tricky: one has to find a William Champain with a wife Agnes, and they must have a daughter named Cecily who was an adult in 1380. There is always the chance of an unrecorded person with the same name, but Professor Braddy's candidate is very satisfactory; there is just one other Cecily, and she can be eliminated because she was a nun.

But if this identification is right, it means that Chaucer raped or seduced the stepdaughter of an old friend who had done him many favors, the former king's mistress, now in disgrace and entirely out of the picture. Or it means that his old friend's stepdaughter brought against him a vindictive accusation, for revenge or blackmail or whatever reason. Human nature being what it is, neither meaning is out of the question.

Stepdaughters and stepmothers are often on bad terms. Cecily's step-mother was a famous courtesan with few scruples and an excellent head for business; if they were on good terms, Cecily may have learned a trick or two from her stepmother.

Alice Perrers, however, was very young when she was married to William Champain; Cecily could have been as old as Alice, even older. She came from a respectable London family of the merchant class, so Chaucer would probably have known her anyway. We know that Chaucer and his wife were often parted; he was in his late thirties; in later years, speaking of his sexual prowess (his "muse"), he wrote, "While I was young, I put hir forth in press." It is reasonable to suppose some seductions or affairs in his early years, perhaps many. He may have had an intimate relationship with Cecily and she may, when things went wrong, have threatened to accuse him of rape. Or in the heat of passion or exasperation he may indeed have raped her. Whatever mitigating circumstances there were, Chaucer did not want the matter to go further: in the law of his day, the accused was not allowed to testify in his own behalf, so there was a grave risk that the whole truth, whatever it was, would not emerge. Hence he settled: "rape" was allowed to be named in the release but what it cost him was kept silent.

Cecily's stepmother's ruling passion was possession. Indeed property and money were the ruling passions of all respectable London merchant families: if there had been a rape, Cecily was probably happier to settle for money than to have revenge. This brings us to the two men involved with her in these documents, Richard Goodchild, a cutler, and John Grove, an armorer, both citizens of London. From what little is known of them they were of decent character, so there is no reason to suspect they were accomplices of hers in a blackmail plot, though it is possible. It sounds more likely that they were acting as agents for Chaucer. Almost two months after Cecily Champain's release to Chaucer, on June 28, these two men signed a writ couched in the same formulaic language releasing Chaucer from "actions, complaints, and suits . . . by reason of any breach of contract or nonpayment of debt or any other matter real or personal"—nothing about *raptus*. On the same day Cecily Champain signed a nearly identical document releasing the same two men from any actions, etc. *tam reales quam personales.* And a few days later, on July 2, John Grove signed a recognizance that he owed Cecily Champain £10, which he later paid. These three documents have no witnesses.

All of this looks like a settlement to be guaranteed and transacted by the two agents. The only other possibility is that some new evidence had come to light in the meantime, some three or more months since the "rape." What could it be? Well, it could be that Dame Cecily was found to be pregnant. This would substantially have reduced her claim, because by a maxim of medieval law it was believed that a woman could not conceive if she had not consented!

And indeed there is circumstantial evidence, if very flimsy, that there was a child which Chaucer acknowledged. In 1391 he wrote his *Treatise on the Astrolabe* for "my little son Lowis," who he said was "of the tender age of ten year." This means he would have been born in 1381. There is a later record of a Lewis Chaucer named alongside Thomas Chaucer, but little else is known of him. If the rape or seduction had occurred not long before the release was signed on May 1, nine months would just barely have gone into 1381.

All we really know is that on May 1 there was a possibility Cecily Champain would accuse Chaucer of "rape" and he saw to it that she made a public disclaimer before five powerful witnesses of his acquaintance. We would be better off if we knew more of Cecily Champain's previous or later life, and if we knew what relation she had with Chaucer, but we are in the dark on both counts. It was true, then as now, that many entanglements—of love, of friendship, of trust—ended in violence and threats and lawsuits. Two months later there was a chance that the two London citizens might bring some action against Chaucer and that Cecily Champain might bring one against them; the three parties signed more or less routine releases, both of which refer to grievances *tam reales quam personales,* personal or property damages. A few days later Richard Grove acknowledged a debt to Cecily Champain of £10, a substantial sum, but perhaps only part of what Cecily was to be paid. These documents suggest that the quarrel, going back into the previous April, was settled out of court. In the autumn and during the following year, 1381, Chaucer accumulated a good deal of capital, and he may have done so to pay off a large debt.

The Peasants' Revolt and the King's Marriage

Exactly a year later, on May 1, 1381, a marriage agreement between King Richard II and Anne of Bohemia was drawn up—the romantic date a good deal more appropriate. While the nation was celebrating the betrothal of their monarch, now fourteen, there was afoot a popular movement that erupted a month later, in June—the Peasants' Revolt. The story of the famous invasion of London by an army of peasants and artisans marching from Kent has been told innumerable times, and everyone remembers the terrible violence and massive destruction, and the courage and majesty of the fourteen-year-old king who confronted the mob on a charger and won their cooperation with empty promises.

Chaucer was an eyewitness to the riot, for he was in London during the week beginning Wednesday, June 12, when it took place.

The revolt was one in a series of thirty or more such uprisings on the Continent and in England in the fourteenth century; during the week it happened there were some dozen incidents of violence in towns through-out East Anglia. The conditions leading to these revolts are not hard to see: the poverty of the peasant classes, the power of the feudal lords and rich merchants, the unjust division of wealth, regulation of labor, and taxes, especially the hated poll taxes of 1377, 1379, and 1380. The 1379 tax had been graduated, but that of 1380 only stipulated that the rich should help the poor, then set a flat amount of a shilling per person (*poll* meant "head"). For a family of ten living at the subsistence level the tax was confiscatory. Everyone opposed it, and many evaded it—when it was collected, the population of England appeared to have shrunk by a third.

In *The Parliament of Fowls,* written the year before, Chaucer unwit-tingly foresaw some of the elements of class conflict that erupted in June 1381, in the Peasants' Revolt, expressing them in an undercurrent of social satire mostly at the expense of the "middle" classes. In their talk and behavior Chaucer showed the lesser orders of birds rude and bump-tious. But he then turned the tables by having the noble birds stoop to the same low level. When the representatives of the lower birds speak, some of the noble birds tell them off in equally rude language. "Lo, here a parfit reason of a goose!" cries the Sparrow Hawk, "Such it is to have a tongue loose" —and the "gentil" birds all burst out laughing. So with the Duck's reply to the Turtledove: "Out of the dunghill came that word full right!"* When the Tercelet raises the possibility of a decision by battle, the knightly birds can barely be restrained from whipping out their swords. No doubt the audience at court, having been allowed first a laugh at the expense of the lower classes, laughed merrily over these gibes at their own expense.

Chaucer appeared in this picture as an amused nonpartisan casting a detached eye. The lower birds make us laugh because they don't under-stand the nobility's preoccupations and scruples, but the noble birds make us laugh because they behave as nobles *did* behave, not always nobly. The poem promotes in its noble audience an amused condescension to the lower classes, a more "gentil" feeling than the hostility it depicts. And it

---

*The Merlion's reply to the Cuckoo is couched in clerical language, as if he were a prelate: "Ye, have the glotton filled enough his paunch, / Than are we well!" and he goes on preaching at him, addressing him in *contemptus mundi* parlance ("Live thou soleyn, wormes corruption!") very appropriate for a worm fowl!

creates a cautiously funny, "distanced" picture of the ruling class as elegant and squawking birds of prey—which could, Chaucer may have hoped, promote an amused self-scrutiny. In a poem written for a youthful king, that could be read as a political message. But Richard didn't learn it, nor did anyone else.

The Peasants' Revolt seemed to come out of nowhere; the court and the city were unprepared for it. King Richard was at Windsor. On Monday, June 10, one mob had taken control of Canterbury; another, in Essex, had pillaged the manor house of the treasurer of England, Sir Robert Hales. Reports of the mobs gathering in Kent, starting a rebellion in Dartford, taking the royal castle at Rochester, were seemingly ignored, and no precautions were taken. On Tuesday the men from Kent began marching toward London. The men from Essex meanwhile moved down the north bank of the Thames and into the city, and camped at Mile End, outside the city wall at Aldgate. The mayor ordered the gates locked and the drawbridge on London Bridge raised. Chaucer could have seen the rebel encampment, not from his apartment over Aldgate, which had no window facing east, but from the parapet on the wall. Although he had witnessed sieges in France, it was the first time he had been in a city under siege. And because England was believed settled by the Trojans' descendants and London was called "New Troy," the siege of Troy must have come into his mind—though the scruffy rebels in their encampment made a poor semblance of Greek warriors.

On Wednesday King Richard came to London, where he and his court holed themselves up in the Tower, an impregnable fortification. In the evening the mass marching from Canterbury arrived, led by Wat Tyler, the leading force behind the revolt. Almost nothing is known of him—he may have been an artisan, or a disbanded soldier, or the rebellious younger son of a respectable Kentish family. He was a born leader of unquestioned ability, a powerful orator, a demagogue though not without ideals. He and his followers had freed from the archbishop's prison in Canterbury a vagrant priest named John Ball, under arrest not for the first time for his radical ideas about the equality of all men and the common ownership of property. Ball provided what the movement needed, an ideology; the rebels proposed to make him archbishop of Canterbury—he evidently believed there should be only one bishop in England, himself. Along the way they were met by royal messengers; they told the messengers they were coming to London to destroy traitors and rescue the king, and they asked to speak with the king in the morning at Blackheath, about five miles east of the city on the south bank of the Thames. There they made their encampment.

The rebels arrived in London with a shared sense of purpose and nebulous ideas mostly perhaps picked up along the way from Wat Tyler and John Ball or from each other, concocted of such folklore as the stories of Robin Hood, and other popular beliefs. They believed first that the king was their leader and would take their side, that he would see justice done. They held the belief—a little myth, as it actually was—that he was surrounded and controlled by "traitors," from whom they had come to save him, and that these traitors were the ones who had kept them poor, who had kept their status of villeinage alive, put a ceiling on the wages of laborers, and imposed the hated poll tax. These "traitors" were in fact the great powers behind the young king's throne—William Sudbury, archbishop of Canterbury, and Sir Robert Hales, the treasurer, and John of Gaunt, most hated of all (who was, however, safely in Scotland, negotiating with his powerful friends there)—and the rebels' first act on arriving at Blackheath was to send a petition demanding these traitors' heads.

The other objects of their rage were abstract entities like the law, bureaucracy, taxes, so that on their rampage they destroyed what seemed symbols of these. They took the New Temple and burned the lawyers' records and houses, burned any records of government they could find, like the records of chancery in the archbishop's palace at Lambeth, killed indiscriminately whatever lawyers or tax collectors or officials fell into their hands; if they had known Geoffrey Chaucer as the controller of the Wool Custom, he would have had to talk fast to stay alive. Learning in the abstract, too, they hated, as representing government, the church, and the law, and of course they took from posterity in so many burned records some of our hope of knowing, even, the injustices of which they complained. (In Cambridge a similar mob burned chests containing parchments in the public square, an old woman named Margery Starre crying, "Away with the learning of clerks, away with it" as she hurled the parchments into the fire.) Written documents had special symbolic force to a largely illiterate populace, and, too, a document burns so much more easily than, say, an equestrian statue.

Foreigners they hated also, for taking English wages away from them, and so they slaughtered Flemish whores; took thirty-five Flemings who had taken refuge in the Church of Saint Martin's in the Vintry, Chaucer's parish church when he was a child, and beheaded them in the street outside; left a pile of forty headless bodies at the west end of Thames Street, where the Chaucer family house still stood (and which Chaucer sold that very week). They went after the Italians in Lombard Street. They wanted, so they said, a world in which all men would be equal save the king, where there would be no "lordship" but his. They wanted

the wealth of the church divided among the people, and the hierarchy
abolished save one bishop. They wanted no law "except the law of Winchester," whatever they meant by that. And they wanted the abolition of
serfdom. They were advocating "popular communism," as medieval historians call it, which had its roots in perfectly respectable Christian principles long since compromised by subtle scholastic distinctions; until the
twelfth century the church taught that all property should be held in
common, that private property was tainted with sin. The famous jingle
of the Peasants' Revolt, on which John Ball preached a sermon, according
to the chronicler Walsingham, was

> When Adam dalf° and Eve span°,   *dug / spun*
> Who was then a gentilman?

The next day, Thursday, June 13, was the feast of Corpus Christi,
a major religious holiday on which in most cities the cycles of miracle plays
were performed. In the morning King Richard with some of his council
went down the Thames in a barge, with an escort of four other barges,
to meet the rebels at Blackheath. But when the royal party reached
Greenwich they saw gathered on the south bank, at the bend where the
river dips southward for a mile or so, the vast, shrieking, menacing rabble.
King Richard II had been raised from infancy to the role of leader, to
kingly and courageous deeds, his models for conduct being no less than
his grandfather Edward III and his father, the Black Prince; though he
was not yet fifteen we may believe the chronicle that tells us he was
prepared to go and meet with the rebels. But the chancellor and treasurer
advised against it. After a few demands and promises were shouted at a
safe distance and barely heard, the barge turned slowly about and took its
way back to the Tower.

Those on the royal barge did not of course know they had performed
before the frantic multitude a dumb show of its shared myth. Here was
the king surrounded by the "traitors" of his council, prepared—as they
may have seen from a gesture or sensed in his demeanor—to parley with
them, but turned away on the remonstrances of those same "traitors."
And this incident tripped off the invasion of the city and the rioting. They
clamored west to Southwark, broke open the Marshalsea prison and
released the prisoners, destroying the house of one of the prison marshals.
They proceeded to Lambeth, where they burned the chancery records,
and from there to London Bridge, where they or a city mob probably
forced the two aldermen in charge, John Horn and Walter Sibil, to lower
the drawbridge (Horn and Sibil were later tried as traitors and acquitted).
They ran screaming across the bridge, veered left into Fleet Street, where
they broke open the Fleet prison, then to the New Temple, burning the

lawyers' parchments, and burning houses, one of the treasurer, Sir Robert
Hales, one of the bishop of Lichfield. At length they came to their
destination, the Savoy, palace of John of Gaunt, said to be the most
glorious in the realm—and found, already attacking it, a mob of Londoners, with whom they joined forces.

Gaunt's palace was the focal point of the attack on London, as Gaunt
had been the focus of popular hatred since the time of Edward III and
the Good Parliament. Rumors had flown about London that he sought
power, desired the throne, was friends with corrupt officials. There was
the rumor that he was a changeling: old Queen Philippa had lain on and
smothered a newborn daughter and, fearing her husband's wrath, had
substituted the newborn son of a Flemish woman. This she was supposed
to have confided in the confessional to the bishop of Winchester, who
advised her not to tell the story unless Gaunt got near the throne. Of
course it was false, and Gaunt ignored it. But in other matters Gaunt
could not keep a rein on his hot temper or disguise his enormous arrogance. Twice he infuriated the citizens of London with his loose tongue,
first by muttering at the abortive trial of John Wyclif, 1377, that he would
drag the absent bishop of London from Saint Paul's by the hair, which
produced a near riot. For expediency's sake he was capable of making up
these quarrels, kneeling before the king, giving in public the kiss of peace
to prominent London citizens, making promises. But then in the next
year, hearing that the bishop of London had refused to answer a summons
to the Council at Windsor, he lost his temper and yelled that he would
ride to Saint Paul's and drag him there "in spite of the ribald knaves of
London." So it was war again with the Londoners, and the rumor spread
that he was, having failed in the latest installment of his Castilian war,
going to seize the wealth of the church.

John of Gaunt managed, moreover, to alienate the church by be-
friending Wyclif and paying learned theologians to defend him. At first
he probably did not know about Wyclif's ideas. He certainly did not
follow him in specific matters; for example, Wyclif taught that auricular
confession was superfluous in a contrite penitent, whereas Gaunt went to
confession alarmingly often. He admired the famous Oxford scholar as a
leading intellectual of the day, sided with him because it was expedient,
then remained his patron out of loyalty. Wyclif was twenty years older
than Gaunt and did not become a radical until the later 1370s. Only from
that time—and he died in 1384—did he have heretical followers, called
"lollers" or "lollards" (the word evidently meant complainers or radicals).
In 1377 the pope ordered him held to account for his heresies; the year
after the Peasants' Revolt his followers were forced to recant, though he
himself was not judged.

Chaucer must have known that the mobs were right in blaming
Gaunt for high taxes. He had been behind the poll taxes of 1379 and 1380.
He had, it was said, mismanaged his part in the war with France, which
cost the nation in money and lives; now he had adopted a policy of truce
with France and other enemies so that he could pursue his war in Castile.
Styling himself king of Castile and León, he meant at any cost in taxation
to wage the war that would put him on the throne. In 1380 England had
renewed its alliance with Portugal (a fatal error), and even now, in June
1381, a fleet was leaving England, under Gaunt's brother the earl of
Cambridge, to fight in alliance with Portugal against the usurper of
Castile.

And so the masses from London and Kent broke into the Savoy and
rampaged through its halls, trampled the sumptuous furniture and hangings, the priceless works of art, the silver and gold plate, the jewelry and
clothes, the pitchers and ewers of gold and enamel, the illuminated manuscript books—quite possibly among them the presentation copies of
Chaucer's "ABC" and *The Book of the Duchess* written some dozen years
before. And then they set fire to its ruined halls. There was no looting,
probably on orders from Wat Tyler, but, too, because they imagined
themselves men of virtue come to save their monarch; one poor scoundrel
seen stealing an object of silver was thrown with his booty into the flames.
They found kegs of gunpowder—or possibly the fire itself found the kegs
in storage—which exploded in the flames, leaving the great palace of the
Savoy, where Philippa Chaucer must often have been in attendance, and
Chaucer too, a smoldering heap of rubble.

Other houses were burned, other prisons opened. It was on this day
mostly that the lawyers were killed, and the Flemings. The rebels came
upon Richard Lyons, the rich and ostentatious vintner who had made his
wealth by lending to the crown and had been collector of the Petty
Custom and Subsidy in the early years of Chaucer's controllership—
whose mysterious relationship with Alice Perrers years before had called
forth a writ signed by substantial citizens, Chaucer's father among them,
that he should not go near her—and seizing him, they cut off his head.
By nightfall the city was in flames. The king had made an effort to disperse
the crowd at Tower Hill by addressing them from a turret and offering
them a pardon, which they scorned. But he had the mayor order, "on pain
of life and limb," that everyone between fifteen and sixty should meet him
at Mile End the next morning at seven o'clock, and this they were ready
to do.

Where Chaucer was on this Thursday we do not know, but we know
that while the throng from Kent entered the city across London Bridge
another throng entered through the gate at Aldgate; if Chaucer was home

he saw them run shrieking through it. The gate was opened for them—
so it was said later when accusations were flying about—by an alderman,
William Tonge, either in treachery or fear. One might suppose that at
some point Chaucer had some duty to perform as an esquire of the royal
household, but since neither the court nor the city was very well organized
he may have stayed in the relatively safe refuge of Aldgate or joined the
court in the Tower. Wherever he was, he saw the city burning. "The king
himself," says one of the chronicles, "ascended to a high garret of the
Tower to watch the fires. . . ." Who knew that night if the city would
not burn to the ground? The notion must have crossed the minds of many,
for it was a medieval commonplace that cities rise in history and fall in
cycles according to Fortune's wheel, one taking its beginning from the
ruins of the last. Learned men like Chaucer must have remembered that
dread night scene in Virgil, and the speech of Aeneas, their ancestor:

> I climbed to the roof top
> To cup my ears and listen. And the sound
> Was like the sound a grassfire makes in grain,
> Whipped by a Southwind.
> . . . .
> Dëphobus'
> Great house in flames, already caving in
> Under the overpowering god of fire;
> Ucalegon's already caught nearby;
> The glare lighting the straits beyond Sigeum;
> The cries of men . . .

On Friday morning the rebels had gone to Mile End as planned.
Chaucer could have watched the scene from the city wall at Aldgate. The
king arrived in the company of the mayor of London, William Walworth,
and other dignitaries, and the rebels fell to their knees, acknowledging
their monarch. It was like Virgil's lines,

> When rioting breaks out in a great city,
> And the rampaging rabble goes so far
> That stones fly, and incendiary brands—
> For anger can supply that kind of weapon—
> If it so happens they look round and see
> Some dedicated public man, a veteran
> Whose record gives him weight, they quiet down,
> Willing to stop and listen.

The rebels presented a petition demanding the end of villeinage, fair labor
practices, and the right to have land at fourpence an acre, and Richard

agreed to all. He may even have granted the release of all prisoners. They demanded through a spokesman that he turn over the "traitors" to them, and Richard diplomatically agreed to do so with anyone found a traitor by process of law: he told them, according to the chronicler, "they could go through all the realm of England and catch all traitors and bring them to him in safety, and then he would deal with them as the law demanded." This was of course a clever evasion—but the rebels went straight to the Tower, and, incredibly, got in. The Tower was under the guard of a sizable armed force, of mounted knights and archers, but according to the chronicles the riffraff ran about the royal premises, pulling the soldiers' beards, says Walsingham, and asking the terrified Princess Joan, the king's mother, for a kiss, while the guard did nothing. Some historians think panic and terror paralyzed the government, that they had—to borrow a phrase from Chaucer's contemporary, the anonymous author of *Sir Gawain and the Green Knight*—"slipped upon a sleep." To be sure, many an ordinary citizen felt in his heart a certain sympathy for the revolt, and there were those who aided the rebels or left them unopposed. But the royal guard at the Tower? It sounds as if they were under strict orders to offer no opposition unless the rebels threatened bloodshed. For the royal policy was one of appeasement and conciliation: promise them anything, but get them out of the city and back to their homes. The rebels had no food supply; hunger would get them out in a few days. And the danger of using armed knights in narrow city streets was considerable, for they were unprotected from above.

What cannot be explained is that under the eyes of the royal guard the rebels found in the chapel, at their prayers, some of the "traitors" they sought, and seized them bodily: Sudbury, the archbishop of Canterbury; Hales, the treasurer, two of whose houses they had burned; John Legge, one of the royal tax collectors; and the duke of Lancaster's personal physician, a friar, William Appleton, whose only offense was his connection with Gaunt. And these they beheaded on Tower Hill, carrying their bleeding heads on long spears in a procession through the city and setting them up, as was the custom, on London Bridge. Their chief "traitor," John of Gaunt, was in Edinburgh, far out of their reach. Among the nobles in the Tower, they seized but failed to capture—for he had been hustled out of sight by one John Ferrour, a disabled soldier once in the retinue of the Black Prince—Henry of Bolingbroke, then fourteen, the king's first cousin and John of Gaunt's heir.

The rampaging went on. A leader called "Jack Straw" emerged—on Thursday he seems to have led an attack on the Flemings, on Friday his band set fire to the treasurer's new house in Highbury. He was later tried and executed. Chaucer remembered his name, for years later, when its emotional associations were reduced, he mentioned it humorously in the Nun's Priest's Tale (line 4584) to describe the noise the local villagers made running after the fox:

> Certes, he Jacke Straw and his meinee
> Ne made never shoutes half so shrille
> Whan that they wolden any Fleming kille
> As thilke day was made upon the fox.

He must have remembered it because Jack Straw led the slaughter of the Flemings in the Vintry, the world of his childhood.

On Saturday the scene shifted to Westminster Abbey. In the morning a band of released prisoners stormed in and seized Richard Imworth, head of the Marshalsea prison, the hated torturer, who had taken sanctuary there, dragged him bodily out of Saint Edward's chapel, the abbey's holy of holies, to Cheapside, and there cut off his head. In the afternoon the king's party came to the desecrated shrine to pray. From here, wearing shirts of mail under their clothes, they went to Smithfield to meet with the rebels. And now the spokesman was Wat Tyler himself. Tyler's unaccustomed role as leader, the dizzying swirl of destruction that had raged almost continuously since Wednesday night, and sheer fatigue seem to have unbalanced him (and he may have been unbalanced enough to begin with): he addressed the king with oaths and rude language, shook his hand like an equal, called him brother. His demands were the familiar ones: the abolition of villeinage, no law but the "law of Winchester," all men equal save the king, the church's estates divided among the people, only one bishop. All, of course, was suavely granted—thirty clerks had been writing out parchments of pardon and freedom since the day before. Tyler was ordered to return with his followers to his home.

What happened then happened so fast that none could agree about it afterward. Tyler and the king were both mounted. By one account, one of the king's party hurled an insult at Tyler and Tyler ordered his men to seize him; by another, Tyler spoke first. The nobles around Richard became nervous, voices were raised. The mayor, possibly perceiving a threat to the king's person, or acting on the king's orders, dragged Tyler from his horse. As Tyler lay on the ground, one of the king's squires, named Standish, ran him through. The crowd of rebels, seeing their leader killed before their eyes, roared in outrage. Bows and arrows were raised.

Then the king, trained from childhood for a moment such as this, spurred his horse and rode out before the rebel crowd, crying, "Sirs, will you shoot your king? *I* am your captain. Follow me." He walked his horse away from the scene, and they followed—like sheep, says one chronicler —to Clerkenwell Fields, a few hundred yards north. Tyler was taken to a nearby hospital. The mayor galloped into the city and returned with an armed force, which surrounded the bedraggled mass, but the king made a show of ordering them to do no violence, pardoned the rebels, and bade them go home in peace.

Tyler, found dying in the hospital, was taken outside in the public square and executed. His head was put up on London Bridge in place of Archbishop Sudbury's. The mayor, who may have saved King Richard's life and saved the day with his armed men, was knighted on the spot at Clerkenwell Fields, along with two of Chaucer's friends, John Philipot and Nicholas Brembre, and some sources say the squire Standish. Peace was restored. The promises made to the peasants and artisans were nullified as made under duress, and though it was dying of its own accord villeinage remained the law of the land. "Villeins ye are and villeins ye will remain," Richard is supposed to have said later. But the poll tax was abandoned for more than a century.

The Peasants' Revolt had its impact on literature. Chaucer's friend John Gower had already begun his long allegorical satire in Latin, *Vox Clamantis*, about England's toils and troubles, and he revised what he had written so that it began with a dream in which he sees the peasants of England turned into animals. The revolt is alluded to in *Piers Plowman*, and there is a handful of poems about it. But Chaucer never mentions it except in the passage naming Jack Straw quoted above. How did he feel toward it? As an official of the royal government he undoubtedly felt little sympathy, if any, for the crazed behavior of the insurgents or for the more extreme of their demands. No man of sense in his time could have taken seriously the notion of distributing the church's wealth among the people or having but a single bishop.

The equality of all men, however, had a certain theological respectability: all *are* equal in God's eyes, and at birth, and as they face death. Some of the art of the period after the Black Death depicts the various estates of society, the pope, a king, a cardinal, a bishop, a nobleman, a peasant all equally beset by a skeleton with a spear—Death. Chaucer probably thought the poll tax unjust and may have disagreed with the Statutes of Labor. Pity for the poor was a phase of Christian charity, and in his works he almost always shows the poor in a sympathetic light.

But mob rule he detested, and he echoes several times the classical idea that a mob is a many-headed monster, that "the people" were, as he put it in a stanza of the Clerk's Tale (lines 995 ff., in his own words, added to his source), stormy, unstable, faithless, indiscreet, fickle, gullible. In *Troilus and Criseyde* it is popular opinion that turns the love story into a tragedy: when Criseyde has been exchanged for Antenor and is to be sent to her father among the Greeks, Hector's speech would have reversed the council's decision had it not been for what Chaucer calls "the noise of people" (4: 183)—which by an interesting association he describes as starting up as fierce "as blaze of *straw* y-set on fire."

At the time of the Peasants' Revolt, Chaucer may already have begun working on his adaptation of Boccaccio's *Filostrato*. If not, he began it soon after. The riots gave him a sense of what it was like in a besieged city and how it would have felt to see Troy burning in its final hours. England now, since the end of the 1360s, had fallen on bad times. The Peasants' Revolt, at least to Gower, symbolized the danger of England's fall because of the vices of her various estates, and to that topic he turned his energies. And in somewhat this way Chaucer made the tragedy of Troilus a cautionary tale for England.

When King Edward had died, the presence of a child on the throne was an anxiety: people were painfully aware of what the Scriptures said, "Woe to thee, O land, when thy king is a child" (Chaucer discreetly omitted the text from his translation of *Melibee*, where it was quoted). But now the king had shown himself great in personal courage, in discretion, in presence of mind, in majesty. In his comportment throughout the revolt, King Richard—already at fourteen tall and handsome like his father and his uncles, with thick blond hair and the Plantagenet nose—had displayed qualities that brought to mind King Edward III and the Black Prince.

His queen, Anne of Bohemia, arrived in England the following December. Her large entourage, according to Froissart, came through Brussels and she stayed there a month or more with her uncle the duke of Brabant. The delay was occasioned by the fear that her ship might be intercepted by Norman vessels lying in wait for it, as part of a plan—so it was rumored—of the French king to halt the marriage. The duke of Brabant sent a delegation to the French court, and it returned with a safe-conduct for her and her party as far as Calais. So the party went on, stopping at Ghent, Bruges, and Gravelines; from there it was accompanied to Calais by the earls of Salisbury and Devonshire with an armed guard of knights and archers. At Calais they set sail on the first favorable wind, on a Wednesday, and arrived at Dover the same day. Here the Lady Anne rested two days, then proceeded to Canterbury, where she was met by the earl of Buckingham and escorted to London.

The marriage took place on January 14, 1382, in the chapel of the palace at Westminster; she was then crowned queen of England by the archbishop of Canterbury. There were elaborate feasts and tournaments. Richard had just turned fifteen when they married; Anne was sixteen. At first the marriage was not popular. Far from bringing a dowry, she had been purchased at a high price, as several chroniclers said—£4,500 along with expenses and loans, plus the ongoing cost of the impoverished Bohemian nobles who made up her train. These extravagances, arranged before the Peasants' Revolt, were not calculated to please beleaguered taxpayers. And in the long run the marriage was a poor bargain: Bohemia never joined in the war against France, and the queen never produced an heir.

But Richard, who had not laid eyes on her until her arrival, loved her deeply. It says something in her favor that she was able to win the English to her side: she was "good Queen Anne," was always spoken well of, even by the king's enemies. One should not think of her as a Bohemian or a German; she was an international figure, the sister of the Holy Roman Emperor, able to read Latin and German as well as Bohemian, and said to be versed in sacred writings (Archbishop Arundel said she was more diligent in reading godly books than the English prelates). She doubtless became fluent in French and English if she were not already. She was for Richard a perfect companion—it is said he rarely let her leave his side. In certain ways she calls to mind Queen Philippa of Hainault. The day after her marriage she pleaded for an amnesty to those involved in the Peasants' Revolt, and she interceded for others in the years that followed. Unlike Queen Philippa she died young, not yet thirty. The idealized effigy on her tomb in Westminster Abbey shows a round-faced and wide-browed gentlewoman with flowing hair, slightly plump, probably quite attractive by medieval standards of female beauty—a placid, kindly face that bespeaks a towering dignity and tender humanity. A funeral effigy in wood, made from a death mask, shows Slavic features—a long nose and high cheekbones, the face thin, youthful, and aristocratic.

So the king had now a proper court with a great lady for his queen —legend has it that she introduced into England the elegant fashion of riding sidesaddle. A new age seemed to be dawning, perhaps as glorious as the bygone days of Edward III that Chaucer could remember from his teens. After the king's wedding, Chaucer turned or returned to *Troilus and Criseyde* determined to depict Troy at its height in a golden age of chivalry, just before Fortune brought its fall.

The Court of Richard II During the *Troilus* Years

Chaucer had been reappointed to the Wool Custom when King Richard came to the throne, and in April 1382 he was also made controller of the Petty Custom, an office he'd held temporarily in 1374–75, and given a deputy. This means his income was greater—how much greater is not clear—but, thanks to the deputy, his work not substantially increased.

There were complaints that such positions were sinecures, and complaints of extortion—in 1376 even the powerful Richard Lyons had gone to jail on that account.

Some think Chaucer got out of the Customs in 1386 to escape a scandal or worse, but there's no evidence to support the suspicion. If his job was a sinecure of sorts, it was given to him with that understanding. The whole system of appointments was geared to bestow favor, and he was in favor. He was hard at work on his great poem of Troy, reason enough (as *we* can see) for him to have a deputy. A deputy, Thomas Evesham, had been appointed to replace him in the Wool Custom in 1377 while Chaucer was abroad, and another, Richard Barrett, in 1378 while he was in Lombardy. Deputies were generally men with experience in the Customs who had been or would become the controller; Chaucer's successor in the Wool Custom, Henry Gisors, was his deputy for a month in 1384 during an absence Chaucer requested for personal reasons, perhaps to work on the *Troilus*. The responsibility remained his, and the records show he gave annual testimony in person at the Exchequer concerning the collectors' accounts. Shortly after that he requested a permanent deputy, and the request was granted in February 1385; there's no record of his appointing one, but we can assume he did—he was asking for time at a point when he was bringing *Troilus and Criseyde* to a close.

So it appears that the poet had sufficient patronage to allow him a settled life, privacy, a good income, and time to write. The old idea was that the patronage came from John of Gaunt, but as we have seen Gaunt had no hand in the pitcher of wine a day, or the controllership, or the gatehouse at Aldgate. All that had been King Edward's doing; and King Richard was pleased to continue his grandfather's largesse. Queen Anne arrived in England late in 1381, after Chaucer had started the *Troilus*; she was a woman of considerable learning, and it may be that he managed to ingratiate himself and enlist her aid. For evidence there is the enigmatic address to women at the end of *Troilus* and the prologue to *The Legend of Good Women*.

Just before Chaucer was first set up in the Customs, Gaunt had returned from France and retired to brood over his military failures. In what appears to have been an extended period of depression, he busied himself with routine matters. He took a genuine interest in preparing his nephew Richard for the throne. His hot temper and arrogance, and his rigidity in personal loyalties, as in the case of Wyclif, had turned the people and the church hierarchy against him. In court politics he was adept and discerning, but as a politician who needed to curry support from various factions and social groups he had no gift at all; his son, Henry of Bolingbroke, developed those skills, perhaps in reaction to his father's lack of them. You can say Gaunt saw the world through the eyes of his illustrious father and his legendary elder brother, the Black Prince, and was uncompromising in matters he thought they would have insisted on. Or you can say he led his life competing with his elder brother, who if he had lived would have been king. Gaunt, knowing he would never be king of England, was obsessed with being king of Castile—by his lights he *was* king of Castile and bound by honor to expel its usurper.

But his military career was a series of disasters. In the summer of 1378, while Chaucer was in Lombardy, Gaunt had taken up arms to put a stop to French raids on the south coast of England; with two French allies he embarked in pursuit of the French admiral, Jean de Vienne, but never found him. So he decided to besiege the walled town of Saint Malo, important as the strongest French port on the north coast; and having brought no horses or equippage for land battle, he had to mine it—to dig a tunnel under it and then ignite the tunnel's supports, making tunnel and fortress collapse. But the tunnel collapsed on its own during a night attack, and Gaunt, in no position to start over again, sailed back to England in humiliation.

In England he found continued fighting on the Scottish border. He went north as a negotiator, succeeded in establishing a truce by making friends with powerful Scottish nobles—he was there, luckily for him, at the time of the Peasants' Revolt. As things then stood, in 1380–1381, Enrique, the usurper of Castile, in alliance with the king of France, had captured the Isle of Man and ransomed its inhabitants, even sailed up the channel and burned the town of Gravesend, twenty-odd miles from London. The time was judged ripe for England to invade Castile. Just before the Peasants' Revolt a fleet had embarked against the French and Castilian forces, under Gaunt's younger brother, Edmund Langley, earl of Cambridge.

In this expedition to Castile Gaunt made two fatal errors: putting his force under his incompetent younger brother, and contracting an alliance with Fernando, king of Portugal. On the arrival of the English fleet, Beatrix, Fernando's nine-year-old daughter and heiress of his kingdom, was betrothed to Edward Plantagenet, the earl's eight-year old son, who was present on the expedition. Little Beatrix had already been twice betrothed and unbetrothed, first to the king of Castile's brother, then to Enrique, the heir of Castile. But no sooner was the betrothal taken care of than Fernando began to complain, justly, that England had promised to send John of Gaunt and instead sent his inexperienced younger brother, that the English force was not large enough for an invasion, and that John of Gaunt, who was to join them with a larger force, never arrived—he was still in London dickering with Parliament. The English soldiers became impatient, sacked a town or two in boredom, had their pay withheld as a punishment, and mutinied. The earl, to quiet them, demanded that the fighting begin. Instead, Fernando followed a most unchivalric scheme: he canceled the betrothal with Edward Plantagenet and promised his daughter to the king of Castile's second son, thus making peace with the enemy without his ally's knowledge. The earl of Cambridge could do nothing but protest this palpable act of bad faith and sail back to England; he arrived at Christmastime, 1382. His own fleet had been captured by the Castilian navy, and to make his humiliation complete, he arrived in merchant ships borrowed from Castile.

While Chaucer was writing *Troilus and Criseyde* England was suffering such setbacks as these, which might have seemed to him like Troy's last days. The armies left London for the Continent, like the Trojan forces on their way to the Greek encampment, and returned in defeat, not as often but on a larger scale. Yet this is not how he portrayed the Trojan war in the poem; he showed the Trojans fighting on, showed Troilus and others in great feats of arms, and only implied that the war was not going in their favor. On the fateful day when Antenor is taken and a truce is declared for the exchange of prisoners, we learn (4: 43) that in the final encounter the Trojans conducted themselves badly and fled home under the cover of night. It's one of the places in Chaucer where he gives a sense of the violence and harshness of medieval warfare, of its futility:

> The longe day, with speares sharpe y-grounde,
> With arrwes, dartes, swerdes, maces felle°,   *dreadful*
> They fight and bringen horse and man to grounde,
> And with hir axes out the braines quelle.
> But in the laste shour°, sooth for to telle,   *encounter*
> The folk of Troy hemselven so misledden
> That with the worse° at night homeward they   *in defeat*
> fledden.

It is, as *we* know, the beginning of the end. But what Chaucer represented in the poem was what he saw in wartime London, the capacity of people to keep up their spirits and hopes, in part by blinding themselves to the reality of imminent defeat.

Chaucer showed the Trojan defeat proceeding from a wrong decision made in the Trojan "parliament," a decision swayed by "the noise of people." Of such "noise," i.e., fickle public opinion, England in these years had to live through a most embarrassing example. In the Parliament of October 1382, the bishop of Hereford made a stirring speech favoring two "crusades" that could save England; Pope Urban VI had offered plenary indulgences to the supporters of both. One was Gaunt's invasion of Castile; it could be dignified as a crusade because the usurping Castilian government had declared allegiance to Clement, the Avignon pope.

The other "crusade" was an invasion of the Continent against all Clementists, to be led by Henry Despenser, the bishop of Norwich. He was about Chaucer's age, the younger son of an illustrious family, and his ruling passion was battle. As a young man he had fought in Italy in the service of Pope Urban V, and the pope in return made him bishop of Norwich in 1370; his reward for prowess was to be buried ten years in diocesan bureaucracy and cut off from military exploits—and possibly the Holy Father knew what he was doing. Then during the Peasants' Revolt this warrior bishop raised in haste an armed force and expelled the invaders from East Anglia. His victory over a rabble led him to see himself as a crusader, and destiny created the need: in Flanders, a French army had taken several cities. Charles VI had entered Bruges as conqueror late in November, seized the wares of English merchants, and declared an end to commerce with England. All of this spoke loud in favor of the "crusade," which Parliament granted early in 1383.

The militant bishop, capitalizing on the reigning hysteria, had argued that his crusade would be financed by the alms of the faithful and cost the government little. The commons, with mercantile interests at heart, supported him, as did the clergy; the lords remained skeptical. Norwich became the jingo hero of the hour, and by selling indulgences, partly through pardoners, collected ample donations—the greater part, it was said, from women—largely of stray coins and personal objects, "nobles, or sterlinges," as Chaucer put it in the Pardoner's Tale, "Or elles silver brooches, spoones, ringes." Indulgences were remissions of sin, not just for the living but for the dead, who it was claimed could be released from Purgatory and would ascend to heaven on their relatives' donations to the crusade.

So the bishop sailed on the sixteenth of May. At the eleventh hour the king recalled him, but he ignored the order. His forces were in large measure clergy bearing arms, or mercenaries masking as crusaders. Later, new recruits sent from London were a crew of apprentices and ne'er-do-wells with booty on their minds. Despenser's forces captured or sacked some coastal cities and laid siege to Ypres; it mattered to him not at all that the count of Flanders was an Urbanist—the land, he insisted, was in the control of Clementist France and must be taken. His unruly captains turned the crusade into a pillaging expedition; some, it was said, were in league with the enemy. All discipline was lost. Under the advance of a French army Despenser took refuge in Gravelines (which he had earlier sacked), and there went down to defeat; the French, at the intervention of the duke of Burgundy, and perhaps not without a certain Gallic irony, let him return to England.

Now, of course, the English thought his crusade a shocking waste of funds and lives; the commons, who had supported him, and the "people," who had given to his cause their silver brooches, spoons, and rings, turned against him. He had slaughtered a few thousand fellow Christians in an Urbanist nation and wasted troops John of Gaunt needed for his own "crusade" against Castile. When he got to England, he was impeached before the autumn Parliament of 1383 on four counts; the proceeding was carried out before the king and the duke of Lancaster (no mention is made of the commons). His sentence was the seizure of his properties, and he was even made to foot the cost of masses for the souls of those whose deaths he caused. But the bishop was of the upper nobility, and class solidarity prevailed: the king consoled him after his sentence was pronounced, and in two years he had his properties back.

One can see how this national disgrace reverberates in the last two books of *Troilus,* in its pictures of popular opinion and cumulative defeat, but otherwise it makes no appearance in Chaucer's writings except for a single line in *The Canterbury Tales.* The Squire in the General Prologue, twenty years of age, is said to have been

> . . . sometime in chivachy°,   *cavalry raid*
> In Flaundres, in Artois and Picardy,
> And born him well, as of so litel space. . . .

Chaucer was writing this about 1386–1387, when the bishop's "crusade" was only three or four years in the past. There had been other campaigns in Flanders, Artois, and Picardy, but this was the most recent one; the audience would have seen that the Squire's first experience in battle, when he was at the proper age, about sixteen or seventeen, had been on the Norwich campaign. It would be interesting to know how they reacted. One can imagine them in a burst of laughter. Or one can imagine them squirming.

The Death of the Princess Joan

John of Gaunt, furious at his younger brother's incompetence and the bishop of Norwich's waste of funds and troops, went ahead with his plan for a Castilian invasion. To get the money out of Parliament, he had to allay their misgivings about England's relations on the Continent. In 1383 he began trying to make peace with France, and the result was a truce to expire in late September 1384. Further and more elaborate negotiations were under way in 1384, with nearly all involved powers represented, but the disappointing result was an extension of the truce through May 1385. Meanwhile, in February, the truce in Scotland expired and fighting broke out at once. Who but Gaunt could intervene? He marched with an army to Edinburgh during an exceptionally cold spring; there was little destruction of lives or property, and he left in April, having made a pact with Henry Percy to defend the Scottish border. Late in April, Parliament convened at Salisbury.

The purpose of the Salisbury Parliament, 1384, was to discuss the war. But orderly discussions were hampered by personal feuds and factional intrigue, among them harsh words between Richard and the earl of Arundel. The court parties at this time were complicated by multiple loyalties and later shifts, but they were roughly four. First, the king's party: Richard and his two closest friends, Thomas Mowbray and Robert de Vere. Then, the opposition: the king's youngest uncle, Thomas of Woodstock, earl of Gloucester, and his two chief allies, the earls of Arundel and Warwick, who were to set themselves up as the king's "protectors." There was in addition a moderate party: Lord Scrope and Sir Michael de la Pole (who was made chancellor in 1383). And there was the Lancastrian party: Lancaster, as a palatinate with special rights of self-government, had power so enormous that it could never belong to any party—it *was* a party.

As for the king's party, Richard's two intimates, often called his "favorites," de Vere and Mowbray, were both highborn nobles. De Vere, ninth earl of Oxford, was some five years older than the king. Orphaned when he was nine, he was made the ward of Enguerrand de Coucy, to whose second daughter, Philippa, he was married at about sixteen. He had been knighted by Edward III with other youngsters of the high nobility when he was eleven; during the Peasants' Revolt he was with the king in the Tower. It is thought Sir Simon Burley encouraged their friendship; de Vere gave Burley, sometime before 1384, one of his manors in Herefordshire, for reasons unknown. De Vere claimed that he and his wife hadn't the means to support their estate, and Richard showered on them various properties, one of which had belonged to Gloucester's wife; the gift did not endear him to Gloucester. Richard made de Vere a member of the privy council and a knight of the Garter. When in the next year the English colony in Ireland called for the king's help, he made him the marquis of Dublin with almost regal powers, even promising him that lands he captured not previously owned by the crown would be his and his heirs' free of rent or service. Walsingham maliciously charged that there was an "obscene familiarity" between them. Parting with this closest of his favorites so he could take his post in Ireland was another matter; Richard sent a deputy.

Mowbray was the same age as Richard. He was the second son of the eleventh Baron Mowbray, and was of the blood royal through his mother, which made him the king's distant cousin. When he was seventeen his elder brother died and he became twelfth baron. Richard shortly bestowed on him the title earl of Nottingham, and in the same year made him knight of the Garter. Before the Scottish invasion of 1384 he made him earl marshal of England for life, an office held by his great-grandfather. In the next year, at nineteen, he married one of Arundel's sisters.

Michael de la Pole was older and of a different background. When he was made one of two "governors" of the king in 1381, he had just turned fifty. His family, from Hull, had been of the merchant class and drew the attention of the court by lending money to the Crown. He had fought extensively in the French wars, serving as an admiral, and had been one of Gaunt's retainers. Not a "favorite" of Richard's, he took a detached, judicious view of court affairs; the other governor, Richard, earl of Arundel, was a dour, impatient militarist whom Richard despised. De la Pole won the king's affection through his fairness, his competence, and his hand in arranging the marriage with Anne of Bohemia. He was made chancellor in time to impeach the bishop of Norwich, and Richard named him earl of Suffolk in 1385.

During the Parliament at Salisbury there were two fantastical attempts, engineered by de Vere, to discredit and eliminate Lancaster. Though he was the king's intimate, it is not clear how much the king knew of these machinations. One day a Carmelite friar, after saying mass before the king, came forward and told him he possessed information that John of Gaunt was leading a conspiracy. Richard, now eighteen, flew into a rage, during which he threw his hat, and then one shoe after the other, out a window. He ordered Gaunt killed at once. Richard's rages had become predictable, and this was doubtless what the masterminds of the plot had counted on. After he calmed down, an effort was made to get factual details in writing from the friar, a demand for which the friar was altogether unprepared. At this point, John of Gaunt entered to fetch the king to the cathedral, where the court was waiting; his amazement at the story and his sincere denials so turned Richard's overwrought emotions that he ordered the friar killed on the spot. Gaunt averted this and the friar was led away; he was intercepted by some knights of mixed sympathies, none from de Vere's party, who tortured him with unspeakable cruelty but got nothing from him; while still being questioned, he fell into a coma and died a day or two later.

The following Christmas at Westminster the king's favorites attempted a more carefully thought-out plot against John of Gaunt. There was to be a meeting of the Council at Waltham; when the duke arrived, he would be seized and tried for treason before a bench of judges already chosen, who would find him guilty. About this Richard must have had at least an inkling, for the plan leaked out to Gaunt's supporters. Gaunt boldly went to Sheen, with an armed escort and chain mail under his clothing, and confronted the king, not implicating him but warning him about his choice of intimates. This time, Richard heard his uncle with perfect calm and agreed to follow his advice. The Princess Joan, as she often did, brought about a reconciliation between Gaunt and the conspirators. Gaunt, it was plain, was the injured party; public hostility shifted to de Vere and the others, and sympathy flowed to Gaunt even from the most powerful of his former enemies, like the archbishop of Canterbury. Once more Chaucer observed the fickleness of public opinion—and this was about the time he was writing Book 4 of *Troilus*.

The Princess Joan, the "Fair Maid of Kent," died the following year, 1385, at fifty-seven; it was said she died of a broken heart over the failure of what was her last venture in making peace among the warring males of the royal household. In that year, when the truce with France expired, the French took Scotland as an ally and planned an invasion of England from the north. The English assembled an army; on the way, near York, the followers of Sir John Holland fell into a brawl with the followers of the earl of Stafford, and one of Holland's squires was killed. Holland, one of the knights responsible for torturing the Carmelite friar, was the son of the Princess Joan by her first husband and so the king's half brother. The Staffords took sanctuary and Richard refused to let them be seized. So Holland sought revenge: he provoked a quarrel with Stafford's son, Ralph, killed him with a single blow, and fled into sanctuary.

The murdered Sir Ralph Stafford, about the same age as the king, had been brought up in the royal household. We have to remember that Richard's favorites, like Mowbray and de Vere and such of his childhood friends as the younger Stafford, were his contemporaries, in their late teens, with the close "bonding" among them of youths that age. Richard was inconsolable at the death of his friend; he swore that Holland, though his half brother, would be treated as a common murderer. Princess Joan tried to intervene with one son on behalf of the other, but Richard was adamant. Although Holland in fact lived on for many years, the princess, grown obese in her later days, and in poor health, died that August, at Wallingford Castle.

Joan of Kent was a figure from England's golden age. She had been the wife of the Black Prince, and was the last of the circle of Edward III's court when it was in its glory. Her death, with its powerful associations, marked the end of an era. It was in the air as Chaucer was finishing the *Troilus*. On September 10 he received along with other esquires of the royal court the customary black cloth for mourning. The princess was buried in Lincolnshire the following January, 1386, when the king had returned from Scotland.

Philippa Chaucer and the Lancastrian Court

In their march through Scotland the English army, on Gaunt's advice, had planned to cut off the enemy's retreat. De Vere, once again trying to stir up trouble, accused Gaunt of duplicity when he recommended a dangerous course; the king lost his temper, called his uncle a traitor, and told him to march off wherever he would. But Gaunt, knowing now that meekness affected the king as rage could not, answered him as a loyal subject, and once again there was a reconciliation—the figment and emblem of Richard's unstable dependency. This incident may have been what inspired a plan to resolve the tensions between de Vere and Gaunt by getting Gaunt out of the country; Gaunt would be sent at last on his "crusade" to win the throne of Castile.

When Gaunt's fleet sailed on July 9, 1386, he had a new alliance with the new king of Portugal, João I. Fernando had died three years before, so his daughter Beatrix was now, at fourteen, the queen of Castile. Gaunt brought with him his wife, Costanza, the rightful queen of Castile, and his three daughters, leaving his son by Blanche, Henry of Bolingbroke, earl of Derby, age twenty, to oversee his affairs and be his lieutenant in the Palatinate of Lancaster. Chaucer's eldest son, Thomas, now eighteen or nineteen and already in John of Gaunt's service, sailed with the army.

None of Gaunt's four children by Katherine Swynford accompanied the party, nor did Katherine herself. In Gaunt's absence she was at Kettlethorpe, the estate in Lincolnshire she had inherited from her late husband. A wealthy woman in her own right through gifts from Gaunt, Katherine lived during these years either at one of Gaunt's Lincolnshire manors or her own. Her four children by Gaunt, surnamed Beaufort, ranged in age from about seven to thirteen and were with her in Lincolnshire. With her too was her sister, Philippa Chaucer, whose annuities, records show, were paid through Lincolnshire officials from 1379 to 1383. Katherine's first son, Thomas Swynford, had been in the retinue of Henry, earl of Derby, as early as 1382, so we may assume he stayed in England with Henry to oversee the Lancastrian estates. Philippa's son Thomas, as we've said, was with Gaunt's army; her daughter Elizabeth was already a nun at Barking, but she still had two young children—her son Lewis (if he was her son, not Cecily Champain's) would have been six, and her daughter Agnes (if she was her daughter) could have been a baby. She was constantly with her sister, both being in the retinue of the Duchess Costanza; now, with the duchess abroad, Katherine's surroundings seemed more suitable for two small children.*

For twenty years Philippa Chaucer had had a connection with Gaunt's household. You can believe, if you want, that she had been his mistress before her sister had, that her eldest daughter and son, Elizabeth and Thomas, were really Gaunt's children. Whether you believe it or not, Philippa and Katherine had both been raised in the royal household as wards of Queen Philippa. It was the queen who had arranged Katherine's marriage to one of Gaunt's retainers and had arranged Philippa's to Chaucer. Philippa had received an annuity from King Edward in 1366, probably by way of a wedding gift. After the queen's death in 1369, the year after the Duchess Blanche died, King Edward and his sons felt an obligation to the two Hainaulter sisters. Katherine was made governess to Gaunt's children and became his mistress about 1371, and Philippa was made damsel to the Duchess Costanza in 1372. Chaucer received an annuity from John of Gaunt, partly (it said) in recognition of his wife's services to Queen Philippa, in 1374, on the day after he took the oath as controller, probably by way of congratulation. In 1373 Philippa appears on a list, drawn up some months in advance, of New Year's gifts to be given to various members of the Lancastrian court, hers a buttonhook and six buttons of silver-gilt, not an especially lavish gift compared to others, but the list suggests she would be spending the holidays with the Lancaster household, and it says not a word of Master Geoffrey.

We can conclude that Philippa had an intimacy with the Lancastrian circle that Chaucer did not. She and her sister, much attached to each other, were of the court in an intimate, familial way, as Chaucer was not. And they probably had an interest in court matters that Chaucer did not share. Whether it was a source of friction we have no way of knowing; it could have been a source of amusement. As we've seen, Chaucer in his poems often does mention, as a kind of in-joke, his "unlikeliness" in courtly love—he is the outsider to gentilesse. They were ladies and probably snobs; he was a professional courtier not really interested in social climbing.

In February 1386, just a few months before Gaunt sailed, Philippa

*Philippa, we know, had lived in Lincolnshire in 1379 and probably at other times. After some twenty-five years of marriage, Chaucer and his wife were not, however, completely estranged, for he continued to collect her Exchequer annuity. She died the year after Gaunt sailed, but we know nothing of her death or burial.

was admitted to the confraternity of Lincoln Cathedral. Membership was reckoned a spiritual benefit, and was socially very prestigious. John of Gaunt had himself been made a member of the confraternity in infancy, along with his father and his two older bothers and the old earl of Lancaster, "blind Harry," the Duchess Blanche's grandfather. Evidently Katherine was already a member, for the Swynfords themselves were local nobles and had their own connections with the cathedral. Those inducted with Philippa were her two nephews—Katherine's son Thomas Swynford, and her oldest son by Gaunt, John Beaufort; her niece, Joan Beaufort, with the young man she was betrothed to; and—he was evidently the instigator of the induction—the duke's son, Henry of Bolingbroke, earl of Derby. It was a family occasion for both Gaunt's and Katherine's families—significant because two of the illegitimate children were there with the legitimate ones. Since their Aunt Philippa was there she was of course included. But there was apparently no reason to send for Uncle Geoffrey.

If Chaucer was outclassed by his wife and her circle, it was probably because he preferred it that way. He knew them all, he was well placed at court, but he had his own world—he was a poet, an intellectual, a valued royal officer, well paid, of a solid mercantile family. Money and comfort and position mattered to him, and the time and freedom for his art. In a total summing up, he was not far below his wife socially, if at all, but he was very far below the Lancastrian women and children who were her constant companions. They may have been mostly the milieu in which he saw his wife and children in these later years. They may even have been a little "court," a baronial court—even a royal court, since Costanza was queen of Castile—to which he read poems aloud, the Lincolnshire court of Queen Costanza, who did not understand English.

Was it felt *at court* that Philippa was more significant on the social scale than her husband? There is the smallest piece of evidence in one of the dreariest documents, a routine assignment of payments to the customs collectors and the controller. The clerk who wrote the order named the controller "Philippus Chaucer," and the error was carefully preserved on all three existing copies. Oh, it is just a slip, to be sure, perhaps just involving a shift of gender, with appropriate adjustment of the case ending. But its meaning lies in its substitution of Chaucer's *wife's* name for his own. It could mean any of a dozen things, but one is that to a certain anonymous clerk in the Exchequer, a young clerk, perhaps, not yet acquainted with the names of the thousands of royals and nobles of the realm and the vast personnel of royal esquires and officials, the name Philippa Chaucer meant something, but the name Geoffrey Chaucer did not.

Whatever his wife and her Lancastrian intimates thought about Chaucer, we would rather know what he thought about them, and what, if anything, he learned from them or used about them in his writings. It may explain how he knew so much about the world of women, about how women behaved with one another at this level of society—as Criseyde behaves with her ladies in Book 3 or with her dreadful consoling women friends in Book 4—and how they talked. It may also explain how he became so conversant in upper-class social interactions: he may have been an inveterate observer of their mentalities, one mentality belonging to the king and his uncles and intimates and their ladies, another to lesser nobles like his wife or Katherine. This clash of mentalities was something he used in the interaction between Troilus the prince and Criseyde the sooth-sayer's daughter.

The use of models from real life was some centuries away from the literature of Chaucer's age, but Chaucer in his public life did know and observe young royals and nobles of Troilus's rank and age, insecure, arrogant, maturing painfully: King Richard himself, and those favorite friends of his age like Mowbray and de Vere and the younger Sir Ralph Stafford, or Gaunt's son, Henry of Bolingbroke. And, in his domestic life, he could observe less exalted youths of that age, like Katherine's son Sir Thomas Swynford or his own son Thomas. Of younger, attractive widows of the lesser nobility there were fewer, but there was Katherine Swynford, and there had been Alice Perrers. They were both rather forward women, like Boccaccio's Criseida; Chaucer saw that for the story of *Il Filostrato* to work, *his* beautiful young widow needed to be timid, "slyding of corage," and to have an older man for a go-between, an avuncular figure with a gift for language and a fund of worldly wisdom, a man of learning, an official of the king's court—a single man with something askew in his love life—for whom Chaucer himself was, it is now agreed, chiefly the model.

12

Troilus
and Criseyde

In the early lines of the *Troilus*, Criseyde is described as being matchless in beauty "Right as our firste letter is now an A" (1: 171), and this line, generally thought a compliment to Queen Anne, could not have been written much before the marriage settlement was signed in May 1381, the month before the revolt. Of course he could have added it to an already existing draft, or to a plan that as yet existed only in his head. Chaucer did think and plan before he set pen to paper, the way rhetoricians advised. And if the poem was still in the planning stage, the Peasants' Revolt, reinforcing its epic and tragic dimensions, helped make it what it is—Chaucer's masterpiece, finished and complete as *The Canterbury Tales* is not, brought flawlessly to a close. It is the first and greatest narrative poem of love in the English language, the triumph of medieval courtly poetry, so far above its predecessors as to have earned Chaucer the name among his contemporaries of a "philosophical" poet.

Chaucer's beginning is, unlike Boccaccio's, the formulaic opening of an epic. The poet states his theme, "The double sorrow of Troilus"—the initial sorrow of unrequited love and the final one of being forsaken—and invokes his Muse, the cruel Fury, Thesiphone, "goddess of torment." The unbearable sadness of Troilus's story, the turning of Fortune's wheel "Fro woe to wele and after out of joye," and the narrator's own overpowering sorrow (the verses themselves weep, he tells us, as he writes them) set the tone. He tells us chillingly at the outset that Troilus' story will move "Fro woe to wele, and after out of joye." The ending is not to be merely the unhappy outcome of a love affair or the death of a hero but the fall of a civilization. Troilus' name itself—some editors spell it "Troylus"— suggests the ancient doomed city. The epic dimension is emphasized by a stanza naming Homer, plus the authors of two medieval prose narratives about the fall of Troy, Dares and Dictys (1: 141):

> But how this town come to destruccion
> Ne falleth naught to purpose me to telle;
> For it were here a long digression
> Fro my mattere, and you too long to dwelle.°   *delay*
> But the Trojan gestes,° as they felle,   *deeds*
> In Omer, or in Dares, or in Dite,
> Whoso that can may read hem as they write.

The Audience in the Poem

Chaucer's initial reaction to Boccaccio's *Il Filostrato* was to this Trojan setting, for Troy was England's ancestral city. The medieval tradition was that Troy fell because of excessive sensuality—moral weakness born of lust and wantonness. This implication is not present in the *Filostrato*, whose moral only warns young men in love of women's fickleness. But Chaucer wanted to make it a cautionary tale for his nation, wanted to make his readers feel that England too could fall from its own weaknesses.

When he started reading the *Filostrato*—and by June 1381 he had surely read the whole several times—he would have taken it for a romance, though a very strange one. If some Italian acquaintance explained to him that it was a *cantare*, not a romance, this would not have raised his estimate of it. The *cantare*, new in Italy in Boccaccio's day, was, to quote David Wallace,

> a fast-moving narrative with a strong story-line and little lyric elaboration. It meets a taste for spectacular combats and fantas- tic adventures, often in exotic settings with women of high sensual beauty and sharp sexual appetite . . . [The *cantari*] encourage the fascination of a popular audience with the distant world of aristocratic manners. Of course, their realization of this

world bears little relation to actual aristocratic practice, or to its representation in authentic courtly literature.

This explains why *Il Filostrato* seems to us so stark and truncated. The *cantari* were popular entertainments, recited or sung aloud, comparable to the "bourgeois romances" known in England. They made much of *cortesia*, but in a watered-down sense that would have seemed bizarre to a courtier: the word, Chaucer found, might even be applied to a horse!

Chaucer was looking for materials, not forms, and certainly not popular forms; he never had any interest in writing for a popular audience, though he was interested in bringing popular traditions into courtly literature. Boccaccio was himself trying to elevate the literary status of the *cantari*, but, again to quote Wallace, he "remained an outsider to the courtly world; his conception of *cortesia* is inevitably impoverished and debased." When Boccaccio wrote *Il Filostrato* he was, we should remember, barely over twenty, an unknown poet in Naples, where he had been raised, trying to attract the attention of the Angevin court. Chaucer, on the other hand, had a courtly education and extensive exposure to courtly ways, and he understood the conventions of courtly culture quite well enough to see that Boccaccio had them wrong. This was probably why he never mentioned Boccaccio by name; there may have been other reasons, but this was reason enough.

Chaucer addressed his poem to a courtly audience—as he indicates in the poem itself. There is a painting in a Cambridge manuscript showing a middle-aged man standing at a lectern or pulpit before an audience, often thought to represent Chaucer reading his poem to the court of Richard II. It is the frontispiece to a luxurious manuscript of the *Troilus* made in the first quarter of the fifteenth century, whose remaining illustrations—for which blank pages had been left—were never painted. The man reading has no book before him, and so appears to be speaking or reciting. It may be more nearly a medieval abstract picture of an experience: courtiers fashionably dressed troop with ceremony down from two castles in the background into a garden, where the figure at the lectern addresses them in the posture of a preacher or teacher. The picture is very stylized and we cannot be sure that the courtiers are identifiable, or that the man in cloth of gold directly in front of the poet, who has no face, is Richard II; the face may have been rubbed off by someone with Lancastrian sympathies, or left blank for a prospective patron. Chaucer's face looks not unlike other portraits of him. The picture shows us that a decade or two after his death Chaucer was still thought of as an oral poet, and his audience was still thought of as a court.

The audience implied in the *Troilus* is unmistakably an audience of courtiers who understand the ways of love. Elsewhere the poet may address the "reader" (e.g., 5: 270), but he *depicts* an audience and makes us believe we are part of it (2: 29):

> And forthi° if it happe in any wise   *therefore*
> That here be any lover in this place . . .

He even presents himself as pointing to individuals in the audience:

> Eek scarcely been there in this place three
> That have in love said like°, and done, in all;   *alike*
> For to *thy* purpose this may liken *thee*,
> And *thee* right nought . . .

He anticipates possible responses from the audience and replies to them; someone might say, he suggests, that *he* wouldn't behave that way in love, or someone else might say, "This was a sudden love" (line 667). At times he shares the audience's emotion, as at the cliff-hanging end of Book 2, with Troilus in his sickroom and Criseyde about to enter, where the narrator asks us, "O mighty God, what shall he saye?" At other times, he presents himself as uninformed, an outsider or a *naïf*, and suggests that it is up to us to deduce or surmise or imagine. He thus enlists his audience in creating the poem's reality. There are women in this audience, for he addresses them directly at the end. Whether the poem's fiction of a court audience corresponds to its actual audience is another question: part of Chaucer's audience were his literary and intellectual friends like Gower and Strode (whom he names at the end) and professional courtiers like himself whose origins were in the merchant class—and of course we, an unknown posterity, are part of his audience. The poem flatters us as being responsive and knowledgeable; it makes us play courtier.

Boccaccio began *Il Filostrato* with a convention which Chaucer himself had used in his dream visions, that of the poet as suffering lover. Boccaccio began with a long, ardent address in prose to his poetical lady,* praying that Troiolo's sad story will make her take pity on him. And he added more of the same in the first five stanzas, where he names his lady as his Muse. Chaucer in his dream visions had only given hints of his own distress in love; he presents himself in the *Troilus* as one who "serves the servants of the God of Love" (a phrase used of the pope) but dares not pray to Love on his own behalf, "for myn unlikelinesse." Boccaccio was

---

*This element of supposed autobiography in Boccaccio's early Italian poems used to be thought veridical; details of the writer's early entanglements, for which there was no other evidence to speak of, were until quite recently used to depict his life. We now think these are conventional fictions used as "framing" devices.

an outsider playing the insider; Chaucer, perhaps in reaction, though much more an insider, chose to play the outsider.

When Chaucer first read the *Filostrato* he found certain conventions of courtly writing missing from Boccaccio's poem. He missed "psychological allegory," the way of looking at love as an experience of interior faculties, in which he had been schooled by the *Roman de la Rose*. He missed the historical detail appropriate to a romance that dealt with the "matter of Rome," the rhetorical flourishes of courtly writing, the high style, and the doctrine or morality expected in serious literature. And he missed a focus on love: he would have viewed *Il Filostrato*, whose story interested him greatly, as naïve and vulgar, for its focus was on lust, on *caldo disio*, "hot desire"—a phrase repeated over and over, often at the ends of stanzas, vivified with images of heat and flame. The subject was Troiolo's anguished passion. The plot was an assignation and an affair. The story was not seen from a Christian or a moral viewpoint—its moral was *women are fickle* and its ending was an appeal to the poet's own lady. It was not Chaucer's idea of what a court poem should be.

Transformations

In adapting *Il Filostrato* Chaucer everywhere enhanced and vivified details, made it more dramatic and in some respects more extravagant, more pagan, more shocking, but at the same time more moral and more Christian. We can tell in a general way what Chaucer *wanted* to do by comparing his finished version with the *Filostrato* and other sources. But in describing what he "really" did, we have to interpret his motives for the changes he made. It was once thought the surviving manuscripts* revealed three successive versions and so showed many revisions; but what we have in the surviving manuscripts, we now know, is a single, completed work.

Chaucer's first adjustment was to change the picture of the storyteller. He wanted a narrator that could behold the action as the reader does and comment on it like a chorus, not one with a lady of his own and an ax to grind. So he removed the narrator's connections with the author

---

*The twenty manuscripts (four of them only fragments) break down into three families, called *alpha*, *beta*, and *gamma*. At one time it was thought these went back to different versions or revisions—the alpha being the earliest, the beta the final revision, and the gamma based on a manuscript postdating alpha. In recent times it has seemed almost a certainty that the gamma version is the final revision. The earlier alpha manuscripts lack some passages like Troilus' song to love in Book 3 and his speech on predestination in Book 4, which may mean that Chaucer added them later—but then, the alpha manuscripts could represent scribes' efforts to shorten the work.

and supplied the figure who says he is like a priest or bishop in the religion of Love, who bids us (using the Christian convention of the "bidding prayer," 1: 22) pray to the God of Love for various sorts and conditions of lovers. This clerkish narrator is swayed by emotion as he tells his story —he is like a member of the audience *inside* the poem, and he reacts as Chaucer himself could not possibly have reacted, even at one point (3: 1319) wishing enviously that he had bought such joy with *his* soul! That we know the narrator is *not* Chaucer, or, if you prefer, that he is Chaucer playing a role, makes us aware of the living poet behind this mask, whom we always sense and who will emerge at the end.

The narrator is, like us, a reader, poring over an "old book," sometimes deeply involved with the story, sometimes turning to us to comment. He claims that his "old book" is by "Lollius," not a code name for Boccaccio but a deliberate fiction. There seems to have been a legend during the Middle Ages—it was based on a misreading of a line from Horace*—of a lost writer, Lollius, the greatest of those who wrote about the Trojan War. Chaucer's narrator claims to *possess this lost book.* So at times he draws aside to consult his source and we are suddenly alone with him at his desk. Then we are plunged back into ancient Troy, and he seems to sit down with us to watch. But at any moment he may intrude to comment, apostrophize or exclaim, give more information, even tell us what the characters are thinking.

What the narrator does with his old book, Chaucer was doing with a shelf of them. It was the medieval way of composing to draw on carefully chosen models, and Chaucer brought to his adaptation of the *Filostrato* ideas and actual passages from the *Teseida,* Dante, Ovid, Virgil, Statius, and others. He aspired in the *Troilus* to leave the company of "makers" and join these more elevated "poets." To him Troilus was at base the brilliant youthful warrior he found in the *Aeneid*; but as a lover Troilus was the youth he found in the *Filostrato*—plus the abstraction he found in the *Roman.* When we first see Troilus we see a youth never before in love, making fun of lovers. This doesn't mean—as critics sometimes say —that he is a virgin or an adolescent; it means that he doesn't yet know the experience of falling in love that he laughs at so defensively. (In Boccaccio, Troiolo is *disillusioned*—love's joys are nothing, he says, com-

---

*The misreading about Lollius resulted from a misspelling in *Epistles* 1: 2, 1, "*Troiani belli scriptorem, Maxime Lolli, / Dum tu declamas Romae, Praenesti relegi.*" Horace was addressing an actor: "While you, Maximus Lollius, are declaiming in Rome, I have been rereading the writer of the Trojan War [i.e., Homer] here in Praeneste." Medieval readers, not realizing that Maximus was Lollius's first name, took it for an adjective, "the greatest." In some manuscripts *scriptorem* ("writer") was incorrectly copied *scriptorum* ("of the writers"). Hence they thought it meant "You, Lollius, the greatest of the writers of the Trojan War . . ."

pared to its torments.) When Cupid strikes him down for his pride by making him fall in love with Criseyde at first sight, he is "converted" to Love's religion. He goes off by himself and suffers the griefs of traditional love melancholy—he sighs, he weeps, he grows pale, he cannot eat; he assumes the lady could love no such wretch as himself, and he keeps her name secret lest he give scandal.

Chaucer's Troilus is by temperament an idealist, who would have gone to his death in miserable silence if his friend Pandarus had not persuaded him, with numerous ingenious arguments, to tell who the lady is. And the argument that makes him reveal her name is the most idealistic one. There are lovers, says Pandarus (1: 810), who have suffered in love for twenty years, and whose ladies knew of their love, yet they never once kissed the lady's mouth—knowing that to serve her is its own reward, a thousand times more than he could deserve. Of *that* word, we are told, Troilus took heed.

Chaucer did all he could to make his hero believable and sympathetic, chiefly in Book 1 where we watch him fall under Love's sway. And here we must accept as best we can all that Chaucer's audience would have taken for granted: the picture of Troilus struck through the eye with Cupid's arrow, forming a deep mental impression of his lady, giving to Love full assent as a convert would (or a sinner), composing a philosophical song to her (which Chaucer adapted from Petrarch's sonnet *S'amor non è*), and suffering a form of madness. While we must make this historical effort, however, we may still laugh at him a little. Chaucer himself calls him "sely Troilus," as we might say "poor fool." Love was for the young, and part of the convention was that as we outgrow this phase of life we can look back on lovers' extravagances with amusement. So does Troilus himself—when he is dead.

For this heroic prince of ancient Troy, so close to the ideals of chivalry and courtly love, Chaucer had to create a suitable lady. Boccaccio's Criseida was a widow who, having tasted love's joys, is not less ardent than her princely suitor but must protect her reputation; once assured by her cousin Pandaro, she agrees to a nocturnal tryst. From here it all becomes very practical: she sends the servants to bed, Troiolo enters by a secret door, she appears on the staircase with a torch, they kiss a thousand times, enter her chamber, disrobe, and get in bed. She keeps on her "last garment," murmuring that the newly wed are bashful on the first night: he begs her to remove the garment and she does so, wrapping herself in his arms until they experience "the last pleasure of love."

Chaucer made her an altogether different character. Criseyde's father, the soothsayer Calkas, having foreseen Troy's downfall, has deserted Troy and gone over to the Greeks, leaving his daughter behind. When we first see Criseyde we see a woman alone with no one to talk to, "well nigh out of hir wit" over her father's shame, and fearful for her own safety —the people have cried out that Calkas's kin should be burned to ashes. Her first act is to ask Prince Hector for protection. She wears a widow's habit of black silk, and we are told she was the fairest in Troy—of angelic beauty, like a heavenly, perfect creature. Hector agrees to give her all protection and honor, and she goes home and stays there, quiet and wary, with a proper household of servants and, as it appears later, of "ladies," companions who are relatives or friends.

Criseyde is more intriguing than Boccaccio's businesslike widow because Chaucer made her mysterious. It is not quite clear in the beginning if she and her father are Trojans: we learn (line 64) that Calkas "was dwelling" in the town, yet we are told (line 97) that she had no friend to turn to. Before long we find out that her uncle, Pandarus, is a Trojan nobleman of high status, a friend of Troilus and a counselor to King Priam, and it is curious—but perhaps revealing—that she did not think to turn to him. Nor do we ever learn whether Uncle Pandarus is her father's or mother's brother. Nor whether she had children: where Boccaccio made a point of letting the audience know that she "had never been able to have one," Chaucer only says (line 132),

> But wheither that she children had or noon,
> I read it naught, therefore I lat it goon.

He does not, he later tells us, know her age. And we never get a physical description of her until toward the end. Part of the creation of this great literary character, the first developed portrait of a woman in English literature, is left to our imaginings or assumptions.

In April—again, we do not know how long a time has elapsed—the Trojans by ancient custom observe the feast of Palladion, a statue (Chaucer calls it a "relic") of Pallas Athena on whose preservation they believe the city's safety depends. To the temple all the people go to hear the service, "many a lusty knight," and "many a lady fresh and maiden bright," and among them is Criseyde, "in widow's habit black." This rather cinematic introduction affords our first impression of her character. Boccaccio had attributed to her a gesture of arrogance: with "ladylike hauteur" (*donnesca altezza*) she threw back the mantle before her face and pushed aside the people to make room for herself. But Chaucer did not want her to be arrogant. He had, this early, decided she should be constitutionally timid—she is, as he says later, "tender-hearted, slyding of corage" (5: 825). Altering the tiny detail of his source, he had her stand alone, "low and still," "always in fear of shame," *behind* the other people, and *near the door*. She is, as we see her this second time, dignified and

reticent, simply dressed, gracious in manner, with an air of assurance—
but she is one of those people who never quite get all the way into a room.

And this is when Troilus sees her. Chaucer greatly embellished the
details he found in Boccaccio to enforce the image of Love's irresistible
power and Troilus's subjection, adding passages of intense lyricism to
remind us that it was the Law of Nature operating (1: 238), that the
experience increased Troilus' virtue (line 252), that on first sight of her
he was stunned (line 274). Keeping his feelings to himself, he goes off to
his palace alone, and there we observe the agonizing effects of love on him,
hear the song he composes, hear him pray for a "friendly look" from her
and see him almost drown in tears.

Trojan Paganism and Its Spokesman

Chaucer added to Boccaccio's version much imagined detail about Troy,
especially its religion; he meant to parade paganism before us. When we
see the people flock to the temple of Pallas Athena, we have the awesome
thrill of watching pagans in the Age of Nature worship a pagan goddess,
or rather, a pagan "relic." A part of their religion is the actual worship
of Venus and Cupid. Medieval "courtly love" thus became in Chaucer's
hands a living part of ancient paganism. He made this paganism convincing with familiar Christian notions like the relic, or a bishop, or penance,
or theological ideas like consent or grace; but he took great pains, in the
speeches of the pagan characters, to allow no such anachronisms. He
meant us to keep in mind that the pagans of his story know nothing of
revealed truth. *We* know that Troy will fall, Aeneas found Rome, the
West be settled, Christianity spread through Europe. But the characters
in the story are in darkness.

Along with the religion, Chaucer supplied a pagan philosophy.
While working on the *Troilus* he was translating Boethius's *The Consolation of Philosophy**; Boethius used pagan philosophy to support a Chris-

---

*It is assumed Chaucer was working on both at the same time because he mentioned them
together in the poem called "Adam Scrivein," playfully scolding his scribe for careless
copying.

Adam scrivein°, if ever it thee befalle	*scribe*
Boece or *Troilus* for to writen newe,	
Under thy long lockes thou must have the scalle°,	*itch*
But after my making° thou write more true.	*writing*
So oft a day I mot thy werk renewe	
It to correct, and eek to rub and scrape—	
And all is through thy negligence and rape°!	*carelessness*

He wishes on Adam an itching disease of the scalp, so that he will have to scratch and
rub his (error-filled) head as Chaucer must rub and scratch at the ink in his copies to insert

tian consolation for human misery, and in doing so he introduced into Western literature the goddess Fortune. Fortune is chance seen from the human view; from God's view it is part of the order of things and all its workings are right. Fortune can betray us only if we climb upon her wheel and desire her gifts, for mutability is the character of those gifts. Indifference—"contempt of the world"—is the great remedy against Fortune's disappointments. Such is the philosophy *Troilus and Criseyde* teaches: the principal characters all echo it, often in passages drawn directly from Boethius's text, as if struggling dimly with fragmented philosophical ideas they cannot fully grasp without the Christian revelation. And such is the message articulated at the end of the poem.

Apart from this true philosophy, there is a false philosophy that Chaucer extrapolated from Boethius and such eclectic works, from collections of philosophical sayings, and from his helter-skelter knowledge of ancient texts. From such reading he had the raw material for an imaginary pagan philosophy—not anything systematic or historically accurate, but a concoction of ancient ideas that does sound like and has the spirit of pagan thinking and classical humanism. And this fictionalized ancient philosophy Chaucer attributed to Criseyde's uncle Pandarus. In this he made an intellectual effort to guess what philosophical thought was like before Truth was revealed; it is a *forbidden* philosophy, exotic and thrilling, as non-Christian as the image of men and women swearing oaths by, believing in, and worshiping Venus and Cupid. It is, he suggests, the philosophy that lies beneath the medieval "religion of love" and the philosophy that gave Troy its reputation for sensuality and decadence.

Pandarus, the spokesman of this philosophy, is the most extraordinary creation in the poem, one of the great literary characters, as complex as any figure in James, as colorful as any in Dickens. Boccaccio's Pandaro was Troiolo's contemporary, a friend, by chance Criseida's cousin, and his name meant "I will give all"; he was the wily go-between and confidant, level-headed, earnest, endowed with street wisdom and an earthy pragmatism. Chaucer made him Criseyde's *uncle,* an older man, as he made him seem, and a figure of importance in Troy. In the *Filostrato* Pandaro's street wisdom took sometimes the form of proverbs and little aphoristic utterances, and Chaucer expanded this: in *Troilus and Criseyde* Pandarus is full of proverbial wisdom—and we must remember that proverbs in the Middle Ages were not old saws and bromides, as we tend to think of *our* proverbs, but lapidary formulations of traditional truth.

---

corrections. Nothing, unhappily, is known about the identity of Adam, though there have been conjectures. The name may have been used figuratively, the biblical Adam having been the source of human error.

Pandarus's proverbs are in large measure a part of his book-learning, and he is always respectful of "clerkes wise" and the "olde lered." In Book 1 when he talks with Troilus he overwhelms us with his store of aphorisms, with elaborate analogies, with logic, rhetoric, and argumentation; he is the glib proprietor of language, and we watch in awe as he breaks down Troilus's resistance. Where Boccaccio's Pandaro reminded Troiolo that widows are more lustful than the inexperienced, Chaucer's Pandarus with greater *delicatesse* quotes learned wise men that there was never man or woman who wasn't apt to experience love's heat, whether celestial or earthly—and then adds (line 983) with a certain cynical wit that, given her beauty and youth, it doesn't suit her "to ben celestial / As yet"!

With all his literary flair, his learning, and his gift of language, Pandarus bears a similarity to the narrator and to Chaucer himself. At the end of Book 1, when Pandarus is planning to approach Criseyde, Chaucer injects a stanza that describes the act of planning by comparing it to building a house—and the simile is translated from the opening lines of the rhetorician Geoffrey of Vinsauf's *Nova Poetria*, where it describes the planning of a poem. Pandarus plans and manipulates events inside the poem as Chaucer the poet does with events outside it. Pandarus's "poem," the love affair of Troilus and Criseyde, is his masterpiece; when things go wrong he is as powerless as is the builder if the house collapses.

Until recent times Pandarus was regarded as a figure of dignity and goodwill. William Godwin, writing in 1803, said he "comes elevated and refined from the pen of Chaucer: his occupation loses its grossness, in the disinterestedness of his motive, and the sincerity of his friendship." In our century C. S. Lewis called him "a friend according to the old, high code of friendship, and a man of sentiment." But others have seen him as a depraved, self-centered, and unprincipled exploiter (at the fringe a few think him a devil or priest of Satan leading the lovers into sin.) He has sometimes been compared with Polonius: but Polonius is now most often played as a dignified statesman advanced in years, wise to the point of suspicion, adept in rhetoric to the point of tediousness, but well meaning. In these respects Pandarus *is* like Polonius; both are professional statesmen, who were required to be masters of the arts of ceremonious blandishment and rhetorical ornamentation—as was Chaucer himself in his career as a diplomat.

Pandarus promotes the love affair of Troilus and Criseyde because he believes in it. Chaucer shows him as filled with concern for his young friend the prince, aware that the liaison would bring joy to Criseyde, and that in her heart she wants it. What he urges is consistent with his philosophical beliefs, whose shortcomings we see only later. To him everything is in constant change, rather like the Heraclitean flux of ancient thought, and change is in the power of Fortune. Hence he is a skeptic and a pragmatist. He believes there are certain moments of opportunity that we must grasp while we may, knowing they will pass. This is very like Horace's *carpe diem,* and indeed Pandarus says to Criseyde (in 2: 291) about her "good aventure": "Cacch it anon, lest aventure slacke." If nothing else makes good fortune "slacken," age will do so, and he warns Criseyde (line 393), echoing Horace again, that no one will want her when she is old:

> Think eek how elde° wasteth every houre   *old age*
> In eech of you a partie° of beautee;   *portion*
> And therefore, ere that age thee devoure,
> Go love, for, old, there will no wight of thee.

He is against intellectualizing and procrastination. He tells Criseyde that if a house is on fire you don't stop to ask how the candle fell in the straw (3: 855–859). And he is against self-absorption. He tells Troilus, in 1: 762,

> Swich is delite of fooles, to beweepe
> Hir woe, but seeken boote they ne keepe

—such is the pleasure of fools to cry over their woe, but they take no trouble to seek a remedy. He warns that we must put as much "craft" into *keeping* good fortune as into seizing it (3: 1625), and must be prepared to lose it. Pandarus's motto is "Alle thing hath time"—there is a time for everything, and that time will pass. Avoiding extremes is all. He believes in a middle course, like the "golden mean" (1: 687):

> . . . bothe two been vices—
> Mistrusten all, or elles alle leve°.   *believe*
> But well I wot, the mean of it no vice is.

Our collective name for the value system of the ancient world is humanism. Pandarus believes that humanity is in the favored position among the hierarchy of creatures. Of angels or other superior beings he knows nothing. Pandarus refers with disdain to "bestiality" (line 735) and praises "so noble a creature / As is a man" (5: 384–85). To him, man is the measure. This humanism includes what is to us Pandarus's least appealing tenet. For he does seem to believe that the end justifies the means, that we can say what we please to get what we want and reverse ourselves later if it serves our purposes. He lies, we know, to promote the love affair, and advises Troilus to find another lover when Criseyde has deserted him. He thinks nothing of contradicting himself. He tells Troilus (at 4: 393) that he should be glad he has had his desire, yet earlier, warning him about Fortune, he said the worst misery is to remember prosperity when it has passed (3: 1625–1628)—Troilus himself notes the contradiction in 4: 481–483. He is cynical, but his ideas of behavior are grounded in classical thought. Nor are his manipulations without restraint: before he brings Troilus and Criseyde together for the consummation of their love, he exacts assurances from Troilus of his honorable intentions. In this pagan world with its "humanistic" values, fleeting pleasure is a legitimate end and marriage is not a consideration—though in fact the lovers probably *have* a secret marriage, made between themselves to each other without witnesses but with vows and rings.

In putting these beliefs into practice Pandarus shows two failures of *understanding*: he does not really understand Troilus and does not fully understand himself. There are times when he recommends to Troilus a kind of cynicism he would be incapable of. There are times when he warns Troilus (as after the consummation) that such joy cannot last, but Troilus in his obsessional way does not hear these warnings. *He* thinks that if he behaves properly all will be well (3: 1639):

> I hope . . . that I shall so me bear
> That in my guilt there shall nothing be lorn.

This is not entirely a matter of temperament. Troilus is a prince, raised in the world of the court where manipulating or wheedling are *infra dig*; Pandarus is a politician.

Neither does Pandarus understand himself. He puts all his energy into fostering the love affair, and his motives are generous. He is happy when Troilus and Criseyde are happy and warns them with concern to tread lightly in their happiness. But he himself is unhappy in love. For some years he has been unrequited in his love for a particular woman. To his friends he makes a joke of it: when he first finds Criseyde with her ladies in Book 2 (line 94) and asks them what they are reading, he adds, "Is it of love? Oh, some good ye me leere"—teach me something useful. Criseyde answers, "Uncle, your maistresse is nat here," and they all laugh. He says he is so in love that he can't eat *every other day*—his joke makes fun of the convention that a lover loses his appetite, but also of Pandarus's love, which it implies is only half serious. We never learn *why* he is unhappy in love; it appears that he himself doesn't know. At the beginning of Book 2 (it is the fateful day, May 3) we see him fall into a fit of love melancholy and wake next morning from a bad night's sleep to remember it is the very day he was to begin his "great emprise" involving Troilus and his niece—and the thought raises his spirits. But of this motive he is unaware.

Chaucer invented this element of the story to show that Pandarus's interest and pleasure in the love affair are in part vicarious. There is

nothing necessarily unhealthy about it. By our standards he is in the best
of mental health: his "defenses," as might be said in modern parlance,
"are excellent." When Criseyde leaves and never returns, we see that he
does not put the energy into consoling Troilus that he put into making
him "seeken boote." Something has gone out of him. But even here his
defenses don't desert him: he hates Criseyde, he says, and wishes her dead.
The outburst may only serve the emotional needs of the moment; he can
change his mind tomorrow.

Criseyde's Choice

Chaucer made the nine parts of Boccaccio's poem into five "books,"
beginning all but the last with a proem expressing the theme and mood
of the book to follow and sustaining the epic manner. The proem of Book 1
introduces the tragic story and the priestly narrator. The proem of Book 2
introduces the "tempestuous mattere / Of disespeir that Troilus was
inne" and calls upon Clio, muse of history; it reminds us that speech and
customs have changed in a thousand years—that "In sondry londes,
sondry been usages"—and that we must approach what follows with a
certain cultural or historical relativism, must suspend our disbelief. It
addresses us, one critic remarks, as "humanists rather than courtiers." The
proem of Book 3 is addressed appropriately to Venus, and (in the last
stanza) to Calliope, muse of epic. Its style is heightened, with majestic
complex sentences and poetic inversions: it addresses us as courtiers once
more, praising Love's universal law, its power to make lovers dread shame
and shun vice. In it Chaucer is asking us to prepare for a scene filled with
joy and glory, what one writer has called "the first great night of love in
our literature."

Although Chaucer set out in Books 2 and 3 to spiritualize and
magnify the celestial heights of love, he was making the characters less
like conventional courtly lovers and more like living people with whom
the audience can empathize. He was almost the first poet, certainly the
first English poet, to set out on such a path. In Book 2 we see Criseyde
not, as before, wary and guarded in a public place, but in the privacy of
her home. When Pandarus greets her, she speaks up in colloquial English
with an interjection ("Ey!"), grasps his hand and holds it up in the
immemorial gesture of hospitality and honor, then seats him on a bench.
In a moment, Pandarus is suggesting that she remove her "barbe" (the
linen cloth that partly covered a widow's face—in medieval England of
course, not ancient Troy), leave her book, and come dance to honor May.
Dignified Criseyde is taken aback:

"I? God forbede!" quod she, "be ye mad?
Is that a widow's life, so God you save?
By God, ye make me right sore adrad°!"   *frightened*

It would be more appropriate, she says, for her to pray in a cave and read saints' lives, and let the younger women do the dancing. Pandarus keeps promising good news, then backing off. While her curiosity increases and she asks him repeatedly to tell, Criseyde is accustomed to his games and keeps her head. The scene, almost entirely original with Chaucer, goes on for some five hundred lines. Pandarus leads up to the good news he has announced, then changes the subject, praises Troilus, and starts to leave. She urges him to stay, and he again advises an end to her mourning. When she asks why, he prefaces his answer with a rhetorical flourish, disclaiming like Polonius that he uses any art and announcing he will come straight to the point. He urges that when "good aventure" comes along one should "cache it anon." And he urges her not to be afraid. In unbearable curiosity she *begs* him to tell.

So Pandarus announces that Troilus loves her, that he will die if she not have pity—adding that if Troilus dies, he will die too! Criseyde thinks, "I shall feelen what he meaneth, ywis" and asks him what he advises; he answers: to return Troilus's love. And here he adds his Horatian sentiment, that age wastes part of beauty every hour and that when she is old no one will desire her. Criseyde begins to weep, lamenting that he, her best friend, is advising her to love, who should be advising against it. Pandarus protests that he will come back no more this week, being so mistrusted. We are reminded that she was the most fearful creature there could be (line 450); we hear her in her thoughts say that she must play his game with caution. Then she tells him she will choose the lesser of two evils (line 470): she won't lead Troilus on or love against her will, but, saving her honor, she will do her best to *please* him from day to day, and she demands that Pandarus expect no more.

They agree and change the subject. But soon she asks, "Tell me how first ye wisten of his woe? Wot none of it but ye? . . . Can he well speak of love?" Pandarus smiles, tells a dressed-up version of how Troilus revealed his passion and did his penance to the God of Love, ending his speech with a passing reference to a time "When ye been his all whole, as he is youre"—to which Criseyde replies, "Nay, thereof spak I nought, ha, ha!" Pandarus in feigned surprise apologizes, says he "mente naught but well," and is gone.

Then, in a remarkable passage (lines 596–931), we watch what happens in Criseyde's mind. We enter into her stream of thoughts and imagery, and at last into her dreams. In Boccaccio the lady remained undecided until later she saw Troiolo and was swept off her feet. But Chaucer at the beginning of the scene has Troilus pass her window, returning from battle; she notes in a soliloquy his good qualities and high rank, says that his loving her is no dishonor, that there is measure in all things, that she is one of the fairest of women (so men say), that she is "her own woman," "right young," and without ties—for husbands are always jealous or overbearing or fickle. Then a "cloudy thought" terrifyingly reverses her thinking: if she lets herself love him she will lose her freedom and security, there will be the danger of gossip, and of male fickleness. There is always woe in love, and all that a woman can do with that woe is "weep and sit and think" (line 783)—women's sad lot, she says, is to *drink their own woe.*

Chaucer achieved in this passage something few writers have achieved, the sustained scrutiny of a character's interior world during a secret turning point of moral determination. And to make it more remarkable, it is a male author's imaginative flight into the interior world of a woman. He had for precedents the tendency of medieval narrative, evident in Boccaccio and Boccaccio's sources, to portray a character's thoughts by indirect discourse or soliloquy; and, as in the *Roman de la Rose,* the tendency of "psychological allegory" to look inside the mind by personifying its faculties, emotions, or reactions. Such tendencies were themselves modeled on the tendency of the Old Humanism to scrutinize in detail the inner mechanics of decision making* in order to show how one chooses virtue or vice.

Approaching Criseyde's decision with such models in mind, Chaucer did something that seems original to us because it is like a novelist's accomplishment. To medieval readers it seemed original too, but for a different reason: the scene depicted a decision being made before the Age of Grace. Criseyde has only natural reason, beclouded by original sin, to guide her, and we see her make a moral choice with no benefit from revealed truth, no concepts of law, sin, the corruption of the flesh, salvation, life eternal. Reason's warnings come to her as practical considerations. Chaucer invents a pagan equivalent for the Christian idea that sexual pleasure limits freedom by increasing desire: he has her think that

*It was believed a sin was committed or avoided through a mental process that began with suggestions from without (from "the world, the flesh, and the devil") and ended with reason giving or withholding its consent. The intermediate state between suggestion and consent, experienced in the will, was "delectation," the pleasurable contemplation of the act, which tended to break down rational resistance. One of the great moral issues of the thirteenth century had been whether "delectation" was itself culpable—whether its involuntary aspects were a part of sinning. Was it sinful to salivate upon seeing or smelling food? was it sinful to "feel the urge" on seeing physical beauty? or have involuntary sexual fantasies, as in dreams?

love restricts one's freedom, makes one vulnerable (line 771). Her thoughts vacillate. She thinks that "He which that nothing undertaketh / Nothing n'acheveth, be him loth or deere" (line 808)—the same idea Pandarus used in 2: 281–291 (later we hear Diomede repeat a similar proverb). Then we learn that "with another thought her herte quaketh," and so back and forth—

> Than sleepth hope, and after dread awaketh,
> Now hot, now cold, but thus, betwixen tweye,
> She rist her up, and went her for to pleye.

Having made no decision, she has left herself at the mercy of any chance influence. And now Criseyde joins her women in the garden to hear Antigone sing a "Trojan song." Since medieval tradition held that Troy fell because of sensuality, we are prepared for a Trojan song to favor sensual indulgence; this one, which is "a heaven to hear" (Chaucer adapted it from Machaut's *Paradis d'Amour*) tells of a woman who offers herself wholly to the God of Love because he gives her joy without fear. Those who say love is thralldom do not know the experience; she, knowing it, knows it will last forever, that "there is no peril inne."

Chaucer wanted to emphasize here the power of lyric to touch our feelings at the deepest level, and he did so with a bit of underplayed dialogue. Criseyde asks who wrote the song and if there can be such bliss among lovers, and Antigone—who could after all have said, if Chaucer wanted, that love songs are only constructed of codes and conventions—answers in the most forceful way that the song was made by the loveliest young noblewoman in Troy, who led her life in joy and honor, that there *is* such bliss among lovers, that *they know*; one must, she says in a potent anachronism, ask saints if heaven is fair and ask fiends if hell is foul. To these words Criseyde only says that night is coming on (line 899),

> But every word which that she of hir herde,
> She gan to printen in hir herte faste,
> And ay gan love hir lesse for t'agaste°	*frighten*
> Than it did erst, and sinken in hir herte,
> That she wex somewhat able to converte.

Her ladies escort her to bed, and in the nocturnal silence she lies thinking of all that has happened, until she sleeps and, sleeping, dreams.

In her dream we see that she has already made her choice. Early in Book 2, when Pandarus first rose to pursue his "great emprise," there was a reference to Procne's song: because Procne's husband Tereus raped her sister Philomel, Procne was turned into a sparrow and Philomel into a nightingale, singing forever their sad mythic songs of love, incest, and rape. As Criseyde falls asleep she hears the nightingale sing, and it cheers her. She dreams that a white eagle tears out her heart and puts his own in its place, yet the act does not frighten or hurt her. The eagle, a royal bird, stands for Troilus: her feelings toward him, which had so disturbed her when awake, bring neither fear nor pain. It is what Antigone's song had argued. Later, in bed with Troilus, she will declare (3: 1210) that she has already yielded to him, and we know then it was in her dream that the balance shifted from hesitation to surrender. The lines are sometimes called the most beautiful in Chaucer:

> A nightingale, upon a cedir greene,
> Under the chamber wall thereas she lay,
> Full loude song ayein the moone sheene,
> Peraunter°, in his bridde's wise, a lay   *as it happened*
> Of love that made hir herte fresh and gay.
> That herkned she so long in good intente,
> Till at the last the deade sleep hir hente°.   *seized*
> And as she sleep, anon-right tho hir mette°   *dreamed*
> How that an eagle, fethered white as bone,
> Under hir breast his longe clawes sette,
> And out hir herte he rente, and that anon,
> And did° his herte into hir breast to gone,   *made*
> Of which she nought agroos°, ne nothing smerte°;   *feared / hurt*
> And forth he fleigh° with herte left for herte.   *flew*

"The First Great Night of Love"

It is Criseyde's fortune, which at first seems like *good* fortune, that these chance circumstances dispose her to return Troilus' love. Her fears are legitimate ones and chance might equally have made her act on them. When on her first encounter with Troilus she is led into the room where he is feigning illness, Chaucer reminds us that she is "All innocent of Pandarus' intent" (2: 1723). She is astonished to find Troilus alone, and reticent to say the words Pandarus presses on her. Even when he bullies her, mimicking her "I! what?" and almost ordering her to say she has pity on Troilus, her answer is "I wold him pray / To telle me the fin of his intent" (3: 124). And speaking then to Troilus (line 170) she lays down strict conditions:

> A kinge's son although ye be, ywis,
> Ye shall namore han sovereignete
> Of me in love, than right in that case is.

In the next book she is hesitant to read Troilus's letter or answer it, and Chaucer takes pains to remind us that hers was no sudden love.

Chaucer evidently wanted to depict in her and Troilus an example of gentilesse in the abstract, without a tinge of Christian precept. Because they are guided only by a pagan philosophy, their freedom of will falls prey to their temperaments or the determining myths of their lives. Pandarus, their philosopher, manipulates them both, but since Troilus is already in love Pandarus needn't tamper with his intentions except about concealing his lady's name. Criseyde's intentions, however, are to "love him unwist, if she mighte, / And guerdon him with nothing but with sight"—to reward him only with the sight of her and let him worship from afar. Pandarus says to himself that she won't hold this opinion two years (2: 1296):

> . . . it shall not be so,
> If that I may; this nice° opinion   *silly*
> Shall not be holden fully yeares two

—his phrase "if that I may" might be translated "if *I* have anything to do with it."

Pandarus, who never lies to Troilus, lies to Criseyde with abandon. Readers can believe Criseyde is duplicitous if they want, but until she has left Troy there is never a line we can lay our finger on and say "That is a lie." Of Pandarus this is far from the case—we can *count* his lies.* And Troilus knows of these lies and does not object to them. He believes Pandarus's scheme is his only hope, so he hides in a small room and watches Pandarus and the ladies dine, lets Pandarus lead him into her room through a trapdoor, and stands silently by as Pandarus tells her his preposterous lie about a rumor Troilus has heard that she loves someone named Horaste. Indeed, in the first instance, when he pretends to be sick, he and Pandarus equivocate, probably in a joking way. "Thou seemest sick, sooth to say," says Pandarus (line 1516), and in a minute "For, parde, sick is he that is in sorrow." Troilus answers that he needn't feign sickness because he really *is* sick (i.e., with love), so much so that he is almost dying for the pain, to which Pandarus coolly observes that then he'll have less need to pretend!

*He tells Deiphebus that certain men are trying to get Criseyde's possessions (2: 1416–1421—the lie is acknowledged at line 1496); he tells Criseyde that Troilus is sick; he tells her in Deiphebus's house that Helen is waiting for her (line 1714) when of course it is Troilus who is waiting. At dinner in his own house he tells her that Troilus is not present (3: 570) though he is there concealed; swears to her repeatedly that all will be well (line 589; see also lines 652, 696, 710); says Troilus has just now come in the night through a secret passage (line 787) in a troubled state; and claims Troilus has heard she loves another (line 796–798).

After Troilus's entrance into Criseyde's bedroom, with all its excitement and wit, after he has fainted and been delivered into her bed for revival, after his guilt and her forgiveness have been reiterated, and after Pandarus has left them, she exacts from him certain unnamed vows, and we are told "for every wight, I guess, that loveth well, meaneth but gentilesse" (3: 1147–1148). Now she tells him to explain his jealousy over "Horaste" or else she'll accuse him of making it up to test her, and here we are told that he must obey her and, as the lesser of two evils, lie: "And for the lesse harm, he moste feyne" (line 1158). He makes up a story about how she failed to look at him at a feast, the narrator deprecating it as of no importance. To be sure, it's a "white lie," but it shows us that while Troilus must passively indulge Pandarus's outrageous lies to get in her bed, once in her bed he must tell lies on his own.

With Pandarus asleep ambiguously in or out of the room, with the narrator interrupting to envy and moon at their joy, we are drawn into their full intimacy. We hear their whispered trifles, Troilus's prayer to Cupid and Venus ("O Love, O Charity"); we sense the rhythms of their sensual joy. They exchange rings, they talk, they embrace, the night is passed "in joy and bisynesse / Of all that souneth into gentilesse" (line 1413). The mystique of courtly love is permitted to rise to its most ethereal heights. The irony, a mere reverberation here, is that its heights last but one night at a time. When dawn comes the lovers exchange conventional dawn songs lamenting the end of their night's joy. When Troilus parts—and this is meant to have a cautionary tone—we learn, at line 1546, that

> Desire all new him brende°, and lust to breede   *burned*
> Gan more than erst°, and yet took he none heede.   *formerly*

In an aftermath, most of it, too, of Chaucer's devising, Pandarus comes to Criseyde in the morning with sly hints about a sleepless night, and asks her how she is. "Never the bet for you, / Fox that ye been!"—none the better for *you*—is her reply, and she covers her face with the sheet, blushing. He puts his hand beneath the sheets, under her neck, and kisses her; and she forgives him. The scene reveals again the vicarious or sublimated eroticism beneath Pandarus's designs; to this our attention is drawn when we read, "Pandarus hath fully his intent."* Pandarus warns

*A fringe of interpreters finds here the innuendo that Pandarus seduces or rapes his niece; in fact he kisses her in a sufficiently avuncular way, but as elsewhere Chaucer reveals an erotic component. When he tells us that Pandarus has "fully his intent," it is to underscore the vicariousness of his desires and the nature of them. Procne and Philomel, singing of love, sing of rape and incest.

Troilus again, that same day, that good Fortune is as hard to keep as to get, that "worldly joy halt nought but by a wire." Troilus ignores the warning, observes the increase of his desire ("I had it never half so hot as now"), and reports a "new quality" in his feelings. The lovers meet again, "many a night" (line 1713),

> And thus Fortune a time led in joye
> Criseyde and eek this kinge's son of Troye.

Book 3 ends with Troilus raised to a new height of perfection by his love. But the narrator, addressing Venus, Cupid, and the Muses, who have thus far guided his poem, warns us they will now depart.

The Wheel Turns

The proem at the beginning of Book 4 is but four stanzas long, not in the high style like the others but in brief, unadorned sentences. It states almost with cruel bluntness that such joy as the lovers have experienced does not endure: Fortune turns her wheel, and laughs, and makes a *moue* at her victim, and from Troilus she has now turned, cast him out of his lady's grace, and set up Diomede on her wheel. The narrator's pen quakes for fear of what he must write: Criseyde forsook Troilus or "was at least unkind." Again he calls on the Furies, and on Mars (in whose hand lies Troy's fall),

> This ilke ferthe° book me helpeth fyne°,   *fourth / end*
> So that the loss of life and love yfere°   *together*
> Of Troilus be fully showed here.

The passage makes us dread to read the remaining two books, a single grim sequence with no proem for Book 5 save a lone stanza on fate. What C. S. Lewis said of it is true: "All men have waited with ever-decreasing hope, day after day, for some one or for something that does not come, and all would willingly forget the experience. Chaucer spares us no detail of the prolonged and sickening process to despair: every fluctuation of gnawing hope, every pitiful subterfuge of the flattering imagination, is held up to our eyes without mercy. The thing is so painful that perhaps no one without reluctance reads it twice."

The turn of Fortune's wheel begins with a Trojan setback in battle on the day the Trojan hero Antenor is captured. During a truce declared to exchange captives, Calkas begs the Greeks for his daughter. The Greeks propose to exchange her for their captive Antenor (who later betrays the city). The exchange is put before the Trojan parliament when Troilus is present, but he keeps silent—for he must not act without her consent. Hector speaks against the exchange, reminds them that she is no prisoner, that Trojans do not sell their women, but his words have no effect. "The noise of people" rises like ignited straw—"as breme as blase of straw y-set on fire" (4: 185): they want Antenor back and are prepared to surrender Criseyde. Chaucer here, very likely with the Peasants' Revolt in mind, adds two stanzas (lines 197–210) of his own devising on the people's ignorance.

Troilus, as before in Book 1, complains against Fortune, sees himself dying in misery. Pandarus—here most unappealingly pragmatic—tells him he has had his joy and should be content to find another woman, even offering to find one "fairer than swiche twelve." When Troilus rejects the offer, Pandarus suggests he take Criseyde away by force; Troilus ticks off five reasons why it would be dishonorable, adding that he would never carry her off unless she agreed—and chameleon Pandarus claims that was what he meant. Criseyde meanwhile plans to starve herself to death when she leaves Troy—characteristically picking the least decisive way, the one most easily reversed—and envisages herself and Troilus reunited in death. There follows an interview between her and Pandarus, most of it from Boccaccio. To it, however, Chaucer adds an offhand remark by Pandarus, that since "Women been wise in short avisement" she should either find a way to avoid going or else go and come back (line 933). This is the hint that gives Criseyde her plan. When she proposes it to Troilus (line 1261), she begins by echoing Pandarus, "I am a woman, as full well ye woot, / And as I am avised soddenly . . ."

Why does she ignore Pandarus's alternative, to *avoid going,* and respond instead to his less feasible suggestion of going and returning? Some think she is seeking a way to get out of Troy and has already decided not to return, but the thought is never attributed to her. And it is consistent with her chronic hesitancy that going away seems easier than staying. She tells Troilus that since old men are greedy, she will tell her father his Trojan friends want to send their possessions to him, huge quantities, which can be sent only through her. She spins out these fantastical notions at almost compulsive length—one senses desperation in her speech. Chaucer adds that it is written she said all this with a good intent, that on leaving she nearly died for woe, and that she was "in purpose ever to be trewe" (line 1420). It is worldly and rather cynical for her to conceive such a plan, as if in imitation of her uncle. Troilus must force his heart to trust her. Then, with hope awakened, they "began for joy th'amorouse daunce"—they make love. But afterward he begs her to keep her promise, almost as if by instinct he knows she will not (line 1440):

And seyde her, "Certes, if ye be unkinde,
And but° ye come, at day set, into Troye,   *unless*
Ne shall I never have hele, honour, ne joye."

Then he asks her not to go. Her father, he says, would see through her
tricks, and would for shame never return to Troy. He imagines that her
father will want to push her into a marriage with some Greek, that he'll
say the Trojans are doomed, that she'll believe him and see other knights
among the Greeks who will make her forget the Trojans. He suggests—
what he had opposed before for high-principled reasons—that they elope.
And now Criseyde opposes it for different high-principled reasons, again
with a tone of desperation. She begs him to be patient, swears she will
return. Agreeing reluctantly, he turns about and suggests once more they
steal away: at this last moment, the scruples of a royal family, which are
for him the dictates of reason itself, turn to dust—his heart tells him to
desert Troy with her, and he now wants to follow his heart.

To Criseyde this means he doesn't believe her. In their discussion
Troilus expressed doubt that Troy would win the war; his doubts may be
what plant in her mind the notion of staying among the Greeks. Twice
she swears by the moon—the inconstant moon, connected with the
worldly realm of change, and swears by Juno, who has opposed Troy. Yet
it is like her to swear in sincerity while picking the ambiguous and reversible oath—rather like her picking the slowest and most reversible way of
suicide. When Troilus agrees that she leave, she says she will live up to
his trust, that she first loved him not for rank or riches or worldly things
but for his "moral virtue, grounded upon trouthe" (line 1673), for his
gentle heart and manhood, and because *his reason controlled his desires*.
And so she swears again to keep her promise. Troilus, dressing, looks at
her and feels cold death upon him. He knows what will happen without
knowing he knows it. No one can imagine, the narrator says, and no
tongue can tell, his sorrow and pain. Then, in what we must reckon a
novelistic touch, he leaves the room without a word.

The Ending

In Book 2 we watched Criseyde's inner world of thoughts, watched an
idea take root, something we scarcely ever watch in real life. With Troilus
she indulged her wishes at the expense of her fears, and made her decision
in her dreams. With Diomede she will indulge her fears: one assumes that
she stumbles toward a determination in much the same way she had done
with Troilus—but she speaks of staying with Diomede in a somber,

resigned way, with regret, sorrow, and guilt (5: 1058–1085). She has chosen the practical solution, and the choice makes her a traitor.

Diomede is pragmatic and opportunistic like Pandarus, but less appealingly so because he has no humor: he has a soldier's gambling spirit, not a philosophy. We hear him say to himself, "For he that nought n'assayeth, nought n'acheveth" (line 784). Criseyde's similar notion, learned from her uncle, was about *undertaking* something; his is about *assaying*: in the same utterance he says, "For to assay, it nought ne greeveth"—it does no harm to take a chance. It is a callous pragmatism without the ideals and principles of Pandarus's view, though to Criseyde it may sound the same. Anyway, it is this view that keeps her from returning; she has learned how to "cope," and she has learned it from the men.

What she has not learned is Pandarus's regard for honor and dignity, for "meaning well." This humane side of his thinking is a set of precepts very like the medieval code of honor: he appears to think that no action should violate dignity and that excessive actions (like Troilus's despair in Book 1 or Criseyde's undue fear) do so. Criseyde ignores this side of his thought; pragmatism and compromise suit her timidity, but not the "olde wise." She *makes* herself ignore this humane side, makes herself break faith by behaving maliciously in what can be called a kind of masochism. She gives to Diomede the brooch Troilus gave her on parting ("And that was littel need," says the narrator). She writes a letter as harsh and callous as one can imagine, accusing Troilus of being selfish, claiming she has heard gossip that he is only leading her on; she promises to return though she cannot say "what yeer or what day." She ends by saying that they can be friends anyway and regretting that her letter isn't longer! Is it any wonder Chaucer ended up apologizing to the ladies in his audience for giving women a bad name? What we see in her is *dehumanization*. She has descended into that "bestialitee" that Pandarus despised.

This dehumanization is what Troilus sees in his dream: a boar with great tusks sleeping in the sun—in its arms, "kissing ay, his lady bright, Criseyde" (line 1241)—and wakes crying out to Pandarus "I n'am but dead!" Pandarus, with his customary skepticism toward the supernatural, asks why the boar in the dream might not be her dying father. Troilus's sister Cassandra* interprets the dream to him, explaining that he must first "a few of olde stories heare, / To purpose, how that Fortune overthrowe / Hath lordes old" (line 1459–1461); the dream means that "Di-

---

*Cassandra's fate, in mythology, was always to speak what was true but never to be believed. Chaucer makes an interesting interpretation of the myth by showing how, in her certainty about her prediction, she shows no tact and employs no rhetoric, thus rousing Troilus's hostility.

omede is in, and thou art out." It is not what he wanted to hear, and he denounces her as a sorceress.

In the remainder of the poem we watch his ominous dream come true and see him accept that truth in anguish. Pandarus tries to distract him; on the tenth day, waiting on the wall, Troilus sees Criseyde coming, and Pandarus must tell him it is only a cart that he sees. He then divines the reasons why she is late. Fortune turns her wheel, Hector dies in battle, Criseyde's dreadful letter comes. Troilus finds in it the beginnings of change but chooses not to believe what he finds. Then he sees on Diomede's captured outer garment, inside the collar, the brooch he gave Criseyde on the day they parted. In a soliloquy he sees that she has cast him out of her mind, and laments that he can never "unlove" her. He becomes possessed, the courtly *virtù* that love engendered in him becomes poisoned, he seeks vengeance on Diomede and seeks his own death in arms. His last words, about what she has done, are "I have it nat deserved."

Pandarus, in sorrow for his friend and shame for his niece, is "still as stone; a word ne coude he saye." For him, the voluble master of speech, this is the ultimate defeat. About his niece's treason he can only say he would change it if he could. He hates Criseyde, he cries, and always will; he wishes she were dead. He says that he did all Troilus asked without regard for his own honor—but in fact Pandarus was the first to ask anything, and once into his plan he *did* have a care for his own honor. His way with words has lost its moorings in reality, and we hear him talking nonsense. Perhaps it is one of his effective defenses that he can lie to himself in such a circumstance. His last words are, "I can no more saye."

Boccaccio's ending disappointed Chaucer in the extreme: he had Troiolo die, then complained of women's fickleness. Chaucer, rejecting this, follows Troilus into death. It is the great moment when Chaucer emulates Dante, in passages taken from the *Commedia,* including its final lines. Yet he took the actual scene from the description of Arcite's death in Boccaccio's *Teseida,* and he had in mind Cicero's *Dream of Scipio* as well. Dante would have placed Troilus in a particular niche of the *Inferno* chosen from the viewpoint of Christian justice; Chaucer, following Boccaccio, gives him a *pagan* death. Troilus's disembodied "ghost" passes blissfully into the heavens, beyond the four elements to the outer edge of the eighth sphere in the Ptolemaic universe, just beneath the *primum mobile;* from here he can see the seven planets and hear the harmony of the spheres, and look down on "This littel spot of earth." Then he is taken away by Mercury, leader of souls into the afterlife, and he goes—Chaucer tells us no more—wherever Mercury "sorted him to dwell."

What Troilus sees in this last vista is the temporal world that he has left behind, the sublunary world subject to time, made of the four elements. He is not in heaven; he has passed into a higher and toward an ultimate reality. This is medieval science rather than religion, though the two were never quite separate. When Troilus sees the little spot of earth "that with the sea / Embraced is," he is looking at the "island of the earth" (*orbis terrarum*), the land mass of three continents that was believed to sit upon the terrestrial globe surrounded by a vast ocean. Troilus, thus "distanced" in this science-fiction way, as it must seem to us, sees as a "little spot" the great island that was to its inhabitants as yet a barely charted wilderness. He sees what "Geffrey" would have seen in *The House of Fame* if the Dantean eagle had flown higher—and Geffrey had kept his eyes open.

As Troilus sees how small and insignificant the *earth* is, he comes to "despise this wretched world." The *world* was the realm of human activity that stood between man and nature—it was the condition fallen man was born to, and was what Christians renounced at baptism. "Despise the world" Englished the term *contemptus mundi*; Chaucer had in mind the many writings that urged disdain of the physical and temporal because they are, as he says (line 1837), all vanity compared to the pure felicity of heaven. This does not mean Troilus is in heaven or is going to heaven; it means that he can see the world from the perspective of the universe, from *afar*. His felicity is that of being above human vanity.

And here, with a kind of telescopic vision we can believe souls have, Troilus looks down upon the place where he was slain, sees his mourners weeping woefully for his death, and *laughs*. We are told he rejected all that follows blind pleasure, and Chaucer adds "And sholden all oure heart on heaven caste," the grammatical ellipsis making it unclear whether this is Troilus's thought or the narrator's. It is a pagan release from the misery of the human condition: the conception, which Chaucer had from Lucan and Dante, is not that the soul lives after death (though that is implied) but that *the dead can laugh*.

Just before the stanza on Troilus's death, Chaucer placed one major digression (lines 1765–1799) whose effect is to disperse reality, to introduce an element of disorder and burgeoning chaos. He tells us in an almost businesslike way that he set out to write of Troilus's love, that he has not written enough about his battles and feats of arms, which, however, the reader can read elsewhere. Then he asks the ladies in the audience not to blame him because Criseyde was untrue, for the story is in other books as well and was not his invention. He says he will the more gladly write, if they wish, about Penelope's faithfulness and about Alceste, a reference to, or an announcement of, his next poem, *The Legend of Good Women*.

And now, still addressing the ladies, he says he is not just talking about men betrayed by women, but *most* about women betrayed by men— "God give hem sorrow, amen!" And he tells them to beware of men and listen to *him*! The joke, assuming it is a joke, may be his way of telling the ladies in his audience that they can think Criseyde was the one betrayed if they want to think it.

At the end Chaucer addresses the poem he has written: "Go, littel book, go, littel myn tragedye . . ." (line 1786). He asks that God "send yet to your maker, before he die, the ability to compose in the manner of some kind of comedy." This is a reference to *The Canterbury Tales* at a time when it was barely an idea. We know this by process of elimination —his only other major work was to be the *Legend of Good Women*, which he has already mentioned and which he would not have called a "comedy" but (as he did) a "legend." Some interpreters think he is referring to the remaining stanzas of *Troilus and Criseyde*, that the poem, so far the tragedy of a hero who dies unhappily, will become a "comedy" in Dante's sense—will show the hero in the universal order of things and thus end happily. But this is not what it shows. Chaucer shows us Troilus beyond the eighth sphere laughing, he shows Mercury taking him away, but of his place in the order of things he shows nothing. The end of the *poem* looks to the Christian world order, but Troilus's end is only a dark voyage.

The Achievement of the *Troilus*

Troilus and Criseyde is Chaucer's masterpiece. To us *The Canterbury Tales* is greater because it is more diverse, more ambitious, more original, but to Chaucer it seemed the lesser achievement because it was miscellaneous, experimental, and unfinished. Chaucer had much greater ambitions for the *Troilus*. In the last lines, which used to be called the "epilog," he addressed his completed book, asked that it not "envy" other writings but take a place of subjection to "alle poesy." He would have it kiss the steps where the greatest poets of antiquity walk—Virgil, Ovid, Homer, Lucan, and Statius.* And having said that, which is saying quite a lot, he expressed a simple, though not humble, hope. In his time the accurate copying of secular texts had no priority at all. For Chaucer, the anxiety of his age about the diversity of English dialects and spelling,

*By "steps" he means footsteps: the image is of a path, not a stairway to the stars. It is not a hierarchy he is speaking of, but a literary tradition: the present in this instance joins the past. "Poesy" is intended as an honorific term; this is the only place Chaucer uses the word—but he uses "poetry" six times in his works, always too in an honorific sense.

which could (and did) cause his words and sentences to be distorted and his sense obscured, prompts him here to pray that no one miscopy what he has written or get the meter wrong. His last and most fervent prayer, which may be reckoned the *magna carta* of Chaucer criticism, was that his poem be understood.

After Troilus is dead, Chaucer exclaims, as Boccaccio did, that such was the end of Troilus's love, his worthiness, his royal status, and so on; but where Boccaccio ended the sentence with "Troiolo's false hope in villainous Criseida" Chaucer ends it with the "false world's brittleness" (line 1827)—its *fragility*. Then he asks "yonge, fresshe folkes" to turn to God, to remember that "all n'is but a faire / This world, that passeth soon as floweres faire" (lines 1840–1841). And he asks them and us to reject "the cursed old rites" of pagans, the wretched appetites of this world, the worship of Jove, Apollo, Mars, or such "rascaille"(the word, ancestor of "rascal," might be translated "trash") and to reject the "form of old clerks' speech in poetry," if we study their books. His moralizing overextends itself into a condemnation of antiquity, which was after all so interesting to Chaucer and his audience; not ten stanzas ago, he had sent his poem to follow in the steps of ancient poets. With irony he takes the moral to the point where we are uncertain of its seriousness.

The last twelve stanzas have perplexed interpreters; the discussion was begun by a critic writing in the 1920s who said that the "epilog" (the last lines, from "Go, littel book" to the end) is "dramatically a sorry performance" because it "suddenly denies and contradicts everything that has gone before." Such a view of the "epilog" as a detachable faux pas inspired so many rebuttals that now the dominant interpretation is the opposite: the poem's Christian and "Boethian" ideas prepare for a valid ending, not an epilogue, making the poem an integral whole and the last stanzas its inevitable and sublime conclusion.

But some critics have come to question this unity and finality. The ending *says* all the right things but ironically undercuts them. First the narrator is sending us to read other books, then he is announcing his next poem, then addressing his book, then his copyists. And when he has finally described Troilus's death, he begins to draw a moral and goes further than he meant. At last, after asking his friends Gower and Strode for their criticism and corrections, he loses himself in contemplating the mystery of the Holy Trinity. The narrator falls into a kind of panic or confusion at the end, casting about in perplexity for the right last word, rather like Pandarus talking hokum in his last speech. Everything is canceled out: Troilus is dead, Criseyde gone, Pandarus silenced, Troy doomed. And now the narrator disappears, for we find suddenly in his place the historical Chaucer, announcing his next work and addressing by name living contemporaries who were his personal friends. The role playing is over and the poet, his poem about to fall in disorganized tatters, retreats into the privacy of prayer.

The ending is like a literary and linguistic apocalypse inside the poem, prefiguring the Last Judgment, from which certain values of the transitory world are saved. The moral is stated and at once unstated. Such is the end of worldly vanity, we are told; we should turn our faces to God, we should think the world is like a fair, and passes like a flower. But indeed we know that while a fair is soon over and while flowers die, the joy and beauty of them were real. Earthly loves, though they are to be rejected, had beauty while they lasted. Pagan antiquity is to be rejected, but the monuments by which we know it deserve still to be admired and studied.

The "dedication" to Gower and Strode is similarly equivocal. Gower and Chaucer had by this time parted company artistically: Gower was still writing medieval complaint with its explicit moralizing, and he disapproved of Chaucer's satire, with its ironic stance. Strode was an opponent of Wyclif's necessitarian beliefs and would, as J. S. P. Tatlock put it, have been "an uncompromising critic" of Chaucer's determinism: he had shown in *Troilus and Criseyde* how much we are in bondage to chance and temperament, how hard we must struggle to make conscious reason bridle impulse, desire, or habit. Asking for correction was conventional; if Gower or Strode had had a real chance to "correct" Chaucer's poem, they would, like reviewers of all ages, have wanted it to be a different book from what it is. Chaucer, having asked them for correction, retreats into the mystery of things where they cannot pursue him with their lists of errors.

We read Chaucer's masterpiece as a triumph over the medieval, a breakthrough into the literature of objective representation and ironic distancing, into the modern. But Chaucer made this breakthrough by using the literary tradition he knew; tradition was his fulcrum. Boccaccio, whose scholarly writings were to be for centuries the great repository of learning about classical antiquity, wrote in the *Filostrato* a work of great originality, and Chaucer, with the instincts of a genius, saw what it was. This does not mean that modernity was the perennial goal of literary history, that what was medieval was gross and to be fled. In recent years even scholars with the strongest vested interest in medieval *arcana* have granted Chaucer's modernity. Professor Wimsatt, the ranking authority on the French courtly background of Chaucer's poems, has analyzed Chaucer's *Troilus* in the light of epic tradition and Dante, of French romance, especially that of Machaut, and of Boethian philosophy; and he finds, by his own summary, this:

[Chaucer] suggests alternately and sometimes simultaneously that the narrative of *Troilus* presents heroic love or ideal lovers, or that it amounts to an indictment or defense of Providence. He does not sustain these suggestions, however, thoroughly undermining them with irony. What he does sustain, after negating all such pretensions, is realism, which he builds up with circumstantial detail, unidealized incident, psychological interaction, and a love story that unfolds according to a common and natural pattern. This realism makes *Troilus* a new kind of literature; the claim of the older critics that it is the first modern novel makes a certain amount of sense.

Chaucer achieved this because he became so deeply immersed in his story. He *lived* it in the six years or so he was writing it, and he imagined striking small details because they were part of that vicarious experience —details that astonish us for their truth to human nature or individual character. This realistic element of the *Troilus* is something *we* respond to as natives to the tradition of the novel. For instance, there is no reason why a hero should not faint, but it was hardly conventional. Boccaccio had Troiolo faint when, in the parliament, he hears the proposal for Criseyde's exchange. Chaucer has him faint not in public but in private—at the moment when he is most (and most unbearably) in private, alone with his lady in her bedroom under a set of false pretenses. It seems amusing that he faints at this particular moment, and we are permitted to be amused during that scene, though our laughter is diverted to Pandarus. But Chaucer also makes us take Troilus's fainting seriously by describing in precise medical terms what happens in his body, in his "vital spirits" and the flow of blood from his heart, that makes him lose consciousness.

Or again: in Boccaccio, Criseyde weeps when she hears that Troiolo is the one who loves her. It is not unimaginable or unmotivated, but Chaucer wanted her feelings—fear and suppressed desire and frustration —to come out not over the fact of the prince's loving her but over the question of whether the love can come to fruition: Pandarus reminds her that beauty is always fading and no one will want her when she is old, and it is the implicit "now or never" that brings the tears. She would rather evade and delay.

Or again: Pandarus, instructing Troilus how to write his love letter, adds cynically that he ought to blot it with his tears a little. He is thinking of tears artfully placed, possibly squeezed from a towel. But Chaucer shows us (in 2: 1086) that as Troilus writes he sheds real tears; and when it is time to seal the letter and he must wet his seal ring so it will not stick in the wax, he *wets it with the tears on his face.* They are real, and they show in the letter not as sprinkled blots but as feelings.

All this we call novelistic and modern. And there is every reason to admire it. Yet the truth is, *Troilus and Criseyde* remains a very medieval poem; it has medieval features as archaic as gargoyles or plainchant. Much of this "gothic" element of the poem has been discovered recently. Such features tend to make a medieval poem seem strange and inaccessible— a notion many critics want to promote. There are for example symbols based on details in Scripture that had symbolical meaning; horses symbol- ized lechery, so Chaucer's reference to "horse's law" in Book 1, used to suggest the hierarchy of creatures, is thought by some to warn against lechery. And there are, supposedly, puns. The word *quaint* or *queint* in Middle English meant "strange," "curious," or "precious," as it still does; it was also the past participle of the verb to *quench*. In addition, it is thought (wrongly) the equivalent and ancestor of the taboo word *cunt*; but it can be used as a euphemism for the female part in the sense of something curious or precious. Chaucer, not once but several times, seems to pun on this word. Troilus, looking at Criseyde's empty house in Book 5, says, "O thou lantern, of which queint is the light" (line 543), and some think that Chaucer, speaking of the lady's empty house as a lantern quenched or put out, meant to imply a sexual meaning. All this is contro- versial and dubious. But if it is there at all, we would be obliged to remember that puns had a different status in the Middle Ages—they were not jokes or displays of cleverness. Strange, dark truths were concealed in puns and etymologies—they had the power to startle and provoke, some- what as "Freudian slips" do for us.

Or again: there was a tradition in medieval literature of disposing the parts of a poem so that the number of lines in a structural unit, or between one point and another, could have a meaning in arithmetic symbolism and be in meaningful ratios with other units. Some still think this study of "tectonics" is a modern fantasy, like Shakespearean cyphers, and indeed it is strange that there are no treatises or manuals about it; but the most spectacular demonstrations work out with such precision that they seem impossible to deny. Such number symbolism has been found in works as far apart as the *Chanson de Roland* and the poems of Edmund Spenser; in Chaucer's time in *Sir Gawain and the Green Knight* and in the *Troilus*. This, if correct, makes the poem a curiously Gothic artifact, brings it into a realm of Pythagorean mysticism, presents us with a world whose minute mathematical rightness, known fully to God, can be worked out by a poet in part through the arts of arithmetic and geometry and incorporated in his poem as part of its shape and meaning.

Or again: Troilus's story consists in his coming to know a truth too harsh almost to be known. Chaucer uses (as we still may) the metaphor "to see" meaning to know or understand: Troilus sees the tragic ending take shape, then in death sees the comic truth about the world. Chaucer extrapolates the image of Troilus's eyes and makes the image hover over the end of the poem like a dreadful, sepulchral emblem. His eyes, which first met Criseyde's when he fell in love, and through which Cupid's arrow passed, are now, when deprived of the sight of her, like empty holes through which he weeps but does not see. He laments that he will end his life like Oedipus in darkness (4: 300), and continues:

O woeful eye two, sin° your disport   *since*
Was all to seen Criseyde's eyen brighte,
What shall ye doon but, for my discomfort,
Standen for nought, and weepen out your sighte.

In this passage Chaucer alludes to a medieval image mentioned in Dante, *Purgatorio* 23: 31–33, of a man's two eyes as zeroes ("nought"), the nose and eyebrows like an M between them, spelling *omo* (Latin *homo*, Italian *uomo*, "man"). Written out in an emblem with a medieval Gothic letter embracing the O's, it makes a ghostly figure of a face with empty eyes, an image of man powerless before destiny:

Such an image dominates the ending of the *Troilus*. Pandarus remarks that "in thine head thine eyen seemen dead" (4: 1092). Troilus sees phantoms and illusions, like the cart he believes is Criseyde; in his dream he sees the truth, too awful to believe. To Criseyde he writes (line 1373),

Mine eyen two, in vain with which I see,
Of sorrowful teeres salt aren woxen° welles.   *have become*

Yet this medieval aspect of Chaucer's imagery, arcane and odd as it may seem on first glance, is possibly easier for us to respond to than it was for readers of earlier times. If we look for a feature in modern art forms that will help us respond to such emblems, our minds leap to the cinema: it has become a convention of the cinema for seemingly irrelevant "background" images to carry with them a mounting suggestiveness that makes them emblematic. We may be able to intuit (better than any readers since the time of Milton) what Chaucer was *really* doing with such literary devices.

Chaucer, having completed his poem and set it in the footsteps of "all poesy," saw it not as medieval or Gothic or even "new," but as part and member of a tradition going back into antiquity. Perhaps it was the fundamental myth of Chaucer's life to escape oblivion in the company of those *poetae* whose works outlasted their lives and their civilizations. And if this is so, he realized that hope in the *Troilus* while still in his early forties.

13

The Worst
of Times—
the 1380s

Chaucer described in the *Troilus* an unusual astronomical event, Saturn and Jupiter joined in Cancer, which actually occurred on May 13, 1385; he made it the cause of the frightening storm that kept Criseyde from leaving Pandarus's house on the night of the consummation. So it is generally assumed that the poem was finished after that date, but before the end of 1386, when things were getting so bad at court and in the Parliament. If the poem was read aloud after its completion, when and where could the reading have taken place? From June 1385 the king was in Scotland; Joan of Kent died in August at Wallingford, where the king had sent her in his absence, attended by some of Chaucer's friends. After her death there would have been a period of mourning during which such a court entertainment was inappropriate—and she wasn't buried until the king returned in January 1386. The following July, John of Gaunt left for Castile taking the Duchess Costanza, his two daughters, and most men of fighting age. Hence the *Troilus* could have been presented in the summer of 1385 before Joan of Kent; before the king and the Lancastrian party in May 1385 or in the spring of 1386 before Gaunt sailed for Castile;

and after that, before the king and what was left of his court. It could have been presented anytime to an audience chiefly of ladies.

All this tells us only that probability favors the story suggested at the end of *Troilus* and repeated in the Prologue to the *Legend of Good Women,* that the audience included or largely consisted of the ladies of the court, who thought Chaucer gave women a bad name by telling Criseyde's story, and that the queen assigned him the penance of writing about *good* women. The protest was no doubt an ironical courtly game that must have pleased Chaucer. The queen may have administered a mock scolding at the behest of the other ladies, but Chaucer may have made up the "penance" himself as part of the poem's fiction—or, as seems more likely, made it up and put it in the ladies' heads, or in the queen's.

The *Boece,* the Boethian Poems, and *Melibee*

During these years the *Troilus* was Chaucer's central undertaking, but he worked too on several related projects—the translation of Boethius and some shorter poems on Boethian themes. It is commonly supposed that his purpose in translating Boethius's *Consolation* was to make it accessible as a source of philosophical ideas used in the *Troilus.* But he didn't need to make a translation for this reason—he read Latin easily and had used many Latin works in the original; he made it because he felt there was a need for one or because someone asked him to do it. The best guess, Professor John Fisher's, is that he was asked to prepare it as part of the education of young King Richard. Of Richard's two tutors we hear little of Guichard D'Angle, but Sir Simon Burley comes through as a warm, spirited man, and he and Chaucer knew each other. Many of Chaucer's casual writings of this period could have been written for the king at Burley's urging.

In hard times, the *Consolation* was a solace, reason enough for Chaucer's translation, but it is also a very political work. Boethius was a Roman senator and later sole consul, whose two sons were also consuls; in A.D. 522 the Emperor Theodoric accused him (with others) of plotting against the imperial power, and he was sent into exile, where he wrote his famous book. One of its themes is how a ruler can govern when he cannot control human nature or events. It is a book about the order of things, about power, about the place of randomness in the governance of a society. King Alfred translated it into Old English for his own use, and Queen Elizabeth I translated it for hers. It was essential reading for a monarch.

Chaucer went about the task in a serious way. He used a commentary by Nicholas Trivet and a French translation by Jean de Meun, and probably other ancillary texts; he included glosses on difficult passages or puzzling usages, which suggests that the king was to study it in his early adult years, between fourteen and twenty—i.e., between 1381 and 1387.

Compared with Chaucer's other prose writings the *Boece* is somewhat graceless. There was no literary prose in Chaucer's century. There was a tradition of artful prose for sermons, epistles, and certain kinds of moral treatises (from which he profited in the Parson's Tale); otherwise prose was practical and instructional—it had no more artistic status than it has to us in a technical manual or a cookbook. And some of Chaucer's prose *was* technical: in later years he wrote what has been called the first treatise in English about a scientific instrument, the *Treatise on the Astrolabe*, to teach a child how to use the instrument. Chaucer may have written another such treatise, *The Equatorie of the Planets*, though many experts doubt that it was his.

Possibly he would have viewed Boethius's *Consolation* as a technical book of philosophical inquiry. Possibly. But the form of Boethius's book cannot have escaped him. That form, the *prosimetrum*, alternated passages of philosophical dialogue with poems, called "meters," in different stanzaic patterns, each fitting perfectly the drift of the thought and the mood; the meters create moments for reflection, for letting the argument sink in at the level of feeling. Boethius calls attention to them and has Lady Philosophy explain why she uses them. Chaucer, himself a poet, failed to translate them into verse, but he must have entertained the idea: his poem "The Former Age" is translated from Boethius, Book 2, meter 5. It begins as a free translation, then becomes an extended meditation, a poem in its own right with bits and snatches from Ovid, the *Roman*, possibly Virgil and Tibullus. There are only two surviving manuscripts of "The Former Age," and one of these appears in an early fifteenth- or late fourteenth-century copy of Chaucer's *Boece* along with the Latin and with many notes and glosses; Skeat thought it was copied direct from Chaucer's original. "The Former Age" is placed just after the meter from which it is translated (with another poem, "Fortune"). It's in eight-line stanzas, but some lines are imperfect and one missing, and it must be that what we have here is a copy of a "Boethian" poem Chaucer drafted and revised with the notion of translating Boethius's meters, at least this one, in verse, but never finished.

The "former age" or "golden age" of classical thought was, for the Middle Ages, the period in history after the Fall of Man. People in it led a simple, primitive kind of existence; the implication was that all of subsequent history went in two directions—men had to use the arts of civilization to improve on fallen nature, but in doing so they became more corrupt and greedy. The medievals believed that the world was in decline. The earliest peoples ate simple food and drank clear well water and were satisfied, nor were their lives hampered with the complications introduced later—plowing the land, using fire or tools or weapons. On the other hand their simple life *needed* the arts of civilization to lighten its hardship. Chaucer made a poem of this by changing Boethius's classical images (like Tyrian dye) to images his audience knew (like grinding spices in a mortar) and by adding more examples of primitive simplicity ruined by later invention. Early man had not begun to mine metals or seek gems in rivers, and therefore knew no greed. There were no weapons or armor, no palaces, no sheets or comforters, yet they slept in safety; there was no pride, envy, avarice, no lords or taxes or tyrants. All of this leads up to a powerful last stanza on the wickedness of the present age:

> Alas, alas! Now may men weep and crye!
> For in our dayes n'is but covetyse,
> Doubleness, and treason, and envye,
> Poison, manslaughter, and murder in sundry wise.

This pessimistic ending suggests that "The Former Age" was written in response to the bad times of the later 1380s when there *was* duplicity and treason and when some of Chaucer's friends were unjustly put to death. The images are commonplaces of medieval verse, and the times furnished occasion enough for using such commonplaces. Unfinished as it may be, "The Former Age" has the power to move us still, to inspire pessimism about the world and waken the desire to reform it.

The poem "Fortune," preserved in the same manuscript and written out without a break as if it were part of "The Former Age," is a dialogue between a "plaintiff" and Fortune. The influences on it other than Boethius are entirely French. Manuscript associations suggest it was started in the early 1380s, but its envoi refers to a statute of 1390. It sounds as if Chaucer resurrected it about 1390 and by adding the envoi turned it into a "begging poem" asking the king for "some better estate." That it was addressed to the king would explain why it is so deliberately courtly and why it has been preserved in nine more copies than its companion "The Former Age," which is a much better poem.

From this period come two "moral ballades" also containing Boethian ideas. The first, "Gentilesse," declares that "the first stock" was the "father of gentilesse." This "first stock" is contrasted (not identified) with "the first fader in majestee," i.e., God or Christ. The sense is, "Whoever wants to be 'gentil' must love virtue and flee vice, because our personal worth pertains to moral virtue, not to inherited rank; and this is so whether one wear the bishop's miter, the nobleman's crown, or the king's or emperor's diadem." The poem is not arguing (as modern readers tend to assume) that any ordinary person is potentially noble if his character is good, but that everyone, in the rank to which God assigned him, must be worthy of his place. The virtues of the "first stock," from whom subsequent nobles descended, were those of the Golden Age when people were uncorrupted. An evil man can inherit wealth, but no one can inherit inner virtue, for virtue belongs ultimately to the "first father in majesty," God, whose heirs are those that please Him, whether they wear the miter, crown, or diadem. It is like a sophisticated way of saying, "Whan Adam delved and Eve span, / Who was then the gentleman?"—an appropriate lesson for a king.

The second moral ballade, known as "Truth," survives in twenty-four manuscript copies and six early printings, a surprisingly large number. The refrain line, "truth thee shall deliver," is from John 8: 32, "the truth shall make you free." But "truth" meant being true to one's word and obligations; in a universe hierarchically conceived, as the Middle Ages conceived it, keeping one's bond and obligation to those beneath and above one, all the way down to one's serfs and up to God, was the essence of social stability. At base the poem teaches "contempt of the world": there is a moral danger in worldly things, so we should desire only what we need, and we should learn to rule ourselves. "Truth" ends with the familiar medieval commonplace that the world is a wilderness and life a pilgrimage:

> The wrastling° for this world asketh a fall.   *striving*
> Here n'is no home, here n'is but wildernesse:
> Forth, pilgrim, forth! Forth, beast, out of thy stalle!
> Hold the high way, and let thy ghost thee lede°;   *lead*
> And trouth thee shall deliver, it is no drede.

In the comparison of man going forth as a pilgrim like a beast from a stall, Chaucer had in mind the "chain of being": it is for man to follow salvation as for the lower beasts to follow man, and this image of life as a pilgrimage to eternity was to be the guiding image of *The Canterbury Tales*.

In one manuscript only, "Truth" has an envoi, addressed as it would appear to Chaucer's friend Sir Philip de la Vache, who fell on bad times between 1386 and 1389 when he was out of favor. It looks as though Chaucer added a humorous envoi and sent him a copy of the poem, picking it for its phrase "beast, out of thy stall" because Vache meant cow! It tells his friend only as much as Chaucer, also out of favor, could have said to himself—don't be enslaved by the world, but rely on God, and "truth" will deliver you.

Another of Chaucer's prose works written during these years, the *Melibee*, turns up in *The Canterbury Tales* as one of the two stories Chaucer himself bumblingly tells. It is a quite faithful translation of a French work, *Le Livre de Melibée et de Dame Prudence*, which is in turn a condensation and adaptation of a work in Latin, the *Liber Consolationis et Consilii* by Albertanus of Brescia (died 1270). There is a single piece of evidence about its date: it omits, after line 1199, a passage that speaks against having a boy for a king. Chaucer obviously omitted it so as not to give offense, which dates it after 1376 when it was clear Richard would have the succession, and enough after that for Richard to be old enough to read a work of its difficulty.

The *Melibee*, like Boethius's *Consolation*, is a useful book for a ruler. It deals with some of the imponderables that those of the ruling class must face: how to choose advisers, whose advice to take or ignore, when to declare war. The work is framed as an allegory with personified figures, after the medieval fashion, but all its practical advice somewhat shoves the allegory out of the way. The advice is good, some of it useful even today. Dame Prudence, an allegorical figure comparable to Boethius's Lady Philosophy, recommends that one ignore the advice of flatterers (whose advice is self-serving), of fools, of former enemies reconciled, of one's own servants, and of drunks, the wicked, and the young. When trying to decide whether or not to declare war, you must decide whether to seek revenge, gamble on Fortune, or bear adversity with patience. Revenge should be according to the right, that is, to the law; you should never confuse it with defense. There is a long digression about riches, arguing that they are good if used well, and adding that you should never enter into war trusting in your own riches.

The remainder of the work is about making a just peace. It is not, as is sometimes thought, a pacifist argument, for the possibility of a just war is granted. Its great lessons are those of Christian charity and forgiveness: the means to a just peace is arbitration practiced with prudence and common sense. The work has occasionally been interpreted as a satire on such treatises, but the opinion does not hold up against careful reading or the background of the times. It was not intended for John of Gaunt, as has been argued, but all the political figures of the age could have profited from it, and especially the king.

Chaucer as J.P. and M.P.

On October 12, 1385, a month or so after the Princess Joan died, while the king was still in Scotland, Chaucer was appointed one of the ten justices of the peace for the county of Kent, replacing a member who had died the month before. Such commissions were charged with enforcing the statutes for keeping the peace, taking surety for good behavior from those who threatened bodily harm or arson, and hearing by sworn inquest all manner of felonies, trespasses, ambushes, and the like. They passed sentence only on lesser offenses. The commissions sat four times a year, for three days if necessary, and each justice was paid 4s. a day for up to twelve days. Sessions were held in various towns, with two or three justices and a clerk attending. The justices, acting on their own outside of the sessions, had such duties as taking mainprise or surety (in which citizens would undertake, under penalty of a certain sum of money, to guarantee the good behavior of a suspect), dealing with breaches of the peace, or arranging local elections. Chaucer was on the commission for almost four years.

The post was prestigious. The peace commission for Kent was traditionally headed by the constable of Dover Castle, who at this time was Sir Simon Burley. The commissioners were chosen in more or less equal proportions from the magnates, the lawyers, and the gentry. The four magnates were lords of importance, and the six lawyers were all sergeants-at-law, the highest legal rank. Those of the gentry, like Chaucer, were landowners and knights who had served at one time or another on commissions or as justices of the peace or members of Parliament. Except for the lawyers, most were residents of Kent, though residency was not a requirement.

Within a year, Chaucer moved to Kent. On October 5, 1386, a lease was issued to Richard Forster, citizen of London, for the dwelling over Aldgate. In November Chaucer signed as mainpernor for his brother-in-law Simon Manning, of East Greenwich, guaranteeing that Simon would appear in court the following January 27 to answer a charge of debt. Twenty years before, Chaucer's sister Katherine had evidently inherited property in Greenwich from their father, which she and her husband sold, and Chaucer may have inherited property there as well. The three manuscripts of his poem to Scogan, written about 1392–1393, have "Greenwich" written in the margin beside a reference to where he lives, and his name appears in some Greenwich records. And, too, in *The Canterbury Tales*, when the pilgrims pass Greenwich, Chaucer has the Host say "Lo, Greenwich, ther many a shrew is inne" (where there's many a scoundrel), which must be a joke on himself.

In August, Chaucer had been elected to the "Wonderful Parliament," as future ages wrongly called it, one of two members from Kent. A petition put before this Parliament, which met on October 1, had to do with the controllers in the ports of the realm: it asked that the lifetime appointments of some controllers be canceled because of their extortions. The king, who had made seven lifetime appointments, replied that his council would look into the behavior of controllers and remove any wrong-doers; about life appointments he would seek the advice of his council. Nothing seems to have come of it, but in 1388 a similar petition was introduced and the king agreed to cancel life appointments. Chaucer did not have a life appointment, but one notion is that he saw the handwriting on the wall and got out of the Customs before an investigation started. The chief enemy of the king and the leader of the rebellion was the duke of Gloucester, Thomas of Woodstock, the youngest of the king's uncles. Gloucester held an assignment of £500 on the Customs (that is, he had been granted the sum, to be paid to him out of Customs proceeds in half-yearly installments), and while Chaucer was controller these pay-ments had fallen in arrears. That could have been the collectors' fault, yet there was no upheaval among collectors at the time. Chaucer may have been caught in a squeeze between Gloucester and someone else with a claim on the funds. There is no reason to suspect Chaucer of extortion, although it is true that extortion was a way of life in the fourteenth century where public office was concerned. Rather, the king's enemies were in power, and Chaucer either was forced out by them or resigned before a storm developed.

The circumstances suggest that he resigned. He feared that he'd be falsely accused, and he probably would have been. On December 4, 1386, Adam Yardley was appointed controller of the Wool Custom, and ten days later Henry Gisors, who had briefly been Chaucer's deputy, was appointed controller of the Petty Custom. If Gloucester blamed Chaucer and had decided to dismiss him, he had the first of his appointees on the books within a week of the close of Parliament, which presupposes an efficiency in government not previously noted. Moreover, if Chaucer had not been leaving the Customs, he wouldn't have left the gatehouse at Aldgate, which was convenient and free; but his successor's lease was drawn up five days after the *beginning* of the Parliament, on October 5.

The move made a dent in Chaucer's income, and during these years he fell on bad times financially. He still had his and his wife's annuities, but as a J.P. he received at most £2. 8s. a year, if indeed that was paid, plus perhaps certain fees and, conceivably, gifts. On April 7, 1386, he received from the Crown a "prest" of £10 (a prest was an advance that might be treated as a loan and called back, or be treated as a gift and exonerated—this one was exonerated). In November 1386 he was paid £24 9s. for his days in Parliament, a substantial sum. Yet about a year later he received a prest for £1! And it was carried on the Pipe Rolls for some ten years—evidently he never repaid it, and, whatever was involved, it may reveal a stubborn streak. He took, as he often had, advances on his Exchequer annuities or other moneys owed him, and apparently lived on credit most of the time; perhaps everyone of his rank did. He must have been paid for serving on a commission to investigate an abduction in 1387, and in the same year for accompanying Sir William Beauchamp, captain of Calais, to Calais in the king's service for purposes unknown, but such assignments were not lucrative, sometimes even required the individual to borrow until the royal bureaucracy paid off his expenses.

Pretty soon he began to be sued for debts. In April 1388 the Court of Exchequer brought an action against him for over £3 owed to John Churchman, a London merchant and collector in the port of London; the suit was subsequently transferred to Kent. In November, one Henry Atwood, a London innkeeper, brought a suit for £7 13s., and this continued to be pressed for over a year—Chaucer didn't show up in court on the appointed dates, a common tactic of evasion. It must have been settled out of court early in 1390, when it disappears from the records. We may guess that Chaucer had run up this Falstaffian bill with an innkeeper by staying at his inn on trips to London, but it is just a guess. He was in the habit of living comfortably and seems to have spent money with abandon. It may tell us something about his personality or about the times he lived in that he assumed money would always come from somewhere, that thrift was no solution in matters of personal finance. The government had men like him in a position of total dependency; with government payments it was easy come, easy go. He worried about money when he was short of it, yet he managed to stay in debt the rest of his life and get out of scrapes by making shrewd maneuvers or writing "begging" poems.

On May 1, 1388, he assigned his Exchequer annuities to John Scalby. Scalby was, like Chaucer, an esquire of the king, who held a lifetime forestership. While such transfers in annuities were not uncommon as a way of raising ready money, there was another reason why he might have surrendered them: the "Merciless Parliament" of 1388 passed a law that certain lifetime annuities containing the phrase "until such time as we will have provided otherwise for his circumstances" were to be canceled if the grantee had received a later grant. It was grossly unfair: a later grant could have been meant as a supplement, not a replacement. But there it was. One of Chaucer's grants contained the clause, and another might have been vulnerable. So he found someone willing to traffic in annuities, as a personal favor or as a speculation. In 1391 Scalby converted Chaucer's annuities into a single one of equivalent value to be paid in the county of Lincoln; Scalby was still holding this annuity in the reign of Henry IV.

What Chaucer had in return is of course not a matter of record. It sounds as if the maneuver was a deft measure to protect his annuities during a political crisis, but he must have taken a loss.

The Parliament of 1386, of which Chaucer was a member, was a turning point in English history. Gaunt had just sailed for Castile, and in his absence Richard, now nineteen, increased his favors to de Vere and to Michael de la Pole, now his chancellor. A new opposition took shape: at its head, as before, Gloucester, the youngest of Richard's uncles, who was now in his early thirties. Gloucester was a competitive and surly man; the youngest son of a glorious king, whose elder brothers mostly outshone him, he had little wealth of his own, and little power—it isn't hard to see his hatred of Richard as an expression of personal discontent. His allies, as before, were Thomas Arundel, bishop of Ely, and Thomas Beauchamp, earl of Warwick. They managed to attract to their party—along with three prelates, Courtenay, Wykeham, and Brantingham—Thomas Mowbray, now Arundel's brother-in-law, and Henry of Bolingbroke. Mowbray and Bolingbroke were moderates in the opposition party; Mowbray was the last to join it and the first to leave.

Bolingbroke and Gloucester were married to the two Bohun sisters, and the circumstance did not make for easy relations. Just before Edward III died, Gloucester had married Eleanor Bohun, who brought to their marriage a vast inheritance that included the earldoms of Hereford, Essex, and Northampton. Having thus gained an enormous family fortune in the right of his wife, Gloucester planned a career in a nunnery for her sister, Mary, who would otherwise take half. John of Gaunt rescued Mary with a payment of 5,000 marks to the king (who had the charge of orphaned heirs and heiresses), and thus provided his son with a most fitting heiress. They were married in 1380, when he was fourteen and she ten; she continued to live with her mother until she was of age, the duke of Lancaster paying her mother for her upkeep. Gloucester probably kept his counsel out of deference to Gaunt.

When Parliament met, the opening speech by the chancellor asked support for a war with France, and the king then withdrew to Eltham to await the outcome. Gloucester's party, finding convenient scapegoats for the prevailing anxiety about war, demanded the dismissal and impeachment of the treasurer, John Fordham, and the chancellor, Michael de la Pole. The king sent word that he would not dismiss a kitchen boy on their account. But he invited a deputation of forty knights to come to Eltham, and meanwhile, in a colossal gesture of contempt, made de Vere the duke of Ireland. Gloucester and Arundel went to Eltham in place of the deputation and demanded that the king attend the Parliament, reminding him that by an "ancient Statute" (which did not exist) Parliament could disperse after forty days if the king were absent. Richard replied that if rebellion was afoot he would seek the help of the king of France; Gloucester answered that if the king of France entered England it would be to destroy him, not help him, and went on to hint at the fate of Edward II as a precedent in this case of the king's negligence.

Gloucester's policy was not to attack the king but to claim that he had received bad advice and then attack his advisers. On October 23 the king appeared in Parliament, with no choice open to him but appeasement. He agreed to the dismissal of Fordham and de la Pole and their replacement with members of the Gloucester faction. And no sooner was Sir Michael dismissed from office than the Commons brought their charges against him. The king defended him and he himself presented a convincing defense; three of the charges were dropped, and the question of his guilt on the others is a matter of degree. His impeachment ended with a relatively light sentence: he was to forfeit irregular grants made to him, pay a fine, and be imprisoned during the king's pleasure. When Parliament was dissolved the king turned the imprisonment to house arrest at Windsor Castle, remitted the forfeiture and fine, and held Christmas at Windsor with de la Pole as guest. He traveled about with the king and remained his chief adviser during the following year.

The other action of the Parliament was to set up a Commission of Government for one year, demanding that the king surrender to it the Privy Seal. To make Richard's humiliation complete, the commission was to take charge of his possessions and have the right to enter his properties at will.

So much Geoffrey Chaucer saw with his own eyes during his one session in Parliament. It is almost certain that his poem "Lack of Steadfastnesse" was written in these dark years, its envoi addressed to the king probably after he declared his majority and took power. Though it is an expression of hope and genuine relief, we sense in its first and last stanzas the burden of those years and feel the poet's outrage.

Lack of Steadfastnesse
Some time the world was so steadfast and stable
That mannes word was obligacion.
And now it is so false and deceivable
That word and deed, as in conclusion,
Is nothing like. For turned up-so-down
Is all this world for meed° and willfulnesse,   *reward*
That all is lost for lack of steadfastnesse.

And the envoi:

> O Prince, desire to be honourable,
> Cherice° thy folk, and hate extorcion,
> Suffer nothing that may be reprevable°
> To thine estate doon° in thy region.
> Show forth they swerd° of castigacion,
> Dread God, do law, love truth and worthinesse,
> And wed thy folk again to steadfastnesse.

cherish
offensive
to be done
sword

The Scrope-Grosvenor Testimony

While Parliament was meeting at Westminster, the famous Scrope-Grosvenor case came to trial in the High Court of Chivalry. In 1385 Sir Richard Scrope, who had been treasurer and twice chancellor, most recently in 1381–1382, had brought an appeal against Sir Robert Grosvenor challenging his right to bear the arms *azure bend or*—a simple design, a gold stripe on an azure background, easily arrived at twice by coincidence, which had been challenged before. He had been in Lancaster's service since his youth, and his loyalty to Gaunt put him out of sympathy with Richard; he had even withheld the seal, possibly at Gaunt's urging, from the king's extravagant gifts—and that was the end of his chancellorship. Once out of office, though he sided with Gloucester's party, he was a moderate; when the king gained full power Scrope was given diplomatic assignments and the like, and he was pardoned in the king's last year for his association with Gloucester. He had fought in Scotland in 1384 and 1385, and while there challenged Grosvenor's arms. He brought an appeal before the High Court of Chivalry when it met at Newcastle-on-Tyne in August 1385; the case was adjourned to Westminster and depositions were ordered. It was a cause célèbre that went on until late in 1391, with hearings held before the two chief military officers, the constable and marshal, and sometimes the king himself.

Sir Richard Scrope's grandfather, the son of a lawyer, came from an obscure Lincolnshire family and had been knighted in the field in the last decade of the previous century, all of which came out in the trial. Scrope's merchant-class origins may have endeared him to Chaucer, and both were Lancastrians and in the royal household, though Scrope was many rungs higher. The Grosvenors, on the other hand, could trace their title back to the Conquest, but they were known better locally than nationally; so the Scropes, prominent in national politics, won. The trial was of course about their right to the arms, not about which family was older; the question, in medieval fashion, came down to which family had better connections and more power, and the Scropes had. A substitute arms was proposed for Sir Robert, but he would have none of it. Finally, at the court's suggestion he adopted *azure garb or* (it had a sheaf instead of a bar), from the arms of the earls of Chester, with whom the trial had established a kinship. A formal reconciliation was held in November 1391 before the king. The costs, upward of £466, were to be borne by Grosvenor, but Sir Richard Scrope chivalrously forgave them.

Chaucer's deposition was taken on October 15, 1386, during the time when he was attending Parliament at Westminster. His testimony, as was said earlier, is the principal source of evidence about the date of his birth. It is also the only place where his actual words are recorded, though at second or third hand. His testimony, given orally, was first taken down by a clerk, not in shorthand (for there was no stenography in the fourteenth century) but in a highly abbreviated script that could have preserved a fair amount of what he actually said. This clerk, or another, then prepared, in the stylized Anglo-French of law courts, a third-person account of the questions and Chaucer's answers. If we sort out the legal mannerisms of the written language from those of the spoken language, put the third-person narration back into the first and second persons as it was spoken, and then translate the Anglo-French into modern English, we have something like Chaucer's spoken discourse, the only indication of it in any record.

> **Q**: *Do the arms* azure bend or *belong, or should they belong, to Sir Richard by right and heritage?*
> **A**: Yes. I saw them armed in France before the town of Rethel, and Sir Henry le Scrope in the same arms on a white label and on a banner, and Sir Richard armed entirely in the *azure bend or,* and I saw them armed thus throughout the whole campaign until I was taken prisoner.
> **Q**: *How do you know that the said arms belong to Sir Richard?*
> **A**: By hearsay—from old knights and squires, and that they have always continuously possessed those arms, and that in all *my* time these have always been reputed to be their arms, as common fame and public voice urges and has urged. And when I saw those arms on banners, on stained-glass windows, on paintings, and on clothing, they were commonly called the arms of Le Scrope.
> **Q**: *Did you ever hear it said who was the first ancestor of the said Sir Richard who bore those arms?*

A: No, nor did I ever hear other than that they were handed down from ancient ancestry and ancient noblemen that held those arms.

Q: *Did you ever hear it said how long ago Sir Richard's ancestors had used the said arms?*

A: No, but I've heard said it goes back before human memory.*

Q: *Did you ever hear of any objection or challenge made to the said Sir Richard, or to any of his ancestors, by Sir Robert Grosvenor or by his ancestors or anyone speaking in his name?*

A: No. But one time I was in Friday Street in London, and as I was walking along the street I saw hanging outside a brand-new sign that had those arms on it, and I asked what household that was that had those arms—of Scrope—hung outside it, and somebody answered me and he said, "Oh, no, sir, they're not at all hung out there for the *Scrope* arms, nor painted there for those arms, but they're painted and hung up there for a knight from the county of Chester, and that man is named Sir Robert Grosvenor." And that was the first *I* ever *heard* of Sir Robert Grosvenor or his ancestors, or of *anyone* having the name of Grosvenor.

What can we say about this surviving scrap of Chaucer's speech? We can say, first, that his answers are clear and brief; as a professional officer of the royal court, trained in law, he knew to answer yes or no first and to distinguish between what he saw and what was hearsay. His diction is precise and specific—saying he saw the arms, he tells *on what*. The grammar is sometimes elliptical, as in speech (and sometimes in Chaucer's writings). He comes across as a cooperative, agreeable, informed, and experienced witness. He probably knew the questions in advance, for they were much the same for all deponents.

When asked if he knew of any challenge made to Scrope's use of the arms by Sir Robert Grosvenor, Chaucer told an anecdote—one that didn't answer the question, but that made a point implicit in his other answers, that *everyone* knew and always did know whose arms they were. There can be no mistaking which side he was testifying for. In the anecdote, he presents a character, a nameless man in Friday Street, who hears or overhears his question, Whose house is that with the Scrope arms? If (as he said) he had, before this encounter, heard of the Grosvenors, he wouldn't have been aware of any controversy with them over the Scrope

*"Before human memory" meant the earliest time that could be remembered by the oldest living person—i.e., about a century. The rest was considered "time out of mind." At the end of the thirteenth century the date was set for legal purposes at the beginning of the reign of Richard I.

arms. And so he wouldn't have had any reason to ask who lived in a house that bore the arms of Scrope. The exchange may have been a little fiction made up for this testimony. He has the man give a very circumstantial answer, stated repetitiously with many negatives and much emphasis, and leading up to the revelation of the name Grosvenor. And although the document is in law-court French the man sounds just the way one would expect a fourteenth-century man in the street to have sounded—uneducated, forthright, perhaps a little cheeky, and, even now, rather like a Cockney.* One can imagine Chaucer mimicking his speech—it was probably very funny. And when the laughter died down, Chaucer added, in his best understated manner, naïvely, like the narrator in one of the dream visions or the General Prologue: "that was the first I ever heard tell of Sir Robert Grosvenor or his ancestors or anyone else having the name of Grosvenor." It's the one sample we have of Chaucer's native gift as a storyteller when reporting *viva voce* something that happened, or that he claimed happened.

In testifying for Scrope, Chaucer was supporting someone he probably had known at court for many years. Possibly he never *had* heard of the Grosvenors, or had heard very little about them. But if he had come from Lancashire or Cheshire he would have known all about them, for they were an ancient family of renown in their own part of the country. His little narrative displays the Chaucerian technique of putting words in others' mouths and himself playing the naïf; his use of it on the witness stand suggests that it was a habit of mind, a part of his personal style. But this does not mean it was the origin of the persona or narrator in his poems. It's just as likely that he developed the device in his writings, based on rhetoric and his reading, and that it then became a mannerism of his spoken discourse. It's a simple kind of role playing that comes naturally to a good storyteller; but in his testimony it wasn't a persona—it was Chaucer speaking in his own person and playing dumb.

Chaucer could have known or found out about the Grosvenors, but it was better not to. His testimony told what he had seen at Rethel twenty-seven years before and what he had heard; Sir Robert Grosvenor was on the same campaign, but this did not come up. If Chaucer had reasons to doubt what he had seen and heard, now was not the time to advance them. Chaucer was a member of the establishment, and he had little choice but to do what was expected of him. Here he brought to those expectations a touch of his skill as a *raconteur*. The pose of the naïf, which must have been in part a defensive posture when dealing with those above

*Chaucer probably gave his testimony in French, for French was still used in some courts, and one would expect it to be used in a court of chivalry. Even in French, the repetitious mannerisms might have suggested lower-class speech to English listeners.

him socially, was also the product of his sense of belonging to the court and the court party, of being on the right side and secure in his sense that his audience understood what he was implying.

Whether there was ever a man in Friday Street we cannot know any more than those present at the trial would have known. Such evidence wouldn't have stood up in any court if its members had been on Grosvenor's side. The trial went on five years and came out predictably for Scrope. One could view it as a drawn-out ritual triumph of the royal court over the old landed baronial interests, and of city over country. Chaucer's ironical little tale may have disguised a certain skepticism or resentment he felt at having to behave under oath like a puppet.* At just this time he must have been experimenting with the General Prologue, beginning to get the feel of the stance or role he would adopt: the wide-eyed, uncritical observer with little going for him but his memory of things seen and heard.

The Legend of Good Women

There is another occasion, this one in his writings, where a real-life conversation seems to come through. It is at the end of *Troilus* where he addresses each lady in the audience, asking that, although Criseyde was untrue, "for that guilt she be not wroth with me" (5: 1775)—that they not be angry with him for her guilt, for they can read about it in other books than his. And he adds,

> And gladlier I will write, if you leste,
> Penelopeë's trouth and good Alceste.

He adds that he's speaking "most" about women betrayed by men, which moves him to warn them, *watch out for men, and listen to me!* The joke relies on our sense of his communicating with the women of his audience, turning upside down the implication of his story that women are fickle and false. To see the humor of it, we have to imagine him winking at the ladies, so to speak, and them grinning wryly. But we imagine this because we are led to assume a prior conversation: the ladies of the court have complained to him that he has given women a bad name by depicting Criseyde's faithlessness. He replies that he would more willingly write about faithful Penelope, the wife of Ulysses who during his twenty-year

---

*Chaucer in fact has the Host in *The Canterbury Tales* use the word "poppet" when asking the poet to tell a tale; it had more the sense of a pet or doll and its use in the modern sense was not recorded until later. But the association that allowed it to mean a dummy or marionette was already present.

absence avoided by various ruses marrying another, or about good Alceste, an ideal of femininity in medieval lore. Since he did write of them in *The Legend of Good Women*, we assume that such a conversation between Chaucer and the ladies of the court took place. And the Prologue of the *Legend* indicates that the queen assigned the penance.

Let us assume then that the *Troilus* was finished in 1386 and the *Legend*, announced at the end of *Troilus*, was begun at once. The *Canterbury Tales* was as yet but vaguely in his mind—he mentions it at the end of *Troilus* only as "some comedye." In the *Legend* he returned to the dream vision and to courtly French models. We can find in it the shadow of Froissart's *Paradis d'Amour*, which he had known as early as *The Book of the Duchess*. It is a very Gothic poem, full of symbolism and ideals. He begins by praising books, then says that in spring he leaves his books in favor of the budding flowers. Of these he singles out the daisy, which he several times calls the "flower of all flowers" (the *flos florum* of medieval lore, that designated the perfection of the beloved, of the Blessed Virgin, and of the universe). He goes into the fields and worships this flower; the English word meant "day's eye," for the flower closes at day's end. When it closes he goes home to sleep. The God of Love appears to him in a dream, holding in his hand the Queen Alceste. She is likened to a daisy (lines 224, 242) and stands for perfect femininity. He sings a ballade to her that offers a list of good women—the germ of the legends to follow. Then he sees nineteen ladies approaching, and many more behind, who are all true in love. They kneel down and adore the daisy, symbol of their collective value.

The narrator kneels by the daisy too, and the God of Love challenges his right to be there. Chaucer has done a disservice to Love's folk by translating the *Roman de la Rose*, which makes wise folk withdraw from serving him, and by writing Criseyde's story, which makes men mistrust women (who are, he reminds the poet, true as steel). Queen Alceste interrupts with a garrulous speech in which she argues that Chaucer is after all only a poet who doesn't care what he writes about, and that if he asks for mercy with a sorrowful heart, he should have a hearing; although he doesn't write very well, she says, he has written works that praise the God of Love. And here Chaucer has her give a list of his works as he conceived them about 1386: the dream visions, the story of Palamon and Arcite and the story of Saint Cecile (later put into *The Canterbury Tales* as the tales of the Knight and Second Nun), the lyrics, and the translation of Boethius—plus one of Origen now lost.

She promises on Chaucer's behalf that from now on he will speak well of women, and, with Alceste herself as his mainpernor, he is excused by the God of Love. Chaucer thanks Alceste and explains that he meant to further good faith in love by making the Rose and Criseyde examples of falseness and vice to be avoided, but she brushes him off and gives him his penance: he will, as long as he lives, spend most of his time writing a "glorious legend," a collection of saints' lives, of women who were true in love, and of the men who betrayed them. He will do this *year by year* (line 481). And when the book is done, he will "yive it the queene, / On my behalf, at Eltham or at Sheene" (line 496), referring of course to Queen Anne.

At the end the God of Love tells him the lady he just saw was Alceste, who was turned into a daisy. Then he gives him instructions about his book of legends. The final legend must be that of Alceste because she is the most important of Love's saints, the legends must be brief, the meters may be of his choosing, and the first should be of Cleopatra.

Chaucer wrote nine of the legends, the last breaking off unfinished just before its end. Together they make up a major Chaucerian puzzle, and a cottage industry of scholarship has grown up that is trying to fathom what the stories have in common, what they lead up to, whether they are funny or ironic, whether they show Chaucer progressively getting bored with the undertaking, whether the women seem "good" only because the men are bad, and, of course, why it was left unfinished. Except for the first, all the stories come from Ovid, but other versions existed, by Virgil, or by Italian writers like Guido delle Colonne and Boccaccio, or by Gower. The first, on Cleopatra, comes from Boccaccio's *De Casibus* and the slightly different version in his *De Claris Mulieribus*. The concept of the work, French and courtly as it is, is based on this latter work of Boccaccio's, his collection of stories about famous women. Chaucer's stories are brief, and he tells them skillfully, using standard devices of rhetoric; but he does not "render" them, with dialogue and realistic details, as in *The Canterbury Tales*. They are a "humanistic" collection, all from pagan antiquity. They introduce violence into courtly love material. Most of the women die unhappy deaths, and most of the men are in the wrong.

What exactly *The Legend of Good Women* was meant to be we can never be sure. How could we if we haven't the whole of it? Alceste says it is to be written "year by year" for as long as the poet lives (line 481), then seemingly contradicts herself by saying that when it is finished the poet should bring it to Queen Anne at Eltham or Sheen. From these details no clear picture emerges, but we can build from them a theory. "Year by year" means one a year: Chaucer uses the expression eight times in his writings, usually with this sense of one year after another. If he was to produce one legend a year, and if he wrote the prologue and the legend of Cleopatra in 1386 and a legend a year until 1394, when the queen died, this would be nine legends, the number we have. The last legend, of

Hypermnestra, though almost finished, was apparently abandoned. The theory explains why there are only nine legends and why the last is unfinished; and it accounts for the frequent charge against the work that all the legends sound the same—it wouldn't have mattered if a year passed between each. Whether the queen or anyone else had a continuing enthusiasm for Chaucer's "penance," we don't know. It must have lost some luster after the first few years, and we do find in the later legends little jokes that appear to acknowledge this—for example, the ending of the eighth, the legend of Phyllis:

> Be ware, ye women, of your subtle foe,
> Sin° yit this day men may ensample see;   *since*
> And trusteth, as in love, no man but me.

Since nineteen ladies are listed in the ballade "Hide, Absolon" (line 249) and the number nineteen is stated (line 283), one assumes there were to be nineteen legends. But why nineteen?* It sounds as if Chaucer was frequently changing his mind until he abandoned the work. And yet in the Retraction, written presumably in his last years, he refers to "The Book of the Twenty-Five Ladies." Does this mean he was still thinking of adding more legends? Or is it a scribal error in copying Roman numerals?

A recent discovery by Professor Bernard Witlieb explains these discrepancies. Witlieb found that in 1376 King Edward III introduced a solitary lady into the order of the Garter; she was his daughter Isabella, countess of Bedford, wife of Enguerrand de Coucy. Richard II, the year after he came to the throne, introduced seven more ladies into the order, six more in 1384, including the queen, and five more in 1386, the date we assign to the Prologue. Thus nineteen ladies, the number given in the Prologue.

More names were added to this women's auxiliary in Richard's reign —Katherine Swynford was one of them—and of course some died. The order of the Garter, in the statutes laid down by King Edward, limited the number of knights to twenty-five plus the king, so of course the ladies of the Garter were to be a mirror image—twenty-five ladies plus the queen. The number seems to have been reached in 1390. Richard named eight more in 1399, but by then there had been as many deaths. When Chaucer wrote the Retraction he gave the number twenty-five as the "correct" or ideal number, the number to which membership was limited and with which he would have stopped. How the ladies of the garter were to correspond with the good women in the poem has yet to be explored.

*The Man of Law in the Introduction to his tale names the stories Chaucer has told. He omits Cleopatra and adds names not mentioned in the *Legend*; the list comes almost to nineteen.

An End to Turmoil

After the Parliament of 1386, the Commission of Government proceeded to dismiss a large number of minor officials, of whom Chaucer may have been one of the first, or may have seen what was coming and resigned. Richard, while making his small acts of defiance, took larger measures in the following year. He made a tour of England to raise an army, a difficult enterprise without the Privy Seal or the Great Seal to make the levies official, and without the Exchequer to pay for them, yet a small army was assembled under de Vere's command. He made an appeal to the pope, without success. He framed ten questions touching upon the conduct of Gloucester's party and put them to the chief justices, twice at a week's interval: the justices agreed that the Commission of Government was counter to the royal prerogative, that those who enforced it were liable to the extreme penalty, that the king had time-honored privileges in Parliament, that searching for precedents in records about Edward II was treason, and that the impeachment of de la Pole was an error that could be revoked.

What Richard most wanted from them was a definition of treason. The Treason Statute of 1352 offered a narrow definition, and he wanted one that would include the mystique of "accroaching the king's prerogative." The penalty for treason was enormous: an ignominious death, the seizure of all property, and a "taint" on the blood that forbade inheritance of titles. It could wipe out a noble family. So powerful a weapon, once used, could be turned on the user, and it was not used—partly because the plan was leaked to Gloucester and he took immediate action. In November 1387 he and his party brought forward a charge of high treason against the king's party—the Archbishop Neville, de Vere, de la Pole, the lawyer Tresilian, and Chaucer's friend Nicholas Brembre. Gloucester, as Constable of England, was head of the High Court of Chivalry, and he summoned these five gentlemen before this court, his own court, without regard to Parliament; charges in that court were called "appeals," whence the name given to Gloucester's party, the "Appellants." Richard referred the appeal to Parliament, a deft way of gaining time while de Vere mustered his army. On November 17 the Appellants met with the king in Westminster Hall; he was prepared for a compromise, and signed writs for a new Parliament that would meet on February 3. By now Bolingbroke and Mowbray had become the moderates in Gloucester's party; after the meeting they were invited to stay and dine with the king. The quarrel had a spicy personal side: de Vere had been married to Gloucester's niece, but having conceived a romantic passion for one of the queen's ladies-in-waiting from Bohemia, Agnes Lancecrona, he had been allowed a divorce and had married her, much to Gloucester's indignation. Richard, however, did nothing about arresting his five friends accused of treason, and by the time the Parliament met, four of them had fled.

De Vere marched his newly formed army down the Severn valley in December 1387; the Appellants' army, under the command of Henry of Bolingbroke, intercepted it at Radcot Bridge on the Thames, and defeated it utterly. De Vere, seeing that all was lost, abandoned his troops, threw aside some of his armor, and escaped down the Thames. He stopped in London to see King Richard, was smuggled out of London with the king's aid, and managed to escape to the Continent. He died in a hunt near Louvain in 1392, bitten by a boar; three years later his body was brought back to England for burial.

The defeat at Radcot Bridge wrote an end to any hope of using military force; Richard and what was left of his court retreated to the Tower.

When Parliament convened in February 1388—it was to be known as the "Merciless Parliament"—more names were added to the lists of the guilty, among them the justices who had advised Richard and Sir Simon Burley. Archbishop Neville and Michael de la Pole were by now safely out of the country, never to return. De la Pole went to his native Hull with the king's permission, and from there fled to the Continent—he died in Paris the following year. The archbishop died in Louvain in 1392, a simple parish priest. Sir Robert Tresilian, the sergeant-at-law who had sat on the Commission of Peace with Chaucer, hid in Westminster, where he took sanctuary; he was found—one source claims that Gloucester himself dragged him from the cathedral—and, condemned, was carried through the streets to Tyburn on a hurdle and hanged like a common criminal. To make this shower of deaths the more devastating to Chaucer, his friend Ralph Strode died in 1387, of natural causes. And in the autumn of that year, with troubles coming in battalions, Chaucer's wife, Philippa, died of causes unknown; they had been married for over twenty years.

Of Richard's supporters only Nicholas Brembre stayed in London and tried to rally support. He had long been a friend of Chaucer's. A grocer, he had risen from the same mercantile background, had been an alderman since 1372, had been knighted for his role in the Peasants' Revolt, and was elected mayor in 1383. He was one of the collectors of the Wool Custom during the whole time of Chaucer's controllership. He was arrested late in 1387, and offered to do trial by combat; when King Richard spoke in his favor, gloves piled up at Brembre's feet like snow, says a chronicler, as the Appellants and others hurled down their challenges to trial by combat, which was quickly ruled out. A committee of twelve lords found him not guilty of any capital crime; but their opinion was ignored and he was found a traitor. It was said in his four-day trial that he meant to rename London "Little Troy," that he had planned to make himself "Duke of Troy," and that he had in his possession a block and ax specially made for the execution of his enemies, on which, the chroniclers say, he himself was executed, in February of 1388.

The Appellants had their will of their enemies by virtue of what they called "Law of Parliament." While they decreed that this law was not to be used thereafter as a precedent, they also decreed that its rulings were not to be reversed or set aside. Justice was dead. The king's confessor and the Chief Justices who had advised Richard were found guilty of treason; on the plea of the bishops they were exiled to Ireland. Young Thomas Usk, the author of *The Testament of Love* (once attributed to Chaucer) —an unstable Londoner who had been private secretary to John of Northampton, mayor of London after the Peasants' Revolt, and then betrayed him to the government, had been once exiled and twice imprisoned, and had probably known or at least cultivated Chaucer—was hanged, then cut down while still alive and beheaded, the usual punishment for treason. Sir Simon Burley, now fifty-two, who had fought beside the Black Prince and served the king as his beloved tutor—that discerning and learned man who, as we've said, asked Chaucer for poems and translations used in the king's education—had everyone but Gloucester on his side. Richard tried to save him with persuasion and delay. Henry of Bolingbroke and Thomas Mowbray, both of Gloucester's party, pleaded for him. The duke of York, Gloucester's brother, made a speech to the commons to save him. The queen herself, in Richard's presence, went on her knees before Gloucester to plead for his life—Gloucester curtly told her she would do better to pray for herself and her husband. Burley was found guilty of treason (he was accused of plotting the deaths of the Commission of Government) and was—as with other "Chamber Knights," like Beauchamps and Berners—allowed only the dignity of beheading; Sir John Salisbury, accused of conspiracy with France, was drawn and hanged as a traitor.

And then, suddenly, the worst of days were over. The business of the Parliament was wrapped up in haste. The Lords Appellant voted themselves £20,000 for their expenses, a staggering sum, which ironically, as it would have seemed to Chaucer, was designated to come from the proceeds of the Customs. The Commission of Government was not renewed, though the nation remained in the Appellants' hands—the king was hereafter to submit his personal affairs to a committee of "protectors." Another committee of lords was appointed to clear up the remaining petitions and bills of the Parliament. On June 3, 1388, the lords and commons renewed their allegiance to the king at a ceremony held in Westminster Abbey. A Parliament held in the autumn concerned itself with more substantive issues like sanitation, "livery and maintenance" (the keeping of private armies), and reactionary laws regulating labor.

King Richard pondered his next move for some time. John of Gaunt had renounced his claim to the Castilian throne, had arranged the marriage of Philippa, his daughter by the Duchess Blanche, to the king of Portugal, had arranged the marriage of Catalina, his daughter by Costanza, to the heir of Castile. Gaunt received an indemnity of £100,000 and an annual payment of £6,000 for life. The immense sums and the marriages did not in the end bring peace between England and the Spanish kingdoms, nor win them over to Pope Urban.

Gaunt's return to England would change things, and from this hope Richard took courage. His move was subtly clever, and reveals his flair for drama. It was made at a Great Council, called by Richard to meet in the council chamber at Westminster—not the "continual council" on which the Appellants sat. The date, May 3, 1389, may have been a court festival, a special "Saint Valentine's day" invented by Chaucer, as was said earlier; it had been the date of Richard's betrothal to Anne. And on this cherished day Richard chose to claim his throne.

When the king was seated in the chamber, he began by asking them his age. Surprised and flustered, they paused while someone said he had turned twenty. In fact he was now twenty-two, and he informed them so, adding that this made him "of full age to govern myself, my household, and my realm." "What heir in my realm," he asked, "when he has passed his twentieth year and his parent is dead, is prevented from freely conducting his own affairs? Why therefore deny me what is conceded to others of lesser rank?" So powerful was the idea of kingship that Richard's move withered opposition. It had been the policy to blame not the king but his advisers; he was entitled to what was his by right, and so the Appellants now admitted. They were caught in the logic of their own position. Gloucester was a son of Edward III, a brother of the Black Prince and John of Gaunt; the family was wedded to the principle of the monarch's rightful inheritance, they had fought in Spain for it, the Black Prince had given his life for it. From the throne Richard declared that in his twelve years' reign he had been ruled by others and his people oppressed with taxes, that he now proposed to bring the realm to peace and prosperity, that he would remove his "protectors" from his Council, summon to it whom he wished, and run his affairs as he pleased. He ordered the chancellor to surrender the seal. The seal was handed over and the lords, abashed and silent, bowed their heads before their monarch.

14

The Canterbury Tales— the Plan Takes Shape

In the years between 1385 and 1389, the darkest period of his life, Chaucer began *The Canterbury Tales*. He was in adversity and under emotional stress, and he evidently began the work as an escape from the outward and inward pressures of his life, an escape he would find in the role of the comic bourgeois we call "Chaucer the Pilgrim."

An escape, but also, in its early stages, *The Canterbury Tales* was for Chaucer what Winston Churchill said writing a book is at first: an adventure, a toy, and an amusement. It was not to be the "greet emprise" that the *Troilus* had been, and unlike the dream visions was not written for a court occasion. Chaucer had no expectation of ever reading it in its entirety before an audience. From the state of the manuscripts, it appears that people were circulating the tales in segments while the work was still in progress. The tales and, as it turned out, the groups into which they fell reflected the preoccupations of his mature years. Once he had fixed upon a pilgrimage as its frame, the work had a beginning, it had an end, and it had a middle that would last him a lifetime. In it he could think about and laugh at the very fabric of a society that seemed to be falling in pieces. Things would change for the better after a few years, but by then he had made the bold step, and the book that had been in his thoughts for some dozen years was a reality.

He called it "some comedy" at the end of *Troilus and Criseyde,* by which he meant (for this was the standard usage) a work about ordinary people, written in a plain style, having a happy ending. He may have meant too, as in Dante's usage, a miscellaneous, encompassing work imitating the harmony of the universe. Years later, in the Retraction he appended to it, he called it not "The Book of . . ." as he did his other long poems, but "The Tales of Canterbury," which throws emphasis slightly away from its unity as a book toward its plurality and variety. And while he revoked all his other "secular" works in the Retraction, he revoked only so much of the Canterbury tales as "sownen into sinne." He knew (which *we* sometimes forget) that the *Tales* contained earnest and moral matter as well as "game," and the ending, a treatise on penance, gave that earnest side a final prominence.

The Plan

Chaucer already had on hand the makings of some half-dozen stories, among them his version of Boccaccio's poem about Palamon and Arcite, his collection of short tragedies called "De Casibus Virorum Illustrium," possibly his life of Saint Cecilia, the story of Constance adapted from Nicholas Trivet, the story of patient Griselda adapted from Petrarch's version in Latin, the story of the martyred Virginia adapted from Livy, and the prose work called *Melibee.* For most of these he had had no immediate plans: he would fit them here and there into configurations of tales as his book took shape. Its essential generic conception was that of the story collection or frame story with its background in literature from Ovid to Boccaccio.

What he needed first was a "frame"—a setting, a group activity, and a cast of storytellers. For the setting he came up with a solution so obvious that it is a wonder no one had thought of it before: a pilgrimage. The pilgrimage was the central institution of the medieval church—the "image of medieval religion," a modern scholar calls it. Pilgrimages existed for the purpose of adoring the relics of saints, and relics have been called the "true religion of the medieval church." The great pilgrimage, of which all others were mere types and shadows, was the pilgrimage to Jerusalem—the center of the world, the land where Jesus had died. But the pilgrimage Chaucer chose was local and national—to the shrine of Saint Thomas à Becket, for whose martyrdom King Henry II had done public penance. Saint Thomas was at first a "popular" saint because the people sided with him against the king, but by Chaucer's time his cult embraced all classes. The Black Prince had been especially devoted to him, and Chaucer—now living in Greenwich, through which pilgrims passed along the Canterbury Way—had marched with the cortege that brought the prince's body to his chosen resting place in Canterbury Cathedral, close by Becket's shrine.

The familiar opening passage that students used to memorize, "Whan that Aprille with his shoures sote . . . ," may have been written when the idea was no more fully developed than this. With its high style and grandiloquent sweep, it is a kind of declaration. The style appears to announce a work of high literary pretensions, a courtly work steeped in learned traditions, but after its first sentence, eighteen lines long, it shifts, by steps, into a plain, conversational manner:

> And shortly, when the sunne was to reste,
> So had I spoken with hem everichon
> That I was of hir fellowship anon,
> And made forward°, early for to rise,   *agreement*
> To take our weye, theras I you devise.

The speaker is no longer a courtier but a plain citizen of mercantile London, a returned traveler with little to recommend him but enthusiasm and total recall: he can remember all the nine and twenty pilgrims who told the tales and can remember their tales verbatim.

Storytelling was a common diversion on pilgrimages, and pilgrims were famous for telling whoppers about their travels. Despite the ostensible religious purpose of a pilgrimage, it was also the medieval form of vacation or travel. The institution had its dark, unrespectable underside, against which moralists inveighed and both church and state passed restrictive laws, quite in vain. Pilgrims not only told tales to keep themselves amused, they flirted and gambled, ate and drank to excess, swore, misbehaved even in the shrines themselves: we read of sexual escapades in dark corners, of pilgrims by the thousands carving their names or coats of arms on the tombs of saints. The sin of "curiosity" was an inevitable temptation to which almost all pilgrims gave way; moving from place to place, especially in strange countries, the traveler saw sights that were a distraction to worship. The hundreds of written accounts of the Jerusalem pilgrimage are interesting to read even now because of the writers' nonpious enthusiasm for such wonders as giraffes or elephants—or bananas, called "apples of paradise" and thought to be the fruit Adam and Eve ate, in which medieval travelers, when they cut them apart, saw what they had heard and read they would see, a crucifix.

But the Canterbury pilgrimage had few curiosities. The route, familiar to Englishmen, did not invite descriptions of places or sights. Chaucer needed to describe only his cast of characters and their plan; along the way he barely mentions towns they passed or where they stopped, and it is unlikely he ever thought to add such details. The group gathers at an inn in Southwark, across the Thames from London—a most disreputable setting, for it was the red-light district. There actually was a Tabard Inn, and its innkeeper in Chaucer's day was one Harry Bailly, who is named in *The Canterbury Tales*. It is he who proposes to ride with the pilgrims and preside over a game of tale telling that will "shorten their way." The energetic Host gets the pilgrims to raise their hands and approve his plan before he's proposed it: each will tell two tales on the way to Canterbury and two more on the way back. He makes himself the official critic and judge, and proposes a prize for the winner—a supper "at our aller cost" (i.e., paid by all) that will assure their taking a final meal at his tavern.

The Miller leads the procession out of Southwark playing his bagpipe; as described in the Prologue he is earthy, sanguine of humour, "a loudmouth, a joker" (line 560):

> He was a jangler and a goliardais,
> And that was most of sin and harlotries.

His bagpipe is a salient feature, for the medieval bagpipe was a rude lower-class instrument associated with the country; because it was shaped like a stomach it suggested gluttony, and because it was notably phallic, having but one pipe, it suggested carnal lust. Later we see Harry Bailly, the Host, bandy words with the London cook hired by the London guildsmen to prepare their food. The cook owns his own shop, which the Host describes unappealingly as infested with flies and serving warmed-over pastries. He calls the cook by his name, "Hodge" (a nickname for Roger) of Ware, and we know that even as there was a real Harry Bailly there was a London cook named Roger Ware alive in Chaucer's time. So apparently Chaucer first set out to depict a pilgrimage starting in a local setting among what one critic calls a "tightly knit group of city business-men": he expected some readers—London readers—to recognize the ebullient innkeeper with his small-time ascendancy and self-promoting ways, the cook, and quite possibly others.

People generally assume that the Host's plan was Chaucer's own. But Chaucer amusingly shows the Host biting off more than the group can chew, then backing down. Later, we hear him tell the Franklin that the plan was for each to tell "at the least a tale or two." When they arrive in sight of Canterbury he declares that all the tales have been told but one, and introduces the Parson. Did Chaucer ever mean to have the thirty pilgrims tell two tales each on either leg of the journey and arrive back at the Tabard Inn for the prize supper? Perhaps at first he did, and one could wish he had. What a wonderful bold notion it is, to extrapolate from the great medieval Christian institution of the pilgrimage its fun-loving, tale-telling side and put it at center stage! In the century after Chaucer's death, two writers purported to continue the story where Chaucer ended it, one describing how the pilgrims behaved in Canterbury, the other adding a tale told on the return; both wished Chaucer had carried out the Host's scheme, though they knew he hadn't.

For what Chaucer depicted at the end was the conventional image of a pilgrimage seen from a religious standpoint: a symbolical one-way journey that repeats the course of human life, from one's home on earth to one's true home in the universal order. The destination of every pilgrimage, even the most insignificant shrine, was a symbol of Jerusalem itself, the Holy Land where the Lord had died—and Jerusalem in turn signified eternal life. A pilgrimage on this account was declared over at its destination; the return home was a contingency, not part of the ritual act. There were hundreds of accounts written about the Jerusalem pilgrimage and a few about other pilgrimages, and none do more than mention the return journey. Only at the end of the fifteenth century did a writer see its possibilities, a German Dominican, Friar Felix Fabri, who wrote the longest and most detailed of all pilgrimage narratives. It ends with his return to Ulm: his brothers are at their devotions, and the monastery dog, recognizing his step, barks to welcome him—a detail strangely like the ending of the *Odyssey*. But in Chaucer's time such an ending was still a century away; at the end of *The Canterbury Tales* he cuts short the tale-telling game as the pilgrims approach the shrine and has the pilgrimage end with the Parson rising to speak of penance and salvation:

> —And Jesu for his grace wit me sende
> To shewe you the way, in this viage,
> Of thilke parfit, glorious pilgrimage
> That highte° Jerusalem Celestial.   *is called*

This shape and ending were instinctively understood by readers until the nineteenth century. It was always thought that the pilgrimage took place, as it seems to, on one day; the company leaves Southwark in the morning, passes certain towns during the daytime, and arrives in sight of Canterbury as the sun is setting. Apparently it was felt to be a symbolical day representing human life, as when the Scriptures tell us "In the morning man shall grow up like grass . . . in the evening he shall fall, grow dry, and wither" (Ps. 89:6). Nothing is said about stops for meals or overnight; the journey seems to pass in a spectral way from morning to evening—much is made of the sun's position, the length of the shadows, the turning of the clock.

But in the Victorian era critics began to want Chaucer's poem to be more like the realistic novels then admired. They reasoned that Chaucer *meant* it to be such a work but hadn't time to execute his plan. Having learned from history books that the Canterbury pilgrimage normally took four days, they looked for "days" in the work and even designated tales as intended for the journey home. This way of reading *The Canterbury Tales*—as a vast design left incomplete, like Coleridge's "Kubla Khan" or Wordsworth's *The Recluse*, a characteristically Victorian notion—meant it must be read for what is missing, not for what is there. Only in the 1950s did scholars begin to propose, nervously and tentatively, that *The Canterbury Tales* was not a work of "realism," that the Host's plan was only part of the story, that the ending comes where it is, at Canterbury, the destination of the pilgrimage, and that this image of a pilgrimage is a reference to the symbolical idea that—as Chaucer himself expressed it—

This world nis but a thoroughfare full of woe,
And we been pilgrims passing to and fro.

The first to propose such an idea was a graduate student at Johns Hopkins, Ralph Baldwin, who completed his doctorate in one year (an all-time record) and then left academic life to start an advertising firm. His doctoral dissertation, *The Unity of the Canterbury Tales*, was published in Denmark with the aid of his Ph.D. advisor, Kemp Malone, in a distinguished monograph series, in 1955. While he argued that the ending just outside Canterbury is an allegory of human life, Baldwin then depicted the pilgrims blushing and squirming as they hear their sins mentioned in the Parson's sermon, none of which is in *The Canterbury Tales* at all. He had fallen back into the search for "realistic details." But he opened the door to the possibility of reading Chaucer's poem the way we read other works, by paying attention to what the author wrote, not to what he might have meant to write if he had had more time.

The Audience

Until now Chaucer had been writing poems addressed to a court, even if that court was chiefly in his head. Now, with the court in crisis, and he himself living in Kent, missing London, his home—only a few miles away, to be sure, but he had to travel to it now and be a visitor in its familiar streets—it was feasible to address a new kind of audience, such an audience (so he may first have imagined it) as the well-dressed London Guildsmen and their pretentious wives described in the General Prologue, who represent the social stratum Chaucer himself came from, and perhaps also the bluff Host of the Tabard Inn and the London cook, proprietor of a small shop, hired by the Guildsmen to prepare their meals, both of them living contemporaries. In writing for such an audience he could bring about something in his imagination very palatable to him in these troubled times: he could banish the court from his thoughts and return to the familiar world of his youth.

But if Chaucer had this initial impulse, he soon dropped the focus on London. He came to think of his audience as a national one that would understand the national cross section of the General Prologue—would see that it does not include the royals and upper nobility, nor the serfs, nor (except for the idealized Plowman) the common agricultural workers; that the pilgrims of highest rank are the Knight (a member of the lesser nobility or "gentry," a crusader), his son the Squire, and the Prioress and Monk, who hold offices in their monasteries and, according to certain hints, come from upper-class families; that the lowest of rank are the Manciple (a servant), the Cook, the Reeve (a farm manager), and the Miller. And they would see that there are two pariahs, the Summoner and Pardoner, from a criminal underworld. The group of pilgrims is an audience too—a *depicted* audience who listen to the tales told and react to them. But they are by no means a mirror image of the *intended* audience outside the work and implied in it.

The intended audience, the work implies, takes an interest in this social structure, especially the "middle" classes who make up the majority. *The Canterbury Tales* is not "mercantile" in the way the *Decameron* is: Boccaccio's intended audience and the concerns of most of his tales make his work a "mercantile epic," yet its storytellers, the ten ladies and gentlemen, all come from the same class, a spectral Florentine gentry that shows no signs of mercantilism. Chaucer's storytellers span the social ranks and only some are mercantile. The Wife owns a clothmaking establishment, quite possibly a large one, and the Merchant, Shipman, and Guildsmen all own businesses. But the Franklin is a country landowner (the "country squire" of later times), and the Man of Law a high-ranking legal officer. The minor nobility, farming and country interests, and various kinds and ranks of clergy are represented. We glimpse the crusading fervor of the Knight and the courtly fashionableness of his son, the various infractions of the regular clergy, and the petty hostilities of the commons. But the intended audience is a "middle," literate group, a mercantile group. This is implied by the language of the General Prologue itself, as Patricia Eberle has demonstrated: commerce is its semantic field. The pilgrimage even begins with the pilgrims paying their bills to the Host—and in it Chaucer "creates a new kind of implied audience, by implying that his audience will bring a commercial outlook to bear on his text, for the first time in any of his works, and perhaps also for the first time in any work of English literature."

This intended audience, if chosen or illustrated from among the pilgrims themselves, might include the "gentles" like the Knight or the Guildsmen or worldly clerics like the Friar. One cannot imagine that it would include the Wife of Bath, the Shipman, or any of the "churls," and surely not the Parson or the Plowman. In fact the pilgrims that best reflect Chaucer's actual audience are the ones who have been called the "new men," the ones who represent emerging sectors of the society, men with literary interests and skills whose tales are experimental literary efforts drawing upon new materials in European literary culture—the Squire with his Oriental tale, the Man of Law (who alludes to Gower and Chaucer in his introduction, and tells a tale Gower had used in the *Confessio Amantis*), the Monk with his "tragedies" (and his definition of the genre) modeled on Boccaccio, the Clerk with his tale from Petrarch, and the Franklin with his Breton *lai* that "invites us to admire the capacity of human beings to rise feelingly to new occasions."

As the majority of pilgrims are males, the audience is conceived as a male audience. We see things through men's eyes; even when we see into a woman's world, as in the Wife's prologue, we see from a male viewpoint—indeed the Wife trips off a characteristic male reaction. Until now in his career Chaucer had been writing for a court audience, at which by convention ladies were present, a fact acknowledged in the poems. The ladies' interest and viewpoint were invoked: we were made to see Criseyde's inner world, and the ladies in the *Legend* appear to be presented as to a female audience. But in *The Canterbury Tales*, when Chaucer implied an audience of men, he probably had in mind friends and acquaintances like Gower or Hoccleve, an audience of chamber knights and well-to-do merchants, of people like himself educated to serve the government and the economy—men of affairs who, however, had literary interests, who wrote, who read, who liked to play critic, whether stuffily as the Man of Law does in his prologue, or by invoking traditional tastes of their class as the Knight does when he interrupts the Monk, or in the lowbrow manner of the Host. One observer suggests that the maleness of the audience Chaucer had in mind for *The Canterbury Tales* is what opened it to such tales as those of the Miller or Reeve.

Chaucer's new conception of his audience was different from the older courtly one chiefly because the monarch and the ladies were removed from the picture. The courtly audience included a large peripheral group of gentry, men like Chaucer and his friends. When the king retreated to the chamber, some of these and most of the ladies were left behind. So long as the king's chamber had special significance, such a small, elite, male audience was at the heart of courtly literature. But in time the chamber was eclipsed by the court, and the court's more inclusive audience became the dominant one.

Writing is a solitary occupation, and the audience a writer imagines while he works may not be anything like the audience he will actually have when his work is completed. Nor is the "audience" necessarily a group that listens and watches: the pilgrims in *The Canterbury Tales* are such a group (though riding along on horseback!), but the intended audience sometimes is addressed as readers who can "turn over the leaf and choose another tale."

Chaucer's audience changed its character in the century after his death and has changed it many times since. Of the particular character of his own contemporary audience who first read or heard his tales we can say little. He, or others, may have read tales aloud, or groups of tales; some of these would be appropriate to be read at court, but nothing encourages us to believe such presentations were intended or took place. From the state of the manuscripts it appears that there were many private copies of selected tales, and it is possible to make a statistical approximation of the most and least "popular." It is now generally accepted that an audience grew up during the reign of King Richard that interacted with writers in such a way as to produce a characteristically "Ricardian" style. But it is not necessarily the case that *The Canterbury Tales* is representative of that style.

The General Prologue

The General Prologue is the heart or backbone of *The Canterbury Tales*. It imposes in advance the "outer" structure of the pilgrimage and the "inner" structure of the pilgrims' tales. In introducing the pilgrims Chaucer arranged them so that we can see their relationships and remember them more easily. The Knight rides with his son and a servant or retainer, the Prioress with another nun and three priests, the London Guildsmen with their wives* and hired cook, the crooked Pardoner with his cohort the Summoner. The Sergeant of Law and the Franklin, both great purchasers of land, ride together. Others are described *as if* they rode to-

*The narrator speaks knowledgeably of their wives but does not say they were present; they may be typical aldermen's wives of whom he can assume pretentiousness though they had stayed at home.

gether: Prioress, Monk, and Friar; Clerk and Merchant; Manciple, Reeve, and Miller; Shipman, Physician, and Wife. The Miller rides colorfully in front, tooting his bagpipe; the Reeve, the Miller's enemy, and a suspicious man by nature, rides last.

In this description Chaucer embedded an old-fashioned ideal of social harmony, "the Three Estates." It was thought society consisted of knights, clergy, and commons, "those who fight, those who pray, and those who work." Gower in his *Confessio* began with an explicit statement of this ideal, but Chaucer only included an ideal member of each Estate: the Knight (described as a crusader), the Parson (a self-sacrificing parish priest), and his "brother" the Plowman (who "lived in peace and perfect charity"). The Clerk seems idealized too, though as a student he has not yet defined his place in adult life—he is described in terms of what he does not have or want, what he would like, and so on. The largest number of pilgrims are of the "commons," which reflects the social circumstances of the day: the commons were now stratified into intermediate classes extending up to the rich and powerful, like the Man of Law or the Franklin, and down to the poor and marginal, like the drunken Cook.

Chaucer arranged these groups in a sequence from high to low, divided symmetrically by the ideal portraits. First are the Knight and his small retinue, the Prioress and hers, and the Monk and Friar; next the Merchant, introducing members of the "middle" and merchant class; and last the "churls," introduced first in a lump (lines 542–544), among whom Chaucer wryly includes himself.

To this descending social order he coupled a descending order of morality. He at first hints so delicately at the pilgrims' transgressions that we are not sure we hear him right: some hear him say that the Knight is an ideal crusader, some that he belongs to a part of the knighthood that has ceased to scrutinize its values, some that he is a mercenary. The Knight's son is more a courtier than a soldier, whose one "crusade" has been the bishop of Norwich's disreputable "Glorious Campaign" of 1383 —there is nothing necessarily wrong with him, but the institution he has been raised to has fallen in decay. The Prioress is charming and ladylike, perhaps ever so slightly pathetic, and we respond with human warmth to her elegant dress and manner, her little dogs, her gold jewelry, even while we are aware that these are small infringements against convent rules. The infringements of the Monk and Friar are lechery and avarice, the charges so often brought against them. We recognize medieval "estates satire" creeping into the descriptions. The Lawyer and Doctor use their positions for personal gain; their transgressions are pretentiousness, ostentation, greed. The Shipman makes enemies walk the plank, the Wife of Bath has profited from marrying and outliving her numerous older husbands. The final group of "churls," the Miller, Reeve, and Manciple, possess the same greed and slipperiness but in smaller, meaner ways; at the end come the obnoxious Summoner and Pardoner, feeding upon the simple faith of ordinary people.

The narrator remains throughout a credulous bourgeois of unflagging enthusiasm who admires cleverness and success, even successful thievery, and empathizes with the social climbers and the snobs. Saint Augustine had said Christians must "hate the sin but love the sinner"; the narrator's attitude is like a comic, slightly grotesque charade of this principle—he fails to make the necessary distinction and seems to love their vices too! Beneath the pose of the *naïf* we are aware of the poet himself using the device to satirize his countrymen, but he still makes God's love shine reflected in the narrator's simplemindedness.

The General Prologue seems an original feat of literary ingenuity, but in composing it Chaucer used the form of the dream vision. He wrote first a description of a season, then of a place and a company depicted *seriatim*, after which one of the company not yet described is made leader of the remaining action. But for the conventional dream he substituted a memory. And for the allegorical or stylized personages, the goddesses or talking birds of courtly tradition, he substituted a cross section of his own society. The Prologue *is* dreamlike: at first we seem to be in the Tabard Inn, but we are not, for the pilgrims are described as they ride together along the way. Yet we are not along the way either, for we learn intimate details about the pilgrims' domestic circumstances, their histories, even their private thoughts. We watch the Prioress feeding her dogs in her convent, we observe the monk's horses and stables, we savor the Pardoner's expectancy before he rises to preach. We are in the narrator's memory of what he had seen and heard, what people told him, what he guessed or surmised or imagined. He is not an "omniscient" narrator: he tells us what he doesn't know, for example the Merchant's name (though he knows the Friar's), tells us only as much as he saw, for example the Prioress's puzzling brooch, and tells us things sometimes in ambiguous language, as when he says the Wife had five husbands "withouten other compaigny in youth."*

And this dreamlike quality of the General Prologue is part of its "realism"—for realism is artifice too. The conventional way to describe a person in medieval rhetoric started with the head and proceeded down-

---

*"Without" could mean "not to speak of," so he could mean that she *had* other company in youth or that she did not.

ward, but Chaucer abandoned the convention in favor of his "impression-ism." He tells us he will report about each pilgrim what is "accordant to reason" (line 38):

> . . . all the condicioun
> Of each of hem so as it seemed me,
> And which they weren, and of what degree,
> And eek in what array that they were inne

—the circumstances of each as it seemed to him, which was which, what their rank was, and how they were dressed. He gives us details as one remembers them, helter-skelter and in fragments, by first impressions and associations. The Squire is first described as a "lover and a lusty bachelor," with curly locks, twenty years old; he has been on "chivachie" in Flanders, Artois, and Picardy, which would have been recognized as the scandalous "crusade" led by the bishop of Norwich, now wryly known as "The Glorious Campaign." He wears an embroidered garment, sings all day, wears a fashionable short tunic with long sleeves, can sit a horse and ride, and compose songs—the organization is selective, associative.

The narrator doesn't hesitate to generalize or comment. He says the Prioress is charitable and compassionate, is at pains to emulate the manner of the court, be dignified in her comportment, be held worthy of rever-ence. Certain details are so specific and unexplained that they have almost a sacramental quality. The Prioress's brooch, of gold, with its crowned A and its motto *amor vincit omnia,* is some kind of keepsake, elegant, expensive, probably secular, but ambiguous enough that we can believe *she* believed it was religious.

We know the pilgrims largely by such signs, presented as shared culture traits. For example their names, of which we know only a few, can be subtly characterizing: Eglantine was an elegant name, Alisoun a name (in contemporary songs) for country wenches, Robin and Oswald low-class names. So with clothes: Chaucer understood that clothes are a language designating social status, attitude, psychological fix. "Fashion," as was said earlier, was new in Chaucer's time; it had come a generation or two before, with the invention of tailoring, which encouraged shaping the body into created "looks." The Squire's short embroidered gown with long sleeves identifies a courtly fashion and distinguishes him from his father, who is dressed for battle. The Prioress's wimple is pushed back, against convent rules, to reveal her ample forehead, a sign of beauty. The monk's furs and gold pin with its "love-knot" show he is an aristocrat, a lusty one who we are told "loved venerie." The way they wear their hair (the Reeve's is shorn round about his ears) and the horses they ride help place them in social ranks. We do not very much, in the General Prologue, see into their minds.

In *The Canterbury Tales* Chaucer developed an effect in literary portraiture rather like one that was to emerge in Italian portrait painting in the next century. It is hard to be certain what was the provenance of this effect, for which there is apparently no name. It involves his actual presence in the work as the artist, as opposed to the narrator or persona he uses as a mask. This effect is seen dramatically in the paintings often called "Portrait of a Young Man," a genre of Renaissance art. In them the artist was commissioned to paint the young son of a patron, and it evidently became a tradition for him to paint what he saw, a spoiled aristocrat not yet capable of concealing adolescent emotions. The young subject appears impatient at sitting still for the artist, and looks at him as at a social inferior. We see him through the artist's eyes and then see the artist himself reflected in his facial expression: it is a portrait of an interaction. The painters could have made their subjects smile or show blossoming manhood, innate generosity, nobility of character, but no: they painted them as they experienced them, aloof, preoccupied, self-absorbed. We feel or sense the artist's slight annoyance and perhaps—as never in the young man—his amusement.

Chaucer attains this effect mostly by what he refrains from telling. We are left to puzzle with him over the Prioress's brooch; we can see that she is from a good family but not so good that "chiere of court" is natural to her nor so well traveled that she speaks other than déclassé Anglo-French. We are struck by her "conscience and tendre herte" and by her exiguous vanities. Her mysterious medallion *means* something, and part of what it means is that the author himself has taken special note of it and chooses to hold his tongue about it. We learn about the pilgrims from the naïve narrator and hear his views about them, but we see them through the interacting, discerning, skeptical eye of the poet himself.

With many of the pilgrims the portraits in the General Prologue raise questions: we feel there is more here than meets the eye, we approach their tales on the lookout for something revealing in their choice of subject, or in their characters, the story itself, or the manner of its telling. To be sure some tales offer few surprises and some portraits don't raise questions. The Merchant, as first described, is typical; but then Chaucer added in the prologue to his tale a fact that accounts for his bitter antifeminist story—he has been married two months and has already found his wife a shrew.

Chaucer saw, as apparently Boccaccio did not, that the tale each told could tell a tale about its teller. It is the pilgrims' tales that make us think

we know them. What if the Knight had told the tale of the patient
Griselda adapted from Petrarch, which the Clerk tells, and the Clerk had
told the Knight's epic of classical times adapted from Boccaccio? What
if the Wife had told the cynical tale the Shipman tells (there is some
evidence Chaucer first assigned that tale to her), or if the Prioress or Monk
had told the life of Saint Cecile, the one true saint's legend, told by the
Second Nun? Some critics downplay Chaucer's use of the tales to characterize the tellers, but he grasped the principle: the Wife's tale evokes her
inner wishes as perfectly as if it were a dream, shows us something about
her we couldn't have known otherwise. All agree that the Knight's Tale
is appropriate to the Knight, the Miller's to the Miller, and so on. But
some tales make us see or suspect qualities not yet revealed, like the
Prioress's cruel story about the "wicked Jews" or the Monk's stuffy collection of tragic stories about the downfalls of the great. These tales that
seem to provide a deeper insight into their tellers bring us, however, into
the realm of contradictions or inconsistencies in character, which is itself
mysterious. The realism of *The Canterbury Tales* lies not in the "photo-
graphic" details but in this element of mystery. We are in a society whose
rules we know and about whose small details we feel we can make informed guesses, a milieu of the greatest particularity—where, as in the
world about us, particulars may jar or puzzle.

The First Tales

Chaucer wrote the General Prologue early: it lays a ground plan, introduces the characters, imposes a form. As the tales took shape, he
evidently went back and added or changed details—it's sometimes
thought the "churls" introduced at the end of the General Prologue were
added later, and there are details in it like the Wife of Bath's deaf ear that
couldn't have existed before Chaucer knew about her deafness, which is
explained in her prologue.

   At the end of the General Prologue the narrator tells how lots were
drawn to decide who would tell the first tale and the choice fell, "Were
it by aventure, or sort, or cas," to the Knight. Whether this asserts that
there is order in the universe or means that the Host manipulated the
straws, it shows that Chaucer had decided to put at the beginning the
story of Palamon and Arcite (his adaptation of Boccaccio's *Teseida*) and
have the Knight be its teller.

   And the tale perfectly suits the Knight: it is aristocratic and military
in content, and its moral has to do with fame or knightly glory. Chaucer
did not add to it anything that reflects individual psychology: this didn't

interest him as far as the Knight was concerned—the Knight stands for his class or social group, really *has* no individual psychology. His tale reflects with remarkable penetration the mentality of his sector of the medieval knighthood. It's always said that Chaucer put him first because he was the highest in rank, but this is not saying much: as a knight he is entitled to be called "sir" and may come from a family of the knightly class. Years ago a scholar tried to identify him with Henry, "the Good Duke,"the Duchess Blanche's father, who did go on some crusades, but the identification is absurd. He is a knight of the "gentry," not much above Chaucer himself except for the title, and probably not as high up on the social ladder as, say, the Man of Law or Franklin. What he represents, which they do not, is an *idea* of a superior warrior class. As a reality he is harder to pin down.

Chaucer let a voice intrude itself into the Knight's narration, a voice that talks about writing and rhyming, exaggerates, and lets certain key scenes end abruptly or collapse into farce. The voice is Chaucer's own. It probably got there first as an expression of frustration at condensing Boccaccio's unwieldy narrative, but its effect is to gently poke fun at the story. This may serve as a device for keeping an emotional balance within the tale, but it still makes us draw back and ask how seriously we are to take this story. It questions and gently satirizes a frame of mind that Chaucer in his heart admired. Knights who were soldiers of fortune like this one no longer thought very much about their motives. They fought for just causes, to be sure, but they fought for booty and glory, too, and in large measure for the sake of the fighting itself. There was something creaky and old-fashioned about it that was funny. But this reflected on people, not on the ideals of the crusade or the just glory of knightly deeds.

This element of satire already introduced in the Knight's Tale makes us the less surprised when, after it is finished, the amenities of the tale-telling game are rudely abandoned. The Host calls next on the Monk, trying to observe decorum according to social rank, but aggression and competitiveness take over as the ordering principle. The drunken Miller sets out to "quit" the Knight. He tells a similar tale of two rival suitors, but from among the ordinary people, set not in the romantic past but in contemporary Oxford.

Where the Miller's tale contrasts with the Knight's in manner and subject, the Reeve's contrasts with the Miller's in tone. We see a kind of degeneration take place. The Miller has "quit the Knight's tale" in a buoyant manner and for fun, but the touchy Reeve wants to "quit" the Miller for revenge. The Reeve, once a carpenter, thinks because the older man in the Miller's story was a carpenter the tale was told against him (the Miller invited this by tweaking him at the outset), so he tells a tale about a miller. It has the same basic plot as the Knight's and Miller's tales: two rival suitors, an eligible female or females, an older man. Reeves, being farm managers, had to do business with millers; the millers were out to cheat the reeves, so the reeves had to be on guard. This is reason enough for the Reeve to be suspicious, but character and temperament put the two further at loggerheads—the Miller is sanguine, ebullient, in the prime of life, the Reeve choleric, querulous, old. Each tale lets us see into its teller's emotional world. In the Miller's Tale people push ordinary life out of shape by acting out their fantasies. The circumstance is of a gullible old carpenter in Oxford married to an eighteen-year-old sexpot. We have an Oxford student (hence a "clerk"), Nicholas, who rents a room from them, and a rival suitor, a "clerk" in another sense of the word, Absolon, who performs menial duties in the local parish. Absolon plays at courtly love with absurd preciosity, while crafty Nicholas pursues a forthright sexual goal in exuberant high spirits. He tells John the carpenter that Noah's flood is coming and he must make them tubs to float in. When the three are bestowed in their tubs, which are hung from the eaves, Nicholas and Alisoun sneak off to bed; at that moment appears Absolon for a courtly serenade. Like all fabliaux* it is a tale of sex and violence, but the sex is for fun and the violence is a farcical melee in which Absolon, expecting a kiss from Alisoun, finds himself kissing her "naked ass" (which she has impudently stuck out the window) and getting a fart in return. He gets even by letting them repeat the same trick while he wields a coulter of red-hot steel borrowed from the blacksmith. It is Nicholas's turn to bare his posterior at the window, and the carpenter (when he hears branded Nicholas cry "Water! Water!") believes, as he's been told, that Noah's Flood has come, and cuts loose his tub.

But the Reeve's sour story makes sex an instrument of revenge: the clerks' horse runs off after wild mares, the one clerk as much as rapes the miller's overprotected daughter while the other rapes his wife, and the women *like* it—the wife, the Reeve maliciously remarks, had never had "so merry a fit." Even the settings reflect rivalry: the Miller's story is set in Oxford, the Reeve's in Cambridge!

These two tales, the first of Chaucer's fabliaux—almost the first to appear in English—parody the Knight's Tale and then parody and "quit" each other. It is all raucously and wonderfully funny, everyone knows; but

*The *fabliaux* were popular tales of sex and revenge, having a set theme that can be expressed as "the trickster tricked." They were French in origin, and were in verse. Chaucer was probably following Boccaccio's lead in introducing them into his work, though Boccaccio had turned his fabliaux into prose. The typical fabliau involves a bargain, a marriage, an extramarital suitor, and an act of "quitting" (getting even). Whether they were lower-class or bourgeois in origin, or were aristocratic tales making fun of the lower classes and the bourgeoisie, remains a subject of controversy.

it is a picture of a world gone sour, a world in decline, in which the old ideas no longer hold and the new world taking shape is petty and mean.

There follows the fragmentary Cook's Tale about a sacked London apprentice, a tale of criminal lowlife so scurrilous, perhaps, that Chaucer thought better of finishing it, or suppressed all but its opening. It does not just break off; it ends with a wonderfully funny line about the sacked apprentice's friend, who liked gambling and reveling and disport,

> And had a wife that held for contenance
> A shop, and swyved for her sustenance

—she kept a shop for appearance's sake and "fornicated for her living." So our cast of characters is an apprentice who has been in prison, sacked for wenching, drinking, gambling, and stealing; a friend who is "of his own sort"; and the friend's wife, a whore. Because no source or close analogue to the tale has been found, some think Chaucer meant to tell an actual incident involving London characters as the Cook's Prologue does, and then thought better of it. That the tale would have been so low down suggests how pessimistic Chaucer was at this time about his corner of the world; his attitude may have changed after a time and he may have thought to abandon this pessimistic local-color narrative, whose prologue contains the actual names of the Host and Cook. That last hilarious line may have stayed his hand from throwing away the fifty-seven lines he had written.

These first tales, as Chaucer felt his way and made them into a unit, are held together by parallels in the plots and characters, dramatic interplay among the tellers, and a downward movement from the high-minded to the scurrilous. One could say that the theme is civil behavior, the conduct of people in cities. The cities move from ancient Athens through Oxford and Cambridge to London, and the movement is a moral decline. What we have in the Cook's Prologue and unfinished tale may be the vestige of an early plan to write about London for a London audience. The prologue to the next tale, the Man of Law's, praises rich merchants who travel and bring back stories—he calls them the "fathers of tidings and tales." So this tale too, or its prologue, may go back to a time when Chaucer was thinking of tales centered in the mercantile world of medieval cities. It's worth noting that, having turned to English subjects and a national audience, he never wrote a tale for any of the London Guildsmen.

Before the Miller's Tale there is a surprise switch in the principle that orders the tales, a switch from decorum to aggression. The passage has been compared to the moment in *The Parliament of Fowls* where the debate of the noble eagles degenerates into a squabble among the lower classes of birds. After this switch the Host still calls upon ten of the pilgrims* to tell tales, but there is no further ordering by rank and we are always prepared for a surprise. What we get are unpredictable moments of spontaneous interplay: the Friar and Summoner have at each other before the Wife has even finished, venting long-standing antagonisms between the friars and diocesan officials. The Host makes Chaucer stop in the middle of his "rime," tells him it isn't worth a turd. The Pardoner ends his sample sermon with an effort to fool the Host or get him to go along with a joke, and the Host bursts forth in a gargantuan insult. One tale, the Canon's Yeoman's, is even told by an interloper who joins the pilgrimage late.

But out of this seeming disorder an order takes shape. Tales fall together in pairs and sequences. Chaucer set up fictional premises that made The Canterbury Tales capable of infinite expansion, reflecting the plenitude of the created universe: there could have been a return journey with a prize supper, four tales by each pilgrim, more interlopers, any number of surprises. But if each pilgrim was to tell only one tale, as in fact each does, then only the tales of the Yeoman, Plowman, Guildsmen, and Host are missing. The work, though unfinished, is complete in design and very nearly so in execution.

The Man of Law's Tale

In 1385–1386 John Gower began work on his Confessio Amantis (commissioned by Richard II) and Chaucer began work on The Legend of Good Women (commissioned probably by Queen Anne). He began The Canterbury Tales soon after. All three works are "framed" collections of tales, and there is not a question that the two poets were sharing ideas and tales. Chaucer and Gower knew each other in a legal setting (legend has it they met at the Inns of Court); Gower was some twelve years older, a lawyer and businessman, with connections at court. They both belonged to a literary coterie and had mutual friends who wrote poetry, like Hoccleve. After 1377 Gower was in semiretirement, living at Saint Mary's Priory in Southwark, as a layman. He never married until late in life, when a marriage was arranged as a way of caring for him in old age.

One of the stories the two poets shared was the story of Constance, both taking it from Nicholas Trivet's Anglo-Norman Chronicle, written about 1355. A few influences and one allusion in Chaucer's tale show that Gower's was finished first—it was finished in 1390, revised in 1392-1393

*Man of Law, Prioress, Chaucer, Monk, Nun's Priest, Clerk, Squire, Franklin, Pardoner, Parson.

and again in 1400. Chaucer probably wrote his version in the late 1380s, influenced by Gower's version, which he'd seen in draft. Gower's tale of Constance, like all the rest of the *Confessio,* was in rhyming octosyllabic couplets; Chaucer's was in seven-line stanzas like the *Troilus.*

Chaucer, having finished his version, assigned it to the Sergeant-at-Law, and wrote—perhaps several years later—an introduction to fit it into *The Canterbury Tales.* The manuscripts unanimously put it after the Cook's Tale. It is a traditional story of victimization: Constance, a Christian, is sent to Syria to marry a Moslem sultan, and her new mother-in-law out of jealousy has her cast adrift. Constance ends up in pagan Northumberland, where she marries and converts a nobleman named Alla, is saved from a false accusation by a miracle, and is cast adrift again by her new mother-in-law. She comes upon a heathen castle where the steward tries to rape her, and again she is delivered by a miracle. At last she arrives in Rome and is restored to her father and her husband Alla. Chaucer told the story in a stately way, moving from episode to episode. The stanzaic form tends to slow the movement and "distance" us—we look on the events as from afar. It is a stylized kind of art, pageantlike but not "operatic" as the Clerk's Tale is. The evil characters are prompted by Satan and motivated by stark passions—jealousy, lust, the desire for power, revenge; the good characters are moved from without, by the stars and Providence. Constance is an allegorical figure, indeed a personification since her name means *constantia,* steadfastness. She may be meant to represent the church, centered in Rome, moving from east to west.

The tale is one of several in *The Canterbury Tales* about heroic women, among them the Clerk's Tale of the patient Griselda and the Second Nun's Tale of Saint Cecilia. All are in stanzas.* Chaucer may have originally collected them for *The Legend of Good Women,* but then decided his heroines there should all be pagans. These stories of Christian heroines became "ideal fictions" about victimized women, told in a stanzaic form to make them elevated and abstract (the stories in the *Legend* are historical and do not have this elevated quality—they are concrete and factual). The lawyer's tale, of justice at work in this world, has a sober and rather stiff kind of moralism, and is told with a display of rhetoric and learning; his presentation sounds as if he is pleading a case, and some think he pleads it badly.

Chaucer's introduction to the Man of Law's Tale is curious. It starts

*The Physician's curious tale is different. He tells it in couplets, his Virginia is not heroic but obedient, and the father's idea of virtue is misguided. Such was the reputation of physicians. It has been argued that Chaucer at some point meant the Physician's Tale to follow the Man of Law's, the two professions being in competition for learning and morality.

with a new day, April 18, and offers strangely minute particulars about the
hour, 10:00 A.M. The Host makes a little homily about idleness and
wasting time, and then calls on the Man of Law. But the Man of Law
turns literary critic and condescendingly praises Chaucer in spite of his
weak meters and rhymes because he's told many a story "in such English
as he can manage," if not in one place then in another. He proceeds to
list Chaucer's classical stories—that of Ceys and Alcione in *The Book of
the Duchess*, and those planned for the *Legend*; *Troilus* isn't mentioned,
or the other dream visions. Then he praises Chaucer for *not* telling wicked
tales of incest like those of Canacee or King Antiochus, which were told
by Gower in the *Confessio*. All this is a private joke directed at Gower;
evidently Gower was a sententious and avuncular man (Chaucer called
him "moral Gower" at the end of *Troilus*, with some irony, surely), and
he had apparently admonished Chaucer for including the Miller's and
Reeve's tales after the Knight's. So the Man of Law (at just this point in
the sequence of tales) condemns Gower for telling dirty stories—the
implication is that if Chaucer told of fornication, Gower did worse and
told of incest. An audience of their poetical friends must have found this
funny, and it is funny enough still; whether Gower thought it was funny
is another question. He and Chaucer had a real disagreement, and it may
have caused some tension between them, but the old notion that they
quarreled is clearly not true.

The Man of Law announces that he will "speak in prose" and let
Chaucer make the rhymes. His seeming false humility has made scholars
assume Chaucer originally meant to have the Man of Law tell a prose tale,
probably the *Melibee* or perhaps the translation of Pope Innocent III's
De Miseria, then changed his mind and assigned him the tale of Constance. But he is probably using the word "prose" in a little-known and
obsolete sense meaning a stanzaic verse form, which was thought appropriate for addressing a king (as opposed to quantitative verse or to
"rhyme," i.e., rhyming couplets or such a form as the tail rhyme parodied
in *Sir Thopas*). Hence the Man of Law's remarks are a boast: *he* will tell
his tale in rhyme royal, not in ordinary couplets, like Chaucer or Gower.

This teasing of Gower shows a side of Chaucer's personality we don't
often see, and we can be glad the passage is there, though it joins awkwardly with what follows. The Man of Law begins his tale with a prologue
drawn from Pope Innocent III's *De Miseria* about the miseries of poverty,
ignoring the fact that Innocent paired it with a passage on the miseries
of the rich; he makes it mean what he wants it to, that poverty is
degrading, that it's morally better to be rich. Quoting Scripture, "All the
days of povre men been wikke," he distorts the meaning with the word
"wikke," and suggests that poverty leads to wickedness (rather than to

wretchedness). And he adds, "Be war, therefore, er thou come to that prikke," as if staying rich meant staying honest. Ending the quotation from Pope Innocent, he eulogizes rich merchants. Traveling merchants are the "fathers of tidings and tales." In fact, he says, a merchant long ago told him the tale he will tell. And the tale begins with a company of Syrian merchants going to Rome and hearing praises of the emperor's daughter, Constance.

It seems a strained and roundabout transition. Chaucer may have been lured into this complicated passage by two conflicting *personal* intentions. He wanted to give a humorous answer to Gower, and he wanted to make fun of one Thomas Pinchbeck, a sergeant-at-law. Chaucer and Pinchbeck were the same age, and could have known each other at the Inns of Court. It happens that Pinchbeck's estate in Lincolnshire was close to Katherine Swynford's, where Philippa Chaucer often visited and perhaps Chaucer too. In the late 1380s Pinchbeck had favored Gloucester's party, but he was judicial steward to Thomas Arundel and probably had little choice. In 1388, he signed a writ to have Chaucer arrested for debt. In the General Prologue, Chaucer says none could "pinchen" (find fault) with his documents, which seems a hint about his identity. Some of the details about him have seemed to some commentators sufficient motive for the barbs Chaucer cast in the prologue. He was of great reverence, says Chaucer—"He seemed swich, his wordes were so wise." Or, there was no one as busy as he, "And yet he seemed bisier than he was." They are playful, if roughly playful remarks; it's hard to see in them Chaucer making an effort to pay off a personal debt. It looks rather more like a joke directed at a friend, like his joke on Gower, though there's some hostility in making one's imagined critics sound so pompous.

Carnival and Pilgrimage

Chaucer introduced in the General Prologue and in some of the tales a side of medieval culture now unfamiliar, the carnival world of medieval popular life, which the Soviet scholar Mikhail Bakhtin discerned as the true context of Rabelais. The tradition is still known to us in certain survivals of celebrations and images—carnivals and circuses, clowns faces, and such. Carnival imagery is first placed before us in the General Prologue to prepare us for what follows in the tales. How different this is from the *Decameron*: Boccaccio in his prologue and frame made his ten young ladies and gentlemen examples of perfect decorum, and permitted the carnival world of buffoonery and grotesquerie to appear only in the stories, where we get wild images of an abbess throwing her lover's trousers over her head thinking they're her wimple, or of a lecherous monk led into the public square on a chain disguised as a wild man and there recognized and apprehended, images of popular medieval folk comedy, mocking and overblown. In Chaucer such images, though they appear in the stories too, are associated with the pilgrims themselves, whose behavior on the pilgrimage is itself carnivalesque.

This medieval idiom belonged to folk culture; it was not "theater." In the modern world clowns and fools and jesters are played by actors, but in medieval life they were real crackbrains. "[They] remained," writes Bakhtin, "fools and clowns always and wherever they made their appearance"; by the same token madmen, dwarfs, and blind men were objects of fascination and mirth. There was a whole world of carnival with its own activities and tastes, its own sensibility and imagery, that survived in some places many centuries after the Middle Ages. In 1788 the poet Goethe described in his *Italienishe Reise* the carnival in Rome, preceding Ash Wednesday, no doubt an actual survival of medieval traditions though changed in many ways. The last vestiges survive still, fragmented in grotesque art, circuses with their "freaks" and spectacles, "amusement parks," and in such festivals as Halloween or, closer to the medieval tradition, Mardi Gras. In medieval times carnival was, according to Bakhtin's analysis, "the people's second life," festive, parodic, egalitarian. The carnival spirit, in such medieval traditions as the Feast of Fools, mocked and degraded official life: it put laughter temporarily in place of official seriousness. To medieval people official life meant fear, humiliation, submission to the whims of those in power; the carnival spirit, in reaction, cultivated the misshapen and incongruous, combining images of birth and life with images of death, disfigurement, or dismemberment.

It is not accurate to think of carnival only as a temporary and permitted reaction of the underprivileged. Bakhtin, as a Marxist, overemphasizes this side, but he recognizes the positive side that celebrated human life per se. The best description of carnival from this viewpoint was made by a Christian writer, W. H. Auden, who saw it in juxtaposition against the transcendent and eschatological aspects of Christianity:

> Carnival celebrates the unity of our human race as mortal creatures, who come into this world and depart from it without our consent, who must eat, drink, defecate, belch, and break wind in order to live, and procreate if our species is to survive. Our feelings about this are ambiguous. To us as individuals, it is a cause for rejoicing to know that we are not alone, that all of us, irrespective of age or sex or rank or talent, are in the same boat. As unique persons, on the other hand, all of us are resentful that

an exception cannot be made in our own case. We oscillate between wishing we were unreflective animals and wishing we were disembodied spirits, for in either case we should not be problematic to ourselves. The Carnival solution of this ambiguity is to laugh, for laughter is simultaneously a protest and an acceptance. During Carnival, all social distinctions are suspended, even that of sex. Young men dress up as girls, young girls as boys. The escape from social personality is symbolized by the wearing of masks. The oddity of the human animal expresses itself through the grotesque—false noses, huge bellies and buttocks, farcical imitations of childbirth and copulation. The protest element in laughter takes the form of mock aggression. . . . In medieval carnivals, parodies of the rituals of the Church were common, but what Lewis Carroll said of literary parody—"One can only parody a poem one admires"—is true of all parody. One can only blaspheme if one believes. The world of Laughter is much more closely related to the world of Worship and Prayer than either is to the everyday, secular world of Work, for both are worlds in which we are all equal. . . .

This explains what is, after all, the preponderant aspect of *The Canterbury Tales* until its end. The General Prologue from the start gives attention to almost microscopic details of physical life and the body. Springtime is represented with the microscopic image of sap flowing in twigs and leaves. We are drawn up close to people's faces; the Prioress, though in a nun's habit, displays a graceful nose, gray eyes, a small mouth soft and red, a broad forehead. Noses and mouths, Bakhtin tells us, dominated the medieval popular image of the body, whereas in modern times expressive features like the eyes dominate; even with the Lady Prioress the nose is mentioned first. We are drawn up to their skin and facial hair—the white skin of the Friar's neck, the Merchant's forked beard, the Franklin's white beard and red complexion, the Shipman's browned skin. The Cook's physical appearance is represented with a single grotesque detail, an open sore on his knee. Some physical details, as we move down the social scale, have significance in the light of medieval science: the Wife's being "gat-toothed," it is said, signifies a lascivious character, the Miller's physical traits show him to be of a sanguine complexion, the Reeve's of a choleric one. The dominant detail about the Monk as we encounter him is the jingling bells on his horses, for the image of bells always appears among what are termed "popular festive" images.

The Miller, the first of the "churls" introduced at the end of the General Prologue, is a generic image of carnival man, with gaping mouth and prominent nose. The Miller has on the tip or bridge of his nose a wart or mole, on which is a tuft of hairs, "Red as the bristles of a sowe's eares" (line 556), and his nose has black, wide nostrils. "His mouth," we learn, "as great was as a great furnais"—the conventional carnival image of a hell-mouth. Of the last pilgrims described, the Summoner with his "fire-red" inflamed face has a form of acne possibly associated in the popular mind (as in medical authorities) with leprosy—"whelkes white" (great white pustules), and "knobbes" (boils or running sores) on his cheeks. Reeking of garlic, onions, and leeks, he incongruously wears a large garland of flowers on his head. And with him rides the Pardoner, not so much loathsome as sexually anomalous, spooky: his hair, "yellow as wax," hangs over his shoulders, thin and in strips, and he has glaring eyes like a hare's, a voice as tiny as a goat's, no beard ("ne never sholde have")—the narrator conjectures that he is "a gelding or a mare," a castrated male or a hermaphrodite.

This grotesque element in the imagery of the General Prologue prepares us for the carnival spirit of the pilgrimage itself. The pilgrimage sets out from the tavern in Southwark, a festive banquet setting, and proceeds to Saint Thomas à Watering, a place of execution. Against this menacing background, the Knight is chosen by lot to tell the first tale; the Host then calls on the Monk as the person next highest in rank, but the Miller drunkenly cries out "in Pilate's voice," swearing "By armes and by blood and bones!" As carnival man the Miller behaves in the carnival idiom: his drunkenness, his boisterousness, his oaths by the parts of Christ's body are all characteristic. He swears he will tell his tale or go his way, and the Host in resignation says, "Tell on, a devil way! / Thou art a fool." Chaucer even takes occasion to make a brief, ironic apology (line 3167): he will, he regrets to say, have to tell the churl's tale or else falsify his "mattere." Addressing us directly, he assures us he does not speak with evil intent. If we don't care to hear it, "Turn over the leaf and chese another tale"—and don't blame me, he adds, if you choose amiss.

Some dozen of the tales are an extension of the carnival spirit introduced through particular pilgrims. There is parody of official culture in Sir Thopas, the Nun's Priest's Tale, and elsewhere. The carnival imagery in the tales goes beyond that of the General Prologue—we get gross images of excrement, fornication, and farting (in the Reeve's and Miller's tales and others), of great oaths especially by the parts of God's body (as in the Host's speeches or the Pardoner's sermon), of a comic devil (in the Friar's Tale), of dismemberment (in relics, the true ones of Saint Thomas à Becket or the Pardoner's false ones), of lechery (in the Merchant's Tale and elsewhere), drunkenness (in the Cook's fall from his horse in the Manciple's Prologue. And gluttony: the banquet image of popular-festive forms, where gluttony triumphs, notable in Rabelais, hovers over the whole of *The Canterbury Tales*: the prize supper at the Tabard Inn, planned at the beginning, is the pilgrims' ostensible goal. When the work actually ends just outside Canterbury, the last image in the last tale, the Manciple's, is the key carnival image of the gaping mouth—this one, very appropriate to the end of a tale-telling game, with a wagging tongue.

Such imagery stands out more in Chaucer's work than in the *Decameron*. While Boccaccio did of course include tales of official culture, of pathos and heroism and patient suffering, Chaucer included a broader spectrum: from him we have a romance of aristocratic idealism, a tale of Oriental wonders, a saint's legend, a pious tale of martyrdom, a didactic allegory, even a prose "meditation" on penance—he shows more of official life. And while Boccaccio altogether excluded the carnivalesque from the refined company of his prologue, Chaucer lets it emerge by stages or degrees among the pilgrims until it becomes preponderant.

But in the end Chaucer turned the carnival tradition on its head. There was a whole side of it that he pointedly mitigated, what Bakhtin calls the "material bodily lower stratum." Such imagery descended from head to bowels or genitals, from earth to hell; it involved fights and beatings, swabbings of the body, debasement. "Carnival celebrates the destruction of the old and the birth of the new world—the new year, the new spring, the new kingdom," Bakhtin observed. The material world was always the focus: the future lay in the next generation, not the other world, and death was viewed as the other side of birth. Carnival showed the defeat of fear by laughter: its images of hell—as in Bosch and the elder Breughel—were grotesque, absurd, and extreme. The idiom produced gross contradictions—mixtures of praise and abuse, the praise of folly, images of things upside down, inside out, bottoms up. In *The Canterbury Tales* the material world is the focus and the lower stratum is by no means ignored. We have the "mooning" or "bum-baring" in the Miller's Tale, elsewhere the upside-down abuse of official life and religious custom, a comic devil and comic hell in the Friar's Tale, excremental imagery in the Summoner's Prologue (the friars' place in hell is in the devil's ass), possibly a scatological satire of Pentecost at its close, where a fart is to be divided in twelve, and the Host's praise of Bacchus at the end of the Manciple's Tale. The last tales before the Parson's meditation may present images of this kind: the Canon's Yeoman's Tale, about false and swindling alchemy and the impossibility of turning base metals into gold is an upside-down image of transcendental and eschatological ideas, and the Manciple's Tale is about the debasement of language, the very stuff of which the work is made.

But *The Canterbury Tales* ends with the image of the cathedral on the horizon, symbol of the Heavenly Jerusalem. It is the reverse of the banquet image of carnival tradition, the prize supper at the Tabard that has until now been the presumed destination. Carnival mocks official culture on certain licensed occasions; but pilgrimage reverses forever the pilgrim's sense of his true destination and ultimate home.

The Ordering of the Tales

Among the tales we see groups internally linked, one coming first and one last, and these groups permit us to reason about the plan or idea of the whole. But the text that comes down to us has many small inconsistencies and loose ends. Most arguments about the order of the tales* are based on their order in the Ellesmere manuscript at the Huntington Library; lavishly produced in the early fifteenth century, it seems the most finished and its order makes the most sense. Recently interest has turned to the Hengwrt manuscript at the National Library in Wales; it is thought written by the same scribe who wrote the Ellesmere, yet it has everything hopelessly fragmented—prologues and links are split off from the tales they go with, and the Canon's Yeoman's Tale is missing. Some hold that this is as close as Chaucer came to an authentic order, and that the scribe then imposed the "Ellesmere order" as an imaginative feat. If so, he discerned that order by a series of sound deductions made from the links between tales and from references to time and place, and he may have had further evidence from other manuscripts or from an informant. He was the first Chaucerian scholar-critic.

There is, however, a long-standing preference among some Chaucer scholars for the chaotic and inexplicable. It is easier to say "we know nothing, there is no evidence" than to follow the arduous process of hypothesizing and reasoning. The Hengwrt manuscript suggests that when Chaucer died he had the parts of his work all hopelessly out of order. This is like a heap of dinosaur's bones to a paleontologist—it's all one has to go on. But does it mean Chaucer meant to keep his fragments that way, in a heap? When we *read* the Hengwrt fragments, we find links between the tales, in the prologues or introductions, that reveal Chaucer's plans for putting some tales together into groups. The initial group following the General Prologue—Knight, Miller, Reeve, and Cook—is followed regularly in the manuscripts by the Man of Law, even in the Hengwrt manuscript. After this, the order must depend on how tales are linked internally, and there *are* missing links. But since the poet didn't alter the

*On the order, see Appendix B.

existing prologues or introductions, or the "head links" and "end links" that join some tales to the prologue or tale that follows (though a few of these were canceled), he left no evidence that he was contemplating a change. Of course every author may change his mind while writing a book, and every dead author *might* have changed his mind and altered his book if he had lived longer. But when Chaucer died, *The Canterbury Tales* had a beginning sequence in which the pilgrims depart and begin telling tales, a middle sequence consisting of several *groups* of tales in an uncertain order, and an ending sequence leading up to the arrival at Canterbury— quite enough to show us its shape and its plan.

15

The Canterbury Tales— Making a World of Story

The "Discussion of Marriage"

Chaucer had been working on *The Canterbury Tales* for about a year when his wife, Philippa, died, in the twenty-first year of their marriage. She was in her middle forties. Of her death nothing is known. She drops from the pages of history by virtue of dropping from the pages of the Issue Rolls: Chaucer collected, as he customarily did, the payment of her annuity on June 18, 1387. The next payment, due the following November 7, was not made, nor any payment after. Where or how she died is beyond conjecture. As we've said, she was probably with her sister Katherine in Lincolnshire. John of Gaunt was in Spain, the Duchess Costanza with him. In July Chaucer was sent to Calais on the king's business, in August to Dartford on a commission investigating the abduction of a young woman. It is hard to imagine that he would have been sent on such commissions in the first months of mourning, so her death must have come in the autumn.

We do not know if Chaucer was with Philippa when she died, nor even what terms they were on in the last years of their marriage. Unless the Cecily Champain affair, which can hardly have been kept secret, were altogether innocent, their relations were probably strained. So when we come to the sequence in *The Canterbury Tales* that Kittredge called "Chaucer's discussion of marriage," which begins with the Wife's expressions of nostalgia and regret, not to say of her wish for a sixth husband, it's hard to escape the conclusion that this striking literary conception was in part occasioned by Philippa Chaucer's death. Chaucer was suddenly a widower; after a time he was thinking of marrying again. In a poem he wrote to his friend Scogan (circa 1393), he reveals with good humor that he is beginning to see himself as beyond the age of love and marriage; and in a poem addressed to his friend Bukton (circa 1396), he indicated, again with humor but here with a sharp edge, that he had decided against remarriage. Experience will teach his friend not to fall into the "trap of wedding," for it is hard, he declares, to be "bond"—to be enslaved. And he cites the Wife of Bath as an authority!

The "marriage group," as this sequence of tales is generally called, could have been an outlet for very complicated emotions. In it he could look back with regret, perhaps remorse, upon his marriage and with uncertainty toward his future. That he projected his widower's feelings on a female character is not especially surprising; it helped distance those feelings, of whose expression he may have remained quite unaware. Medieval poetry was never knowingly used for "self-expression," but the best poetry has in it—witness Dante—the deepest feelings of the writer, and such feelings are by nature personal. Chaucer had the makings of the Wife and her prologue at hand in the long monologue of the Duenna in the *Roman de la Rose*. And there *were* Englishwomen like the Wife who ran prosperous businesses and had a cheeky independence. Perhaps trying to see his marriage through his dead wife's eyes, trying to assess some of his own shortcomings as a husband, he hit upon the remarkable notion of a garrulous woman from the merchant class who knew what the church fathers had said about women and marriage, knew the Church's antifeminist lore and its position about "perfection" in matters of sex and marriage, and was prepared to offer a rebuttal. How could any medieval woman know all that? A woman like the Wife of Bath might have great native intelligence and a retentive memory, and some women of this class could read—but the church fathers, who wrote in Latin? Yet she could know them *if her husband read to her aloud.* He imagined a characteristic medieval *florilegium* composed of such writings, and then imagined a young husband, the Wife's fifth, once an Oxford clerk (he has the cliché clerk's name "Jankyn") who had such a "Book of Wicked Wives" and took a perverse delight in reading to her from it.

Chaucer had the Wife of Bath begin her discourse with a question that was on *his* mind: Is it better to remarry or not to remarry? The Church's answer was that there were "grades" of perfection and in the sexual sphere chastity was highest. If one married, it was better to marry once and, if the spouse died, never again, a state called "widowhood." Beyond that, it was allowable to marry more than once, but to do so put you lower on the ladder of perfection. The Wife is in this lowest state, which she embraces with a certain questionable gusto—"Welcome the sixth!" Chaucer was in the intermediate state, "widowhood," and there may have been times when he thought "Welcome the second." He has the Wife summarize quite accurately the doctrines he must himself have been mulling over (it is plain he had been reading Saint Jerome): the saints are specially called to the highest state, and we should not envy them. We are only counseled to be perfect, not commanded, but we are commanded to "go forth and multiply" ("That gentle text can I well understand!" cries the Wife). There could be no virgins if no seed were sown. Nature gave us organs of generation to this purpose, and we are expected to "pay the marriage debt." Yet the Wife, championing "engendrure," never says anything about her having children, which suggests she was barren. This could indicate certain feelings at a deep level that Chaucer had about himself, feelings of emptiness or futility or unfulfillment. On the other hand, he may have kept silent about whether the Wife had children for the same reason he did so with respect to Criseyde, to avoid those aspects of a woman's experience a man finds hard to imagine. And too, if his son Thomas was really the bastard son of John of Gaunt and Philippa, and his son Lewis was his bastard son by Cecily Champain, perhaps the subject of children was better not raised.

In line 154 of her prologue the Wife changes the subject and never returns to this question of remarriage and "perfection." Unless Chaucer meant to pick it up later in the Second Nun's Tale, which depicts a chaste marriage dedicated to the Church, the subject is permanently dropped. The Wife turns to her second question, which must also have been Chaucer's: What kind of a marriage does one want? And here she sets forth her thesis that the woman should have the upper hand in marriage and the man have the "tribulacioun." This gets an immediate rise from the Pardoner; claiming he was about to wed a wife but now thinks better of it, he eggs her on. She begins with her first three husbands, who were old and rich, and whom she harassed for their putative slanders against women—which produces a remarkable and very funny compendium of antifeminist notions. There follows the bitter story of her fourth husband, who deserted her. And yet she interrupts this harsh recital with those nostalgic, yearning lines that shimmer with her indomitable *joie de vivre* and her toughness—some of Chaucer's best lines, which must express a

feeling he knew, perhaps about the earlier years of his marriage before
things went awry:

> But, Lord Christ! whan that it remembreth me
> Upon my youth and on my jollitee,
> It tickleth me about myn hearte° roote.   *heart's*
> Unto this day it dooth myn hearte boote°   *comfort*
> That I have had my world as in my time.

Her tale ends with the story of the young fifth husband, Jankyn, over
whom at last she gains what she calls "the governance of house and land,
and of his tongue, and of his hand also." After they fought and she
pretended to be dead, she made him burn his book on the spot. And after
his submission, she says, they fought no more: she was always kind to him
and true, and so was he to her. The implication is that if the husband
submits to the Wife's sovereignty, the result is mutuality, a marriage as
between equals.

The "Marriage Group" is the most focused of the groups of tales,
and it begins with such a flourish, moves with such dramatic intensity, and
ends so ambiguously, that one can imagine it came to Chaucer all at once
as a fully integrated concept. He envisaged the Wife's whirlwind discourse, her five husbands, Jankyn and his book, their fight, her deaf ear,
her argument for women's "sovereigntee," and the explosion of male
reactions that would follow. He wrote the description of her in the
General Prologue, or added to it her deafness in one ear, and he found
for her a tale—the tale of the ugly old hag who knows what women really
want—more appropriate and far more revealing than the one he had
originally assigned her, which became the Shipman's.

Chaucer followed her tale with a medley of characteristic male responses: the Friar courteously suggests that she leave these ideas to
"preaching and to school eek of clergye," and the Summoner lets go a
burst of wrath at the Friar*—their squabble epitomizes the male rage in
the air.

Chaucer's Friar, as described in the General Prologue, is charming
and sexy, but scheming, greedy, unprincipled. To complicate this picture
and give it depth, Chaucer has him show real theological learning in his
tale: a summoner traveling the countryside comes upon a yeoman dressed
in green, who quickly lets him know he is a devil. The summoner, noncha-

---

*Friars and Summoners were natural adversaries, like Reeves and Millers, and the two
swear they will tell tales against each other. Later, the Friar explains the enmity between
them when he boasts that the friars were exempted from the jurisdiction of such officers.
"So were the whores!" cries the Summoner—and it's true that at this time the prostitutes
were licensed and exempt from church control.

lant, falls into league with the courteous devil, who, we learn, has higher principles than the summoner, a better sense of legality and a better understanding of theology. Trying to extort something from a poor widow, the summoner so exasperates her that she curses him ("upon her knees"): may the devil take the summoner's body and the pan he wants from her as well. The devil won't take the pan because he knows she didn't mean it, but he takes the summoner off to hell. The Friar ends by praying aloud for summoners!

Friars were a universal object of satire, and Chaucer doesn't let the Friar win the exchange. Instead he has the repugnant Summoner satirize friars from the viewpoint of a gross mentality arrested at the level of preadolescent scatology. First depicting the friars' place in hell (up the Devil's "arse"), he launches into a raw story of dividing a fart in twelve: his point (based on a classic English pun) is that friars are so greedy they'll take the twelfth part of a "fart-hing." Chaucer lets this absurd notion gain an iota of legitimacy by hinting at a comparison with certain old learned diagrams of the Twelve Winds, or certain arcane ecclesiastical traditions about Pentecost, or the fact that a "convent" of friars numbered twelve plus the abbot, in imitation of Christ and the Apostles.

After this interruption comes the Clerk's idealistic tale, a direct reply to the Wife of Bath, about a peasant woman married to a nobleman (it is Boccaccio's tale of the patient Griselda, in Petrarch's version), which ends with the Clerk's ironic acknowledgment that the idea of patient wives is dead. We know that Chaucer was thinking about remarrying, that in 1393 (in "Scogan") he was imagining others calling him "old gray-beard," and that by 1396 he had renounced the idea. If through the Wife he expressed expectancy and hope, and good humor about the "tribulations" of marriage, he seems in the Clerk's final song to express some second thoughts. The song is called "L'envoy de Chaucer" in manuscripts, and may go back to a time when the tale was presented before a male audience without the marriage group tales that surround it.

And after the Clerk comes the Merchant with his bitter story of the foolish old knight, January, and his ill-conceived marriage to a young woman, May. Chaucer introduced into the Merchant's Prologue a detail, rather like the Wife's deafness, that gives him a motive for telling such a tale: having lately married, he has found within a matter of weeks that his wife is the worst of shrews. His tale is a projection of his circumstances, revealing with acid details his hatred of women and contempt for himself. The Merchant's "self-lacerating" portrait of deluded January cuckolded before his own eyes may be a fossil of moments when Chaucer felt strong discontent with himself and his life.

Next the Squire tells a meandering Oriental tale of fantasy, about talking birds, one of them a lady bird betrayed by a faithless lover. The tale breaks off when the Franklin diplomatically interrupts it with compliments (for the Squire shows no sign of ending it) and goes on at the Host's urging to tell his own story. Kittredge believed the Franklin's Tale was "what Chaucer thought about marriage." It begins with a proposal for a marriage based on mutual concession—the lady takes the man as "husband and lord," the man swears never to take "maistrye" (mastery) but to follow her will in all things, retaining only the *name* of sovereignty lest he be thought of lower rank. She agrees to be his "humble, true wife." The Franklin tries to concoct a compromise that will satisfy every viewpoint so far expressed. He holds that "maistrye" is inimical to love, that patience is the key; his formula combines the ideals of courtly love and Christian wedlock, so that the husband is "Servant in love, and lord in marriage."

The husband in this ideal alliance returns from the wars and finds that his wife, Dorigen, has pledged herself to a young squire Aurelius, who has fallen in love with her. She has promised *in play* that she will be his lover if he can make the rocks along the coast disappear—for they were what most endangered her husband's return, and are a sort of objective correlative of her anxiety. Aurelius, in a literal-minded spirit, finds an astrologer who creates an *illusion* that the rocks disappear. The wife, horrified, sees that she must keep her bargain. And the husband, when he hears it, declares in tears that "truth" (keeping an agreement) is the highest thing, expresses some hope that all may yet be well, then *takes* the sovereignty and issues orders to her "on pain of death" that she keep the incident silent. At the end, all *male* parties withdraw their claims and an agreement is reached by mutual concession, the admired principle on which the marriage was based at the outset.

Is such compromise possible? Perhaps the Franklin answers this question by making the event that causes Dorigen's dilemma, the disappearance of the rocks, an illusion. Perhaps the bargain itself is an illusion based on a misunderstanding: Dorigen makes her promise in a tone of aristocratic irony or courtly "dalliaunce," knowing its impossibility, but Aurelius takes it literally. Perhaps the vivid "memorial" images, the fearsome rocks, the courtly garden where the heroine spends her hours and meets Aurelius, represent a world of illusion, and the key to the strange story is the lady's chance meeting with Aurelius *in a busy street,* in the quotidian atmosphere where the realities of everyday life are attended to. The Franklin himself in the General Prologue is affluent, generous, jolly, the archetype of the affable country squire; to such a figure Chaucer might well have assigned a key tale (its source is a tale Boccaccio told twice, in the *Filocolo,* Ques. 4, and the *Decameron* 10: 5) that reveals the secret

of success in marriage. But it is possible to see the Franklin as naïve and
so to read his optimistic tale with skepticism.

But what sort of emotions about marriage *was* Chaucer expressing,
if unconsciously, in the tales that make up the marriage group? It appears
that he was expressing conflicted, ambivalent emotions that no amount
of storytelling could resolve. The Wife raises a question about "the woe
that is in marriage": How is it to be avoided? By having the husband resign
his power, she answers. But at the end of her prologue she suggests that
the goal is mutuality, a balance of power. The Clerk's and Merchant's
tales negate this: the Clerk argues that there was once an ideal of wifely
conduct but it is dead, the Merchant that women are awful and men, who
are fools to think otherwise, can be happy in marriage only through willful
self-deception. The Franklin thinks compromise is the secret, but he
presents the notion with a naïve awe of working agreements and kept
promises. The ambiguous Franklin's Tale is a clear-headed, positive notion about mutuality in marriage—ironically pushed away in caution or
in doubt.

There is a strain that runs through the Marriage Group reminding
us, in a characteristic medieval fashion, that things are not what they used
to be, that there is a kind of impossibility in all our hopes and fantasies.
The Wife begins her story telling how in the old days of King Arthur there
used to be *incubi* that lay with women and impregnated them with
otherworldly children; now there are only friars. The Clerk ends his tale
with the harsh reminder that the Griseldas of yore have lost the moral
quality they had—he calls them *alloys*: he is alluding to the medieval idea
of "the world grown old," in decline from an age of gold down through
silver, bronze, and so on. The Merchant's Tale, peopled with pagan gods
who oversee the sudden loss and restoration of January's sight and give
May her credible retort, is like a myth of marital relations that must
remain forever static: the woman will always have the gift of gab, the man
will always be deluded. The Squire's Tale refers to the great knights of
Arthurian days as dead and gone, perhaps figments to begin with; Who
could tell such a story? he asks, and answers, "No man but Lancelot, and
he is dead" (line 287), and he speaks the same way of Gawain, "Though
he were comen again out of Fairye" (line 94). The Franklin's Tale takes
place in pre-Christian Brittany in a land of enchantment that must be,
like this land of "fairye," a thing of the past.

Probably in the end the Wife's Tale remains the most revealing
element of the Marriage Group. It is of a rapist knight condemned to
death; the ladies of the court will stay his execution if he can return to
court in a year and tell them *what a woman really wants*. His violent act
against womankind is striking as part of the Wife's fantasy or of her

storytelling repertoire, for it is not in any of the known sources—and the more striking if Chaucer had been guilty of rape. The women must think they've assigned the knight an impossible task. The wise old hag who has the answer is of course a projection of the Wife herself. And when the young knight turns in loathing from her, calling her ugly, old, and lower class, she delivers an interminable harangue about "true gentilesse," adding a few feeble words in defense of age and ugliness. Then she gives him a choice: he can have her old and ugly and she will be faithful, or he can have her young and beautiful and take his chances on her fidelity. And he can't decide. Once she has in this way gotten the "maistrye"—for he leaves the choice up to her—she is magically turned into a beautiful young woman and he is "bathed in a bath of blisse." But the surprise comes in the next line. Having gained a token submission,

> She obeyed him in every thing
> That mighte doon him plesance or liking.

The Wife ends by reiterating that she wants a husband meek, young, and "fresh abed" and wants to outlive him. But what the tale shows about her fantasy is its uncertainty: she wants to dominate and she wants to submit. She wants her husband to obey her, but then *she* wants to obey and please. This may express Chaucer's idea—a man's idea—of what women really want: they want it both ways, want the opposite of what they say they want. And of course it expresses something about human nature itself— we all want to demand our way as we did when we were little children, and at the same time want to be passive, nurtured, and cared for. It may express *au fond* Chaucer's own confusion about his own desires. When he was young he may have been confident and greedy in sexual matters, may not have treated his marriage as he should have, or his wife, or women in general; when he was older and his wife was dead, he was free, but the confidence wasn't there anymore, or the opportunities.

The Inner Workings of the Plan

So the work progressed by fits and starts among the vicissitudes and interruptions of his life, from the middle 1380s into the 1390s. If we suppose a point when he had finished the initial group of tales and the "Marriage Group," he had on hand certain tales already written that he meant to revise and include. One of these was the story, drawn from Livy and the *Roman de la Rose*, of a young maiden appropriately named Virginia whose chastity is threatened by the machinations of a wicked judge. Her father, Virginius, in an almost operatic scene of Chaucer's devising, slays her in cold blood to preserve her chastity. Chaucer probably came upon the story in the course of looking for "legends of good women," and may have made his adaptation with that work in mind. What he thought of the grisly story doesn't show through, but he must have known what Saint Augustine wrote about such legends of women who killed themselves to preserve their chastity, that such deaths were meritorious but unnecessary because chastity is of the spirit, not merely of the body; but murder, indeed infanticide, performed to this end is an entirely different issue, which explains why Chaucer never put the story into the *Legend of Good Women.* Later, it occurred to him that the cold, bloodless story would suit the Physician, inured to death as a Physician must be who has gotten rich on the plague. To the Physician, chastity *is* of the body and murder an acceptable way to preserve it. Chaucer may have thought to put the tale after the Man of Law's Tale because physicians and lawyers were often in competition and fancied themselves moralists, but it remained apart. In later years he linked it, for reasons still obscure, to one of his masterpieces, the Pardoner's Tale.

Chaucer also had on hand some tales that he linked together into a small anthology of literary types, what we now designate as Fragment VII. It begins with the Shipman's Tale, left over now from the time it had been assigned to the Wife. It suits the Shipman well enough because shipmen and merchants were natural adversaries, like millers and reeves, or friars and summoners; he must have meant to have the Shipman and Merchant tell tales against each other. The Shipman tells how a merchant is duped by his clothes-crazy wife and a lecherous monk. It's a funny story with a counterpart in the *Decameron* 8: 1, and the Shipman takes open delight in its immorality.

Chaucer followed it with the Prioress's Tale: the Host calls on the Prioress perhaps to clear the moral air, and she begins with a prayer and tells a miracle of the Virgin, handsomely in stanzas as if it were a "rime" she had by memory. The story is of a seven-year-old Christian boy who walks daily on his way to school through a Jewish ghetto, singing a Latin hymn to the Virgin, the *O Alma Redemptoris Mater,* which he has proudly learned by rote. The Jews are prompted by Satan (who, the story tells us, has his wasp's nest in the hearts of Jews!) to take offense at what they suppose is open mockery; they hire an assassin to cut the child's throat and throw the corpse in a privy. The child's mother searches the body out, and it begins to sing the Christian hymn. The Jews who know of the murder are—without a trial—tortured, drawn behind wild horses, and then hanged "by the law," and the dead child's singing is silenced by a holy abbot. While the Shipman consciously flaunted the immorality of his tale, the Prioress's immorality is entirely unconscious: to her it's a pious story, whose grim significance doesn't even occur to her. How Chaucer meant this irony to be taken remains a subject of controversy.

Then Chaucer followed this pair of tales with a pair by a surprise pilgrim, himself. The Host looks at Chaucer and asks a better question than he knows: "What man art thou?" He observes that Chaucer is forever staring at the ground, as if looking for a hare; that he's shaped in the waist "as well as I," a good puppet for any woman to embrace; that he looks "elvish"—"otherworldly," i.e., abstracted—and doesn't talk to others. The only story he knows, Chaucer replies, is a "rime" he learned long ago. This is "The Tale of Sir Thopas," a parody of a type of English metrical romance that had degenerated from courtly poetry into bourgeois or popular entertainment. The humor of it is in its singsong rhythm, its wooden rhymes, its clichés and incongruities, for the knight who is its hero is a coward, a simpleton, and a bourgeois. The Host interrupts it after some two hundred lines, calls it "doggerel," declares it not worth a turd, and asks for something else.

Chaucer suggests he might tell "a little thing in prose," the *Melibee*. In *The Canterbury Tales* it makes up the final part of a subtext—which began with the Knight's Tale—addressed to the court and the ruling class. The *Melibee* might be thought a counterpart to the one other prose work included, the Parson's Tale, addressed to the believing Christian: it is addressed to the ruling class, the warrior class. In it, as one observer remarks, he was later to write that "there is full many a man that crieth 'Werre! Werre!' that wot full little what werre amounteth." Yet it is not as some claim a "pacifist" work. Based on a treatise by Albertano of Brescia, it deals with questions like when war should be resorted to, how it should be decided on, and whose advice a lord should take in such matters, but it takes the position that there *are* just wars. Elsewhere Chaucer treats war as serious business; some of the airs and pretenses of knights, their too great eagerness for battle, and some conventions of knighthood and knightly literature are the butt of his humor, but warfare never. He understood the "glory" that medieval nobles saw in warfare, could admire—and describe—the gleaming sword, the drawn-up regiments, the rush and thrill of battle or hand-to-hand combat, the noble idealistic comportment that was chivalry. He knew the harsh side of war too—the cruel imprisonment of Arcite and Palamon "without any ransom," the pillaging of dead or half-dead bodies on a battlefield, widows mourning, the noise and confusion, the danger, the bloodshed. He includes this treatise in the *Tales* for reasons that remain obscure, but it seems as if he wanted to reveal this deliniation of the thin line between arbitration and war as one he held in his own person.

The Host then calls on the Monk, teasing him unmercifully about his sexual prowess. The Monk stands on his dignity, casts about for something grave and moral like "The Life of Saint Edward," then announces he will tell some "tragedies" and gives a definition. Chaucer here includes the collection of stanzaic stories called *De Casibus Virorum Illustrium* he had begun late in the 1370s. To the pilgrims the Monk's offering seems repetitious, long-winded, and lugubrious: the Knight interrupts him, says that "little heavinesse / Is right enough," and praises stories that end happily. The Host chimes in, ridicules the Monk, and pointedly suggests he tell about "hunting," but the Monk quietly bows out. Chaucer didn't have to rewrite his "tragedies" to suit the Monk: they suit him for their cheerlessness. He is of an aristocratic family and has never left behind the nobleman's interests—horses, hunting, clothes, jewels, women. For the scholarly work a monk must do he collects stories about the rich and powerful, the great rulers of history who fell from power, which compensates for his lack of secular estate and worldly power.

These five tales suit the pilgrims' characters and even add further dimensions, and, linked as they are, they have continuity. They alternate between funny and serious, secular and religious; various critics have found in them a running thesis about literature, or a set of surprises, or a theme about individual conduct. But as they stand, they don't *go* anywhere or teach anything. John Gower, bringing the first version of the *Confessio* to a close about 1390, thought there was no morality to Chaucer's frame narrative. And perhaps he was right: in the tales of Fragment VII what was written up to this time would be only a various and diverting sequence if Chaucer hadn't come up with a tale that could encompass them all, give them unity in retrospect, represent a quintessentially Chaucerian spirit that the five tales seem to be leading up to.

This was the Nun's Priest's Tale. One writer calls it "*The Canterbury Tales* in little," another thinks it the most Chaucerian of the tales. It used to be thought that Chaucer suffered an artistic decline in his later years and wrote his best works earlier, but it seems more apparent that experience gave him better ideas and a surer hand. And he revised his work constantly. It's hard not to suppose that the Nun's Priest's Tale was written, in its final revision, in Chaucer's later years, say between 1391 and 1397—not later than that, for in his last years he seemed to turn to somberer topics.

The Nun's Priest's Tale takes place in a widow's barnyard; its characters are a cock, a hen, and a fox. Such stories had a tradition in France, and the audience would have known that the plot might involve the clever fox tricking the strutting rooster, a chase, and then a turnabout. Chaucer chose as its teller an almost faceless figure, the priest who accompanies the two nuns; he's not described in the General Prologue or characterized in the prologue before his tale except with a display of enthusiasm. Chaucer avoided having a strong personality intervene because the spirit of the tale is so much like his own.

Talking birds were conventional, but here Chaucer outdid himself. The Priest begins his tale with a slow-moving description of the poor widow's house and barnyard, which we recognize at once as a parody of a rhetorical description; the whole of the tale is told with a playful eye on rhetoric, and leads up to the moment when the teller, bewailing the rooster's fate with orotund apostrophes, apostrophizes Geoffrey of Vinsauf himself, master rhetorician. The hen, Pertelote, is a courtly lady; the rooster, Chaunticleer, a courtly lover. The story begins with him groaning in his sleep as if deeply troubled. The lady, frightened, addresses him in courtly parlance—"Herte deere! What aileth you?"—in which address Chaucer managed to find the one courtly phrase, "dear heart," which when pronounced in Middle English with the *r*'s flapped or trilled sounds exactly like a hen clucking.

Much of the humor of the tale involves our hearing the grand rhetorical speeches of Pertelote and Chauntecleer, and following their intricate medieval arguments, replete with "exempla" and "authorities," then being abruptly reminded that they're barnyard animals. In the midst of their strutting and posturing they make barnyard noises or perform barnyard actions like "flying down from the beam." Chaunticleer's dream was of a strange creature who set upon him and would have killed him (*we* know it's a fox, and that what's involved is the theory of "animal magnetism"); he can't resist romanticizing his dream—it is a *somnium celeste*, he believes, a warning from on high, and makes him a noble spirit. His lady is not sympathetic. Her notion is the medical one, that the dream is caused by an imbalance of humors and that he needs a laxative—and other medications too, which conveniently grow in their barnyard: "Peck hem up right as they grow and eat hem in!" This pumps up Chaunticleer's vanity the more, and he proceeds with a long speech giving examples and proofs and authorities of noble spirits warned in dreams, through which after nearly two hundred lines he concludes that he does *not* need a laxative.

Chaunticleer fails to heed his own warning because after his long speech he flies down from the beam, and there is beautiful Pertelote: sex undercuts his pretensions. "When I see the beautee of your face," he says to her, "Ye been so scarlet red about the eyen. . . ." And so he "feathers" her twenty times and "treads" her as often. Then, pleased with himself, he prances about like a grim lion, walking on his toes: he didn't deign to set his foot to ground, says the Nun's Priest, remarking at once that he *chukketh* when he finds a corn. At this point the fox appears, flatters him into singing, and when he has his mouth wide open and his eyes shut, grabs him and flees, the townspeople chasing after. But Chaunticleer, borne along in the Fox's mouth, suggests that the fox hurl out some words of defiance at the people giving chase; the fox says "It shall be done," by opening his mouth releases his grip, and Chaunticleer flies into a tree.

This basic story affords the occasion of one of the great masterpieces of satiric and parodic writing. Courtly love, theories of dream interpretation, rhetoric, exempla, authorities, even the theology of predestination come up in the Nun's Priest's discourse. At one point medieval antifeminist ideas creep in, until the Priest becomes aware of the Prioress's presence and backtracks—"Thise been the cocke's wordes, and not mine." The tale even pokes fun at *The Canterbury Tales* itself—there are sly references to the Prioress's theme of "murder will out," a slanting reference to the *Melibee,* a direct hit at the Monk's stories of Fortune, even a reference to the fateful day of the Knight's Tale, May 3. But while all these are subjects of mirth, they're not really objects of satire. Satire is corrective, aims to improve by ridicule. Some like to call the tale a universal satire of medieval fads and conventions, but the real object is the spirit in which people took those fads—a spirit too serious, too pompous, too roosterlike. Chaucer preferred his fads to be taken up with a little more modesty and discretion, a little more irony, a sense of humor. That is the endearing lesson of the tale. It teaches a frame of mind very like Chaucer's own, one wants to think, when he was at his best. But its effect isn't available from reading it alone. It can't be explained to a novice reader—so many phases of medieval life come up in it that the explaining spoils the fun. It has to be read in the totality of Chaucer's work, and against the background of his life and times, to have its full effect.

And the moral? Most people move toward abstractions when they try to describe it—it's about "flattery," they say, or, adopting Chaucer's terms, "jangling" or "winking," or pride, or vanity. Many ingenious efforts at political and religious allegory have tried to squeeze from the tale some circumstantial moral; their authors mostly sound like Chaunticleer—and one would like to think Chaucer planned it this way. The nun's Priest states the moral as clearly as it can be stated, but virtually everyone misses it—which may tell us something about what is being satirized. The big mistakes occur when the rooster closes his eyes to sing and the fox opens his mouth to scoff; the moral is that you are better off to keep your eyes open and your mouth shut:

> For he that winketh° whan he sholde see,   *close the eyes*
> All willfully, God lat him never thee°!   *prosper*

So concludes Chaunticleer, and the Fox agrees:

> Nay [quod the fox,] but God yeve him mischaunce
> That is so undiscreet of governaunce
> That jangleth° whan he sholde hold his peace.   *chatters*

The Phases of the Poem's Making

The form of *The Canterbury Tales* as a whole was in Chaucer's mind, and certain passages in the completed text allow us to glimpse his mental image of it. To us, the form looks like a list or table (see Appendix B); not so to the medievals. They lived before the time of the printed book; reading, because of the abbreviations commonly used and the differences in handwriting, was more laborious, and closer to speech. Memory was different too: using a system passed down from the ancient world called "artificial" memory, they trained themselves to hold in memory a structure such as a church and then to construct vivid images representing the concepts to be remembered, "placing" them on that remembered structure.

Medieval readers accordingly conceived and remembered a narrative in a more visual way than we do. Certain images were commonplaces having a shared meaning in people's experience. A recent writer argues that these images, which had a life of their own in the visual arts in a secular as well as a religious iconography, would have been part of the medieval experience of *The Canterbury Tales*. The image of the prison garden in the Knight's Tale, or the flood in the Miller's Tale, or the runaway horse in the Reeve's Tale, would, he thinks, have stood out as dominant and been recognizable to medieval readers. Their memory of the work would have involved such images, and that memory would have represented for them the structure of the work.

One such image was the Labyrinth or "House of Daedalus," as mentioned in *The House of Fame*, lines 1920–1921—what we call a maze. It was a circular design with an entrance to a winding path redoubling many times upon itself (but with no dead ends, as in modern mazes) and coming at length to the center. It is thought that these designs, inscribed on the walls or pavements of Gothic cathedrals, may have been used as substitute pilgrimages, with the pilgrim tracing "the Way" through many turnings until he reached the middle. Inscriptions placed on them in later years identify the center as *ciel* or *Jérusalem* and the path as the way or pilgrimage of human life. Chaucer may have envisaged the

General Prologue, the sequences of tales, and the ending as a design of
this kind.

In such ways medieval readers experienced poems differently from
the way we do, and the differences make medieval poetry seem to us
arcane and foreign. To hear some people talk, you'd think that anyone
who reads Chaucer and finds funny characters and absurd situations,
pathos, wit, insight into people's minds, or "realism," is reading him the
wrong way. True, there are symbols and images, as there are words or
idioms, that we would not recognize or understand without the benefits
of research. They are there, they are real, they enhance our understanding.
But there is a large irreducible element of common sense, shrewd observation, wisdom, and comedy in Chaucer that is not hard for us to grasp
because it is part of life still.

The Canterbury Tales contains a spectrum of medieval literary
genres, some of them realistic, comic, or sentimental tales of kinds we still
admire; but the whole collection is given a "shape" different from what
we are used to. The great challenge to twentieth-century criticism has
been to recapture the medieval taste for *un*realistic, ideal, allegorical, and
stylized literary forms. The realistic tales, the raucous and sexy ones, the
ones that seem to involve true-to-life motivations or circumstances, retain
their power to move us. For the others, teachers used to fetch up analogies
with nonrealistic art of our own time—expressionism or surrealism—or to
stylized art forms like ballet or opera, and even so students used to smirk
and shrug. But since the late 1950s literary tastes have changed, partly
because of new narrative modes and techniques in fiction and film. A rich
literature of fantasy has captured the imagination of a whole generation;
the uncanny and unmotivated, along with the stylized and symbolical,
have become part of our aesthetic frame of reference. Kafka, Tolkien,
Robbe-Grillet, Nabokov, and others have made it easier to read fantastical
stories like the Squire's or Manciple's tales, stories of abstract victimization like the Man of Law's, Clerk's, or Physician's tales, even a saint's
legend like the Second Nun's Tale in which motivations come not from
within but from above. Readers of student age seem to understand these
tales without analogies. We are probably in a better position now to read
the tales as Chaucer intended them than people have been at any time
since the fifteenth century.

And this shift in modern tastes has made the ending of *The Canterbury Tales* accessible. Until a generation ago, the customary response was
to assume, as Tatlock wryly put it, that *The Canterbury Tales* was "a kind
of foundling asylum for the waifs and strays of [Chaucer's] earlier beget-
ting." What the tales' critics didn't like or understand they treated as
leftovers, earlier efforts that Chaucer didn't know what do with. Such tales

were thought lumped in the final sequence. Now we realize that these final tales, stranger to us than most others, were gathered (and some written) late in Chaucer's life as components of an ending.

Chaucer worked on *The Canterbury Tales* for some fourteen years, from about 1386 until his death in October 1400. His labors fall into three phases. First, as we've said, he wrote the General Prologue and then the tales attached to it—the Knight's Tale, the three fabliaux (Miller's, Reeve's, Cook's), and, though in a different fragment, the Man of Law's Tale. That would be Phase One.

In the tales of this first phase we find literary effects not found in his earlier works. The scattershot "impressionistic" descriptions of the pilgrims in the General Prologue are one such development in his art. Another is his control over the voice or "register" in the tales: he begins the General Prologue in the "high style," then slips by degrees into a plain, colloquial manner. We can find both styles in his earlier works, but not such ease in modulating from one to the other (more often such changes had been a surprise, as with the first speeches of the birds in *The Parliament of Fowls*). Another new effect, which we see in the Knight's Tale, is what we might call the "intrusive narrative voice": one voice, the Knight's, is telling the tale, yet as he tells it we are aware of a second voice, the poet's, that speaks of writing and rhyming, complains about all the detail he must omit from his source, and sometimes comments humorously on the story, as at line 2815:

> Arcite is cold, ther Mars his soule gie°!   *guide*
> Now will I speaken forth of Emelye.
> Shrikte Emelye.

("Arcite is cold, so Mars guide his soul. Now I will speak of Emily. Emily shrieked.") Few critics agree about how much this voice is meant to be playful or satiric, but few insist that it is the Knight's voice.

Another effect emerges in Phase One: Chaucer displays the full artistry of the accomplished medieval rhetorician in passages that he then puts in the mouths of uncouth characters. He has it both ways. No one reads *The Canterbury Tales* so literally as to suppose that the Miller, say, is natively gifted in turns of phrase or parallel sentence structures, let alone rhymed couplets. We accept the poetic artistry and accomplished rhetoric because it is there, not because it is part of the impersonation of the pilgrim in his dramatic monologue. Here is the Miller getting on with his story in the bluff, lower-class way one can imagine he would have spoken (line 3271):

> Now, sire, and eft, sire, so bifel the case,
> That on a day, this hende Nicholas . . .

But the artistic properties of his tale, the wonderful plays on words, the biblical allusions, the echoes of key lines from the Knight's Tale, the hilarious dialogue, the bold "tee-hee," Absolon's misuses of conventional courtly-love language, and (when he has gotten a fart for a kiss) his abrupt transformation to a man of action bent on revenge, belong to Chaucer; no one supposes the Miller himself possesses such cleverness.

In Phase One, Chaucer for the first time in English literature, perhaps in any literature, used dialect. He began the Reeve's Prologue having the Reeve speak in an approximation of East Anglian dialect. We get enough of this to *imagine* he goes on speaking in dialect, though in fact he lapses into standard English and, as elsewhere, tells his tale with a kind of literary sophistication (as in the parody of compline on their retiring) that is not part of the presentation of his character. Then Chaucer went a step further: while we may still imagine the Reeve's Tale being told in East Anglian, he has the two clerks speak a broad northern dialect, imitated with surprising accuracy. It appears that in this sequence of tales, which degenerate in their tone and morality, Chaucer wanted to show language itself degenerating, splitting apart into mutually incomprehensible varieties—far, far beyond Babel. It was one of the anxieties of Chaucer's time that dialect variants made English cumbersome as the national language,* and it was one of Chaucer's personal anxieties that copyists, turning his poems from his own dialect into theirs, would "miswrite" or "mismeter" them "for defaut of tongue" (*Troilus* 5: 1795).

The next phase, which included the "discussion of marriage," probably came after a period of mourning—a year or two, perhaps more, after his wife died, in the late 1380s. In 1389 the king declared his majority and took the reins of government; Chaucer was appointed Clerk of the King's Works, a post of great importance that probably took up most of his time until he resigned it in 1391. Then he continued writing the tales about marriage and worked on other tales. Between 1393 and 1396 he apparently gave up the idea of marrying again; it is not out of the question that there had been a woman in the picture. That would be Phase Two —from 1389, say, until 1396.

In Phase Two he continued to use techniques and effects of Phase One, but new dimensions opened up. The tales of Phase Two relate to each other through the personal and social interactions of the pilgrims, as before, but now, rather than merely parody or "quit" each other, they

*William Caxton, the first English printer, told in the preface of his *Eneidos*, a paraphrase of the *Aeneid*, of a merchant asking a housewife for eggs: "And the good wife answered, that she could speak no French. And the merchant was angry, for he also could speak no French, but would have had eggs, and she understood him not. And then at last another said that he would have *eyren.* Then the good wife said that she understood him well. Lo, what should a man in these days now write, eggs or *eyren*?"

become elements in an extended discussion. The natural adversary relationships of people in social roles, as between the Miller and Reeve, continue to direct the sequence of tales (witness the Friar and Summoner), but new kinds of relationships crop up: the Wife's discourse threatens *all* the men—the battle of the sexes is invoked—and the Clerk's apparently idealistic tale of a former age when wives were patient and submissive is followed by his biting song, which ends his tale on a negative note and cancels his own argument. The Merchant's cynical tale that follows may cancel itself out by ending on a positive note: we last see January stroking May's "womb"—in Middle English the word could mean either vagina or belly, so we don't know if he is last seen as a doting lecher or a happy expectant father. The Wife had introduced the question of perfection, only to drop it and move to the question of "maistrye." That question, which the Franklin purports to settle, may be left up in the air because the Franklin himself remains an ambiguous character. These tales about marriage have contradictory, inconclusive, and ambiguous qualities that we don't find in the tales of Phase One.

In Phase Two, Chaucer began to write another new kind of tale—what we may call the "tale ineptly told." It is the obverse of the principle that a pilgrim's tale may be told with a literary art he wouldn't be capable of, and it has its precedents in passages where Chaucer intentionally made a character speak awkwardly for comic effect—Juno in *The Book of the Duchess*, or himself in *The House of Fame*, or the second Tercel in *The Parliament of Fowls*, or (in the Knight's Tale) the passages where the Knight's rhetoric gets out of hand and we sense ridicule of the story. Of such tales the most extreme example is Chaucer's own tale, "The Tale of Sir Thopas," which parodies "bourgeois romance" with howler clichés, singsong rhythm, and wild incongruities. It may be that Chaucer meant the Prioress's Tale to be such a tale: if so it is a good deal more subtle, for its stanzas are skillfully written and its story well told—it is only that the Prioress unknowingly violates the spirit of such miracle tales with mindless hate, which Chaucer underscores in ironic passages, as where he draws attention to the illegality of the vengeful punishment decreed by the biased judge (line 1822):

> "Evil shall have that evil wol deserve";
> Therefore with wilde horse he did hem drawe°,   *had them drawn*
> And after that he heng hem° by the lawe.   *hanged them*

Or again, in the Squire's Tale, whose narrative material intrigued Spenser and Milton, and can intrigue us still as part of the "Matter of Araby" new in his time, Chaucer depicted the Squire as unable to handle the complex tale he began. He overuses the rhetorical "modesty topos" (excusing one's inadequacies), gets woefully sidetracked—he spends eight lines (401–408) making the point that he is getting to the point!—and tries to make fantastical details credible by the unlikely resource of repeating them (as witness the claims made for the magic sword, lines 156–67). This of course does not parody the tale but the rhetoric; it's part of the tale's charm that the Squire can't manage it, and one can believe that when the Squire breaks off, just after the rubric has announced *pars tercia* with no end in sight, the Franklin's speech is intended as a kindly interruption to get the Squire out of the labyrinth he has entered. The Monk's Tale is in a sense one of these "clown poems," as the late John Gardner called them: the Monk's stories, perfectly well told, are interrupted and denounced because they're cheerless and tedious. Chaucer didn't write them with this in mind, as he wrote the singsong verses of *Sir Thopas,* but capitalized on the fact that they *would* be boring if told one after another in this relentless way.

It has always been understood that Chaucer wrote such "clown poems," but the understanding has led some critics to find clowning where it is not. Gardner thought the *Melibee* and the Physician's Tale were such works, yet both are adaptations of serious writing by eminent writers, without distortions or exaggerations that invite amusement. Most of the serious tales in *The Canterbury Tales* have been thought a joke by one critic or another; but Chaucer was at base a serious man—he always had a serious side even at his most humorous, and this side took on a somber quality in his last years.

What can we say was the sum of Chaucer's achievement in *The Canterbury Tales*? He left some eight tales unlinked, and left a few pilgrims without a tale (the Knight's Yeoman, the Guildsmen, the Plowman, and the Host, but they may not all have been meant to tell a tale). By 1395–1396 he had probably finished most of the tales that fall into dramatic and thematic units. In his last years he probably put together the last tales (the Second Nun's, Canon's Yeoman's, and Manciple's tales) to lead up to the end of the storytelling game and the arrival at Canterbury. From that point the concern is with the end of life's pilgrimage and the life to come; he must have finished the Parson's treatise on penitence in those years, and put finishing touches on the Pardoner's Tale.

The General Prologue is what makes *The Canterbury Tales* tick. It gives coherence to the whole, hovers over the arrangement of the tales and their assignment to appropriate tellers. The tales and tellers are uniquely a group in a complex dramatic relationship—a society in little —who gravitate toward each other on principles of class and group solidarity, or fall into competition because of traditional enmities or differences of temperament, age, and sex. Group dynamics direct their alliances and aggressions, which in turn direct the "plot" of the pilgrimage through debates on issues like marriage, parodies of others' tales, or personal animosity and revenge. Chaucer's achievement is a dramatic one, for the essence of drama is interplay and conflict; but in drama his great achievement was the *Troilus*. The achievement of *The Canterbury Tales* is better called novelistic, for Chaucer introduced into its concerns an in-depth curiosity about people's motives and mentalities. When people like his pilgrims hear or read a tale, each will find something different in it; they will see the characters with reference to their familiar worlds or their selves, and twist the plot to serve their fantasies. The pilgrims tell tales they have been drawn to, have remembered, and have chosen to tell; each choice reveals an interest or inclining, a mentality—each tale tells a tale about its teller.

These circumstances can be called "psychological" in a general way. Emily, the female figure in the Knight's Tale, is the demure, silent young noblewoman that someone like the Knight would envisage—quite different from Boccaccio's more talkative and flirtatious Emilia. The female figure in the Miller's Tale is a pert sexpot, ebullient and earthy like the Miller himself; and the two women in the rival Reeve's Tale—the prim, sour wife and the overprotected, pathetic daughter—are projections of the Reeve's choleric and querulous character. In these variations Chaucer no doubt captured elements of personal psychology, but more often he captured differences of mentality based on social background, status, and group membership. In some cases he even experimented with figures not described in the General Prologue about whom we know only their identity and their tale. The Second Nun tells a tale of a female saint, of whose character a certain churchly mentality is all we get. The Nun's Priest, contrariwise, tells a tale so witty and humane and fun-loving, so intelligent and balanced, that we discern in him a mentality we can aspire to. Or take the Franklin. We have a sense of him, see in him the stereotypic "country squire," are intrigued by the spirit of evenhandedness and common sense embodied in his tale. His public spiritedness and generosity, and his consciousness of status, were probably characteristic of such men, but the traits don't add up to an individual psychology. Nevertheless, there are pilgrims in whom temperament, personal reaction formations, and individual quirks account for character. They are among Chaucer's most interesting storytellers, and their tales reveal their characters. The Prioress and the Monk are examples, and, supremely, the Wife of Bath and the Pardoner. With them we have the wherewithal to see inside their minds.

The tales told in this familiar social world are, however, written texts. The fiction is that they are spontaneous oral presentations, and their "voiceness," if we may call it so, is sometimes indicated by token passes

at dialect (in the Reeve's Tale), or free association (in the Wife's Prologue), or other characteristics of spoken language. Yet they are told on
horseback in open country, or on absurdly frequent stops by the wayside.
They are in rhyming verse, they reflect literary traditions and rhetorical
conventions, they show a level of wit and artistry and learning of which
few of the pilgrims would be capable. The fact is, they are texts. For all
our talk about the "voices" of author, narrator, and pilgrims, the tales exist
on paper, we hold them in our hands, turning the leaves, selecting—they
are in our power, and we must be participants in making them an experience.

Seen this way the tales possess a relatedness of their own within a
world of other texts. They can be understood only with reference to shared
formulas of language or generic traits; as stories, they belong to a world
of story. The Knight's Tale is adapted from a longer tale in another
language, belonging to a different genre. Immediately on its completion
it becomes the object of a literary parody in which the same essential plot
is treated in the Miller's Tale from the viewpoint of a different social class
and a different mentality. Then *this* tale is parodied in the next one, the
Reeve's Tale.

This "intertextuality" is paraded in the text itself: some pilgrims
announce their actual source (the Physician identifies his story as taken
from Livy) and others announce a fictional source (the Franklin says he
tells a "Breton lai," though the tale is actually from Boccaccio's *Decameron*). We learn something of each pilgrim's character by observing what
he or she likes to read or hear. And we are kept aware that each story is
derived from an older story. In this way the tales bring together an
international spectrum of literary relations and backgrounds, real and
fictional. They come from Italy (the Knight's and Monk's tales from
Boccaccio, the Clerk's from Petrarch, Chaucer's "little thing in prose"
from a treatise by Arnold of Brescia); from France (where the fabliaux
came from, though Chaucer represents them as popular tales of the
English countryside); from as far as the Orient (the Squire's Tale), and
from close to home (the Man of Law's Tale, drawn from the fourteenth-
century English chronicler Nicholas Trivet, and from Gower); from the
body of ancient Christian legend (the Second Nun's Tale from the *Acta
Sanctorum*), and from ancient pagan writers (the Manciple's Tale from
Ovid). Chaucer characterized the world of story as a world unto itself that
knows no bounds of language or of nation.

These relations, which exist among the tales Chaucer had completed
by the mid-1390s, are the great achievement of Phase Two. They give
The Canterbury Tales the unique character of a hall with many mirrors
set not facing each other in infinite reflection but at various angles, so that

we see each component of the picture reflected in multiple views from
different vantage points, see the wide-eyed narrator seeing it all, glimpse
beneath his mask sometimes the role-playing author, and find ourselves
in the picture trying to see it clearly.

By the time he had completed this much, Chaucer was old by
medieval standards, and evidently in poor health. In the "Complaint to
Venus," written probably after 1393, he wrote:

> For elde°, that in my spirit dulleth me,   *old age*
> Hath of enditing° all the subtilté   *composing*
> Well nigh bereft out of my remembraunce.

But, though he may have thought this, there is no reason to think his
artistic powers were in decline. He wrote less, wrote more slowly, worked
on projects already begun, and had no new artistic plans. His writings of
these last years were more reflective, and are to us more haunting. They
show a preoccupation with the essential values of life, with renunciation,
idealism, truth, silence, with age, with death, and with the "art of dying."
By putting the Parson's Tale at the end, and preparing for that end with
tales thematically related, Chaucer arranged a final angle of vision: all that
we have seen so far in sequences that follow from and relate to the General
Prologue we see now again in retrospect, leading toward the Parson's
"meditation." That final shift of viewpoint was the achievement of Phase
Three, which was to be the last.

16

A New Age—
the 1390s

The Court of Richard II

When King Richard laid claim to his realm in 1389, there were certain moves he wanted to make at once, and few of his intimates were left to advise him. John of Gaunt, having made his Castilian compromise, had gone off to Gascony as king's lieutenant; and did not want to come home —it made a difficulty for him that his son Henry had been one of the Appellants, the king's opponents, though he was a moderate. Finally Richard ordered John of Gaunt to return. When he arrived in November, the king rode in state to meet him, granted him the duchy of Aquitaine for life and made his palatinate of Lancaster hereditary through the male line—an ironic twist, since Henry of Derby, who inherited it, usurped the throne.

By the time Gaunt arrived, Richard had completed his shake-up in a surprisingly conservative way, and with no bloodbaths or reprisals. He chose a council chiefly of venerable elders. He replaced Archbishop Arundel, the chancellor, with the very conservative William of Wykeham, bishop of Winchester, founder of two Oxford colleges. As treasurer he appointed the aged bishop of Exeter. Sir John Holland, the king's half brother, with whom Richard had quarreled some four years back as their mother tried in vain to reconcile them, and who was now Gaunt's son-in-law, was made the earl of Huntingdon and named admiral and captain of Brest, replacing Thomas earl of Arundel. Richard made what turned out to be a brilliant choice by appointing Edmund Stafford the keeper of the Privy Seal; a year or two younger than Chaucer, he was second cousin to the Sir Ralph Stafford whom Holland murdered. He was a churchman of great learning, now dean of York; in him the king gained a devoted public servant whom he made chancellor in 1396, and who was retained on the council of Henry IV.

Richard's former enemies took the turnover in stride. They had never had any idea of deposing the king, and they knew that when he came of age they could go on as his "protectors" only with his consent. They may have thought him too weak-kneed or mercurial to assert his right, but when he did they knew he had called their bluff. They retreated with equanimity—one scholar thinks, with relief. It tells us something about Richard's demeanor and their sense of their circumstances that none fled for his life. The king having proclaimed that he would rule the better for the advice of his council, the Appellants proclaimed themselves well-wishers and bowed out of public life. The earl of Warwick retired to his country properties. The earl of Arundel planned a crusade or pilgrimage to the Holy Land, but never left; Henry of Bolingbroke went on a crusade to Prussia against the king of Lithuania; his uncle Gloucester followed him soon after, but his ship was turned back by storms. Mowbray, who had been the most moderate of the Appellants, quickly returned to the king's favor. In 1389 Richard sent him to Scotland, appointed him to a commission to make a truce, and made him warden of the east Marches. In 1390 the king proposed a pension for him, which set off a dispute in the council and the following year he made him captain of Calais for six years. And in 1394 he went to Ireland with Richard's army.

All was chivalry and gentilesse. Richard deferred a part of the recent subsidy (the tax on merchandise), which pleased the merchant class, and, incredibly, allowed to be paid the huge sum the Appellants had claimed for themselves. Continuity was his keynote: the measures of the Merciless Parliament were confirmed, and no impeachments, it was announced, would be instituted for any of its actions. Nor did Richard, as was feared, make any effort to recall his friends from exile. In due course he even restored Arundel, Warwick, and Gloucester to the council—and Arundel replaced Wykeham, after several years, as chancellor. All was appeasement and tranquillity.

Richard's policies, in which Gaunt collaborated, were intelligent and on the whole successful. He instituted—with a magnificent tournament held at Smithfield in October 1390—an effort to make permanent peace with France. The negotiations, begun in the next year with Gaunt as ambassador, started out with outrageous demands (the French wanted the surrender of Calais and the razing of its fortifications; the English, not to be outdone, wanted King Jean's ransom paid). The talks went on with many compromises and interruptions until May 1394 when the Truce of Lelighem was signed. It brought peace, as things turned out, for some time to come. Later in his reign Richard turned his attention to Ireland, went there himself with an army, and made some headway in organizing that part of his kingdom, introducing English chivalry to the Irish knight-hood like a missionary.

In 1392 the king had a fearsome clash with the citizenry of London. The Crown constantly borrowed money from the city, but on this occasion the city government turned down a request, and when a Lombard merchant provided the loan instead, a band of Londoners assaulted him. The king's reaction was extreme: he canceled the city's traditional liberties, deposed the mayor (Chaucer's friend John Hend, for whom he had stood surety in 1381), fired the sheriff, Henry Vanner (also a friend of Chaucer), and moved the royal court to York. John of Gaunt and Queen Anne prevailed on him to settle with the Londoners, which, however, cost the city £13,000. At Christmas there was a great celebration (the citizens gave the king among other gifts a camel), but the end result was the king's loss of friendly relations with the city.

The following year there was an uprising in Cheshire, of enough consequence to make Gaunt interrupt the peacemaking mission and return to England. It and a similar revolt in Yorkshire were by-products of peace with France: England was full of unemployed soldiers, and their discontent was extreme. Gaunt solved the problem by recruiting them for service in his duchy of Aquitaine and even pardoned their leaders. The uprisings, seemingly spontaneous, revived English paranoia—there was talk that they were instigated by Arundel and Gloucester, by the pro-war party, even by Richard himself, and these outrageous accusations were signals, not perceived at the time, of latent rage and discontent.

Richard's behavior in taking the reins of government was almost suspiciously estimable. He had been schooled in kingship and politics by the best possible teachers, he had a flair for the dramatic—he *knew*, one can argue, in the depths of his being, how he should stage-manage his assumption of full regal power, knew public interests must take precedence over private motives, and was prepared to compromise and forbear. Almost certainly "good Queen Anne" helped bring out and foster these abilities. Gone were the sudden outbursts and unstable turnabouts of his earlier years. One notion is that he had above all else learned how to *wait* —that during his years of powerlessness he had coldly, single-mindedly worked out a master plan to have revenge, that he adopted, in one historian's words, "a purposeful policy of ultimate revenge." Yet he did know how things had to be done, and he showed he was capable of compromise in the public interest. Richard was, one can argue, a brilliant and erratic young man who at twenty-two had assimilated the lessons of a lifetime spent as heir presumptive and then heir apparent among the privileged and powerful, and who might have been a ruler of genius if Fortune had not turned her wheel when he was twenty-seven.

Richard never forgot the humiliations he had suffered, and certain small incidents reveal how much the past was with him. Shortly after he declared his majority he ordered sent to Westminster Abbey the gift of a pair of slippers—red velvet slippers with floral designs composed of precious stones. They were to replace the slippers of Edward the Confessor, one of which had fallen from Richard's foot at his coronation, while Sir Simon Burley was carrying the weary ten-year-old through the crowd on his shoulders. Why was it still on his mind? People had thought it an ill omen, and it was, at least, the first of many misfortunes—he might in some dark recess of consciousness have thought the gift could turn his luck. Or, remembering the incident, he may have felt it as a failing in himself to have tired of the arduous ceremonies, to have let go his control. The gift, seen one way, was a rather touching act of making up for something lost or lacking. But seen another way, it was an act of inflated grandeur: he was replacing no ordinary article of footwear but the traditional coronation slippers, and the slippers he sent would be used in the coronations of the kings to follow him. At the center of the memory was the figure of his tutor, Sir Simon Burley, executed by the Appellants despite the king's pleas and his queen's, Bolingbroke's, and Mowbray's. Regarded as a conscious gesture, the gift was like a vow to avenge Burley, but it may have been a much more complex act, revealing how the king's hopes for the future were tied to the father surrogate of his childhood and adolescence. Three years later he arranged with the monks of the Abbey of Saint Mary Graces near the Tower of London, where Burley was buried, to hold an anniversary observance of his death and add his name to their list of martyrs. And he made a sustained but unsuccessful effort on behalf of Edward II, his deposed ancestor, now venerated in some quarters as a saint, to have him canonized.

Another signal that he had not forgotten the humiliations of the past was to come in 1394. Richard canceled Gloucester's life appointment as justice of Cheshire and North Wales and gave the post to Thomas Mowbray.

Chaucer as Clerk of the King's Works

King Richard is known as a patron of the arts. It is argued that his reign brought a renaissance to England—brought a new "Ricardian style" in literature; a new concept of "public poetry" addressed not to the court but to a public and dealing with national, not court concerns; and a surge of activity in painting, sculpture, architecture. Some think this notion of a Ricardian renaissance is exaggerated, that Edward III did more in such respects, that Henry IV was more of an intellectual, that Richard was not directly responsible for the activities going on during his reign. Unlike the other men in his family, he was not fundamentally a warrior—he fought in jousts and headed an army in Ireland, but his policy was for peace abroad and prosperity at home. And developments in the arts did take place during his reign, some at his instigation, some with his encouragement. Richard's reign, however, could not sustain a renaissance until 1389, when his troubles were over. When Queen Anne died in 1394, the loss seems to have changed him. His reign was a five-year period of glory followed by a declining aftermath, but there *was* activity in the arts and Geoffrey Chaucer was a part of this "Ricardian" movement, as a poet, of course, and as an administrator in the king's building program.

Some nine weeks after Richard assumed the powers of kingship, he appointed Chaucer the Clerk of the Works—the date on the papers is July 12, 1389. Chaucer held the post almost exactly two years. It was an arduous job, one usually held by clerics, and must have consumed most of his time. Some think he was dismissed, but it's more likely he asked to be released. Two years was not a short term: several clerks in Richard's reign served only one year, and the longest term was seven. Most held the office "during their pleasure," that is, as long as they were willing, which may have meant as long as they could stand it. Chaucer's office was conferred "as long as he conducts himself in that office well and faithfully," not an unusual condition if one had no previous experience in the job. But he had had plenty of experience in accounting, probably the most important of his functions—for the clerks of the Works had to deal with very large sums of money.

There was more than one clerk at a time. Each was assigned to superintend the upkeep, repair, or building of specific royal properties. The clerk hired the craftsmen and workers for a project, conferred with the architects, saw to the purchase of materials and the sale of "dead stock" (i. e., junk—right down to the branches and bark from trees cut down for timber), paid the workers and his staff of deputies and clerks, kept the books (not necessarily in his own hand), chased after workers who left their jobs without permission, and held sworn inquests about the disappearance of materials. A controller, William Hannay, was appointed to audit his accounts; Hannay had himself been Clerk of the Works for, among other things, Richard's coronation. Chaucer was paid the traditional salary, 2s. a day (which remained the same until the seventeenth century); it came to over £36 a year if Sundays were counted—a very high salary, twice that of the great architect Henry Yeveley. Chaucer's predecessor, one Roger Elmham, the one other layman to hold the post in Richard's reign, had more responsibilities than Chaucer did, but Chaucer's were extensive enough: they included Westminster Palace, the Tower, the castle of Berkhampstead, the manors of Kennington, Eltham, Clarendon House in Wiltshire, Sheen, the manor of Byfleet, King's Langley, Feckenham, Hatheburgh Lodge in New Forest, and their various lodges, gardens, millponds, structures, etc. It may have amused the author of *The Parliament of Fowls* and the Squire's Tale to know he was also in charge of the mews for the falcons. On the anniversary of his appointment he was also made clerk for the repair of the collegial chapel of Saint George at Windsor Castle, then on the point of ruin.

Some of the projects Chaucer administered were by Henry Yeveley, the leading architect of Chaucer's time, a genius whose work epitomizes the Perpendicular Style, which he perfected in England. Twenty or more years Chaucer's senior, he died the same year Chaucer did. In the 1360s he worked for the Black Prince, and made the alabaster tomb of the Duchess Blanche; in the following decade he worked on the Palace of the Savoy, only to see it destroyed in the Peasants' Revolt. It was probably he who designed the tombs of the Black Prince, Edward III, and Richard II. Famous in his own time, he was a royal esquire and held the title Master Mason of Westminster: after the earthquake of 1382 he had commissions to repair Saint Paul's Cathedral, Canterbury Cathedral, and the Tower of London. In the 1390s he designed Westminster Hall as we see it today, with its magnificent wooden roof (designed by his colleague Hugh Herland). There was scarcely any English artist who left a greater mark on that age, unless it was Chaucer himself; it must tell us something about Richard's reign that they worked together.

One of Chaucer's assignments was to supervise the building of the lists at Smithfield for the tournaments in May and October 1390, the spectacular overture of Richard's successful effort to establish peace with France. It was a major work of construction, and a gigantic piece of conspicuous waste, since it was used but once. There were scaffolds for the king and queen and other dignitaries, and a large area for the combats walled about with such materials as could withstand the weight of armed men and horses. It's often remarked that Chaucer's experience with this great tournament, a throwback to the glorious days of Edward III, may have inspired, at least in some details, the tournament he described in the Knight's Tale.

Chaucer was summoned to an audit a little sooner than was customary, in February 1391. He was to submit his accounts up until the previous Michaelmas. When this audit was almost complete, in June, he received orders to turn over his office to John Gedney. Evidently the already existing audit was updated at the end of his term and one inclusive audit made. It showed a surplus of £21 that the government owed him. There was a further sum of £66 on assignment from Sir William Thorpe that was uncollected when Thorpe died. Chaucer had listed the sum in his accounts as paid, so that it constituted a fictitious loan to the government —a common device for balancing the books. The debt was assigned to Chaucer and he collected it, but not until May 1393.

There are very good reasons to think Chaucer *asked* to be relieved. He had served almost two years. The job paid well, and it was prestigious —he seems now to have been called Sir Geoffrey, as a onetime member of Parliament and as Clerk of the Works, not because he was knighted but because it was customary for those holding these high offices. But it was also terribly demanding. He had to administer thousands of small details in several locations at once, and had to travel constantly. Here was the author of *Troilus and Criseyde,* some four years into his next work, a book of tales told on a Canterbury pilgrimage, and his time was taken up with endless talk and paper work, dispensing and collecting money, and keeping or supervising accounts.

And it was dangerous. He had to travel alone with large sums of money on him, and medieval roads crawled with thieves. On September 3, 1390, Sir Geoffrey was set upon by highwaymen and robbed of £20 of the king's money plus his horse and other property. The incident happened at a place called the Foul Oak at Hatcham, a hamlet outside Deptford in Kent, on the road Chaucer was traveling from London to the manor of Eltham, probably to pay workers. The robbers must have been watching him and learning his habits, for three days later he was robbed of £10 while in Westminster and on the same day, again at Hatcham, of £9 and 40-odd pence. A commission was appointed to look into the robberies—two of its members, as one might expect, had sat with Chaucer on the Commission of the Peace in Kent. The robber, named Richard Brierley, was apprehended and he confessed; he was a member of a gang that wandered through a number of counties. In jail he named his confederates, a William Huntingfield, former member of a Surrey gang, who had joined the Brierley group just before Chaucer was robbed, an Irishman called "Broad" (a cleric whose real name was Thomas Talbot), and his clerk Gilbert. They all had records; they were hardened criminals, and there was violence, for Chaucer is reported to have been wounded. They were tried in the Court of King's Bench before Sir Walter Clopton, lord chief justice, who had also sat on the Kentish Commission of the Peace with Chaucer. All were jailed or hanged eventually for one crime or another; Brierley was hanged after losing a judicial combat with one of his confederates who challenged him, and Talbot, who pleaded clergy, was turned over to the archdeacon of York as a clerical criminal.

For Sir Geoffrey this was the last straw. He had risen well above the average lot of a royal esquire, was exceptionally well paid, was in charge of many projects, was respected and trusted by the king. But when he reached this height he didn't like the work, or the danger, or the tedium. It was one thing to travel abroad with some colleagues and an armed escort, and represent with rhetorical flourish the king of England's desires, bargain in a foreign tongue, be entertained courteously and exposed to the customs, buildings, and books of a foreign culture. Traveling about hiring and paying stonemasons and carpenters and laborers, being robbed and beaten up by gangs of highwaymen and left without a horse to find safety, testifying at the numerous trials of the tawdry underworld characters— all that was a different story. And perhaps on the government's side his misfortunes and discontents were taken as signs he wasn't suited for the job. The lesson of Fortune was not to love worldly vanities because they will disappoint and betray you: Fortune had given him rank and riches, but they had not made him happy, and at length he decided to defy Fortune and request another post.

So Chaucer wrote a poem asking for "some better estate"—a better position, or better circumstances. He took a poem written earlier, "Fortune," one of the "Boethian" poems from the early 1380s, and added an envoi stating his request. The poem was a dialogue between a Plaintiff and Fortune, relevant to his circumstances only in a general way: the Plaintiff, declaring "Fortune, I thee defy," says Fortune cannot harm the man who has mastery over himself. Fortune agrees: he who possesses himself has enough—for no one is wretched unless he thinks he is. Fortune says thrice in a refrain that the poet "still has his best friend alive"; he answers that she cannot take his best friend from him. She concludes that she has given him riches and then taken them away, and she reminds him that she is executing God's will, that by nature the world is "ever restless travail." The "best friend" seems therefore to have meant himself, that is, his own good counsel.

But the envoi Chaucer added, spoken by Fortune, has a much more specific application, and here the "best friend" is the king:

Princes, I pray you, of your gentilesse,
Let not this man on me thus cry and plaine,
And I shall quitte° you your bisinesse — *repay*
At° my request, as three of you or twaine. — *attention to*
And, but° you list releve him of his paine, — *unless*
Prayeth his beste friend, of his noblesse,
That to some better estate he may attaine.

When Fortune says she'll "repay your attention to my request, three of you, or two," the reference is to an ordinance of the Privy Council passed in March 1390 in an effort to curb Richard's extravagant gifts, which decreed that his grants or gifts had to have the consent of his uncles, the dukes of Lancaster, York, and Gloucester, or any two of them. So we know the poem was written after March 1390, and—if the robberies were a phase of Chaucer's discontent—after September. The last sentence is puzzling, but seems to mean "And, unless it please you yourselves to relieve him of his discomfort, ask his best friend [to do so], of his nobility, so that he may attain to some better position." In June of 1391 he was directed to turn over his office to John Gedney. He was free.

Sir Geoffrey in Semiretirement

And after that he was in semiretirement, which meant a sharp drop in income. He was variously employed in minor capacities, and for the rest, we can suppose, returned to his writings. He had sold his Exchequer annuities to his friend Scalby two years before but may have still had income from them, and he still had the annuity of £10 per annum he received from John of Gaunt in 1374.

While he was Clerk of the Works, on March 5, 1390, a disastrous storm blew down more than a hundred oak trees at the king's manor at Eltham, which Chaucer had charge of. Along the banks of the Thames the marshes in Kent were flooded, a peril to farmlands. Walls and ditches to prevent flooding were the responsibility of individual landowners under the "law of the Marsh," and Chaucer was appointed within a week of the storm to a commission charged with overseeing their repair. The ditches were drainage canals, sometimes as much as 15 feet deep and 48 feet wide, that could serve as waterways for boats; they were called "sewers" (the modern meaning of the word was not to develop for two hundred years), whence the mistaken notion that Chaucer served on a sanitation commission. What he served on was a commission to hold hearings and determine responsibility (*oyer et terminer*), and to order repairs; it had power to levy fines up to £1,000. There were two lawyers on the commission, both of them sergeants-at-law, and four members, including Chaucer, who had vested interests in Kentish property, among them Chaucer's old friend Sir Richard Stury, now a member of the royal council.

Chaucer received, in 1390–1391, the post of subforester in the forest of North Petherton held jointly with one Richard Britte; he was reappointed alone in 1397–1398. The land belonged to Roger Mortimer, earl of March, then a minor. Sir Peter Courtenay, who was "farming" the property (collecting its income for a fixed payment), had a lawsuit pending against the Mortimers; possibly they appointed Chaucer to represent their interests. He held the post continually until his death, and his son Thomas was appointed to the same or a similar post in 1405. The records are extremely obscure; since it wasn't a government position, there was no bureaucracy to record it several times in French and Latin. He was appointed by the family, and the only evidence was a manor roll seen in the seventeenth century and reported two generations later, happily by a reliable writer. Chaucer's salary was not mentioned.

The records afford otherwise only brief glimpses of Sir Geoffrey in semiretirement. In 1392 he received a loan of 26s. 8d. (2 marks) from Gilbert Mawfield, a London merchant and moneylender whose clientele included John Gower and Henry of Bolingbroke, the future king, in fact everyone—bishops, knights, the mayor, the chamberlain, the city of London, even the king and the duke of Lancaster. At the time of his death Mawfield was heavily in debt to the Crown—his property was seized and his revealing account book went into the public records, which is how it survived and how we know of Chaucer's little loan. The loan was made on a Sunday in July for payment within a week (he evidently paid it) and was taken out just two weeks after he collected more than £13 still due on the accounts of the clerkship. In the fall of 1393 he was being sued for a debt of £3 6s. 8d. by William Venour, a London grocer, who was lending money, quite a lot of it, on the side. Another grocer in the next year was suing him for £2 4s. for unpaid bills. Chaucer's seeming poverty is a puzzle. Granted, a credit economy was like a new toy in the fourteenth century—banks and checkbooks lay in the future, and large amounts of cash invited theft. It may have been a habit among people of middle status to borrow small amounts and pay them off when they came by a large amount. Even so, it does appear that Chaucer was irresponsible about money. He was an expert accountant, who had kept the books of the Customs for twelve years and handled the enormous accounts of some dozen major projects when he was Clerk of the Works, but in his private finances he seems to have treated money as if it were not real. He was sued for debt over and over, and he paid for the most part, but he often ignored the orders to appear in court. He left the debt of a pound on the books of the Exchequer for a dozen years, until it was declared desperate, and after that until he died (perhaps in this instance there was some rancor; perhaps he claimed it wasn't owing).

Possibly his lax financial habits only reflect the government's own insouciance about credit. But one must consider whether he was a compulsive spender; or whether he was one of those people who think money will always come from somewhere (as for him it generally did, though not without his asking for it); or whether the picture of him that Harry Bailly draws, staring at the ground, withdrawn, incommunicative, didn't turn, as he grew older, into a picture of one so long in government service that he was quite capable of putting his debts out of mind along with courts, lawsuits, or any nuisance, in quiet little acts of passive aggression.

Soon his luck turned. In 1393 he received a gift of £10 from the king and in the following year a grant of £20 a year for life as a reward for good service. In 1395–1396 he was given a scarlet gown lined and trimmed with more than £8 worth of fur by Henry of Bolingbroke, earl of Derby, for what service is not clear. During these years Chaucer fairly often witnessed documents in Kent, some of them involving figures as significant as the archbishop of York. He was appointed an attorney of Gregory Ballard, one of the king's butlers, to take formal possession on his behalf of certain properties that had fallen to him when Arundel's estates were forfeited. Such services were often done by friends for friends; but these men were not, so far as we know, friends of Chaucer's, and he may have been charging fees for his services as a free-lance attorney.

Chaucer's social and private life during these years is as obscure as his finances. After his wife's death in 1387 he no doubt withdrew for a time. The following year was the horrid year of the Merciless Parliament; the year after that he was made Clerk of the Works. He had been thinking about remarrying; now, relieved of the clerkship, he must have had further thoughts in that direction. And apparently there was an involvement with some woman: in his poem to Bukton (1396) he indicates that he doesn't want to fall again into such "dotage"—and this can hardly be a reference to his marriage. "Dotage" meant senility, and when it was used, as here, to mean folly, it meant the folly of old age, not a marriage contracted in one's twenties. Chaucer's folly must have been to want to marry again, and probably to have had a particular woman in mind. There are a few short poems touching matters of the heart that might have been written about this time, but we can't be sure they're by Chaucer or have anything to do with his personal circumstances. Among them is "Against Women Unconstant"; it is modeled on a poem by Machaut and borrows his refrain —"Instead of blue, ye may well wear all green" (blue symbolized fidelity, green infidelity). It is a complaint against a faithless woman; she is, the poet says, worse than Delilah or Candace (who betrayed Alexander the Great), or Criseyde. The lyric has a genuinely harsh tone—the jilting lady is likened to a mirror's image and a weathercock, and she is told off in such terms as to make her little better than a whore; her only consistent quality is her changeableness and no one can wipe that defect from her heart— if she loses one lover, she'll get two. But the poem, if Chaucer wrote it, doesn't show us anything except that he was thinking along these lines, and in poetry of the French tradition such lines were a set theme.

Another poem, called "The Complaint of Venus," a triple ballade with an envoi addressed to "princes" or "princess,"* is loosely adapted from three ballades by the Frenchman Oton de Graunson, a knight from Savoy or Burgundy. In the envoi he apologizes for the paucity of rhyme in English (which makes translation word by word impossible), and addresses Graunson as the flower of poets in France. Graunson, who was about Chaucer's age, had long-standing connections with England and had been there as early as 1372. In 1391 he had been named as an accessory in the death of the count of Savoy, and now, two years later, his properties in Savoy had been seized. Having fought on the English side, he came to England in 1393 and swore allegiance to King Richard. The poem is thought to have been written for this occasion. Richard gave him an annuity of £126 13s. 4d., which could have made Chaucer envious —but then Graunson was a nobleman. Being a nobleman, he returned to France in 1397 to fight a judicial duel in defense of his honor, and was killed.

These are traditional French-style courtly poems done with skill, and they show us that Chaucer never left that mode behind him. The first two stanzas of the triple roundel called "Merciless Beautee," quoted above in chapter 2 as an example of the conventions Chaucer observed in his early poems, could have been written almost any time in his adult life,† and the abrupt transition to a third roundel joking about himself is a typically Chaucerian anticlimax. Its suddenness has made some critics question whether it could have been by Chaucer; Brusendorff thought the imagery of the third roundel was not like Chaucer's "ripe comic power" but crude after the manner of "more primitive forms of humour employed by lesser

*Some think Chaucer's poem, like Graunson's, was addressed to Isabella, daughter of the king of Castile and sister of the Duchess Costanza, who was now the duchess of York, and concerns a court intrigue. But the speaker in the poem is a woman and its circumstances have no bearing on Isabella. The line doubtless begins "Princes," and the poem was meant for a public court occasion welcoming Graunson.
†Some lines bear similarities to some poems of Deschamps that were brought to England by Chaucer's friend Sir Lewis Clifford about 1393–1394, which is proposed as the date of the poem; but the lines are commonplaces of courtly poetry.

men"—one wonders what he thought about the Reeve's Tale! But, as Alfred David remarks, "probably no English poet but Chaucer" could have written the splendid line, "Your eyen two woll slee me soddenly." One can fantasize that the first two roundels were written early and the third added later: the third rejects courtly love traditions as inapplicable to one who has developed a paunch, and his middle-aged paunchiness is then celebrated as his escape from Love's miseries:

> Syn° I fro Love escaped am so fat,   *since*
> I never think to been in his prison leane.
> Sin I am free I count him not a beane.
>
> He may answer and saye this and that,
> I do no fors°, I speak right as I meane.   *don't care*
>   Syn I fro Love escaped am so fat,
>   I never think to been in his prison leane.
>
> Love hath my name y-strike° out of his slate,   *erased*
> And he is strike out of my bookes cleane
> Forevermo, there is none other meane°.   *way*
>   Syn I fro Love escaped am so fat,
>   I never think to been in his prison leane.
>   Syn I am free, I count him not a beane.

In these lines Chaucer is thumbing his nose at the convention that lovers must be lean and suggesting that their leanness comes from their sighs and sleeplessness and loss of appetite: he describes himself jovially as fat and free, says Love has erased him from his slate and he has erased Love from his books (accounting books, they probably are) forever.

Making fun of courtly love conventions was part of the tradition. For example, the poem "To Rosemunde" presents the typical circumstance of a courtly song. The woman is "the shrine of all beauty" to the ends of the *mappamonde* (the medieval maps or drawings of the three continents), and her name is "Rosemunde" (*rosa mundi*, "rose of the world," that is, the essence of perfection, like a rose window design); the man is her worshiper, even though, as the refrain tells us, "ye to me ne do no daliance"—she doesn't talk with him or respond to his advances. This paragon, we learn, has round, red cheeks and a squeaky voice, rather like a child. It used to be thought she stood for the eight-year-old Princess Isabelle of France who was married to Richard II after the death of Queen Anne; but the poem is much too flip to be about a royal marriage (unless it was a private joke among Chaucer and his friends carefully kept from the king's eyes). It can be compared with Shakespeare's "My mistress' eyes are nothing like the sun," which is in the same tradition of parody;

but while Shakespeare concluded that he loves his unpromising mistress all the same, Chaucer concludes his mock praise of her by making fun of himself—seeing her dance is like an ointment for his wound, he weeps a vat full of tears, he is like a fish (not the fish on a hook, which was conventional, but a *cooked* fish wallowing in a sauce), and therefore he is "Tristan the Second," burning with amorous pleasure.

These poems, parodying the clichés of love poetry and the extravagances of courtly love (which was by definition *young* love), have the feel of a man's middle or later years, when men nurture such humorous defenses—that love is foolishness, that we now can laugh at youthful folly, that we have grown plump and can't be bothered.

Of course love was one thing and marriage another; a man of fifty in the role of lover was a comic figure, but it wasn't incongruous for a widower to remarry. In a verse epistle to his friend and fellow poet, Henry Scogan, dated 1393 by its reference to the torrential rains of that year, Chaucer describes what his feelings were about love and marriage as he entered his fifties. Scogan was some twenty years younger, one of the royal esquires, and at that time, as the poem indicates, in the royal household. "The Envoy to Scogan" humorously chides the younger man for having broken all the laws of Love: the seven gods (the planets) are weeping and wailing, Venus has drenched us with her tears in a "deluge of pestilence," and it's all Scogan's fault because, when his lady failed to see his distress, he gave her up and called on Cupid to witness it—probably in a poem he had sent to Chaucer.

He knows, he says, that his friend will say "Lo, old grisel list to ryme and playe!" (old graybeard likes to rhyme and joke), but no, he'll not excuse himself in rhyme:

> Ne think I never of sleep to wake my muse,
> That rusteth in my sheath still in pees°.   *peace*
> While I was young, I put it forth in press—
> But all shall pass that men prose or ryme.

Does this mean he's done with writing poetry? It sounds that way, but then he's writing a poem as he makes the statement, and what he says is "all shall pass that people write about in prose or rhyme. . . . Take every man his turn." The envoi of the poem changes the subject: Scogan is kneeling at the head of the stream (at Windsor, say the manuscript glosses) and here is Chaucer at its end (in Greenwich), as "dull as dead," forgotten in a "solitary wilderness." He asks Scogan to have a thought for his friend—and, oh yes, he adds, see to it you don't defy Love again. Suddenly the poem turns into a "begging poem," the whole matter about Love is brushed under the carpet, and the younger courtier is asked to put in a word for him. And Chaucer *was* awarded an annuity the following February.

It's a wonderful poem, crisp and witty and,well, *kittenish.* It's epistolary and personal, Horatian in its manner, amusingly evasive. Did he write it to enlist young Scogan's aid, using his defying Love as a pretext? Maybe so; one can't imagine Chaucer passing up a chance to increase his income. But the message that really emerges is of friendship, the special friendship of a shared world and shared interests; the jokes about defying Love, having gray hair and a round shape, writing poems, needing money, getting older reveal two men who have spent their lives in the common world of the king's court—their comradeship and sense of belonging is the real focus. The voice here is intensely personal, relaxed and humorously open: this is no "persona" but Chaucer himself addressing a trusted younger friend.

The abrupt change in the envoi, however, indicates that he has said enough. He has just said he won't defend himself in rhyme, won't wake his muse from its sleep—my muse, that is still *rusting in peace in my sheath.* It has been argued that this refers to a fallow period in his artistic life, just after which he started the Marriage Group—but does it sound like a poetical muse? Perhaps, some say, it is a Horatian figure and means his pen, his pen is rusting—an odd thing for a quill pen to do, but then the classical idea was that a satirist's pen is like a sword. Neither muses nor pens have sheaths; knives and swords have sheaths, and the knife or sword was a common figure for the penis in Middle English; in the next line he says "While I was young, I put it forth in press / But all shall passe"—all shall pass that men write of in prose and rhyme. He felt a connection between his sexual and his poetical powers, and knew that while both would pass, his writings would last longer and could outlive him. Here, in his last years, he seems to have been harboring the hope of the Italian humanists, that fame would confer a measure of immortality on earth. But there is an undertone of anxiety. The "muse" that he put to use when he was young is now rusting like a knife in a sheath ("*my* sheath"). He has fear of impotency on his mind, a not unusual fear in men of this age, and it becomes a symbol for the loss of other powers, but it is said with courtly wit, in mellow friendship and with humorous resignation.

Three years pass and Chaucer writes a similar verse epistle, "The Envoy to Bukton," to another friend, probably Sir Peter Bukton, eight years younger than Chaucer, who was in the service of the house of Lancaster and later a favorite of Henry IV; or possibly Sir Robert Bukton, who was in the king's service. Both were of the class of civil servants to which Chaucer belonged; and he addresses Bukton with the same intimate tone he took with Scogan. The poem can be dated from late 1396 by its reference to an expedition against Friesland in the autumn of that year. The implied circumstance is that Bukton is about to marry and has asked Chaucer's counsel; Chaucer says he promised to express "the sorrow and woe that is in marriage" (an echo of the Wife of Bath's Prologue) but doesn't really dare to write anything condemning it too strongly, "Lest I myself fall eft in swich dotage"—unless I fall into that senile folly myself a second time. This, if taken literally, suggests that Chaucer still had marriage on his mind, and "dotage" can't refer to his former marriage— it must suggest his recent thoughts or a recent effort at a second marriage. He proclaims marriage the devil's chain, by which if one is freed one would wish never to be bound again, and the "doted fool" that would *choose* to be chained again has it coming to him. In his advice to his friend he quotes Saint Paul, as the Wife of Bath did:

> But yet, lest thou do worse, take a wife;
> Bet° is to wed than bren° in worse wise.   *better / burn*

But, he adds, you'll have sorrow, and be your wife's thrall, and, if the Bible isn't good enough, "experience shall thee teach" (shades of the Wife again) that you'd rather be captured in Friesland than fall a second time into wedding's trap. The Frieslanders had, that very year, refused to ransom their countrymen and killed their English prisoners, so being captured there meant death—so much for marriage. In the envoi he tells his friend that if he has security he shouldn't take a risk. And he adds,

> The Wife of Bath I pray you that ye reade
> Of this mattere that we have on honde°.   *are discussing*
> God graunte you your life freely to leade
> In freedom; for full hard is to be bonde°.   *enslaved*

It's a teasing poem, like the one to Scogan, and its antimatrimonial sentiments were—to an extent still are—stock humor among men. If you listen to what women say among themselves, Chaucer implies, it will confirm the arguments against marriage, and he cites the Wife of Bath as if she were a church father. Her prologue and tale were finished by now and had been circulating, and perhaps through them he had persuaded himself that it was better not to remarry. In the poem to Bukton he's still talking wittily to a fellow courtier, taking pleasure in their common world and their friendship. But the subject is marriage, not love, and he calls it sorrow and woe, the devil's chain, a prison, a trap, slavery. Yes, it was a conventional joke not to be taken too seriously, but there is a harshness

of tone that cannot be overlooked. He can speak now as one free of
marriage, and the reader does, as Derek Brewer remarks, "sense a real
relief in it." It is as if between 1393 and 1396 Chaucer had grown old.

The Deaths of the Ladies: 1394

In those years, between 1393 and 1396, England itself underwent a
transition. On March 25, 1394, as John of Gaunt was preparing to leave
for France, the Duchess Costanza died. Her younger sister, Isabella, who
had married Edmund, duke of York, and led a rather scandalous life in
the English court, had died two years before; but at forty, Costanza's life,
unlike her sister's, had been morose and isolated, consecrated to an obsession about her father, a life of religiosity practiced in part as an escape.
Though she had been an exile in England over twenty years, she had made
little effort to learn English or adapt to English life. She had come to
England in her teens to find her grown-up husband provided with a
mistress. Her son, John, died in infancy; her daughter was now queen of
Castile. She was but half a wife to the duke: Katherine Swynford's relation
with Gaunt was now acknowledged and accepted—she attended court
affairs with him and played the hostess in his household. It is the classic
example of the fact that for medieval noblemen love was a private affair
and marriage a political one. Costanza had taken, and perhaps preferred,
a back seat. Philippa Chaucer had been in her service, and Chaucer would
have known the duchess, possibly wrote poems for her or read his works
before her court. He must have had a feeling for her that others at court
didn't have, for in his writings he shows an almost inborn sympathy for
women exiled and alienated, left to their own devices in a man's world.
He could not have foreseen that Gaunt, a stickler for proprieties, would
marry Katherine Swynford two years later and prevail on the king to
legitimize their children.

Then, on July 4, Mary, countess of Derby, wife to Gaunt's son
Henry, died in childbirth. Henry had returned from his pilgrimage the
year before, having left in 1390. She was twenty-four. She had borne him
six children, four sons and two daughters, of whom the oldest, born in
1387, was to be the legendary "Prince Hal," later King Henry V.

In the same year John of Gaunt had asked Parliament to reconsider
the question of the succession; the earl of March had laid claim to the
throne nine years before, and his claim was accepted. The succession had
become a matter of general anxiety because Richard and Anne had still
produced no heir, and it seemed apparent that they would not. Gaunt
came up with a mad story—that Edward Crouchback (son of Henry III)

had been true heir to the throne but was put aside because of his deformity, in favor of Edward I; this put Henry of Bolingbroke in a direct line through his mother Blanche. Gaunt produced a forged chronicle to help resolve the matter, but left for France with it still unresolved. Henry did not remarry until the throne was his.

Between these two deaths, on June 7, 1394, Queen Anne died at Sheen, of a sudden illness, in her twenty-eighth year. Richard, always volatile in expressing his emotions (most often rage), now fell into an agony of grief, notable even in an age when men were given to strong feelings and not ashamed to weep in public. He was dependent on her in the profoundest way; all the kingdom had come to love her for the sweet nature that her effigy displays, and Richard got from her a kindly tenderness and understanding that he needed. Daughter of the emperor, Anne was well educated and well read, and had absorbed from her upbringing a political sense; in Richard's darkest hour, when his friends were dead and exiled and John of Gaunt abroad, it must have been she who helped him plan his course. It was said he never let her leave his side— perhaps no great exaggeration, for he went through his adolescence and his twenties with her as his confidante. That she bore him no children, a great failing in a medieval queen, did not mitigate his or his people's love for her; the reason for their infertility was and is a mystery. Her body lay in state at Sheen until August 2, when it was taken in procession to Westminster Abbey, and there she was buried with long and solemn rites.

The funeral was marred by the hostile comportment of the earl of Arundel. He failed to join the procession and came late to the obsequies, then asked to leave early, as he said, for urgent private reasons. Richard, enraged by the churlish insult, grabbed a staff from a verger and knocked him to the floor, drawing blood and therefore desecrating the sanctuary; the rites were halted while the necessary prayers were said, and Arundel was dragged off to the Tower. In a week he was ordered before the king at the archbishop's manor in Lambeth to take an oath of good behavior, with his brother the archbishop and nine magnates and nobles as mainpernors—his surety was the humiliating sum of £40,000.

Chaucer must have been present at the queen's funeral. One would suppose he went also to the funeral of the Duchess Costanza, though she was buried in Saint Mary's, Leicester, about a hundred miles from Greenwich, no short journey. The deaths of the three great ladies of that time put the court into a melancholy mood, and Chaucer was beyond a question deeply affected; two of them may have been his patronesses, and all had surely heard him read his poems. The queen, if we may take his word for it, assigned him to write the *Legend*. All three of them were among the nineteen ladies of the Garter mentioned in the *Legend of Good*

Women. Their deaths would have brought to Chaucer from the still halls of memory the deaths of the Duchess Blanche and Queen Philippa—which occurred, like these, in a single year—and the death of his wife. For all his fascination with women, his fondness for them and attraction to them, his ability to have them for companions, care about them, see into their minds, and depict them in his writings—for all this, his relationships with women had been, in retrospect, disappointing. The deaths of the ladies impressed it on him, too, that he was beyond the age of love or marriage. In the same year he learned of the death of Sir John Hawkwood, the English mercenary with whom he had negotiated in Milan in 1378. These deaths of 1394 set him to brooding on his own. His spirits turned to morose preoccupations with the brevity and vanity of human life. The image of the grimly smiling skeleton with a spear came back to him from the plague years of his childhood, and with it the great lesson of that time: *beth ready for to meet him evermore.*

When Queen Anne died Chaucer abandoned *The Legend of Good Women,* leaving the last few lines of the ninth legend unfinished. If our dates are right and if the legends were produced one a year, he would have been working on that ninth one at the time. Conceivably, each legend was meant to be dedicated or addressed to one of the ladies of the Garter. Having abandoned the legends, he made a revision of the prologue that has survived in a single manuscript. The two versions of the prologue are called F and G after two Cambridge manuscripts. In recent years it has been established that G is the later, revised one. The F version is closer to the sources, whereas G omits a number of conventional details and has a number of lines that echo phrases from *The Canterbury Tales* (not begun, or barely, when F was written). And G adds several references to old age, which as we have seen began to preoccupy the poet about this time. Most tellingly, the G version omits references to Queen Anne, especially the lines where Chaucer is told to bring his poem to her "at Eltham or Sheen"—they would have been too painful for the bereaved king, whose enormous grief could not have borne a reference to his lady's favorite manor, Sheen. The chronicler Adam of Usk reports that Richard ordered it destroyed, "by reason that that lady's death happened therein."

Some readers prefer the earlier prologue, mostly because of the magnificent passage where the poet worships the daisy; in the later version it is shorter and comes inside the dream, not before it. Chaucer, wanting to displace emphasis from ideal femininity to the more concrete theme of good women, added thirty or so lines to Love's accusation against him that explain why he was assigned this theme. The ladies themselves, rather than the narrator, sing the ballade "Hide, Absolon." And the narrator wakes up before the legends start, so that the legends are presented as history; in the earlier version they were part of the dream. The revised version shows us that Chaucer had the discipline to cut passages of poetic dazzle for the sake of focus.

Why did he go on revising the prologue to the *Legend* when its occasion was a thing of the past? He may have started the revision earlier, but its date, on internal evidence, is after Queen Anne's death. It is uncertain that he meant to present it to the king, to whom even the revised version could have been upsetting, and the best guess is that he went on to finish it out of devotion to her memory, or to keep his promise, or for his own satisfaction. He had reason to be grateful to the king, who had given him, in February of that year, the annuity of £20 for life, possibly as a reward for writing the legends so far completed.

And why did he want to work at the *Legend* now when he was busy with *The Canterbury Tales*? For this there is a feasible explanation having to do with the writer's art. In *The Canterbury Tales* he was doing something bold, something never done before; it may have created a kind of interior balance for him to be writing at the same time another frame narrative that is a conventional courtly dream vision. The frame of the *Legend* is pure introduction, the introduction of a theme; the tales are not told by tellers but by himself in the role of court poet, and they do not relate to each other but are in a string, each related only to the theme. For a writer to achieve an inner balance in such a way is not unusual; one might call a work written for this reason, or on this instinct, a "blotter work"—a work that a writer uses as a foil to another work of a different kind. It would be why Henry James wrote plays, why scholars write detective stories, or novelists book reviews. Chaucer may have found in a conventional dream vision actually written for the court a means of working out his revolt against courtly tradition.

Richard II: 1394–1399

A few months before the queen died, Richard had taken away from Gloucester his life appointment as justice of Cheshire and North Wales and bestowed it on Thomas Mowbray. Mowbray, it will be recalled, was the same age as the king, and had been, with de Vere, one of those closest to him. But in 1385 Mowbray had married a sister of Arundel, and accompanied his new brother-in-law on a successful expedition against the French, Flemish, and Spanish. When he returned, de Vere wouldn't speak to him and the king was cool. He retired to his estates. Though a moderate and the last to join the Appellants, Mowbray had been with the army that routed de Vere at Radcot Bridge, and had been removed from the privy council with the other Appellants when Richard declared his majority. But it was in Richard's interest to win him over, and within a few months Mowbray was back, the first to be reconciled. Richard's cousin Henry of Bolingbroke was soon back on the council too, and both were given major responsibilities. The shake-up reveals Richard's aims toward Gloucester; and it may reveal his secret longing for the close, intense friendships of his youth.

After Costanza's death, John of Gaunt returned to France until the Truce of Lelighem was signed in May; in the fall, Richard went on his first expedition to Ireland, taking Mowbray with him. They were there eight months. Henry of Bolingbroke stayed in England, a member of the council that ruled in the king's absence. He was now twenty-nine. He had done all the things one was supposed to do—married, fought in the lists, gone on a crusade and on the Jerusalem pilgrimage. He was a warrior, as Richard was not. But he did not have the dazzling intelligence Richard had; where Richard was brilliant and erratic, Henry was, already before his thirties, stodgy.

On returning from Ireland, the king had the body of Robert de Vere, whom he had in happier days made the duke of Ireland, brought from Louvain to be reburied in his family tomb at Earls Colne in Essex. There was an elaborate funeral. At one point Richard ordered the coffin opened and gazed long and with indecipherable emotion at the face of the embalmed corpse, grasping the hand of his dead friend and, according to one account, placing a ring upon one of the fingers. The gesture, if it occurred, may have been a conscious pledge of vengeance; but it may have been an impulsive, theatrical act of devotion, which itself helped to fuel a vengeance long held under check.

In that year, 1395, Richard appointed Edmund Duke of York, his son, the earl of Rutland, Mowbray, and others, to a commission charged with negotiating a final peace and alliance with France. The means to this end was of course a royal marriage to the French princess, Isabelle, who was eight years old. Richard had, it appears, learned the lesson of *The Parliament of Fowls* very well: other brides were proposed, but political advantage pointed to the French child bride, even though it would further delay the birth of an heir. Richard's grief over Anne's death probably made a child bride more feasible than an adult, even preferable. The truce was signed in March 1396 and the proxy marriage held a week later. The following autumn the marriage itself was performed at Calais in a lavish celebration with ostentatious fashions and much exchanging of gifts. In November the princess came to London in a grand ceremonial entry; she was crowned on January 7, 1397. The whole production of truce and marriage is said to have cost over £200,000, but it was cheaper than another war. As things turned out, Richard *loved* the little princess—the chroniclers comment on his fondness for her, the devotion he lavished on her. Leaving again for Ireland he bade her a tender and emotional farewell. He had no children, she was of an age to be his daughter, and he longed for affection since Anne's death.

The day before the child queen's coronation was the king's birthday: he had just turned thirty. By modern theories, young men between twenty-eight and thirty-three are in a transition: having entered adult life they face a period of settling down, and the upheaval often involves a withdrawal from the mentors of one's twenties. But Richard during his twenties had suffered extreme deviations from the usual life pattern. His chief mentor, Burley, was put to death by self-appointed protectors of an abusive and cruel nature, and his closest friend, de Vere, five years older than he, was forced to flee the country. Apart from John of Gaunt, who was out of the country much of those years, there were few if any mentors to outgrow; for him the "age thirty transition" was a time to even scores. His seven years of full reign were something he could take pride in; he had almost universal support among the peerage, he had established lasting peace with France, and his reign was a small golden age in building and the arts. He had every reason to feel confident of support, to have faith in his power and in his mystical ideals of kingship. In that year he was approached by two of the electors of the Holy Roman Emperor to discuss the possibility of his replacing Wenceslas, his former brother-in-law; the overtures, part of a scheme of Pope Boniface's, came to nothing, but they inspired Richard with ambition and a sense of kingly grandeur.

So the time was ripe to act on impulses he had forced himself to rise above. And Fortune picked this time to lay opportunity before him. Richard had made an agreement with the duke of Brittany about the fortress at Brest, captured by Edward III in 1342: England gave it back and the duke pledged the use of it for the duration of the war—for a sizable loan from England and the grant of certain English properties. Brest was a territory at the westernmost coast of France, on the Cape of Finistère, administered from the fortress (it included at its southern extremity Penmarch, scene of the Franklin's Tale). The agreement was an equitable one that met no opposition. But in April, during the final course of a dinner in Westminster, the duke of Gloucester turned the conversation to the plight of soldiers returning from Brest. The king assured him of what would be done for them. Gloucester pursued the matter, saying the king ought first to risk his life capturing a city before he started giving away the ones his ancestors captured. The king made him repeat the remark, then asked his uncle heatedly if he took him for a merchant or a traitor. The evening ended with civilities, but the rift did not close.

In August the Appellants of 1388—Gloucester, the earl of Arundel and his brother Thomas (now archbishop of Canterbury), Warwick, Thomas Mowbray, and Henry of Bolingbroke—dined at Arundel Castle. They swore, so it was said, to stand together until the king and the dukes of Lancaster and York were imprisoned and the other lords of the king's council executed; but it seems impossible Henry of Bolingbroke could have taken such an oath against his father. Mowbray told the king about the plot, and the king issued orders for the arrest of Warwick and Arundel; he went himself, with a strong armed guard of knights and archers, to have the pleasure of arresting Gloucester, whom he found on a sickbed. They told Gloucester he was needed at once in the council and so got him inconspicuously out of the castle. Once out of sight he was taken prisoner and turned over to Mowbray, who was captain of Calais, to be imprisoned there. Arundel and Warwick, arrested in similar fashion, were imprisoned in the Tower.

All was ready for a trial before the autumn Parliament. It was to follow, with exquisite irony, the format of the Merciless Parliament. There were eight nobles (Mowbray was one) who were to accuse the three arrested men of treason. A temporary structure was made for the Parliament, Westminster Hall being under reconstruction. The king's Cheshire Archers and the armed retainers of others made it a display of military power; at one point there was a small agitation, and the king's archers created a panic by drawing their bows, until Richard ordered them at ease. The eight accusers appeared in red silk robes to make their accusations. Arundel was tried first; he demanded trial by battle but it was refused him —as it had been refused to Brembre in 1388. He had tart answers for various charges, but at length the king asked him if he and his fellows had not, against the king's word that there was "no cause of death in him," slain Sir Simon Burley. He gave no answer. John of Gaunt, as seneschal of England, sentenced him to a traitor's death and the forfeit of his properties. The king magnanimously allowed him to be beheaded (rather than the hanging and mutilations traditional for traitors). According to Froissart, his son-in-law, Mowbray, put the blindfold on him. One chronicler claims that his head was chopped off on the same spot where Burley was beheaded.

Warwick's trial was quite otherwise. Adam of Usk says he confessed "like a wretched old woman . . . wailing and weeping and whining." Asked who had tempted him to treason, he named Gloucester and some others, and the king, taking this for an admission of conspiracy, exclaimed that his confession was more pleasing to him than all the lands of Gloucester and Arundel. Warwick forfeited his possessions and was sent into exile on the Isle of Man—then in short order to the Tower, and there he remained until he was freed by Henry IV.

When it was time for Gloucester's trial, the king had it announced —he had known it all along—that the duke had died in prison. A confession, purported to have been obtained from him by Sir William Rickhill, was read aloud; in it he begged for mercy. His estates were forfeited— Richard had already split them up (as he did Arundel's and Warwick's) and bestowed them on various people. Possibly Gloucester died, as was announced, of the sickness he already had, which could have been exacerbated by poor treatment. But it is no less possible that he was murdered there on the king's orders. For his murderer there are four suspects, one of them his jailer Mowbray. For the motive, probably the king feared a confession and plea for mercy might get him leniency; and murder was simpler—if he had been convicted, John of Gaunt would have had to pass sentence on his own brother. Then too if we remember Gloucester's treatment of Burley and his nasty words to Queen Anne, murder was what Richard had in his heart.

Thus the king had his revenge, and it came closer to justice than the acts of the Merciless Parliament had, for it was a personal action of the king's against particular individuals. Archbishop Arundel, who had been involved only because of the earl his brother, forfeited his properties and was sent into exile. As for the other Appellants of 1388, Mowbray had been reconciled with the king and had given evidence against the conspirators, and Bolingbroke, as Gaunt's son, was untouchable.

After the revenge there had to be rewards. Arundel's estates were given to Mowbray and he was made duke of Norfolk; Henry of Bolingbroke was made duke of Hereford; Rutland was made duke of Albermarle or "Aumerle," and so on. When Henry triumphed, they lost these titles and went back to their former ones. This mountain of confusing detail passed from the chronicles of Chaucer's time to Holinshed and from him to Shakespeare; it is what makes most histories of those years so frustrating, and what makes *Richard II* so hard to sort out but so authentic as a view of late medieval life.

There is no reason to think Chaucer witnessed any of these events of 1397. He was feeling old, was probably in ill health; the year before he had written the verse epistle to Bukton with its melancholy view of remarriage. Nor is there any passage in his writings that suggests these events. Of their cause he had vivid memories, for he had sat in the Merciless Parliament of 1388. He was on the king's side, had received a generous annuity from him two years before. He had by now retired from court life, but when he heard the details of Arundel's beheading, Warwick's imprisonment, and Gloucester's murder, he must have heard them with approval.

"The King is Dead, Long Live the King"

Parliament met again at Shrewsbury the following January. Roger Mortimer, earl of March, heir presumptive to the throne, was summoned to take the oath of loyalty to Richard—he had been absent from the last Parliament, when the others had done so, because he was in Ireland as king's lieutenant. He took the oath on his first day there and returned at once to Ireland. That same year he was killed in battle by Irish rebels, and Richard recognized his eight-year-old son Edmund Mortimer as heir presumptive.

At this Parliament, news broke of a quarrel between Henry of Bolingbroke (then the duke of Hereford) and Thomas Mowbray (then duke of Norfolk). Bolingbroke told the story and made the accusation: when they had met on the road to London a month before, Mowbray made a remark about the danger they were in as the two remaining Appellants and claimed that Henry's father, Gaunt, was also on the list of those to be destroyed. When Henry protested that he and Mowbray had been pardoned, Mowbray replied "So were Arundel and Gloucester," and suggested they take steps before it was too late.

Bolingbroke later said that Gaunt advised him to tell the king, which he did. But betraying a fellow knight's confidence was against the code of chivalry, and one may doubt that Gaunt advised it. For Richard it was a dilemma: if Henry were shown a liar he would be disgraced, but if he were believed Mowbray could be given a traitor's death. Richard, not knowing which opportunity to seize, made an effort to reconcile them, announced that the quarrel would be brought before the Parliament, and had them both arrested. Henry, with the vast Lancastrian wealth behind him, produced bail; Mowbray, unable to put up bail, was confined to Windsor Castle. Parliament had adjourned, and the case was heard by the usual committee appointed to finish up its business. Bolingbroke added two further points to his accusation—that Mowbray had murdered his uncle Gloucester (as quite possibly he did) and had misused public funds. The committee decided in advance that if Henry could not prove his allegations the matter would be settled by judicial combat; in April it declared he had not proved them, and the combat was set for Coventry on September 16.

This was the famous Coventry Lists of Shakespeare's opening scene.

They were publicized all over England and Europe. The king made his armory available to the two contestants, Bolingbroke sent to Milan for armorers, Mowbray to Germany. When the day came, with a huge crowd and lavish pageantry, it was quite as dramatic as Shakespeare's version. Henry, duke of Hereford, as the challenger, entered first, on a white courser banded with green and blue velvet cunningly embroidered with gold figures of swans and antelopes. Then the king with the peers of the realm entered in solemn procession. At last Thomas Mowbray, duke of Norfolk, the defendant, entered on a horse banded with crimson velvet embroidered with lions and mulberry trees. The trumpets sounded, the combatants began to charge at each other. At once the trumpets sounded a different call. The king had thrown down his staff to signal a stay. The armed knights turned their horses, dismounted, and took seats while the king consulted with the peers and the audience fidgeted. It was two hours before the king's secretary announced that Henry of Bolingbroke was sentenced to exile for ten years, and Mowbray to exile for life and the confiscation of his properties. Both would receive an allowance. Richard apparently decided that to have one of them die and one live was not what he wanted; this way, he was rid of them both. The judgment looked like a snap decision, but it may have been thought out carefully in advance, even discussed with certain peers. The announcement of it, made suddenly before an international audience, is an example of Richard's predilection for the dramatic. He turned a great chivalric contest into an anticlimactic shambles at the last possible minute, and it must have given him a wonderful sense of power. But his capriciousness, which seemed childish in former days, now begins to seem unbalanced.

Richard may have meant to bring Henry back after the dust settled, and he did reduce the years of his exile to six on Gaunt's plea. But he had little reason to hasten Henry's return. Mowbray took ship for Holland and traveled from there to Italy. A year later he was dead, in Venice—various accounts have him about to leave for or just returned from the Jerusalem pilgrimage. Henry, duke of Hereford, was seen off by a huge crowd of weeping Londoners—an image that must have impressed itself upon him —and proceeding to Paris was entertained at the French court. He was given twice the allowance Mowbray was, £2,000 a year, and was guaranteed the inheritance of his father's estate. This last was an oversight: he was to inherit vast wealth and almost regal powers, and his father was now advanced in years. Richard was not rid of him at all.

John of Gaunt died at Leicester after a long illness on February 3, 1399, exactly a year after he had made his will. His death left Henry of Bolingbroke sole inheritor of the vast estates and palatine powers of Lancaster. Gaunt had behaved honorably and nobly to Richard, and

Richard, finally loving him for it, rewarded him with an excess of generosity that now gave to his heir more power than any monarch could tolerate. Therefore on March 18 Richard took an unbelievable step, by which he sought to eliminate this colossal threat and, incidentally, fill his coffers: he extended Henry's exile to life and confiscated the Lancastrian estates.

About the consequences he had not thought enough; to his mind, it was the only course and the best one, and he shut his eyes to the apprehension it would cause in all landowning barons and the reaction it would provoke in Henry, which he did not wait to learn. In April, Richard made out his will; at the end of May he embarked on his second Irish expedition. It's hard to believe he left the country vulnerable to an invader at this moment, but, puffed up with a sense of his own omnipotence or obsessed with his Irish goals, he did just that. His only precaution was to take hostages, among them Henry Beaufort, now bishop of Lincoln, who was Chaucer's nephew, and Bolingbroke's son Henry, "Prince Hal," then eleven.

Almost immediately, at the end of June, Henry set sail for England. He had with him about a hundred supporters in three ships. They sailed up the east coast of England, stopping here and there to sound out what sort of support they might expect, and landed at Ravenspur. They occupied several Lancastrian properties, making their headquarters at Pontefract Castle. Here they rallied their allies—Northumberland, Hotspur, Westmoreland—and conducted a campaign of propaganda. Nasty rumors were spread about Richard; Gaunt's story about Edmund Crouchback was revived; Henry of Bolingbroke piously claimed he had only come to reclaim his inheritance. Recruits arrived in abundance—more than could be used. Richard's regency government sent a messenger to Ireland to inform the king, but failed to underscore the danger; most of them in their hearts supported Henry's claim. The war-loving bishop of Norwich raised a force to support his sovereign, but other military powers were sparse, and there were desertions and surrenders. Within weeks Henry had massive support; to all intents and purposes he had taken England.

When the news reached Ireland, Richard called his council at once. Salisbury was sent ahead to rally the loyalists in Cheshire, and the army marched to South Wales to take ship for England. But by the time they arrived, Bolingbroke was in control. Richard suffered massive desertions from his army; his only choice was to go and meet Salisbury at Conway Castle. He rode in haste the 160 miles to North Wales, only to find that Salisbury had been unable to hold together a loyalist army in the king's absence. All but a handful had gone home.

Henry, learning the king's whereabouts, marched to Chester with a gross treachery planned. Richard sent two ambassadors to him, who were to offer him his inheritance; Henry seized them as hostages. In turn he sent ambassadors to Richard, offering more or less reasonable terms, and Richard after several days accepted (his council at Conway taking careful note that the decision was made under duress and could be withdrawn). At the conclusion of the talks, the king and his followers rode along with Henry's ambassadors toward Chester. When they entered the forest they were aware of armor and weapons flashing among the trees: in a terrible breach of chivalry, they were ambushed by Henry's army. Richard was taken prisoner by Northumberland, who had only the day before sworn on the Blessed Sacrament that Henry meant no treason. Along the way an attempt to rescue the king failed. He was taken to London, on a pony and in an ordinary black gown, to Westminster Palace. In the morning he heard mass in the Abbey that he loved and then was removed to the Tower.

In the late Middle Ages the sanctity of kingship had obtained almost a mystical character, and to that idea Richard subscribed with all his heart. This medieval "political theology" held that the king's earthly body is incorporated, at his coronation, and especially in the anointing, into a spiritual "body politic" of which he is the head. From this spiritual position he cannot be removed against his will except by death, when his heir replaces him. It is the basis of the phrase "The king is dead, long live the king": when the king dies in his earthly body, his people acclaim the spiritual kingship that passes to his heir. What it meant was that Richard must abdicate before Henry could take the throne, unless he could be proved a rex inutilis—one not fit to reign. Henry pressed his claim on the grounds of his father's story, supported by a forged chronicle, that Edmund Crouchback had been the true heir; if it were so, he inherited the kingship from Henry III through the line of his mother, the Duchess Blanche—which meant the three Edwards and Richard II were not true kings. This hereditary right was his first argument; second, he claimed the throne by conquest. Henry was an opportunist: he came to England, as he said, to claim what was his own, but when he saw that he could claim the throne, he proceeded. He asked Parliament to support his claim, but he carefully avoided anything that suggested Parliament controlled the kingship.

Richard, confronting Henry, asked several times for a fair and public trial, but he received none. Henry suavely explained that the council wished him kept confined until Parliament met; when he asked to see his wife, Henry said the council forbade it. When the estates and the people (technically not Parliament) met at the end of September, Henry had in his hand an abdication signed by Richard. They accepted it. After this a long list of Richard's alleged wrongs was read. They agreed to it. Henry then rose, made the sign of the cross, and, speaking in English, claimed the throne by descent, showing a signet ring he said Richard gave him in the Tower. Those assembled accepted his claim. In this meeting (but this was omitted from Lancastrian accounts) the bishop of Carlisle, Thomas Merke, boldly spoke against condemning the king without a hearing. He called upon them to bring him in and "hear what he has to say, and to see whether he be willing to relinquish his crown to the duke or not"—for which the bishop was thrown into prison.

As for the abdication, the Lancastrian versions have Richard cheerfully agree to it—which does not sound like Richard. He was never again seen in public. On the day following, October 1, Parliament sent messengers to inform him of the act of deposition and the withdrawal of allegiance. When they said he would have to renounce the dignities of kingship, he replied that he could not renounce the mystical nature of kingship imparted by his anointing. When they said he had admitted he was unworthy to reign, he denied it. If in Richard's discourse there was anything like the sonorous speeches Shakespeare wrote for an actor, they were spoken in prison, while he was dining, and reported by Adam of Usk: "My God, a wonderful land is this, and a fickle; which hath exiled, slain, destroyed, or ruined so many kings, rulers and great men, and is ever tainted and toileth with strife and variance and envy."

Henry was crowned on October 13, 1399. It seems likely that Chaucer attended the ceremony as a retired official of the court. What he thought about Richard's fall and Henry's coronation we can only guess. As we shall see, he won the favor of the new monarch with a poem, in which he gave him his allegiance. He would have known both these young men, now in their early thirties, from former days, and would have had fond memories of each. Richard, born in Bordeaux, was not brought to England for several years, and by then was heir presumptive: his life was sequestered in the closed world of the royal household, but Chaucer, through Sir Simon Burley, became involved with Richard's preparation for kingship when the king was still a child. Henry, Gaunt's eldest son by the Duchess Blanche, was raised in the Duchess Costanza's court by a governness, the Lady Katherine, Chaucer's sister-in-law.

Later, though Chaucer had known the youthful king to misbehave in disappointing ways, he had seen him treated with barbaric indignity by Gloucester and the Appellants, and he had seen him claim his throne and rule with kingly grace. It was a happy ending, and Chaucer could take satisfaction in what he had contributed, through his writings, to the formation of Richard's character. In his heart he must have applauded the king's revenge on the Appellants, for he had suffered, too, in those dark years. That Bolingbroke was one of the Appellants surely disappointed

Chaucer—as it evidently disappointed or embarrassed John of Gaunt. Chaucer would have seen the two young men in very different ways. Richard had a more lively intellect, was articulate and theatrical, had a poet's instincts; he admired and patronized poetry, including Gower's and Chaucer's, promoted the arts and brought—or seemed to bring—to England for a time a renaissance in building and architecture, painting, the crafts of the goldsmith or enameler. One wouldn't have seen interests of this kind in Bolingbroke. When suddenly he returned from exile and took the nation by storm in a matter of weeks, Chaucer, though out of court life, would have heard all the tidings from Westminster. One must assume he felt disgust at the crass, tyrannical behavior of Henry toward Richard, and sorrowful that Richard's shortcomings, among so many virtues, had brought his fall.

Henry's coronation was not the grand affair young Richard's had been. He was at pains to observe every precedent, as any usurper must be. There was no hint of any change in government or kingship—it wasn't revolution but destiny, he meant to convey. As for the sacred mystery of kingship that Richard still claimed was imparted to him by the coronation anointment, Henry's public relations experts managed to come up, and just in time, with the true sacred oil vouchsafed by the Virgin to Saint Thomas of Canterbury and discovered by Edward II. A rumor went around, possibly started by Henry's party, that King Richard had meant to have himself recrowned, using it. It was found in an eagle-shaped receptacle, lost so long that none remembered it. And with this superior oil Henry of Bolingbroke was anointed.

Two weeks after the coronation Richard was removed from the Tower disguised as a forester. At Christmastime, there was an armed uprising of Richard's supporters, but Henry's forces crushed it. In February 1400 Richard was dead. The pro-Lancastrian chroniclers say he starved himself to death, the French chroniclers that he was murdered by Sir Piers Exton. If he was killed, care was taken that his death seem natural, easily managed in a winter prison. The body was sealed in lead with the face exposed and taken slowly to London; at every town people gazed on it, had the ocular proof of his death that Henry wanted them to have.

There was a rumor that Richard escaped to Scotland, insane, and died there in later years, and one small detail gives curious support to it. When Henry was told of the uprising of Richard's supporters, Richard was supposedly in prison; but Henry is reported to have said "if I meet him, one of us shall die," seeming by a slip to have acknowledged the escape. Some think the face shown to so many was that of a look-alike, possibly Richard's secretary Maudeleyn, who was said to resemble him strikingly. But probably he was starved to death on Henry's command. Adam of Usk says he died in chains, brokenhearted and "tormented by starving fare," and names as his jailer and murderer Sir Thomas Swynford, Chaucer's nephew.

17

The End
of the
Pilgrimage

Chaucer died on October 25, 1400. The date, recorded on his tombstone, is more probable than others that have come down to us because it falls within the limits of possible dates set by other records. On June 5, 1400, he had drawn a payment on his Exchequer annuity. That is the last record we have of him as a living person. No further payments on the annuity were recorded (the next would have been due in November), and his house in Westminster was leased to a new tenant sometime in the fiscal year that began September 28.

He was buried in Westminster Abbey at the entrance to Saint Benedict's chapel, the farthest southwest of the chapels surrounding the high altar, where King Richard had buried many of his family and friends. The tomb that survives today was not erected till 1556, not quite on the spot but near it, along the east wall of the south transept. Though an altar tomb, there is no reason to think it contains Chaucer's remains. In the early seventeenth century this part of the abbey, because Chaucer was buried there, came to be called the Poets' Corner; it contains the graves or memorials of major English writers that the tourist sees today. When Dryden's grave was dug, the old simple stone at Chaucer's original grave was uprooted and used to mend the pavement.* In the four-hundred-odd years since the later tomb was erected, its inscriptions and coats of arms have eroded to illegibility, like the names carved in ice beneath the House of Fame.

Chaucer's Last Years

John Leland, Henry VIII's librarian, who had available to him materials since lost in the dissolution of the monasteries and the Great Fire of London (1666), and who was always careful about evidence, wrote that Chaucer "grew old and white-haired, and felt 'old age itself to be a sickness'" (*senectus ipse morbum est*, a proverbial expression going back to Terence, which may suggest either depression or resignation). Leland went on to say that Chaucer's sickness grew worse and he died while taking care of his business in London—which seems to suggest a protracted illness or general debilitation with low spirits, and then a sudden death. Although by medieval reckoning "old age" began at fifty, many people lived past seventy; a man in good health in his fifties needn't have expected to die soon, but Chaucer's writings of this period reveal a pervasive gloom and a preoccupation with death.†

Chaucer adjusted with difficulty to the idea of being old. He had always admired youth and vigor and taken a negative view of old age. In the Knight's Tale he leads us expectantly up to words of wisdom from old Egeus, Theseus's father, then gives us senile platitudes—"No one ever lived who didn't die, and no one ever died who didn't live *in some degree!*" The carpenter in the Miller's Tale, a stereotyped old man in a world of healthy youths, is shown as a gull and a laughingstock. The old Reeve is petulant, self-pitying, and mean, the Wife's old husbands are wimps, January a fool. Where are the venerable wise older men in Chaucer, of the kind he might have wanted to be himself in advancing years? The Franklin, perhaps, but he is depicted as white-haired and mature, not really old. And there is the quasi-allegorical old man of the Pardoner's Tale, knocking on the earth with his staff and begging "Leve moder, let me in," who speaks words of existential wisdom. But in 1393, in the "Envoy to Scogan," he imagines his friend calling him "old graybeard"

*When Browning's grave was dug, at or near the spot where Chaucer had been buried, some bones were found that were thought to be Chaucer's, and were reported as having been measured by the coroner of the Abbey, but the story was apparently a hoax.

†Unfortunately for the biographer no will has been found, or, if Chaucer died intestate, no administrative documents. An extensive search was carried on early in the present century by experts who knew exactly what to look for, even though they knew that such documents for those years are mostly lost.

("grisel," line 35), and adds about his youth that "all shall pass." During the time of what we would call his midlife transition, in his forties, Chaucer had to pass through that nightmare period of the Appellants, and it may have made the transition harder. When he reached his fifties, he wasn't acclimated to his age. Erik Erikson has said people undergo at this time of life a crisis between integrity and despair. Chaucer achieved integrity in his writings, which reflect the sober thoughts of maturity; he did not really turn to despair, though a modern observer might see it so. In his era, despair of the world's toils and troubles, which was what Erikson had in mind, could lead the soul to rise above those cares, to embrace faith and hope; "despair" in Christianity meant to lose hope of salvation.

In his last years, the records seem to show that Chaucer's annuity of £20 from King Richard was renewed by Henry IV on his coronation day, along with a renewed barrel of wine per year* and an added annuity of 40 marks, and that Chaucer, now well provided for, took new lodgings in Westminster for which he signed a lease on the day before Christmas, 1399. The dwelling was generally leased to men who had an official connection with the court—Chaucer's son Thomas inhabited it in later years. It was evidently a small house in the garden outside the Lady Chapel of the Abbey; the houses had gardens of their own, which other tenants (but not Chaucer) rented, and it commanded a higher rent than nearby houses. It sounds like a peaceful retreat where he could write and study, next to a cathedral and among the Benedictine monks whose abbey it was. Where he had been living before is not known; he continued to have business in Kent, and it's possible the Westminster lodging was in the nature of a pied-à-terre. Chaucer was presumably still employed by the court, for he had been issued a safe-conduct on May 4, 1398, protecting him while going on the king's "arduous and urgent business" in England, guaranteeing him security from enemies and lawsuits. And yet an exhaustive search has failed to produce any business on which the king employed him.

This picture of a peaceful retirement in the shadow of the Abbey became rather less idyllic in 1967, when a scholar of such documents showed that the handsome annuity given to the poet by Henry IV had

---

*In December 1397 King Richard had granted Chaucer a barrel of wine a year, which the poet never received. On October 13, 1398—appropriately the feast of Saint Edward the Confessor, an important date in Richard's court—Chaucer petitioned to receive it. Two days later, October 15, Richard granted it retroactively to December 1397; the order was back-dated to October 13, the feast of Saint Edward, with an identical document that added *per ipsum regem* (by the king's own order), possibly at Chaucer's request, for whatever reason. Henry IV, following Richard's example, chose October 13 as the day of his coronation.

been backdated. The date, October 13, 1399, the feast of Saint Edward the Confessor, was the day Henry chose for his coronation. But the grant to Chaucer is found in the patent rolls not in October, where it should belong, but among documents dated in February 1400. Evidently—and it was not a unique instance—Chaucer's payment on his Exchequer annuity due September 29, 1399, was not paid because Richard, who granted it, was no longer king; the royal bureaucracy routinely canceled all such grants when the government changed hands until they were validated by the new monarch. It must have been a bleak time for those in government service, who would have had to borrow money in the interim; Chaucer was in debt already, and hadn't been paid since July.* In December he leased the dwelling in Westminster—possibly, it has been suggested, because it could provide sanctuary from his creditors.

The sanctuary afforded by the abbey went back to the time of Saint Edward the Confessor, and it made Westminster much less Trollopian than we may imagine. The majority of those taking sanctuary were murderers, and most of the rest were thieves. They were under the protection of the Church, as sanctioned by the state, and could not be arrested. There were stringent regulations they had to follow—in some places they had to confess their crime to the prior and wear a black robe with a yellow cross, and after a certain time they could be asked to renounce the kingdom and even be escorted to a port to take ship. If there was no ship, they had to go into the sea each day up to their knees and cry "Passage, for the love of God and the king's sake!" One of the streets nearby was called Thieves Street, indicating why its inhabitants sought to be near the abbey. All this explains one particular irony of medieval life, that certain cathedrals or holy shrines, as places of sanctuary, were magnets for a criminal underworld. Not a promising atmosphere for a courtier-poet, but then Chaucer had a respectable house that would normally have been rented by a public servant like himself. His living there does not mean he had taken sanctuary. Yes, he had that writ from the previous May, which protected him against lawsuits, but since it was signed in Richard's reign it was no longer valid. It's unlikely he would have needed to take sanctuary, given his shrewdness in keeping out of financial scrapes, but he was only a few steps from a cathedral door and the possibility surely crossed his mind.

By February 1400 the government got around to his case and the king rewarded him generously for his services with renewed annual grants of £20 plus the annual barrel of wine, and an additional 40 marks (about

---

*On the day in September his annuity would have been paid, the negligible advance of £1 made to him almost twelve years before was transferred to a separate roll of "desperate" debts.

£27). These were dated back to the day of Henry IV's coronation, giving Chaucer some four months of retroactive pay. The cumbersome process of renewing his grants would normally have taken longer; something must have hurried it up, and for once we know what—a humorous poem Chaucer addressed to King Henry, called "The Complaint of Chaucer to His Purse." It is possibly the last poem he wrote. It is a parody of a courtly ballade, a love song to his purse. He says his purse is "light," meaning empty, but *light* also meant loose in morals: the purse emerges as a mistress or a whore (and "purse" of course had a sexual meaning). When he says "unless you make me heavy cheere" (a sad face), he has the purse's physical heaviness in mind! He had always made a joke of his ill success in love, and now, as Alfred David puts it, "he carries on the old jest but with the wry acknowledgment that the purse *is* the true lady of a bourgeois official and poet who depends upon the smiles of his noble patrons." The poem starts out in the courtly vein and goes downhill to reality: the lady's traditional golden hair becomes the clinking golden coins he needs, and the language becomes slangy: he says he's "shaved as close as a friar" —friars, who lived in poverty, had shaved tonsures, and "shaved" meant "broke."

Quite possibly it's a poem Chaucer had written in previous years, to which he added, sometime between October 1399 and February 1400, the envoi addressed to King Henry. He made it a spoof of courtly love traditions, one of which used courtly conventions to describe the Virgin Mary; there's a hint of this in his phrase "Queen of comfort," applied to his purse! He takes the religious undertone so far as to call his purse his "savior, as down in this world here"—the saucy implication being that we need salvation in eternity, but in *this* world we need cash. And he adds a prayer that the purse, through its power, help him "out of this town," a line that was always a "crux": before the discovery of the correct date of his annuity, people thought it meant he wanted to get out of wherever he was and move to peaceful Westminster. Now it seems to mean he wanted to get *out* of Westminster.

Chaucer added an envoi that is, unlike the poem itself, not playful. It makes a strong and quite explicit political statement:

> O conquerour of Brute's Albion,
> Which that by ligne and free eleccion
> Been verray king, this song to you I sende.
> And ye that mowen all our harms amende
> Have mind upon my supplicacion.

"Brute's Albion" is ancient England going back to its founding by Felix Brutus, and the king is greeted as being in that true ancient line ("ligne")

of kings—Henry was, like Richard, Edward III's grandson. His main rival
had been Roger Mortimer, son of Prince Lionel's daughter and therefore
Edward III's great-grandson through the female line. This was thought
the stronger claim; and the Mortimer family claimed direct descent from
Brutus, the founder of Britain. (When Roger Mortimer died in 1398, it
made the question one of idle theory; his son was a child, and of child
kings England had had enough.) Chaucer further greets Henry IV as king
by the free choice (*eleccion*) of his subjects, referring to the act of
Parliament that acclaimed him. After Richard's deposition it was desirable to believe the king reigned by the consent of the governed. By calling
Henry "conquerour" Chaucer suggests that Henry took the throne by
right—it's the only hint that Chaucer favored the deposition. There were
powerful arguments on either side, and Chaucer as an intellectual saw
both sides clearly. He had seen the worst of Richard's comportment, and
Henry was, after all, John of Gaunt's son by the Duchess Blanche. While
the poem is a classic example of a court poet telling a monarch what he
wants to hear, Chaucer was probably satisfied that he believed what he
said. He was of that new breed of civil servants whose loyalty was to
government, not individuals. Besides, at the moment he was in no position
not to shift his loyalty.

His poem got him what he wanted, but he did not live to enjoy it.
While the king more than doubled his annuities, the glacial process of
payment couldn't be hastened. Immediately he managed to collect £10,
as a gift from the king, representing the arrears on his annuity from King
Richard. He collected £5 of his new grant in June, and that was all.

His Last Writings

In the revised prologue to *The Legend of Good Women* Chaucer altered
the list of his works that Queen Alceste offers in his defense. One would
expect a reference to *The Canterbury Tales,* but he does not mention it;
this must mean it was still too far from being finished to be considered
a work. In the retraction he called it *The Tales of Canterbury,* but he
didn't call it a "book" as he did other longer poems. In Alceste's speech
he keeps the phrase "the love of Palamon and Arcite" although by now
it was part of *The Canterbury Tales.* At this time, about 1395, he must
still have been uncertain how his tales would take shape when brought
together.

Chaucer added to this list a work that he called "Of the Wretched
Engendering of Mankinde / As man may in Pope Innocent y-finde" (G
Prologue 414–415), a translation of the *De Miseria Humane Conditionis*

by Pope Innocent III, which he must have worked on since the earlier prologue, written about 1386. Pope Innocent's work was written in the last years of the twelfth century and was commonly known by the generic title *De Contemptu Mundi*. One of the classic works of the later Middle Ages, it was translated into almost all European languages, is preserved in hundreds of manuscripts, and remained a classic until the seventeenth century. It was twice translated into English during the Elizabethan period, both translators carefully obscuring its papal authorship. Its importance or popularity is a puzzle—to us. Why would Chaucer want to translate anything so morbid? Although Pope Innocent in his preface said he could as easily write a treatise on the dignity of man, he preferred to anatomize human misery in three books, treating its "ingress, progress, and egress"—i.e., the nature of the human condition at birth, our sins during life, and the death and damnation of sinners. Chaucer's title, which uses the word "engendering," probably refers only to the first book, which is the gloomiest; the second, on sins, gets into social satire and implies a need for reform, and the last is about death and damnation. The first book is about the wretchedness of human life in all its aspects—our birth "between dung and urine," miseries specific to children and old people, rich and poor, serfs and masters, the married and the single, the good and the evil; the vileness of the body; life's terrors and worries, its brevity, and its ugliness.

His choosing to translate this work, and perhaps only this particular book of it, may indicate a mood in which society and the afterlife were less on Chaucer's mind than the sheer wretchedness of life itself. Reading such works as Pope Innocent III's *De Miseria* was an outlet and release; it gave one the satisfaction of learning not to care. Chaucer needed to learn that at this time in his life, when he saw himself (so we learn from his poems) as unmarriageable, old, and gray, failing in his sexual powers and perhaps in his poetical and intellectual ones.

This preoccupation with death and the wretchedness of human life is the prevailing mood in the writings of his later years. In the Man of Law's Prologue and the Pardoner's Tale are many echoes of the *De Miseria*—all three books of it—which suggests that he began these prologues and tales while translating Pope Innocent. He *said* he translated it; if he had been given to naming works as finished that he was still writing, he would have mentioned *The Tales of Canterbury* too. The *De Miseria* wouldn't have been mentioned in the retraction, where he gives the names only of his secular writings. He may have abandoned it. But it may have been lost, whether finished or not, and there remains the possibility that it may be found, in an attic or on a library shelf, uncatalogued, or catalogued as if it were a copy of the Latin version.

The *De Miseria* could have been begun in the later 1380s when everything looked so bleak, and it may at first have been intended for the king. By the 1390s the king was happy and the kingdom settled, but things were not well with Chaucer, and he may have worked on it for his own sake as an exercise in renunciation.

Another prose translation from Latin, the treatises on sin and penitence, which, combined, became the Parson's Tale, was—according to a recent reexamination of the evidence—written in Chaucer's later years, when *The Canterbury Tales* was substantially completed. Preceded by three other tales (the Second Nun's, the Canon's Yeoman's, and the Manciple's), it comes at the end of *The Canterbury Tales*; to it Chaucer added the paragraph in which he revokes his secular works and asks the reader to pray for his soul.

The Pardoner

When he died, the order in which Chaucer meant to put his "tales of Canterbury" was for the most part clear in his mind. The exception was the Pardoner's Tale. Because it quotes many lines from the *De Miseria*, it was probably written about the time he was translating that work, in the mid 1390s; one scholar believed its place was undecided when he died. It is linked, for reasons we can only guess, to the Physician's Tale; but the resulting fragment is unconnected at either end—it is often called "floating." This is perhaps because it relates to the overarching idea of *The Canterbury Tales*, not to any particular tale or group of tales. It is a commentary on the pilgrimage itself. The Pardoner stands for the central complex of medieval institutions Chaucer chose as his setting—saints, relics, indulgences, pilgrimages—and he reveals its corrupted side. The tale is so dramatic, so startling, and so unlike anything else in *The Canterbury Tales* that in almost any position it would spoil something else. That it is linked to the Physician's Tale shows Chaucer was trying to fit it in. Its unique ending (the Pardoner and Host yelling at each other, the Knight intervening) is hard to link with another tale. One writer, with perhaps too much ingenuity, argues that by some mysterious serendipity it is where it belongs, floating outside the structures of the tale-telling game and the pilgrimage. One might compare the marginal world of medieval aesthetics, the lewd or quotidian drawings in the margins of serious manuscripts, the gargoyles on the outer surfaces of Gothic cathedrals—an antiworld of corrupted nature, which was to become the world of Bosch and Breugel.

In the General Prologue, the Summoner and Pardoner, the bizarre pair who make up part of the carnivalesque atmosphere of *The Canterbury Tales,* are presented last. The Summoner has a disfiguring disease, "alopicia," thought in the Middle Ages to be a form of leprosy; it gives him a bright red face with great "knobs" and "whelkes." He drinks strong red wine and likes garlic, onions, and leeks. He carries a cake with him like a shield, and wears on his head an outsized garland of flowers. His companion, the Pardoner of Roncivale, is a traveling preacher who collects offerings in return for indulgences; it was an ecclesiastical way of raising funds for worthy causes like hospitals or crusades. Such efforts were sometimes farmed out to laymen, who took a percentage of what they gained, and there were fake pardoners who took all. That the Pardoner travels with the Summoner suggests he is of this latter kind. The Summoner can use his position to get him entrée to the archdiocese; they are in cahoots. As they ride, the Pardoner sings a popular song, "Come hider, love, to me," and the Summoner "bar to him a stiff burdoun"—a strong bass accompaniment. Because "burdoun" could also mean a staff and thus suggest a phallus, some think this line hints at a homosexual tie between them; strained as the notion is, it is often accepted as a fact.

The physically repugnant qualities of this duo are a counterpart of their moral depravity. They are perverters of religion, exploiting the church and feeding upon the naïve piety of simple people. The Pardoner, like the Summoner, has a disorder: his symptoms are stringy yellowish hair hanging in bunches, glaring eyes, a "small" voice like a goat's; he has no beard and, says the narrator, never would have—to which he adds, "I trow he were a gelding or a mare." This evidently means he was either a castrated person or someone born with female secondary sex characteristics. Viewing these symptoms in the light of modern medicine has produced one diagnosis that he is a "testicular pseudo-hermaphrodite of the feminine type" and another of Klinefelter's syndrome. The popular conception is that "mare" was a slang term, now obsolete, meaning a feminine man, hence a homosexual; there is, however, no evidence that "mare" was ever used that way—but many *want* the Pardoner to be a homosexual and take this plus the "stiff burdoun" as proof. Probably the most revealing fact is that the eunuch (whether by castration or birth) had an allegorical significance in medieval thought: the "eunuch of God" would be one who practiced voluntary chastity, the "eunuch not of God" would be a sinner deprived of God's grace, that is, one who is damned. The Pardoner's androgynous quality can call to mind the medieval tradition of a male-female Christ, and from this viewpoint he may be an Antichrist figure, comparable to other such figures introduced in the last tales.

In the General Prologue Chaucer points up the Pardoner's evil

trickery—his false relics, his preaching for gain—but reminds us that he
was a brilliant orator, an actor, an evil genius with an artist's gifts and
instincts. We are meant to be overwhelmed by the cleverness of his
oratory and the fascination of his tale, are meant to be amused by his
candor in admitting that he preaches only for gain, that his relics are
counterfeits, that he can make people repent though he cares nothing for
their souls. We are meant to be horrified at the extent of his evil—
horrified and fascinated. His mockery of goodness exposes the weaknesses
of society—he laughs at the "good citizen," turns us back upon ourselves.
The Pardoner is an archetypal figure, one of those figures we encounter
in dreams, a grotesque man-woman whose evil reveals to us, like a mirror,
the evil in ourselves* and warns us of its punishment.

The Pardoner's Prologue is his confession; his tale is the sermon he
gives as he goes about the countryside. Sermons did normally have an
exemplum, an illustrative story. Knowing, as he has told the company,
that "lewed [ignorant] people loven tales olde," he lets the tale swallow
up the sermon and does his sermonizing in digressions, diatribes against
various sins, which include the borrowings from Pope Innocent III. His
text, "The desire of money is the root of all evils" (1 Tim. 6: 10) lets him
denounce avarice to make them give—and namely, as he says, to him.

His sermon begins with another archetype, powerful in Chaucer's
time because it came out of the Black Death. It too was an image Chaucer
retained from his childhood, the image of Death as a figure with a spear
stalking the land. Three "rioters" are in a tavern one morning, drunk, and
they see a corpse carried to its grave. One of them asks his boy who it was
and is told it was an old fellow of theirs,

> And suddenly he was y-slain tonight°,   *last night*
> For-drunk. As he sat on his bench upright,
> There came a privee theef° men clepeth° Death   *thief / call*
> That in this countree all the people sleeth,
> And with his spear he smoot his heart a-two,
> And went his way withouten wordes mo.
> He hath a thousand slain this pestilence°.   *plague*

The image of Death furnishes the occasion for the tale because the three
rioters mistake the personification for a reality and drunkenly make a pact
to slay Death. The boy, with youthful innocence, tells them what his
mother taught him, always to be ready to meet Death. In a moment they
come upon an old man, whom they menace; he is wrapped up and
carrying a staff, the conventional medieval image of Old Age. He says the

*Jean-Paul Sartre's *Saint Genet: Actor and Martyr* is an exploration of this archetype, using
Jean Genet as its exemplar.

earth is his mother, but though he knocks on it with his staff and says "Leeve moder, let me in," she will not let him die. He tells them they should respect old age, echoing the Golden Rule:

> Ne doth unto an old man none harm now,
> Na more than that ye wolde men did to you
> In age, if that ye so long abide°.   *live*

When they demand to know where Death is, he points them to a "Crooked Way" and disappears. They find there some eight bushels of gold florins. The youngest of the three is sent after wine; with it he buys poison and puts it in two of the wine bottles, so he can have all the gold himself. But when he returns, the other two kill him—for the same reason —drink the wine, and die too. The Pardoner winds up:

> . . . And lo, sirs, thus I preche.
> And Jesu Christ, that is our soules leeche°,   *physician*
> So grante yow *his* pardon to receive,
> For that is best, I wol you nat deceive.

Just where his memorized sermon ends is a matter of debate. One interpretation is that it ends when he says "lo, sirs, thus I preche," that he then gives sincere expression to his agonized conscience, and that this burst of sincerity frightens him, so that he turns about and in wild jesting tries to make them offer money to his relics. He casts about for someone who will go along with him, gambles on the Host, urges that he kiss the relics. But the Host, whether in anger or as a coarse joke, refuses with vehemence and adds,

> I wold I had thy coillons° in mine hand   *testicles*
> Instead of relics or of seintuarie°.   *holy objects*
> Let cut hem off, I wol thee help hem carrie—
> They shall be shrined in an hogge's turd.

The Host, knowingly or not, has insulted him on the one matter he would have kept secret. The Pardoner falls into an angry silence, the Host declares he won't play with an angry man, and the people laugh. Then the Knight intervenes. He gets them to give each other the kiss of peace:

> Anon they kissed, and riden forth hir waye.

After the ritual act of charity and forgiveness, they join the larger pilgrimage of human life—the Pardoner, one scholar writes, "is absorbed into the pattern of existence and the universe goes on undisturbed."

This dreamlike, allegorical tale, which has so much that is mysterious and uninterpretable, deals with the fundamental Christian lessons of charity and forgiveness, of preparing for death and eternity. Until the unaccountable happening at the end we are on the Host's side, are outraged at the Pardoner's monstrous evil even as we laugh at his trickery and listen in fascination to his tale. Saint Augustine taught that we should "hate the sin but love the sinner"; the tale is contrived to make us do the opposite, laugh at the sin but hate the man himself. No literary artist ever manipulated his readers more successfully: now, almost six centuries later, critics still write of the Pardoner sometimes almost with crazed vituperation, then turn and admit if grudgingly that, yes, he could still repent and be saved. The ending, when the Host without words embraces the Pardoner and gives the emblematic kiss, makes us reverse our feeling—we react with rational distance and noninvolvement, feel charity waken in us. In postmedieval literature, this would make an effective ending for *The Canterbury Tales*, and Chaucer is in tune with modern thought for having written it. But for the end of *The Canterbury Tales* he had already decided on a "meditation"—and he made everything lead up to a final utterance by the Parson as the pilgrims stand in sight of the shrine. Whether those last words were intended to be poetical and stirring—as much so as the Pardoner's Tale—we do not know. It is reasonable to think so. But time was getting short, and Chaucer put here at the end the prose treatise on penitence he had begun in earlier years.

The Last Tales

To link the Parson's Tale with the rest of *The Canterbury Tales*, Chaucer gathered three tales to lead up to it: the Second Nun's, Canon's Yeoman's, and Manciple's. Explicit statements in the Canon's Yeoman's Prologue and the Manciple's Prologue put them in that order. In the Manciple's Prologue the pilgrims are at the east end of Harbledoun ("under the Blean," line 3), which abuts the west end of Canterbury. In the Parson's Prologue the pilgrims are "entering at a thrope's ende," entering [it] through the outskirts of a small village. The implication is that they are at the destination.

These three tales preceding the Parson's seem at first to have little in common, and it used to be thought they were leftovers for which Chaucer had found no place. The Second Nun's Tale was probably written some years earlier; since it has no link or prologue, we wouldn't know who the teller is except for the rubrics in the manuscripts. Her tale is the legend of Saint Cecilia, an early Christian heroine (she is the patron saint of music). She married a pagan knight and converted him; their marriage was a chaste one, devoted to missionary enterprise in the world, and it ended with their martyrdom. The tale is drawn from the *Acta Sanctorum.* There is no tinge of irony; the Nun, not described in the General Prologue, is a figure whose personality cannot be found reflected in her story. The tale may look back to the Marriage Group by depicting a marriage of an extreme kind, a marriage without sex dedicated to the promulgation of the faith. It is a story about ideal conduct in the active life. Here, as elsewhere, Chaucer in religious matters takes little interest in spiritual growth. Saint Cecilia's virtue in the world is missionary action; facing martyrdom, it is renunciation.

The Second Nun's Tale depicts an ideal; the Canon's Yeoman's Tale that follows depicts a *failed* ideal. The Canon, an alchemist, rides up with his Yeoman to join the pilgrimage at this late hour, and the Yeoman tells the Host that his master is an alchemist, praising him with youthful enthusiasm. In response to questions from the Host he begins to reveal the Canon as a fraud—and the Canon rides away in shame. Then, outraged, the Yeoman tells a tale revealing the swindles and confidence games with which alchemists raise money to support their quest for the secret of turning base metals into gold. He is torn between idealistic hope and grieved disappointment. Alchemy in Chaucer's time was one of the shabby leavings of the Old Humanism, "scientific" humanism. One notion was that the ancients really had the secret but had wrapped it in enigmas to keep it from misuse; some said it might be recovered, others said it was lost forever. The Canon may be a figure representing the devil or the Antichrist, introduced in the eleventh hour of the pilgrimage. His Yeoman proclaims alchemy a part of forbidden knowledge and thinks the quest should be renounced, but he remains in the grip of its ideals. There was in fact a kind of spiritual alchemy that sought to raise the mind above the level of the mundane, and symbolized the quest of man for God. Its degeneration from a sacred mystical or gnostic practice to a mere confidence game is the theme of the tale. Putting the tale after the Second Nun's Tale, as the end of the pilgrimage approaches, Chaucer may have meant alchemy to stand for Christianity itself, the noble faith corrupted by the greed and vanity of its own officialdom.

While these two tales represent the world in decline from the saintly practices of the primitive church and the superior knowledge of the ancient world, the Manciple's Tale that follows descends almost to nihilism. In his prologue the Manciple plays a cruel joke on the drunken Cook, then admits that because he is known to cheat his masters, the learned lawyers in one of the Inns, the Cook could easily get even. His prologue establishes him as a cynic; his tale with its moral about keeping quiet suits his circumstance, but its final encomium to silence has a broader meaning. The Manciple tells the story of Phebus, god of poetry, and his talking white crow. When Phebus, solicitous and jealous of his wife, goes away, the wife brings in her lover, a "man of littel reputatioun," and brazenly cuckolds her husband in his own bed. The talking white crow, who has the ability to mimic and can imitate the speech of any man "when he should tell a tale" (line 135), sees it all, and when Phebus returns, he cries out "Cuckoo!" (in medieval bird lore the cry meant "cuckold"). The crow gives further details and proofs, and Phebus in a rage murders his wife, destroys his musical instruments, tears apart his bows and arrow—then regrets his acts. Now he believes she was faithful, blames himself for his lack of trust and his impetuosity, plans to kill himself, and then vents his anger on the truth-telling crow; he calls him a false thief, and deprives him of his song, his white feathers, and his power of speech.

The tale is about telling tales—and about telling the truth. If you have a truth to tell, you must persuade your audience to hear and believe it. Since people believe what they want, the truth must be made palatable with rhetorical ornament and diplomacy—and to the extent that it is, it is falsified or sugar coated. The Manciple pursues this observation with two examples. If a noblewoman and a poor woman both give their bodies to a man, the noblewoman is called "his lady as in love" but the poor woman is called "his wench or his lemman"—yet the man, adds the Manciple, lays the one as low as the other. Or another example: a tyrant has power, so we call him a captain, but we call an ordinary outlaw a thief. Language used artfully blinds us to reality—that is the harsh view the Manciple takes. If you tell the unvarnished truth, you get in trouble; rhetoric coats the bitter pill, whence every tale teller is a liar—and one is better off to hold one's tongue.

Of this fact about rhetoric Chaucer the diplomat was painfully aware. His disillusionment comes out at the end of his last work, after a tale of sainthood and a tale of thwarted idealism. And he turns the thought into a bloated utterance about keeping quiet. The moral is like the end of the Nun's Priest's Tale, but the spirit is the opposite. "Thus taughte me my dame," the Manciple says. The expression ("My mother taught me") meant it was plain good sense, but he takes the expression literally: we get an absurd carnival-like picture of his mother haranguing him—"Keep well thy tongue and keep thy friend" she begins, and goes on with a display of seventeen proverbs, interspersed with her repeated, didactic "My son,—" We hear again and again the words "tongue" and "jangling." Thus the end of the last story told on the pilgrimage is an overlong speech commending silence. And its last image is a wagging tongue making meaningless noise.* With this Chaucer brings the tale-telling game to a close.

Now the pilgrims have their first sight of their destination. The Host says that only one tale is lacking—"Fulfilled is my sentence and my decree," and the Parson says his tale will "knit up all this feast and make an ende" (line 47). Chaucer in his later years translated or adapted the Parson's Tale from a Latin (or French) original, a bit at a time, perhaps at the behest of someone and in part as a spiritual exercise. When it was finished, he added at its end his retraction, addressing those who have heard or read "this little treatise," meaning the Parson's Tale.

The Parson's Tale is a reversal from all that has gone before. It is in three divisions with various subdivisions, not a "tale" at all but a "treatise" to be heard or read, studied, learned from, a book not of "mirth" but, somewhat discouragingly for us, of "doctrine." It demands of the reader a massive shifting of gears. The teller of this "meditation" is the ideal Parson of the General Prologue, devout, self-sacrificing, guilty of no infractions. The actual Parson of the pilgrimage is a different character, a crusty, rather sharp-tongued man who at one point scolds the Host for swearing; here, when asked for a tale, he replies "Thou gettest fable none y-told for me"—you don't get a story from me. He thinks stories are lies and lies are sinful. His idea is to tell a morally instructive "meditation," as he calls it. The Host and company agree, somewhat reluctantly, to hear him out. Until that point, we have had a sequence of stories in a storytelling game; now we return to the Way.† We have had talk, talk, talk; now we have vision, at the end of the Parson's meditation—"the sight of the perfect knowledge of God."

To a medieval reader this treatise would have been like a how-to manual about acknowledging and paying for one's sins, which is the way to salvation. Chaucer's version is a distinguished piece of Middle English prose, written before prose was a literary medium. Profiting from a tradition of sermons and religious writings, it has the qualities we ask of good prose—economy, clarity, concreteness, parallelism, variety in sentence rhythm based on the rhythms of speech. It covers many abstract, difficult,

---

*Boccaccio, at the end of the *Decameron*, makes a defense of himself in which the last image is *his* tongue, the implication being that ladies have praised it not just for storytelling but for kissing.

†The Parson's Tale is based on two Latin prose works, joined by Chaucer or an unknown predecessor. One is on the three parts of penitence: contrition, confession, and satisfaction. To the middle part, on confession, is added a treatise on the Seven Deadly Sins, which swells it to over twice the length of the first part. Many such treatises were written after the Fourth Lateran Council (1215), when auricular confession was declared mandatory, to teach parish priests the relevant moral theology or to serve laymen as a guide; in recent years a small chain-gang of scholars has produced a partial list of some nine thousand such treatises.

and often controversial medieval ideas, giving examples to make them concrete, and the examples afford a sense of the daily life of medieval times: the "kiss-pax," a piece of wood or metal passed around at mass for the kiss of peace, or the painted castles of paper that covered dishes at medieval banquets, mentioned in *Sir Gawain and the Green Knight,* or kinds of penance still palatable to us (giving food, clothing, and shelter, visiting the sick or imprisoned, burying corpses, giving alms) or kinds not palatable (vigils, fasting, wearing hair shirts or coarse wool or armor next to the skin, scourging), or fashions in clothes, inveighed against here in almost Rabelaisian detail. This specificity about the world is like an anticarnival in which worldly life is not celebrated but submitted to the demands of moral probity. Here, translated into modern English, is a small scolding about men's fashions (line 416)—the decorations and hose and codpieces we see in fifteenth-century paintings:

> The first of these sins is excess in clothing, which makes it expensive, to the disadvantage of the common people—not just the cost of embroidering, flashy scalloping, or making designs of stripes, waves, vertical bars, coils, bands, and similar waste of cloth, all for vanity's sake; but also the costly fur added to their gowns—so much punching of holes with blades, so much trimming with scissors. And too, the excessive length of these gowns —of men as well as women—trailing behind in dung and mire, on foot or horseback, so that all that trailing cloth is wasted. . . . On the other side, to speak of the terrible and improper *scantiness* of clothing, as with those short loose jackets or tunics that fail to cover men's shameful parts, for wicked reasons. Why, some of them display, in the way their hose clings, their bulging outline and shocking tumescent member that looks like a hernia; and their buttocks look like the hind part of a she-ape in the full of the moon.

Clothes were described in the General Prologue to characterize the pilgrims—they had meaning in social and individual terms; here, we see them in moral terms. The human comedy of the beginning and middle is seen again from a different viewpoint at the end. But Chaucer's treatise is too general and philosophical to have been meant as a retrospective survey of one pilgrim and then another as their besetting sins are touched upon. We look back only upon the whole of the pilgrimage, from a higher moral perspective. Some have wanted to read the Parson's Tale as ironic, and therefore *not* a turnabout from what has gone before. But Chaucer, facing the end of his life, meant at the end of the work to turn the carnival world of his frame narrative solemnly on its head.

". . . That Shall Be Saved"

In these last years of the fourteenth century its two most famous portraits were painted. One is the Wilton Diptych, showing King Richard at his coronation: about him, in complex symbolism and iconography, we see three guardian saints painted, it is believed, to represent Edward II, Edward III, and the Black Prince—the king's lineage. It used to be thought the painting was done for the king's coronation; now it is established that it was painted in the last years of his reign, a nostalgic look back at the moment of his becoming king, and an argument for his right as inherited monarch. The other portrait is of Chaucer, a small manuscript painting, the "Hoccleve portrait," executed in the margins of books. The original is lost, but the copies we have still show the artist's skill—it is said to be the first English example of portrait art as we know it. We can believe Chaucer looked in these last years as he is depicted, with remarkable realism and mobility, in the Hoccleve portrait, white-haired, with a sensitive, controlled, and slightly jaundiced eye, an expression benign but weary—and with a rosary in his hand. This seems the Chaucer we know: kindly, slightly removed, making a storyteller's gesture. Hoccleve wrote in the accompanying verse that he had had Chaucer's resemblance painted so that he would live in the memory of others. Where the Wilton Diptych looks back, Chaucer's portrait looks forward into our time.

We sometimes glimpse in the records of his life what Chaucer was like as a person, and we can see certain sides of him in his poems, rather much as we can gaze on his portrait. We can see stages or seasons in his life—a period of youthful ambition in his twenties, a period of quest early in his thirties, a peak period of artistic creativity in his late thirties and forties. In his fifties, while he was writing some of his best work, we see him possibly in poor health, weary, and depressed. We would like to think he had the support of his friends in his last years, and indeed there was Hoccleve. But of Chaucer's friends and colleagues the larger number were now dead. Strode died in 1387, Brembre and Usk, and Simon Burley, were executed in 1388. John Clanvowe, who was almost exactly Chaucer's age, died in Constantinople in 1391; he was there on a pilgrimage or, less likely, a crusade, with his friend Sir William Nevill, who died of grief two days later. From others he had grown apart; his relations with William Beauchamp, as with Gower, seem not to have been resumed with intensity after 1388; and Gower was by this time retired and sickly. If you had asked Chaucer now, as the stranger in *The House of Fame* had asked him in his thirties, whether he were seeking fame, would he still have said, "No, I know best how I stand"?

In Chaucer's work we see the ineradicable stamp of genius, and a genius is by definition independent, imaginative, discerning; the genius thinks and talks at a level beyond the rest of us—sees connections we don't see, associates general ideas to particular observations in ways we do not, finds significance we don't notice. In conversation with a genius you would both be talking about the same thing but thinking on different levels and often moving in different directions. On this account, geniuses usually seem quirky and uncommunicative. And because they must live to such an extent in a world of their own, they often are eccentric in mannerisms or speech or habits. The genius, by the nature of the case, must live an insular existence, cut off from "the main." Oliver Sacks, writing of autistic children, asks, "Is there any 'place' in the world for a man who is like an island, who cannot be acculturated, made part of the main? Can 'the main' accommodate, make room for, the singular?" Comparing the circumstances of the genius, he adds that of course he does not mean all autists have genius, "only that they share with genius the problem of singularity."

This was surely what made Chaucer depict himself in *The House of Fame,* when he was in his thirties, as being out of communication with his neighbors, not interested in flying among the stars but in seeking "what in mine head y-marked is," or, in *The Parliament of Fowls,* approaching forty, as one isolated in a wintry world from the simple springtime pleasures; or, in his forties, in the *Troilus,* as a love poet with no personal experience of love, who lives his life in books; or, in his fifties, as in *The Canterbury Tales,* staring at the ground, "elvish" and withdrawn.

But in his last years this singularity and removal, which had been a posture, a defense, turned in the direction of real loneliness.

In most of his work Chaucer makes himself unreachable—he is role playing with a mask of his own invention, making the reader guess what is behind the mask. But there are a few moments in his works when we feel we are in his actual presence—in the last lines of the Miller's Prologue, where he says somewhat nervously that he is going to tell things as they were and invites us to turn over a leaf if we do not like what we find; at the end of the Nun's Priest's Tale, where the priest, never described, suddenly seems to have a personality and set of attitudes strangely like Chaucer's own; at the end of the Pardoner's Tale, where he has the swindled pilgrims move like spectral figures along the way of life's pilgrimage, and the quarreling Pardoner and Host, making a gesture of peace and joining with them, "riden forth hir way."

This sense of closeness to Chaucer occurs—almost—in the Parson's Prologue, as the shadows fall and the day comes to an end, with the pilgrims in sight of the cathedral. The Parson rises to preach; his "medita-tion" on penitence remains, if only vaguely and on principle, part of the fiction that it is the Parson's utterance—we are, we know, really in Chau-cer's study with a book open before us, being asked to turn our thoughts to the idea of penitence as the link between all worldly activities and the life eternal. Penitence, the Parson says in his last sentence, will bring us to "the sight of the perfect knowing of God," and this perfect state must be purchased by spiritual poverty, by lowness, by hunger and thirst, by travail, and by death and mortification of sin.

But at its end, in Chaucer's "retractions," as he called the passage echoing Saint Augustine's term, we hear the voice of the poet himself speaking to posterity, simple and direct. It may be the only passage in Chaucer's works where such directness occurs. He writes without a pose or stance or a persona, and with no work at his elbow from which he translates or adapts, as if in a letter. The only passage like it is the opening of *The Treatise on the Astrolabe*, addressed to "little Louis my son," in which he appears—this once—in the role of a loving father teaching his child how to operate an instrument for navigation, the astrolabe, ancestor of the sextant. The work is the first treatise in English on a scientific instrument, yes. It is also the first user's manual in English—and possibly the clearest.*

The retraction occurs in all complete manuscripts of *The Canterbury Tales* and there is no question of its authenticity. Its meaning is another matter. It is taken at one extreme to be a deathbed utterance written in a moment of panic; at the other extreme, an instance of Chaucer's humor. It is very carefully crafted: not a word is wasted; it has the power of simplicity and is in its own right a small monument of Middle English prose. Of its date, we can say only that it was written sometime in the later years of Chaucer's life. It is a deathbed utterance *written in advance*:

> Now pray I to hem all that harken this littel treatise or read, that
> if there by anything in it that liketh [pleases] hem, that thereof
> they thanken our Lord Jesu Christ, of whom proceedeth all wit
> and all goodness. And if there be anything that displease hem,
> I pray hem also that they arrette it to the defaut of mine
> unkonning [charge it to my ignorance] and not to my will, that
> would full fain have said better if I had had the konning. For
> our Book saith, "All that is written is written for our doctrine"
> —and that is mine intent.Wherefore I beseech you meekly, for
> the mercy of God, that ye pray for me that Christ have mercy

*There is another manual of this kind, *The Equatorie of the Planets*, about another instrument, but it is not certain that it was by Chaucer.

on me and forgive me my guilts, and namely of my translations and enditings [compositions] of worldly vanities, the which I revoke in my retractions—as is the book of Troilus, the book also of Fame, the book of the XXV Ladies, the book of the Duchess, the book of Saint Valentine's Day of the Parlement of Briddes [Birds], the tales of Canterbury thilke that sounen into sin; the book of the Lion*—and many another book, if they were in my remembrance, and many a song, and many a lecherous lay; that Christ for his great mercy forgive me the sin.

But of the translation of Boece *De Consolatione,* and other books of legends of saints, and homilies, and morality, and devotion, that thank I our Lord Jesu Christ and his blissful mother and all the saints of heaven, beseeching hem that they from henceforth unto my life's end send me grace to bewail my guilts and to study [give attention] to the salvation of my soul, and grant me grace of very [true] penitence, confession, and satisfaction to doon in this present life, through the benign grace of Him that is King of kings and Preest over all preestes, that bought us with the precious blood of His hert, so that I may been one of hem at the Day of Doom that shall be saved.

Some think its conventionality precludes its being a "personal" or "autobiographical" utterance, but this is nonsense. Would we argue that every word spoken in the confessional, say, was a conventional act and therefore not relevant to a person's biography? Such conventions call upon the individual to say or write something particular and earnest—and we must ask exactly what it was that Chaucer wrote.

The last words of the retraction, "that shall be saved," though not necessarily the last he put to paper, are the last English words of his last work—after them, the Latin formula for ending a prayer. In some part of his mind, when he wrote them, he meant them as an epitaph to his life's work. It is hardly a surprising wish for a medieval Christian, that he might be saved, but the wish is preceded by a list of his *works,* those he would retract and those he wished preserved. "Saved" is the key word of the passage, used at the end referring to his salvation, but with a subliminal suggestion of preservation: he would have what does *not* "sounen [tend] into sin" in *The Canterbury Tales* saved for posterity. He makes a display of renouncing his secular works by name and what in them may tend to sin, yet he names among them works like the *Troilus* that do, in plain fact, have a Christian moral. One scholar thinks the retraction is "a

*"The Book of the Lion" is a lost work, thought to have been an adaptation of Machaut's "Dit dou Lyon."

last earnest appeal to the reader to believe in the good intentions of the poet and to read all the poems in this spirit." And Chaucer is very careful to name all these secular works lest any be overlooked; he had made similar lists in the Man of Law's Prologue and the Prologue to *The Legend of Good Women*, and there—as here too—he was concerned with establishing his canon. When he comes to his religious writings he does not, except for the *Boece*, name any; he lumps them as "other books of legends of saints, and homilies, and morality, and devotion," as if to let them fend for themselves.

We may see him here faltering, in a moment of confusion, possibly fear. He has, in his last hour, one eye on God and the other on posterity, one on salvation and the other on fame. The contradictions in the passage are not different in kind from the contradictions in all his writings: with his ironic self-effacement he turns to meet his Maker, carefully reminding the reader of the exact titles of those works he would "retract," by which he means to ask for our best intentions in reading them; and they are the works for which, six centuries later, we do remember him.

Chaucer had a religious reason to "retract" his successes, his art itself, because it was of and about the world. Facing death, one revokes the vanities of life. This was the "art of dying," a conscious discipline on which hundreds of treatises were written—the original and most widely read of them (often called "the" *De Arte Moriendi*, as if it were the only one or the most important) was written during or shortly after Chaucer's lifetime, in the aftermath of the Black Death. It was part of the new religiosity of Chaucer's generation, the first generation of those who survived the plague. The art of dying, we now know, was more of a Renaissance than a medieval phenomenon, for such treatises remained standard reading until the Victorian era. It was an art practiced on one's deathbed or in preparation for it; a process, moving from the practical to the spiritual—disposing of one's affairs, making a will, reviewing the errors of one's life and repenting them, forgiving one's enemies, and so on. It was a way of letting go of life, of embracing death—a *style* of death belonging to an age that had few painkilling drugs and no doubt of the soul's immortality. One died, according to the art of dying, in bed, by steps and stages, receiving extreme unction and the last sacrament, with the priest and all one's family standing about in a vigil. We do not know that Chaucer died this way. Of sudden, violent, or accidental death the art of dying took scant notice; to die, like Hamlet's father, sent to his account with all his imperfections on his head, was the ultimate misfortune, which the Elizabethans thought a punishment since it left no moment for the impulse to repent, or for last words or gestures. The belief of Chaucer's age that dying can be an art reveals, more than anything else,

its new feeling about art. Death is no longer only the beginning of eternal
life; it is one's last moment of artful glory in the world.

Chaucer could say—as he does say in the retraction—that in the end
all that is written is written for our doctrine, and that *that was his intent.*
In moral theology and law it was a standard argument that one did not
speak evil if one spoke by way of example to exalt the good. Chaucer used
the argument himself facetiously in *The Legend of Good Women* (F
Prologue 470–474) to excuse his "sins" against the God of Love:

> . . . What so mine auctor mente,
> Algate°, God wot, it was mine intente   *at all events*
> To furthren truth in love and it cherice°,   *cherish*
> And to ben ware fro falseness and fro vice
> By swich ensample; this was my meaning.

He implies as a corollary of his retraction such an argument about "intent." It resembles Boccaccio's argument at the end of the *Decameron,*
that "like all other things in this world, stories, whatever their nature, may
be harmful or useful, depending upon the listener." But where Boccaccio
threw the moral burden on the listener's intention, Chaucer at the end
of his life claimed as his own the intention to write for the reader's
"doctrine."

It was the personal slant of his religion, as we remarked in speaking
of his religious writings, that he viewed extreme virtue, "saintliness," not
as growth but as renunciation. Here in these last words of his retraction,
from that pious side of his mind, is his last effort to renounce the world.
But from the side of him that viewed fame as the reward of endeavor, an
earthly immortality in the stream of human lives, here is his effort to
surrender his works to the world that will live on after him. He wished
still, on the deathbed of his imagining, what he had wished for *Troilus
and Criseyde*:

> . . . read whereso thou be, or elles sung,
> That thou be understonde, God I beseeche!

Petrarch, who had been crowned with laurel on the Capitoline, had said
in contemplating his death that mortal man must care first for mortal
things, and that to things mortal things eternal shall succeed. One must
think of the world while one is in the world; facing eternity, our thoughts
become closed within the self, our words become silence, and all our works
upon this little spot of earth seem like the waves of the sea.

Chronology,
Appendices,
Reference Notes,
and
References

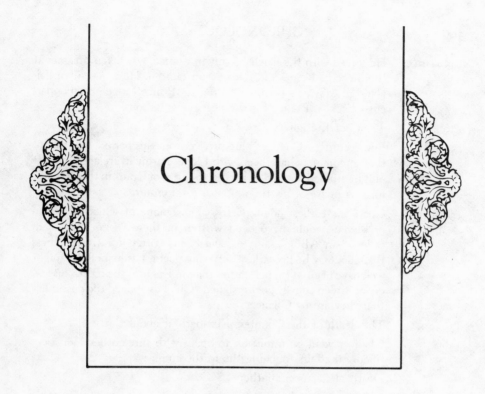

Chronology

1327–1377	REIGN OF KING EDWARD III
1342?	Geoffrey Chaucer was born in London, not later than the early months of 1343, the son of John Chaucer, importer of wines, and his wife, Agnes. His father and grandfather both held public office. The family was well to do and had connections with the royal court and the Lancastrian court.
1346	The English victory at Crécy.
1347	The fall of Calais.
1348–1349	The Black Death
1349–1350	Chaucer began his formal schooling at Saint Paul's cathedral school, London, under the headmaster William Ravenstone, an early adherent of the New Humanism.
1356	The victory at Poitiers; King Jean of France was captured, taken prisoner, and held under luxurious house arrest in London at the Palace of the Savoy.
1357	At fourteen, Chaucer was sent to serve as a page in the household of Lionel, earl of Ulster, second son of King Edward III, and his wife the Countess Elizabeth. This was the beginning of his education as a courtier.

1359–1360	He served with the English army in France, was taken prisoner at the Siege of Reims and released on ransom. He was sent to England in May as a personal courier for Prince Lionel, then apparently back to France for the peace negotiations.
1360	Treaty of Brétigny.
1360–1366	Few records of Chaucer's life survive from this period. For part of the time he may have been with Lionel's army in Ireland; for part of it he studied law and finance at the Inns of Court in their earliest form, a phase of his training as a royal esquire.
1360–1368	Chaucer's earliest adult poetry, almost none of which has been preserved, would have been written in these years. The poem called "An ABC," said to have been written for the Duchess Blanche, may be his earliest surviving poem. His first efforts might well have been in French rather than in English; the recent discovery of fifteen courtly poems signed "Ch" has opened the possibility that they are by Chaucer.
1363	The death of the Countess Elizabeth at about thirty.
1366	Chaucer went on a mission to Spain with three others not identified, on affairs touching the forthcoming war.
	Death of Chaucer's father.
	Chaucer married Philippa Roet, elder daughter of Sir Gilles de Roet, the queen's retainer from Hainault. She appears to have been in the Countess Elizabeth's service with him, in which case they would have known each other ten years. The marriage was arranged by the queen, who was Philippa Roet's guardian. She received an Exchequer annuity of 10 marks a year for life, presumably as a wedding gift. The Chaucers had, it appears from the records, three children. Thomas was born in the early years of the marriage, Lewis in 1381. An Elizabeth Chaucer, a nun, may have been their eldest.
1367	January 6: birth of Richard at Bordeaux.
1366–1367	First Invasion of Castile. April 3, 1367, the battle of Nájera; the beginning of the Black Prince's illness.
	Chaucer, now in the service of King Edward III as Esquire of the Royal Household, received on June 20, 1367, from King Edward an Exchequer annuity of 20 marks a year for life.
	Chaucer went to Milan, with the wedding party of Prince Lionel, for his marriage to Violante Visconti. Chaucer was sent home to England with messages and then back again to Milan.
	September: the death of the Duchess Blanche. *The Book of the Duchess* begun.
	October: the death of Prince Lionel.

1369	The war with France resumed.
	August: death of Queen Philippa. On September 1 Chaucer and his wife received liveries of mourning.
1370	To the Continent, possibly on matters touching the war with France.
1371	September: John of Gaunt was married to Costanza, heiress of Castile and León. He had by now taken as his mistress Katherine Swynford, younger sister of Chaucer's wife, Philippa, who now entered the service of the Duchess Costanza.
1372	Philippa Chaucer received an annuity of £10 for life from John of Gaunt.
1372–1373	Chaucer went to Italy: first to Genoa to negotiate the use of an English port by the Genoese merchant fleet, then to Florence to negotiate loans. This was Chaucer's introduction to Italian culture during the early period of Renaissance humanism. The influence of Dante, then of Petrarch and Boccaccio, dates from this journey. He left England on December 1, 1372 and arrived back on May 23, 1373.
1374	April 23: the king awarded Chaucer a pitcher of wine a day for life. The gesture, possibly a reward for the success of his Italian mission, was made at Windsor at the annual feast of the Garter, and appears to have been a harbinger of the king's favor.
	May: Chaucer took up residence in the gatehouse at Aldgate.
	June 8: he was made Controller of the King's Custom and Subsidy of Wools, Hides, and Wool Fells in the Port of London.
	June 13: he received an annuity from John of Gaunt of £10 a year for life, conceivably a reward for *The Book of the Duchess*.
	In these years Chaucer assimilated the Italian poetry he knew, especially Dante, and began writing *The House of Fame*. It is in part an ambivalent commentary on the Italian humanists' obsession with fame.
1376	June 8: death of Edward the Black Prince.
1376–1377	Chaucer went to the Continent, at least three times, on matters touching the negotiations for peace and the king's marriage.
1377	Chaucer went to France (Paris, Montreuil, and elsewhere), February to June, on a commission negotiating for the marriage of King Richard with one of the French princesses; according to Froissart.
	June 21: death of Edward III.
1377–1399	REIGN OF KING RICHARD II
1377	June 22: the coronation. King Richard confirmed Chaucer's annuities and offices.

1378   March–April: King Richard renewed Chaucer's annuities, converting the pitcher of wine a day to an annuity of 20 marks.

Chaucer went to Lombardy, on business touching the war with France. In Milan he met with Bernabò Visconti and with Sir John Hawkwood, the famous expatriate English mercenary captain. It is to be assumed that some feelers were made about a marriage between Caterina Visconti and the king. On this trip Chaucer probably acquired the manuscripts of works by Boccaccio and Petrarch that he was to use in his poems.

1379   *The House of Fame,* begun earlier and adapted for the occasion of the king's marriage to Caterina Visconti, was abandoned when the marriage plans were canceled.

1380   Chaucer was released by Cecily Champain from any legal action *de meo raptu*—concerning her "rape" or her "abduction." Chaucer may have paid her a large sum of money. Two London merchants also signed a release to Chaucer for any legal action, and Cecily Champain signed a release to them on the same day; a few days later one of them signed an agreement that he owed her £10. The nature of the incident remains obscure.

The Parliament of Fowls, written for the occasion of the king's marriage to Anne of Bohemia, was completed during a delay in the negotiations; it is a humorous, quasi-philosophical poem about the special character of a king's marriage.

1381   May 3: King Richard II officially engaged to Anne of Bohemia in a proxy ceremony.

June: the Peasants' Revolt.

Death of Chaucer's mother. The family home in the Vintry was sold to Henry Herbury, Vintner, who had been leasing it.

Lewis Chaucer born.

1381–1386   *Troilus and Criseyde* was begun in these years and worked on steadily. The translation of Boethius was written about this time, and some poems based on Boccaccio's *Teseida,* especially the early poem on Palamon and Arcite, later to become the Knight's Tale.

1382   January 14: marriage of Richard and Anne.

Chaucer was appointed Controller of the Petty Customs on wine and other merchandise in the port of London, in addition to the controllership he already held.

1385   October. Appointed justice of the peace in Kent, he took up residence in Greenwich. He was permitted a deputy in the Wool Custom.

1385–1389   Second Invasion of Castile.

1386   *Troilus and Criseyde* completed.

The Legend of Good Women begun. The notion of writing it, and of writing "some comedy," i.e., *The Canterbury Tales*, is mentioned at the end of *Troilus*. In its Prologue Chaucer indicates that he was assigned by Queen Anne to write first a prologue and the legend of Cleopatra, and then to write one legend a year.

Chaucer, elected knight of the shire, sat in the "Wonderful Parliament" the one session of 1386. The office was secured by the king's influence. Gloucester's party was at this time gaining control over King Richard.

October: Chaucer's testimony in the Scrope-Grosvenor trial.

Chaucer ended his service at the Customs and left the gatehouse over Aldgate, probably in a political shake-up involving Gloucester's party. Certain lifetime appointees, Chaucer among them, were threatened with the loss of their annuities. Chaucer evidently resigned to avoid this, and sold or loaned out his annuities.

The Canterbury Tales, "Phase One": the General Prologue and the tales that follow it, the Knight's, Miller's, and Reeve's tales, the unfinished Cook's Tale, and perhaps the Man of Law's Tale.

1387   Chaucer went to Calais, on a mission whose purpose is unrecorded.

Death of his wife, Philippa Chaucer.

1388   The "Merciless Parliament." Certain of Chaucer's friends and acquaintances, partisans of the king, were executed: Sir Robert Tresilian was hanged like a common criminal, Sir Nicholas Brembre was beheaded, as were Thomas Usk and Sir Simon Burley, the king's tutor.

1389–1393   *The Canterbury Tales*, "Phase Two": the "Discussion of Marriage" and the collection of miscellaneous tales beginning with the Shipman's Tale and ending with the Nun's Priest's, now comprising "Fragment VII."

1389   May 3: Richard II declared himself capable of ruling without "protectors" and took the full powers of kingship. In July he appointed Chaucer the Clerk of the King's Works, an administrative office of importance. Chaucer probably came to be called Sir Geoffrey after this, though he was not knighted. As Clerk of the Works he was in charge of building and repairing specified royal properties; he had many workmen under his jurisdiction, worked closely with famous architects like Henry Yeveley, and was responsible for large amounts of money.

1390   March: he was appointed to a royal commission for the repair of walls and ditches after a disastrous storm and flood.

September: he was robbed of public funds twice in a day and once assaulted by the same highwaymen, who were brought to trial. He resigned the commission in June of 1391.

1391   June: appointed deputy forester of the royal forest of North Petherton, not a royal appointment but one made by the Mortimer family. Chaucer's son Thomas was to hold the same post in later years.

1391-92   The *Treatise on the Astrolabe* written for his ten-year-old son, Lewis.

1393   "Envoy to Scogan."

1393-1399   *The Canterbury Tales*, "Phase Three": the Pardoner's Tale, coupled with the Physician's Tale written earlier, and the tales that lead up to the ending: the Second Nun's, the Canon's Yeoman's, and the Manciple's. For the ending Chaucer finished a treatise on penitence begun earlier and made it the Parson's Tale, adding to it his "retractions."

1394   Death of Queen Anne. Chaucer abandoned *The Legend of Good Women*, leaving the ninth legend unfinished; later he wrote a new version of its Prologue.

Death of the Duchess Costanza.

1396   John of Gaunt married Katherine Swynford, his mistress of more than twenty years, who was Chaucer's sister-in-law.

"Envoy to Bukton." Chaucer declared he would not marry again, referring to "such dotage," a suggestion that he had been involved disappointingly with a woman.

1397-1399   King Richard carried out what appears to have been a carefully wrought plan of revenge on his enemies. Gloucester's estates were forfeited and he was secretly murdered. The earl of Arundel's property was forfeited and he was beheaded. Warwick, who confessed, was imprisoned in the Tower.

1399   February: death of John of Gaunt. He was buried in Saint Paul's beside the Duchess Blanche.

October 13: coronation of King Henry IV.

1399-1413   REIGN OF KING HENRY IV

December: Chaucer took a long-term lease on a house in the garden of Westminster Abbey. His financial circumstances were not good. His poem "Complaint to His Purse" (or the envoi added to it) written at this time, asked the king to renew his annuities.

1400   January: an unsuccessful conspiracy to restore King Richard to the throne.

February: King Henry renewed Chaucer's annuities, backdating them to the day of his coronation and adding an annuity of 40 marks.

February: murder of King Richard II. Some held that he escaped to Scotland and lived on, insane.

October 25: the traditional date of Chaucer's death. He was buried in Westminster Abbey and in the Renaissance, the "Poets' Corner" grew around his tomb.

Appendix A

On Chaucer's Language

Between Chaucer's time and Shakespeare's, the pronunciation of English changed, so much so that Chaucer's poems no longer sounded right. He was admired for his rhetoric and his "philosophy," his skill as a storyteller, and as the "first finder of our fair language," but his rhythms were a puzzle and his rhymes did not sound true. People tolerated Chaucer's "rough" verses and assumed he had a tin ear. Henry Peacham, writing in 1622, found "under a bitter and rough rind," a kernel of "conceit and sweet invention." Dryden said there was in his verse "the rude sweetness of a Scotch tune"—"natural and pleasing, though not perfect."

Because Chaucer satirized certain corruptions of medieval religion, Elizabethans thought of him as a sort of proto-Protestant; then, thinking this, they attributed to him old poems on religious subjects that couldn't possibly have come from his pen. Milton always refers to "our Chaucer," praising him as the originator of the English poetic tradition; but his favorite tale was the "Plowman's Tale," an alliterative poem not by Chaucer at all, and it sounds as if he hadn't read *Troilus* or the Knight's Tale, or even (strangely) the Clerk's Tale.

A few writers in the sixteenth and seventeenth centuries insisted Chaucer's meter was regular. In the eighteenth century certain men of letters proposed that one could reconstruct the pronunciation of fourteenth-century English. Thomas

Gray, writing about 1760, suggested that if the final -e in Chaucer, and some e's within words, were pronounced, it would make his verses scan. And he was right. Not only different pronunciations but a different system of rhythm had existed in Chaucer's time. The old system disappeared during the lifetime of Sir Thomas Wyatt (1503–1542), whose editor, Tottel, "smoothed out" his old-fashioned rhythms.

Students are still taught that the final -e in Chaucer is always pronounced at the end of a line and pronounced within a line if it makes the line scan. And for the most part it works. But there were several different kinds of final -e's in Middle English and not all were pronounced; for example, there were "scribal" e's, written to indicate the length of a preceding vowel—a spelling convention that still exists in pairs like *hope* and *hop*—or written because they looked good, and these were not pronounced. There were also e's within words that have been slurred out of existence since Chaucer's time: a past tense like *bathed* would have been pronounced as two syllables, and a word like *Engeland* (derived from Old English *Engla-lond*) would have been pronounced as three. Because of these variations, the old spellings are not much help as a clue to pronunciation.

Probably one secret of Chaucer's rhythm is not so much in pronouncing these phantom e's as in *hearing* them. When we drop a vowel out of ordinary speech, we continue to spell it—and to hear it too. The pronunciation of "national" in modern American colloquial speech is most often in two syllables, like *"nashnul."* In the following couplet it seems to scan only if pronounced in three:

> Saying everything twice
> Is our national vice

—but try pronouncing it in the colloquial two-syllable way and you'll see that it *still scans.* Evidently there is a fossil space or pause left that we can hear, but it may be left in our "ear," not in our speech. We "hear" the syllable even when it is not actually sounded. The e's in Chaucer probably involved a similar circumstance. There were mental or auditory spaces for them, and you could hear them in poetry when you needed to. Practically speaking, this means that in a line like "The tender croppes and the younge sunne," though we are schooled to sound the e's in 'croppes,' 'younge,' and 'sunne,' these may have been "unpronounced but heard," like the middle vowel sound of "national" in modern English.

Recently Professor Jack Conner, in *English Prosody from Chaucer to Wyatt,* 1974, has proposed that until Wyatt's time final consonants in English were sounded with "audible release." Any word ending in a consonant had, after that final consonant, a neutral vowel or a small puff of breath: "meet" would have sounded like *meet-tuh,* as if in an Italian accent. The sound would normally be elided with a following vowel, unless it came before a pause. In poetry the practice would produce "weak" syllables that a poet could capitalize on for metrical subtleties. Conner's is an altogether different theory from the older theory of etymological "syllabic" e's, and as a theory probably a good deal more appealing.

There are other differences between Chaucerian English and modern English that also had an effect on rhythm.

For one thing, Middle English had long and short vowels. These are rare in modern English, and distinctions of meaning almost never depend on them, but you can hear a vestige of the distinction in "I can do it" (*I'm able*) and "I can peaches" (*I preserve peaches in tins*), or in "hoarse" and "horse." But vowel length was a common feature of Middle English. "Hat" was pronounced with the modern "broad *a*" as in "father" (better yet, like the flat "Hahvud yahd" in a Harvard accent) and "hate" was pronounced the same way, but the first was short and the second was long (hence they developed different pronunciations in modern English). But we don't know how long the Middle English long vowels were; certain British dialects today have very long vowels, which give them their "brogue"-like quality, but we have no idea if this was so in Chaucer's London.

Then, during the century after Chaucer's death, a curious change took place in the pronunciation of the long vowels. (Short vowels remained the same, except for short *a* as in "that," pronounced like "thaht," and short *u* as in "but," pronounced like modern "put.") This shift in the long vowels is called the Great Vowel Shift; before it took place, English vowels had their "Continental values" —i.e., were pronounced as in Germanic or Romance languages. Evidently the change began when two long vowels pronounced in the front of the mouth, *u* and *i*, became diphthongs. (Middle English "mouse" and "mice," pronounced like "moose" and "meese," came to be pronounced in two component vowels, as they are today.)

The vowels in a language are a system of meaningful contrasts, and when the places in that system were deserted by these two changed sounds, they were filled by words normally pronounced the way the two changed sounds had been pronounced. Once the two long "front" vowels became diphthongs, the other long vowels shifted regularly forward in the mouth, like dominoes. The system itself remained intact.

Learning to pronounce Chaucer so that he scans and rhymes properly is chiefly a matter of restoring the original "Continental" values to the long vowels. As for consonants, most were the same as they are now, and the rest were pronounced as they were spelled: the "l" was sounded in *folk*, the "g" in *gnat*, the "k" in *knight*; the "gh" was pronounced as in modern German or Scots with a guttural sound, initial "h" was silent in words of French origin, and "r" was trilled or flapped.

Middle English pronunciation is described in any text of Chaucer, and there are many recordings available. It was pieced together on the evidence of rhymes, puns, spellings, and occasional remarks or jokes about pronunciation. But it is still only an approximation. We don't, for example, always know where the stress fell in words. Some French words brought into English since the Norman Conquest retained their French stress (like *li- coúr*), but the historical tendency of English is for stress to fall back toward the beginnings of words. Words ending in *-ing*, especially at the end of a poetic line, could have the stress on the *-ing*: in the line "And of the feest that was at hir weddinge" (Knight's Tale, line 883), the last word was pronounced "wed-díng-e," but in the line "For there he wolde her wedding apparaille" (*Legend of Good Women,* line 2473), the same word is pronounced *wéd-ding* in what has become the normal way.

Nor do we know anything about Middle English intonation—the patterns of pitch and pause. Chaucer's voice may have risen and fallen, in questions or for emphasis, in what would seem an outlandish fashion today, but such aspects of speech leave no evidence behind. Finally, we don't know what Chaucer would have sounded like when he *performed* his poetry. We know oral reading was a form of entertainment and that poets did perform their own verses. But we haven't a clue about what such a performance would have sounded like. We may imagine Chaucer to have been a wonderful mimic, and to have been able to bring his verses alive in performance by playing the roles that seem so lifelike when we read them today, yet the very idea of such representational performance—"acting" in the modern sense—wasn't known in Chaucer's day or even in Shakespeare's. Scholars infer that medieval oral performance made no effort to be realistic—that it was a form of declamation modeled on public address and directed *at* an audience.

And yet, in spite of all we *don't* know about it, Chaucer's language lives. The characters speak to one another or the narrator to us, and we have the feeling that we hear them, that their speech is natural and colloquial, and that despite some changes it is still our language.

Appendix B

Further Reading

TRANSLATIONS AND EDITIONS

For the reader who wants to read more Chaucer, nearly all his works are very capably translated into modern English in three Penguin Books: *The Canterbury Tales* (revised ed., 1958) and *Troilus and Criseyde* (1971), both translated by Nevill Coghill; and *Love Visions* (1983), translated by Brian Stone.

Of course something is always lost in translation. An easy way to tackle the original language is to use an edition in which the variant spellings of medieval scribes are consolidated into normalized, consistent spelling as nearly as possible like modern spelling:

The Canterbury Tales: A Selection. Edited by Donald R. Howard and James Dean. New York: Signet, 1969.

Chaucer's Poetry: An Anthology for the Modern Reader. Edited by E. T. Donaldson. 2d ed. New York: Ronald Press, 1975. An inviting book with all of Chaucer's verse in single columns, expansive margins, and the editor's insightful essays.

Standard editions of Chaucer's works:

The Riverside Chaucer, 3rd ed. General editor, Larry D. Benson, based on *The Works of Geoffrey Chaucer.* Edited by F. N. Robinson. Boston: Houghton Mifflin, 1957.

The Complete Poetry and Prose of Geoffrey Chaucer. Edited by John H.
Fisher. New York: Holt, Rinehart and Winston, 1977.
Chaucer's Major Poetry. Edited by Albert C. Baugh. Englewood Cliffs, N.J.:
Prentice-Hall, 1963.

REFERENCE BOOKS

A Chaucer Glossary. Edited by Norman Davis et al. Oxford: Oxford Univer-
sity Press, 1979. All editions have notes and glossaries of some sort, but
this separate paperback glossary is complete and very helpful.
A Concordance to the Complete Works of Geoffrey Chaucer. Edited by
John S. P. Tatlock and Arthur G. Kennedy. 1927: Reprint, Gloucester,
Mass.: Carnegie Institute of Washington, 1963.

BIBLIOGRAPHIES

Larry D. Benson. "A Reader's Guide to Writings on Chaucer." In *Writers
and their Background: Geoffrey Chaucer,* edited by Derek Brewer.
Athens, Oh.: Ohio University Press, 1975. The best brief account of
writings on Chaucer.
Chaucer: A Bibliographical Introduction. Edited by John Leyerle and Anne
Quick. Toronto: University of Toronto Press, 1986. The best overall
selective bibliography (about 900 entries).
Chaucer. Edited by Albert C. Baugh. Arlington Heights, Il.: Goldentree
Bibliographies, 2d. ed. AHM Publishing, 1977. An older and longer
selective bibliography (about 3,000 entries).

A complete bibliography of all writings on Chaucer was begun in *Chaucer:
A Bibliographical Manual,* edited by Eleanor Prescott Hammond (1908). It has
been supplemented in *Bibliography of Chaucer 1908–1953,* edited by Dudley
David Griffith (1955); *Bibliography of Chaucer 1954–1963,* edited by William
R. Crawford (1967); and *A Bibliography of Chaucer, 1964–1973,* edited by
Lorrayne Y. Baird (1977); an update for 1974–1983 will appear in 1987.

An annual bibliography appears in *The Chaucer Review* (since 1966; uneven
in coverage), and an annual annotated bibliography in *Studies in the Age of
Chaucer* (since 1979).

There is in preparation a series of complete, detailed, and annotated bibliographies, published by the University of Toronto Press; the first volume to appear,
by Russell A. Peck, *Chaucer's Lyrics and "Anelida and Arcite": An Annotated
Bibliography 1900 to 1980* (1983), is of a very high quality.

Another collaborative project of this kind now in preparation, published by
the University of Oklahoma Press, is *A Variorum Edition of the Works of
Geoffrey Chaucer,* edited by Paul G. Ruggiers and Donald C. Baker, projected
in eight volumes consisting of a staggering total of forty-four parts, each sepa-

rately bound. The few volumes that have appeared are uneven in quality, but Volume 5, Part 1, *The Minor Poems,* edited by George B. Pace and Alfred David (1982), is excellent.

HANDBOOKS OF CRITICISM

Writers and their Background: Geoffrey Chaucer. Edited by Derek Brewer. Athens, Oh.: Ohio University Press, 1975.

Companion to Chaucer Studies. Edited by Beryl Rowland. Rev. ed. Oxford: Oxford University Press, 1979.

Both consist of essays on various assigned topics by various scholars. The former has Benson's "Reader's Guide," mentioned above; the latter has individual bibliographies for each chapter.

COLLECTIONS

Chaucer and Chaucerians. Edited by D. S. Brewer. London: Thomas Nelson and Sons, 1966. A selection of essays by modern scholars, commissioned to survey the field.

Geoffrey Chaucer. Edited by J. A. Burrow. Middlesex, Eng.: Penguin Books, 1969. The selection goes back to Chaucer's contemporaries and up to the present.

Chaucer's Mind and Art. Edited by A. C. Cawley. Edinburgh and London: Oliver and Boyd, 1969. The selections were chosen for quality more than coverage; a good select bibliography.

Geoffrey Chaucer. Edited by George D. Economou. New York: McGraw-Hill, 1975. A collection of original articles, more advanced than those named above.

Chaucer's Troilus: Essays in Criticism. Edited by Stephen A. Barney. Hamden, Conn.: Archon Books, 1980. Selected essays on *Troilus and Criseyde,* most of them previously published, a few new.

BIOGRAPHY

Brewer, Derek. *Chaucer and His World.* New York: Dodd Mead, 1978. A personal account of Chaucer's life and times, distinguished by handsome color reproductions.

Chaucer Life-Records. Edited by Martin M. Crow and Clair C. Olson. Austin, Tex.: University of Texas Press, 1966. The invaluable source materials for any biography of Chaucer.

Chute, Marchette. *Geoffrey Chaucer of England.* New York: E. P. Dutton, 1946. A short popular biography, now dated.

Gardner, John. *The Life and Times of Chaucer.* New York: Knopf, 1977. A biography by the well-known novelist.

CRITICISM

A brief survey of criticism in our century can be suggested by looking at some important books on *The Canterbury Tales*. Similar histories could be written for Chaucer's other works, and are suggested above in the chapters or sections of chapters devoted to these works, and in their notes.

In the nineteenth century the tendency was to consider Chaucer's works as if they were realistic Victorian novels. This older, realistic estimate, that the *Tales* is an incomplete account of a true-to-life pilgrimage, is best represented by George Lyman Kittredge, *Chaucer and His Poetry* (1915). Subsequent critics tried to see the book against the background of its time as its contemporaries would have seen it: for example, John Livingston Lowes, *Geoffrey Chaucer* (1934). Such a view, applied to *The Canterbury Tales*, produced books like Walter Clyde Curry's *Chaucer and the Mediaeval Sciences* (1926; rev. 1960), still informative. It also produced books like John Matthews Manly's *Some New Light on Chaucer* (1926), which attempted to find living prototypes of Chaucer's characters. Manly was right that the Host and Cook, and possibly also the Man of Law, were real people that Chaucer knew. A further way of seeing the work in a historical light was to ask what works Chaucer was adapting or imitating in the *Tales*. This "source hunting" produced *Sources and Analogues of Chaucer's Canterbury Tales*, edited by W. F. Bryan and Germaine Dempster (1941), which reprints the sources or analogues in their original languages, offers commentaries on each problem, and is still a standard work.

There was, of course, a reaction against this historical approach, and it went in two directions. One was that of the "new criticism," which ignored history in favor of the "text" or "the work itself," insisting that a work's structure and language direct us to what is significant as "background." Such close attention to individual works is best exemplified by the essays of E. Talbot Donaldson, in *Speaking of Chaucer* (1970) or in the commentaries in his edition mentioned above. Works of the New Criticism often proceeded from beginning to end in a "reading," e.g., Trevor Whittock, *A Reading of the Canterbury Tales* (1968), or isolated a problem, e.g., Peter Elbow, *Oppositions in Chaucer* (1975).

The other direction was to redefine history, to think less about persons, events, and society and more about ideas, aesthetics, art forms, sensibilities. An important step in this direction was taken by Ralph Baldwin in *The Unity of the Canterbury Tales* (1955): he argued that the work has unity of style and intent, and is not so fragmentary as it may seem—the pilgrimage is a metaphor for human life and the work itself therefore has an appropriate ending in the "meditation" the Parson preaches as the pilgrims approach Canterbury.

Such a thesis depends partly on a notion about how medieval rhetoric and literary theory influenced writers. That influence on Chaucer was studied by Robert O. Payne in *The Key of Remembrance* (1963). It also depends on a notion of what kind of meaning audiences found in literature. The importance of allegory in medieval theories of literature, and of religion in medieval life, is the theme of D. W. Robertson's *A Preface to Chaucer* (1962). The history of literary styles was the focus of Charles Muscatine's *Chaucer and the French Tradition*

(1957), which showed how Chaucer adapted a style from the courtly and bourgeois styles of French literature. Behind styles lies an aesthetic, and Robert M. Jordan in *Chaucer and the Shape of Creation* (1967) argued that the medieval aesthetic did not seek "unity" or admire organicism as the modern aesthetic does —that we must expect a medieval book like *The Canterbury Tales* to be "Gothic" after the manner of medieval cathedrals, that is, disjunctive in its form, multi-structured, and complex.

Literary tradition—the relationship among texts as they influence or react against one another—is a special aspect of literary history. There have been attempts, mostly in England, going back to John Speirs's *Chaucer the Maker* (1951), to assess the poet's place in English literary tradition. One study, Jill Mann's *Chaucer and Medieval Estates Satire* (1973), narrows the problem to the General Prologue and the tradition to social class satire. The endnotes to chapters 14, 15, and 17 of the present book suggest current subjects of discussion.

Appendix C

The Order of
*The Canterbury
Tales*

One subject of never-ending discussion is the order in which Chaucer meant us to read the tales. When he died, the work had a beginning and an end, but some of its middle was still missing. In some manuscripts the order is helter-skelter: the Hengwrt manuscript in the National Library of Wales has the General Prologue and the sequence Knight-Miller-Reeve-Cook at the beginning and the Parson's Tale at the end, but it puts the Manciple's Tale early, between the Summoner and the Nun's Priest, puts the Second Nun's Tale between Franklin and Clerk, and omits the Canon's Yeoman's Tale. Its links sometimes belie its order.

Our notion of the shape of *The Canterbury Tales* as a whole is based on the order of the Ellesmere manuscript in the Huntington Library, generally thought the most authoritative. It was probably compiled by the same scribe who compiled the chaotic Hengwrt manuscript; he rearranged tales on the evidence of the links between them, and if we possessed only the Hengwrt manuscript, we could make from it the same deductions the Ellesmere scribe made. What appear to be the most carefully compiled manuscripts of *The Canterbury Tales* give us an unfinished work in ten fragments (traditionally referred to in roman numerals) in a tentative order. The only sure evidence for the order is the "links" that acknowledge the preceding teller or tale and introduce the next. After the first sequence there are eight tales without such links, so we have nine sequences in which the tales are linked to one another, as in the following list (the hyphens stand for the links):

     I   General Prologue—Knight—Miller—Reeve—Cook
    II   Man of Law
   III Wife of Bath—Friar—Summoner
   IV Clerk—Merchant
    V   Squire—Franklin
   VI Physician—Pardoner
  VII Shipman—Prioress—Sir Thopas—Melibee—Monk—Nun's Priest
 VIII Second Nun—Canon's Yeoman
 IX–X Manciple—Parson—Author's Retraction

There is a consensus that the Man of Law's Tale (II) belongs where it is because it stands there regularly in manuscripts; that III, IV, and V comprise the group of tales about marriage, and that VIII, IX, and X are linked by references to place. The result is a set of five groups, some having traditional names, that would look something like this in the minds of most Chaucerians:

   I–II   *Beginning*: Knight—Miller—Reeve—Cook; Man of Law
 III–V ("The Marriage Group"): Wife of Bath—Friar—Summoner; Clerk—
           Merchant; Squire—Franklin
    VI ("The Floating Fragment"): Physician—Pardoner
   VII Shipman — Prioress — Sir Thopas — Melibee — Monk — Nun's
          Priest
VIII–X *Ending*: Second Nun—Canon's Yeoman; Manciple—Parson—Re-
          traction

For the order in which those three middle groups should be read there is no evidence. Each has order and unity in itself, a relation to the whole, and a kind of theme, but as they stand they can be read interchangeably.

The abrupt, unlinked beginnings of the four groups after the first reveal Chaucer thinking ahead. Anticipating a part of his plan perhaps newly conceived, he left off the link or prologue of the initial tale until he knew how the resulting group would fit his larger plan. When we read these headless beginnings we have a sense of excitement and anticipation. Who is speaking? What is the tale going to be? What tale will come after? They make effective beginnings—reason enough, perhaps, why the poet never got around to writing prologues for them. As the groups came to have topics or themes, he may have wanted, rather than string all the tales together, to keep them in discrete units, like the days in Boccaccio's *Decameron* or the books of Gower's *Confessio*.

Appendix D

Chaucer's Reputation

When Chaucer died his manuscripts, it is traditionally assumed, were in a chest, with possibly one tale or a group of *The Canterbury Tales* on his desk. These were his authentic writings, in his own hand or copied by a scribe with his corrections. None of these holograph manuscripts, or the contemporary copies made from them, is known to survive.

What survives are manuscripts of a third generation, and later generations copied from the third or from earlier ones. After the printing press was introduced in England in 1477, there were three fifteenth-century printed editions of *The Canterbury Tales* and one of the *Troilus*; in the sixteenth century there were four printed editions of Chaucer's collected works.

Chaucer was recognized as a major poet in his own lifetime. He was praised over and over as a "philosophical" poet, a great rhetorician and translator; he was imitated by lesser poets like Usk and Hoccleve, and in the fifteenth century, especially in the north, by Henryson, Dunbar, and other "Scottish Chaucerians." During the Renaissance he was more read than imitated; Reformation England viewed him as an early reformer, at heart a Protestant, the originator of "our" English poetry—"our Chaucer," they called him. In the Restoration and eighteenth century he was translated by distinguished poets such as Dryden and Pope; and he was studied—scholars like Urry and Tyrwhitt began editing his poems with care and raising questions about his prosody and pronunciation. A few eighteenth-century intellectuals realized that the early English poets must have had a different system of rhythm and a different way of pronouncing English, but this didn't change the way he was read. Again, it wasn't known until 1775 that *Troilus* was adapted from a work by Boccaccio, and even at that people didn't believe it until a parallel-text edition, *Chaucer's Troylus and Cryseyde . . . Compared With Boccaccio's Filostrato*, William Michael Rossetti, ed. and trans., Chaucer Society, 1st series, 44 (London, 1873), was published almost a hundred years later. They feared that this would make him "derivative"; and they felt they needed to show the *Filostrato* an inferior product in order to reveal Chaucer's success in adapting it. In the nineteenth century, new and careful editions were made, the authentic works were weeded out from inauthentic ones, the sources and analogues were identified. It began to be possible to take Chaucer's works seriously and study them with rigor.

At the beginning of our century, attitudes toward the Middle Ages changed, and with them the image of Chaucer. The old idea that he was simple, refreshing, and naïve was altered to the more sensible idea that he was ironic: "A naïf collector of Customs," wrote Professor Kittredge, "would be a paradoxical monster." The poet's self-presentation was dissociated from his historical self and viewed as a *persona* or "naïve narrator" created as a mouthpiece, behind which we sense a presence that is the author. There emerged a sophisticated, a learned Chaucer. In our time there have been Chaucer the ironist and social commentator, the gloomy Chaucer, the pietistic Chaucer whose writings are all allegories; there is also a super-literary Chaucer whose works are all pronouncements or inquiries about poetry. The Chaucer you have been reading about was a fourteenth-century civil servant who wrote poems, a most complicated man, an enigma in a mystery, and most of the sides of him that have been extrapolated from his writings probably *were* phases of his character when he walked upon the earth.

Modern readers feel disappointed when they learn how much in Chaucer's dream visions comes word for word from Machaut or Deschamps or Froissart, or that the *Troilus* is an adaptation of a preexisting poem, or that the Canterbury tales have identifiable sources. But a medieval poem was generally a collage of passages drawn nearly verbatim from other poems; it could still stand on its merits and not be thought unoriginal. A generation ago, the constant theme of Chaucer scholars was that Chaucer *improved* on what he borrowed; it was claimed that in the "frame" of *The Canterbury Tales* "what he could have borrowed from others is slight in comparison with what he certainly created himself." Now critics like to show how his version of a preexisting work is a different kind of work that called for different treatment. The "idea" of each of his works is a composite of preexisting ideas drawn from literary conventions and social customs, something Chaucer and his readers could have taken for granted and never thought about. But each idea is none the less original for that.

Reference
Notes

The publishers wish to express their gratitude to Mr. Thomas Moser, Jr. and Mr. Steven Kruger, graduate students of Professor Howard's at Stanford University, who, at short notice and in difficult circumstances, took on the responsibility of reading, in proof stage, the Reference Notes and References.

References are given by page number and catch phrases placed in the order of their appearance on the page. Subtitles are given only when substantive.

Works cited in two or more chapters are abbreviated according to the table that follows. Certain works with long or complicated titles, as for example chronicles, are listed here if cited at all. Works cited in one chapter only are generally given a full reference on their first appearance and thereafter by the author's last name and a short title.

On selection of references, see p. 517.

Many of the works cited have been published both in Great Britain and in the United States. I have given the place of publication and date of the edition I used with the place and date of any other editions available.

ABBREVIATIONS USED FOR WORKS BY CHAUCER

BD	*The Book of the Duchess*
CT	*The Canterbury Tales*
HF	*The House of Fame*
LGW	*The Legend of Good Women*
PF	*The Parliament of Fowls*
TC	*Troilus and Criseyde*

ABBREVIATIONS OF WORKS CITED IN MORE THAN ONE CHAPTER

Adam of Usk   Adam of Usk, *Chronicon Adae de Usk A.D. 1377–1421.* 2d ed. Edited by Sir Edward Maunde Thompson. London, 1904.

Anonimalle   Galbraith, V. H., ed. *The Anonimalle Chronicle 1333 to 1381.* Manchester, 1927.

Armitage-Smith   Armitage-Smith, Sydney. *John of Gaunt.* 1904. Reprint. London, 1964.

Barber   Barber, Richard W. *Edward, Prince of Wales and Aquitaine.* New York, 1978.

Barnie   Barnie, John. *War in Medieval English Society.* Ithaca, N.Y., 1974.

Baugh   Baugh, Albert C., ed. *Chaucer's Major Poetry.* Englewood Cliffs, N.J. and London, 1963.

Boitani   Boitani, Piero, ed. *Chaucer and the Italian Trecento.* Cambridge, Eng., 1983.

Braddy   Braddy, Haldeen. *Geoffrey Chaucer: Literary and Historical Studies.* Port Washington, N.Y., 1971.

Branca   Branca, Vittore. *Boccaccio: The Man and His Works.* Translated by Richard Monges and Dennis J. McAuliffe. New York, 1976.

Brewer, *Background*   Brewer, Derek, ed. *Writers and their Background: Geoffrey Chaucer.* Athens, Ohio, 1975 and London, 1974.

Brewer, *Heritage*   ———, ed. *Chaucer: The Critical Heritage.* Vol. 1, 1385–1837. London, 1978.

Brewer, *World*   ———. *Chaucer and His World.* New York and London, 1978.

Brusendorff   Brusendorff, Aage. *The Chaucer Tradition.* 1925. Reprint. Gloucester, Mass., 1965.

Cassell   Cassell, Anthony K., trans. and ed. *The Corbaccio.* Urbana, Ill., 1975.

CE   *College English*

Chamberlin   Chamberlin, E. R. *The Count of Virtue: Giangaleazzo Visconti, Duke of Milan.* New York, 1965.

ChauR   *The Chaucer Review.*

Chron. Ang.   "Monk of St. Alban's," *Chronicon Angliae, ab Anno Domini 1328 usque ad Annum 1388.* Rolls Series 64. Edited by Edward Maunde Thompson. 1874. Reprint. 1965.

Clemen   Clemen, Wolfgang. *Chaucer's Early Poetry.* Translated by C. A. M. Sym. 1963. Reprint. London, 1968.

Condren   Condren, Edward I. "The Historical Context of *the Book of the Duchess*: A New Hypothesis." ChauR 5 (1971), 195–212.

Cook   Cook, Albert Stanburrough. "Chaucerian Papers—I." *Transactions of the Connecticut Academy of Arts and Sciences* 23 (1919): 1–63.

Cooper   Helen Cooper, *The Structure of The Canterbury Tales.* London and Athens, Ga., 1983.

Cosman   Cosman, Madeleine Pelner. *Fabulous Feasts: Medieval Cookery and Ceremony.* New York, 1976.

Court and Poet   Burgess, Glyn S., ed. *Court and Poet.* Liverpool, 1981.

Cox   Cox, Eugene L. *The Green Count of Savoy: Amadeus VI and Transalpine Savoy in the Fourteenth Century.* Princeton, 1967.

CPR   *Calendar of the Patent Rolls* Preserved in the Public Record Office (London 1891–1948)

Cummings   Cummings, Hubertis M. *The Indebtedness of Chaucer's Works to the Italian Works of Boccaccio.* Diss. Princeton, 1916. Reprint. New York, 1967.

Daiches   Daiches, David and Anthony Thorlby, eds. *The Mediaeval World.* London, 1973.

David   David, Alfred. *The Strumpet Muse: Art and Morals in Chaucer's Poetry.* Bloomington, Ind. and London, 1976.

De Sanctis   De Sanctis, Francesco. *History of Italian Literature.* Translated by Joan Redfern. 2 vols. 1931. Reprint. New York, 1959.

Donaldson ed.   Donaldson, E. Talbot, ed. *Chaucer's Poetry: An Anthology for the Modern Reader.* New York, 1958, 2d ed., 1975.

Donaldson   ———. *Speaking of Chaucer.* New York, 1970.

DMA   Strayer, Joseph R., ed. in chief. *Dictionary of the Middle Ages.* Vols. 1–. New York, 1982–.

DNB   Stephen, Sir Leslie and Sir Sidney Lee, eds. *Dictionary of National Biography.* 63 vols. New York and London, 1885–1900.

Du Boulay	Du Boulay, F. R. H. *An Age of Ambition: English Society in the Late Middle Ages.* London, 1970.
Du Boulay ed.	Du Boulay, F. R. H. and Caroline M. Barron, eds. *The Reign of Richard II: Essays in Honour of May McKisack.* London, 1971.
E & S	*Essays and Studies.*
Economou	Economou, George D. *The Goddess Natura in Medieval Literature.* Cambridge, Mass., 1972.
EETS	Early English Text Society
EHR	*English Historical Review*
EIC	*Essays in Criticism*
ELH	*ELH* [*English Literary History*]
ELN	*English Language Notes*
Emerson	Emerson, Barbara. *The Black Prince.* London, 1976.
English Court Culture	Scattergood, V. J. and J. W. Sherborne, eds. *English Court Culture in the Later Middle Ages.* London, 1983.
ES	*English Studies.*
Esch	Esch, Arno, ed. *Chaucer und seine Zeit.* Zeitschrift für englische Philologie 14. Tübingen, 1968.
Favent	Favent, Thomas. *Historia . . . Mirabilis Parliamenti . . .* Edited by Mary McKisack. Camden Society, 3d ser., 37. *Camden Miscellany* 14. London, 1926.
Ferris	Ferris, Sumner. "Chaucer, Richard II, Henry IV, and 13 October." In Rowland, ed., 210–217.
Fisher	Fisher, John H. *John Gower.* New York, 1964.
Fisher ed.	———, ed. *The Complete Poetry and Prose of Geoffrey Chaucer.* New York, 1977.
Froissart	Froissart, Jean.* *Chronicles of England, France, Spain, and the Adjoining Countries.* Translated by Thomas Johnes. New York, 1855.
Frye	Frye, Northrop. *Anatomy of Criticism.* Princeton and London, 1957.
Fyler	Fyler, John M. *Chaucer and Ovid.* New Haven and London, 1979.
Gardner	Gardner, John. *The Life and Times of Chaucer.* New York, 1977.
Giffin	Giffin, Mary. *Studies on Chaucer and His Audience.* Hull, Quebec, 1956.

*Froissart is cited in this edition of the Johnes translation because it is the one I used. The book numbers are Froissart's; the chapter numbers were added later and are not authentic. The authoritative complete edition of the French is that of Kervyn de Lettenhove, 17 vols. (Brussels, 1867–1872), which I have sometimes consulted.

Green — Green, Richard Firth. *Poets and Princepleasers: Literature and the English Court in the Late Middle Ages.* Toronto and Buffalo, 1980.

Hammond — Hammond, Eleanor Prescott. *Chaucer: A Bibliographical Manual.* New York, 1908. Reprint, New York, 1983.

Harvey — Harvey, John. *The Black Prince and His Age.* Totowa, N.J. and London, 1976.

Higden — Higden, Ranulph. Polychronicon Ranulphi Higden. 9 vols. Rolls Series 41.

Historia Vitae — Stow, George B. Jr., ed. *Historia Vitae Et Regni Ricardi Secundi.* Philadelphia, 1977.

Hist. Rel. — Amyot, Thomas, ed. "An Historicall Relation . . ." *Archaeologia.* London, 1829. 204–284. [British Library: Harley 6217, an Elizabethan translation from the *Chronicle of St. Albans.*]

Howard, *Idea* — Howard, Donald R. *The Idea of the Canterbury Tales.* Berkeley and London, 1976.

Howard, *Writers* — ———. *Writers and Pilgrims: Medieval Pilgrimage Narratives and Their Posterity.* Berkeley and London, 1980.

Hulbert — Hulbert, James Root. *Chaucer's Official Life.* Menasha, Wis., 1912. Reprint, New York, 1970.

Hutchison — Hutchison, Harold F. *The Hollow Crown: A Life of Richard II.* London, 1961.

Innocent III — Segni, Lothario dei (Pope Innocent III). *On the Misery of the Human Condition: De Miseria Humane Conditionis.* Edited by Donald R. Howard, translated by Margaret Mary Dietz. Indianapolis, 1969.

JEGP — *JEGP (Journal of English and Germanic Philology)*

JMRS — *Journal of Medieval and Renaissance Studies*

Kay — Kay, F. George. *Lady of the Sun: The Life and Times of Alice Perrers.* London, 1966.

Keen — Keen, Maurice. *Chivalry.* New Haven and London, 1984.

Kern — Kern, Alfred A. *The Ancestry of Chaucer.* Baltimore, 1906.

Kirkstall — Taylor, John, ed. *The Kirkstall Abbey Chronicles.* Leeds, 1952.

Kittredge — Kittredge, George Lyman. *Chaucer and His Poetry.* Cambridge, Mass. and London, 1915.

Kolve — Kolve, V. A. *Chaucer and the Imagery of Narrative: The First Five Canterbury Tales.* Stanford, Calif., 1984.

Levinson   Levinson, Daniel J., et al. *The Seasons of a Man's Life.*
                      New York, 1978.

Lewis, *Allegory*   Lewis, C. S. *The Allegory of Love.* Oxford, 1936. Re-
                      print. New York, 1958.

Lewis, *Image*   ————. *The Discarded Image: An Introduction to
                      Medieval and Renaissance Literature.* Cam-
                      bridge, Eng., 1964.

Loomis   Loomis, Roger S. "Chaucer's Eight Years Sickness."
                      MLN 59 (1944): 178–180.

Loomis, *Mirror*   ————. *A Mirror of Chaucer's World.* Princeton,
                      1965.

LR   *Chaucer Life-Records.* Edited by Martin M. Crow and
                      Clair C. Olson from materials compiled by John
                      M. Manly and Edith Rickert, with the assistance
                      of Lilian J. Redstone et al. Austin, Tex. and Ox-
                      ford, 1966.

MAE   *Medium AEvum*

Manly   Manly, John M. *Some New Light on Chaucer.* New
                      York, 1926. Reprint, Gloucester, Mass., 1939.

McFarlane   McFarlane, Kenneth B. *Lancastrian Kings and Lollard
                      Knights.* Oxford, 1972.

McKisack   McKisack, May. *The Fourteenth Century 1307–1399.*
                      The Oxford History of England, edited by Sir
                      George Clark. Vol 5. Oxford, 1959.

Middleton   Middleton, Anne. "Chaucer's 'New Men' and the
                      Good of Literature in *The Canterbury Tales*." In
                      *Literature and Society: Selected Papers from the
                      English Institute,* NS No. 3 (1978), edited by
                      Edward W. Said. Baltimore and London, 1980,
                      15–56.

Minnis   Minnis, A. J. *Chaucer and Pagan Antiquity.* Totowa,
                      N.J., 1982.

MLN   *Modern Language Notes.*

MLR   *Modern Language Review.*

MP   *Modern Philology.*

Muscatine   Muscatine, Charles. *Chaucer and the French Tradition.*
                      Berkeley and London, 1957.

N & Q   Notes and Queries

NS   New series

OED   *Oxford English Dictionary.*

Olson   Olson, Glending. *Literature as Recreation in the Later
                      Middle Ages.* Ithaca, N.Y. and London, 1982.

Oman   Oman, Charles W. C. *The Great Revolt of 1381.* Ox-
                      ford, 1906. New edition. Oxford, 1969.

OS   Old series

Packe   Packe, Michael. *King Edward III*. Edited by L. C. B. Seaman. London and Boston, 1983.

Painter   Painter, Sidney. *French Chivalry: Chivalric Ideas and Practices in Mediaeval France*. Baltimore, 1940.

Palmer   Palmer, J. J. N. "The Historical Context of the *Book of the Duchess*: A Revision." ChauR 8 (1974): 253–261.

Palmer ed.   Palmer, J. J. N. *Froissart: Historian*. Totowa, N.J. and Woodbridge, Suffolk, 1981.

Parr   Parr, Johnstone. "The Date and Revision of Chaucer's *Knight's Tale*." PMLA 60 (1945): 307–324.

Payne   Payne, Robert O. *The Key of Remembrance: A Study of Chaucer's Poetics*. New Haven and London, 1963.

Perroy   Perroy, Edouard. *L'Angleterre et le Grand Schisme d'Occident*. Paris, 1933.

PMLA   *PMLA: Publications of the Modern Language Association of America*.

Power   Power, Eileen. *The Wool Trade in English Medieval History*. Oxford, 1941. Reprint, London and New York, 1942.

PQ   *Philological Quarterly*

Pratt   Pratt, Robert A. "The Order of the *Canterbury Tales*. PMLA, 66 (1951): 1141–1167.

Redstone   Redstone, V. B. and L. J. "The Heyrons of London: A Study in the Social Origins of Geoffrey Chaucer." *Speculum* 12 (1937): 182–195.

Register 1372–   Armitage-Smith, Sydney, ed. *John of Gaunt's Register 1372–1376*. 2 vols. Camden Society, 3rd. ser., 20–21. London, 1911.

Register 1379–   Lodge, Eleanor C. and Robert Sommerville, eds. *John of Gaunt's Register, 1379–1383*. 2 vols. Camden Society, 3rd ser., 56–57. London, 1937.

RES   *Review of English Studies*.

Robertson, *London*   Robertson, D. W., Jr. *Chaucer's London*. New York, 1968.

Robertson, *Preface*   ———. *A Preface to Chaucer: Studies in Medieval Perspectives*. Princeton, 1962.

Robinson ed.   Robinson, F. N., ed. *The Works of Geoffrey Chaucer*. 2d ed. Boston, 1957.

Rolls Series   *Rerum Brittanicarum Medii AEvi Scriptores, or Chronicles and Memorials of Great Britain and Ireland during the Middle Ages*. Rolls House, 1858–1911.

RomR   *Romanic Review*

Roskell Roskell, John Smith. "Thomas Chaucer of Ewelme." In *Parliament and Politics in Late Medieval England*, Vol. 3. 151–191. London, 1983.

Rot. Parl. *Rotuli Parliamentorum ut et petitiones, et placita in parliamento* (Parliament Rolls). 6 vols. London 1767–1777.

Rowland, *Companion* Rowland, Beryl, ed. *Companion to Chaucer Studies*. Rev. ed. New York, 1979.

Rowland ed. ———, *Chaucer and Middle English Studies in Honor of Rossell Hope Robbins*. London, 1974.

Russell Russell, P. E. *The English Intervention in Spain and Portugal in the Time of Edward III and Richard II*. Oxford, 1955.

Rymer Rymer, Thomas. *Foedera conventiones, literae, et cujuscunque generis acta publica.* 2d ed., 20 vols. London, 1726–1735.

SA Bryan, W. F. and Germaine Dempster, eds. *Sources and Analogues of Chaucer's Canterbury Tales*. Chicago, 1941. Reprint. Atlantic Highlands, N.J., 1958.

SAC *Studies in the Age of Chaucer.*

Salzman Salzman, L. F. *English Trade in the Middle Ages*. Oxford, 1931.

Sandquist Sandquist, T. A. and M. R. Powicke, eds. *Essays in Medieval History presented to Bertie Wilkinson*. Toronto, 1969.

Schless Schless, Howard H. *Chaucer and Dante*. Norman, Okla, 1984.

Seward Seward, Desmond. *The Hundred Years War: The English in France, 1337–1453*. New York and London, 1978.

Skeat ed. Skeat, Walter W., ed. *The Complete Works of Geoffrey Chaucer*. 6 vols. Oxford, 1894.

Southern Southern, R. W. *Medieval Humanism and Other Studies*. Oxford, 1970.

SP *Studies in Philology*

Spearing Spearing, A. C. *Medieval Dream-Poetry*. Cambridge, Eng. and New York, 1976.

Speculum *Speculum: A Journal of Medieval Studies*

Steel Steel, Anthony. *Richard II*. Cambridge, Eng., 1962.

Stevens Stevens, Martin. "The Royal Stanza in Early English Literature." PMLA 94 (1979): 62–76.

Stow Stow, John. *The Annals of England* . . . London, 1592.

Tatlock	Tatlock, John S. P. *The Development and Chronology of Chaucer's Works*. Chaucer Society, 2d ser., No. 37. London, 1907.
Thrupp	Thrupp, Sylvia L. *The Merchant Class of Medieval London, 1300–1500*. Chicago and London, 1948.
Tout	Tout, T. F. *Chapters in the Administrative History of Mediaeval England: The Wardrobe, the Chamber and the Small Seals*. 6 vols. Manchester, 1920–1933.
Traison	Williams, Benjamin, ed. *Chronicque de la Traïson et Mort de Richart Deux Roy Dengleterre*. English Historical Society. Vol. 22. London, 1846.
TSLL	*Texas Studies in Language and Literature*.
Tuchman	Tuchman, Barbara. *A Distant Mirror: The Calamitous Fourteenth Century*. New York, 1978.
Unwin	Unwin, George, ed. *Finance and Trade under Edward III*. Manchester, Eng., 1918. Reprint. New York and London, 1962.
UTQ	*University of Toronto Quarterly*.
Vale	Vale, Juliet. *Edward III and Chivalry: Chivalric Society and its Context 1270–1350*. Woodbridge, Suffolk, 1982.
Var. 5: 1	Pace, George B. and Alfred David, eds. *A Variorum Edition of the Works of Geoffrey Chaucer*. Edited by Paul G. Ruggiers and Donald C. Baker. Vol. 5, Part 1. *The Minor Poems*. Norman, Okla., 1982.
Wallace	Wallace, David. *Chaucer and the Early Writings of Boccaccio*. Dover, N.H. and Woodbridge, Suffolk, 1985.
Walsingham	Walsingham, Thomas. *Historia Anglicana*. Edited by Henry Thomas Riley. 2 vols., Rolls Series No. 28, vol. 2, parts 1–2. London, 1863–1864.
West. Chron.	Hector, L. C. and Barbara F. Harvey, eds. *The Westminster Chronicle 1381–1394*. Oxford, 1982.
Williams	Williams, George. *A New View of Chaucer*. Durham, N.C., 1965.
Wisdom of Poetry	Benson, Larry D. and Siegfried Wenzel, eds. *The Wisdom of Poetry: Essays in Early English Literature in Honor of Morton W. Bloomfield*. Kalamazoo, Mich., 1982.
Wood	Wood, Charles T. "Coming of Age in Europe: Confirmation, Crowning, and Kingship in Medieval England and France." American Historical Asso-

ciation Proceedings, Session 63. Washington, D.C., 1982.

YES   *Yearbook of English Studies.*

Zacher   Zacher, Christian K. *Curiosity and Pilgrimage: The Literature of Discovery in Fourteenth-Century England.* Baltimore and London, 1976.

References

PREFACE

xii   in Florence: Systematic searches by Professors Larry D. Benson and William Coleman had negative results.

xii   document found in Spain: LR, 64–66. It is a safe-conduct for one "Geffroy de Chauserre" (or Chanserre, *u* and *n* being indistinguishable in most Gothic hands) and three companions to Navarre in 1366. It was published in 1890, but was called a safe-conduct for "Geoffroy de Sancerre, English squire," and so went unnoticed until 1955.

xiii   "the drought of March": A. Stuart Daley, "Chaucer's 'Droughte of March' in Medieval Farm Lore," ChauR 4 (1970): 171–179, who gives references to earlier studies.

xiii   "Little Ice Age": Tuchman, 24.

xiii   date of *The Book of the Duchess*: Condren, 195–212; Palmer, 253–263. For Condren's reply, ChauR 10 (1975): 87–95.

xiv   day of Richard II's coronation: Wood, esp. 1–2; Ferris, 212.

xv   "no real biography . . .": Howard, *Idea*, 24.

xv   "prism of history," an "X-ray moving picture": I cite these phrases in homage to Tuchman's *A Distant Mirror* and Kenner's *The Pound Era*, both models for the present book.

Part One: Into the King's Service (1342–1372)

1. MEMORIES

3   earliest record of Chaucer's life: LR, 14; others on 13–18. It is sometimes argued that Chaucer could have been in the countess's service several years and would by now be sixteen and a yeoman rather than a page. Records of years before 1356 are lost. Chaucer shows up first in the entries for 1357. He is granted less money than some others, which signifies lower status. The one time he is called "Geoffrey Chaucer of London" is in 1357; although the form was used somewhat randomly, it seems more likely to have been used of a relative newcomer. There is this much evidence that he came to the countess during the season 1356–1357; there is no evidence that he came before then.

4   served her as a page: This is assumed from his apparently youthful age; at sixteen or seventeen he would have become, as he did, a *valettus* (yeoman); see LR, 16–18. For an argument, in my opinion strained, that he was not a page, based on the recorded cost of his paltock (tunic), from which his diminutive size is inferred, see Williams, 11–12.

4   evidence of Chaucer's birth: LR, 370.

4   royal clerk . . . got most of them wrong: See Samuel Moore, "Studies in the Life Records of Chaucer," *Anglia* 37 (1913): 1–26.

5   possibly a year or so before: There had been no campaigns for a young English soldier to go on during the three years before the campaign of 1359–1360. His age, if calculated from 1343, would mean "no younger than," but the dates thus derived fit a characteristic picture and it is hard to imagine him retained in the Ulster household five or six years without someone finding him better employment. After he was captured and ransomed in the campaign of 1359–1360 he was sent to England by Prince Lionel as a courier: it has been argued (Williams, 16) that because such a responsibility would not have been given to a "mere stripling," he must have been older. But this is nonsense; if at seventeen he was old enough to fight, he was old enough to carry letters—in all likelihood not official documents but private family business (LR, 20).

5   John Chaucer: LR, 1–7 passim.

5   Agnes Westhall: Vincent B. and Lilian J. Redstone, "The Heyrons of London: A Study in the Social Origins of Geoffrey Chaucer," *Speculum* 12 (1937): 185; Kern, 47–58, 139.

6   attempted coup: See McKisack, 100; LR, 3.

6   cousin of the same name: LR, 3–4; Redstone, 186.

7   real estate: LR, 4–5, 8–10.

7   Chaucer's mother: LR, 7–8.

7   married about 1340: Kern, 93.

7   married before: Kern, 94, 160–161. She would have been an in-law of William de Northwell, keeper of the king's wardrobe. The marriage is inferred from a feoffment to "John de Northwell, son of Agnes Chaucer of London."

7   London . . . a merchant city: Thrupp, ch. 1 and passim.

8   "mainprise": LR, 292–293.

8   surety . . . for Richard Lyons: LR, 5.

8   Alice Perrers . . . about sixteen: Kay, 23.

8   Richard Lyons . . . one of the wealthiest merchants: Kay, 85, 135–137; Thrupp, 134, 354.

9   Chaucer . . . knew Alice Perrers: Haldeen Braddy, "Chaucer and Dame Alice Perrers, *Speculum* 21 (1946): 222–228, repr. in Braddy, 107–115.

9   Sir Richard de Perrers: Kay, 18–20.

9   owned no land: Thrupp, 126–127.

10   Thomas Pynchbek: Manly, 151–157.

10   Harry Bailly: Manly, 77–83.

10   Roger Ware: Edith Rickert, "Chaucer's Hodge of Ware," TLS, Oct. 20, 1932, 761.

10   pretentiously with silver knives: Various sumptuary laws limited the wearing of silver knives to those of higher status or those worth at least £500, but such laws were ignored. J. Wilson McCutchan, "A Solempne and a Greet Fraternitee," PMLA 74 (1959): 313–317, believes the guildsmen are from a craft fraternity and men of eminence, but the livery they wear suggests otherwise; see Thomas Jay Garbáty, "Chaucer's Guildsmen and Their Fraternity," JEGP 59 (1960): 691–709.

11   family home on Thames Street: LR, 8–12; Thrupp, 130–143.

11   coat of arms: Thrupp, 247–256.

11   servants. Ibid., 151–152.

11   Chaucer coat of arms (note): LR, 542–543.

11   seals (note): Kern, 97–99.

12   Black Death: Anna Montgomery Campbell, *The Black Death and Men of Learning* (New York, 1931); Johannes Nohl, *The Black Death: A Chronicle of the Plague Compiled from Contemporary Sources* (London, 1961); Philip Ziegler, *The Black Death* (New York, 1969); George Deaux, *The Black Death, 1347* (London, 1969); *The Black Death: The Impact of the Fourteenth-Century Plague*, ed. Daniel Williman (Binghamton, N.Y., 1982); Robert S. Gottfried, *The Black Death* (New York and London, 1983).

12   "the nearest approach . . .": A. L. Maycock, in Campbell, *Black Death and Men of Learning*, 5.

12   first in the southern ports: McKisack, 331; Ziegler, *Black Death*, 119–129. But the actual directions taken by the plague are very hard to document.

12   deputy butler: LR, 4.

13   "mice and animals . . .": in Campbell, *Black Death and Men of Learning*, 35.

13   at Avignon: Ziegler, *Black Death*, 66–67, 95.

13   "it was so contagious . . .": Campbell, *Black Death and Men of Learning*, 3.

13   the cause of the disease: Ibid., 37–58.

14   "aerial spirit . . .": Ziegler, *Black Death*, 23.

14   disease to be prevented: Campbell, *Black Death and Men of Learning*, 60, 65–77.

14   knew no cure: Ibid., 77–92.

15   "Others . . . maintained that . . .": *The Decameron*, trans. G. H. McWilliam (Baltimore and Harmondsworth, Middlesex, 1972), 52.

16   "He hath a thousand slain . . .": Pardoner's Tale, 679-683.

16   "Nothing is more certain . . .": Campbell, *Black Death and Men of Learning*, 174.

17   friars had developed them: James M. Clark, *The Dance of Death in the Middle Ages and the Renaissance* (Glasgow, 1950).

17   "On Saturday . . ." *The Portable Medieval Reader*, ed. James Bruce Ross and Mary M. McLaughlin (New York, 1949), 176.

18   archbishop of Naples: Campbell, *Black Death and Men of Learning*, 174.

18   Black Death and literature: Olson, esp. ch. 5.

19   "all that is written . . .": Rom. 15: 4, "*quaecumque enim scripta sunt ad nostram doctrinam scripta sunt,*" a quotation sometimes misidentified as 2 Tim. 3: 16 ("*omnis scriptura divinitus inspirata et utilis ad docendum, ad arguendum, . . .*" etc.) where the reading of Scripture is referred to. But the text from Rom. 15 was used to justify reading in general.

19   "celebrate pure aesthetic pleasure . . .": Olson, 230.

20   Prices . . . wages: McKisack, 331–336.

20   "children" until puberty: C. H. Talbot, "Children in the Middle Ages," *Children's Literature* 6 (1977): 17–33.

20   "They think only . . .": Ibid., 18–19.

21   "as doth the mother . . .": used of January's roaring and cry in the Merchant's Tale, 2365, when he sees his young wife cuckolding him in a most unseemly manner. But the simile would be neither true nor funny if such grief were not acknowledged as extreme.

21   primer: George A. Plimpton, *The Education of Chaucer Illustrated from the Schoolbooks in Use in his Time* (London and New York, 1935), a book so full of errors that its every word is suspect, but such a primer is reproduced and discussed, 18–35.

21   French: On the bilingualism of the period, see Albert C. Baugh and Thomas Cable, *A History of the English Language*, 3rd ed. (Englewood Cliffs, N.J., 1978), 126–157.

22   "lords, barons, knights . . .": Ibid., 139 (reported by Froissart).

23   "no more French . . .": Ibid., 150.

23   "Escript a Hereford . . .": Ibid., 151 n. 1.

23   Chancery: John H. Fisher, "Chancery and the Emergence of Standard Written English in the Fifteenth Century," *Speculum* 52 (1977): 870–899.

23   Mandeville . . . an Englishman: Josephine Waters Bennett, *The Rediscovery of Sir John Mandeville* (1954; repr. New York, 1971), esp. ch. 5, 13–14.

24   Chaucer family . . . owned a few books: Thrupp, 160–163.

24   decline in the quality of education: See William J. Courtenay, "The Effect of the Black Death on English Higher Education," *Speculum* 55 (1980): 696–714, esp. 706–707.

24   medieval grammar school: Clara P. McMahon, *Education in Fifteenth-Century England* (Baltimore, 1947), 99-122.

25   Almonry School at Saint Paul's: Edith Rickert, "Chaucer at School," MP 29 (1932): 257–274, and *Chaucer's World* 121–126. Writing of classical works in the school's library, Prof. Rickert remarked, "I have examined many lists of school and college libraries and found nothing comparable to that of St. Paul's Almonry at so early a date" ("Chaucer at School," 272).

25   poor scholars: McMahon, *Education*, 101.

26   Seven Liberal Arts: Ibid., 101–107; Plimpton, *Education of Chaucer*, 93–114. On the general subject see *The Seven Liberal Arts in the Middle Ages*, ed. David L. Wagner (Bloomington, Ind., 1983), esp. ch. 1 and 2.

26   Geoffrey of Vinsauf: Charles Sears Baldwin, *Medieval Rhetoric and Poetic* (to 1400), (New York and London, 1928), 187, characterized Geoffrey's work as a "museum for boys," i.e., presumably a work for students. Though its influence has been contested, we know that Chaucer knew it because he quoted it and named the author.

27   Renaissance of the Twelfth Century: Charles Homer Haskins, *The Renaissance of the Twelfth Century* (Cambridge, Mass., 1927), and see C. S. Lewis, *De Descriptione Temporum* (Cambridge, Eng., 1955).

27   "made a leap . . .": Kenneth Clark, *Civilisation* (New York, 1969), 33.

27   One theory: Lynn White, Jr., *Medieval Technology and Social Change* (Oxford, 1962), 57–78.

27   Another theory: Henri Pirenne, *Les villes du moyen age* (Brussels, 1927); and see Henri Focillon, *The Year 1000* (repr. New York and London, 1969), 80–81.

28   "medieval humanism": R. W. Southern, *Medieval Humanism and Other Studies* (Oxford, 1970), 29–60.

28   in the monasteries: The discovery of Giles Constable in an unpublished essay.

29   "Man, being the . . .": Southern, *Medieval Humanism,* 40.

29   "partly a ground plan . . .": Ibid., 41.

30   circular designs: Howard, *Idea,* 199–209, 325–332.

30   "Europe then entered . . .": Southern, *Medieval Humanism,* 58.

30   Thomas Aquinas . . . vision: *New Catholic Encyclopedia* (New York McGraw-Hill: 1967), 14: 109.

31   Petrarch: *Petrarch's Secret,* trans. William H. Draper (London, 1911), 192.

31   Pandarus and the Pardoner: *Troilus and Criseyde,* 4: 1505, and the Pardoner's Tale, 539.

32   whether Chaucer knew nominalist ideas: Russell A. Peck, "Chaucer and the Nominalist Questions," *Speculum* 53 (1978): 745–760.

32   obsolescence: Cf. Howard, *Idea,* 89–92.

33   Chaucer . . . mentions . . . Alain de Lille: *Parliament of Fowls,* 316; the reference is to *De planctu Naturae.*

33   Richard de Bury: See p. 215.

34   the great fairs: Salzman, ch. 8.

34   speculative financiers: Power, 119.

35   Derek Brewer: See Brewer, *World,* e.g., 41–44, where Chaucer's retraction of "all his non-religious poems" is put forth as evidence of a father "normally easy-going, but in the end strict." Perhaps. But such an exercise is extremely vulnerable. We can't be sure Chaucer really meant to condemn his secular poems, or in what spirit he wrote the passage in which he seems to do so. David Wallace points out to me that his retraction may have sprung from a Catholic sense of *propriety.* Nor must such strictness show paternal influence in an age when priestly father figures were in such abundance. Then, too, some react *against* their fathers: one could make as strong a case that his retraction was a self-destructive act betokening unresolved Oedipal conflict, or an overly dutiful act that suggests a rejecting father, or a competitive act. Brewer uses adjectives applied to mothers and fathers in Chaucer's works as a hint of his parents' characters —an interesting thought. But such characterizations, often conventional, could indicate what Chaucer wished his parents had been, not what they were, or how he viewed himself and his wife

as parents. Nearly all such passages apply to fictional fathers and mothers seen through others' eyes, and all can be thought stereotypes. In such matters it has seemed to me better, when nothing is known, to say nothing.

35   John Heron: J. M. Manly, "Mary Chaucer's First Husband," *Speculum* 9 (1934): 86–88 and Redstone, "Heyrons," *Speculum* 12: 182–194.

35   Uncle Simon [Chaucer]: Kern, *Ancestry*, 79–80.

35   Simon Manning: LR, 288–289; Alfred A. Kern, "Chaucer's Sister," MLN 23 (1908): 52.

35   mainpernor: LR, 285 ff.

35   Katherine inherited: LR, 288 and n. 7.

36   most often at thirteen or fourteen: Thrupp, 196.

36   Derek Brewer: "Love and Marriage in Chaucer's Poetry," MLR, 49 (1954): 461–464.

37   pressure . . . to "take up knighthood": Du Boulay, *Ambition*, 66.

37   Geoffrey Darsham: LR, 6.

37   sued for debt: LR, 6.

37   In 1350: McKisack, 137; Armitage-Smith, 6–8.

38   Froissart's account: Froissart, 1: 163 (pp. 105–106).

38   she was in London: LR, 18 n. 4. The money paid Chaucer on May 20 was paid at London. For the amount, 2s., LR, 13.

39   Christmas, 1357: LR, 18; Armitage-Smith, 10–11.

39   necessaries against the feasting: LR, 15.

39   marriage . . . to Blanche: Armitage-Smith, 11–15.

2. A YOUNG MAN'S WORLD

41   "new man": See Middleton, 15–56. On the concept, Donald R. Howard, "Chaucer the Man," PMLA 80 (1965): 337–343; D. S. Brewer, "Class Distinction in Chaucer," *Speculum* 43 (1968): 290–305; and Paul Strohm, "Chaucer's Audience," *Literature and History* 5 (1977): 26–41.

42   Pages continued . . . schooling: Joseph and Frances Gies, *Life in a Medieval Castle* (New York, 1974), 111; Green, 85.

42   only a passable Latin scholar: Bruce Harbert, "Chaucer and the Latin Classics," in Brewer, *Background*, 137–153.

42   Seneca . . . passages he cites: Robert A. Pratt, "Chaucer and the Hand that Fed Him," *Speculum* 41 (1966): 619–642.

43   what books were available where: cf. Green, 94. On Edward III's court as a patron of literature and the arts, see Vale, ch. 3.

44   "Your eyen two . . .": Var. 5: 1: 171–178. The poem survives in a single ms. and there is no strong reason for believing it is by Chaucer; see Brusendorff, 440. But if it is not by Chaucer, it is a very successful Chaucerian imitation.

44   a French song: See Fisher, ed., 578, note to *Parliament of Fowls* 677, and the notes in Robinson, and Baugh. Skeat remarked it was hard to see how Chaucer's five-stress line could be sung to music for an octosyllabic line.

44   "Now welcome, summer . . .": *Parliament of Fowls*, 680–692.

45   an alienated man: Brewer, "Class Distinction," *Speculum* 43: 290–305.

46   Henry Herbury: LR, 9 and n. 6; for the deed itself, LR, 1–2.

47   Easter spent in London: LR, 18.

48   Prince Lionel: McKisack, 267.

48   king's policy: Tout 3: 252.

48   heir presumptive: LR, 17 n. 3.

48   Keeper of England: Tout 3: 164.

48   finances were reorganized: LR, 18.

48   about twenty-five: George E. Cokayne, *Complete Peerage* (London, 1959), 12: 180.

49   compensatory maternal feeling: Kay, 63.

49   annuity of £100: LR, 17.

49   betrothed to Edmund Mortimer: LR, 18.

49   In a royal household: See esp. Gies, *Life in a Medieval Castle*; and *The Secular Spirit: Life and Art at the End of the Middle Ages*, intro. by Timothy B. Husband and Jane Hayward (New York, 1975).

50   symbolical or allegorical treatment: Marcelle Thiébaux, *The Stag of Love: The Chase in Medieval Literature* (Ithaca, N.Y. and London, 1974).

51   Tournaments: Sidney Painter, *French Chivalry* (Baltimore and London, 1940), 45–53, 156–157; Keen, ch. 5 and 11; Vale, ch. 4.

51   "expended and laid waste . . .": Henry Knighton, *Chronicon*, in Barnie, 84.

52   rhythms of a day: Gies, *Life in a Medieval Castle*, ch. 6.

53   drunkenly saying goodnight: E.g., Squire's Tale, 347 ff.

53   courtesy books of the period: Frederick J. Furnivall, ed., *Early English Meals and Manners*, EETS OS 32 (London, 1868) is a collection of such works.

53   John Russell's *Book of Nurture*: in Furnivall, *Early English Meals*, 1–123.

54   main meals: Cosman, 11–20 and passim.

55   dinner for a fish day: Furnivall, *Early English Meals*, 50–53; Cosman, 25.

56   Subtleties: Cosman, 33.

56   "excess of divers . . .": Parson's Tale, 444 ff.

57   Reading aloud: Green, 97–100.

57   "placed on . . .": Green, 99.

58   frontispiece: See p. 347.

58 Colle: *House of Fame,* 1277–1281, and James F. Royster, "Chaucer's Colle Tregetour," SP 23 (1926): 380–384.

58 mimes . . . plays: E. K. Chambers, *The Mediaeval Stage,* 2 vols. (Oxford, 1903) 1: 89–389.

58 playing the flute: "floyting" could also mean whistling, but the latter would be an unconventional detail and no accomplishment for a courtier.

59 Memory: Frances A. Yates, *The Art of Memory* (Chicago and London, 1966), esp. ch. 3 and 4.

59 visual picture of the universal order: See Lewis, *Image,* the best short treatment of the medieval world order.

59 Felix Fabri: Howard, *Writers,* 45–46.

59 "the Goddess Natura": Economou, esp. ch. 1 and 2.

60 "the Goddess Fortuna": Howard R. Patch, *The Goddess Fortuna in Mediaeval Literature* (1927; repr. New York, 1967), and Willard Farnham, *The Medieval Heritage of Elizabethan Tragedy* (1936; repr. Oxford, 1956).

61 Saint Thomas Aquinas: See Dom Odon Lottin, *Psychologie et Morale aux XIIᵉ et XIIIᵉ siècles,* 6 vols. (Louvain and Gembloux, 1942–1960) 2: 588–589.

61 Satan: Jeffrey Burton Russell, *Satan: The Early Christian Tradition* (Ithaca, N.Y., 1981).

62 old feudal ceremonies: For a wonderful example, if an extreme one, see Tuchman, 23.

63 "soft" existence: The distinction between "soft and hard primitivism" was developed by Arthur O. Lovejoy and George Boas, *Primitivism and Related ideas in Antiquity* (Baltimore, 1935), esp. ch. 1.

64 *three ages . . . seven* ages: See Gerhart B. Ladner, *The Idea of Reform* (1959; rev. New York, 1967), 222–238, and George Boas, *Essays on Primitivism and Related Ideas in the Middle Ages* (1948; repr. New York, 1966), 177–193.

65 mythology of its own: Keen, ch. 6.

65 *chivalry*: Ibid., esp. ch. 1 and 2, but the whole of Keen's masterful book is the definitive treatment of chivalry as an idea and a behavioral code.

65 "Prowess": Painter, 29 and passim.

65 "Glory": Painter, 34–37, 153–155.

65 for booty too: Painter, 156–158.

66 "storial thing . . .": Miller's Prologue, 3179.

68 "English Gaufred": *House of Fame,* 1470.

68 mnemonic verses: Thrupp, 248, mentions "the kings of England versified."

69 not quite into the twelfth: Cf. the anthropologists' observation that family histories never go back more than seven generations;

Robert Kanigel, "Storing Yesterday," *The Johns Hopkins Magazine*, June 1981, 32.

69   In 1359 the glory: This account of the campaign of 1359–1360 is chiefly based on LR, ch. 3, and Oliver Farrar Emerson, "Chaucer's First Military Service—A Study of Edward Third's Invasion of France in 1359–1360," RomR 3 (1912): 321–361. Emerson compared chronicle accounts of the campaign with an eye to Chaucer's experience, and I know no one who has improved on his work. Possibly he used Froissart more than a historian would today, but possibly he was right. Froissart distorted facts out of chivalric sentiment and nostalgia, but these feelings he shared with men of his day, for whom he was creating a myth, and they are part of the historical picture. See also Edouard Perroy, *The Hundred Years War*, trans. W. B. Wells (New York, 1965), 136–142, and Seward, 96–101.

71   They waited: According to one account they made a futile one-day effort at an assault; see Emerson, "Chaucer's First Military Service," RomR 3: 351 n. 105.

71   at Cormicy: Froissart 1: 209 (p. 128).

71   Derek Brewer: Brewer, *World*, 76–79.

71   captured and imprisoned: LR, ch. 3.

72   Machaut . . . Deschamps: LR, 27 n. 9. Most scholars assume Chaucer could not have known Machaut was here. For the idea that he was detained in Reims I am indebted to a conversation with James I. Wimsatt.

72   Maison des Musiciens: George G. Williams, "*The House of Fame* and the House of the Musicians," MLN 72 (1957): 6–9; Georges Boussinesq and Gustave Laurent, *Histoire de Reims* (Reims, 1933), 1: 348–350.

73   earl of March: Ramona Bressie, "Was Chaucer at the Siege of Paris?" JEGP 39 (1940): 209–221. Others listed with Chaucer were with one exception all ransomed on January 12 or thereafter, when the English had left the area of Reims. Chaucer, with one other (Richard Dulle, archer, ransomed April 8), is listed as captured *in partibus Francie*. See LR, 24, table. Rouvray was in semi-independent Burgundy, so possibly the phrase indicates they were captured before the army entered that region. The editors of LR, 28 n. 1, think it probably has no significance, and probably they are right. Prof. Bressie did not raise the issue. Passage between Reims and Guillon would not have been easy for a ransomed soldier, to be sure, but then a soldier discharged at Rouvray would have found it no easier to get home.

73   "it seemed . . .": *Chronicle of London*, in Emerson, "Chaucer's First Military Service," RR 3: 356.

73   king vowed: Froissart 1: 212 (p. 130).

73   Treaty of Brétigny: LR, 19–20.

74   Lionel in Ireland: LR, 21; McKisack, 231–233.

74   Inner Temple: LR, 12 n. 5. Edith Rickert, "Was Chaucer a Student at the Inner Temple?" *The Manly Anniversary Studies in Language and Literature* (Chicago, 1923), 20–31, and D. S. Bland, "Chaucer and the Inns of Court: A Re-examination," ES 23 (1952): 145–155.

74   William Buckley: Rickert, "Was Chaucer a Student?" *Manly Anniversary Studies*, argued too that Buckley had no motive for making up Chaucer facts to feed to Speght, unless to reflect credit on the Inner Temple, as this story does not. Still, assuming Master Buckley was a Protestant, his story does slightly reflect the view of Renaissance Englishmen that Chaucer was a sort of proto-Protestant; it could have been a trick of memory, something both these Elizabethans would have enjoyed believing. Even so, I still agree that it sounds authentic.

74   three-fourths of offenses: Rickert, "Was Chaucer a Student?" *Manly Anniversary Studies*, 24–25.

75   received a stipend: Green, ch. 1.

75   records show: Rickert, "Was Chaucer a Student?" *Manly Anniversary Studies*, 28–29.

75   in the Ulster household: LR, 17, 21, 24, 69, 95, 99–102, 106–109. For much more extensive evidence of this kind, see Hulbert, 6–36.

75   Agnes Archer: LR, 69 gives the date of this marriage as 1343, which would make him a generation older than Chaucer. Possibly two people of the same name are involved. Or he could have been transferred back and forth, for this was not unusual. If it is one person, he was a valettus for an alarmingly long time.

75   Geoffrey Stukely: Tout 4: 348.

75   John Prior . . . son of a London merchant: Thrupp, 361, lists a prominent John Prior who could have been his father, but the name is not an uncommon one.

76   "noriture" . . . "lettrure": Green, 73–91.

76   taught at the Inns of Court: W. Herbert, *Antiquities of the Inns of Court and Chancery* . . . (London, 1804); Robert R. Pearce, *A History of the Inns of Court and Chancery* (London, 1848); John Bruce Williamson, *The History of the Temple, London* (London, 1924). All such treatments of education at the Inns are based on later documents; in Chaucer's time their educational system was beginning to evolve. How far along it was in this evolution by the 1360s is not known. But it seems reasonable to argue, as I do in what follows, that its development *began* with the teaching of law and that polite accomplishments were added under the influence of the royal court. Their taking in students

may have been a matter of economic necessity: since the courts
met only some dozen weeks of the year, they were empty most
of the time when they were literally inns. See S. E. Thorne,
"The Early History of the Inns of Court with Special Reference
to Gray's Inn," *Graya* 50 (1959): 79–97. In these matters I am
indebted to conversations with and an unpublished essay by
Prof. George D. Gopen.

76   they existed: Tout 3: 202 n. gives the earliest date of a record of
lawyers in the Inns as 1356, and it is ambiguous; a sure connection of the Inns with "prentices" of the law is not found until
1381. Stow, *Chronicles,* reported that during the Peasants' Revolt the rioters "took out all the books and remembrancers that
were in the hatches of the prentices of the law, carried them into
the high street, and there burnt them," Pearce, *History of the
Inns of Court,* 213–218. Possibly this is the record Tout refers
to. But even here, "prentices" does not necessarily mean students. The source of much information of this sort is Sir John
Fortescue, who took pleasure in pointing out that some features
of education were modeled on practices of the king's court; see
Green, 71–72.

76   "in terms": General Prologue: 323–324; see Howard, *Idea,* 147–148
n. 27.

77   "Take, for example . . .": Rickert, "Was Chaucer a Student?" *Manly
Anniversary Studies,* 30.

77   those educated in the common law: Tout 3: 202.

3. THE BEST OF TIMES—THE 1360s

79   Jean Froissart: F. S. Shears, *Froissart: Chronicler and Poet* (London,
1930), ch. 2.

80   left no visible marks: This from Geoffrey le Baker; he adds that he
was beaten and starved, which would have been visible enough.

80   attended her funeral: LR, 18.

81   the claims of the time: The imputation of a homosexual relation
between the king and Piers Gaveston was apparently gossip of
a later time, which was then much later made a "factoid"
through Marlowe's play; patronage is the more likely explanation of their closeness, and canon-law reasons for deposing a king
may explain the origin of the rumor. See Jeffrey Scott Hamilton,
"Piers Gaveston, Earl of Cornwall, 1307–1312," Ph.D. diss.,
Emory University, 1982.

82   *myn biddinye*: Kay, 59. Edward had the name embroidered on a
bodice given to her on the occasion of their daughter Isabella's
marriage to Enguerrand de Coucy, with another embroidered
"Ich wrude muche" (her motto, "I work hard"). The gift on the

occasion of her child's marriage seems an indication of his tenderness toward her. For the meaning of the phrase I'm indebted to my colleague Orrin Robinson, who adds that *biddinye* ("helper") would have had a certain connotation of servile status.

83   In youth she had: The description is based on the bishop of Exeter's report written when she was nine; there is some question whether it may apply to one of her sisters, but the family resemblance still probably makes it applicable enough. See G. C. Coulton, *Chaucer and His England* (New York and London, 1908), 181–182.

83   her large debts: Tout 4: 174–175, 5: 250–259, 278–284.

83   "Countess of Salisbury": Emerson, ch. 6, and see Harvey, 88. See Margaret Galway, "Joan of Kent and the Order of the Garter," *Univ. of Birmingham Historical Journal* 1 (1947): 13–50, held the quite mistaken idea that Joan of Kent was the countess of Salisbury. On the founding of the order of the Garter, see Packe, 170–174; on the story of the rape of Alice Brotherton by King Edward, recorded by the chronicler Jean le Bel but omitted and denied by Froissart, see Packe, 105–123, who argues that the violence was done her nine years later and by her own husband, Edward Montagu. On Froissart's treatment, Palmer ed., 22, 71.

83   legendary beginning of the order of the Garter: On its actual beginnings, Vale, ch. 5. And see Barber, 85–87.

84   Prince of Wales: McKisack, 266.

84   Isabella, resisted all efforts: Tuchman, ch. 9; Tout 3: 253.

85   Blanche was the daughter: Marjorie Anderson, "Blanche, Duchess of Lancaster," MP 45 (1948): 152–159; Armitage-Smith, esp. 19–20; McKisack, esp. 254–255.

86   Gaunt's career: Armitage-Smith, ch. 2.

88   "An ABC": Fisher ed., 673–676, and see his introductory remarks on 668–669; see also notes in Skeat ed., and Robinson ed. (Skeat prints the French original); Clemen, 175–179; Brusendorff, 238–241.

88   surviving manuscripts bear this out: George B. Pace, "The Adorned Initials of Chaucer's *ABC*," *Manuscripta* 23 (1979): 88–98.

88   entries in the papal registers: Anderson, "Blanche," MP 45: 154–155.

90   vivid words: The only ordinary words Chaucer uses for the initial "alphabet" lines of stanzas, "He" (meaning God), "I," and "Even," have stark existential referents that make them germane to the poem's purpose.

90   concrete and specific: Chaucer adds to his source the *flos florum* motif, "the flower of flowers," (line 4) referring to the perfection of the Blessed Virgin. See Peter Dronke, *Medieval Latin and the*

Rise of European Love-Lyric (Oxford, 1968) 1: 181–192, and Howard, *Idea,* 206–207.

90   Its language is heightened: Clemen, 175–176, shows that there are more abstract nouns of romance origin in it than in Chaucer's other poems; and Romance words are, to English ears, more elegant.

90   religion of resignation: See p. 493.

90   better piece of religious verse: See Rossell Hope Robbins, "The Lyrics," in Rowland, *Companion,* 395. This does not of itself argue that it is a later work. Chaucer could have stumbled this early on the "pentameter" line, and a genius can do things in youth that others can't do at any age. Alfred David, "An ABC, To the Style of the Prioress," in *Acts of Interpretation,* ed. Mary J. Carruthers and Elizabeth D. Kirk (Norman, Okla., 1982), 148–150, argues for an early date on the assumption that one style must be used at one time in a writer's life. The consensus is that the poem is "probably [the] earliest of his surviving writings"; see Pace, "Adorned Initials," *Manuscripta* 23: 95.

91   letter in Latin: LR, 67–68.

91   wife's maiden name: LR, 68 n. 5.

91   Nine months later: See Williams, 45; but this interpretation would seem to discredit Williams's notion that this child was not Chaucer's.

91   Gilles de Roet: LR, 69; Manly, 49–56; Cook, 55–63. Little is known of him. He was buried in Saint Paul's cathedral and his tombstone is said to have reported that he died in the reign of Edward III. The source is somewhat unreliable; its author was Major Payne Fisher, poet laureate to Oliver Cromwell, said to be inaccurate as a scholar of antiquities. See Payne Fisher, *The Tombs, Monuments, &c. visible in S. Paul's Cathedral . . . Previous to its Destruction by Fire A. D. 1666,* ed. G. Blacker Morgan (London, 1684; privately repr. 1885) 46, 66–67.

92   "Philippa Pan" (note): LR, 16–17; Manly, *Light,* 57–63; Margaret Galway, "Philippa Paṅ, Philippa Chaucer," MLR, 55 (1960): 481–487, and "Walter Roet and Philippa Chaucer," N & Q NS 1 (Feb. 1954): 48–49.

92   evidence . . . has to do with money: LR, ch. 5 and 6.

92   June 13, 1374: LR, 271.

92   Chaucer's father died: LR, 6–7.

92   Chaucer's sister . . . inherited: LR, 288 and n. 7.

93   four children: LR, ch. 30.

93   Elizabeth "Chausier": LR, 545–546. "Chaucy" was a spelling of Chaucer's name sometimes found used of him, along with "Chausier" and the like. The nineteenth-century notion that she was Chaucer's sister is preserved in Robinson, p. xix, along

with the more general assumption that she was his daughter. For the conjecture that she was the illegitimate daughter of John of Gaunt, see Williams, 45–47.

93   eldest son, Thomas: Roskell, 152.

93   second son, Lewis: The age is given in the introduction of the treatise itself, line 24 as numbered in Robinson ed., 545.

93   record of Thomas and Lewis Chaucer: LR, 544–545.

94   Thomas Chaucer . . . the bastard son of John of Gaunt: Williams, 44–55, whose notes give references to his precessors in these conjectures, Russell Krauss and Margaret Galway. Gardner, 152–167, supported the idea. Roskell, 151–153, ignores it. Martin B. Ruud, *Thomas Chaucer*, Research Publications of the University of Minnesota, Studies of Language and Literature No. 9 (1926), ch. 7, concluded that there is no reason to doubt Thomas Chaucer's legitimacy. On the arms, see E. A. Greening-Lamborn, "The Arms on the Chaucer Tomb at Ewelme," *Oxoniensia* 5 (1940): 78–93, who dismisses the notion that Thomas was Gaunt's son (84).

94   B. J. Whiting: Review of Krauss, *Three Chaucer Studies*, in *Speculum* 8 (1933): 535.

95   One biographer: Gardner, 167.

95   "the transaction . . .": Du Boulay, 96.

95   marriage in the late fourteenth century: Du Boulay, 88–101.

97   Coleridge: *Table Talk*, Sept. 1, 1832.

98   "It seems impossible . . .": J. W. Hales in DNB under Chaucer, p. 158.

99   the specified number of years: Roger S. Loomis, "Chaucer's Eight Years Sickness," MLN 59 (1944): 178–180.

99   One scholar: Margaret Galway, "Chaucer's Hopeless Love," MLN 60 (1945): 431–439.

99   less than complimentary to Philippa: See Brewer, *World*, 187.

99   his later songs: Notably the envoys to Bukton and Scogan, and "Merciless Beaute," Var. 5: 1: 139–160, 171–178.

103 move medieval readers . . . to tears: See A. S. Cook, "The First Two Readers of Petrarch's Tale of Griselda," MP 15 (1918): 633–643.

103 God grante you . . .": Var. 5: 1: 144–148.

103 "To Rosemunde": Var. 5: 1: 161–170.

103 fish caught on a hook: Mark E. Amsler, "Mad Lovers and Other Hooked Fish: Chaucer's *Complaint of Mars*," *Allegorica* 4 (1979): 301–314. The notion is apparently based on the Latin pun *Amor / Hamor*.

104 C. S. Lewis's four characteristics: *Allegory*, esp. 12–23.

104 but one of many interpretations: For a summary, and my own interpretation, Howard, *The Three Temptations* (Princeton, 1966),

83–103. Those mentioned are the interpretations of Wechssler, Denomy, Moller, and Robertson. A good overview of the subject is Elizabeth Salter, "Courts and Courtly Love," in Daiches, 407–444.

104   Georges Duby: *Medieval Marriage: Two Models from Twelfth-Century France*, trans. Elborg Forster (Baltimore and London, 1978).

105   "While I was young . . .": "Envy to Scogan," 40, in Var. 5: 1: 159.

106   adultery was the norm: Lewis, *Allegory*, 13–18, gives a summary of theological positions.

106   "inborn suffering": the phrase was Andreas Cappellanus's, in *De Amore*.

106   John of Garland: John M. Steadman, "Courtly Love as a Problem of Style," in Esch, 1–33.

4. THE WHEEL TURNS

109   "accustomed winter and summer . . .": *Liber Niger* [of the household of Edward IV], in Fisher ed., 958.

110   diplomatic betrayal: Barnie, 13 f.

110   "They danced . . .": Richard Barber, ed., *The Life and Campaigns of the Black Prince* (London, 1979), 104.

110   Round Table: Barnie, 66 f.

111   "fashion": See Anne Hollander, *Seeing through Clothes* (New York, 1978), 17, 90, 132–133; and Stella Mary Newton, *Fashion in the Age of the Black Prince* (Woodbridge, Suffolk, and Totowa, N.J., 1980).

111   expediency in warfare: Charles W. C. Oman, *The Art of War in the Middle Ages: A.D. 378–1515* (1885; rev. ed., John H. Beeler, ed., Ithaca, N.Y., 1953), 124–132. On other reasons for the English victory, see Barber, 70–73.

112   ". . . pomp of the French race": Barber, *Life and Campaigns*, 46.

112   social inferiors: Cf. Barnie, 70.

112   "like a stouthearted soldier . . .": Geoffrey le Baker, in Barber, *Life and Campaigns*, 82.

113   common servant: Froissart 1: 252 (p. 179), by which is probably meant a *valletus* (yeoman), not a *villain*; the English, Froissart says, grumbled that the mission was worthy of a prelate or a baron.

113   profit motive: Barnie, 71; Painter, 34–37.

113   "Let the boy . . .": Froissart 1: 129 (p. 82).

113   his father loved her first: On this notion, now discredited, see Margaret Galway, "Joan of Kent and the Order of the Garter," *Univ. of Birmingham Historical Journal* 1 (1947–48): 13–50.

114   campaign of propaganda: P. E. Russell, "The War in Spain and
       Portugal," in Palmer ed., 83–100, esp. 89.

115   issued a safe-conduct: LR, 64–66. See Thomas J. Garbáty, "Chaucer
       in Spain, 1366: Soldier of Fortune or Agent of the Crown?"
       ELN 5 (1967): 81–87, and Albert C. Baugh, "The Background
       of Chaucer's Mission to Spain," in Esch, 55–69.

116   African king: Froissart 3: 76 (pp. 437–438).

117   "Thou knowest . . .": Froissart 1: 241 (p. 166).

118   marriage . . . arranged for Prince Lionel: A. S. Cook, "The Last
       Months of Chaucer's Earliest Patron," *Transactions of the Con-
       necticut Academy of Arts and Sciences*, 21 (1916): 1–144.

118   city of Arezzo: Tuchman, 410.

120   poisoned by the younger two: Chamberlin, 26; note the conflicting
       reports.

120   Chaucer accompanied the English party: LR, 29–30. Margaret Gal-
       way, "Chaucer's Journeys in 1368," TLS, Apr. 4, 1958, 183;
       Edith Rickert, "Chaucer Abroad in 1368," MP 25 (1928): 511–
       512.

121   marquis of Montferrat: Cox, 310–313.

122   "shrouded in a dark mist . . .": Howard, *Writers*, 39.

123   one scholar argues: Palmer, 253–261.

123   others that it was not: Esp. Condren, ChauR 10, 87–95.

123   wrote to Count Louis de Male: Palmer, 253–255.

125   The prince . . . asked du Guesclin: Froissart 1: 244 (pp. 170–171).

125   denying ransom: William Askins, collecting references about denied
       ransoms, found none about the English, which speaks for their
       good record.

125   On August 15: Froissart 1: 273 (p. 190).

125   what contemporaries called dropsy: Agnes Strickland, *Lives of the
       Queens of England* (Philadelphia, 1848), 2: 201 says a "dropsi-
       cal malady"; Loomis, *Mirror*, no. 15, says, I think in error,
       plague. Dr. Thomas Ainsworth suggested congestive heart fail-
       ure.

125   Froissart reports: Froissart 1: 273 (pp. 189–190).

126   "march out of the town . . .": Froissart 1: 145 (pp. 90–91).

127   10 marks yearly to Alice Perrers: Kay, 67–70, source not given.

127   liveries for mourning: LR, 85.

127   a daughter named Blanche: Kay, 79.

128   July to November 1369 . . . Chaucer was with him: LR, 31.

128   In June 1370: LR, 31–32.

128   Sir John Chandos . . . was slain: Froissart 1: 278 (p. 193), but various
       writers interpret details differently. See Barber, 222.

128   "with great pleasure . . .": Froissart 1: 290 (p. 201).

129   cirrhosis of the liver: Emerson, 231.

129   "the undisciplined populace . . .": Walsingham, in Barnie, 77–78.

130 "It was a most melancholy business . . .": Froissart 1: 290 (p. 200).
     It is sometimes objected that Froissart wrote this passage after
     he had begun to show pro-French sympathies. But it should be
     weighed that his sympathies shifted from England to France in
     part because England's days of chivalry seemed to be at an end.
     On his treatment of the Black Prince, see Richard Barber, "Jean
     Froissart and Edward the Black Prince," in Palmer ed., ch. 2;
     and Harvey, 25–26.

130 Costanza was sixteen when they married: Williams, 54.

131 English fleet was intercepted: Russell, 186–195.

131 The . . . venture cost £900,000: Walsingham 1: 315, but probably
     an inflated figure.

5. THE EAR WITHIN

132 *babble* and *doodle*: Frye, 270–281.

133 "first finder of our fair language": Thomas Hoccleve, in Brewer,
     Heritage, 63.

133 Some writers: George Gascoigne (1575) claimed that the poetic line
     "which hath in it fewest syllables shall be found yet to consist
     of words that have such natural sound as may seem equal in
     length to a verse which hath many more syllables of lighter
     accents." See Brewer, *Heritage*, 110. Speght in his edition of
     1598, reprinted in 1602 and 1687, insisted that Chaucer's meter
     was regular.

133 one Henry Peacham: Brewer, *Heritage*, 149.

133 Dryden said: Ibid., 1: 165.

133 Thomas Gray: Ibid., 1: 215–220.

133 The editor Thomas Tyrwhitt: Ibid., 1: 232.

134 discovered by . . . James I. Wimsatt (note): *Chaucer and the Poems
     of 'CH' in University of Pennsylvania MS French 15*, Chaucer
     Studies IX (Cambridge, Eng. and Totowa, N.J., 1982).

135 poet Martin le Franc: Green, 98.

136 "Womanly Noblesse": Var. 5: 1: 179–186.

139 the standard principles of medieval rhetoric: See Alan M. F. Gunn,
     The Mirror of Love (Lubbock, Tex., 1952).

140 The pictures are lively and elegant: See John V. Fleming, *The Roman
     de la Rose: A Study in Allegory and Iconography* (Princeton,
     1969) for such an argument; for the objections, see the review
     by Alfred David in ELN 9.2 (December 1971): 134–139.

140 The Middle English translation: On the text, see the introduction to
     Ronald Sutherland, *The Romaunt of the Rose and Le Roman
     de la Rose: A Parallel-Text Edition* (Berkeley, 1968).

143 "major" stresses: These are the "maximal" stresses described by Mor-
     ris Halle and Samuel Jay Keyser, "Chaucer and the Study of

Prosody," CE 28 (1966): 187–219. On Chaucer's debt to the
"main tradition of medieval verse," "its measurement of the line
by syllables, counted and variously grouped," see John Stevens'
"The 'Music' of the Lyric: Machaut, Deschamps, Chaucer," in
Medieval and Pseudo-Medieval Literature, ed. Piero Boitani and
Anna Torti (Cambridge, Eng. and Tübingen, 1984), 109–129
esp. 125–129.

148 Jean de La Mote: Constance L. Rosenthal, "A Possible Source of
    Chaucer's Booke of the Duchesse—Li Regret de Guillaume
    by Jehan de la Mote," MLN 48 (1933): 511–514, and see
    Baugh, 4.

148 completed it within a matter of weeks: Palmer, *Duchess,* 259.

148 September 1371: Armitage-Smith, 93.

148 criticism of Gaunt's second marriage: Palmer, 258–259. Gaunt's liai-
    son with Katherine Swynford was established by the time he
    married Costanza. In the poem Gaunt is referred to as the earl
    of Richmond, a title he surrendered along with the castle before
    July 1371; but he might have been referred to by what was his
    title then, at the time of Blanche's death. Similarly he seems to
    be referred to as a king in line 1314, and he styled himself king
    of Castile and León only after his marriage to Costanza. But
    "king" might refer back to "Octavian" (who is, however, called
    an emperor); or it might refer to Gaunt as the king in the
    metaphorical game of chess in which the queen is lost. But these
    two bits of evidence are not as persuasive as Palmer's argument
    from the *tone* of the poem.

149 when or how it was *presented*: On such presentations, see Green,
    63–65 and passim.

149 commemorations of the duchess's death: Condren, 195–200. On the
    commemorations, see Armitage-Smith, 77–78.

149 sixth anniversary, 1374: N. B. Lewis, "The Anniversary Service for
    Blanche, Duchess of Lancaster, 12th September, 1374," *John
    Rylands Library Bulletin* 21 (1937): 176–192.

150 no acknowledgment of the queen's death: There is at least one
    analogue, Froissart's lines from *Le Joli Buisson de Jonece,* writ-
    ten at a time when he could look back on both deaths, in which
    he couples the queen's death with the duchess's. See Condren,
    211–212 n. 21.

150 refer to any number of things: The conventional language would have
    named love, whereas it is only implied here. Some have argued
    that the sorrow is not love but mourning, or a state of sin, or
    an intentional puzzle.

150 Chaucer got it out of Machaut: Loomis, 178–180. Of course Chaucer
    might not have felt justified in using the detail unless it had
    some historical relevance. Counting back exactly eight years to

late 1360 does not yield a relevant event, but a poet might count in a loose or general way or like the rest of us not remember accurately how long ago an event happened. For example, by inclusive reckoning there were eight years since the death of Blanche's father, Henry, the Good Duke, surely a key moment in Lancastrian affairs. Or one might count eight full years of married happiness since Gaunt's marriage in May 1359, starting with 1360; if Chaucer's narrator is a mirror image or alter ego of John of Gaunt, this could have been relevant. Such conjectures seem to me farfetched (the two just offered have never to my knowledge been proposed), though they make Chaucer's expropriation of Machaut's figure seem less arbitrary.

150   Chaucer translated these lines: His translation may reveal certain particular conceptions of his own that differ from Geoffrey of Vinsauf's; see Howard, *Idea*, 135–137.

151   "O sorrow! . . .": *Poetria Nova*, trans. Margaret F. Nims (Toronto, 1967), 30.

151   *Dit de la Fonteinne Amoureuse:* On Chaucer's use of this and other sources in BD see James I. Wimsatt, "Chaucer and French Poetry," in Brewer, *Background*, 119–130; and *Chaucer and the French Love Poets: The Literary Background of the Book of the Duchess* (Chapel Hill, 1968).

152   According to one editor's count: Fisher ed., 543.

153   proper form in which to address royalty: Stevens, 62–76.

153   poem . . . successfully dreamlike: Kittredge, 68–71.

153   The dreamer's horse: Stephen Manning, "That Dreamer Once More," PMLA 71 (1956): 540–541.

154   a mirror image of Blanche's death: See Angela Carson, "Easing of the 'Hert' in the *Book of the Duchess*," ChauR 1 (1967): 157–160.

154   series of contrasts: See J. Burke Severs, "Chaucer's Self-Portrait in the *Book of the Duchess*," PQ 43 (1964): 27–39.

156   narrator cannot understand . . . the complaint: For the explanation adopted here, see W. H. French, "The Man in Black's Lyric," JEGP 56 (1957): 231–241. Earlier critics, and some since, thought the dreamer intentionally failed to understand in order to induce the Knight to unburden his sorrow. But this was Chaucer's intention, not the dreamer's.

159   religious consolation: The poem was long understood as one of consolation with precedents in courtly literature; see for example John Lawlor, "The Pattern of Consolation in *The Book of the Duchess*," *Speculum* 31 (1956): 626–648. The religious emphasis was introduced in Robertson, *Preface*, 463–466 and passim; Bernard F. Huppé and D. W. Robertson, *Fruyt and Chaf: Studies in Chaucer's Allegories* (Princeton, 1963), ch. 2; and in Robertson's article "The Historical Setting of Chaucer's *Book of the*

Duchess," *Medieval Studies in Honor of Urban Tigner Holmes, Jr.* ed. J. Mahoney and J. E. Keller (Chapel Hill, 1966), 169–195. Less allegorical treatments are by Rodney Delasanta, "Christian Affirmation in *The Book of the Duchess*," PMLA 84 (1969): 245–251, and John B. Friedman, "The Dreamer, the Whelp, and Consolation in the *Book of the Duchess*," ChauR 3 (1969): 145–162. Joerg O. Fichte, "*The Book of the Duchess* —A Consolation?" *Studia Neophilologica* 45 (1973): 53–67 has argued that it is not a consolation at all but a monument based on the belief that the "memory of things lives on in books." And see James I. Wimsatt, "The *Book of the Duchess:* Secular Elegy or Religious Vision," in *Signs and Symbols in Chaucer's Poetry,* ed. John P. Hermann and John J. Burke (University, Ala., 1981), 113–129.

160 Is Octavian mentioned: For these details, see R. A. Shoaf, "Stalking the Sorrowful H(e)art: Penitential Love and the Hunt Scene in Chaucer's *The Book of the Duchess*," JEGP 78 (1979): 313–324.

161 the passing of a way of life: Cf. Stephen Manning, "Chaucer's Good Fair White: Woman and Symbol," CL 10 (1958): 97–105, and John Fyler, "Irony and the Age of Gold in the *Book of the Duchess*," *Speculum* 52 (1977): 314–328.

162 thoughts about how old he is: John Winter Jones, "Observations on the Origin of the Division of Man's Life into Stages," *Archeologia* 35 (1853): 167–189. See also Henry Green, *Shakespeare and the Emblem Writers* (London, 1870), 406–409.

162 Dante's reckoning: *Convivio* 4: 24: 34, a work Chaucer knew, though probably not yet.

162 young men in their twenties: Levinson, esp. ch. 5 and 6; on previous theories and the universality of the concept, 317–326.

162 John Gower: Fisher, 204–208; on the date of Gower's birth, ibid., 46, 59.

164 developed much of a sense of humor: Cf. Muscatine, 107.

Part Two: To Italy (1372–1380)

6. FLORENCE, 1373

169 Jacopo Provano: See Wendy Childs, "Anglo-Italian Contacts in the Fourteenth Century," in Boitani, 74. For the Italian names conjectured from the anglicized spellings of the records, I am indebted to my colleague John Freccero.

170 Italian banks: E. B. Fryde, "Loans to the English Crown, 1328–31," EHR 70 (1955): 198–211

170   downfall . . . of the great Florentine banks: Unwin, 98–99.

170   he could speak Italian: Schless, 184–188 and passim.

171   a colony of Italians . . . a community of Genoese: LR, 39; Redstone,
       193–194; and see Alwyn A. Ruddock, *Italian Merchants and
       Shipping in Southampton, 1270–1600* (Southampton, 1951),
       40.

171   *read* Italian with great accuracy: Wallace, esp. ch. 6.

171   off to an unfortunate start: LR, 37–38, esp. 38 n. 1.

171   king owed him money: See Unwin, 126 and n.

171   The route: George B. Parks, "The Route of Chaucer's First Journey
       to Italy," ELH 16 (1949): 174–187.

172   Crossing the Alps: George B. Parks, *The English Traveler to Italy*, 2
       vols. (Stanford, 1954), 1: 179–185.

172   lead the frightened horses: In fact there are good reasons to suppose
       they rode mules; but accounts call them horses for the sake of
       elegance.

172   Adam of Usk: Edith Rickert, comp., *Chaucer's World* (New York
       and London 1948; repr. New York, 1962), 278.

172   The way they *pictured* a journey: Leo Bagrow, *History of Cartogra-
       phy*, rev. R. A. Skelton (Cambridge, Mass., 1966), 61–73.

174   an "invention": Edmundo O'Gorman, *The Invention of America*
       (Bloomington, Ind., 1961). On Columbus see Howard, *Writers*,
       107–109.

174   "a manner Latin corrupt": Man of Law's Tale, 519.

176   wars . . . in Milanese territory: Tuchman, 252–259.

177   On Genoa's prominence, see Robert S. Lopez and Irving W. Ray-
       mond, *Medieval Trade in the Mediterranean World* (New York,
       1955), 69–70; on its buildings and history, Robert W. Carden,
       The City of Genoa (London, 1908). On the route taken, Parks,
       "Route," ELH 16: 178–179.

177   40,000 inhabitants: These figures for the population of Genoa and
       Florence, revised downward somewhat from previous estimates,
       were kindly provided by my colleague Judith Brown.

177   alum: Ruddock, *Italian Merchants*, 40.

178   English "gentry": Fritz Rörig, *The Medieval Town* (Berkeley, 1967),
       67.

178   maritime insurance: Lopez and Raymond, *Medieval Trade*, 255–256.

178   the English thought them more serious: Salzman, 416.

178   Porta dell'Olivella: Samuel Eliot Morison, *Admiral of the Ocean Sea*
       (Boston, 1942), 9.

179   del Mare was back in Bruges: LR, 38 n. 1. Professor William E.
       Coleman has discovered at Genoa a document that he has not
       yet published, dated Oct. 22, 1374—well after Chaucer had
       returned to England—detailing a quarrel over money between
       Provano and del Mare. Records show (LR 36, 38) that on March

23, 1373 Provano had issued 220 florins to Chaucer, presumably in Florence. So while del Mare had returned to Bruges by March, Provano must have gone on to Florence with Chaucer or met him there.

179   Florence: The standard history remains Ferdinand Schevill, *History of Florence* (New York, 1936); see esp. ch. 14–19. On the buildings, Paul G. Ruggiers, *Florence in the Age of Dante* (Norman, Okla., 1964), esp. ch. 2 and 3. On the nature and importance of the mission, Cook, 39–44.

180   normal route: Parks, "Route," ELH 16: 182–183.

180   *The Triumph of Death*: See Millard Meiss, *Painting in Florence and Siena After the Black Death* (Princeton, 1951), esp. 74–75 and n. 3.

181   "the Katherines of the one lordship . . .": *Information for Pilgrims unto the Holy Land* (1498; repr. London, 1824), cited in Howard, *Writers*, 22.

181   gestures of repayment: Unwin, 129–131.

181   Bardi merchants got special treatment: Ibid., 102–103.

183   Petrarch and Boccaccio studied Greek: Branca 33–34, 115–119.

183   "civic" humanism: Marvin B. Becker, *Florence in Transition*, 2 vols. (Baltimore, 1967–1968), 2: 25–92 and passim; Hans Baron, *The Crisis of the Early Italian Renaissance* (rev. ed. Princeton, 1966).

184   pasta was eaten: Francesco Zambrini, ed., *Il Libro della Cucina del sec. XIV*, in *Scelta di Curiosità Letterarie*, 40.

184   a strange new instrument, the fork: Cosman, 16.

184   Some women dressed: Sibylle Harksen, *Women in the Middle Ages* (New York, 1975), plate 102.

184   sumptuary laws: Cassell, Appendix, 153–164.

185   ". . . sat in the seats of power": Schevill, *History of Florence*, 261.

186   "something so novel and ominous . . .": Ibid., 267.

186   Italian literary culture: On this subject see the very suggestive essay by David Wallace, "Chaucer's Continental Inheritance," in *The Cambridge Chaucer Companion*, ed. Piero Boitani and Jill Mann (Cambridge, Eng. and New York, 1986), 19–37.

187   Chaucer knew some Italian literature: Schless, 188–197, and Paul G. Ruggiers, "The Italian Influence on Chaucer," in Rowland, 160–184; Wendy Childs, "Anglo-Italian Contacts," in Boitani, esp. 80–84.

188   Petrarch . . . had been crowned laureate poet: Ernest H. Wilkins, "The Coronation of Petrarch," *Speculum* 18 (1943): 155–197, and *Life of Petrarch* (Chicago, 1961), 24–29; Morris Bishop, *Petrarch and His World* (Bloomington, Ind., 1963), 160–171.

188   "the most famous private citizen . . .": Wilkins, *Life*, 29.

190   whether Chaucer met Petrarch: Parks, "Route," ELH 16: 182–186,

discusses in minute detail the possible routes and concludes that a visit to Petrarch was physically possible but unlikely. Cf. Wilkins, *Life*, 238.

190   Petrarch was in Padua: Wilkins, *Life*, 234.

190   Petrarch . . . translation of the Griselda story: Ibid., 236–237.

190   Petrarch . . . was in failing health: Bishop, *Petrarch*, 365–368; Wilkins, *Life*, 229–238 passim; the scabies is mentioned in Branca, 174.

191   Boccaccio was at Certaldo: Branca, 176–177.

191   "mercantile epic": Ibid., 276–307 and passim; and see Vittore Branca, *Boccaccio Medievale* (rev. ed. Florence, 1970), ch. 5. For a general survey of the matter, Aldo D. Scaglione, "Boccaccio, Chaucer, and the Mercantile Epic," Daiches, ch. 17.

191   *Decameron* . . . written in mercantile hands: Branca, 197–201, and *Boccaccio Medievale*, 3–5; and Branca's detailed treatment in "Per Il Testo del 'Decameron'—La prima diffusione del Decameron," *Studi di filologia italiana* 8 (1950): 29–143, esp. 134–142.

191   Boccaccio was in ill health: Branca, 174–175, 181.

192   "magister" and "pater": Ibid., 173.

193   "and other bookes took me to . . .": PF 695–696.

193   "On bookes for to read . . .": LGW 30–31, 33–34.

193   living like a hermit: HF 658–659.

194   Boccaccio was working on: Branca, 176.

195   messengers had been sent . . . to London: See LR, 34–36, esp. the "tribus nunciis" mentioned on 36. Some writers suggest that the messengers were hired in Italy, but it seems more likely that they were trusted members of the king's messenger service. See Mary C. Hill, *The King's Messengers 1199–1377* (London, 1961).

195   Albertano of Brescia: The translation is that of William Askins, which the author kindly provided to me in manuscript. Prof. Askins has discovered that there are some four hundred known mss. and thirty early printings, far beyond what had previously been thought.

196   brevity of speech: Brewer, *Heritage*, 39–42.

196   the language of gesture: A subject of recent interest. See Barry Windeatt, "Gesture in Chaucer," *Medievalia et Humanistica* 9 (1979): 143–161, and Robert G. Benson, *Medieval Body Language: A Study in the Use of Gesture in Chaucer's Poetry*, Anglistica Vol. 21 (Copenhagen, 1980).

196   The weather that year was good: I owe this piece of intelligence to Prof. Judith Brown.

197   he would have seen a countertendency: Meiss, *Painting in Florence and Siena*, ch. 3.

197   *Meditationes Vitae Christi*: Brewer, *World*, 130. See Elizabeth

Salter, "Nicholas Love's *Myrrour of the Blessed Lyf of Jesus Crist,*" *Analecta Carthusiana* 10 (Salzburg, 1974).

197   the Blessed Virgin knitting a shirt: Harksen, *Women in the Middle Ages,* plate 100; the painting is on wood panel, ca. 1390.

198   *legends . . . myths*: Cf. Spearing, 74.

198   a different "mode": Cf. Frye, 33–67.

199   *Trionfi*: Wilkins, *Life*, 118, 244–245.

7. TO THE GATEHOUSE

200   The ships commandeered . . . : Armitage-Smith, 102–105. According to chronicles there were 15,000 mounted soldiers of whom 6,000 were archers, doubtless an exaggerated figure.

201   "Lancaster's midsummer madness": Ibid., 102.

201   collect the money owed him: LR, 34–37.

201   an advance of £10: LR, 108–109.

201   received 220 florins: LR, 36, 38.

202   Thomas's age: Russell Krauss, *Chaucerian Problems* (New York, 1932), 158–161. See ch. 3, p. 93. Roskell, 152 gives 1367 as his birth date without offering evidence.

202   Gaunt had had one bastard child: Armitage-Smith, 460–462. This was the daughter of Marie de St. Hilaire, named Blanche; the name, judging from the customs of the time, suggests he was engaged or married to Blanche of Lancaster when she was born.

202   assigned to go to Dartmouth: LR, 40–42; Manly, *Light*, 169–181.

203   Black Prince . . . in the House of Lords: Emerson, 252.

203   Alice Perrers: Kay, 80–116 passim; Braddy, 107–115.

205   Her father was Sir Richard Perrers: This is the best guess from among several possibilities. See Kay, 11–21.

205   William Champain, a . . . London baker: Haldeen Braddy, "Chaucer, Alice Perrers, and Cecily Chaumpaigne," *Speculum* 52 (1977): 906–911. The daughter Isabel, if William Champain's, would have been over seventeen at this time. She is named in *Hist. Rel.*, an Elizabethan translation of the *Chronicle of St. Albans*, according to Braddy, "Chaucer, Alice Perrers," 908. This must have been Stow's source, *Stow's Annals or Chronicle* (London, 1606), 429, for he reports the same in identical language.

205   Sir William of Windsor: See S. Harbison, "William of Windsor, the Court Party and the Administration of Ireland," in *England and Ireland in the Later Middle Ages: Essays in Honour of Jocelyn Otway-Ruthuen,* ed. James Lydon (Dublin, 1981), 153–174.

205   a child whom he knighted: Emerson, 243; Margaret Galway, "Alice Perrers's Son John," EHR 66 (1951): 242–246.

205   "Geoffrey Perrers": Braddy, "Chaucer, Alice Perrers and Cecily

Champaigne," *Speculum* 52: 906–911, 11–12. The document is CPR 15: 490.

206   "by their good and noble governance . . .": *Rot. Parl.*, in Armitage-Smith, 113.

206   King Edward . . . reprimanded him: Armitage-Smith, 117; but the source is Christine de Pisan, who was hostile to Gaunt.

206   tournament at Smithfield: Kay, 116, source not given.

206   Gaunt had landed at Dartmouth: Register 1372–, 1: 247, no. 667.

206   the Palace of the Savoy: Ibid., 1: 252, no. 682.

206   a pitcher . . . of wine a day: LR, 112–116.

206   an amount per day is rare: LR, 113, but see the grant to William Cressingham (LR, 116), which comes out like Chaucer's with an odd pitcher, signifying that it was granted by the day. The grant to John Weston (LR, 113) was for a gallon a day for life.

206   reward for presenting a poem (note): Manly, 67–69; Gardner, 204–206.

207   Richard II commuted it to cash: LR, 115, 304–305.

208   connections with the group of Hainaulters: The proposal was made by Thomas Garbáty, "Chaucer, the Customs, and the Hainault Connection," in a paper presented at the New Chaucer Society, Philadelphia, 1986.

208   The gatehouse at Aldgate: LR, 144–147; Ernest P. Kuhl, "Chaucer and Aldgate," PMLA 39 (1924): 101–122. See J. M. Manly, "Three Recent Chaucer Studies," RES 10 (1934): 257–273, who agrees (p. 264) that Gaunt had no part in Chaucer's preferments of 1374.

208   appointment to the controllership: LR, 148–158.

208   Petty Custom: LR, 160.

208   "also for the good service . . .": LR, 271.

208   Gaunt ordered alabaster: Register 1372–, 2: 212–213, no. 1394.

209   nearly £70 a year: Figured as follows: £11 or more as the basic pay of a squire (see Hulbert, 20–22), 20 marks from the Exchequer annuity of 1367 (LR, 123-125), £10 as wages of the controllership plus 10 marks bonus (LR, 151), £10 from the 1374 annuity from Gaunt (LR, 271), 10 marks from Philippa's Exchequer annuity of 1366 (LR, 67), £10 from Philippa's 1372 annuity from Gaunt (LR, 85).

209   her servant had board and lodging (note): Thrupp, 142–143.

209   plan of Aldgate: W. R. Lethaby, "The Priory of Holy Trinity, or Christ Church, Aldgate," *The Home Counties Magazine* 2 (1900): 45–53.

210   On the controllership of the Customs, see LR, 148–270; Hulbert, 42–47; *The English Government at Work 1327–1336*, ed. James F. Willard et al., 3 vols., Mediaeval Academy of American Publications No. 37, 48, 56 (Cambridge, Mass., 1940–1950)

2: 168–200, esp. 176–177; 3: 13–33, and Eileen Power, *The Wool Trade in English Medieval History* (Oxford, 1941).

210   the oath required: LR, 157–158.

211   Richard Lyons . . . the "farmer" of the Petty Custom: *Calendar of the Patent Rolls Preserved in the Public Record Office* (London, 1891–   ); Edward III, vol. 15: 323–324, 319, 382; Unwin, 292. And see A. R. Myers, "The Wealth of Richard Lyons," in *Essays in Medieval History presented to Bertie Wilkinson,* ed. T. H. Sandquist and M. R. Powicke (Toronto, 1969), 301–329.

211   Chaucer received £71 4s. 6d.: LR, 269–270.

211   controllers . . . did take bribes: LR, 151, 209 n.1.

212   "cocket" seal: Hilary Jenkinson, *Guide to Seals in the P. R. O.* (London, 1954), 9–10.

213   One memorandum in French: LR, 164.

213   these wardships . . . could be purchased: LR, 294–302; Tout 4: 122–125, 309; and see *The English Government at Work,* 3: 13.

214   Medieval books: G. S. Ivy, "The Bibliography of the Manuscript-Book," in Francis Wormald and C. E. Wright, *The English Library before 1700* (London, 1958), 32–38; James Westfall Thompson, *The Medieval Library* (Chicago, 1939; repr. New York, 1957), 630–646; Warren Chappell, *A Short History of the Printed Word* (New York, 1970), 12–16. Jesse M. Gellrich, *The Idea of the Book in the Middle Ages* (Ithaca, 1985) treat the cultural changes taking place in Chaucer's time with respect to the book.

215   Richard de Bury: *Philobiblon,* trans. E. C. Thomas, ed. Michael Maclagan (Oxford, 1970); see Zacher, ch. 4.

215   Men said that his quarters: Zacher, 62.

215   About 1,500: Roberto Weiss, "The Private Collector and the Revival of Greek Learning," in *The English Library,* ed. Wormald and Wright, 113–115.

216   English prelate, Adam Easton: Giffin, ch. 2.

217   One theory: Giffin, ch. 4, esp. 79–88.

217   There were droughts: McKisack, 385.

217   Stories began to circulate: Ibid., 393; Armitage-Smith, 138–144.

217   Until the spring of 1375 Gaunt . . . : Armitage-Smith, 117–120.

218   On the "Good Parliament," see ibid., ch. 6; McKisack, 384–397; George Holmes, *The Good Parliament* (Oxford, 1975).

219   free-for-all of insults and threats: Armitage-Smith, 152.

219   the Black Prince died: Harvey, 116–121; Emerson, 242–261.

220   "of all mortal men . . .": in Emerson, 256.

220   replaced by . . . replicas in 1956: The replicas were made by the Tower Armoury; the date (given incorrectly in various books) was kindly furnished by A. M. Oakley, archivist of the cathedral.

221   "son of Dame Alice Perrers": Anonimalle, 106. See Galway, "Alice Perrer's Son John," EHR 66: 242–246.

221   On the coronation of Richard, see McKisack, 397–399; Armitage-Smith, 186–195; Hutchison, 20–24. The principal chronicle accounts are Walsingham 1: 329–340 and Anonimalle, 107–115.

221   ". . . the morrow of . . . Saint Swithun": John of Gaunt himself, in his formal report of the coronation, is the authority for the choice; see *Munimenta Gildhallae Londoniensis*, ed. Henry Thomas Riley, Rolls Series 12 (London, 1860) 2: 2, *Liber Custumarum*, p. 456. That it was the eve of Saint Kenelm, the boy king, was an invention, actually a malicious one, of later chroniclers. By the saint and the white garments signifying innocence, Gaunt meant to suggest that he wanted to be regent/tutor to the king, which indeed he was, though not officially. See Charles T. Wood, "Coming of Age in Europe: Confirmation, Crowning, and Kingship in Medieval England and France," American Historical Association Proceedings, Meeting 97 (Washington, 1982), session 63.

221   court of claims: *Calendar of Close Rolls Preserved in the Public Record Office (1272–1485)*, 45 vols. (London 1892–1954). Richard II, vol. 1 (1377–1381), 1–5.

222   crown . . . held above his head: Anonimalle, 114.

222   On Chaucer's four or more journeys, see LR, 44–53.

223   Sir Thomas Percy: Hulbert, 49–50.

223   a deputy was appointed: LR, 162.

223   Froissart says: LR, 49–51. Froissart's account, written from hearsay many years later, varies in different versions and is probably not reliable.

223   those receiving mourning attire (note): LR, 52, 105.

223   "a daughter of his adversary . . .": LR, 49. This entry in the Issue Roll referring to "journeys to France to treat of peace in time of Edward III, and in time of Richard II to discuss marriage," etc., is often taken to signify that marriage was not discussed in the earlier missions; but any discussion of peace at this time could not have avoided the question of a marriage.

223   Three later missions: LR, 53 and n. 1.

223   Princess Marie: Braddy, 6–11; see the subsequent controversy between Braddy and J. M. Manly, "Three Recent Chaucer Studies," RES 10: 267–272 and 11 (1935): 209–213, who argued that Marie died in January, not in May.

224   commission was sent to Milan: LR, 53–61; Braddy, 16–19 and J. M. Manly, "Chaucer's Mission to Lombardy," MLN 49 (1934): 209–216; E. P. Kuhl, "Why Was Chaucer Sent to Milan in 1378?" MLN 62 (1947): 42–44.

224 "certain affairs . . .": LR, 56.
224 Sir Edward Berkeley: Hulbert, 49.
224 Richard Barrett: LR, 164.
224 Richard Forester: LR, 54, 60; Hulbert, 52–53.
225 his friend John Gower: Fisher, 59–61.
225 marriage alliance . . . to be explored: Hulbert, 48; cf. Braddy, 7 and Gardner, 249.
225 Milan in the fourteenth century: Chamberlin, 11–74; Cox, 309–316.
225 It was said in the previous century: Bonvesino da Riva, in Chamberlin, 12–14.
225 the historian Sachetti: Chamberlin, 15.
226 Secondotto, already notorious: Cox, 310–313; Chamberlin, 62.
226 "stabbed through": *Stow's Annals*, 423.
226 Visconti emblem: Chamberlin, 16.
227 "learned in the Decretals": Ibid., 27.
227 "Don't you know, fool . . .": Ibid., 67.
227 Sir John Hawkwood: John Temple-Leader and Giuseppe Marcotti, *Sir John Hawkwood (L'Acuto)*, trans. Leader Scott (London, 1889), 1–45, 125–131 and passim.
228 "warm, eager, and practiced . . .": Villani, in Chamberlin, 52.
228 "our dear and loyal John Hawkwood": LR, 54.
228 Hawkwood . . . at Monzambano: Robert A. Pratt, "Geoffrey Chaucer, Esq. and Sir John Hawkwood," ELH 16 (1949): 188–193. While Hawkwood was in Milan, a representative of the lord of Mantua made the three-day journey to discuss damages done by Hawkwood's men back where his army was encamped; hence it can be assumed he stayed at Milan for most of the period.
228 Galeazzo Visconti died: Chamberlin, 23–31, 38.
228 founder of the great Visconti libraries: Robert A. Pratt, "Chaucer and the Visconti Libraries," ELH 6 (1939): 191–199; William E. Coleman, "Chaucer, the *Teseida*, and the Visconti Library at Pavia," MAE 51 (1982): 92–101. Rodney K. Delasanta, "Chaucer, Pavia, and the Ciel d'Oro," MAE 54 (1985): 117–121, adds that Pavia's famous church, in which Augustine and Boethius were buried, may also have been the burial place of Lionel, which provides a further reason for Chaucer's having gone to Pavia.
229 ". . . the very manuscripts in question": Pratt, "Chaucer and the Visconti Libraries," ELH 6: 197.
230 Hawkwood failed to rescue him: Temple-Leader and Marcotti, *Sir John Hawkwood*, 188–189.
231 messages from Hawkwood: LR, 61.
231 Hawkwood remained in Italy: Temple-Leader and Marcotti, *Sir John Hawkwood*, 80–84, 172, 263–294.

231   "marriage contract between our person . . .": Rymer, 7: 213; Perroy,
           138.

8. *THE HOUSE OF FAME*

232   dates from . . . 1376: Larry D. Benson, " 'The Love-Tydynges' in
           Chaucer's *House of Fame*," *Chaucer in the Eighties*, ed. Julian
           N. Wasserman and Robert J. Blanche (Syracuse, N.Y., 1986),
           3–22. Benson reviews all evidence about the date; I find his
           conclusions entirely convincing.

233   grew in layers: On these components and their sources, the best
           treatment is J. A. W. Bennett, *Chaucer's Book of Fame* (Oxford
           and New York, 1968).

233   court gossip (note): One scholar thought the gossip was about
           Gaunt's appearing in public with his mistress, Katherine Swyn-
           ford (Frederick Carl Riedel, "The Meaning of Chaucer's *House
           of Fame*," JEGP 27 [1928]: 441–469); another that it was un-
           specified but consistent with the "texture" of the poem (Ber-
           trand H. Bronson, "Chaucer's *Hous of Fame*: Another Hypoth-
           esis," *Univ. of California Publications in English* 3 [1934]:
           171–192 and *In Search of Chaucer* [Toronto, 1960], ch. 2, esp.
           49–50); or that it was about John of Gaunt (whom the eagle
           stands for) at a time when he may have been planning to desert
           Katherine Swynford (Williams, ch. 6), or related to Chaucer
           himself (a revival of a nineteenth-century theory—see A. Inskip
           Dickerson, "Chaucer's *House of Fame*: A Skeptical Epistemol-
           ogy of Love," TSLL 18 [1976]: 171–183). None of these authors
           comes up with more than a conjecture, and none answers the
           objection that the poem's sources suggest a royal marriage as its
           subject.

233   Dido and Aeneas: The best treatment of Chaucer's sources in Ovid
           and Virgil is Fyler, ch. 2, esp. 30–41; he points out that medieval
           commentators held Virgil's account inaccurate.

233   they become moving images: The notion may be based on Dante's
           "visibile parlare," in *Purgatorio* 10: 95. See lines 1068–1082,
           where speeches in Fame's house take on the images of those who
           spoke them. Paul G. Ruggiers, "Words into Images in Chau-
           cer's *Hous of Fame*: A Third Suggestion," *MLN* 69 (1954):
           34–37, thinks the notion derives from *Paradiso* 4: 37–48, where
           Beatrice explains to Dante how paradise can be visible. On this
           effect in Chaucer, see Kolve 24–42.

234   "What are these tidings . . ." (note): Koch radically emended it to
           "that bring thee hider, and these things / That thou wilt heer";
           see Brusendorff, 155–156. In fact the mss. read *"why* are these
           tidings," noted by Skeat but the emendation to "which" is

generally accepted. Possibly, though, the line was supposed to mean, "Why are these tidings the ones that bring you here?"

235   "Atte last I saw": "Nevene" (name) is the emendation of Skeat and Koch, now generally used in editions, probably because it is thought the line as given in mss., "which that I nought ne kan" ("whom I don't know"), doesn't scan, though by some accounts of Middle English prosody it does.

235   missing at the end: Bennett, *Chaucer's Book of Fame*, 185, may be cited as the extreme statement of this view; while he does not deny that something is missing, Bennett argues that the ending as it is suffices to make the poem whole: "In any case the quizzical preface to the poem ought to have half-prepared us for an unusual or unorthodox close. We may feel cheated: but the cheating may be deliberate, and its purpose to suggest that the true conclusion is to be found in the poetry that was to follow."

235   the poem . . . was a prologue (note): Originally proposed by John M. Manly, "What is Chaucer's *Hous of Fame*?" in *Anniversary Papers by Colleagues and Pupils of George Lyman Kittredge* (Boston and London, 1913), 73–81. The notion is accepted, if reservedly, by John Leyerle, "Chaucer's Windy Eagle," UTQ 40 (1971): 236–265.

235   a joke on the court: Donald K. Fry, "The Ending of the *House of Fame*," in *Chaucer at Albany*, ed. Rossell Hope Robbins (New York, 1975), 27–40, argues that Chaucer left the poem without an ending to surprise his audience when reading it aloud; Benson, "Love-Tydynges," *Chaucer in the Eighties*, accepting this view, provides a credible motive and circumstances.

235   ending got detached: Brusendorff, 148–166, esp. 156.

235   Caxton made up twelve lines (note): Brusendorff, 152–154. Thynne's printing of 1532 was based on Caxton's version but supplemented by material from another manuscript now lost. Thynne suppressed Caxton's disclaimer and so created the impression that Caxton's added lines were genuine.

235   "man of greet auctoritee": On the various proposed endings see Kay Stevenson, "The Endings of Chaucer's *House of Fame*," ES 59 (1978): 10–26; she concludes that Chaucer would have ended the poem, as he ended others, by retaining and not resolving the oppositions set up in it, and so "did not need to go on."

235   identifies the man . . . as Christ: see B. G. Koonce, *Chaucer and the Tradition of Fame* (Princeton, 1966), 265–279, one of several "Robertsonian" readings that find in the symbolism of the poem a Christian message.

235   identifies him as Boethius: Paul G. Ruggiers, "The Unity of Chaucer's *House of Fame*," SP 50 (1953): 16-29, and Gardiner Still-

well, "Chaucer's 'O Sentence' in the *Hous of Fame,*" ES 37 (1956): 149–157.

235   harbinger of Harry Bailly: Leyerle, "Chaucer's Windy Eagle," UTQ 40: 260, is surely right that the context of the ending is too farcical to introduce such solemn figures as Christ or Boethius.

236   Boccaccio: R. C. Goffin, "Quiting by Tidinges in *The Hous of Fame,*" MAE 12 (1943): 40–44, and Robert J. Allen, "A Recurring Motif in Chaucer's *House of Fame,*" JEGP 55 (1956): 393–405, both very tentatively urged; Donald C. Baker, "Recent Interpretations of Chaucer's *Hous of Fame* and a New Suggestion," *Univ. of Mississippi Studies in English* 1 (1960): 97–104, accepts Allen's notion but thinks it is, rather than a recurring motif, the central theme.

236   God of Love: Pat Trefzger Overbeck, "The 'Man of Gret Auctorite' in Chaucer's *House of Fame,*" MP 73 (1975): 157–161.

236   poet . . . as authority: James Winny, *Chaucer's Dream-Poems* (London and New York, 1973), 108–112.

236   child not yet twelve: Baugh, ed., 27 f. makes this point, and I am not aware it had been made before.

236   "new things": On Froissart, see Brusendorff, 158–160; in Dante the phrase occurs seven times, most notably in *Purgatorio* 2: 54, just following one of the passages about the heavenly eagle that Chaucer is thought to have had in mind, and in *Purgatorio* 10: 94, which mentions the concept *visibile parlare,* "they become moving images." The passage, in Singleton's translation, is: "He who never beheld any new thing wrought this visible speech, new to us because here it is not found."

236   Ovid's passage: *Metamorphoses,* trans. Rolfe Humphries (Bloomington, Ind., 1955), 286–287.

237   Virgil: *Aeneid,* trans. Robert Fitzgerald (New York, 1983), 102.

237   *confer* fame: On the concept of Fame in Western history see the encyclopedic treatment by Piero Boitani, *Chaucer and the Imaginary World of Fame* (Totowa, N.J. and Cambridge, Eng., 1984), esp. ch. 3 on the Italian concept; on the Italianness of Chaucer's conception, 155–156. J. L. Simmons, "The Place of the Poet in Chaucer's *House of Fame,*" MLQ 27 (1966): 125–135, thinks the man of authority was to be a poet and the poem was to be essentially a plea for patronage. Since most court poetry is implicitly a plea for patronage, this argument doesn't counter any other argument about the poem's meaning, and indeed Simmons thinks the announcement at the end would have been "court news."

237   Petrarch's *Triumph of Fame:* Brusendorff, 161 n.; Bennett, *Chaucer's Book of Fame,* 108–110.

237   Boccaccio's . . . *Amorosa Visione*: Bennett, *Chaucer's Book of Fame*, 135.

237   On Chaucer's relation to Dante, see Howard Schless, "Chaucer and Dante," in *Critical Approaches to Medieval Literature*, ed. Dorothy Bethurum (New York, 1960), 134–154, and his recent encyclopedic treatment *Chaucer and Dante* (Norman, Okla., 1984). My notion that Dante influenced Chaucer because Chaucer reacted against him, while not new, is hardly orthodox. In the past decade or so, the traditional idea of poetic influence as a master-pupil relationship has been altered by the writings of Harold Bloom, who has made it plain that ambivalence must inevitably enter into a "strong" poet's feelings toward his poetical mentors. My notion that Dante and Chaucer belonged to different eras separated by a major cultural and intellectual change is essentially that of R. W. Southern, discussed above in ch. 1. For my earlier notions, Howard, *Idea*, 37–45.

238   "Had Chaucer been able . . .": Fisher ed., 211.

238   "Thought, that wrote . . .": Line 523; cf. *Inferno* 2: 8.

238   parody of *The Divine Comedy*: A very old theory, now discredited; for references see Robinson ed., 778. That there is an element of parody is of course evident; see Fyler, 41–56.

238   reference to Chaucer's wife: Skeat ed., note to line 562.

238   parody of Gower: Fisher ed., 211 f.

239   Eagles in medieval lore: Leyerle, "Chaucer's Windy Eagle," UTQ 40, esp. 252–254. On eagles as kings of the air, Reginald Berry, "Chaucer's Eagle and the Element Air," UTQ 43 (1974): 285–297; as symbols of thought or contemplation, John M. Steadman, "Chaucer's Eagle: A Contemplative Symbol," PMLA 75 (1960): 153–159; as symbols of rhetoric, William S. Wilson, "The Eagle's Speech in Chaucer's *House of Fame*," *Quarterly Journal of Speech* 50 (1964): 153–158.

240   Medieval poetry was expected: See Edgar De Bruyne, *The Esthetics of the Middle Ages*, trans. Eileen B. Hennessy (New York, 1969), 40–41, 160–162, 197–209.

240   "all this newe science . . .": PF, 25.

240   "key of remembrance": LGW, F Prologue 26.

240   nominalism: On the skeptical strain in the poem, see Sheila Delany, *Chaucer's House of Fame: The Poetics of Skeptical Fideism* (Chicago and London, 1972); Laurence Eldredge, "Chaucer's 'Hous of Fame' and the 'Via Moderna,'" *Neuphilologische Mitteilungen* 71 (1970): 105–119, argues that the Eagle represents the skeptical position of Occam—that we know only through experience—and that Geoffrey takes a doubtful view of the idea.

241   Boethius's *De Musica*: Chaucer may have had it second hand from

Vincent of Beauvais, Macrobius, or Vitruvius; see Fyler's note
in the forthcoming third edition of Robinson, kindly lent me in
manuscript by the author.

242   Lydgate, a century later: "The Fall of Princes," Pro. 302 f., in Brusendorff, 148–149.

243   kinds of dreams: See Lewis, *Image*, 54, 63–65, and Francis X. Newman, "*Hous of Fame*, 7–12," ELN 6 (1968): 5–12. That Chaucer identifies Book 1 as a "sweven" and Book 2 as an "avisioun"
is, so far as I know, my own observation. One must add that in
Book 2 he also calls his dream a "dreem" (line 527), but
"dreem" was the general term for any dream (see Newman,
"*Hous of Fame*, 7–12," ELN 6: 11).

243   famous passage in Macrobius (note): *Commentary on the Dream of
Scipio*, trans. William Harris Stahl (New York and London,
1952), esp. 52–55 on Chaucer's knowledge of the work and
87–92 for the famous statement about the types of dreams.
Lewis argues that the sixth kind of dream, the "revelation,"
came from Chalcidius, but cf. Saint Paul's *visiones et revela-
tiones Domini* (2 Cor. 12: 1, a passage from which Chaucer
quotes in line 981) and *Roman de la Rose*, 18479–18480.

244   a comical work on contempt of the world: This interpretation is close
to those mentioned earlier that name a "Boethian" moral as
central to the poem, notably Ruggiers, "Unity," SP 50: 16–21;
Stillwell, "Chaucer's 'O Sentence,' " ES 37: 149–157, and to an
extent Bennett, *Chaucer's Book of Fame*. A more recent article
taking such a view, with great subtlety, is Ann C. Watts,
" 'Amor Gloriae' in Chaucer's *House of Fame*," JMRS 3
(1973): 87–113. The emphasis on a "Boethian" moral in these
articles is prompted by the fact that Chaucer was, at about this
time, probably working on his translation of Boethius's *Consolation*. But Boethius's work is in a tradition of moderated, rational
"philosophy"—which *The House of Fame* parodies, perhaps,
but does not adopt. Chaucer, on his own testimony in LGW,
G Prologue 414 f., also translated the classic work on contempt
of the world, Pope Innocent III's *De Miseria Humane Conditionis* (see below p. 613); he names it directly after naming his
translation of Boethius and before his legend of Saint Cecilia.
These lines were added to the later version of the Prologue,
written after 1394; he must have been working on the translation of *De Miseria* in the later 1380s and early 1390s, some ten
years after he wrote *The House of Fame*, but it shows that the
interest was there. To turn such an interest in the direction of
comedy was immanent in the medieval worldview.

244   Lothario dei Segni: Pope Innocent III, *On the Misery of the Human*

Condition, trans. Dietz, ed. Howard (Indianapolis, 1969), 2: 29 (p. 54).

244   inspired by . . . the *Roman de la Rose*: Bennett, *Chaucer's Book of Fame,* 104.

245   "Trust rather in letters . . .": As in the widely known *contemptus mundi* poem "Cur mundus militat," which Chaucer probably had in mind here. "Plus crede litteris scriptis in glacie / quam mundi fragilis vanae fallaciae . . ." *The Latin Poems Commonly Attributed to Walter Mapes,* ed. Thomas Wright (1841; repr. New York and London, 1968), 147 f., and see Bennett, *Chaucer's Book of Fame,* 107–108. The poem, very widely known in the Middle Ages, has two "ubi sunt" stanzas about the famous men of ancient times.

245   Dutch pipers playing dance tunes: The presence of musicians here might have been inspired by a passage from a French romance, *Libeaus Desconneus,* and the Maison des Musiciens, with players of instruments adorning the niches of its exterior, that Chaucer may have seen at Reims. See Bennett, *Chaucer's Book of Fame,* 120–124, who cites B. J. Whiting, " 'The Hous of Fame' and Renaud de Beaufeu's 'Le biaus Descouneüs,' " MP 31 (1933): 196–198.

245   "Colle": James F. Royster, "Chaucer's 'Colle Tregetour,' " SP 23 (1926): 380–384; he was a necromancer at Orléans, mentioned in a French conversation book composed in 1396.

245   windmill under a walnut shell: This meaning of the curious figure was the discovery of Mr. Robert Watson.

246   "English Gaufride": Geoffrey of Monmouth, twelfth-century writer whose *History of the Kings of Britain,* in Latin, dealt with early legendary kings like Lear and Arthur. In his first chapter he preserved the legend that Britain was founded by Brutus, who was descended through Aeneas from the Trojans; interestingly, he remarked that the deeds of those he wrote about deserved everlasting praise. The mention of him here is evidently part of Chaucer's program of naming a modern and British figure in each category, probably modeled on Petrarch's *Trionfi,* which mentioned famous moderns, among them the duke of Lancaster. Chaucer was evidently hard pressed to come up with an English author of a "Troy Book," but he may have come up with "Gaufride" (Geoffrey) as a humorous hint that he himself might be a candidate. Watts, "Amor Gloriae," JMRS 3: 111–113, pointing out that more is made of Troy in *The House of Fame* than of other civilizations, conjectures that Chaucer may already have had *Troilus and Criseyde* in mind and hoped it would bring him fame.

248   labyrinth: See Howard, *Idea,* 327–332; Robertson, *Preface,* 373;

Koonce, *Chaucer and the Tradition of Fame*, 248–258; Boitani, *Chaucer and the Imaginary World of Fame*, ch. 6. See page 441 and n. The inscriptions mentioned are said to be later additions, but they might have been added to explain their cultural significance at a time when it was coming to be forgotten. We cannot prove that labyrinths were substitute pilgrimages. But no one has suggested what else they may have been.

249   earliest germ of *The Canterbury Tales*: See above, note to p. 235, "the poem . . . was a prologue."

250   art of poetry: See Laurence K. Shook, "The *House of Fame*," in Rowland, 414–427; Allen, "Recurring Motif," JEGP 55: 393–405; Baker, "Recent Interpretations," *Univ. of Mississippi Studies in English* 1: 97–104; Payne, 129–139; Donald R. Howard, "Chaucer's Idea of an Idea," E & S n.s. 29 (1976): 39–55, and "Flying Through Space: Chaucer and Milton," in *Milton and the Line of Vision*, ed. Joseph Anthony Wittreich (Madison, Wis. and London, 1975), 3–23. Joseph A. Dane, "Chaucer's *House of Fame* and the *Rota Virgilii*," *Classical and Modern Literature* 1 (1980): 57–75, argues that the three books treat respectively the Virgilian genres (epic, didactic, pastoral / lyric) and their corresponding levels of style (high, middle, and low).

251   *novelle*: See Goffin, "Quiting by Tidings," MAE 12: 40–44, and his later observation, in N & Q NS 8 (1961): 246, that "tidings" translates French *nouvelles* in the Middle English RR, 6038 and 7478, and means "stories" rather than "news": "Here surely in fact is the original sense of Boccaccio's *novella.*" One may add that "tidings" translates *nouveles* in the *Ovide Moralise* 8: 1610–1611; cf. HF 1956–1957. TC 2: 1112–1113 affords evidence of a distinction between "newe thinges" (news) and "tidinges" (report). For this and other evidence I'm in the debt of Prof. Bernard Witlieb.

251   chance . . . in poetic invention: Cf. Howard, *Idea*, 134–137; the lines are TC 1: 1065–1069.

252   Aventure: Stevenson, "Endings," ES 59: 19, remarks that Aventure is connected with both houses, as the mother of tidings (line 1983) and as the principle on which the gate of Fame's castle was carved (line 1297).

252   "the most personal of all Chaucer's poems": Brusdendorff, 160 n.

252   "the occasionally uneasy . . .": Spearing (Cambridge, Eng., 1976), 87.

253   "Drink it all": For the proverb "He who brews . . . ," see Robinson, ed., note to 1: 1879–1880; cf. Gower, *Confessio Amantis* 3: 1626, and Bartlett Jere Whiting, *Proverbs, Sentences, and Proverbial Phrases from English Writings Mainly before 1500* (Cambridge, Mass., 1968), 405. Chaucer uses the favorable connotation in *Melibee*, 1409–1411.

254   shrine of Saint Leonard: See Robinson's and Baugh's notes on line 117. The association with marriage is based on *Roman de la Rose*, 8833–8838 where Saint Leonard's role as patron of prisoners is associated with marriage as bondage, but there is no reason why that association should be applicable to this passage. Chaucer in fact lived two miles from the Convent of Saint Leonard, which all the more makes the reference seem a personal or private joke. See H. M. Smyser, "Chaucer's Two-Mile Pilgrimage," MLN 56 (1941): 205–207, who remarked (206) that "the true purport of the allusion would probably have been clear only to Chaucer's circle."

254   Chaucer had not read Boccaccio: There are a few passages that could, but need not, reflect a reading of Boccaccio's *Amorosa Visione* (there's no firm evidence elsewhere in Chaucer that he knew this work), and no indication that he yet knew *Il Filostrato*.

254   "played almost as a child . . .": John Livingston Lowes, "The Prologue to the Legend of Good Women Considered in its Chronological Relationships," PMLA 20 (1905): 850–851.

255   ". . . where fame was recognized . . .": Williams, 118–119; the quoted passage is Robert Kilburn Root, *The Poetry of Chaucer* (Boston, 1906), 130.

255   John Gower: See Fisher, esp. 204–215.

256   "the decadence of late Gothic art": Muscatine, 114, 246.

256   Laura Kendrick: "Chaucer's *House of Fame* and the French *Palais de Justice*," SAC 6 (1984): 121–133. With a scholar's caution she reminds us that the French royal palace doesn't correspond with Chaucer's image in every detail, was only part of his inspiration, and doesn't contend with his literary sources. Nevertheless, the correspondence is the more remarkable because when Chaucer saw these architectural monuments he was on a commission that discussed a marriage alliance with King Richard.

256   Sainte Chapelle: Mary Flowers Braswell, "Architectural Portraiture in Chaucer's *House of Fame*, JMRS 11 (1981): 101–112.

256   "swept up to heaven": Jean de Jandun, in Kendrick, "Chaucer's *House of Fame*," SAC 6: 130.

257   "its walls reverberated . . .": J. H. Shennan, *The Parlement of Paris* (Ithaca, N.Y., 1968), 102, in Kendrick, "Chaucer's *House of Fame*," SAC 6: 127.

257   Caterina Visconti: Benson, "Love-Tidings," *Chaucer in the Eighties*, 14–19.

257   two Milanese ambassadors: Perroy, 138 and n. 1–2.

257   following December: See ch. 7, p. 230.

258   commission to France: Rymer 4: 70–71. Another commission was sent Apr. 1, 1380 (Rymer 4: 83).

9. READING BOCCACCIO

260   "Palamon and Arcite": Robert A. Pratt, "Chaucer's Use of the *Teseida*," PMLA 62 (1947): esp. 613–614. See also Parr, 307–324 and Pratt's reply, "Was Chaucer's *Knight's Tale* Extensively Revised after the Middle of 1390?" PMLA 63 (1948): 726–736.

260   assumed by Tyrwhitt (note): Hubertis M. Cummings, *The Indebtedness of Chaucer's Works to the Italian Works of Boccaccio* (Menasha, Wis., 1916; repr. New York, 1967), 123.

260   William Godwin (note): Brewer, *Heritage*, 247.

260   Ten Brink (note): Cummings, *Indebtedness*, 123–124.

261   a notion since discarded (note): Tatlock, 45–66.

261   Lydgate (note): "The Fall of Princes," Pro. 284–285, Brewer, *Heritage*, 53.

261   "version made by Boccaccio . . ."(note): Ibid., 1: 246.

261   Ralph Waldo Emerson (note): Ibid., 2: 35. On "Trophee" see Skeat ed., 2: lvi n. and note in Robinson ed., to Monk's Tale 2117, where Chaucer uses the name as if it were an author (possibly Guido delle Colonne, since "trophy" meant "ancient monument" in earlier English, whence columns, translating *Colonne*).

261   A doctoral dissertation: Alfons Kissner, *Chaucer in seinen Beziehungen zur italienischen Litteratur* (Marburg, 1867).

261   parallel-text edition: W. M. Rossetti, ed., *Chaucer's Troylus and Cryseyde compared with Boccaccio's Filostrato*, Chaucer Soc. 1st ser. 44 (London, 1873). See Hammond, 398–399.

262   "the perfection of everything . . .": W. P. Ker, *English Literature; Medieval* (London and New York, 1912; repr. 1925), 237.

262   "unsurpassed indeed . . .": Clemen, 198.

263   episode at the English court: See Robinson ed., 788.

263   One theory holds (note): Boyd A. Wise, *The Influence of Statius upon Chaucer* (Baltimore, 1911), 67–68. Cf. James W. Bright, "Chaucer and Lollius," PMLA 19 (1904): xxii f., and W. G. East, "Lollius," ES 58 (1977): 396–398. But Douglas Bush, "Chaucer's 'Corinne,' " *Speculum* 4 (1929): 106–107, afforded a less fanciful account.

263   manuscripts at Pavia: William E. Coleman, "Chaucer, the *Teseida*, and the Visconti Library at Pavia: A Hypothesis," MAE 51 (1982): 92–101.

263   French in origin: See James Wimsatt, "*Anelida and Arcite*: A Narrative of Complaint," ChauR, 5 (1970): 1–8.

263   five-stress line: Bernhard ten Brink, *Chaucers Sprache und Verskunst* (Leipzig, 1884), showed that Chaucer's rhyming decasyllabic couplets differed from such verses in French in most of the ways those in Italian did.

266   "rhyme royal": Stevens, 62–76.

266   influence from the *dolce stil nuovo*: Brusendorff, 269–270.

267   saved by mistake: Ibid., 273.

267   annual merchant feast, the "Puy": Stevens, 63–66; Fisher, 76–83.

268   "The Complaint of Mars": Perhaps more correctly called "The
        Brooch of Thebes"; see Brusendorff, 263. Here one should re-
        cord the opinion of Brusendorff and others that "The Com-
        plaint of Mars" and "The Complaint of Venus" are two parts
        of a single poem called "The Brooch of Thebes." To me they
        seem disparate in verse form, style, and tone, and the reasons for
        dating the latter poem in the 1390s seem strong. For the argu-
        ments on the other side, see Rodney Merrill, "Chaucer's *Broche
        of Thebes*: The Unity of 'The Complaint of Mars' and 'The
        Complaint of Venus,' " *Literary Monographs* 5 (1973): 3–61,
        187–195.

268   Others have claimed (note): Merrill, "Chaucer's *Broche*," *Literary
        Monographs* 5: 8.

269   *copulare*: Chauncey Wood, *Chaucer and the Country of the Stars*
        (Princeton, 1970), 147. So too when Venus flees to a cave,
        "cave" translates a technical term for "degree."

269   moral lesson: Ibid., 154–160, discusses Mars' ridiculous posture at the
        end, finding perhaps too solemn a lesson in the ending.

270   exact number of lines as the *Aeneid*: Robert A. Pratt, "Chaucer's Use
        of the *Teseida*," PMLA 62 (1947): 599 n. 3.

270   closer to a medieval romance: Ibid., 601–603.

271   this mock-epic quality: This element of humor has often been noted,
        probably first by Henry Barrett Hinckley, *Notes on Chau-
        cer* (Northampton, Mass., 1907), 113. Hinckley, like others,
        thought such passages were out of place, being lapses of taste or
        decorum. On the other side, see Paul T. Thurston, *Artistic
        Ambivalence in Chaucer's Knight's Tale* (Gainesville, Fla.,
        1968), and my review in MLQ 31 (1970): 112–115; Edward E.
        Foster, "Humor in the *Knight's Tale*," ChauR 3 (1968): 88–94;
        Howard, *Idea*, 227–237.

272   One estimable critic: Muscatine, 187.

273   arriving at Christian moral doctrine: Minnis, ch. 4.

274   principal source of the Franklin's Tale: SA, 377–383.

274   *Corbaccio*: See Margery L. Brown, "The *Hous of Fame* and the
        Corbaccio," MLN 32 (1917): 411–415, and Cummings, *Indebt-
        edness*, ch. 4. The traditional date of the work is 1355, but it
        may have been written a decade later; see Cassell, xxvi.

274   Lodovico Bartoli: Cassell, xxi n. 22.

274   "swamp-faced . . .": Ibid., 54.

274   references to Boccaccio's age: Ibid., 23; the reference is to his father's
        not approving of his studies in philosophy.

274   sumptuary laws: Cassell, 153–164, and passim.

275   "Do you think . . .": Cassell, 26–27. A much closer source for the
         Wife's harangue in her prologue has been shown to be Des-
         champs's *Miroir de Mariage*; see John Livingston Lowes,
         "Chaucer and the *Miroir de Mariage*," MP 8 (1910–11): 165–
         186, 305–334, and SA, 207–222.

275   "language worthy of Plautus": De Sanctis, 1: 324. Boccaccio owned
         a manuscript of Terence and at least knew about Plautus.

276   adapted from works he knew: On his knowledge of Statius see Wise,
         Influence of Statius, esp. 60–137; on Troy books, C. David
         Benson, *The History of Troy in Middle English Literature*
         (Woodbridge, Suffolk, 1980), esp. ch. 1 and pp. 138–143 where
         it is proposed that the concept of the narrator was inspired by
         Guido delle Colonne's treatment.

276   to Boccaccio, Troy held little interest: Wallace, 74.

276   evidently used its title: SA, 615—616.

277   Certain lines and passages: SA, 616.

278   he singled out the Monk: With this account of the writing of the
         work and its chronology, cf. Tatlock, 164–172, who believed it
         was written for *The Canterbury Tales*.

279   Chaucer turned to *Il Filostrato*: Chaucer may have written or at least
         begun *Troilus and Criseyde* before he wrote the "Palamon and
         Arcite" poem, but he read the *Teseida* before he read the
         Filostrato, as we know from its earlier presence in his work; see
         esp. Pratt, "Order," PMLA 62: 608–620.

279   history like its sources: Wallace, 73–74.

279   C. S. Lewis: "What Chaucer Really Did," E & S 17: 60.

279   something he could not have expected: Wallace, 93–94.

280   why he never named Boccaccio: Wallace, 151–152 and passim. On
         the *cantari* see Armando Balduino, ed., *Cantari del Trecento*
         (Milan, 1970), and Wallace, ch. 5, who compares them most
         interestingly with English tail-rhyme romances.

281   "we must . . . continue to doubt": Cummings, *Indebtedness*, 198–
         199.

281   Harold Bloom: *The Anxiety of Influence: A Theory of Poetry* (New
         York, 1973) and *A Map of Misreading* (New York, 1975).

282   "be unoriginal": Larry D. Benson, "Chaucer Learns to be Unorigi-
         nal," paper presented at the New Chaucer Society, Washing-
         ton, D.C., 1978.

10. BOCCACCIO AND THE BIRTH OF FICTION

283   new genre or "mode": See Frye, 303–314.

283   collections of [*novelle*]: Janet Levarie Smarr, *Italian Renaissance
         Tales* (Rochester, Mich., 1983), esp. the very good introduction.

See also Robert J. Clements and Joseph Gibaldi, *Anatomy of the Novella* (New York, 1977), 4–5, 40, and passim. On the word itself and its association with news and gossip, see T. Atkinson Jenkins, "On Newness in the Novel," PMLA 42 (1927): xliii–lix.

284   "This Story Is . . .": Smarr, *Italian Renaissance Tales*, 8.

285   "I say, then . . .": Giovanni Boccaccio, *Decameron: The John Payne Translation*, ed. Charles S. Singleton, 3 vols. (Berkeley and London, 1982), 1: 8.

285   "first novel . . .": Kittredge, 109.

286   letter to Petrarch: It is known only from Petrarch's reply, *Epistolae Seniles* 1: 5; see *Petrarch: The First Modern Scholar and Man of Letters*, trans. J. H. Robinson and H. W. Rolfe (New York, 1898), 384–396.

286   revised version of the *Decameron*: Vittore Branca, *Boccaccio: The Man and His Work*, trans. Richard Monges (New York, 1976), 172–173, who dates the revision 1370–1371. See *Decameron: Edizione diplomatico-interpretativa . . .*, ed. Charles S. Singleton (Baltimore and London, 1974), ix–xiii and Petrucci's "Note codicologiche e paleografiche," 647–661, and see *Giovanni Boccaccio, Decameron*, ed. Singleton, 3: 927–930. Another and independent confirmation was made by Vittore Branca and Pier Giorgio Ricci, *Un Autografo del Decameron* (Padua, 1962), which concludes that it was a luxurious presentation copy prepared from a rough draft of a revision.

287   it has been argued: See note to p. 297.

287   Boccaccio returned to Florence: Branca, *Boccaccio*, 50–54; Thomas G. Bergin, *Boccaccio* (New York, 1981), 38-39.

288   Boccaccio as his disciple: Branca, *Boccaccio*, 89.

288   hospitality of the Visconti: Ibid., 98.

288   Niccolò Acciaiuoli: Ibid., 103–107, 133–139; Bergin, *Boccaccio*, 57–58. Acciaiuoli has had at least one defender (for references see Branca, *Boccaccio*, 148 n. 9) but the matter need not concern us; Boccaccio no doubt overreacted, but it is hard to suppose he imagined it all.

288   eight years later: Branca, *Boccaccio*, 133–138.

289   offered a chair: Ibid., 90–91.

289   sent Petrarch a magnificent gift: Ibid., 102, 106–107.

289   "That distinguished gentleman . . .": Cited in Branca, *Boccaccio*, 102: *Hoc immensum opus donavit michi vir egregius dominus Johannes Boccaccii de Certaldo poeta nostri temporis, quod de Florentia ad me pervenit 1355 aprilis 10.*

289   "the blessed Petroni": Branca, *Boccaccio*, 129–131; Bergin, *Boccaccio*, 55–56. Petrarch's letter, *Epistolae Seniles* 1: 5, dated May 28, 1362, describes the message of the Sienese stranger and

refers to Boccaccio's "consternation and grief." Evidently Boccaccio proposed to sell his books and gave Petrarch first choice.

289   an ecclesiastical benefice: Branca, *Boccaccio*, 120.

289   offering to buy it himself: *Epistolae Seniles* 1: 5; see Robinson and Rolfe (trans.), *Petrarch*, 394–395.

290   "Your book, written . . .": Ibid., 17: 3; 191–192.

290   imitated each other: Branca, *Boccaccio*, 92.

290   revised the *Trionfi*: Ibid., 173.

291   Acciaiuoli sought a copy: Ibid., 134 and n. 6.

291   "nothing in common . . .": *Boccaccio on Poetry*, ed. and trans. Charles G. Osgood (1930; repr. Indianapolis and New York, 1956), 49–50.

291   "Prince Galeotto": It is a pun; *galeotto* also meant "pilot" or "steersman." Boccaccio in his commentary on Dante glossed it *mezzano*, "go-between." There is no evidence that it had undergone semantic degeneration at this time and meant "pimp." See Karla Terese Taylor, "Chaucer Reads the *Divine Comedy*" (diss., Stanford, 1983), 51, 86–87 n. 19.

293   truth can be grasped through falsehoods: See Charles S. Singleton, *Dante Studies* 1: 62–65, who cites the remarkable passage in Saint Augustine, *Soliloquia* 2: 10 (PL 32: 893). Cf. Howard, *Idea*, 195–196.

293   regimen doctors actually prescribed: Olson, esp. ch. 5.

293   names are suggestive: A well-known effort to weave an allegory from the supposed meanings of the characters' names is Angelo Lipari, "The Structure and Real Significance of the *Decameron*," *Yale Romanic Studies* 22 (1943): 43–83.

294   The author's story: His story makes a total of 101 tales and so makes the fifty-first, the last tale of the fifth day, numerically central: that central story contains, like the *Decameron* itself, tales within a tale. And it is about a father who keeps his son from women until he realizes that he cannot protect the boy from nature. See Donald R. Howard, "Fiction and Religion in Boccaccio and Chaucer," *Journal of the American Academy of Religion* 47 (1979) Supplement, 318–319, from which some of the present section is taken with the journal's kind permission.

295   "revaluation of instinctive life . . .": Aldo D. Scaglione, *Nature and Love in the Late Middle Ages* (Berkeley, 1963), 64.

295   to desacralize the institution: Joy Hambuechen Potter, *Five Frames for the Decameron* (Princeton, 1982), ch. 2.

296   idea that fiction is a mass: The notion derives from its recognition as a genre; Boccaccio used the generic term *fabula* for all invented narrations, of which he distinguished four kinds. The fourth, containing "no truth at all," neither mystical nor historical, is what I am calling fiction; presumably Boccaccio, who did

not give it a name, had in mind the *novelle* of his time. In English "fiction" is used as a mass or uncountable noun in this sense, but the idea of the relatedness of fictions in a category predates the usage.

296   "only by the common purpose . . .": Erich Auerbach, *Mimesis*, trans. Willard Trask (Princeton, N.J., 1953), 228.

296   emerges . . . an ethos: Cf. Scaglione, *Nature and Love*, ch. 4; Branca, *Boccaccio*, part 2, ch. 3.

297   "On *Meaning* in the Decameron": See Singleton, "On *Meaning* in the Decameron," *Italica* 21 (1944): 117–124; written in reply to Lipari, "Structure," *Yale Romanic Studies* 22: 43–83; a subsequent exchange was in *Italica* 22 (1945): 101–108. For a short history of the reading or reception of the *Decameron*, see Judith Powers Serafini-Sauli, *Giovanni Boccaccio* (Boston, 1982), 127–130. For a survey of modern criticism, Aldo D. Scaglione, *Nature and Love in the Late Middle Ages* (Berkeley, 1963), 48-53. Modern critical controversy is in essence a reaction to Francesco De Sanctis, *History of Italian Literature*, (trans. Joan Redfern [2 vols., 1931; repr. New York, 1959], 1: 336), which, though not published until 1870–1871 reflected the medievalism of the Romantic era; setting the *Decameron* beside the *Divine Comedy*, he bemoaned the loss of medieval faith and transcendency: "This world of Nature, empty and superficial, devoid of all the inner powers of the spirit, has no seriousness at all of means or of end. The thing that moves it is instinct—natural inclination; no longer God nor science, and no longer the unifying love of intellect and act, the great basis of the Middle Ages: it is a real and violent reaction against mysticism." De Sanctis reacted less against Boccaccio than against his era, and made some perceptive and admiring observations about his works.

297   meaning in the frame: More accurately, "frames": see Potter, *Five Frames*, ch. 4 and 5.

297   "none of the attempts I have seen . . .": Ibid., 114.

298   "As a story's superficial aspect is . . .": *Boccaccio on Poetry*, ed. and trans. Osgood, 48–49.

298   "I count as naught . . .": Ibid., 50. Singleton (122) speaks as though Boccaccio does reject it: "There were kinds of fiction worthy of students (and of humanists and scholars) and there was a kind that was not. Boccaccio knew this when he wrote the *Decameron* and he knew it when he wrote the *Genealogia*. The *fact* had not changed. *He* had." But he wrote this before it was known that Boccaccio revised the *Decameron* in his last years.

299   Various critics have argued: These are the views respectively of Branca, *Boccaccio;* Scaglione, *Nature and Love;* and Potter, *Five Frames;* and of Mark Musa and Peter E. Bondanella, "The

Meaning of *The Decameron,*" in their edition (New York, 1977), 322–331.

299   Critics have found patterns: Lipari, "Structure," 22: 43–83; in recent years Joan M. Ferrante, "The Frame Characters of the *Decameron*: A Progression of Virtues," *Romance Philology* 19 (1965): 212–226, and "Narrative Patterns in the *Decameron*, ibid., 31 (1978): 585–604. For a structuralist analysis, Tzvetan Todorov, *Grammaire du Décaméron* (The Hague, 1969). Millicent Joy Marcus, *An Allegory of Form* (Stanford, 1979) argues that Boethius and the theme of consolation is central and that this is underscored by the Griselda story at the end. All seem convincing, yet the work defeats any effort to unlock its central meaning.

299   Wesley Trimpi: *Muses of One Mind: The Literary Analysis of Experience and its Continuity* (Princeton, 1983). This extraordinary book incorporates the author's earlier long articles, especially for our purposes "The Quality of Fiction: The Rhetorical Transmission of Literary Theory," *Traditio* 30 (1974): 1–118.

300   "legal fictions": Lon L. Fuller, *Legal Fictions* (Stanford, 1967).

300   establishes a middle ground: This is the *tertium quid* of which Quintilian speaks. Trimpi, *Quality*, points out (80), that there was a *psychological* middle ground (the probable, which lies between the true and the false) and a *judicial* middle ground ("equity," which lies between the general and the particular). The two became increasingly interdependent in medieval thought.

301   *exempla* were the originals of fictions: See Salvatore Battaglia, *Giovanni Boccaccio e la Riforma della Narrativa* (Naples, 1969), esp. 1–81. The word *exemplum* came to have a broader sense when the ancient word *hypothesis* became restricted to a single kind of story; from this viewpoint, what they called an *exemplum* was virtually synonymous with "fiction." See Trimpi, *Muses*, Appendix A.

302   How clearly medieval thinkers understood: On Chaucer, see Trimpi, *Muses*, 387–390. A partial understanding is suggested by their use of terms and their practices.

Part Three: Into Our Time (1380–1400)

11. CHAUCER AT FORTY

307   England had opened negotiations: Larry D. Benson, "The Occasion of *The Parliament of Fowls*," *Wisdom of Poetry*, 123–144. For a more detailed account, Perroy, ch. 4.

307   twenty thousand gold florins: Rymer, 7: 290–302. Specifics about

money are not mentioned in the marriage treaty itself but are detailed in a separate agreement signed the same day. The day, chosen in courtly sentiment, was May 1, 1381.

308   no principal source: On sources and analogues of various passages, the best treatment is J. A. W. Bennett, *The Parlement of Foules* (Oxford, 1957). Phillip W. Damon, *"The Parlement of Foules and the Pavo,"* MLN 67 (1952): 520–524 discovered a possible source or close analogue in a thirteenth-century Latin poem by Jordanus of Osnabruck. Haldeen Braddy, *Chaucer's Parlement of Foules in Its Relation to Contemporary Events* (1932; repr. New York, 1969) thinks it may have been modeled on Graunson's "Songe Sainct Valentin," but the evidence is by no means conclusive. Nicolai von Kreisler, "Bird Lore and the Valentine's Day Tradition in Chaucer's *Parlement of Foules,"* ChauR 3 (1968): 60–64, pointed to an analogue that shows the preexistence of a body of bird lore having many similarities with details of Chaucer's poem, of which Valentine's Day, however, is not one.

308   Valentine's Day poem: These poems are all set in the spring, but February was reckoned a spring month in medieval lore. On Chaucer as the inventor of the tradition, see Jack B. Oruch, "St. Valentine, Chaucer, and Spring in February," *Speculum* 56 (1981): 534–565. On the Lupercalia and the possible twelfth-century tradition, Alfred L. Kellogg, *Chaucer, Langland, Arthur* (New Brunswick, 1972), ch. 8. Haldeen Braddy, *Chaucer and the French Poet Graunson* (1947; repr. Port Washington, N.Y., 1968), ch. 5, presents evidence that Graunson wrote his Valentine poems in the early 1370s and thinks Chaucer was indebted to him for the convention. See Gardiner Stillwell, "Chaucer's Eagles and Their Choice on February 14," JEGP 53 (1954): 546–561.

308   Saint Valentine of Genoa: Henry Ansgar Kelly, *Chaucer and the Cult of St. Valentine,* Davis Medieval Texts and Studies No. 6 (Leiden, 1986), ch. 6.

308   the day Richard was betrothed to Anne: Ibid., ch. 7, esp. 120 ff.

308   May 3 had further meanings (note): George R. Adams and Bernard S. Levy, "Good and Bad Fridays and May 3 in Chaucer," ELN 3 (1966): 245–248; John P. McCall, "Chaucer's May 3," MLN 76 (1961): 201–205 (who cites Ovid, *Fasti,* 4: 943–948 and 5: 183–378).

308   Chaucer had lately read . . . *Dream of Scipio*: Benson, "Occasion," *Wisdom of Poetry,* 126, thinks that it was known to few in Chaucer's audience and that Chaucer read it as a mirror for princes, 129–130.

309   The two entrances: On the subtlety and complexity of the passage,

see Bennett, *Parlement,* 65–67. Thomas Jay Garbáty, "Andreas Capellanus and the Gate in the *Parlement of Foules,*" *Romance Notes* 9 (1968): 325–330, pointing to analogous passages in Andreas's *De Amore* which Chaucer probably had via Boccaccio, thinks the inscriptions present a choice between love and infertility. But Clemen, 139–140, reminds us that it is a single entrance with two inscriptions: this points up its ambiguous nature but does not suggest that a choice must be made. Francis J. Smith, "Mirth and Marriage in *The Parlement of Foules,*" *Ball State University Forum* 14 (1973): 19, remarks that the gates mean that the happy in love and the unhappy start at the same point. Laurence Eldredge, "Poetry and Philosophy in *The Parlement of Foules,*" *Revue de l'Université d'Ottawa* 40 (1970): 441–459, perceptively shows that the concept of Nature is based on moderate realism (species and genera are inherent in individuals) while the concept of Venus is based on nominalism (each individual is unique): Chaucer meant to show that real love requires individualism—Nature without Venus has only to do with propagating a species.

310   good Venus: Economou, 85–91. Ian Robinson, *Chaucer and the English Tradition* (Cambridge, 1972), 52–62 and J. A. Kearney, "The Parliament of Fowls: The Narrator, the 'Certeyn Thyng' and the 'Commune Profyt,' " *Theoria* 45 (1975): 55–71.

310   Will: In Boccaccio, Volluta, "Pleasure," daughter of Cupid. Chaucer's ms. might have read (for the variant form *voluttade*) *voluntade*; or he might have written "Well," i.e., well-being, rather than "Will." Bennett, *Parlement,* 84–85, thinks he meant "Will" in the sense of "impulse" or "desire."

310   temple made of brass: Boccaccio in the *Teseida* has copper, the metal sacred to Venus. But copper and its alloys were easily confused. See the note in Brewer's edition, *The Parlement of Foulys* (1960; repr. Manchester, 1972), 109.

310   lustful Venus: On the iconography, Bennett, *Parlement,* 93–100, and Economou, 136–139, and see Robert Hollander, *Boccaccio's Two Venuses* (New York, 1977), esp. n. 44 on pp. 158–160 and the notes on p. 186. Howard Schless, "Transformations: Chaucer's Use of Italian," in Brewer, *Background,* 199–207, demonstrates detailed changes from Boccaccio's original.

310   Alain de Lille: See Richard H. Green, "Alan of Lille's *De Planctu Naturae, Speculum* 31 (1956): 649–674.

310   *sodomia*: Curtius, 117–119. John Boswell, *Christianity, Social Tolerance, and Homosexuality* (Chicago, 1980) reports its meaning generally in the Middle Ages as "any emission of semen not directed exclusively toward the procreation of a legitimate child within matrimony," adding that "the term included much—if

not most—heterosexual activity" (202–205); cf. 93 n. 2. The word itself may have become specialized by Chaucer's time, but what he has in mind as "unnatural" is the more general conception he found in Alain.

310 "Formel" meant "female" (note): Roger Smith, "Boece and Chaucer's 'Formel,' " a paper presented to the Medieval Association of the Pacific, University of Washington, 1984, argues that the word was not previously used of eagles and that Chaucer appropriated it here with reference to Platonic forms, to buttress the Boethian thought in the poem.

310 lower-class birds only choose a mate: The contrast of "lady" and "mate," with one code for the upper-class birds and another for the rest, was remarked on by Macdonald Emslie, "Codes of Love and Class Distinctions," EIC 5 (1955): 1–17. Cf. Kearney, "Parliament," *Theoria* 45: 68.

311 hanging . . . was lower class: Cf. Robinson, *Chaucer and the English Tradition,* 65.

313 female Duck: So one may infer from the fact that the male of the species is called a *drake* in line 360.

314 sing a roundel: Chaucer comments that the tune was made in France, which suggests that the pleasantly intricate little poem was indeed meant to be sung. The song is lacking in most mss., and the most nearly complete version was added in a later one. This may mean that the poem *was* performed and the song was actually sung, hence not in the poet's copy.

314 celebrated a court marriage: That of Richard and Anne was first demonstrated by John Koch, "The Date and Personages of the 'Parlement of Foules,' " in *Essays on Chaucer,* Chaucer Soc. 2d ser. 18 (1878), 400–409; Koch identified Friedrich of Meissen correctly but thought the third suitor was William of Hainault. Oliver Farrar Emerson, "The Suitors in Chaucer's *Parlement of Foules,*" MP 8 (1910): 45–62, identified the third suitor as the future Charles VI. For other identifications of the marriage, see Robinson, p. 791. An ingenious suggestion by Lydia Alix Fillingham is that the Formel stands in fact for Richard II—or for the monarchy—and the three suitors are three nations who had made a bid for a marriage with the king: Milan, Luxembourg, and France. Braddy, *Chaucer's Parlement of Foules in Its Relation to Contemporary Events,* argued that the occasion was the negotiations for Richard's marriage with Princess Marie of France, 1376–1377; but the historical circumstances do not match the details of the poem in as startling a way as do those of the negotiations with Luxembourg, and the accomplished use of the five-foot line, the more extensive borrowing from the

Teseida and general similarities with later poems discourage so
early a date.

314   future Charles VI: Perroy, 142–145.

314   J. M. Manly: "What Is the Parlement of Foules?" *Studien zur en-
        glischen Philologie*, 50 (1913): 278–290.

314   Edith Rickert: "A New Interpretation of the *Parlement of Foules*,"
        MP 18 (1920): 1–29. She went on to propose that the poem
        was about John of Gaunt's plans for the marriage of his daughter
        Philippa to three possible suitors (Richard II, William of Hai-
        nault, and John of Blois), but the proposal never gained much
        acceptance.

314   its content of ideas: These emphases date from the 1930s; in later
        years they were promoted, but were not first inspired, by the
        New Criticism. They are all perfectly valid ways of looking at
        the poem even when it is viewed as an occasional poem, but they
        were for the most part urged as alternatives to that view.

        The notion that the poem has a religio-philosophical or
        moral meaning was introduced by R. C. Goffin, "Heaven and
        Earth in the 'Parlement of Foules,' " MLR 31 (1936): 493–499;
        he specifically set aside the notion that it is about a royal mar-
        riage, arguing that it is about true felicity as revealed in the
        Somnium and false felicity as revealed in the Garden (which he
        thought represents the transitory world). The thesis was picked
        up twelve years later by R. M. Lumiansky, "Chaucer's *Parle-
        ment of Foules*: A Philosophical Interpretation," RES 24
        (1948): 81–89, who saw the conflict of the poem as a more
        personal one, Christianity vs. writing love poetry, a conflict
        unresolved at the end, though the narrator hopes to find the
        answer in books.

        Reacting against this notion, two authors argued in 1955
        that the poem is not moral but ironical and open-ended. Doro-
        thy Everett, *Essays on Middle English Literature*, ed. Patricia
        M. Kean (Oxford, 1955), 97–114, did not deny a topical allusion
        but thought the poem an ironical meditation on love, courtly
        and natural; Charles O. McDonald, "An Interpretation of
        Chaucer's *Parlement of Foules*," *Speculum* 30 (1955): 444–457,
        saw "genial irony" and an unresolved and comic *demande
        d'amour* treated with "sympathetic understanding and broad
        humor." Such a view is at the heart of the admirable and de-
        tailed book by Bennett (1957), and of the interpretation offered
        by Brewer in his edition (1960), 13–25.

        Some critics have proposed themes other than love, not
        unrelated to the foregoing but treated less tentatively, e.g., natu-
        ral law (Gareth W. Dunleavy, "Natural Law as Chaucer's Ethi-
        cal Absolute," *Wisconsin Academy of Sciences, Arts, and Let-*

ters 52 [1963], 177–187); the futility of earthly love (Huppé and Robertson [1963], 101–148); order and disorder (Robert W. Uphaus, "Chaucer's *Parlement of Foules*: Aesthetic Order and Individual Experience," TSLL 10 [1968], 349–358); the relation of nature and culture (Spearing, p. 100); cycles of time vs. the concretes of experience (Robert L. Etzminger, "The Pattern of Time in *The Parlement of Foules*," JMRS 5 [1974], 1–11); the active life as the basis of an ordered state governed according to natural law (Bruce Kent Cowgill, "The *Parlement of Foules* and the Body Politic," JEGP 74 [1975], 315–335—cf. Paul A. Olson, "*The Parlement of Foules*: Aristotle's *Politics* and the Foundations of Human Society," SAC 2 [1980], 53–69).

Since 1960 various writers have furthered the argument that the poem, being as Muscatine (p. 116) put it about "the comic, contradictory variety of men's attitudes toward love," is ironic, equivocal, and unresolved. See for example John P. McCall, "The Harmony of Chaucer's *Parliament*," ChauR 5 (1970): 22–31; James Winney, *Chaucer's Dream-Poems* (London, 1973), 113–143; Smith, *Ball State Univ. Forum* 14: 15–22; David Aers, "the *Parliament of Fowls*: Authority, the Knower and the Known," ChauR 16 (1981): 1–17. Such a view is now the consensus; I share it myself, but it is not inconsistent, as I have tried to show, with the work's status as a court poem about arrangements for King Richard's marriage.

314   its structure and unity: The seminal essay was Bertrand H. Bronson, "In Appreciation of Chaucer's *Parlement of Foules*," Univ. of California Publications in English 3 (1935): 193–223; he was intent on demonstrating the esthetic value of the work, arguing for its conventionality. Bronson did not take seriously the notion that it is an occasional poem (though this was conventional too), but he allowed it was a satire having several objects. Gardiner Stillwell, "Unity and Comedy in Chaucer's *Parlement of Foules*," JEGP 49 (1950): 470–495, rejected the notion that the poem has a moral and argued that it is a "comedy of medieval manners and ideas . . . light, witty, and impartial." Robert Worth Frank, Jr., "Structure and Meaning in the *Parlement of Foules*," PMLA 71 (1956): 530–539, argued that its three parts—*Somnium*, garden, debate—present three clashing attitudes, each treated with sympathy; a sense of love's power emerges. Robert M. Jordan, "The Question of Unity and the *Parlement of Foules*," *English Studies in Canada* 3 (1977): 373–385, argued that the poem has unity of a nonorganic, disjunctive kind characteristic of the Middle Ages, whence the debate fails to achieve the resolution expected in the modern concept of unitary order: the poem has not a center but a circumference, the "all-embrac-

ing idea of love." Cf. Larry M. Sklute, "The Inconclusive Form of the *Parliament of Fowls*," ChauR 16 (1981): 119–128, who claims the form is intentionally inconclusive, expressing a "pluralistic vision of reality" that relies on individual choice rather than valid opinion—a vision carried out in *The Canterbury Tales*. One of the most penetrating ideas about the structure of the work was presented briefly by Muscatine, 123—that the poem reverses the structure of *Troilus*, putting the palinode first and ending with lived experience; in the *Troilus* the palinode is a lesson learned from experience.

314   its satiric intention: First raised, again as an alternative to the topical interpretation, by Rickert, MP 18: 26–28, who proposed that the birds of ravine stood for the nobility, the water birds for the great merchants, the seed birds for the country gentry, and the worm birds for the working classes, and that the poem satirized the lower orders. David Patrick, "The Satire in Chaucer's *Parliament of Birds*," PQ 9 (1930): 61–65, proposed that it satirizes rather the pretensions of the aristocracy and their failure to grasp the common sense of the lower classes. Lewis, *Allegory*, 171–174, reacted against this idea, arguing that the humor doesn't make for satire, that laughter and cynicism are accorded a place in the poem as it is said one makes a revolutionary safe by giving him a seat in Parliament. Robert E. Thackaberry, "Chaucer's 'Parlement of Foules': A Re-interpretation" (diss., Iowa, 1937) was evidently the first to argue that both upper and lower classes are satirized for failing to work for the common profit. Stillwell, "Unity and Comedy," JEGP 49: 482–488, thought that the birds only roughly correspond to the peasant and merchant classes; in "Chaucer's Eagles," JEGP 53: 546–561, he argued that the lower birds with their common sense don't understand the upper-class birds, who are not so different from their inferiors as they think. Clemen, 165, thought they are not identifiable by class but are part of a satire of parliamentary procedures. Olson, "Parlement," SAC 2: 53–69, identifies on the basis of certain analogues the fowls of ravine with the nobles, the turtle with the clergy, the water foul with the commons, and the cuckoo and worm fowl with selfish curial officials; he thinks the song at the end is a "hymn to civic charity."

315   Professor Benson: "Occasion," *Wisdom of Poetry*, 123–144.

315   Hamilton Smyser: "A View of Chaucer's Astronomy," *Speculum* 45 (1970): 359–373.

315   Alan Lazarus: "Venus in the 'north-north-west'? (Chaucer's *Parliament of Fowls*, 117)," in *Wisdom of Poetry*, 145–149.

316   ". . . a sober philosophical tract": Muscatine, 122. Cf. Clemen, 123.

316   solitary, alienated figure: See James J. Wilhelm, "The Narrator and

His Narrative in Chaucer's *Parlement*," ChauR 1 (1967): 201–206; Wilhelm observes that Donaldson alone (Donaldson ed., 1120) has pointed to the seriousness of this ending.

317   document signed by . . . Cecily Champain: LR, 343–347. The question of this and its accompanying documents was opened up and dealt with in detail by a legal historian, P. R. Watts, in "The Strange Case of Geoffrey Chaucer and Cecilia Chaumpaigne," *Law Quarterly Review* 63 (1947): 491–515.

317   minors or wards . . . kidnapped: Chaucer sat on a panel to investigate such a case; see LR, 375–383. For a good summary of evidence for the meaning of the word, see Paull F. Baum, *Chaucer: A Critical Appreciation* (Durham, N.C., 1958), 41–43.

317   eminent legal historian: T. F. T. Plucknett: "Chaucer's Escapade," *Law Quarterly Review* 64 (1948): 33–36, in a reply to Watts's article, ibid., 63: 491–515.

318   D. W. Robertson: *Chaucer's London* (New York and London, 1968), 99–101.

318   "that Chaucer seduced Cecily . . .": Plucknett, "Chaucer's Escapade," *Law Quarterly Rev.* 64: 35.

318   the woman consented and regretted it later: Cf. Brewer, *World*, 150.

318   Alice Perrers's stepdaughter: Haldeen Braddy, "Chaucer, Alice Perrers, and Cecily Chaumpaigne," *Speculum* 52 (1977): 906–911.

318   she was a nun: LR, 346 n. 3.

319   "While I was young . . .": "L'envoy de Chaucer a Scogan," line 40.

319   testify in his own behalf: Watts, "Strange Case," *Law Quarterly Rev.* 63: 502.

319   two men involved with her: LR, 346–347.

319   signed a recognizance: LR, 345.

320   Chaucer accumulated . . . capital: I.e., apart from regular payments of annuities and the like. In November he collected the balance owed him for his journey to Lombardy two years before; LR, 59–60. The following March he was given a gift of £22 for his journeys to France in the time of Edward III to treat of peace and in the time of Richard II to negotiate for a marriage with the French princess; LR, 49. In May he was assigned £16 in fines owed the crown; LR, 320. In June he sold his father's house in London to Henry Herbury; his mother had leased it to Herbury, but the date of her death is not known; LR, 1–2.

320   Peasants' Revolt: R. B. Dobson, ed., *The Peasants' Revolt of 1381*, 2d ed. (London, 1983) is a collection of primary documents with commentary. Charles Oman, *The Great Revolt of 1381* (1906; repr. Oxford, 1969) remains a standard treatment, and see McKisack, 406–423.

320   army of peasants and artisans: Rodney Hilton, *Bond Men Made Free* (London, 1973), 9–11, 25–40.

321   Chaucer in London: Chaucer was there on May 24 to receive payments of annuities—see the tables in LR, ch. 5 and 13; he was there on June 19 to sign a quitclaim to his father's house in Thames Street—see LR, 1–2, and there is no reason to believe he left the city between these two dates.

321   thirty or more such uprisings: See Dobson, ed., *Peasants' Revolt*, 36–44.

321   population . . . shrunk by a third: McKisack, 407.

322   led by Wat Tyler: Maude Clarke, *Fourteenth Century Studies*, ed. L. S. Sutherland and M. McKisack (Oxford, 1937), 95–97 suggest it was the Culpeper family.

323   sense of purpose and nebulous ideas: See V. H. Galbraith, "Thoughts about the Peasants' Revolt," in *The Reign of Richard II*, ed. F. R. H. DuBoulay and C. M. Barron (London, 1971), 56.

323   Margery Starre: McKisack, 417.

323   forty headless bodies: Dobson, ed. *Peasants' Revolt*, 210.

324   ". . . Law of Winchester": Dobson, ed., *Peasants' Revolt*, 164 n. 2. They may vaguely have had in mind Edward I's Statute of Winchester, which held that all men from fifteen to sixty should possess arms to defend the realm. The law of Winchester made mutilation or blinding, rather than hanging, the punishment of serious felonies. Since hanging was the lower-class form of execution, it's interesting that the rebels chose to behead their captives, if only for efficiency.

324   private property was tainted with sin: Southern, 53–55.

324   believe the chronicle: Anonimalle, 139.

325   trial of John Wyclif: Armitage-Smith, 148–152.

325   war again with the Londoners: Ibid., 152–159.

325   alienate the church: Ibid., 160–183.

326   meet him at Mile End: Dobson, ed., *Peasants' Revolt*, 159 n. 1.

326   through the gate at Aldgate: Ibid., 220.

327   William Tonge: Ibid., 220, 225.

327   "The king himself . . .": Anonimalle, Ibid., 160.

327   "I climbed to the roof top . . .":*Aeneid* 2: 302–305, 310–313 trans. Robert Fitzgerald (New York, 1981), p. 44.

327   "When rioting breaks out . . .": *Aeneid* 1: 148–152, ibid., p. 8.

328   "they could go through all the realm . . .": Anonimalle, in Dobson, ed., *Peasants' Revolt*, 161; cf. McKisack, 412 n. 1.

328   rebels went straight to the Tower: According to Walsingham a contingent was already at the Tower while the meeting was going on; see Dobson, ed., *Peasants' Revolt*, 171.

328   John Ferrour: McFarlane, 18; Hutchison, 234.

329   addressed the king with oaths . . . : Anonimalle, in Dobson, ed., *Peasants' Revolt*, 164. Other chroniclers are less exact, but several bear out Tyler's disrespect, ibid., 203, 207.

329   "Sirs, will you shoot your king? . . .": McKisack, 413, paraphrasing the more verbose utterance reported by Walsingham.

329   they followed—like sheep: Anonimalle, 149.

331   "Woe to thee, O land . . .": Eccl. 10: 16.

331   Anne of Bohemia arrived: Hutchison, 85–87; Steel, 109–111; McKisack, 427; Perroy, 143–156.

331   she was then crowned queen: *Chron. Ang.* 332-333.

332   £4,500: See McKisack, 427 n. 1.

332   Archbishop Arundel: Hutchison, 87 n. 2.

332   reappointed to the Wool Custom: LR, 158.

332   made controller of the Petty Custom: LR, 159. Normally he would have been made controller of the Petty Subsidy as well, since both were collected from the same merchants, but at this time the income from the Petty Subsidy was designated for defense; see LR, 161–62.

333   Richard Lyons: LR, 160 n. 7.

333   Some think Chaucer: E.g., Gardner, 250–251, 274–275.

333   absence Chaucer requested for personal reasons: LR, 165–168. There is no indication of his being on an assignment; the leave was granted at such time as he could find a suitable deputy, which suggests a personal reason.

333   requested a permanent deputy: LR, 168-170. In cases where men of great influence were appointed controller (one had been chamberlain of the Exchequer) they were released from performing the controller's actual duties, but this was not the case with Chaucer. It was the nature of his job that he had to take personal responsibility as auditor; that is why the appointment called for the books to be kept in his own hand.

334   Edward Plantagenet: Armitage-Smith, 264. Russell, 311, gives his age as six; the DNB gives his year of birth, with a question mark, as 1373.

335   merchant ships borrowed from Castile: Armitage-Smith, 267. Russell, 343, says the earl needed little more than a dozen ships to bring back the army that came in forty. The English fleet had already been sent home; see Russell, 313–314, 321, 337.

337   Squire in the General Prologue: Alan Gaylord, "A85–88: Chaucer's Squire and the Glorious Campaign," *Papers of the Michigan Academy of Science, Arts, and Letters* 45 (1960): 341–361.

338   Sir Simon Burley encouraged their friendship: Rot. Parl., 3: 242.

338   "obscene familiarity": Walsingham 2: 148.

340   the princess . . . died that August, at Wallingford Castle: Margaret Galway, "Chaucer's Sovereign Lady," MLR 33 (1938): 145-199, thought Chaucer was there to present the *Legend*, but he is not named in the records. It seems more likely that if he

presented anything it would have been the *Troilus*, but at best it is only a speculation.

341   black cloth for mourning: LR, 103–105. The gift of cloth for mourning was traditional at court. Chaucer's name is in a separate column that was added, as if overlooked. Among other of his friends are listed Clifford, Vache, Sturry, and the poet Clanvowe. The gift of black cloth does not necessarily mean he attended the funeral, which was put off until January, but he probably did; see Edith Rickert, "Chaucer at the Funeral of the Princess of Wales," TLS, August 11, 1927, 548.

341   Chaucer's eldest son, Thomas: Roskell, 153.

341   gifts from Gaunt: Armitage-Smith, 462–463.

341   Lincolnshire manors or her own: LR, 87–88.

341   Beaufort: The name was after a town in France granted to Gaunt by the Black Prince and long since lost; see Armitage-Smith, 199.

341   Philippa . . . paid through Lincolnshire officials: LR, 87–88.

341   Thomas Swynford: Armitage-Smith, 461.

342   her son Lewis: LR, 541–546. See Robinson ed. 867–868; his age is given as ten in *Astrolabe*, line 24.

342   her daughter Agnes: LR, 546 n. 4. She is listed as lady-in-waiting at the coronation of Henry IV (1399), and would have had to be fourteen or more; it is to be noted that Agnes was Chaucer's mother's name.

342   Philippa . . . had lived in Lincolnshire (note): Her Exchequer annuity was paid there in 1379 through John Yarburgh, sheriff of Lincolnshire, as was her annuity from Gaunt. See LR, 77–78, 80.

342   Chaucer continued to collect her Exchequer annuity (note): LR, 77–78.

342   annuity from King Edward in 1366: LR, 69.

342   became his mistress about 1371: Armitage-Smith, 462–463.

342   damsel to the Duchess Costanza: LR, 86–87.

342   annuity from John of Gaunt: LR, 271–272.

342   New Year's gifts: LR, 88–91.

343   confraternity of Lincoln Cathedral: LR, 91–93.

343   routine assignment of payments: LR, 236–237.

12. *TROILUS AND CRISEYDE*

345   compliment to Queen Anne: But the phrase may have been proverbial; Brewer, *World*, 73, mentions a poem in the Vernon ms. in which this is one of the points Christ explains to the Pharisees.

345   Chaucer did think and plan: See Wallace, ch. 6, for evidence drawn from close analysis of Chaucer's principles or ground rules in translating phrases from Boccaccio.

345   "philosophical" poet: Brewer, *Heritage*, 1: 39–43, 58–59, 62–64.

346   Trojan setting: C. S. Lewis, in "What Chaucer Really Did to 'Il Filostrato,' " E & S 17 (1932): 56–75, said Chaucer would have viewed the work as "a new bit of the Troy Story" (57).

346   excessive sensuality: See John P. McCall, "The Trojan Scene in Chaucer's *Troilus*," ELH 29 (1962): 263–275, n. 4, repr. *Chaucer's Troilus: Essays in Criticism*, ed. Stephen A. Barney (Hamden, Conn., 1980), 101–113.

346   to quote David Wallace: Wallace, "Chaucer and Boccaccio's Early Writings," in Boitani, 157.

347   to a horse!: Ibid.

347   "remained an outsider . . .": Ibid., 159.

347   never mentioned Boccaccio by name: Ibid., and Wallace, ch. 5.

347   painting in a Cambridge manuscript: Margaret Galway, "The 'Troilus' Frontispiece," MLR 44 (1949): 161–177, believed the figures were identifiable as particular members of the royal court; she thought the face of the king had been scratched off, perhaps by someone of Lancastrian sympathies. An alternative theory is that it was left blank for the face of a patron. No one I have read reports having looked at the face with a magnifying glass or under ultraviolet light to see if there are knife marks. Chaucer has brown hair and a forked beard and looks about the age he would have been when he completed the poem; his face may be modeled on the Hoccleve portrait. Brusendorff, 19–23, argues that the painting is based on a late fourteenth-century picture and thinks, as Galway did, the figures are identifiable. On the iconography, Elizabeth Salter and Derek Pearsall, "Pictorial Illustration of Late Medieval Poetic Texts," *Medieval Iconography and Narrative*, ed. Flemming G. Andersen et al. (Odense, Denmark, 1980), 100–123; they think the upper register suggests Criseyde leaving Troy, arguing on a comparison with "scenes of ceremonial procession and meeting," but they do not analyze the scene, which many think shows courtiers arriving at the scene below. See their earlier treatments: Pearsall, "The *Troilus* Frontispiece and Chaucer's Audience," YES 7 (1977): 68–74, and Salter, "The 'Troilus Frontispiece,' " *Troilus and Criseyde: A Facsimile of Corpus Christi College, Cambridge MS 61* (Cambridge, Eng., 1978), 15–23. I am indebted here to an unpublished paper by the art historian Katie Solomonson, and to another unpublished essay by Laura Kendrick, "The Troilus Frontispiece and the Dramatization of Chaucer's *Troilus*," of which the author kindly sent me a copy; she argues that the two well-dressed figures in front of the man on the platform are miming the action as the poem is recited, and that the occasion is a "Puy."

348   audience implied in the *Troilus*: The relation of the *Troilus* frontispiece to Chaucer's relationship with his audience was explored in David, ch. 1. See Dieter Mehl, "The Audience of Chaucer's *Troilus and Criseyde*," in *Chaucer and Middle English Studies in Honour of Rossell Hope Robbins*, ed. Beryl Rowland (London, 1974), 173–189; repr. in *Chaucer's Troilus*, ed. Barney, 211–229. And see ch. 14, pp. 407–409.

349   conventions of courtly writing missing: Cf. Lewis, "What Chaucer Really Did," E & S 17: 58–74.

349   surviving manuscripts revealed: The original theory was that of Robert Kilburn Root, in *The Textual Tradition of Chaucer's Troilus*, Chaucer Soc. 1st ser. 99 (London, 1916) and in his edition (Princeton, 1926). On the state of present knowledge, see Barry Windeatt, "The Text of the *Troilus*," in *Essays on Troilus and Criseyde*, ed. Mary Salu (Totowa, N.J. and Cambridge, Eng., 1979), 1–22.

350   The misreading about Lollius (note): Robert Armstrong Pratt, "A Note on Chaucer's Lollius," MLN 65 (1950): 183–187. Cf. George Lyman Kittredge, "Chaucer's Lollius," *Harvard Studies in Classical Philology* 28 (1917): 49–56.

350   youthful warrior . . . in the *Aeneid*: Winthrop Wetherbee, *Chaucer and the Poets* (Ithaca, N.Y. and London, 1984), 87–92.

351   form of madness: Mary F. Wack, "Lovesickness in *Troilus*," *Pacific Coast Philology* 19 (1984): 55–61.

352   if she and her father are Trojans: Later Calkhas says he was a Trojan (4: 71–72) and Criseyde says she was born in Troy (5: 956–957), but only later.

353   imagined detail about Troy: See McCall, "Trojan Scene," ELH 29: 263–275. See also J. S. P. Tatlock, "The Epilog of Chaucer's *Troilus*," MP 18 (1921): 640–658; Lewis, "What Chaucer Really Did," E & S 17: 59–61; Howard, *Idea*, 111–124.

353   no such anachronisms: See Morton W. Bloomfield, "Chaucer's Sense of History," JEGP 51 (1952): 301–313.

353   "Adam Scrivein" (note): Var. 5: 1: 133–137.

354   an imaginary pagan philosophy: See esp. Morton W. Bloomfield, "Distance and Predestination in *Troilus and Criseyde*," PMLA 72 (1957): 14–26; and Donald R. Howard, "The Philosophies in Chaucer's *Troilus*," in *Wisdom of Poetry*, 151–175. On paganism in the poem see John Frankis, "Paganism and Pagan Love in *Troilus and Criseyde*, *Essays*, ed. Salu, 57–72, and Minnis, ch. 3.

354   Criseyde's *uncle*, an older man: We are meant to assume this. In Boccaccio Pandaro and Troiolo are contemporaries. We do not know if Pandarus is Calkhas's brother or Criseyde's mother's brother, and we know nothing of their families or ages. Of

course it is possible to have an uncle one's own age or younger, but most are older; and the avuncular manner that Pandarus displays is that of an older man talking to younger people. Chaucer makes Pandarus *seem* older. Where his Italian counterpart is a street-wise swain, Pandarus is well-read, learned, articulate, an adviser to the king, who has been unsuccessfully in love for some years. Pedagogical and sententious, he *talks* like an older man, has an older man's world-weariness and cynical wit.

354   sometimes the form of proverbs: On the taste for proverbs and their status, see Howard *Idea,* 186–188 and Karla Taylor, "Proverbs and the Authentication of Convention in 'Troilus and Criseyde,'" *Chaucer's Troilus,* ed. Barney, 277–296.

354   think of *our* proverbs: Although we are in general nowadays condescending to proverbs of the Poor Richard variety, we do have certain classes of proverbs that have a magic about them not unlike what they had in the Middle Ages: these would be dire existential sayings ("The Impossible has already happened"), familiar maxims ("Power corrupts"), slogans of the bumper-sticker variety ("Make love, not war"), and familiar quotations.

355   "clerkes wise": 1: 961, 976.

355   Pandarus bears a similarity: The notion goes back at least to Nevill Coghill, *The Poet Chaucer* (Oxford, 1949), 75–76. See Howard, "Literature and Sexuality: Book III of Chaucer's *Troilus,*" *Massachusetts Review* 8 (1967): 446–448, and E. Talbot Donaldson, "Chaucer's Three 'P's: Pandarus, Pardoner, and Poet," *Michigan Quarterly Review* 14 (1975): 282–301.

355   "comes elevated and refined . . .": Brewer, *Heritage,* 1: 242.

355   "a friend according . . .": Lewis, *Allegory,* 191. Eugene Slaughter, "Chaucer's Pandarus: Virtuous Uncle and Friend," JEGP 48 (1949): 186, said his role was meant to "be ideal, and wholly commendable; Pandarus acts always within the limits set by the classical ideal of friendship." See Robert G. Cook, "Chaucer's Pandarus and the Medieval Ideal of Friendship," JEGP 69 (1970): 407–424.

355   seen him as a depraved: Robert Kilburn Root, *The Poetry of Chaucer* (Boston and New York, 1906), remarked that he was "wholly destitute of moral elevation" (119) and characterized him as "a middle-aged cynic" (121). Cf. Alan Gaylord, "Uncle Pandarus as Lady Philosophy," *Papers of the Michigan Academy of Science, Arts, and Letters* 46 (1961): 571–595.

355   a few think him a devil: D. W. Robertson, Jr., "Chaucerian Tragedy," ELH 19 (1952): 16–17; Charlotte D'Evelyn, "Pandarus a Devil?" PMLA 71 (1956): 275–279, refuted the notion.

355   compared with Polonius: Root, *Poetry of Chaucer,* 119.

356   the worst misery: The idea occurs in Boethius, *Consolation of Philos-*

ophy, 2: prosa 4, and Dante, *Inferno* 5: 121–123. It might be added here in defense of Pandarus's consistency that he is advising Troilus *not* to remember by finding something to make him forget.

357   a secret marriage: See Henry Ansgar Kelly, "Clandestine Marriage and Chaucer's 'Troilus,' " *Viator* 4 (1973): 435–457, and *Love and Marriage in the Age of Chaucer* (Ithaca, N.Y. and London, 1975).

358   "humanists rather than courtiers": John M. Ganim, *Style and Consciousness in Middle English Narrative* (Princeton, 1983), 88.

358   "the first great night of love . . .": Sanford B. Meech, *Design in Chaucer's Troilus* (Syracuse, N.Y., 1959), 72.

359   Then, in a remarkable passage: It is based on a soliloquy in Boccaccio (2: 68–77) one-fourth the length, that reports her vacillating thoughts. The present analysis is condensed from my article "Experience, Language, and Consciousness: *Troilus and Criseyde*, II: 596–931," in *Medieval Literature and Folklore Studies: Essays in Honor of Francis Lee Utley*, ed. Jerome Mandel and Bruce A. Rosenberg (New Brunswick, N.J., 1970), 173–192.

361   Procne's song: On the parallel of the two songs, see Charles A. Owen, Jr., "The Significance of a Day in 'Troilus and Criseyde,' " *Mediaeval Studies* 22 (1960): 369. And see the suggestive article by Marvin Mudrick, "Chaucer's Nightingales," *Hudson Review* 10 (1957): 88–95, repr. *Chaucer's Troilus*, ed. Barney, 91–99.

364   Pandarus seduces or rapes his niece (note): Haldeen Braddy, "Chaucer's Playful Pandarus," *Southern Folklore Quarterly* 34 (1970): 71–82.

365   "All men have waited . . .": Lewis, *Allegory*, 195.

366   with the Peasants' Revolt in mind: Carleton Brown, "Another Contemporary Allusion in Chaucer's *Troilus*," MLN 26 (1911): 208–211.

368   in its arms, "kissing ay . . .": The line makes it ambiguous whether the boar is kissing her or she kissing it; possibly Chaucer intended this ambiguity, but I have placed commas so as to suggest the more unpleasant image, that Criseyde is kissing the boar.

369   Chaucer emulates Dante: Cf. Wetherbee, *Chaucer and the Poets*, 242, speaking of the last lines in Book 5: "they speak here with one voice." But Wetherbee goes on to say very rightly that the allusion was inspired by Boccaccio.

371   "send yet to your maker . . .": See Howard, *Idea*, 30–45. For the opposite notion, that the lines refer to the remaining stanzas of the *Troilus*, see Middleton, 35, and Wetherbee, *Chaucer and the Poets*, 225.

371   Troilus's end: John M. Steadman, *Disembodied Laughter: Troilus*

and the Apotheosis Tradition (Berkeley and London, 1972), esp. ch. 7.

372 critic writing in the 1920s: Walter Clyde Curry, *Chaucer and the Mediaeval Sciences* (1926; 2d ed., New York, 1960), 294. The year before Curry's treatment, Karl Young had argued that the ending is ambiguous after the manner of Andreas Capellanus; see "Chaucer's Renunciation of Love in *Troilus*," MLN 40 (1925): 270–276. It is tempting to conclude that in the criticism of the poem we have come full circle, returning to Young's position but with a better knowledge of the rhetorical tradition, especially the *argumentum in utramque partem*, and schooled in the notion of deconstruction.

372 dominant interpretation is the opposite: From reactions to Curry there emerged the standard notion, certainly borne out by the particulars of the work, that the philosophy behind the ending was that of Boethius. Howard R. Patch, "Troilus on Determinism," *Speculum* 6 (1931): 225–243; James Lyndon Shanley, "The *Troilus* and Christian Love," ELH 6 (1939): 271–281; and J. S. P. Tatlock, "The People in Chaucer's *Troilus*," PMLA 56 (1941): 85–104. In the context of this question, whether the poem is philosophically of a piece, some have viewed the story as an exemplum of which the last lines were the moral: see esp. D. W. Robertson, Jr., "Chaucerian Tragedy," ELH 19: 1–37, who treated the characters as sinners, and T. P. Dunning, who treated them as pagans, Troilus following a "natural religion" shown to be insufficient—see "God and Man in *Troilus and Criseyde*" in *English and Medieval Studies Presented to J. R. R. Tolkien* . . . , ed. Norman Davis and C. L. Wrenn (London, 1962), 164–182.

372 question this unity and finality: In much of the criticism, the figure of the narrator was the focus of ideas about the poem's unity. In this view it was argued that the narrator's speeches at the end do not necessarily "cancel" the value of worldly life but affirm "the real validity of human values"; see Donaldson, ed., 1129–1144 and his later "Criseide and Her Narrator" and "The Ending of 'Troilus,'" in Donaldson, ch. 5 and 6. In the same year as the Donaldson ed., 1958, appeared Robert M. Jordan's "The Narrator in Chaucer's *Troilus*," ELH 25 (1958): 237–257; Jordan later argued that "organic unity" is a modern conception, that the disjunctive and paradoxical were a part of the medieval aesthetic—see his *Chaucer and the Shape of Creation: The Aesthetic Possibilities of Inorganic Structure* (Cambridge, Mass. and London, 1967), esp. ch. 4. That the ending falls apart and its realities are dispersed, a notion implicit in Donaldson, is one strain in recent criticism. I argued in *The Three Temptations*

(Princeton, 1966), 144, that the narrator is unmasked at the end and revealed to be Chaucer (see 5: 1799–1801), an opinion held also by Jordan; and see my bolder remarks in *Wisdom of Poetry,* 170–175.

372   Some treatments of narrator and ending that proceeded in various ways from Donaldson's treatment: Alfred David, "The Hero of the *Troilus,*" *Speculum* 37 (1962): 566–581; Stephen A. Barney, "Troilus Bound," *Speculum* 47 (1972): 445–458; John M. Fyler, "The Fabrications of Pandarus," MLQ 41 (1980): 115–130; Sherron E. Knopp, "The Narrator and His Audience in Chaucer's *Troilus and Criseyde,*" SP 78 (1981): 323–340; Richard H. Osberg, "Between the Motion and the Act: Intentions and Ends in Chaucer's *Troilus,*" ELH 48 (1981): 257–270; Bonnie Wheeler, "Dante, Chaucer, and the Ending of *Troilus and Criseyde,*" PQ 61 (1982): 105–123; Richard Waswo, "The Narrator of *Troilus and Criseyde,*" ELH 50 (1983): 1–25; James Dean, "Chaucer's *Troilus,* Boccaccio's *Filostrato,* and the Poetics of Closure," PQ 64 (1985): 175–184.

373   retreats into the privacy of prayer: Bloomfield, "Distance and Predestination," PMLA 72: 26: "In the last stanzas, Chaucer the narrator escapes from Troilus to where the pagan cannot follow him; he escapes into the contemplation of the mysteries of the Passion and the Trinity, the supreme paradox of all truth, which is the only possible way for a believing Christian to face the facts of his story."

373   "dedication" to Gower and Strode: Howard, "Philosophies," *Wisdom of Poetry,* 172–174.

373   still writing medieval complaint: Fisher, 3, 153, 206–207.

373   Strode was an opponent: On Chaucer as a predestinarian, see Bloomfield, "Distance and Predestination," PMLA 72: 22–26. The view goes back to Curry, 241–298, and Patch, "Troilus on Determinism," *Speculum* 6: 225–243. Cf. Tatlock, "Epilog," MP 18: 635 ff.; for the quotation, 656 n. 2.

373   Chaucer's modernity: See James Wimsatt, "Medieval and Modern in Chaucer's Troilus and Criseyde," PMLA 92 (1977): 203–216. The article quoted is his "Realism in *Troilus and Criseyde* and the *Roman de la Rose,*" in *Essays,* ed. Salu, 43–56.

374   what happens in his body: See *Troilus and Criseyde and Selected Short Poems,* ed. Donald R. Howard and James Dean (New York and London, 1976), xxii; my notion was that the stoppage of emotion, which Chaucer describes in medieval medical terms, is caused by his guilt and results in his fainting. Jill Mann, "Troilus' Swoon," ChauR 14 (1980): 319–335, interpreting in modern psychological terms, thinks the swoon demonstrates

"his subjection to Criseyde and to his love of her" (328) and
marks their mutual yielding to one another.

375   warn against lechery: Robertson, *Preface*, 472–502 and passim, and
see also his "Chaucerian Tragedy," ELH 19: 1–37.

375   puns: See Larry D. Benson, "The 'Queynte' Punnings of Chaucer's
Critics," *SAC Proceedings*, 1 (1984): 23–47.

375   Such number symbolism: See Russell A. Peck, "Numerology and
Chaucer's *Troilus and Criseyde*," *Mosaic* 5, 4 (1972): 1–29, and
Thomas Elwood Hart, "Medieval Structuralism: 'Dulcarnoun'
and the Five-book Design of Chaucer's *Troilus*," ChauR 16
(1981): 129–170.

376   a face with empty eyes: On the medieval emblem, see *The Divine
Comedy* ed. Charles S. Singleton, 6 vols. (Princeton, 1973), the
note to *Purgatorio* 23: 32–33. Of many other images of eyes, see
e.g., 3: 1354–1355 where Criseyde's eyes are compared to nets,
and 5: 813 where her brows are joined as in pre-Boccaccian
versions (reckoned a sign of beauty in ancient times); in 4: 869,
Criseyde's eyes have purple rings, Troilus's eyes are streaming
tears in 4: 246–247, as are Pandarus's eyes in 4: 872–873.

13. THE WORST OF TIMES—THE 1380s

378   before the end of 1386: Tatlock, 141–142, thought *The Canterbury
Tales* was conceived in 1385 and begun in 1387 and put *Troilus*
much earlier, about 1377. See Robinson, ed., 810–811, for references to the replies of Lowes, Kittredge, and Brown, who argued
that the poem was being written in the early 1380s. For the
argument that it was completed in 1385–1387, based on astronomical allusions, see Robert Kilburn Root and Henry Norris
Russell, "A Planetary Date for Chaucer's *Troilus*," PMLA 39
(1924): 48–63, but see John J. O'Connor, "The Astronomical
Dating of Chaucer's *Troilus*," JEGP 55 (1956): 556–562. The
strongest argument for the date 1386 shows how contemporary
events and Chaucer's experience as an M.P. are reflected in the
poem; see John P. McCall and George Rudisill, Jr., "The Parliament of 1386 and Chaucer's Trojan Parliament," JEGP 58
(1959): 276–288.

379   shorter poems on Boethian themes: *Boece* and *Troilus* are mentioned
together in the poem "Adam Scrivein" as being copied at the
same time. Most of Boethius's influence on Chaucer shows up
in work written then or thereafter, i.e., the *Troilus*, the shorter
"Boethian" poems, the Knight's Tale and some other of the
Canterbury tales.

379   Professor John Fisher's: Fisher ed., 814.

380   "The Former Age": See Var. 5: 1: 91–101 for the information about manuscripts, etc., presented here, and the text quoted.

381   The poem "Fortune": Var. 5: 1: 103–119.

381   entirely French: Brusendorff, 241–245. See James I. Wimsatt, "Chaucer, Fortune, and Machaut's 'Il m'est avis,' " *Chaucerian Problems and Perspectives: Essays Presented to Paul E. Beichner, C.S.C.,* ed. Edward Vasta and Zacharias P. Thundy (Notre Dame, Ind., 1979), 124–129.

381   by adding the envoi: Howard R. Patch, "Chaucer and Lady Fortune," MLR 22 (1927): 377–388.

381   "Gentilesse": Var. 5: 1: 67–76.

382   "Truth": Var. 5: 1: 49–65.

383   *Melibee*: On the date, Tatlock, 188–197; he thought it was written for Richard II (192). See Paul Strohm, "The Allegory of the *Tale of Melibee,*" ChauR 2 (1967): 32–42, which emphasizes the religious side; and Gardiner Stillwell, "The Political Meaning of Chaucer's *Tale of Melibee,*" *Speculum* 19 (1944): 433–444. William Askins, at the New Chaucer Society meeting, Philadelphia, 1986, presented in a paper called "The *Tale of Melibee* and the Crisis at Westminster, November, 1387" a view of the *Melibee* as recommending arbitration during the events of 1387.

383   a satire on such treatises: Lloyd Jean Matthews, "The Latent Comic Dimensions of Geoffrey Chaucer's *Tale of Melibee*" (diss.; University of Virginia, 1971). Cooper, 173–176, argues for a "hint of subversion."

383   not intended for John of Gaunt: J. Leslie Hotson, "The *Tale of Melibeus* and John of Gaunt," SP 18 (1921): 429–452.

384   justices of the peace: LR, 348–363.

384   residency was not a requirement: LR, 363.

384   Richard Forster: LR, 145–146. The indenture was delivered to Forster on November 6, but the editors of LR seem to feel, without saying why, that the property would have been vacated by the date of the lease. The terms of Forster's lease, like Chaucer's, granted the house for life.

384   Chaucer signed as mainpernor: LR, 285–289.

384   manuscripts of his poem to Scogan: Var. 5: 1: 159 n. 43–46.

384   Greenwich records: See LR, 288–289, 512–513. For a summary of the evidence that Chaucer lived in Greenwich, see Margaret Galway, "Geoffrey Chaucer, J.P. and M.P.," MLR 36 (1941): 1–36, esp. 16–17.

384   "Wonderful Parliament": LR, 364–369. The sheriff of Kent was ordered to arrange the election of two "knights of the shire" to attend Parliament at Westminster on Oct. 1. The election took place in the shire court. Representatives of counties were called

"knights," though Kent like most rarely put up anyone who had actually been dubbed a knight.

384   lifetime appointments of some controllers: LR, 269.

385   saw the handwriting on the wall: Gardner, 266, 272–275.

385   payments had fallen in arrears: McCall and Rudisill, "Parliament of 1386," JEGP 58: 277–278.

385   forced out by them or resigned: On his leaving the Customs, see LR, 268–269. According to the extravagant guess by Galway, "Geoffrey Chaucer, J. P. and M. P.," MLR 36: 1–36, Richard relieved him of the Customs job and sent him to live at one of his favorite estates, Eltham or Sheen, or at Greenwich nearby, both in Kent; Chaucer would, in this scenario, have been made justice of the peace to look out for the king's interests in Kent and been put in charge of the upkeep and remodeling of the king's estates at a time when the king was away on a military campaign (in Scotland) and the queen was having her "first experience of solitary state." Later, when the king regained power, it was natural for him to make Chaucer the Clerk of the Works. Galway thought the king got Chaucer, now already in Kent, elected to the Parliament of 1386. She did not answer the objection that if he was secretly in the king's employ he would not have been in such bad financial straits.

385   Adam Yardley: LR, 244–246, 268–269.

385   Henry Gisors: LR, 165–167, 268–269.

385   at most £2 8s. a year: LR, 356. Gardner, 250–251, 272–275, thought extortion was the expected way of gaining income from the position, and he states without evidence that Sir Simon Burley took bribes. The sergeants-at-law were said to grow rich on extortions. Probably Chaucer was too cautious to take a bribe even if tempted, though there may have been certain gifts that he might take without incurring suspicion of bribery. But if he had done much of this sort of thing, one would expect him to be richer than he was.

385   "prest" of £10: LR, 119–120.

385   paid £24 9s.: LR, 367.

385   prest for £1!: LR, 330–334.

386   commission to investigate an abduction: LR, ch. 19.

386   to Calais in the king's service: LR, 61–62.

386   sued for debts: LR, 384–401. The Henry Atwood who brought suit was not evidently related to the Robert Atwood of Deptford, to whom Simon Manning owed money; see LR, 285–289, esp. 288 n. 6.

386   John Scalby: LR, 336–339; on Scalby's identity, LR, 336 n. 1.

387   Gaunt rescued Mary: Kirby, 17–18.

388 His impeachment ended with: J. S. Roskell, *The Impeachment of Michael de la Pole* (Manchester, 1984), esp. 11–55.

388 "Lack of Steadfastnesse": See Var. 5: 1: 77–79 for the most probable date.

389 Scrope-Grosvenor case: LR, 370–374. See R. Stewart-Brown, "The Scrope and Grosvenor Controversy, 1385–1391," *Transactions of the Historic Society of Lancashire and Cheshire* 89 (1938): 1–22.

390 highly abbreviated script: See Christian Johnen, *Geschichte der Stenographie* (Berlin, 1911), 280–281. I'm indebted to my colleague George Brown for his advice about this apparently obscure point. He asked the three top experts in such matters, Professors James John, Richard H. Rouse, and Malcolm Parkes. The last kindly enclosed a copy of a lecture he had given, "Tachygraphy and Writing Techniques." All three supported my contention that tachygraphy, i.e., rapid, abbreviated writing (as opposed to shorthand, not revived until the sixteenth century) was in use in law courts and could have preserved something close to a deponent's actual words.

391 "Before human memory" (note): M. T. Clanchy, *From Memory to Written Record: England, 1066–1307* (Cambridge, Mass. and London, 1979), 123. But see G. D. Squibb, *The High Court of Chivalry* (Oxford, 1959), 179–183, where it is argued that "time immemorial" in the Court of Chivalry was the Conquest, 1066, and not 1189.

392 Grosvenor was on the same campaign: Stewart-Brown, "Scrope and Grosvenor Controversy," *Transactions . . . Cheshire* 89: 16.

394 Alceste, an ideal of femininity: See Lisa J. Kiser, *Telling Classical Tales: Chaucer and the Legend of Good Women* (Ithaca, N.Y. and London, 1983), esp. ch. 2; she argues that Alceste is an ideal figure but does not emphasize femininity.

394 *Troilus* was finished in 1386: McCall and Rudisill, "Parliament of 1386," JEGP 58: 281–288, argue that Chaucer's experience in Parliament is reflected in the poem, which would of course date it at the end of 1386 or after. Possibly this element, like the astronomical reference, could have been added to a version already completed; but the political reference is less tangible than the astronomical one and can be otherwise explained.

394 *flos florum*: See Peter Dronke, *Medieval Latin and the Rise of European Love-Lyric*, 2d ed. 2 vols. (Oxford, 1968), 1: 181–192, and Edgar De Bruyne, *The Esthetics of the Middle Ages*, trans. Eileen B. Hennessy (New York, 1969), 70.

395 Alceste . . . turned into a daisy: This was evidently Chaucer's invention; see Kiser, *Telling Classical Tales*, 58–59, 139.

395 Chaucer wrote nine: Ibid., ch. 4. The legends themselves remain a

bafflement; it is hard to know on what principles they were chosen or what kind of treatment they receive. The notion that a sort of trick or joke is involved is not now taken seriously.

395   introduce violence into courtly love material: Robert Worth Frank, Jr., *Chaucer and The Legend of Good Women* (Cambridge, Mass., 1972), ch. 2, esp. 34–36.

395   "Year by year": To my knowledge no one has proposed this but myself. "Year by year" is normally taken to mean "year after year, continually," but Chaucer uses the phrase eight times in his works, in some instances with the sense of "every year." See OED, "year," 7a.

396   Since nineteen ladies are listed: Eighteen plus Alceste (who is not named) or, alternatively, nineteen counting "Hypermnestra *or* Ariadne" (268) separately. The passage reflects a certain indecision on the poet's part.

396   A recent discovery: Bernard Witlieb, basing his information on George Frederick Beltz, *Memorials of the Most Noble Order of the Garter.* . . (1841; repr. New York, 1973). On the Ladies of the Garter, see James L. Gillespie, "Ladies of the Fraternity of Saint George and of the Society of the Garter," *Albion* 17 (1985): 259–278, which does not make the connection with Chaucer's poem. One wonders why in revising the Prologue after the queen's death Chaucer let "nineteen" stand, for by then there were twenty-five ladies. Perhaps he decided first to keep the number as he had meant it when he wrote, but later in the Retraction decided to make it what it would have been if he had finished it.

398   De Vere, seeing that all was lost: Hutchison, 113, 131 n. 1.

398   Ralph Strode died in 1387: Fisher, 62.

398   gloves piled up . . . like snow: Hutchison, 178 cites Favent, 16.

399   block and ax: Hutchison, 119, cites Walsingham, 2: 174.

400   date of Richard's betrothal: See ch. 11, p. 308.

400   "of full age . . .": Walsingham 2: 181, in Hutchison, 127.

14. *THE CANTERBURY TALES*—THE PLAN TAKES SHAPE

402   half-dozen stories: See ch. 9, and Tatlock, 142–197.

402   story collection or frame story: See esp. Cooper, ch. 1.

402   What he needed first was a "frame": See esp. Morton W. Bloomfield, "*The Canterbury Tales* as Framed Narratives," *Leeds Studies in English* N.S. 14 (1983): 44–56. It has been supposed that the setting of Sercambi's *Novelle* was a pilgrimage, but it is only a trip around Italy to escape the plague and does not follow the pattern of a pilgrimage; see Howard, *Idea*, 28 n. 11. DeGuille-

ville's *Pelerinage de la Vie Humaine* used the pilgrimage as a frame, but for an allegory.

402 "image of medieval religion": The phrase is Jonathan Sumption's, in *Pilgrimage: An Image of Mediaeval Religion* (Totowa, N.J. and London, 1975).

403 The sin of "curiosity": Christian K. Zacher, *Curiosity and Pilgrimage* (Baltimore and London, 1976).

403 accounts of the Jerusalem pilgrimage: See Howard, "Writers," and Jean Richard, "Les Récits de Voyages et de Pelerinages" in *Typologie des Sources du Moyen Age Occidental* No. 38 (Turnhout, 1981).

404 Harry Bailly: Manly, *Light,* 77–83.

404 His bagpipe: G. Fenwick Jones, "Wittenwiler's *Becki* and the Medieval Bagpipe," JEGP 48 (1949): 209–228; Edward A. Block, "Chaucer's Millers and their Bagpipes," *Speculum* 29 (1954): 239–243; and see Robertson, *Preface,* 128–133 and fig. 15.

404 Roger Ware: Edith Rickert, "Chaucer's 'Hodge of Ware,' " TLS, Oct. 20, 1932, p. 761.

404 "tightly knit group . . .": R. M. Lumiansky, *Of Sondry Folk* (Austin, 1955), 237.

404 thirty pilgrims: This is taking Chaucer at his word in 1: 24 that there were nine-and-twenty not counting himself, but it is hard to be sure how he counted. There are twenty-nine not including Chaucer if you count only one of the "preestes three" mentioned in 1: 164 (the other two might mean the Monk and Friar, whose descriptions follow). Otherwise thirty is a round number, and there is a latecomer, the Canon's Yeoman, to complicate the matter.

405 two writers purported to continue: Lydgate in *The Siege of Thebes* and the anonymous author of *The Tale of Beryn.* See A. C. Spearing, "Lydgate's Canterbury Tale: *The Siege of Thebes* and Fifteenth-Century Chaucerianism," in *Fifteenth-Century Studies,* ed. Robert F. Yeager (Hamden, Conn., 1984), 333–364.

405 took place . . . on one day: Howard, *Idea,* 166–168.

406 "This world nis . . .": Knight's Tale, 1: 2847–2848.

406 Ralph Baldwin: *The Unity of the Canterbury Tales, Anglistica* 5 (Copenhagen, 1955).

407 The intended audience: On the general problem of what an "audience" was, see Paul Strohm, "Chaucer's Audience(s): Fictional, Implied, Intended, Actual," ChauR 18 (1983): 137–145—the opening of an excellent symposium on the subject, Ibid., 137–181. See also Strohm, "Chaucer's Audience," *Literature and History* 5 (1977): 26–41.

407   Patricia Eberle: "Commercial Language and the Commercial Out-
        look in the *General Prologue*," ChauR 18 (1983): 161–174.

408   "invites us to admire . . .": Middleton, 43.

408   ladies were present: Richard Firth Green, "Women in Chaucer's
        Audience," ChauR 18 (1983): 146–154.

408   maleness of the audience: Ibid., 153.

409   more inclusive audience became the dominant one: Paul Strohm,
        "Chaucer's Fifteenth-Century Audience and the Narrowing of
        the 'Chaucer Tradition'," SAC 4 (1982): 3–32.

409   most and least "popular": Ibid., 24–28.

410   The Clerk seems idealized: See Middleton, 46.

410   divided symmetrically by the ideal portraits: Howard, *Idea*, 151, thus:

        Knight: Squire, Yeoman, Prioress, Monk, Friar, Mer-
                           chant
        Clerk: Man of Law, Franklin, Guildsmen, Shipman,
                           Physician, Wife of Bath
        Parson/Plowman: Miller, Manciple, Reeve, Summoner, Pardoner,
                           Host

410   "estates satire": Jill Mann, *Chaucer and Medieval Estates Satire*
        (Cambridge, Eng., 1973).

411   "hate the sin . . .": Augustine, Letter 211, J.-P. Migne, *Patrologia
        Latina* 33: 962.

411   form of the dream vision: J. V. Cunningham, "Convention as Struc-
        ture: The Prologue to the Canterbury Tales," in *Tradition and
        Poetic Structure* (Denver, 1960), 59–75.

411   realism is artifice too: Ibid., 75.

414   Chaucer first assigned that tale: See Hammond, 285.

414   element of mystery: Morton W. Bloomfield, "Authenticating Real-
        ism and the Realism of Chaucer," *Thought* 39 (1964): 335–358.

414   lays a ground plan: Some earlier scholars, Furnivall and Skeat, be-
        lieved the General Prologue was written later. Tatlock, 142–150,
        argued that it was written after the first tales (Knight, Miller,
        Reeve).

414   suits the knight: The final moral of the tale, after its famous "Boe-
        thian" passage about order in the universe, is that a man does
        better to die young at the height of his knightly glory than when
        he is "appalled for age." This is the ideal of knightly glory and
        fame, a prime motive of the medieval knighthood; Chaucer's
        interest in Boccaccio's epic may well have been that it reflected
        the Renaissance humanists' fascination with fame.

415   As a reality he is harder: For example, Terry Jones, *Chaucer's Knight:
        The Portrait of a Medieval Mercenary* (Baton Rouge and Lon-
        don, 1980), argues that the presentation of the Knight is a biting
        satire. His book is vastly learned and his argument not to be
        brushed aside, but his treatment of the literary evidence is ten-

dentious. When the Knight is praised in the General Prologue, Jones supposes Chaucer is being ironical and means the opposite of everything he says. And when he finds the Knight's mercenary mentality reflected in his tale, he has to twist or exaggerate: the enmity between Palamon and Arcite over fair Emily is "a barrack-room brawl dressed up in the fine rags of pageantry" (153). Some of the naïve and exaggerated quality of the fight between the friendly rivals *does* reflect the Knight's mentality, but the pageantry and exaggerated courtliness reveal an idealism and romanticism in the Knight that raise him above the level of the ordinary mercenary. He has fought in Crusades for what must be—at least in part—idealistic motives. That his son has joined him, and that the son is a courtier with all the proper courtly accomplishments, strongly suggests the Knight *is* of the knightly class.

The ranking authority on medieval chivalry, Maurice Keen, in "Chaucer's Knight, the English Aristocracy and the Crusade," *English Court Culture*, 45–61, has demonstrated that men of the knightly class, and of noble and royal families too, *did* go on crusades—many of them the same ones mentioned in connection with the Knight. Jones assumes going on crusade in the fourteenth century was disreputable, as if crusading had fallen entirely into the hands of mercenaries; Keen shows this was not true. Then too, knights were paid and booty was part of their reward—gain entered into the motives of all knights. In this sense a mercenary soldier was different from other soldiers only because fighting was his only means of livelihood, and because he fought in an army whose leader would sell its services to any buyer.

415   keeping an emotional balance: Muscatine, 187, calls it a "deftly administered antidote for tragedy."

417   suppressed all but its opening: This possibility could be accounted for if the last page of the Reeve's Tale or the Cook's Prologue (if Chaucer meant to keep it) were on the recto side of a manuscript page; the opening of the Cook's Tale would have been on the verso side and thus retained though the remaining pages would have been removed. But it would be rather much of a coincidence that the last lines of that verso page happened to be the splendidly funny couplet about the wife's "swiving for her sustenaunce."

417   Because no source or close analogue: SA 148–154.

417   compared to the moment in *The Parliament of Fowls*: Cunningham, *Tradition and Poetic Structure*, 70–71.

418   *Confessio Amantis* (commissioned by Richard II): Fisher, 9–10, 116.

418   A few influences and one allusion: Ibid., 27, 290–292.

418   Gower's was finished first: Ibid., 116.

419   put it after the Cook's Tale: On the date of the Man of Law's tale, see Tatlock, 172 ff.; it was probably not written before 1386 or it would have been mentioned in the Prologue to LGW. Its use of Pope Innocent III *De Miseria* suggests a date in the late eighties or early nineties.

419   "ideal fictions": J. V. Cunningham, "Ideal Fiction: *The Clerk's Tale,*" *Shenandoah* 19: 2 (1968): 38–41.

419   pleads it badly: So it was argued by George D. Gopin in an unpublished paper, "Legal Education in Medieval England and Chaucer's Sergeant-at-Law."

419   Such was the reputation of physicians (note): Mann, *Chaucer and Medieval Estates Satire*, 91–99.

419   to follow the Man of Law's (note): Beryl Rowland, "The Physician's 'Historial Thyng Notable' and the Man of Law," ELH 40 (1973): 165–178; she thought the two were paired and that the Physician's tale was "an exemplum which adroitly subverts the arguments of all those who asserted that law was nobler than medicine" (177).

420   *Troilus* isn't mentioned: But see the reference to Brixeida, line 71.

420   the old notion that they quarreled: Fisher, 27–36.

420   The Man of Law announces: The Man of Law seems to say it doesn't matter if he comes after Chaucer with plain fare ("I recche nought a bene / Though I come after him with hawebake," 2: 94–95); since Chaucer hasn't told a tale, one would think "come after" might be used metaphorically to mean "be second to." But the phrase "come after" seems to be used only once elsewhere by Chaucer, and in the temporal sense. It appears to me from the context that "with hawebake" (they are hawthorne berries, by the way, very plain fare indeed) is in a phrase with "him," not "come after," so that it means "come after one who offers hawebake."

420   using the word "prose": Stevens, 62–76; and see OED under "prose."

421   Thomas Pynchbeck: Manly, 131–157, esp. 151–156.

421   have Chaucer arrested for debt: LR, 386.

421   the carnival world: Mikhail Bakhtin, *Rabelais and His World*, trans. Helene Iswolsky (Cambridge, Mass., 1968). This aspect of European culture, which survived well after Rabelais's time, has been studied as an aspect of various periods. See for example Natalie Zemon Davis, "The Reasons of Misrule," *Past and Present* 50 (1971): 41–75; in later English literature, C. L. Barber, *Shakespeare's Festive Comedy* (Princeton, 1959); in the eighteenth century, Terry Castle, "The Carnivalization of Eighteenth-Century English Narrative," PMLA 99 (1984): 903–916. David, esp. 94–95, 105–106, was evidently the first to remark on its

importance in Chaucer studies. John Ganim is writing on the subject, and Laura Kendrick in a book to be called *Chaucerian Play*. Carl Lindahl, in "The Festive Form of the *Canterbury Tales*," ELH 52 (1985): 531–574, has surveyed carnivalesque and other "festive" elements in Chaucer; his thesis, that whereas Renaissance authors reshaped folk forms into literature, Chaucer reshaped literature into festival, "crafting a frozen representation of a lively play form," seems to me wrong-headed: Chaucer did exactly what later writers did—he included folk forms in a literary artifact. The carnival element is only part of the larger form of *The Canterbury Tales*, the fun and games on the framing pilgrimage.

422	"They remained . . . fools and clowns . . .": Bakhtin, *Rabelais*, 8.
422	official seriousness: Ibid., 95.
422	W. H. Auden: "Concerning the Unpredictable," in *Forewords and Afterwords*, ed. Edward Mendelson (New York, n.d.), 471–472.
423	Noses and mouths: Bakhtin, *Rabelais*, 315–321.
423	the image of bells: Ibid., 214–215.
424	image of a hell-mouth: Roy J. Pearcy, "Does the Manciple's Prologue Contain a Reference to Hell's Mouth," ELH 11 (1974): 167–175. The gaping mouth, though a carnival image, was also part of the iconography of the Last Judgment, and as such appeared in the medieval drama.
424	Saint Thomas à Watering: Robertson, *Chaucer's London*, 58; Francis Watt, *Canterbury Pilgrims and Their Ways* (London, 1917), 68–69.
424	a comic devil: Bakhtin, *Rabelais*, 41.
424	dismemberment: Ibid., 349–350 and passim.
424	the banquet image: Ibid., ch. 4.
425	the gaping mouth: Ibid., 184, 317, and passim.
425	"Carnival celebrates . . .": Ibid., 410.
425	satire of Pentecost: Alan Levitan, "The Parody of Pentecost in Chaucer's *Summoner's Tale*," UTQ 40 (1971): 236–246.

15. *THE CANTERBURY TALES*—MAKING A WORLD OF STORY

428	wife, Philippa, died: LR, 83–84.
428	John of Gaunt was in Spain: Armitage-Smith, 310 ff.
428	sent to Calais: LR, 61–62.
428	in August to Dartford: LR, 378.
430	reading Saint Jerome: Samuel Moore, "The Date of Chaucer's Marriage Group," MLN 26 (1911): 172–174.
430	feelings at a deep level: This is of course the kind of conjecture on which a biographer can base nothing. Yet probably his other most striking character, the Pardoner, who was in Chaucer's

mind at this time (for he interrupts the Wife in her Prologue), is described in the General Prologue as a "gelding or a mare," and whatever else this may mean, it means that he lacked the ability to father a child.

431   became the Shipman's: This reassignment is commonly accepted; see Robinson's notes, 732, and Tatlock, 208–209. The reason is a passage, lines 1201–1209, clearly spoken by a woman. It is possible, however, that the passage is supposed to have invisible quotation marks around it, as if the Shipman were mimicking the characteristic complaints of women.

432   presented before a male audience: The stanza is missing in one family of manuscripts and was probably added later when the tale was made part of the Marriage Group. In the earlier version the Envoy ended at line 1200. See Fisher ed., 165 n. to 1170.

432   Merchant with his bitter story: That the bitterness inheres in the speaker's language was demonstrated by E. T. Donaldson, ch. 3.

433   promised *in play*: Line 988; the phrase is Chaucer's addition.

433   a tale Boccaccio told twice: SA, 377–385.

434   "the world grown old": See James Dean, *The World Grows Old* (diss., Johns Hopkins, 1971).

436   Saint Augustine: *City of God*, 1: 16–19. See Anne Middleton, "The *Physician's Tale* and Love's Martyrs," ChauR 8 (1973): 9–32.

436   physicians and lawyers: See p. 419.

436   Prioress's Tale: See Florence H. Ridley, *The Prioress and the Critics* (Berkeley and Los Angeles, 1965).

437   as one observer remarks: Seward, 98, quoting *Melibee* 1036.

438   lack of secular estate and worldly power: Middleton, 44–46, says that in the Monk's hands the tales become "laments for the passing of human greatness."

438   various critics have found: Alan Gaylord, "*Sentence* and *Solaas* in Fragment VII of the *Canterbury Tales*," PMLA 82 (1967): 226–235, called it the "literature group" and thought it alternated funny and serious tales. Paull F. Baum, *Chaucer: A Critical Appreciation* (Durham, N.C., 1958), 74–84, called it the "surprise group" and thought the tales after the Shipman's are surprises because each is other than what is anticipated; he thought all were parodies. Howard, *Idea*, 271–288, styles them "tales of private conduct."

438   there was no morality: Fisher, 286.

438   "*The Canterbury Tales* in little": Charles Muscatine, "*The Canterbury Tales*," in *Chaucer and Chaucerians*, ed. D. S. Brewer (London and University, Ala., 1966), 111.

438   the most Chaucerian of the tales: On its quintessentially Chaucerian character, see Donaldson ed., 1104–1108.

441   form of *The Canterbury Tales*: Howard, *Idea*, ch. 4 and 5, and
       Cooper, esp. ch. 5 and 6. Traugott Lawler, in *The One and the
       Many in the Canterbury Tales* (Hamden, Conn., 1980) ap-
       proaches the matter of form by exploring the manner in which
       Chaucer took the diverse materials of the world and found a
       oneness among them in accordance with nature as conceived in
       Platonic traditions.

441   "artificial" memory: Frances A. Yates, *The Art of Memory* (Chicago
       and London, 1966), ch. 3–5.

441   A recent writer: Kolve, esp. ch. 1 and 2.

441   Labyrinth: See above p. 248 and n. On the design itself, see W. H.
       Matthews, *Mazes and Labyrinths* (1922; repr. New York, 1970),
       esp. ch. 9. Penelope B. R. Doob, *The Idea of the Labyrinth:
       Studies in the Life of a Sign* (forthcoming) will be the definitive
       study.

442   "a kind of foundling asylum . . .": Tatlock, 189.

444   parody of compline: Robert M. Correale, "Chaucer's Parody of Com-
       pline in the *Reeve's Tale*," ChauR 1 (1967): 161–166.

445   May's "womb": Rossell Hope Robbins, "January's Caress," *Lock
       Haven Review* 10 (1968): 3–6.

445   "Matter of Araby": Dorothee Metlitzki, *The Matter of Araby in
       Medieval England* (New Haven and London, 1977).

446   "clown poems": Gardner, 290–292.

446   Pardoner's Tale: On the date of the Pardoner's Tale there is little
       agreement. Hammond, 257, thought it was written early, Skeat
       and Ten Brink that it was written late (see Hammond 320).
       Tatlock did not take up the question. My reasoning is that
       Chaucer translated one of the influences on it, Pope Innocent
       III's *De Miseria*, between 1386 and 1394, adding the reference
       to it in the later G Prologue to LGW (ca. 1394). Tatlock,
       188–197, showed that the *Melibee*, also an influence on the
       Pardoner's Tale, was written in the later 1380s. So the Par-
       doner's Tale was started in the 1390s, and very likely after 1394.
       Its gloomy mood and preoccupation with death suit that part of
       Chaucer's life, but I am dating it from its literary relations, not
       its mood.

447   each choice reveals an interest: Some argue that not all tales reveal
       or even suit the pilgrim, but the principle is clearly established
       and we must assume it *can* hold in all instances. The most
       striking instances are ones where an unexpected side of the
       pilgrim is revealed in his tale, which makes such tales the most
       arguable. The least arguable are those most obviously suited to
       the teller, like the Second Nun's Tale, a saint's legend.

448   "Breton lai": See Kathryn Hume, "Why Chaucer Calls the *Frank-
       lin's Tale* a Breton Lai," PQ 51 (1972), 365–379.

16. A NEW AGE—THE 1390s

451   one scholar thinks, with relief: McKisack, 463.

451   Arundel planned a crusade or pilgrimage: Ibid.

452   John Hend: LR, 281–284.

452   Henry Vanner: LR, 490–493. Vanner served with Chaucer on the commission for walls and ditches, 1390.

453   "a purposeful policy of ultimate vengeance": Hutchison, 131.

453   red velvet slippers: Higden, 9: 222.

453   vow to avenge Burley: Hutchison, 168.

453   anniversary observance of his death: N. B. Lewis, "Simon Burley and Baldwin of Raddington," EHR 52 (1937): 662–669.

454   King Richard . . . patron of the arts: The view was probably most fostered by Gervase Mathew, *The Court of Richard II* (London, 1968) and John A. Burrow, *Ricardian Poetry* (New Haven and London, 1971). On "public poetry," Anne Middleton, "The Idea of Public Poetry in the Reign of Richard II," *Speculum* 53 (1978): 94–114, and her unpublished essay "Chaucer as a Ricardian Poet," and Laura Kendrick, "Rhetoric and the Rise of Public Poetry: The Career of Eustache Deschamps," SP 80 (1983): 1–14.

454   Edward III did more: J. W. Sherbourne, "Aspects of English Court Culture in the Later Fourteenth Century," in *English Court Culture*, 1–27.

454   Henry IV was more of an intellectual: McFarlane, ch. 1.

454   Clerk of the Works: LR, ch. 21. See also John H. Harvey, "The Medieval Office of Works," *Journal of the British Archaeological Assoc.* 3rd ser., 6 (1941), 20–87.

454   Two years was not a short term: LR, 411.

454   "as long as he conducts . . .": LR, 404.

454   staff of deputies: LR, 417–419.

455   the same until the seventeenth century: Howard Montagu Colvin, ed., *The History of the King's Works*, 6 vols. (London, 1963), 1: 193.

455   Henry Yeveley: John Harvey, *English Mediaeval Architects* (1954; rev. Gloucester, 1984), 358–366; Harvey has written a separate biography, *Henry Yeveley, c. 1320 to 1400: The Life of an English Architect* (London, 1944). See also Harvey, "Medieval Office of Works," *Jour. Brit. Archaeological Assoc.* 3rd ser., 6: 42–49 and "Henry Yeveley Reconsidered," *Archaeological Journal* 108 (1952): 100–108.

455   lists at Smithfield: LR, 472–473.

456   the tournament . . . in the Knight's Tale: Parr, 317–323.

456   summoned to an audit: LR, 461–462.

456   further sum of £66: LR, 441 n. 5, 462, 469.

456   called Sir Geoffrey: Cook, 38–39.

456   set upon by highwaymen: LR, ch. 22. See W. D. Selby, *The Robberies of Chaucer*, Chaucer Soc. 2d ser. 12 (1875), and E. P. Kuhl, "Chaucer and the 'Fowle Ok,'" MLN 36 (1921): 157–159.

457   reported to have been wounded: See LR, 477; the document reports he was beaten and wounded. Some think there was only one robbery, which the records make look like three.

457   "Fortune": Var. 5: 1: 103–119; on the date, 103–105.

458   appointed . . . to a commission: LR, ch. 23, and see Virginia E. Leland, "Chaucer as Commissioner of Dikes and Ditches, 1390," *The Michigan Academician* 14 (1981): 71–79.

459   post of subforester: LR, ch. 24, which presents evidence passed down and recorded by Thomas Palmer in the eighteenth century and John Collinson in the nineteenth.

459   Gilbert Mawfield: LR, ch. 25.

459   William Venour: LR, 391–393.

459   Another grocer: LR, 394–397.

460   He left the debt of a pound: LR, 331–334.

460   gift of £10 from the king: LR, 120.

460   grant of £20 a year for life: LR, 514–515.

460   scarlet gown: LR, 275. See J. H. Wylie, *History of England under Henry IV*, 4 vols. (London, 1898) 4: 136. The fur alone cost £8 8s. 4d. (101 pelts at 20s. apiece) and was purchased in February 1395; the gown was presented the following year.

460   witnessed documents in Kent: LR, ch. 26.

460   a few short poems: Robinson, ed., 540–543.

460   "Against Women Unconstant": Var. 5: 1: 187–193.

461   Oton de Graunson: Haldeen Braddy, *Chaucer and the French Poet Graunson* (1947; reprt. Port Washington, N.Y., 1968).

461   some poems of Deschamps (note): Ibid; see John Livingstone Lowes, "The Chaucerian 'Merciles Beaute' and Three Poems of Deschamps," MLR 5 (1910): 33–39.

461   Brusendorff: 439–440.

462   Alfred David: Var. 5: 1: 172.

462   "to Rosemounde": Var. 5: 1: 161–170.

463   "Envoy to Scogan": Var. 5: 1: 149–160; R. T. Lenaghan, "Chaucer's *Envoy to Scogan*: The Uses of Literary Conventions," ChauR 10 (1975): 46–61.

464   Horatian in its manner: John Norton-Smith, "Chaucer's Epistolary Style," in *Essays on Style and Language*, ed. Roger Fowler (London, 1966), 157–165; and see his *Geoffrey Chaucer* (London and Boston, 1974), ch. 7.

464   special friendship of a shared world: Lenaghan, "Chaucer's Envoy," ChauR 10: 46–61.

464   fallow period in his artistic life: Samuel Moore, "The Date of Chaucer's Marriage Group," MLN 26 (1911), 172–174.

464 means his pen: Norton-Smith, "Chaucer's Epistolary Style," *Essays*, ed. R. Fowler, 160–165, cites Horace, *Satires*, 2: 39–44.

464 "The Envoy to Bukton": Var. 5: 1: 139–148.

466 "sense a real relief in it": Brewer, *World*, 187.

466 Duchess Costanza died: Higden, 9: 283.

466 Isabella . . . had died two years before: Armitage-Smith, 357–359.

466 Mary, countess of Derby: Kirby, 42–43.

466 "Prince Hal": J. L. Kirby, *Henry IV of England* (London, 1970), 17–18.

467 forged chronicle: Armitage-Smith, 359–362.

467 hostile comportment of . . . Arundel: Hutchison, 145; Hist. Angl., 2: 215; *Annales Ricardi II et Henrici IV (1392–1406)* in *Chronica Johannis de Trokelowe*, ed. H. T. Riley, Rolls Series 28.3 (London, 1866), 169, 424. On top of this, Arundel attacked Gaunt in the Parliament; Armitage-Smith, 354–355.

468 "by reason that . . .": Adam of Usk, 151; for the Latin, 9.

469 annuity of £20: LR, ch. 27.

470 body of Robert de Vere . . . reburied: Hutchison, 157; McKisack, 476; Annales, 184–185; Walsingham, 2: 119.

470 £200,000: Annales, 194 and Walsingham, 2: 222 both say between 30,000 and 40,000 marks. Hutchison, 164, and Steel, 216 both say £200,000, but neither cites a source.

471 period of settling down: Levinson 57–59.

471 almost universal support among the peerage: See the summary in McKisack, 473–475.

472 where Burley was beheaded: Kirkstall, 75, 119.

472 "like a wretched old woman . . .": Adam of Usk, 161.

473 estates were forfeited: McKisack, 481–482.

473 passage in his writings: Despite the effort of J. Leslie Hotson, "Colfox vs. Chauntecleer," PMLA 39 (1924): 762–781.

475 Gaunt . . . had made his will: See Armitage-Smith, Appendix 1.

477 "political theology": Ernst Kantorowicz, *The King's Two Bodies* (Princeton and Guildford, Surrey, 1957).

477 anointing: On its importance, see Charity Cannon Willard, *Christine de Pizan, Her Life and Works* (New York, 1984), 22.

477 *rex inutilis*: W. H. Dunham, Jr. and Charles T. Wood, "The Right to Rule in England: Depositions and the Kingdom's Authority, 1327–1485," *American Historical Review* 81 (1976): 738–761; and Charles T. Wood, "Celestine V, Boniface VIII and the Authority of Parliament," *Journal of Medieval History* 8 (1982): 45–62. Cf. Wood, DMA under "England 1216–1485."

478 "hear what he has to say . . .": Traison, 70–71, 221–222, in Hutchison, 231.

478 "My God, a wonderful land . . .": Adam of Usk, 182.

479   true sacred oil: See Walsingham, 2: 239. See T. A. Sandquist, "The Holy Oil of St. Thomas of Canterbury," in Sandquist, 330–344.

479   murdered by Sir Piers Exton: This version was the one Shakespeare followed. But when his body was examined in 1871, no marks of violence were found. See Edward King, "Sequel to the Observations on Ancient Castles," *Archaeologia* 6 (1782): 314; Thomas Amyot, "An Inquiry Concerning the Death of Richard the Second," Ibid. 20 (1824): 424–442; Arthur Penrhyn Stanley, "On an Examination of the Tombs of Richard II and Henry III in Westminster Abbey," Ibid. 45 (1880): 315, 316, and Stanley, *Historical Memorials of Westminster Abbey*, 2 vols. (London and New York, 1882), 1.178.

479   ocular proof: In Henry's council of Feb. 8 it was said that if he were dead his body should be shown to the people. Hutchison, 235.

480   by a slip to acknowledge the escape: Hutchison, 236; see Benjamin Williams's introduction to *Traison*.

480   "tormented by starving fare": Adam of Usk, 41.

17. THE END OF THE PILGRIMAGE

481   October 25, 1400: See Hammond, 42–43 and LR, 547–549.

481   other records: One such date is the year 1402, clearly impossible. Another, "A.D. 1400. 4. nonas Junii" (June 2), was three days before the date of his last Exchequer payment. See R. F. Yeager, "British Library Additional MS. 5141: An Unnoticed Chaucer *Vita*," JMRS 14 (1984): 262, 273–277.

481   leased to a new tenant: LR, 537.

481   not erected till 1556: Hammond, 42–43, cites an opinion that the altar tomb is the original tomb and only the canopy was added in 1556; *Athenaeum* 2 (1850): 768. Loomis, *Mirror*, no. 6, accepts this, but others do not. See LR, 549, and W. R. Lethaby, "Chaucer's Tomb," TLS, Feb. 21, 1929, 137.

482   used to mend the pavement: Yeager, "British Library Add. 5141," JMRS 14: 274, cites John Dart, *Westmonasterium* . . . , 2 vols. (London, 1723), 1: 83.

482   some bones were found (note): LR, 549. In *Nineteenth Century* 42 (1897): 336, a letter appeared by Henry Troutbeck claiming that he examined Chaucer's bones "when they were exposed in the digging of Browning's" in 1889. Recent efforts to find a record of the examination have failed; see the letter by Robert M. Penn in *Chaucer Newsletter* 7 (1985): 5, which identifies the Coroner as John Troutbeck, brother of Henry. The original communication seems to have been an eccentric's effort at a leg-pull: the writer objected to Chaucer's having been omitted from a list of "men of genius" and proceeded to comment on his "stature."

482   John Leland: Hammond, 5; see Yeager, "British Library Add. 5141," JMRS 14: 275. The phrase, from Terence, *Phormio* 4: 575, was proverbial; whether in the seventeenth century it implied resignation or melancholia is not clear.

482   no will has been found (note): LR, 548. Roskell, 154–155, reports that his son Thomas inherited from him only a property in Golding Lane, London, worth £8 a year and the lease of the house in the Abbey garden.

483   annuity of 40 marks: LR, ch. 28.

483   new lodgings in Westminster: LR, ch. 29.

483   safe-conduct on May 4, 1398: LR, 62–64.

483   Chaucer petitioned to receive it (note): LR, 116–117; the document must have been composed by Chaucer himself.

483   possibly at Chaucer's request (note): The conjecture of Ferris, 214, is, "Probably Chaucer himself called discreet attention to the fact that, magnanimous though the gift was, it would be even more so if dated on the feast of one of Richard's patron saints." But another member of the court might have made the suggestion. If Chaucer did, it reveals him as sycophantic in the extreme or, which seems more plausible, as having grown fussy and eccentric as he approached sixty.

483   Henry IV, following Richard's example (note): LR, 118–119, 525–528.

483   handsome annuity . . . had been back-dated: Sumner Ferris, "The Date of Chaucer's Final Annuity and of the 'Complaint to His Empty Purse,'" MP 65 (1967): 45–52.

484   negligible advance of £1 (note): LR, 334.

485   "The Complaint of Chaucer to His Purse": Var. 5: 1: 121–132; the text quoted below is based on this edition.

485   "he carries on the old jest . . .": Ibid, 123.

486   Roger Mortimer: Giffin, 89–105.

486   new breed of civil servants: Cf. Hutchison, 223.

486   £10 . . . the arrears on his annuity from King Richard: LR, 530–534.

486   On contempt of the world, see Pope Innocent III, *De Miseria Humane Conditionis*, ed. Michele Maccarrone (Lugano, 1955), and the introductions to *On the Misery of the Human Condition*, trans. Margaret Mary Dietz, ed. Donald R. Howard (Indianapolis, 1969), and *Lotario dei Segni (Pope Innocent III), De Miseria Condicionis Humane*, ed. Robert B. Lewis (Athens, Ga., 1978).

488   recent reexamination of the evidence: Lee W. Patterson, "The 'Parson's Tale' and the Quitting of the 'Canterbury Tales,'" *Traditio* 34 (1978): 331–380, esp. 356–370.

488   undecided when he died: See Pratt, 1162; he hypothesized that Fragment VII was on his desk, but he felt, so he once said, that

Chaucer had not found a place for Fragment VI (Physician-Pardoner) when he died.

488 often called "floating": Two scribes wrote doggerel links trying to fit it before the Shipman's Tale. It is generally conceded that it may go in any of the spaces left by unconnected tales; the term "floating fragment" appears to be first introduced in the Robinson ed. (726).

488 where it belongs: Howard, *Idea*, 338–339.

489 "knobs" and "whelkes": Walter Clyde Curry, *Chaucer and the Mediaeval Sciences*, 2d ed. (New York, 1960), 37–47.

489 garlic, onions, and leeks: Robert E. Kaske, "The Summoner's Garleek, Oynons, and eek Lekes," MLN 74 (1959): 481–484.

489 "testicular pseudo-hermaphrodite . . .": Beryl Rowland, "Animal Imagery and the Pardoner's Abnormality," *Neophilologus* 48 (1964): 56–60.

489 Klinefelter's syndrome: This discovery was first made by Professor Daniel Silvia.

489 "mare": See Monica McAlpine, "The Pardoner's Homosexuality and How It Matters," PMLA 95 (1980): 8–22, esp. 10–15. If we are to posit a lost slang expression, it would make more sense to derive it from the other word *mare*, which survives only in words like "nightmare," that meant an incubus, specter, or hag—rather much the equivalent of modern "fairy." Cf. Judy Grahn, *Another Mother Tongue* (Boston, 1984), ch. 4.

489 "eunuch of God": Robert P. Miller, "Chaucer's Pardoner, the Scriptural Eunuch, and the Pardoner's Tale," *Speculum* 30 (1955): 180–199.

489 male-female Christ: Caroline Walker Bynum, *Jesus as Mother: Studies in the Spirituality of the High Middle Ages*, (Berkeley, 1982), ch. 4.

490 archetypal figure: See Howard, *Idea*, 372–376.

491 One interpretation: Kittredge, 216–217.

491 "is absorbed into the pattern . . .": Alfred L. Kellogg, "An Augustinian interpretation of Chaucer's Pardoner," *Speculum* 26 (1951): 465–481.

492 still repent and be saved: E.g., Derek Pearsall, "Chaucer's Pardoner: The Death of a Salesman," ChauR 17 (1983): 358–365.

492 begun in earlier years: The conjecture of Charles Muscatine in an unpublished paper, "The 20th-Century Chaucer."

492 "entering at a thrope's ende": It is called a "thrope" or "thorp," a small agricultural village; they enter through or by means of it (see OED, under *at*, 1: 10)—the implication being that they here enter Canterbury.

492 written some years earlier: In 1383, according to Griffin, ch. 2.

493 cannot be found reflected in her story: This is somewhat problemati-

cal because a nun would, ideally, *be* without personality. One line only might reflect a sheltered life: ". . . as oft is the man-nere" (142); but cf. LGW 2673.

493   renunciation: Sherry L. Reames, "The Cecilia Legend as Chaucer Inherited It and Retold It," *Speculum* 55 (1980): 38–57.

493   devil or the Antichrist: Bruce A. Rosenberg, "Swindling Alchemist, Antichrist," *Centennial Review* 6 (1962): 566–580.

493   symbolized the quest of man for God: Edgar H. Duncan, "The Literature of Alchemy and Chaucer's Canon's Yeoman's Tale," *Speculum* 43 (1968): 633–656.

493   Manciple's Tale: See esp. Britton J. Harwood, "Language and the Real: Chaucer's Manciple," ChauR 6 (1972): 268–279; Howard, *Idea*, 298–306; and James Dean, "Dismantling the Canterbury Book," PMLA 101 (1985): 746–762.

494   story of Phebus: William Askins, "The Historical Setting of *The Manciple's Tale*, SAC 7 (1985): 87–105.

495   Latin (or French) original: On the sources of the Parson's Tale, see SA, 723–760, and Siegfried Wenzel, "The Source for the 'Remedia' of the Parson's Tale," *Traditio* 27 (1971): 433–453, and "The Source of Chaucer's Seven Deadly Sins," *Traditio* 30 (1974): 351–378. The Parson's Prologue seems to prepare for this final change of manner; it begins, as did the Man of Law's Prologue, with an elaborate measurement of the time of day, and introduces the figure of Libra, the scales of justice. See Chauncey Wood, *Chaucer and the Country of the Stars: Poetic Uses of Astrological Imagery* (Princeton, 1970), 272–297, and Rodney Delasanta, "The Theme of Judgment in *The Canterbury Tales*," MLQ 31 (1970): 302–307.

495   not a "tale" at all but a "treatise": On the terminology see Paul Strohm, "Some Generic Distinctions in the *Canterbury Tales*," MP 68 (1971): 321–328.

495   chain-gang of scholars (note): These would be Morton W. Bloom-field, Bertrand-Georges Guyot, O.P., Thyra Kabealo, and my-self, in *Incipits of Latin Works on the Virtues and Vices, 1100-1500 A.D.*, Mediaeval Academy of America Publication No. 88 (Cambridge, Mass., 1979).

496   hind part of a she-ape: On this fanciful image, see D. Biggins, "*Canterbury Tales* X (I) 424: 'The hyndre part of a She-ape in the Fulle of the Moone,'" MAE 33 (1964): 200–203, and Beryl Rowland, "Chaucer's She-ape (*The Parson's Tale*, 424)," ChauR 2 (1968): 159–165.

496   too general and philosophical: Patterson, "Parson's Tale," *Traditio* 34: 370–380.

496   Parson's Tale as ironic: See John Finlayson, "The Satiric Mode and the *Parson's Tale*," ChauR 6 (1971): 94–116 and Judson Boyce

Allen, "The Old Way and the Parson's Way: An Ironic Reading of the Parson's Tale," JMRS 3 (1973): 255–271.

497 Wilton Diptych: John H. Harvey, "The Wilton Diptych—A Reexamination," *Archaeologia*, 98 (1961): 1–28, and Sumner Ferris, "The Iconography of the Wilton Diptych," *Minnesota Review* 7 (1967): 342–347.

497 "Hoccleve portrait": Howard, *Idea*, 11–13; some years ago the National Portrait Gallery in London had a show of medieval faces, and the portrait of Chaucer, blown up many times, was placed at the end as the first English portrait in the modern sense.

497 indeed there was Hoccleve: The friendship between them may have been something Hoccleve, who was some twenty-five years younger than Chaucer, fancied, whereas it was really the case of an older man being kind to a younger one. They traveled in different circles, and garrulous Hoccleve doesn't speak as if he knew much about Chaucer. See Jerome Mitchell, "Hoccleve's Supposed Friendship with Chaucer," ELN 4 (1966): 9–12.

497 John Clanvowe: *The Works of Sir John Clanvowe*, ed. V. J. Scattergood (Cambridge, Eng. and Totowa, N. J., 1975).

498 Oliver Sacks: "The Autist Artist," *New York Review of Books*, April 25, 1985, 21.

499 The retraction occurs: See James D. Gordon, "Chaucer's Retraction: A Review of Opinion," *Studies in Medieval Literature in Honor of Professor Albert Croll Baugh*, ed. MacEdward Leach (Philadelphia, 1961), 81–96, and William A. Madden, "Chaucer Retraction and Mediaeval Canons of Seemliness," MS 17 (1955): 173–184, who sees in the passage a "tension between the demands of art and the demands of prudence" (184). My view of the ambivalence or "doubleness" of the retraction is a small step in the direction of a "deconstructive" reading of it; I found very agreeable an article in manuscript kindly sent to me by Peter W. Travis, which is just such a reading.

500 "a last earnest appeal . . .": Dieter Mehl, "The Audience of Chaucer's *Troilus and Criseyde*, in *Chaucer's Troilus*, ed. Barney, 225.

501 establishing his canon: Cf. Olive Sayce, "Chaucer's 'Retractions': The Conclusion of the *Canterbury Tales* and Its Place in Literary Tradition," MAE 40 (1971): 245.

501 "art of dying": See Nancy Lee Beaty, *The Craft of Dying: A Study in the Literary Tradition of the Ars Moriendi in England* (New Haven and London, 1970).

501 *De Arte Moriendi*: See Sister Mary Catharine O'Connor, *The Art of Dying Well: The Development of the Ars Moriendi* (New York, 1942), a study, largely bibliographical, of "the" *Ars Moriendi* (Inc.: *Cum de presentis exilii . . .*) that was so widely circulated throughout Europe for so long. She argues that it was written